FREEDOM OF EXPRESSION AND FREEDOM OF INFORMATION

Essays in Honour of Sir David Williams

Edited by

JACK BEATSON

and

YVONNE CRIPPS

OXFORD
UNIVERSITY PRESS

Great Clarendon Street, Oxford OX2 6DP

Oxford University Press is a department of the University of Oxford.
It furthers the University's objective of excellence in research, scholarship,
and education by publishing worldwide in

Oxford New York

Athens Auckland Bangkok Bogotá Buenos Aires Calcutta
Cape Town Chennai Dar es Salaam Delhi Florence Hong Kong Istanbul
Karachi Kuala Lumpur Madrid Melbourne Mexico City Mumbai
Nairobi Paris São Paulo Shanghai Singapore Taipei Tokyo Toronto Warsaw
with associated companies in Berlin Ibadan

Oxford is a registered trade mark of Oxford University Press
in the UK and in certain other countries

Published in the United States
by Oxford University Press Inc., New York

British Library Cataloguing in Publication Data
Data available

Library of Congress Cataloging in Publication Data
Data available

ISBN 0–19–826839–4

1 3 5 7 9 10 8 6 4 2

Typeset in Garamond by
Cambrian Typesetters, Frimley, Surrey

Printed in Great Britain
on acid-free paper by
Biddles Ltd,
Guildford and King's Lynn

Preface

The purpose of this volume, which we are editing as members of the Cambridge Centre for Public Law, is to celebrate Sir David Williams's contribution to public law on the occasion of his seventieth birthday. The range of that contribution can be seen from the survey of Sir David's scholarship by Jack Beatson and Sir William Wade. This book deals with only part of the ground he has covered. Freedom of expression and freeom of information play a central role in modern democracies and they are of particular importance as the Human Rights Act 1998 comes into force and the Freedom of Information Bill approaches enactment.

The fact that leading judges, practitioners and scholars from the United Kingdom, Australia, New Zealand, and the United States not only responded positively to our invitation to contribute to this collection but in fact produced the goods shows not only the strength of Sir David's reputation but also the warmth of the regard felt for him by his professional colleagues and friends. That warmth was shown at the conference convened by the Cambridge Centre for Public Law in February 2000 at which the contributions to this volume were first presented. It was exemplified by one of Sir David's oldest friends and collaborators, Professor Charles Alan Wright of the University of Texas at Austin who, despite serious illness which prevented him from contributing the paper he had planned, travelled to Cambridge from Austin for the conference, chaired one session and participated in others. We were very sorry to learn that Charles Alan Wright died in July.

We owe debts of gratitude to many. Clifford Chance supported the Centre's conference and seminar programme, and Keith Clarke, Michael Smyth and Richard Thomas continue to be good friends of the Centre. The Emmanuel Society very generously supported the conference and in particular the dinner held at Emmanual College. Phillip Greenwood and Felicity Eves of the Centre for Public Law provided administrative support for the conference, aided by staff in the Faculty office, and Felicity Eves also assisted in co-ordinating our large team of contributors and liaising with our publishers. The staff of the Squire Law Library as usual provided invaluable help. Louise Riley Smith allowed us to reproduce a photograph of her portrait of Sir David and Julia Hedgecoe allowed us to reproduce her photographs of Sir David and Lady Williams. Last but not least, the team at Oxford University Press, in particular Mick Belson, saw the project through, kept to the tight timetable, and produced an elegant book.

Cambridge   J.B.
August 2000   Y.M.C.

Contents

List of Contributors

Trevor Allan is Reader in Legal and Constitutional Theory at the University of Cambridge; Fellow of Pembroke College; author of *Law, Liberty, and Justice: The Legal Foundations of British Constitutionalism* (Oxford, 1993).

Alfred C. Aman Jr is Dean and Roscoe C. O'Byrne Professor of Law, Indiana University School of Law, Bloomington. He was Law Clerk to Hon. Elbert P. Tuttle, US Court of Appeals, Fifth Circuit, 1970–2.

Eric Barendt is Goodman Professor of Media Law, University College London. He is author of *Freedom of Speech* (1987), *Libel and the Media* (1997) and *An Introduction to Constitutional Law* (1999), all published by Oxford University Press.

Jack Beatson QC is Rouse Ball Professor of English Law and Director of the Centre for Public Law, University of Cambridge and a Deputy High Court Judge. He is author of *Administrative Law Cases and Materials* (2nd edn 1989) (with M. H. Matthews); *Human Rights: the 1998 Act and the European Convention* (with S. Grosz and P. Duffy); *Anson's Law of Contract* (27th edn 1998); and *The Use and Abuse of Unjust Enrichment* (OUP 1991).

The Hon Michael J. Beloff QC is President of Trinity College, Oxford, Judge of the Court of Appeal of Jersey and Guernsey, Master of the Bench of Gray's Inn and Emeritus Chairman of the Administrative Law Bar Association.

Malcolm Clarke is Professor of Commercial Insurance Law, University of Cambridge. He is author of *The Law of Insurance Contracts* (3rd edn); *International Carriage of Goods by Road* (3rd edn); *Policies and Perceptions of Insurance* (1997).

The Rt Hon Lord Cooke of Thorndon KBE, Lord of Appeal, United Kingdom; Judge of Final Court of Appeal of Hong King, Fiji, Samoa, Kiribati; former President of New Zealand Court of Appeal; Hon. Fellow Gonville and Caius College, Cambridge; Distinguished Visiting Fellow Victoria University of Wellington, former Visiting Fellow All Souls College, Oxford.

Jason Coppel Barrister, 11 King's Bench Walk Temple.

Yvonne Cripps is a barrister of the Middle Temple and Senior Fellow of the Centre for Public Law, University of Cambridge. She holds the Harry T. Ice Chair of Law at Indiana University and is a Visiting Professor at Cornell University. She has served as an adviser to the Royal Commission on Environmental Pollution, the House of Lords Select Committee on Science and Technology and as a member of the Home Office's Animal Procedures Committee. She is the author of *The Legal Implications of Disclosure in the Public Interest* (1994), and *Controlling Technology: Genetic Engineering and the Law* (1980).

Sir Patrick Elias is a Judge of the High Court, Queen's Bench Division, formerly Fellow of Pembroke College and lecturer in law, University of Cambridge.

David Feldman is Legal Adviser to the parliamentary Joint Select Committee on Human Rights, and Professor of Law in the University of Birmingham. He was Barber Professor of Jurisprudence in the University of Birmingham from 1992 to 2000, and Dean of Law from 1997 to 2000. He previously taught at the University of Bristol and the Australian National University. He has written extensively on civil liberties, human rights, police powers and public law generally.

Christopher Forsyth is Assistant Director of the Centre for Public Law, University of Cambridge and Fellow of Robinson College, Cambridge. His books include *Private International Law* (3rd edn, 1996), *In Danger for their Talents: A Study of the Appellate Division of the Supreme Court of South Africa, 1950–1980* (1985) and with Sir William Wade QC, *Administrative Law* (8th edn., Oxford University Press, 2000). He is a barrister of the Inner Temple and an Advocate of the Supreme Court of South Africa.

Ivan Hare is Assistant Director of the Centre for Public Law in the University of Cambridge and Fellow of Trinity College. He is a graduate of the Universities of London, Oxford and Harvard. He is a barrister and member of Gray's Inn.

Bob Hepple QC is Master of Clare College and Professor of Law in the University of Cambridge and Master of the Bench at Gray's Inn. He has written extensively on labour law and industrial relations, discrimination law, and the law of tort.

Rt Hon Sir Kenneth Keith KBE is a Judge of the Courts of Appeal of New Zealand, Samoa, the Cook Islands and Niue; Associé Institut de Droit International; formerly a member of the New Zealand Law Commission, the Victoria University of Wellington Faculty of Law, the United Nations Secretariat and the New Zealand Department of External Affairs, and Director of the New Zealand Institute of International Affairs.

Clive Lewis, Barrister, 4–5 Gray's Inn Square, sometime Fellow of Selwyn College, Cambridge and former Lecturer in Law, University of Cambridge. He is author of *Judicial Remedies in Public Law* (2nd edn) and *Remedies and the Enforcement of European Community Law* (2000).

The Hon Sir Anthony Mason AC KBE is former Chief Justice of Australia. He was Chancellor of the University of New South Wales and the Arthur Goodhart Professor of Legal Science at the University of Cambridge in 1996–7.

Stephanie Palmer is University Lecturer in Law and Fellow of Girton College, Cambridge. She teaches human rights and constitutional law. She is a barrister and member of Middle Temple.

David A. Schulz is chair of the Media Law Practice Group at Clifford Chance Rogers and Wells LLP in New York, and serves as an Adjunct Professor of Mass Media Law at Fordham University School of Law.

The Rt Hon Lord Scott of Foscote is a Lord of Appeal in Ordinary; formerly Vice Chancellor of the Supreme Court 1994–2000; Head of Civil Justice 1995–2000; High Court judge 1983–91; Lord Justice of Appeal 1992–4.

Sir Stephen Sedley is a Lord Justice of Appeal; Hon. LLD of Nottingham Trent, Bristol, Warwick and North London Universities; Chairman, Judicial Studies Board Human Rights Working Group; Honorary Professor of Law, Cardiff and Warwick Universities; Judicial Visitor, University College London; a founding Director of the Public Law Project. He has delivered the Bernard Simons, Paul Sieghart, Radcliffe, Laskin, Morris of Borth-y-Gest and Hamlyn lectures.

A. T. H. Smith is Professor of Criminal and Public Laws and currently Chairman of the Faculty of Law in the University of Cambridge and a barrister (Middle Temple). He is author of *Offences Against Public Order* (1987), *Property Offences* (1994) and, with Sir David Eady, *Contempt of Court* (1998).

Richard Thomas is Director of Public Policy at Clifford Chance, the international law firm. He is responsible for helping the firm and its clients to anticipate, understand and deal with legislative and regulatory developments. He gave evidence to the Public Administration Select Committee reviewing the draft Freedom of Information Bill and is a member of the CBI's Working Party on Freedom of Information.

Sir William Wade QC is Emeritus Rouse Ball Professor of English Law, University of Cambridge, formerly Master of Gonville and Caius College, Cambridge and Professor of English Law, University of Oxford. He is author of *Administrative Law* (8th edn, Oxford University Press) and *Constitutional Fundamentals* (1989).

Derrick Wyatt QC is Professor of Law, University of Oxford, St Edmund Hall, Oxford. He is co-author of Wyatt and Dashwood's *European Union Law* (4th edn., Sweet & Maxwell) and co-editor of Rudden and Wyatt, *Basic Community Laws* (7th edn., Oxford University Press).

Leslie Zines is Emeritus Professor, Law Program, Research School of Social Sciences, Australian National University. He was Arthur Goodhart Professor of Legal Science at the University of Cambridge 1992–3 and Robert Garran Professor of Law, Australian National University 1977–92. His works include *The High Court and the Constitution* (4th edn., 1997) and *Constitutional Change in the Commonwealth* (1991).

List of Abbreviations

AC	Law Reports, Appeal Case (1891–current)
ACLC	Australian Company Law Cases
ACP	African Caribbean and Pacific States
AD	Annual Digest and Reports of Public International Law Cases
Ad & E	Adolphus and Ellis's Reports
Admin LR	Administrative Law Review
AIPAC	Americal Israel Public Affairs Committee
AJCL	American Journal of Comparative Law
AJIL	American Journal of International Law
Alberta LR	Alberta Law Review
ALJ	Australian Law Journal
ALJR	Australian Law Journal Reports
All ER	All England Law Reports
ALR	Australian Law Reports
ALRC	Australian Law Reform Commission
Am B Found Res J	American Bar Foundation Research Journal
App Cas	Law Reports, Appeal Cases (1875–90)
Aust LJ	Australian Law Journal
BA	British Airways
BCCI	Bank of Credit and Commerce International
BCLR	British Columbia Law Reports
BHRC	Butterworths Human Rights Cases
BMA	British Medical Association
BNA Act	British North America Act
Boston UL Rev	Boston University Law Review
BSC	Broadcasting Standards Commission
BUL Rev	Boston University Law Review
Burr	Burrow's Reports
Calif L Rev	Californian Law Review
Cambrian LR	Cambrian Law Reports
Cardozo Arts & Eng LJ	Cardozo Arts and Entertainment Law Journal
CaseW ResJIL	Case Western Research Journal of International Law
CCC	Canadian Criminal Cases
Cd.	Command Papers (1900–18)
Ch	Law Reports, Chancery Division
Chi-Kent LR	Chicago-Kent Law Review
Civil Justice Q	Civil Justice Quarterly

CLJ	Cambridge Law Journal
CLP	Commercial Law Practitioner
CLR	Commonwealth Law Reports
Cm.	Command papers (1986–current)
CMLR	Common Market Law Reports
Cmnd.	Command papers (1957–86)
Colum L Rev	Columbia Law Review
Cox CC	E. W. Cox's Criminal Law Cases
CPR	Civil Procedure Rules
Cr App R	Cohen's Criminal Appeal Reports
CRE	Commission for Racial Equality
Crim LR	Criminal Law Review
Curr L Prob	Current Legal problems
D-MA	Democrat, Massachusetts
D-VT	Democrat, Vermont
Dalhousie LJ	Dalhousie Law Journal
DeG & Sm	De Gex and Smale's Reports
DLR	Dominion Law Reports
DR	Decisions and Reports of the Commission
Duke LJ	Duke Law Journal
East	East's Reports
ECHR	European Convention on Human Rights
ECommnHR	European Commission of Human Rights
ECR	European Court Reports
ECtHR	European Court of Human Rights
E-FOIA	Electronic Freedom of Information Act of 1996 (US)
EGLR	Estates Gazette Law Reports
EHRR	European Human Rights Report
EHRLR	European Human Rights Law Review
EL Rev	European Law Review
EOC	Equal Opportunities Commission
ER	English Reports
ERA	Employment Rights Act 1996
EU	European Union
FA	Football Association
FACA	Federal Advisory Committee Act of 1972 (US)
Fam	Law Reports, Family Division
FEC	Federal Election Commission
FECA	Federal Election Campain Act of 1971 (US)
Fed Comm LJ	Federal Communications Law Journal
Fed L Rev	Federal Law Review
FOI	Freedom of Information
FOIA	Freedom of Information Act of 1966 (US)

Fordham L Rev	Fordham Law Review
FSR	Fleet Street Patent Law Reports
GATT	General Agreement on Tariffs and Trade
GIPPS	Georgetown Internet Privacy Policy Survey: Report to the Federal Trade Commission 9 (1999)
GPS	Global Positioning System
Harv LR	Harvard Law Review
Hastings LJ	Hastings Law Journal
H.R.	House of Representatives
HRA	Human Rights Act 1998
HRLJ	Human Rights Law Journal
ICCPR	United Nations Covenant on Civil and Political Rights
ICJ Rep	International Court of Justice Reports
ICLQ	International and Comparative Law Quarterly
ICR	Industrial Court Reports
ICRC	International Committee of the Red Cross
ICTY	International Criminal Tribunal for the former Yugoslavia
ILC	International Law Commission
ILM	International Legal Materials
ILO	International Labour Organization
Ind LJ	Indiana Law Journal
Iowa Law Rev	Iowa Law Review
IRLR	Industrial Relations Law Reports
ITC	Independent Television Commission
J Marshall J Computer & Info L	John Marshall Journal of Computer and Information Law
JCCP	Joint Committee on Parliamentary Privilege
JCL	Journal of Comparative Legislation
JL & Com	Journal of Law and Commerce
JL & Pol	Journal of Law and Politics
JL & Info Sci	Journal of Law and Information Science
JMLC	Journal of Maritime Law Contracts
JPIL	Journal of Public International Law
Jurimetrics J	Jurimetrics Journal
KB	Law Reports, King's Bench Division
Ld Raym	Lord Raymond's Reports
LDRD Bulletin	Libel Defense Rourse Center Bulletin
LGR	Local Government Reports
LJCh	Law Journal, Chancery (1831–1946)
Ll L Rep	Lloyd's List Law Reports (1919–current: from 1951 Lloyd's Rep)
Lloyd's Rep	Lloyd's List Law Reports (1951–current)
LMCLQ	Lloyd's Maritime and Commercial Quarterly

LQR	Law Quarterly Review
LRC	Law Reports of the Commonwealth
LR QB	Law Reports, Queen's Bench Division
LT	Law Times Reports (1859–1947)
Mac & G	Macnaughton and Gordon's Reports
Media L Rep	Media Law Reporter
Michigan L Rev	Michigan Law Review
MLR	Modern Law Review
NATO	North Atlantic Treaty Organization
NGO	Non-governmental organization
NIAMDD	National Institute of Arthritis, Metabolism, and Digestive Diseases
NSWR	New South Wales Reports
NY Times	New York Times
NZLC	New Zealand Law Commission
NZLC R	New Zealand Law Commission Report
NZLR	New Zealand Law Reports
Ohio St LJ	Ohio State Law Journal
OJLS	Oxford Journal of Legal Studies
OMB	White House Office of Management and Budget
P & CR	Planning and Compensation Reports
PCC	Press Complaints Commission
Phil & Pub Aff	Philosophy and Public Affairs
PIDA	Public Interest Disclosure Act 1998
PL	Public Law
Pub Pol'y & Mktg	Journal of Public Policy and Marketing
POA	Public Order Act 1886
QAR	Queensland Appeal Reports
QB	Law Reports, Queen's Bench Division (1891–1901, 1953–current)
QBD	Law Reports, Queen's Bench Division (1875–90)
R	The Reports
R-Mont	Republican, Montana
RAC	Royal Automobile Club
RSC	Rules of the Supreme Court
Rutgers L Rev	Rutgers Law Review
SALJ	South African Law Journal
San Diego LR	San Diego Law Review
SCC	Supreme Court of Canada
SCR	Canada Law Reports. The Supreme and Exchequer Courts of Canada
SLJ	Solicitor's Journal
Sol Jo	Solicitor's Journal

Stan LR	Stanford Law Review
Syd Law Rev	Sydney Law Review
Temple L Rev	Temple Law Review
TEU	Treaty on European Union
Texas LR	Texas Law Review
Tort & Ins LJ	Tort and Insurance Law Journal
TranspR	Convention relative au Contrat de Transport International de Marchandises par Route Transportrecht
Tulane Law Rev.	Tulane Law Review
TULRCA	Trade Union and Labour Relations (Consolidation) Act 1992
Tulsa LJ	Tulsa Law Journal
U Chi L Rev	University of Chicago Law Review
U Chi Legal F	University of Chicago Legal Forum
U Fla JL & Pub Pol'y	University of Florida Journal of Law and Public Policy
U Pa L Rev	University of Pennsylvania Law Review
U Toronto LJ	University of Toronto Law Journal
UCLA L Rev	University of California at Los Angeles Review
UN	United Nations
UNESCO	United Nations Educational Cultural and Scientific Organization
Vand J Trans'l Law	Vanderbilt Journal of Transnational Law
VUWLR	Victoria University Weekly Law Reports
Wis L Rev	Wisconsin Law Review
WLR	Weekly Law Reports
Wm & Mary	William & Mary Bill of Rights Journal Bill Rts J
WTO	World Trade Organization
Yale JIL	Yale Journal of International Law
Yale LJ	Yale Law Journal

Table of Cases

EUROPEAN UNION

FRANCE

GERMANY

UNITED STATES OF AMERICA

ZIMBABWE

Table of Legislation

Australia

International Legislation

Ireland

Italy

Netherlands

United States of America

Sir David Williams QC, DL

JACK BEATSON QC AND SIR WILLIAM WADE QC

At the conference at which the contributions to this volume were first presented, there were many warm tributes from former pupils and colleagues to Sir David Williams's inspirational qualities as a lecturer, his distinguished contribution to University affairs, culminating with his seven years' service as Vice-Chancellor of the University of Cambridge, and his service on many public bodies, notably the Royal Commission on Environmental Pollution. He might be said to have had two careers, one at the highest level of legal scholarship and the other at the summit of academic government. In both he won many friends and admirers. Many also had cause to be grateful for the warm collegiate atmosphere which he fostered when President of Wolfson College, his abundant hospitality there and his ecumenical outlook which brought so many overseas judges, academics and others as visitors to Cambridge. In whatever activity or office, he enriched the human life around him. He had to give up the Presidency of Wolfson and the Rouse Ball Chair of English Law when he became the first full-time Vice-Chancellor of Cambridge University. He bore the increased burden of that office with conspicuous success. He travelled tirelessly in the University's interests, carrying its name and fame more than once round the world. When he left office he could well be proud of the pre-eminent worldwide standing enjoyed by Cambridge, which owed not a little to his energies and wisdom.

It is Sir David's scholarship, however, to which this volume is a tribute. His commitment to it is shown by the way he returned to it with relish after laying down the office of Vice-Chancellor in 1996. Since then he has contributed significant analyses of the legislative scheme for devolution of power to Wales,[1] the accountability of the police[2] and natural justice.[3] In the following pages we group his contribution under the following headings; civil liberties, particularly freedom of assembly, freedom of expression, and police accountability; official secrets; administrative law, particularly judicial review, tribunals and inquiries and environmental law; and devolution.

The contributions to this book cover the subject of David Williams's two path-breaking books, *Not in the Public Interest; The Problem of Security in Democracy*, published in 1965, and *Keeping the Peace; The Police and Public Order* published in 1967. But in doing so they concentrate on only part of his contribution to legal scholarship and development in the forty-two years since he took up his position as

---

[1] *Constitutional Reform in the United Kingdom; Practice and Principles* (Hart Publishing, 1998), ch. 4, and in Tomkins (ed.), *Devolution and the British Constitution* (1998) 19.

[2] Chapter 14 in D. Butler, V. Bogdanor and R. Summers (eds.), *The Law, Politics and the Constitution* (1999).

[3] 'Lord Cooke and Natural Justice' in Taggart (ed.), *The Struggle for Simplicity* (1997); 'Bias; the Judges and the Separation of Powers' [2000] PL 45.

an Assistant Lecturer in the Department of Law of the University of Nottingham in 1958. Sir David has ranged over nearly all constitutional and administrative law. His historical and contextualized approach to statute and case law brings it to life and shows how exciting the study of public law can be, not least because of the interplay between legal and democratic concepts.

Since Sir David has said that *Beatty v Gillbanks*[4] is his favourite case, we start with civil liberties, police powers and police accountability. *Keeping the Peace: The Police and Public Order* followed a series of articles in the Criminal Law Review dealing with the police, public meetings and public order, the control of obscenity, racial incitement, and the Administration of Justice Act 1960.[5] Its introduction states 'there have been countless serious disturbances in this country during the past three centuries. Many of them have left their mark in case law and statute law. The surprising range and complexity of the laws of public order can best be understood only against a background of the historical environment in which they were created and evolved.' *Keeping the Peace* provides this background.

Keeping the Peace emphasizes a number of important themes in any assessment of public order in England and Wales. These include the dominance of summary trial and the fact that before 1960 there was no appeal to the House of Lords from the Divisional Court of the Queens Bench Division, which heard appeals on points of law from magistrates' decisions. This means that our law has been shaped without much assistance from what is now the Court of Appeal Criminal Division or the House of Lords. Secondly, there is the judicial standard of reasonableness against which the action of the police is judged. *Keeping the Peace* and later work emphasizes the importance of an objective approach to 'reasonableness', and the complex nature of the balancing process between freedom of assembly and freedom of expression on the one hand, and the operational needs of the police on the other. Sir David's verdict is that while at times the courts may have been unduly sensitive to those needs, even where the actions of the police are largely upheld, the importance of cautionary dicta should not be underestimated.[6] Thirdly, there is the piecemeal nature of legislation, often enacted to meet particular problems but which has sometimes been adapted to meet new purposes, albeit with varying measures of success.[7] Sir David is particularly critical of the use of the Incitement to Mutiny Act 1797 against trade union and communist leaders.

The fourth theme concerns the importance of discretion. The uncertainties in the definition of crimes relevant to public order mean that the decision as to whether and for what to prosecute is frequently more important than the decision of a court

---

[4]   (1882) 9 QBD 308.

[5]   'The Administration of Justice Act 1960' [1960] Crim LR 149; 'The Police, Public Meetings and Public Order' [1963] Crim LR 149; 'The Control of Obscenity' [1965] Crim LR 471, 522; 'Racial Incitement and Public Order' [1966] Crim LR 320.

[6]   e.g., most recently in 'Police Accountability: Four Cases and a Statute' in D. Butler, V. Bogdanor and R. Summers (eds.), *The Law, Politics and the Constitution* (1999), 294.

[7]   See pp. 4–5 below for other reservations about legislation as compared with the common law.

itself. Moreover, the judgment of the police as to whether the needs of public order override principles of freedom of assembly and freedom of expression, and the restraint applied by courts when reviewing the exercise of such judgments have been important features of the law. An obvious focus of discussion is the emphasis on preventive action in the area of public order. Sir David's view, first articulated in *Keeping the Peace* but developed in later essays and articles, in particular his reappraisals of *Beatty v Gillbanks*[8] and *Thomas v Sawkins*,[9] is that while the police should be in a position to respond immediately to any public disorder, preventive action should be a last resort. One of his favourite quotations is that from the *Pall Mall Gazette* of 12 February 1886 opposing panic legislation in response to the Trafalgar Square riots of 'Black Monday' on 8 February 1886, that 'to sit on the safety-valve is not the best means of preventing an explosion'. He sees the distinction between prior control and instant response as crucial to the assessment of the long-term significance of *Beatty v Gillbanks*.

Sir David's later writings track the gradual but constant movement to the primacy of prior control. The argument is developed with a keen eye to the historical context in which the cases arose, whether it is protest by suffragettes before the First World War, by fascists before the Second World War, by those demonstrating against the Vietnam War, by Republicans and Unionists demonstrating in Northern Ireland, or by miners during the long strike in 1984 and 1985. His 1970 *Cambridge Law Journal* article 'Protest and Public Order', written against a background of the anti-Vietnam War demonstrations and the civil disturbance in Northern Ireland notes the 'relative success of the British police in preserving order'[10] and seeks to explain it by reference to the determination of the police to adhere to traditional methods of crowd control and the determination of the police to avoid wherever possible any entanglement in protests and demonstrations taking place on private property. Since then, however, he has noted that the claim that the police had used more force than was necessary to quell the 1974 disorders in Red Lion Square concerned in part the role of the Special Patrol Group (established in 1965 as a reinforcement for any police job felt to be beyond the strength of the local police),[11] and the extension of the power to enter private property resulting from Lord Denning MR's endorsement of the wide view of what constitutes a threatened breach of the peace.[12]

His 1987 Criminal Law Review article on the impact of the Public Order Act

---

[8] 'The principle of *Beatty v. Gillbanks*; a reappraisal' in Doob and Greenspan (eds.), *Perspectives in Criminal Law*, Canada Law Book (1984) 105.

[9] (1985) 16 Cambrian LR 116. See also 'Protest and Public Order' [1970] CLJ 96 and 'Prosecution, Discretion and the Accountability of the Police' in Hood (ed.), *Crime, Criminology and Public Policy* (1974) 161.

[10] [1970] CLJ 96, 116.

[11] See 'Freedom of Assembly and Free Speech; Changes and Reforms in England' (1975) 1 University of New South Wales Law Journal 97, 112.

[12] 'Preventive Action and Public Order: the Principle of *Thomas v Sawkins*' (1985) 16 Cambrian LR 116, 123. The endorsement was in *R v Chief Constable of the Devon and Cornwall Constabulary, ex p CEGB* [1982] QB 458, 471, p. 6 below.

1986 on processions, assemblies and the freedom of the individual was not entirely enthusiastic.[13] Sir David notes that the relevant provisions of Part 2 of the Act amount to a considerable extension of the Public Order Act 1936 by providing for advance notice of public processions, the widening of the preconditions for the imposition of conditions on such processions, and the extension of power to impose such conditions on static public assemblies. In particular, conditions may be imposed under the 1986 Act not only where the police have reasonable ground for apprehending serious public disorder but also where they have reasonable ground for apprehending serious disruption to the life of the community or that the purpose of the organizers is the intimidation of others. These provisions were introduced to enable the police to re-route processions to limit traffic and other congestion and to reduce disruption. But the phrase 'serious disruption to the life of the community', as Sir David points out, neglects the fact that the acts of processing and demonstrating may also be seen as part of the life of the community. Moreover he cites with approval Lord Scarman's fear that the new criteria 'could lead the police away from the likelihood of disorder and of violence being caused or provoked into a realm where they would be handling values which they are not better able to assess than any other one of us in our individual capacities and which are not values which ought to determine whether restrictions should be put on the right of free speech, of demonstration and of assembly.'[14]

In Sir David's latest essay on police accountability[15] there is a hint of regret that in *R v Chief Constable of Sussex, ex p International Trader's Ferry Ltd*[16] the Court of Appeal rejected any application of *Beatty v Gillbanks*. That case concerned the activities of animal rights protesters to prevent the export of livestock from Shoreham harbour. The Chief Constable stated that because deployment of police resources was affecting his ability efficiently to police other areas of the community, he would restrict police operations at the harbour, and, if the export could not be accomplished safely with the reduced police presence, issue instructions that lorries be turned back. Since then the judgment of the House of Lords has been delivered. Again the application of *Beatty v Gillbanks* was rejected. Sir David would no doubt agree with Lord Slynn of Hadley that *Beatty's* case does not lay down that the police can never restrain a lawful activity if that is the only way to prevent violence and a breach of the peace.[17] After all, his close examination of the circumstances of *Beatty's* case led him to conclude that the evidence in that case did not give the impression

---

[13] 'Processions, Assemblies and Freedom of the Individual' [1987] Crim LR 167.
[14] *Hansard*, HL (series 5) vol. 476, col. 526 (13 June 1986).
[15] 'Police Accountability: Four Cases and a Statute' in D. Butler, V. Bogdanor and R. Summers (eds.), *The Law, Politics and the Constitution* (1999), 294. See also 'Crime Prevention and Private Security: Problems of Control and Responsibility' (1974) Aust LJ 380; 'The Accountability of the Police: Two Studies', Cambridge-Tilburg Lectures, 1st Series 1978 27, 41.
[16] [1997] 2 All ER 65, CA, [1999] 1 All ER 129, HL.
[17] [1999] 1 All ER 129, 142.

that the police were unable to cope.[18] But his view would probably be closer to that of Lord Cooke of Thorndon who considered (without express reference to *Beatty v Gillbanks*) that a police decision which results in lawless elements acting on the side of protesters prevailing over the rights of a lawful trader 'cannot be justified except for most cogent reasons'.[19] Although Lord Cooke concluded that there were such cogent reasons in that case, his different starting point meant that, whereas Lord Slynn tested the legality of the Chief Constable's decision by applying the *Wednesbury* test, Lord Cooke appeared to exercise a more intensive form of scrutiny.[20]

We have noted his scrutiny of the political and historical context of the events that led to our leading cases. Sir David's contribution to this area of the law is marked by a number of other features. First, his analysis of the relative contributions of legislation and litigation has led him to the conclusion that, given the type of legislation that has been common in the United Kingdom, even in the absence of a constitutional bill of rights, the courts are better equipped to formulate principles than is often recognized.[21] He argues that the judicial response to serious threats to public order has been 'more consistent and formative' than the legislative response.[22] We have noted his view in *Keeping the Peace* concerning the piecemeal nature of legislation. The Public Order Act 1986, while perhaps not piecemeal, is said to be rather a blunt instrument which did not balance the interests of order and freedom of assembly sensitively.[23] What has concerned Sir David has been the absence of a principled legislative framework. It is appropriate that as this book is published, the Human Rights Act 1998 will come into force and will provide the United Kingdom with a legislatively based set of principles from the European Convention on Human Rights.[24] Sir David was one of the earliest commentators in this country to test the adequacy of both case law and legislation by reference to the principles enshrined in the European Convention.

In his view that the courts have on the whole conducted the difficult exercise of balancing the interest in order and the interest in freedom of assembly and freedom of expression reasonably well, Sir David is more complimentary about the contribution of the House of Lords to this area than was Glanville Williams, one of his predecessors

---

[18] 'The principle of *Beatty v Gillbanks*, a reappraisal' in Doob and Greenspan (eds.), *Perspectives in Criminal Law*, Canada Law Book (1985) at 112.

[19] [1999] 1 All ER 129, 158. See further p. 197 below.

[20] ibid. 159.

[21] ibid. at 107.

[22] 'Freedom of Assembly and Free Speech: Changes and Reforms in England' (1975) 1 University of New South Wales Law Journal 97, 101. See also 'Civil Liberties and the Protection of Statute' [1981] Curr L Prob 25; 'Public Interest and the Courts' (1983/84) *Staatkundig Jaarboek (Leiden)* 117.

[23] See [1987] Crim LR 167.

[24] The Convention rights are not directly incorporated as part of English law so as to become part of substantive domestic law but the direction in the Human Rights Act to read and give effect to legislation in a way which is compatible with Convention rights 'so far as it is possible to do so' (s. 3(1)) will mean that the position is substantially the same; Grosz, Beatson, and Duffy, *Human Rights: the 1998 Act and the European Convention* (2000) 7–9.

as Rouse Ball Professor, about its contribution to the criminal law in general. Thus, he approves of what he describes as an unequivocal assertion of the priority accorded by English law to the right of passage on the highway in *Broome v DPP*.[25] He describes as 'salutary' the reminder in *Brutus v Cozens*[26] that s. 5 of the Public Order Act 1936 (now s. 5 of the 1986 Act) 'was never intended to prohibit all speech or conduct likely to occasion a breach of the peace' and that there may be many manifestations of behaviour which will cause a resentment or protest without being insulting.[27] His assessment of the more recent decisions is perhaps more guarded. In *O'Hara v Chief Constable of the Royal Ulster Constabulary*[28] the House of Lords considered the approach in determining whether a constable's suspicion that a person has been concerned in acts of terrorism was based on reasonable grounds. The constable's reasonable grounds were based on a briefing by a superior officer, evidence which the trial judge said was scanty, but their Lordships held that the trial judge was entitled on the sparse materials before him to infer the existence of reasonable grounds for suspicion. Sir David comments that this shows the balancing process the court has to undertake 'is clearly very delicate, and *O'Hara*—irrespective of the result—could be interpreted as a reminder that trial judges should respect that delicacy.'[29]

The contribution of the Court of Appeal is also generally noted with approval. For example, Lord Denning's statement favouring a 'right' of public assembly[30] is welcomed. On the other hand the wide view of threatened breach of the peace which was endorsed by Lord Denning MR in *R v Chief Constable of the Devon and Cornwall Constabulary, ex p CEGB*[31] is not. Lord Denning stated that there 'is a breach of the peace whenever a person who is lawfully carrying out his work is unlawfully and physically prevented by another from doing it' and that such unlawful conduct 'gives rise to a reasonable apprehension of the breach of the peace. It is at once likely that the lawful worker will resort to self-help by removing the obstructer by force from the vicinity of the work so that he obstructs no longer . . .'. In that case the police had declined to intervene in a case where employees of the electricity board where obstructed by anti-nuclear protestors from entering certain land. Notwithstanding his broad approach to what constituted a breach of the peace, Lord Denning dismissed the application for judicial review on the grounds that the decision of the Chief Constable not to intervene was a policy decision. While Sir David sympathizes with respect for policy decisions taken by the police, not least because of the wide-scale ramifications of a single incident of public disorder, he correctly argues that 'respect

25   [1974] 1 All ER 314.
26   [1972] 2 All ER 1297, 1301.
27   (1975) 1 Univesity of New South Wales Law Journal 97, 104.
28   [1997] AC 286.
29   'Police Accountability: Four Cases and a Statute' in D. Butler, V. Bogdanor and R. Summers (eds.), *The Law, Politics and the Constitution* (1999) 284. This also considers *R v Chief Constable of Sussex, ex p International Trader's Ferry Ltd* [1997] 2 All ER 65, CA, on which, see above and [1999] 1 All ER 129, HL.
30   *Hubbard v Pitt* [1976] QB 142.
31   [1982] QB 458, 471–2.

for policy at a general level should not be allowed to spill over into reluctance to question the reasonableness of particular police action'.[32] In this context he emphasizes the objective nature of the concept of reasonableness and 'reasonable cause'.

Sir David's belief in the general ability[33] of the courts adequately to control by reference to the standard of 'reasonableness' is reflected in his welcome for the introduction by s. 13 of the Public Order Act 1986 of a standard of reasonable belief of serious public disorder as the test for prohibiting a procession. Similarly, he comments that the use of subjective terminology in s. 12(1) of the 1986 Act authorizing conditions which appear to senior police officers to be necessary to prevent disorder, damage, disruption or intimidation to be imposed do not 'in principle' inhibit judicial review. On the other hand, he is not unaware of the difficulties of the concept of 'reasonableness'. Thus, pointing to the terms 'reasonable excuse' in s. 39(4)(b) and 'reasonable suspicion' in s. 39(3) of the 1986 Act, he states that such phrases provide the possibility of a beanfeast for the lawyer in court.[34]

The third feature of Sir David's contribution in this area has been to emphasize something that, in recent times with concentration on the judicial review jurisdiction of the courts, has perhaps not been sufficiently recognized, viz. the role of inquiries, investigations, and official advice as instruments for developing principles. Notwithstanding the contribution they have made, the courts, faced with problems of public disorder whether concerned with political expression, industrial picketing, football crowds, or pop festivals, have tended to shy away from statements of principle. Sir David points out that 'the law relating to public order remains an ill-assorted collection of common law offences, statutory offences, administrative powers, police powers, political pronouncements, and official and unofficial reports'.[35] A notable early example of official advice was that offered by the Home Secretary to the Stamford Magistrates in 1881 as a response to attacks on marches by the Salvation Army.[36] Sir David's analysis makes significant use of inquiries, from the report in 1856 on the alleged disturbance of the public peace in Hyde Park on 1 July 1855, and that of Mr Chester Jones into disturbances at Rotherhithe in 1912,[37] to Lord Scarman's inquiries into the disorders in Red Lion Square in 1974[38] and in Brixton in 1981.[39] The continuing significance of such inquiries is illustrated by the impact of the Stephen Lawrence Inquiry.[40]

This section has concentrated on Sir David's principal contribution to the law of civil liberties. But his pre-occupation with freedom of assembly and public order

---

[32] (1985) 16 Cambrian LR 116, 124. See also 'Criminal Law and Reasonableness' in Smith (ed.), *Criminal Law (Essays in honour of J. C. Smith)* (1987) 170.

[33] But cf. his comment (noted above) on *O'Hara v Chief Constable of the Royal Ulster Constabulary* [1997] AC 286.

[34] [1987] Crim LR 167, 177, adopting the phrase used by Lord Hutchinson of Lullington, *Hansard*, HL (series 5) vol. 481, col. 237 (21 October 1986).

[35] 'The principle of *Beatty v Gillbanks*; A Reappraisal' (n. 18 above) 105.

[36] ibid., 109. This is set out in The Times, 11 October 1881 at 6 (1881) 16 Law Journal 480).

[37] Cd. 6367 (1912).   [38] Cmnd. 5919 (1975).

[39] Cmnd. 8427 (1981).   [40] Cm. 4262–1 (1999).

should not obscure his work in other areas. For instance, he has written on contempt[41] and on equal protection,[42] and his work for the Commission for Racial Equality on s. 43 of the Education (No. 2) Act 1986 provides a lucid explanation of the new legal framework to ensure freedom of speech in universities, polytechnics and colleges.[43]

Turning to administrative law, Sir David's writing has extended over most parts of this subject but he has been particularly interested in two aspects of it. The first concerns the effective scope of the judicial review jurisdiction[44] and the extent to which considerations of justiciability affect the control of discretionary power. His essays 'Justiciability and the Control of Discretionary Power'[45] in which the chameleon-like quality of the concept of justiciability and the fact that it 'is inevitably bound up with issues of judicial restraint, judicial techniques, political understandings, and particular controversies'[46] and on 'Prosecution, Discretion and the Accountability of the Police'[47] have been particularly influential in moulding subsequent academic debate.

The second area of concentration concerns tribunals and inquiries. We have already mentioned that in the context of civil liberties Sir David regards the contributions of inquiries into particular incidents of disorder as an important source of principle. More broadly, however, his analysis of the role of tribunals and inquiries, the effect of a developed tribunal system in a particular context on the extent to which recourse may be had to judicial review, and the attitude of the reviewing court itself have been illuminating. In these areas his contributions, which we examine in more detail below, reflect his long service as a member of the Council on Tribunals. But our concentration on those should not obscure his range within this subject. Apart from his co-authorship of the important section on administrative law in the fourth edition of *Halsbury's Laws of England* in 1973, the first time that work contained a separate section on administrative law, he has written extensively on natural justice, most recently in his Harry Street lecture on 'Bias; the Judges and the Separation of Powers'[48] on delegated legislation (where he feels there has been too much judicial restraint),[49] and on remedies.[50]

---

[41] (1969) 27 CLJ 9; (1973) CLJ 15; (1975) 32 CLJ 6; (1980) 39 CLJ 229.

[42] (1985) 59 Tulane Law Rev 959. See also 'Legal effects of Positive discrimination' (1968) 2 *Social and Economic Administration* 242.

[43] Commission for Racial Equality, *Racism and freedom of speech on the campus* (1988) 11.

[44] On public interest immunity, see below.

[45] In Taggart (ed.), *Judicial Review of Administrative Action in the 1980s* (Oxford, 1986) 103.

[46] ibid., 122.

[47] In Hood (ed.), *Crime, Criminology and Public Policy: Essays in Honour of Sir Leon Radzinowicz* (1974), 161.

[48] [2000] PL 45. See also 'Dismissal of a Chief Constable' [1962] Crim LR; 'Lord Cooke and Natural Justice' in Taggart (ed.), *The Struggle for Simplicity* (1997).

[49] 'Statute law and Administrative law' Statute Law Review 157; 'Subordinate Legislation and Judicial Control (1997) 8 Public Law Review 77.

[50] 'Administrative Law in England; the Emergence of a New Remedy' (1986) 27 William and Mary Law Rev. 715; Judicial Review: Institution and Background—The Experience of England and Wales' (1983) 43 *La Revue du Barreau* 141.

His essay 'Justiciability and the Control of Discretionary Power' argues that there is no coherent concept of 'justiciability', and that an appreciation of what is or what is not justiciable may vary sharply in different courts and in different periods so that the matter is better considered in terms of judicial restraint or judicial activism.[51] Developments in the way the judicial review jurisdiction is exercised since that essay was written, for example *R v Secretary of State for the Home Department, ex p Bentley*[52] and *R v Secretary of State for Foreign and Commonwealth Affairs, ex p World Development Movement Ltd*[53] in relation to the prerogative of mercy and the conduct of the foreign aid programme have vindicated his approach. One of us takes the view that the courts' use of the term 'prerogative' to describe any power or right of the Crown which does not derive from statute is an over wide usage, that only powers unique to the Crown should be termed 'prerogative',[54] and that the non-reviewability of powers unique to the Crown was not solely a question of non-justiciability. Be that as it may, Sir David's observations, as early as his succinct but all encompassing note on the *Blackburn* case in 1971[55] both anticipated and reflected developments in the courts.

Justiciability is also a factor in the exercise of the judicial review power in relation to statutory discretions. Sir David notes that the circumscribed view of courts' ability to review prerogative power in the first cases in which such review was considered possible has similarities to the approach taken in particular to statutory powers couched in subjective terms before the landmark decisions of *Padfield, Congreve* and *Tameside*.[56] Elsewhere he points to the fact that the interpretation of statutory discretions is affected both by context and by broad constitutional assumptions affecting the process of statutory interpretation. By context he means the circumstances in which the statute was enacted and the circumstances in which it has to be enforced. His discussion of the less well-known decision *R v Agricultural Land Tribunal, ex p Benney*[57] in which a farmer in Cornwall ultimately succeeded in setting aside a tribunal's decision that the Minister could seek an order turning him off his land, illustrates the role of context vividly. The background of the case was rumbling discontent about the continuation of the wartime policy of detailed control over agriculture, concerns that were reflected in the report of the Franks Committee on Administrative Tribunals and Enquiries.[58]

The broad constitutional assumptions mentioned by Sir David in his address to the Statute Law Society in 1984[59] include not only assumptions or presumptions

---

[51] In Taggart (ed.), *Judicial Review of Administrative Action in the 1980s* (Oxford, 1986) 103, 121–2.
[52] [1994] QB 349.
[53] [1995] 1 WLR 386.
[54] Wade 'Procedure and Prerogative in Public Law' (1985) 101 LQR 180,197.
[55] 'Prerogative and Control' [1971] CLJ 178.
[56] *Padfield v Minister of Agriculture, Fisheries and Food* [1968] AC 997; *Congreve v Home Office* [1976] QB 629; *Secretary of State for Education and Science v Tameside MBC* [1977] AC 1014.
[57] [1955] 1 All ER 123 DC, [1955] 2 All ER 129, CA.
[58] Cmnd 218 (1957), paras 145–52.
[59] 'Statute Law and Administrative Law' [1984] Statute Law Review 157.

about personal freedom, such as access to the courts, rights of property, and personal liberty, but the status of the governmental authorities involved. He notes that 'statutory interpretation is often a highly complex and unpredictable process, leaving the judges with ample discretion to expand or contract the methods of controlling the administration'.[60] The importance of context is well illustrated both in his essay on the role of the courts in welfare law[61] and its assessment of the importance of the volume of cases and alternative controls, such as internal review by superiors and recourse to a complaints procedure such as those in ombudsmen schemes, and in that on prosecutorial discretion, which anticipated the burgeoning of judicial review as a means of controlling decisions to prosecute or not to prosecute.[62] The analysis of *Roberts v Hopwood*[63] in his 1970 essay 'The Control of Local Authorities'[64] and his Ralph Fuchs Lecture in 1993[65] illustrates the way in which assessments of constitutional propriety can determine the scope of review. Although nine of the eleven judges involved in the different courts found in favour of the district auditor and against the Poplar councillors, it is argued that 'quality and quantity should not be too hastily merged'. The two judges who found in favour of the councillors were Atkin and Scrutton LJJ, two outstanding judges, neither of whom could be accused of an inclination to be unduly deferential to administration. Atkin LJ emphasized that the case was concerned with 'powers given to public bodies consisting of representatives elected by the public on a wide franchise for comparatively short periods'[66] and Scrutton LJ spoke of 'the reasonable limits of discretion in a representative body', and of a 'wide margin of error' being allowed for error of judgment.[67]

As noted, Sir David's contribution to the law on tribunals and inquiries was informed by his ten-year membership of the Council on Tribunals, membership of the JUSTICE-All-Souls review of administrative law[68] as well as seven years' service on the Royal Commission on Environmental Pollution, and service on the Commission on Energy and the Environment, the Clean Air Council, the Animal Procedures Committee, and the Senior Salaries Review Body. He also chaired the RAC Foundation for Motoring and the Environment's Advisory Group's first report on 'Cars and the Environment: A view to the Year 2020'.[69]

His generally positive and gradualist approach is reflected in his 1984 article reviewing the Council on Tribunal's first twenty-five years.[70] While noting the desirability of establishing a standing advisory committee concerned with administrative

[60] ibid., 162.
[61] 'Judicial Restraint and Judicial Review; the role of the courts in welfare law' in Partington and Jowell (eds.), *Welfare Law and Policy* (1979) 101.
[62] In Hood (ed.), *Crime, Criminology and Public Policy: Essays in Honour of Sir Leon Radzinowicz* (1974), 161.
[63] [1925] AC 578.
[64] Andrews (ed.), *Welsh Studies in Public Law*, ch. 8 (University of Wales Press, 1970).
[65] [1994] 2 Indiana Journal Global Legal Studies 191.
[66] [1924] 2 KB 695, 725–6.   [67] ibid., 719–21.
[68] *Administrative Justice; Some Necessary Reforms* (1988).
[69] RAC, 1992.   [70] [1984] PL 72.

adjudication with a research capability, this concludes that 'some of the success of the Council at the grass-roots of administrative law may be attributable to the concentration of effort dictated by Parliament'. By 1990, however, it was clear that many of the recommendations made by the Council on Tribunals in its Special Report in 1980[71] (which was the basis for Sir David's earlier commentary) would not be implemented. Even its suggestion that Departments consult the Council not only when such consultation is required by statute but in other cases, for example where the need for an appeal procedure is being considered, had not been taken up by all Departments. It was perhaps this lack of progress that led Sir David to modify his earlier view that 'it is by no means clear that a formal political base would significantly assist the Council [on Tribunals] in the performance of its functions'. In 1990 he suggested that 'the time may well be right . . . for more political steam to be generated, and the Council would doubtless benefit from a link through a select committee in Parliament. A political stimulus might help in securing more realistic resources and, armed with greater resources, the Council would be able to launch new initiatives and examine new proposals with much greater effectiveness.'[72]

Sir David's public service and involvement in environmental administration, in particular the Royal Commission on Environmental Pollution, has been noted. This has enabled him to deploy insights from this context in his writing, particularly in his analyses of public local inquiries and their difficulties in dealing with polycentric policy issues concerning the environment, highway congestion, and safety.[73] His 1980 study of public local inquiries, and the impact of the *Bushell* case[74] which he regards as possibly the most important case arising from a formal administrative adjudication since the Second World War,[75] considers the difficulty of dealing with broad policy issues such as the 'need' for motorways, and the safety of nuclear reprocessing plants. Sir David traces the breakdown in the inquiry process as public dissatisfaction grew, and as the scope of inquiries widened in the wake of aroused concern about energy resources and environmental protection. The tensions revealed in the differences between the approach of Lord Diplock who, for the majority, spoke of the danger of overjudicializing inquiry procedures, and Lord Edmund-Davies who, while recognizing these dangers, took the view that what amounted to fairness in such an inquiry was determined not only by its nature as set out in the statute, but by the issues made relevant by the inspector conducting it, illustrate strikingly the complexity of issues that arise in such cases. Sir David's sympathies appear to lie with the minority. He comments that the weakness of the majority approach is that 'there

---

[71] *The Functions of the Council on Tribunals*, Cmnd. 7805 (1980).

[72] 'The Tribunal System—Its Future Control and Supervision' (1990) Civil Justice Q 27.

[73] See also 'Is Enforcement of Existing Legislation Adequate?' in NSCA, *Clean Air-Ways and Means* (1978); 'Environmental Protection in the United Kingdom' (1981) 12 Journal of Business Administration (UBC) 281; 'The Role of the Courts in Great Britain: Problems of the Environment' (1989) 1 ERPL 329; 'Developments in British Environmental Law' (1984) 24 Natural Resources Journal 511.

[74] *Bushell v Secretary of State for the Environment.* [1981] AC 75.

[75] (1980) 29 ICLQ 701, 715.

is insufficient awareness of the purpose of highway inquiries and the radically changed climate in which they have to operate'.[76]

Our third area, official secrecy, was the subject of Sir David's first book, *Not in the Public Interest; The Problem of Security in Democracy*, published in 1965. That set out the scope of executive secrecy, focusing in particular upon the workings of the Official Secrets Act 1911 and the impact of official restrictiveness upon the press, and the principal means by which executive secrecy is enforced, including a detailed examination of the role of the security services.

Not in the Public Interest traces the 'dramatic extension'[77] of the laws concerned with the preservation of state secrets during the first half of the twentieth century, and the extent to which successive administrations succeeded in operating much of the machinery of governmental secrecy (and especially national security) in a political and legal vacuum. Some argue that the veil of secrecy over the working of central government is so extensive that it defeats its own purpose and that independent scrutiny would promote efficiency. Others argue that the machinery of government would become too slow, too cumbersome, and often too inefficient were it to be operated in a full blaze of publicity. The rival claims are examined, but it is clear that Sir David is in the first camp. Three features of the British system are noted; what some have called its 'passion for secrecy', its adherence to non-statutory instruments, such as the 'D' notice system, the absence until very recently of any regulation of the security services,[78] and a very cautious approach by the courts. His conclusion is that 'it is desirable that as far as possible the workings of the central government should either be subject to publicity or subject to some form of independent scrutiny. Sweeping assertions of executive secrecy ought not to be tolerated in a democratic country.'[79]

Not in the Public Interest does not, however, advocate the 'juridification' of control, but a mixed system in which responsibility for control 'rests in varying degrees with Parliament, the courts of law, the Press (and other media . . .) and the central government itself'.[80] Sir David's later writings comment on changes and further manifestations of the problems.[81] He was one of those who analysed the defects in the law revealed by the so-called *ABC* case in 1978.[82] In his view[83] the trial

---

[76] (1980) 29 ICLQ 701, 718. See also 'The Donoughmoure Report in Retrospect' (1982) 60 Public Administration 273.

[77] Williams, *Not in the Public Interest* (1965) 206.

[78] There has been a partial system in force since the Security Service Act 1989. See also the Intelligence Services Act 1994 and the Security Service Act 1996.

[79] Williams (n. 77 above) 215.   [80] Williams (n. 77 above) 215–16.

[81] 'Official Secrecy in England' (1968) 3 Fed L Rev 20; 'Official Secrecy and the Courts', in Glazebrook (ed.), *Reshaping the Criminal Law* (1978) 154; 'Law and National Security' in *The Cambridge Lectures* 1981 (Butterworths, 1983) 268; 'Lord Denning and Open Government' (1986) Denning Law Journal 117; 'The Spy Catcher Saga' (1989) 12 Dalhousie L J 209.

[82] His confidential advice to the Canadian Commission of Inquiry into the Royal Canadian Mounted Police on national security in the United Kingdom, included an analysis of the ABC case. See *Security and Information* First Report of the Commission of Inquiry (1980).

[83] 'The ABC case and Official Secrecy' (undated ms) 19.

in that case had effectively ensured that reform of the Official Secrets Act would not be confined merely to a repeal and replacement of s. 2 alone. As well as the question of what official information should or should not be protected by the criminal law, the trial raised controversial issues of fair trial ranging from jury-vetting to the burden of proof under the Official Secrets Act. The case also gave rise to difficult and unexpected issues of contempt of court and contempt of Parliament. It focused attention and gave added stimulus to complaints about the inadequacy of Parliamentary accountability.

The scene has fundamentally changed since 1965. We now have a mixed system of accountability of the sort advocated by Sir David. The notorious s. 2 of the Official Secrets Act 1911 has been repealed by the 1989 Act, albeit with new restrictions on unauthorized disclosure of a narrower range of information. Legislation now has a greater role in the regulation of the security and intelligence services: there is independent oversight in the form of a Judicial Commissioner who reports to Parliament, and a tribunal to investigate complaints, albeit with limited powers. Notwithstanding the hiccup revealed in the *Matrix Churchill* case,[84] the courts have taken on an enhanced role in considering claims to public interest immunity. In this last area, Sir David has suggested that, although an area such as public interest immunity inevitably involves the courts in politically sensitive decisions, the case law suggests 'a widening range of judicial competence in a surprising range of problems'.[85] But in other respects Sir David would probably still find the present situation unsatisfactory. For example, the law of confidence has not been put on a statutory basis as he suggested it should in his 1989 Horace Read lecture.[86] Again, and more significantly, the current proposals for a Freedom of Information Act do not afford the full access to courts to enable them to resolve disputes arising from refusals to furnish documents which he sees as part and parcel of judicial control of administrative action.[87] The doubts expressed in the 1970s as to whether 'such essentially political matters could best be determined in the Courts' or even by the Parliamentary Commissioner for Administration,[88] noted by Sir David are still evident in those responsible for the Freedom of Information Bill now before Parliament.[89]

Some of Sir David's writing is concerned with the constitution of the United

---

[84] See Sir Richard Scott V-C, *Report of the Inquiry into the Export of Defence Equipment and Dual-Use Goods to Iraq and related Prosecutions* (H.M.S.O. C. 115) especially vol. 1, chap. 1, and vol. 3, Section G.

[85] 'The ABC case and Official Secrecy' (undated ms) 21. See also 'Lord Denning and Open Government' (1986) 1 Denning LJ 117; 'Lord Wilberforce and Administrative Law' in Bos and Brownlie (eds.), *Liber amicorum for Lord Wilberforce* (1986) 103.

[86] 'The Spycatcher Saga' (1989) 12 Dalhousie LJ 209.

[87] 'Official Secrecy and the Courts', in Glazebrook (ed.), *Reshaping the Criminal Law* 173.

[88] See eg Green Paper on Open Government, Cmnd. 7520 para. 55 (1979); Report of the Committee of Privy Councillors on Ministerial Memoirs, chaired by Viscount Radcliffe, Cmnd. 7520, paras 55, 65 (1976).

[89] On Freedom of Information see Chs. 13–15, 20, 21, 23 below (Mason, Sedley, Palmer, Aman, Keith, Thomas).

Kingdom in general,[90] but in this final section we confine ourselves to his substantial contribution to the subject of devolution, in particular the Welsh perspective, which in comparison with that of Scotland, has been relatively under-analysed. As with many of his contributions on particular issues, he puts this into a broader and principled constitutional context. Again, his analysis is deeply rooted in history and reflects uneasiness at the fact that both the proposals of the Royal Commission on the Constitution in 1973 and the current arrangements of devolution treat Scotland and Wales differently from the English regions and from each other.[91] Commenting on the proposals in the Kilbrandon Commission's 1975 Report, he states that a federal plan would be 'a more honest plan' and that 'neither federal government nor legislative devolution is likely to work satisfactorily under a selective scheme from which England and the regions of England are excluded'.[92] The scheme of administrative devolution enacted for Wales in 1998 is seen as an inferior package to the Scottish one and as 'niggardly'.[93] The lack of rationale for the division of powers between Westminster and the Welsh Assembly and the fact that Westminster is ultimately responsible for the government of Wales are said to be sources of difficulty. Sharing is more difficult than transfer and will make it more difficult for the Welsh Assembly to adopt an integrated approach to policy making. The difficulties are not helped in his view by the fact that the relationship between Whitehall departments, the Secretary of State for Wales, and the Welsh Assembly is not addressed in the legislation but left to non-statutory understandings or 'concordats'. One of the hallmarks of Sir David's work has been to examine the workings of such non-statutory features of the constitution and to point to their limitations. As experience grows, his fears about the adequacy of these arrangements are being borne out.[94]

This cursory survey of Sir David's many writings will at least give some idea of the wide fields which lie within his interests and of the fruitful way in which he has studied and analysed them. Happily his energies show no sign of diminution, so that we may look forward to still more instruction and enlightenment from him.

[90] See e.g. 'The Constitution of the United Kingdom' [1972B] CLJ 266; 'The Independence of the Judiciary in England' (1964) Rassegna dei Magistrati 337.

[91] 'Wales and Legislative Devolution' in Calvert (ed.), *Devolution* (1975), 63; 'Devolution; the Welsh Perspective' in Tomkins (ed.), *Devolution and the British Constitution* (1998) 19; and in *Constitutional Reform in the United Kingdom; practice and principles*, Cambridge Centre for Public Law (1998) 41.

[92] 'Wales and Legislative Devolution' in Calvert (ed.), *Devolution* (1975) at 76, 82.

[93] 'Constitutional Issues Facing the United Kingdom' (1999) 30 Law Librarian 13, 15.

[94] See e.g. Rawlings (2000) 116 LQR 257.

PART I
Freedom of Expression

1

Common Law Constitutionalism and Freedom of Speech

T. R. S. ALLAN

1. INTRODUCTION

In response to H. L. A. Hart's suggestion that all moral and legal thought proceeded on the 'tacit assumption that the proper end of human activity is survival',[1] the American legal theorist Lon Fuller proposed an alternative 'central indisputable element' in human striving, that of effective communication between persons. Freedom of speech or expression was thus the first principle of natural law: 'Open up, maintain, and preserve the integrity of the channels of communication by which men convey to one another what they perceive, feel, and desire.'[2] Freedom of speech was not only a necessary condition of survival, but a means of enriching and expanding the meaning and scope of life itself.

The degree to which speech or expression should be granted special constitutional protection, and the precise justification for such a guarantee, are notoriously controversial questions. I shall defend a view of free speech that locates its value in its role as the servant of truth in the limited, but supremely important, sphere of justice or political morality. From this perspective, freedom of expression is an intrinsic feature of any genuine *constitutional* democracy, in which the power of the majority is constrained by the interests and aspirations of the minority, and where the legitimacy of state coercion depends in every case on its compatibility with a public scheme of just governance, presupposing the fundamental equality of citizens. There are both positive and negative aspects to this view of free speech, reflecting the perspectives of both speaker and listener, and marking the different roles of the citizen as active participant, on the one hand, and as recipient of the state's commands, on the other.

At the heart of freedom of speech, in its positive aspect, lies the citizen's right to participate, as a contributor to political debate, in the collective pursuit of justice. A constitutional guarantee of freedom of speech ensures his ability to assist in the operation and development of institutional arrangements that serve the common good, enabling all members of the community to pursue their various ends in reasonable harmony and co-operation. Since the requirements of justice are invariably contested, reflecting divergent conceptions of the common good, they cannot simply be imposed on selfish or recalcitrant individuals by a wise and benevolent ruler: in a

---

[1] H. L. A. Hart, *The Concept of Law* (Oxford, 1961) 187.
[2] Lon L. Fuller, *The Morality of Law*, revised edn. (New Haven, Conn., 1969) 185–6.

decent society, that acknowledges the equal dignity of all members of the community, the requirements of justice must be determined, and regularly reassessed, by means of well-informed reflection and debate. Freedom of speech serves the end of justice by denying government the ability to stifle moral and political discussion, especially where it concerns the merits of the current conduct of government or the legitimacy of the prevailing distribution of power.

In its negative aspect, the principle of freedom of speech curtails the state's authority to deprive someone of the information necessary to judge its coercive acts. Assertions of governmental authority are not self-validating, and the citizen is sometimes right to deny them, practising civil disobedience. The state may properly punish disobedience when its commands are just; but an autonomous citizen, capable of accepting responsibility for his actions, must ultimately make his own judgment about the truth of the state's claim to act justly. He cannot simply defer to another's interpretation of the scheme of justice that the constitution enshrines, when he has serious cause for doubt: 'There can be no legal or socially approved rendering of these principles that we are always morally bound to accept, not even when it is given by a supreme court or legislature.'[3] Freedom of speech is a necessary consequence of the view that 'a legitimate government is one whose authority citizens can recognise while still regarding themselves as equal, autonomous, rational agents'.[4] Freedoms of thought and conscience should be regarded as absolute—intrinsic components of human dignity—and communication between persons may not be restricted in a way that seriously impairs these fundamental freedoms.

Although this essay will focus mainly on the first or positive aspect of freedom of speech, each perspective is of crucial importance and they should be viewed as complementary.[5] My (qualified) duty to obey laws that I judge unjust is largely (though not wholly) dependent on my freedom to influence their content and interpretation, albeit often only marginally and indirectly. There must be a fundamental equality of citizenship, in the sense that each person is accorded equal opportunity to influence the course of political debate and collective action. As Ronald Dworkin explains the idea of democracy, as 'communal government by equals', each person 'must be offered a role that allows him to make a difference to the character of political decisions, and the force of his role—the magnitude of the difference he can make—must not be structurally fixed or limited by assumptions about his worth or talent or ability'.[6] It is only when freedoms of speech and conscience are secure that the law can be regarded as legitimate, in the critical sense that it can be intelligibly treated as *our* law—that of the community to which we belong and to which we owe duties of loyalty.

---

[3] John Rawls, *A Theory of Justice* (Oxford,1972) 390.

[4] T. Scanlon, 'A Theory of Freedom of Expression', in R. M. Dworkin (ed.), *The Philosophy of Law* (Oxford, 1977), at 161.

[5] For the 'negative' aspect, see Allan, 'Citizenship and Obligation: Civil Disobedience and Civil Dissent' [1996] CLJ 89.

[6] Ronald Dworkin, 'Equality, Democracy, and Constitution: We the People in Court' (1990) 28 Alberta LR 324, at 337–8.

In his essay, *On Liberty*, John Stuart Mill treated freedoms of thought and expression as preconditions of the advance of truth and understanding, which in turn promoted happiness and well-being by enabling people to reject traditional modes of life in favour of more satisfactory alternatives. Fuller objected, however, that Mill's essay proceeded on the basis of a false assumption by treating formal social arrangements, such as laws, customs, and institutions, as imposing limitations on personal freedom; whereas such formal arrangements actually provide the means of collaborative social effort, without which significant individual choice would be impossible: 'Our more important choices are meaningless if there is no way of carrying them over into the larger social order on which we are dependent for almost all our satisfactions. But, to give social effect to individual choice, some formal arrangement, some form of social order, is necessary.'[7] The implicit opposition between freedom and order was a false antithesis. A choice of lawmakers requires some machinery of election; but the form of election adopted will necessarily exclude alternative means of choice. A contract between two parties provides 'the most elementary form of social order by which individual choice can receive social effect': an agreement enables the individual to make his choice effective, but only at the cost of accepting obligations towards the other party.

The contrasting examples of social order provided by elections and contracts illuminate a useful distinction whose neglect was responsible, Fuller thought, for much confused discussion about freedom. Organization by 'common ends' was a fundamentally different form of social order from organization by 'reciprocity'. In the former case, of which the institution of governments is an example, the pursuit of freedom 'starts with the objective of assuring to its members the most meaningful possible participation in decisions affecting the aims of the organization and the methods to be used in realizing them'; the election of representatives and procedures of consultation are the natural means to this end. The reciprocity involved in the exchange of economic goods, by contrast, is secured by the operation of a free market—a type of freedom that cannot be obtained by majority vote or the delegation of authority to an economic planning agency. Fuller reminds us that some of the most important and complex forms of order have not been achieved by 'a single act of creation', but through 'the cumulative effect of countless purposive directions of human effort'. His examples include not only language, economic markets, and scientific theory, but the common law. The distinction between forms of social order is of significance in the present context because, in considering the importance of free speech to democratic government and politics, we are apt to overlook its equal importance to the common law.

Fuller's work not only emphasizes the intimate relationship between individual freedom and the various institutional forms that give it concrete content, but also contains a related theme relevant to the present discussion. Rejecting a purely instrumental view of social institutions and processes, he denied that their significance

---

[7] L. L. Fuller, 'Freedom—A Suggested Analysis' (1955) 68 Harv LR 1305, at 1312.

could be fully understood in terms of extrinsic or independent goals. He insisted on the interdependence of means and ends in the conduct of human affairs, arguing that our choice of institutions and procedures often reflects social values that lie beyond the attainment of immediate tasks or the fulfilment of specific functions.[8] Fuller not merely distinguished various modes of governance or decision-making, appropriate for different social tasks, but regarded them as expressing intrinsic moral values, just as he treated the concept of law itself as having an intrinsically moral character that was incompatible with certain kinds of injustice at the hands of the state.[9] We will attain a better understanding of the special value of freedom of speech, I shall argue, by reflection on the intrinsic value of common law adjudication as a mode of governance in accordance with the rule of law.

2. CONSTITUTIONAL DEMOCRACY AND THE COMMON LAW

Freedom of speech is often prized chiefly for its instrumental value in facilitating and enhancing representative democracy: its preservation enables citizens to participate in government by supporting or opposing political programmes and policies, and by choosing between candidates for election on the basis of adequate knowledge of their opinions and abilities. The standard view of democracy gives pride of place to political debate; and legal argument, concerning matters of legal analysis and interpretation, is treated as a very poor relation, concerned only with the largely technical process of giving loyal effect to the outcomes of the political process, duly embodied in authoritative legislation. It is in the wider political sphere that freedom of speech is all-important, giving citizens access to the public forum and enabling all interests to be represented in a manner that permits the legislative product to claim democratic legitimacy. The implementation of statute, however, is thought to *exclude* political argument (broadly understood) in favour of narrow textual analysis: justice consists in the consistent application of settled legal rules.

The sharp distinction between political debate, on the one hand, and legal interpretation, on the other, is widely regarded as a consequence of the separation of powers. It is, after all, a fundamental tenet of the rule of law that whereas legislation is intended to alter existing law, for whatever reasons may appeal to the legislators, judges should normally adhere to existing law in deciding particular cases, even when they would prefer to change it. Moreover, the legal and political spheres are often treated as radically different in purpose and character: whereas the former may be regarded as a 'forum of principle', in which the highest standards of consistency and rationality can be legitimately demanded, the latter is much less strictly constrained.[10] Politics is sometimes viewed as the arena for a battle of power and

---

[8]   See Kenneth Winston (ed.), *The Principles of Social Order* (Durham, N.C.,1981), 47–64, 249–63.
[9]   Lon L. Fuller, *The Morality of Law*, revised edn. (New Haven, Conn., 1969).
[10]   cf. Ronald Dworkin, *A Matter of Principle* (Oxford, 1985), ch. 2.

influence, where opposing interests and constituencies compete for dominance. These attitudes are, of course, closely related. If politics is properly to be understood in that way, it is particularly important that political discourse should be excluded, as far as possible, from the process of law: adjudication must be insulated from the clash of power and interest that would otherwise corrupt it. Judges and litigants must desist from recourse to the kind of argument that dominates the political arena: the legitimacy of adjudication depends on the maintenance of an impartiality or neutrality to which politics does not even aspire.

The inadequacy of the vision of the rule of law implicit in this account should, however, be as readily apparent to the common lawyer as the impoverished nature of its conception of democracy. Most starkly, its depiction of adjudication and legal analysis wholly neglects the common law. In treating law as primarily the product of the legislative process, it allocates an essentially subservient role to the judiciary by overlooking what in British legal tradition is the very foundation of civil and criminal justice—the common law. The common law is not the product of democratic procedures, in any ordinary sense of those words, yet it forms the chief source of legal values that together 'constitute' the polity, in lieu of any formal or codified constitution. As a corpus of rules of just conduct, primarily governing the relations between private citizens, the common law reflects the spontaneous order of society to which Fuller's notion of reciprocity refers. Since it was not posited in the manner of statute law, it is not the product of any legislative will: it provides and reflects an order of justice, rather than serving particular interests or even governmental ends. In so far as the common law consists of an order of justice independent of government or legislature, it may be regarded as potentially a constitutional barrier to the exercise of state power—as Coke famously viewed it as a bulwark against the attempted encroachments of James I.[11]

Moreover, even in regard to legislation the central role of interpretation, and therefore of competing conceptions of justice, is easily underrated. The truism that statutes should generally be strictly applied by the judges in accordance with their terms, even when their justice or wisdom is regarded as doubtful, neglects the more complex truth that such doubts often infect the reception of a statute's meaning. Since the authors of statutes have no means of resolving uncertainties of interpretation in advance—'ambiguities' revealed by specific instances whose complexities were unforeseen at the time of drafting or enactment—judges have no alternative but to look for reasonable solutions, not merely in the general purposes or policies an Act reveals, but by recourse to more enduring constitutional values, reflected or embodied in the common law. It is quintessentially the judicial task to interpret the law as a whole, ensuring the equal treatment of litigants according to some rational and consistent scheme of justice, albeit at some fairly high level of abstraction. No conception of law that merely emphasizes the faithful application of statutes, considered discretely one

---

[11] See F. A. Hayek, *Law, Legislation and Liberty* (London, 1982), especially vol.1, chs. 4 and 5; vol. 2, ch. 8.

by one, even remotely captures our more reflective understanding of the rule of law.[12]

As an order of social justice, the common law is clearly as dependent on freedom of speech as the democratic process. Although its architects are primarily judges rather than legislators, and are rightly insulated from the pressures of public opinion as it bears on particular cases, and immune from popular recall or ordinary democratic accountability, they are none the less highly visible participants in the moral debate whose health and vigour provide the chief rationale for freedom of speech. It is precisely its capacity for development in response to altered perceptions of justice and enlarged moral insight that gives the common law its special value as a constitutional framework. That capacity crucially depends on the power of moral and political discourse in society at large, so that both judges and litigants are well informed and better equipped both to identify, and then resolve, the questions of justice raised by legal disputes. No quantity of statutes, however large, can settle in advance all the intricate questions of morality and justice that a constantly changing society continuously generates. There is no practical alternative to judicial deliberation, focused on the peculiarities of particular cases, for the satisfactory reconciliation of the numerous moral imperatives that demand accommodation; and the special emphasis of the common law on reasoned argument and elaborate judgments, tailored to the arguments presented, enables it to make a crucial contribution to an effective and attractive moral discourse.

In many respects, moreover, common law adjudication is superior to the legislative process as a means of resolving questions of justice, even when the latter is accompanied by wide consultation to ascertain public opinion and preceded by vigorous political debate. In highly sensitive matters, where moral and ethical opinions are most personal and deeply divided, legislation may be hard to formulate in generally acceptable terms; and a negotiated compromise is likely to produce radically inconsistent results in the various marginal cases. The common law method of reasoning by analogy, where the appropriateness of the suggested analogy is always a matter for closely reasoned argument, may often provide a more sensitive and generally satisfactory mode of decision-making, better able than statute to accommodate all the complex and critical features of specific cases. Fuller was careful to warn that each form of social order possessed its own virtues and defects: none was entitled to claim overall superiority.[13] Moreover, the differences between 'made' and 'implicit' law were ultimately ones of degree, each containing elements of the other. None the less, Fuller warned that in some situations reliance on reciprocity was the safest form of social order: 'Legislative fiat is at least as capable of destroying order as it is of creating it.'[14]

Reflection on the foundational role of the common law, and the freedom of moral

---

[12] cf. Ronald Dworkin, *Law's Empire* (London, 1986).
[13] Lon L. Fuller, *Anatomy of the Law* (London, 1968), Part 2.
[14] Fuller, 'Freedom—A Suggested Analysis' 68 Harv LR 1305, at 1322.

debate on which its healthy evolution depends, can help to resolve a paradox inherent in an exclusive focus on the political domain. If freedom of speech exists chiefly to enhance the democratic process, helping to ensure that the preferences of the majority are accurately ascertained and embodied in legislation, it is not clear why it should be granted any special constitutional protection if the majority are clearly in favour of its suppression. Why should they not have freedom to decide that the public good would be enhanced by the prohibition of certain kinds of discussion, even involving matters of justice? Such a power of censorship may even be thought compatible with British democracy, under a constitution in which parliamentary sovereignty is regarded as absolute and even judicial review of the legality of acts of the executive is justified on the basis of (at least notional) legislative intent.[15] If parliamentary sovereignty is thought to rest ultimately on popular sovereignty, it reinforces the conclusion that any special constitutional protection of speech would be illegitimate.[16] Where Parliament exercises an unfettered legislative power, there can be no effective appeal to constitutional values that a legislative majority is determined to override or reject, and therefore no special role for political speech beyond that acceptable to the current majority.

The paradox can be resolved by rejecting the conception of democracy on which it depends, as well as by achieving a better understanding of the ideal of the rule of law, which underpins the constitutional role of the common law. Once again, Fuller proves a useful guide. He insisted that the virtue of democracy lay not 'in the mere fact that a numerical majority controls at election time', but rather 'in the forces which are permitted to play upon the electorate'.[17] It was only in a constitutional democracy that ideas could flourish according to their intrinsic merit rather than in virtue of their utility for enabling those in office to retain control—mere weapons in a struggle for power. Denouncing conceptions of democracy rooted in moral and intellectual scepticism, which treat majority rule as a necessary substitute for government based on commitments to justice and reason, Fuller insisted on the crucial role of ideas. Reason was essential to the proper development and operation of legal and social institutions, and especially to the health and expansion of autonomous order: 'Some minimum faith in ideas is necessary to give practical significance to the doctrine of free speech and free thought.' From this perspective, democracy is in an important sense dependent on, or even partly constituted by, unimpeded freedom of speech; and judicial protection of the citizen's power to participate in political debate and criticism may be thought not only compatible with British constitutionalism, in its contemporary form, but ultimately critical to its survival.

We should, then, view democracy as a means for the collective pursuit of justice, enabling conflicts of interest to be resolved primarily on grounds of right rather than power or influence. Democratic deliberation should appeal to moral principles that

---

[15]　See e.g. Christopher Forsyth, 'Of Fig Leaves and Fairy Tales: The Ultra Vires Doctrine, The Sovereignty of Parliament and Judicial Review' [1996] CLJ 122.

[16]　cf. Frederick Schauer, *Free Speech: A Philosophical Enquiry* (Cambridge, 1982) 40–4.

[17]　L .L. Fuller, *The Law in Quest of Itself* (Boston, 1966) 123.

facilitate agreement among people who seek the common good, instead of narrow self-interest, in order that the results can be accepted by everyone as amounting to a reasonable accommodation that treats all citizens as equally entitled to concern and respect. Members of Parliament must be understood as having as their principal obligation the duty to fight for justice and a coherent conception of the public good, as opposed to being merely, or largely, the servants of their constituents' or their parties' interests, more narrowly interpreted.[18] Amy Gutmann and Dennis Thompson have elaborated a conception of deliberative democracy by development of John Rawls's principle of 'reciprocity', that requires an order of society amounting to a fair scheme of co-operation between citizens, allowing each to pursue his own ends under conditions that all can reasonably be expected to accept.[19] In their account, democracy consists chiefly in the facilitation of debate over questions of justice, in which people are encouraged to appeal to reasons or principles that their fellow citizens can be expected to share; and where empirical claims are duly consistent with reliable and generally accepted methods of inquiry: 'Deliberation promotes an economy of moral disagreement in which citizens manifest mutual respect as they continue to disagree about morally important issues in politics.'[20]

3. DELIBERATIVE DEMOCRACY AND THE RULE OF LAW

The critical role of freedom of speech, in relation to moral and political discourse, is clearly apparent in the context of the ideal of deliberative democracy. In its essentials, however, that ideal closely corresponds to the overriding constitutional principle of the rule of law. Properly understood, the rule of law entails a requirement of justification for coercive acts of government, whereby every specific interference with individual liberty can be shown to be truly consistent with the general principles of law and justice applicable to everyone. Democracy and the rule of law rest alike on an abstract, but fundamental, notion of equality. The equal status of citizens that justifies universal adult suffrage, equal rights of political expression and equal opportunities to stand for public office, also entails a form of equality before the law that excludes arbitrary discrimination in every sphere of interaction between citizen and state. Interpreted as a principle of constitutionalism, the rule of law requires, not merely formal equality or the absence of arbitrary immunities and dispensations for privileged persons, but a *constitutional* equality, giving substance to the ideal of equal citizenship.[21]

The dissimilar treatment of different persons or classes of persons is not forbidden; but all legislative and administrative classifications and distinctions must be

---

[18] cf. F. A. Hayek, *Law, Legislation and Liberty*, vol. 1, ch. 6; vol. 3, ch. 13.
[19] John Rawls, *Political Liberalism* (New York,1993) 16.
[20] Amy Gutmann and Dennis Thompson, *Democracy and Disagreement* (1996) p.43.
[21] See Allan, 'The Rule of Law as the Rule of Reason: Consent and Constitutionalism' (1999) 115 LQR 221.

properly related to legitimate public purposes. Arbitrariness is excluded by insisting that all forms of discrimination be capable of reasoned justification, according to some coherent conception of justice and the public good that is itself open to public scrutiny and criticism. Equality is ensured by the generality of the laws; and departures from such generality, although inevitable in practice, must be appropriately justified. No legislature in a genuine constitutional democracy, for example, could enact a valid act of attainder, inflicting punishment on specified individuals without judicial trial: such statutes are forms of victimization that flout the ideal of equality inherent in the rule of law.[22] Any purported justification for such a measure would inevitably deny the equal status or dignity of citizens, just as a proposal to limit the franchise to a favoured section of the population would necessarily do so.

Freedom of speech is therefore as much an integral requirement of the rule of law as of democratic governance: it fulfils largely the same role under each ideal. It makes no sense to insist that the laws should be capable of justification in accordance with an intelligible conception of the public good, and that that conception itself be the subject of open critical public appraisal, unless there is freedom to exchange information and ideas relating to the content of the laws and the conduct of government. Freedoms of speech, conscience and association are all intrinsic to the constitutional interpretation of the rule of law: they protect and foster rational criticism of government and support the requirement that laws should be morally justifiable, consistent with justice and the common good. The rule of law may itself be viewed as equivalent to a form of deliberative democracy, in which both politics and the legal process serve the requirements of justice.

When the rule of law is understood as essentially the rule of reason, the special nature of the common law as constitutional foundation becomes clear. For the common law itself is first and foremost a body of reason, reflecting the accumulated wisdom born of the practical experience of regulating social and economic relations, and vulnerable to amendment and reformulation in response to reasoned argument, conducted in the light of changing circumstances. It is a striking feature of common law adjudication, as Fuller observed, that the rule applied to a case and the reason or justification for the rule are often so intertwined in the court's opinion that it is difficult to distinguish between them.[23] It is, of course, that dependence of the rule on its explicit justification that affords courts in subsequent cases the flexibility required for an evolving order of governance: the rule can be modified or distinguished as the context for its application changes. As the force of the reasons for the rule declines, in the light of altered circumstances, so the rule itself can be adjusted accordingly. In that way the judges can keep faith, to the appropriate degree, with the underlying principles—principles whose interpretation is always open to moral argument and public criticism.

Freedom of speech is therefore fundamental to the integrity of the common law:

---

[22] ibid., 234–5. See further Allan, *Law, Liberty, and Justice* (Oxford, 1993) 68–78.
[23] Fuller, *Anatomy of the Law* 127–30.

it could not evolve to meet altered perceptions of justice, or be adapted to the needs of novel circumstances, if moral and political debate were restricted within society at large. The common law is ultimately the common morality, in the sense that it provides the basis for legitimate forms of interaction between citizens and between citizens and government; and its content must therefore reflect widely shared conceptions of justice and right. Its dependence on reasoned deliberation enables it to make the rule of law effective in practice by forcing both citizens and government officials to justify their actions, when challenged on reasonable grounds. No official can escape scrutiny merely by reliance on a settled rule that purports to provide justification, since its proper interpretation is always open to judicial review even when its authority and provenance are clearly established. Legal argument cannot be neatly severed from the moral or political discourse from which it derives necessary sustenance. The distinction between the two modes of discourse is only one of degree; and the point of intersection or division can only be ascertained, from case to case, by reflection on the fundamental ideas and values that inform the polity, viewed as a whole.

It is not sufficient, then, that there be open channels of political communication for the exchange of views and information; there must be equal access to the courts, in which each citizen's ability to defend his legal rights is preserved. The litigant's right to address an independent court, in order to enforce the scheme of justice that enjoys constitutional authority, is itself an aspect of freedom of speech. His access to the court is the counterpart, in the legal system, of his participation in government, enabling him to seek enforcement of what he considers to be the most reasonable understanding of existing law. It is clearly as important that government officials should be made answerable to the litigant in this way as that other citizens should be. Since the rule of law, properly understood, makes the validity of governmental acts and decisions dependent on their compliance with some general scheme of principle, capable of consistent and intelligible defence, they must be susceptible of challenge before independent courts, able to judge whether or not the appropriate standards of justification are satisfied.

The core of freedom of speech, in a constitutional democracy, is the liberty to argue in favour of a specific conception of justice, or more concretely, in support of the particular decisions or arrangements that conception requires. At the political level, it encompasses the freedom to speak in defence of any principle or policy that is consistent with the constitution, or even in favour of constitutional amendment (in the case of a 'written' constitution limiting the powers of the organs of government). In particular cases, which must be determined by existing law, freedom of speech is secured for those directly affected by the principles of natural justice: a person must be free to argue, not merely in support of a view of the relevant facts of his case, but in favour of a specific interpretation of the law that officials or judges are bound to apply. Taken together, legal and political arrangements should secure a fair distribution of influence over official decisions. Whereas legislators are encouraged to listen to anyone whose advocacy can illuminate the general questions of justice that they must resolve, courts and officials are required to attend chiefly to those who can provide information relevant to an application of existing rules, or whose particular circumstances raise new questions about what those rules should be understood to require.

It would be wrong to press the analogy between legal and political discourse too far, or to deny the fundamental distinction between legislation and adjudication. Legal analysis is rightly subject to important constraints of authority and strict rationality that do not apply in politics; no one thinks that a legislator should be bound by precedent in the manner of a court. None the less, the overriding goal of justice imposes similar duties on both judge and legislator: each must acknowledge obligations of consistency based on the responsibility to secure justice for all citizens, according to some coherent account of what that requires in practice. A republican ideal of politics, wherein all strive to articulate and further a conception of the common good, prohibits discriminatory treatment of unpopular minorities or any other form of arbitrary state action, inconsistent with the equal status of persons. It does not follow that legislative supremacy must be wholly rejected: Parliament may well be thought the best judge, in most cases, of what justice truly requires. No plausible interpretation of constitutional justice could embrace absolute supremacy, however: legislation that denied an individual or a minority basic rights or protections accorded to others, without good reason, would inevitably contradict the basic premise of legal equality.

Both the manner in which freedom of speech primarily serves the interests of justice, and the related connection between legal and political forums, are illuminated by reflection on a recent decision of the House of Lords, upholding a prisoner's right of access to a journalist in order to publicize his claim to have been wrongly convicted. In *R v Secretary of State for the Home Department, ex p Simms*, the court held that the prison authorities had acted unlawfully in imposing a ban on oral interviews between a prisoner and a journalist, the latter having declined to give an undertaking not to publish the results.[24] The right to speak directly to a journalist, willing to investigate the safety of the prisoner's conviction, enforced a fundamental common law value. Freedom of speech enabled the prisoner to challenge the basis of his detention and so took priority over the penal consequences of his sentence: it was 'not easy to conceive of a more important function which free speech might fulfil'.[25] The relevant rules had therefore to be construed consistently with the prisoner's 'fundamental or basic right'.

Freedom of speech, in the sense of access to the press and consequent publicity, served the administration of justice by enlisting the resources of the media in an effort to activate formal legal channels of redress. The powers of both the Home Secretary and the Criminal Cases Review Commission to refer a case back to the Court of Appeal were available in the event of a suspected miscarriage of justice; but new evidence was normally required to stimulate the exercise of such powers, and

---

[24] [1999] 3 All ER 400.   [25] ibid., at 408 (Lord Steyn).

only investigative journalism, backed by the necessary resources, was in practice likely to generate new evidence. The analogy between the prisoner's rights of natural justice, or right to a fair trial, and his more general right of free speech is clear: he invokes the latter in the present case in order to further precisely the same interests as the former are intended to protect. His appeal to the public forum has the same character as the exercise of his rights of natural justice or due process within the system of criminal justice: freedom of speech enjoys its special weight in virtue of its purpose in facilitating the attainment of justice.

4. ADVERSARIAL ADJUDICATION AND PROCEDURAL FAIRNESS

The critical role of reason in matters of government and political affairs, when democracy is practised in ways that are consonant with its genuine value, underlies a further aspect of the analogy between legal argument and political debate, illuminated by Fuller's influential writing on law and adjudication. According to Fuller, the 'distinguishing characteristic' of adjudication was its conferring 'on the affected party a peculiar form of participation in the decision, that of presenting proofs and reasoned arguments for a decision in his favour'.[26] Adjudication was concerned with questions of legal right precisely because of its intrinsic dependence on reasoned argument, reflecting the nature of the litigant's participation. A litigant can make a rational appeal for a specific decision only by invoking some general principle; and 'a demand supported by a principle is the same thing as a claim of right'. Fuller's warning that adjudication was not an appropriate method of resolving certain kinds of problem—principally, those that he described as 'polycentric', involving many interconnected and interdependent variables—also reflected his view of the principal characteristic of this form of decision-making. Questions that cannot be reduced to matters of right or general principle cannot be determined by resort to proofs and legal argument, but require a more open-ended and wide-ranging mode of treatment. By the same token, the pivotal role of the litigant is undermined: whatever weakens or destroys the meaning of a litigant's participation in the process destroys the integrity of adjudication itself.

By emphasizing the central importance of the litigant's participation, Fuller's analysis reminds us of the way in which adversarial adjudication, as practised in common law countries, supplements democratic procedures by allowing the parties to shape legal proceedings according to their own needs and convictions. The court must respond to the arguments offered by the parties, rather than making its own independent inquiry into the dispute. The 'peculiarly urgent demand of rationality' that the legal process must be able to satisfy therefore supports a system of deliberative democracy by obliging the state to answer the most pressing complaints of injustice, as they affect the circumstances of individuals. Demands for justification of acts

---

[26] Lon L. Fuller, 'The Forms and Limits of Adjudication' (1978) 92 Harv LR 353, at 364.

and decisions that may receive inadequate answers in the political arena, where innumerable claims and appeals have to be reconciled and compromise may be inescapable, can be reiterated in court, where the most intractable questions of principle must finally be confronted and, at least temporarily, resolved. Even if a litigant's case is held to be incompatible with enactments or administrative orders that satisfy appropriate tests of fairness and rationality, he obtains a fully considered answer to the question of justice it raises: the limit of the authority of statutes or executive decisions is itself necessarily a question of justice that, in the last analysis, depends on interpretation of the basic values and governing principles of the constitution.

It may be objected that the proposed analogy between legal argument and political debate overlooks the mainly strategic and self-serving nature of the former: whereas political discourse is concerned with what justice demands for everyone, legal argument relates to the particular case and focuses principally on the settled rights of the litigants alone. Questions of existing law, however, are always also questions of political morality since the choice between conflicting answers, if it is rational, will inevitably reflect competing conceptions of justice, albeit within a limited range of possible legal interpretations. Fuller rejected legal positivism on the grounds that its insistence on the distinction between the law as it is and the law as it should be betrayed an impractical detachment from the complexities of legal practice. A litigant's claim in court is always an appeal to the requirements of justice: he defends what he considers the most reasonable interpretation of a rule or principle, when set in the context of the general values of the legal system and the polity of which it is part. Necessarily, moreover, he pleads the cause of all those persons who constitute the class or category with which he aligns himself for purposes of the claim—those whose circumstances are sufficiently similar to his own to make them participants by proxy. His case succeeds or falls with theirs.

It is true that the litigant's scope for appeal to ultimate constitutional values will depend on the nature of his dispute; in most cases the pertinent legal issues can be resolved without recourse to abstract principles whose interpretation would invite prolonged and sometimes profound disagreement. However, the moral dimension to legal argument is irreducible: even 'technical' resolutions of legal claims, on the basis of consistency with statute or precedent at a fairly mundane level of analysis, assume the appropriateness in the context of that mode of decision; and its appropriateness can always be questioned when a plausible case can be made on relevant constitutional grounds. It is always the insistent demands of justice, if only in the guise of principled consistency, that guide the constant evolution of the common law, enabling it to meet new conditions and satisfy changing social expectations. Speech, therefore, fulfils essentially the same function in both legal argument and political debate. However selfish the *motives* of the participants may be, their *arguments* must take the form of an appeal to some intelligible conception of justice or the common good; and, in any decent democracy, an advocate's success, in either legal or political forum, should depend, primarily at least, on the moral and intellectual strength of his case. It is, then, the role of reason—which Fuller sought to defend from a debilitating cynicism that attributed every idea to some undisclosed personal motive—that unites legal and political discourse, when constitutional democracy achieves it basic aspirations for decent government.

The fundamental nature of the analogy between legal and political discourse can only be fully appreciated, however, by recognizing the intrinsic, as opposed to merely instrumental, value of freedom of speech. If, as D. J. Galligan argues, the primary object of the litigant's participation is to ensure the provision of information about the case that might otherwise be unavailable, adversarial adjudication has no intrinsic merit that its inquisitorial counterpart lacks; and Fuller's attachment to the common law model of adjudication was narrowly provincial.[27] If the value of natural justice or due process is only instrumental, intended to facilitate the accurate treatment of persons according to authoritative legal standards, then it is misleading to stress the initiative retained by litigants, as regards the detailed nature of their proceedings, as characteristic of adjudication in its pure form. However, there are good reasons for resisting a purely instrumental view of natural justice: the central role accorded the litigant's participation by adjudication, in its traditional common law form, gives the proceedings an intrinsic moral value akin to that of democracy itself.

The purpose of adjudication, as conducted at common law, is not merely to resolve disputes but to *justify* the result to the parties, in accordance with whatever conception of justice the legal and constitutional order embodies. In the case of judicial review of the acts and decisions of state officials, adversarial adjudication meets as closely as possible the demand of the rule of law that such acts and decisions should be justified in terms of an intelligible and consistent conception of the common good. The initiative exercised by the litigants in framing the nature of their dispute enables them to elicit reasons for decision that reflect their particular concerns, sensitive to their own interpretation of the law and the constitution; and, since the parties appeal to the same constitution, whose basic values each may normally be taken to share, even if they favour widely different interpretations in particular instances, there are the strongest moral reasons for acceptance of the decision. Adversarial adjudication places the parties on an equal footing, even where the citizen challenges the action of the state: his responsibility for formulating the nature of his complaint gives him both the power to invoke constitutional fundamentals, according to his own understanding of their tenor, and a basis for acknowledging the outcome as legitimate. Where he has submitted his grievance to an independent and impartial authority, required to respond to the specific arguments he presents, it would normally be wrong to repudiate the decision: his participation, being appropriately guaranteed, provides the grounds of his moral obligation to accept the result as binding.

The analogy between democratic government and the principles of natural justice is ultimately related to a conception of legal obligation, implicit in the ideal of the

---

[27] D. J. Galligan, *Due Process and Fair Procedures: A Study of Administrative Procedures* (Oxford, 1996) 243–6.

rule of law. Inherent in the requirement that laws should be justified in accordance with a coherent vision of the common good, consistently applied, is the assertion of an associated claim to moral authority: legal obligation must be understood as a species of moral obligation that a citizen can freely acknowledge without surrender of his powers of independent moral scrutiny.[28] The binding quality of the decision of a court or tribunal that has met the requirements of natural justice may be compared with the moral authority of a statute, enacted in accordance with a democratic procedure. The chief virtue of democracy is that it affords the opportunity for everyone to participate in the process of law-making; and that opportunity gives reason for all to accept the outcome, at least within reasonable limits.[29] Where opposing views can be freely voiced and heard, and all can vote on the basis of full information about rival candidates for office and their attitudes to questions of justice, there are strong (though not, of course, conclusive) moral grounds for obedience to the laws duly enacted. In a morally divided community, only some form of deliberative democracy can generate legitimate answers to questions of justice, worthy of general acceptance. It is only within a constitutional framework that meets the requirements of the rule of law, permitting vigorous and unimpeded public debate about the requirements of justice, that we can justifiably speak of government by consent. The existence of free elections alone is plainly inadequate.

5. FREE SPEECH AND FAIR TRIAL

If freedom of speech is chiefly valued for its role in securing justice, in a form acceptable to the members of a morally pluralist community, it will rarely constitute an intelligible ground for tolerating conduct likely to impede that overriding imperative. Justice can be attained only when both political and legal processes operate fairly and effectively. The common law rules of contempt of court are therefore generally legitimate restrictions on forms of communication that, by interfering with the administration of justice, would undermine the principal grounds of freedom of speech. It is not merely that encroachments on press freedom and public comment are permissible: they are sometimes required by the prior claims of justice. Publications that present a serious risk of endangering the fairness of a trial, by intimidating or prejudicing witnesses or jurors, should generally be prohibited. There is usually no public interest or redeeming value in the dissemination of material that substantially diminishes the chances of a civil or criminal trial being conducted fairly and impartially: in the absence of special literary or artistic value, such a publication derives no protection from the principle of freedom of speech, which in such circumstances has little or no weight.

---

[28] See Allan, 'Citizenship and Obligation: Civil Disobedience and Civil Dissent' [1996] CLJ 89, at 92–104.
[29] See Allan, 'Procedural Fairness and the Duty of Respect' (1998) 18 OJLS 497, at 507–10.

Accordingly, what may at first appear to be a conflict between equally fundamental principles of free speech and fair trial will often dissolve, on closer analysis. There is generally scope for the balancing of principles—weighing freedom of speech against the needs of the administration of justice—only where the risk to a trial is uncertain or remote. If the risk is real, and cannot be overcome by making reasonable adjustments to the mode or place of trial, temporary and narrowly defined restrictions on public discussion are entirely consistent with constitutional principle. There is, of course, a strong public interest that the conduct of trials and the treatment of litigants should be open to continuous public scrutiny. The public nature of a trial may help to guarantee that the participants will be treated fairly in accordance with the law, reasonably interpreted and strictly applied. The fairness and effectiveness of the administration of justice in general should also be readily susceptible of analysis and criticism. Since such scrutiny and criticism are intended to facilitate the attainment of justice, however, its purpose would be largely defeated if discussion of current proceedings in particular cases, or premature public disclosure of relevant materials, were allowed to undermine the fairness of trials.

In so far as the jurisprudence of the European Court of Human Rights suggests that the principle of freedom of speech has some intrinsic priority, even in cases where restrictions would safeguard the fairness of a trial, it must be subject to serious question.[30] If there is truly a difference between the law of the Convention and the common law approach, the latter is surely to be preferred.[31] The cogency and weight of the principle of free speech always depends on the context in which it is invoked: it cannot be treated as presumptively overriding, when reasons of justice argue against it, without undermining its most reasonable basis in the constitutional fabric of a free society. It is not merely that the principle of freedom of speech is overridden, but rather that its triumph, at the expense of the fairness of legal proceedings, would constitute a deep contradiction within the theory that provides its most plausible justification. (Any preference for the conclusions reached by the European Court over those of the House of Lords, in the *Sunday Times* (thalidomide) case, may be readily attributed to the weakness of the British judges' reasoning, as it applied to the circumstances of the particular case: the relevant publication posed no genuine threat to the administration of justice or the authority of the judiciary.)[32]

Since the principle of freedom of speech ultimately derives from an abstract conception of equality, or equal dignity, that underlies our commitments to both democracy and the rule of law (or so I have argued), its compass and weight are necessarily limited by other dimensions of that abstract ideal. We cannot legitimately sanction departures from equality, thus defined, any more than we can dispense with the rule of law for reasons of competing public interest. (Unjustified inequalities entail breaches of the rule of law.) The ideal of equality, however, imposes require-

---

[30]   See *The Sunday Times v United Kingdom* (1979) 2 EHRR 245, para. 65.
[31]   See *Attorney-General v BBC* [1980] 3 All ER 161, 176 (Lord Fraser).
[32]   See Eric Barendt, *Freedom of Speech* (Oxford, 1985), 229–35.

ments of equal access to the administration of justice and equal protection from prejudicial publicity and improper influence. In that sense, the rule of law invests the litigant with an absolute right to a fair trial. That does not mean that every trial must take place under perfect conditions; but it does mean that no court can properly conduct what, by comparison with the normal treatment of other litigants in similar cases, it regards as unfair proceedings. Any attempt to balance the litigant's right to a fair trial against a general, undifferentiated interest in freedom of speech, where the effect is to sacrifice justice in the particular case, is a denial of the rule of law that cannot be accepted in a free society.

These conclusions are confirmed by reflection on the proceedings in both House of Lords and European Court of Human Rights relating to Thompson and Venables, two children convicted of murder. A majority of the House of Lords held that the Home Secretary had acted unlawfully in giving weight to various communications from members of the public regarding the appropriate length of the boys' detention.[33] In fixing a 'tariff' to reflect the requirements of retribution and deterrence, the minister was performing a judicial function and should therefore act judicially, ignoring public clamour. Despite the difficulty of reconciling this view with any principle of unqualified parliamentary sovereignty, as the speeches of Lord Browne-Wilkinson and Lord Lloyd make clear, it is none the less justified by other considerations of constitutional propriety. From the perspective of the rule of law, one cannot dissent from Lord Steyn's opinion that Parliament should be taken to have entrusted the relevant power to the Home Secretary on the basis that he 'would not act contrary to fundamental principles governing the administration of justice'. We should notice, however, that the conclusion entails a limited and justified curtailment of freedom of speech. Since the purpose of the relevant communications was clearly to persuade the minister to impose a lengthy tariff sentence, his duty to ignore them rendered them ineffective and futile.

A further dimension of the relationship between values of free speech and those underlying the administration of justice is illustrated by the decision of the European Court of Human Rights, holding that the defendants had been denied a fair trial.[34] The court decided that when the public nature of a criminal trial jeopardizes its fairness, by seriously intimidating a child witness, it was right to impose suitable restrictions on access by both the public and the press. Accordingly, the case provides an example of legitimate restrictions on both positive and negative aspects of freedom of speech—rights to influence the treatment of the defendants and rights to information about the details of the criminal proceedings. Recognition of the overriding claims of the administration of justice was, however, quite consistent with the underlying grounds of the principle of freedom of speech. When public opinion is permitted to determine, or influence, the punishment of a particular defendant, who has provoked public outrage and incurred public hostility, or when unfettered access to

---

[33] *R v Secretary of State for the Home Dept., ex p Thompson and Venables* [1997] 3 All ER 97.
[34] *T v United Kingdom* (ECHR, 16 December 1999).

his trial undermines its fairness, the primary purposes of freedom of speech are jeopardised, rather than promoted. When the principle of freedom of expression is understood to reflect the sovereign virtue of justice, the apparent conflict between the values of free speech and fair trial is substantially dissolved.

These conclusions confirm the truth of Fuller's insight, concerning the dependence of freedom on the existence of effective social arrangements, rejecting any fundamental opposition between individual liberty and formally constituted legal order. The restrictions on forms of communication that serve to maintain the integrity of legal proceedings ultimately reflect the ideal of equality that informs the rule of law: they ensure that general principles of justice are fairly and accurately applied to particular cases, insulating the process of reasoned deliberation from extraneous influences that would otherwise corrupt it. The legitimacy of restrictions on speech, then, must always be judged in the light of our primary commitment to constitutional justice. The unfair treatment of individuals, as a result of the pressure of public opinion or the premature revelation of prejudicial information, constitutes a violation of the rule of law and, accordingly, a denial of the fundamental premise of freedom of speech.

2

Freedom of Speech and Representative Government

LESLIE ZINES

In recent decades similar issues of freedom of speech, expression or communication have come before the courts of several countries. The issues have arisen in the context of applying the provisions of constitutions or international conventions and common law principles. The courts include those of the United States, Britain, Canada, Germany, India, Australia, New Zealand and the European Court of Human Rights. In all these cases the courts have accepted that special regard should be had to freedom of communication on matters pertaining to politics and government which, in the words of the European Court of Human Rights, 'is at the very core of the concept of a democratic society'.[1] I shall be referring to only some of these jurisdictions.

1. THE UNITED STATES

The oldest and richest source of experience in matters of freedom of speech is contained in the decisions of the Supreme Court of the United States interpreting the First Amendment and its implied incorporation into the Fourteenth Amendment. Many of those decisions have both attracted and repelled the courts of other countries and commentators in the United States and elsewhere.

The American guarantee is not confined to ensuring sound representative government or democracy in general. That is also true of similar provisions in the constitutions of Canada and Germany, in the human rights legislation of Britain and New Zealand and in the European Convention. Some theories of interpretation of constitutional rights in the United States, such as those of Meikeljohn, Ely and Sunstein, however, would treat the concept of representative government as the prime criterion for construing and applying rights provisions.[2]

The famous footnote four of the otherwise unremarkable case of *United States v Carolene Products Co.*[3] raised the question whether legislation which restricted political processes was to be subject to 'more exacting judicial scrutiny' than other

---

[1] *Handyside v United Kingdom* [1976] 1 EHRR 737, para. 42.

[2] Tucker, 'Representation—Reinforcing Review' in Campbell and Sadurski, *Freedom of Communication* (1994) ch. 8; Meikeljohn, *Free Speech and its Relation to Self Government* (1948); Ely, *Democracy and Dissent* (1980); Sunstein, 'Free Speech Now' in Stone, Epstein and Sunstein (eds.) *The Bill of Rights in the Modern State* (1992).

[3] 304 US 144 (1938).

types of legislation. The heavy emphasis given to the presumption of constitutionality and deference to legislative judgment by the Supreme Court after 1937 rested, in part, on the democratic character of the other arms of government. That reasoning was inapplicable if the democratic process itself was impaired. Freedom of speech was seen as central to that process, although it was never accepted that the guarantee was limited to that purpose. Freedom of the press, speech, and religion guaranteed by the First Amendment was given a 'preferred position' by the judges of the Roosevelt Court on the ground that it was at the heart of free government.[4]

Although one does not hear much in recent times of a 'preferred position', the Court in establishing a hierarchy of speech protection has been most protective of messages concerned with politics or government administration. It has protected a great deal of such communication from legislative and executive interference, but in doing so it has not revealed any underlying coherent theory. If, as the Court has suggested, the maintenance and enhancement of representative democracy is an important constitutional value, it is argued that the Court has not had sufficient regard to the social and economic framework to achieve that object. Much of the criticism of scholars such as Sunstein and, earlier, of Ely is concerned with that aspect. Outside the United States that sort of criticism has been quite familiar.[5] It is further argued that a number of the decisions reveal an attitude to society and to government that is peculiar to the United States or, at any rate, is different from social and political perceptions in some other countries. Basically it is a distrust of governmental power and a comparatively benign acceptance of corporate power in this area.

The most controversial decisions that have given rise to the criticism include those holding invalid the following:

(a) The prohibition of 'hate speech' and racist propaganda.[6]

(b) Provision of access rights to broadcasting.[7]

(c) A statutory right of reply to attacks and criticism made in newspapers, even where the newspaper has a monopoly in an electoral district and the plaintiff was a candidate for election not supported by a newspaper.[8] The Court admitted that the plaintiff could not effectively answer the criticism and allegations without access to the newspaper, yet the legislation was held invalid because it interfered with the freedom of speech of the editor.

---

[4] *Murdoch v Pennsylvania* 319 US 105 (1943).

[5] Barendt, 'Importing United States Free Speech Jurisprudence' in Campbell and Sadurski, *Freedom of Communication*, ch. 8; Barendt, 'Free Speech in Australia: A Comparative Perspective' (1994) 16 Syd Law Rev 149.

[6] *Collin v Smith* 578 F 2d 1197 (1978). See Feldman, 'Content Neutrality' in Loveland (ed.) *Importing the First Amendment*, ch. 8.

[7] *CBS v Democratic National Committee* 412 US 94 (1973).

[8] *Miami Herald v Tornello* 418 US 241 (1974).

(d) Legislation placing limits on campaign expenditure. This was regarded as interfering with the right of wealthy persons to communicate a message and gain political office.[9]

The case that courts in many other common law countries have examined, and which has provided fascination if not agreement, is *New York Times v Sullivan*[10] where it was held that the First Amendment protected false and defamatory speech critical of official conduct unless the plaintiff could prove that the defendant knew that the statement was false or acted with reckless disregard of its truth or falsity. The Court said that the Amendment required debate on public issues to be uninhibited and robust, and might include vehement, caustic and unpleasantly sharp attacks on government and governmental officials. The Court accepted that civil action could have a 'chilling effect' on free speech at least equal to that which could occur by threat of criminal prosecution.

The principle behind this decision requiring the reshaping of defamation law in the interest of representative government came to be accepted in a number of other countries, but none exactly followed the resolution of the issue in the *Sullivan* case.

2. CANADA

The rights set out in the United States Constitution are stated in unqualified terms, yet it is recognized that they are qualified to an uncertain degree in the face of an important social interest, where some 'balancing' has to occur. The Canadian Charter of Rights and Freedoms, on the other hand, has one general limitation clause, which is in s. 1, and provides that the rights and freedoms 'are subject only to such reasonable limits prescribed by law as can be demonstrably justified in a free and democratic society'.

This is intended as the source the judges can use to work out the necessary modifications of the enunciated rights and freedoms, which include, in s. 2(b), 'freedom of thought, belief, opinion and expression, including freedom of the press and other media of communication'. As in the United States, the Canadian Supreme Court has emphasized the special importance of freedom of expression to democratic government.

In Canada there were in fact a number of judicial statements that suggested, long before the Charter was enacted, that freedom of speech was a necessary incident of representative government, which was implied in the British North America Act 1867 (BNA Act). These pronouncements were affirmed after the Charter came into existence and they were to have an effect on the decisions of the High Court of Australia in the 1990s.

---

[9] *Buckley v Valeo* 424 US 1 (1976). See also *Citizens Against Rent Control v Berkeley* 454 US 290 (1981), relating to contributions to referendum committees and *FEC v National Conservative Political Action Committee* 470 US 480 (1985) regarding expenditure by political action committees.

[10] 376 US 254 (1964).

In 1938 it was held that it was beyond provincial power to curtail the right of public discussion because it would interfere with the working of parliamentary institutions as contemplated by the British North America Act. Some of the remarks suggested that the federal Parliament was similarly restricted. Duffy CJC declared that public discussion was 'the breath of life for parliamentary institutions'.[11]

Similar reasoning was used when, in 1957, the Court held invalid a Quebec Act which prohibited the use of any house to propagate communism, and made unlawful the printing and distribution of communist literature. The Court held that the Act was within the subject of 'criminal law', an exclusive federal power. Rand J said that Canadian parliamentary government, declared in the preamble of the BNA Act to be similar to that of the United Kingdom, meant 'a government of free public opinion of an open society' and that it demands 'a virtually unobstructed access to a diffusion of ideas'. Abbot J used similar language and clearly stated that the Canadian Parliament itself could not abrogate freedom of discussion and debate.[12]

These judicial pronouncements seemed to have fallen into the doldrums until they were revived, somewhat strangely, after the Charter of Rights and Freedoms was enacted. In 1985, in a case where on the facts the Charter was inapplicable, the Chief Justice on behalf of the Court said that freedom of speech as an incident of Canadian democratic government was 'a principle of our common law constitution, inherited from the United Kingdom by virtue of the preamble to the Constitution Act 1867' (as the BNA Act had become).[13] In 1986 McIntyre J, speaking for the Court, referred to the remarks on freedom of political discussion in the above cases and added: 'Indeed this Court may be said to have given it constitutional status.'[14] The following year Beetz J was more emphatic that 'the essential structure of free parliamentary institutions could not, apart from Charter considerations, be impaired by federal or provincial legislation'.[15]

While the finding of this implication had some effect on the Australian scene, the course of development of Canadian constitutional and common law in this area naturally concentrated on s. 2(b) of the Charter.

The importance of freedom of expression for representative government has, in the Charter context, been again emphasized by the Canadian Supreme Court in a number of cases.[16] It has been described as the 'linchpin' of the guarantee in s. 2(b).[17] The approach of the Court is to interpret the freedom quite broadly, and then to apply s. 1 for the balancing process, rather than to take account of countervailing

---

[11] *Re Alberta Legislation* [1938] SCR 100, [1938] 2 DLR 87, 107. See also Cannon J at (DLR) 119, (SCR) 146.

[12] *Switzman v Elbling* [1957] SCR 286, 328 [1957] 7 DLR 337, 358, 371. See also *Saumur v City of Quebec* [1953] 2 SCR 299, [1953] 4 DLR 41 holding invalid a Quebec law prohibiting distribution of literature in the streets without the consent of the Chief of Police.

[13] *Fraser v PSSRB* [1985] 2 SCR 455, 462–3.

[14] *SDGMP v Dolphin Delivery Ltd.* [1986] 2 SCR 573, 584.

[15] *OPSEU v Attorney-General (Ont.)* [1987] 2 SCR 2, 57. See also Dickson CJC at 25.

[16] e.g. *Edmonton Journal of Alberta v Attorney-General (Alta)* (1989) 64 DLR 577.

[17] *R v Keegstra* [1990] 3 SCR 697, 763–4.

considerations in interpreting and applying the provision that enacts the right or freedom. For example, in a case involving a provision of the Criminal Code prohibiting the promotion of hatred against racial groups, the Court regarded the prohibited acts as protected by s. 2(b), but then by a narrow majority of four to three held that the prohibition was valid under s. 1. The Court rejected the argument that s. 2(b) should in this case be narrowed by other guarantees including equality (s. 15) and multiculturalism (s. 27).

The issue of which approach to adopt is not purely formal because, in showing that an activity is protected by a right or freedom the onus is on the plaintiff, while the onus of proving that there is a countervailing pressing social interest and that the means chosen are proportionate to the legitimate end is on the defendant, usually the government.[18]

The Canadian Court has at times come under similar criticism to that of the Supreme Court of the United States in not having sufficient regard to the social context and to other elements of a sound system of representative democracy. Moreover the cases in that area are often decided by slim majorities. For example, in *R v Zundel*[19] the Court had to determine the validity of a provision prohibiting the wilful publication of false news that the defendant knew to be false. In that case the news was that there had been no Jewish holocaust. The Court held that the communication was protected by s. 2(b) and a majority of four to three held that the legislation was not saved by s. 1 because it was aimed at the content of the message.

From the viewpoint of representative government it is difficult to see how it is enhanced by the legislature being unable to prohibit deliberate lies. The concept of 'content neutrality' familiar to United States law (and adopted in Australia) is a useful guide in ensuring that government cannot manipulate public discussion but, as Professor Feldman has pointed out, it is not an infallible criterion.[20] Indeed three years later, in a different context, the Court said that false statements were not deserving of much protection.[21]

Quite often the Court has accepted the existence of a pressing social interest in a setting of representative government which requires a restriction on freedom of expression. In some of those cases a law has, nevertheless, been held not to be saved by s. 1 because it goes beyond what is necessary to achieve the particular purpose.

For example in *Osborne v Canada*[22] a federal provision was held invalid in so far as it prohibited members of the federal public service from engaging in political activity. The court accepted the virtues of a neutral public service in a democratic system but held the provisions to be not within s. 1 because they were too drastic. It prevented a public servant from discussing matters that could not reasonably be regarded as threatening to bureaucratic neutrality in federal politics.

---

[18] Hogg, *Constitutional Law of Canada*, 4th edn. (1997) 693–4.
[19] (1992) 95 DLR 202.
[20] Feldman (n. 6 above).
[21] *Hill v Church of Scientology* [1995] 2 SCR 1130.
[22] [1991] 2 SCR 69.

In many cases the Canadian Court has shown greater acceptance than the US Supreme Court of the view that legislative intervention in the area of freedom of expression may be justified to achieve the object of greater equality of opportunity for the expression of views and giving information to ensure a more effective and fairer system of representative government.

In *Libman v Attorney-General (Que.)*,[23] for example, the Quebec Referendum Act required that expenses must be paid from the limited funds of committees authorized to represent certain sides in a referendum. The Supreme Court found that the object of the Act was to promote equality between the options submitted and to promote free and informed voting. It did this by preventing the affluent from exerting disproportionate influence by dominating the debate due to more resources. This made it necessary to control strictly independent spending which could upset the balance.

In the result, however, the legislation was held invalid, despite judicial approval of its object, because it was not a proportionate means to advance that object. It came close to a total ban by, for example, prohibiting payments by independent persons to have posters printed to express their point of view. The Court said that if the Act had limited expenditure to a low amount and prevented third parties from pooling their spending it would have been a proportionate means to fairness and equality.

This case illustrates the careful analysis often undertaken by the Court where political expression is involved and it is accepted that a legitimate object entitles the legislature to limit free expression. It can be contrasted with the American decision of *Buckley v Valeo* referred to above.[24]

This was not, however, the approach taken by the Supreme Court in respect of defamation actions brought by public officials. That Court had adopted the most conservative attitude to defamation of any of the courts considered in this chapter. It was held in 1986 that the Charter had no effect on a common law action for inducing breach of contract by means of picketing.[25] The Court said that 'where private party A sues private party B relying on the common law and where no act of government is relied upon to support the action, the Charter will not apply'.

That view was followed in the defamation case of *Hill v Church of Scientology*.[26] It was said, however, that although the Charter does not directly apply, the Court should interpret the common law in a manner consistent with Charter principles because those principles were to be taken as among the prevailing social conditions and values.[27] The Court held that the Charter and the prevailing common law of defamation were in harmony.

Sullivan was rejected because information about officials and public affairs was polluted by false information and the reputation of a defeated plaintiff might be

---

[23] (1997) 51 DLR 385.
[24] See n. 9 above.
[25] *RWDSU v Dolphin Delivery* [1986] 2 SCR 573.
[26] [1995] 2 SCR 1130.
[27] ibid. 1132.

destroyed by false a statement that could have been avoided if a reasonable effort had been made to investigate the facts. On a more general plain the Court considered that a greater evil than the 'chilling effect' of defamation on communication about governmental affairs was the harmful effect of defamatory statements on the search for truth and the advancement of participation in the affairs of the community. It was said that it would deter sensitive and honourable persons from seeking public positions if qualified privilege was extended to defamatory statements concerning the fitness for office of candidates.

The case did not involve the media and concerned the 'personal integrity' of a Crown attorney, in the Court's view, rather than that of the government. The Court therefore said it did not have to consider the broader issues decided by the Australian High Court in the cases dealt with below. Nervertheless it clearly rejected the view that defamation actions, in which truth was the only defence, detrimentally affected representative democracy. The judges instead emphasized the protection of reputation, described by Cory J as reflecting 'the innate dignity of the individual'.[28] Little regard, if any, was paid to the view that the common law of defamation might result in the suppression of true statements as well as false ones.

3. AUSTRALIA

The Australian Constitution does not contain any provision guaranteeing freedom of speech, expression or communication. Indeed, among common law countries it probably stands alone in having neither a constitutional nor statutory 'bill of rights', at any rate since the passing of the Human Rights Act of the United Kingdom. It, therefore, surprised many people when the High Court held in 1992 that there was implied in the Constitution a freedom to communicate on matters relating to politics and government. The conclusion was derived from finding that the Constitution prescribed in the federal sphere a system of representative government. That in turn was regarded as the result of ss. 7 and 24 of the Constitution, which provide that members of the Senate and the House of Representatives 'shall be directly chosen by the people', s. 64 requiring ministers to be members of Parliament within three months of appointment and s. 128, which provides for a combination of parliamentary action and a referendum of the people to alter the Constitution.

In *Nationwide News Pty. Ltd. v Wills*[29] the Court held invalid a provision making it an offence to bring a member of the Industrial Relations Commission or the Commission 'into disrepute'. A majority held that provision inconsistent with the implied freedom of communication required by representative government because it suppressed justified and reasonable criticism.

---

[28] Hogg, *Constitutional Law of Canada* (4th edn.), para. 40.10.
[29] (1992) 177 CLR 1.

In *Australian Capital Television Pty. Ltd. v Commonwealth*[30] federal legislation prohibited, subject to exceptions, the use of radio and television broadcasting, during election periods, of political advertisements, comment or argument. The exceptions were news and current affairs, talk-back radio programmes, 'policy launches' and provisions for free election broadcasts. A majority of the Court held the provisions invalid for breach of the implied freedom of communication.

It was argued that the Act was consistent with representative government because the provisions were designed (a) to safeguard the integrity of political parties from corruption and undue influence that follows from having to procure large sums to pay for costly broadcasting, (b) to prevent an advantage being given to the wealthy in political broadcasting, and (c) to put a stop to the 'trivialization' of political debate resulting from very brief advertisements.

The High Court accepted that these were legitimate objects, consistent with representative government, which could justify burdens on communication. It was, however, held that the Act went beyond what was appropriate or proportionate to those objects. As is the position in the United States, the majority judges said that, because the ban was based on the political content of the communication, the onus on the Commonwealth was particularly heavy. The main reason for invalidity was that the 'free time' provisions favoured established political parties and candidates, while non-candidates were excluded. However, no inquiry was made into whether, as a practical matter, any other system was feasible for the purpose of fulfilling the legislative objects.

There was much dispute among lawyers and social scientists relating to these decisions.[31] Some argued that the Court introduced American notions based on a fear of government intervention, and had not given sufficient consideration to the deleterious effect on representative government of the evils that the legislation was designed to eradicate or prevent. There are a number of critics, like myself, who would accept the Court's reasoning that the Constitution provides for representative government, which limits the power of the Parliaments and governments, but nevertheless are of the view that the legislation was consistent with representative government, as Brennan J held.

The Court, however, did not reject the relevance of the matters raised by the government, as would probably have occurred in the United States. Where the legislation foundered was on the free-time provisions which were regarded as enhancing the power of existing political interests at the expense of others. Had the Act been amended to deal with that matter it probably would have been upheld. By then, however, the political climate had changed.

The implied freedom in Australia clearly differs from the freedom of speech, expression or communication in the United States, Canada and under the European

---

[30] (1992) 177 CLR 106.
[31] See articles in (1994) 16 Syd LR 145–305; Goldsworthy, 'Implications in Language, Law and the Constitution' in Lindell (ed.), *Future Directions in Australian Constitutional Law* 150.

Convention on Human Rights in that it is limited to what is necessary for representative government. The Australian constitutional framers in the 1890s expressly rejected the concept of a bill of rights. For them, like other British people of their day, freedom was regarded as secured by the common law and parliamentary supremacy. In one sense the approach of the High Court might be regarded as consistent with the reasons of the founders for rejection of a bill of rights, preferring to rely on the democratic process. It is that process, involving as it does freedom of communication on the affairs of government, that provides the moral and political justification for the supremacy of Parliament.

In the Australian context disagreement can of course arise as to whether a particular form of communication comes within the area of constitutional protection. In *Cunliffe v Commonwealth*,[32] for example, there was disagreement in the Court about whether communication for purposes of public administration was covered. That case involved legislation prohibiting all but registered immigration agents from giving certain advice to migrants about entrance applications, which concerned communication with government officials. In *Levy v Victoria*[33] the plaintiff challenged a State law preventing him from going on to an area at the beginning of the duck-shooting season. His purpose was to hold up dead ducks for the television cameras as a protest against the shooting of birds. He lost the case on the ground that even if the activity was within the purview of the freedom, the law was an appropriate means of ensuring public safety. Most of the judges, however, were of the view that such a protest constituted communication on governmental matters. The issue was not, of course, the meaning of 'speech', but the relevance of the conduct to representative government as prescribed by the Constitution.

The significance of *New York Times v Sullivan* came up for consideration by the High Court in *Theophanous v Herald and Weekly Times Ltd*.[34] The Court held that in the light of the implied freedom of communication the existing law of defamation did not comply with the Constitution in its application to communication about political and governmental concerns. The majority agreed with statements in *Sullivan* and in *Derbyshire County Council v Times Newspapers Ltd*.[35] relating to the inhibiting effect that libel actions could have on such communication. However, the *Sullivan* solution was rejected because the placing of the onus of proving deliberate falsehood on the plaintiff did not pay sufficient regard to the protection of reputation. They considered also that the expansion of who were 'public figures' for purposes of the *Sullivan* principle had gone too far. It was held that the publication was not actionable if the defendant proved that it (usually a media corporation) was unaware of the falsity of the statement, did not publish it recklessly and that the publication was reasonable in the circumstances. Reasonable action could be shown either by taking some steps to establish the accuracy of the impugned matters or that it was justified in not taking such steps. One of the majority judges, Deane J, would

---

[32] (1994) 182 CLR 272.   [33] (1997) 189 CLR 579
[34] (1994) 182 CLR 104.   [35] [1993] AC 534.

have gone beyond the ratio in *Sullivan* and (like the minority in that case) expressed the opinion that the constitutional implication precluded completely the application of defamation laws in respect of the publication of statements about the official conduct or suitability of a member of Parliament 'or other holder of high Commonwealth office'. In order to ensure a majority, however, he supported the answers of the other three judges (Mason CJ, Toohey and Gaudron JJ).[36]

Theophanous was decided by a bare majority. The following year Mason CJ retired and Brennan J was made Chief Justice. Gummow J of the Federal Court was appointed to fill the vacancy. A challenge was then made to that case in *Lange v the Australian Broadcasting Corporation*.[37] This time a unanimous Court affirmed the constitutional principle of representative government at the federal level and the implied freedom of communication on governmental affairs as a necessary incident of that principle. There was more emphasis on representative government as *prescribed by the Constitution* rather than as an abstract political concept, but that does not appear to have made much substantive difference.

In the early part of the judgment the Court declared that the freedom was not a positive right but a restriction on legislative and executive power. That seemed to deny any effect on the common law, as had been held in Canada and by minority judges in *Theophanous*. In an apparent disapproval of the latter case, it was said that the issue was not, as in the United States, the creation of a 'constitutional privilege' against the application of State common law. That was because in Australia there was a national common law declared by the High Court as a national court of appeal. The judgment then went on to say that 'of necessity, the common law must conform with the Constitution'.[38] The protection of reputation must admit therefore, as an exception, the constitutional freedom to discuss governmental affairs and politics.

The Court went on to remodel the common law of defamation to make it consistent with the freedom by developing the defence of qualified privilege. In fact the defence was extended beyond constitutional requirements to all communications about governmental matters even if they had no clear connection with the Commonwealth's sphere of government.[39] The new defence was therefore vulnerable to statutory alteration only to the extent that the new common law defence exceeded constitutional requirements.

While qualified privilege usually required only honesty of purpose, that was because the defence had been traditionally restricted to publication to a limited

---

[36]   The principles expounded in *Theophanous* were applied to actions by State members of Parliament in respect of statements made about their official conduct in *Stephens v West Australian Newspapers Ltd.* (1994) 182 CLR 211.

[37]   (1997) 189 CLR 520.   [38]   ibid. 566.

[39]   In *Australian Capital Television* (n. 30 above) it was said that federal representative government required freedom of speech in respect of all political matters even if they were concerned with State or local government affairs, because all such matters were relevant to federal parliamentary debate, federal funding and initiation of constitutional amendment. *Lange* (n. 37 above) suggested that there could be some State, local government or international governmental affairs which did not have a sufficient connection with the Commonwealth to come within the implied freedom.

number of persons. The new extension in respect of political communication, however, related to mass communication. In those circumstances the Court said that reasonableness of conduct was a necessary element of the defence. In most cases that would require the defence to prove the same matters as those included in the 'constitutional defence' under the *Theophanous* principle. It was also said that conduct would not be reasonable if, in normal circumstances, the defendant had not sought a response from the person defamed and published that response.

4. THE EUROPEAN CONVENTION AND THE UNITED KINGDOM

The European Court of Human Rights in a number of cases has emphasized the special importance of freedom of expression to democratic institutions. Discussion of political and governmental affairs has been seen as a prime subject of protection under Article 10 of the Convention providing, inter alia, and subject to qualifications, that 'Everyone has the right of freedom of expression'. In *Lingen v Austria*[40] that freedom was described as 'one of the essential foundations of a democratic society'. The task of the press to impart information and ideas to the public and the right of the public to receive them was recognized. Similarly, the Court said that because of the democratic system a politician must put up with a greater degree of criticism than a private individual. That has some resemblance, of course, to the approach in *New York Times v Sullivan*.

For a number of years Article 10 of the Convention and the notion of freedom of expression as an important legal principle had little, if any, effect on judicial reasoning in Britain. In the *First Spycatcher Case*[41] Lord Bridge, in his dissenting judgment, remarked that he had not hitherto been one of those who advocated adoption in domestic law of the European Convention because he had 'confidence in the capacity of the common law to safeguard the fundamental freedoms essential to a free society including the right of freedom of speech which is specifically safeguarded by Article 10 of the Convention'. He added that his confidence had been seriously undermined by the decision of the majority in that case.

Both the Convention and the concept of freedom of speech as an important principle received short shrift in *R v Secretary of State for the Home Department, ex p Brind*,[42] which upheld the ban by the Secretary of State on the use of the voices (but not the images or messages) of IRA terrorists in broadcasts. The statutory authority was in very general terms. The Court refused to interpret it so as to comply with Article 10 or having regard to a general principle of freedom of speech because the legislation was 'unambiguous'.

The concept of 'ambiguity' is, of course, itself an uncertain one. The extent to

---

[40] (1986) 8 EHRR 407 at 418.
[41] *Attorney-General v The Guardian* [1987] 1 WLR 1248 at 1286.
[42] [1991] 1 AC 696.

which the Convention or common law concepts of freedom can be used in interpretation depends on how ready the courts are to accept that the meaning the Crown is advocating is clear and unambiguous. There is, in any case, a reverse principle of statutory interpretation, namely, that an Act will not be construed so as to interfere with basic common law rights in the absence of clear and unmistakable language.[43]

Nevertheless, in *Brind* Lord Bridge did say, in relation to review of the Secretary of State's discretion, that 'we are perfectly entitled to start off with the premise that any restriction of freedom of speech requires to be justified and that nothing less than an important social interest will be sufficient to justify it.[44] For present purposes, however, it is sufficient to note that the concept of representative government did not play a notable part in the reasoning in that case.

The opposite was the position in *Derbyshire County Council v Times Newspapers Ltd.*,[45] where it was held that neither a local government corporation nor any institution of the central government had a right to maintain an action for defamation. This time there was a specific reliance on freedom of expression as an important legal principle and as vital to a democratic system of government.

Many hailed the decision as a new beginning of a more principled approach by the House of Lords to the subject of human rights. On this occasion the principles involved were seen as transnational and international. Recourse was had to cases and reasoning of the United States Supreme Court and the European Court of Human Rights. The House of Lords relied directly on the public importance of ensuring that democratically elected bodies should be open to public criticism. That policy could be fettered by threat of an action for defamation.

Lord Keith's judgment referred quite extensively to reasoning in the early American case of *City of Chicago v Tribune Co.*,[46] which declared that a civil action could be as great, if not greater, restriction than a criminal prosecution on freedom of speech. That case had been endorsed by the Supreme Court in *New York Times v Sullivan*. Lord Keith went on to say that:

While these decisions were related most directly to the provisions of the American Constitution concerns with securing freedom of speech, the public interest considerations which underlaid them are no less valid in this country.[47]

After then referring to the state of the law under the European Convention, His Lordship said that he found it satisfactory to conclude that the common law of England was consistent with the European Convention on freedom of expression.

On the subject of protection of political discussion and debate, however, the judgment left open a possibility which threatened to undermine the policy on which it relied. Lord Keith said:

---

[43] *Wheeler v Leicester City Council* [1985] AC 1054 at 1065. *Coco v R* (1994) 179 CLR 427 at 436–8.
[44] [1991] AC at 748–9.   [45] [1993] AC 534.
[46] (1923) 139 NE 86.   [47] *Derbyshire* (n. 45) 548.

If the individual reputation of any of these [Councillors] is wrongly impaired by the publication any of those can himself bring proceedings for defamation.[48]

Professor Barendt wrote that Lord Keith did not indicate whether the decision precluded libel actions by public officials. He considered that its extension to politicians was 'inevitable'.[49] Lord Keith's statement seemed to assume that a right of action was available. *Reynolds v Times Newspapers Ltd.*,[50] however, treated the issue as having been left open by *Derbyshire*. If the latter case had extended to actions by individual officials, it would have gone considerably further than the majority in *Sullivan* and would have embraced the view of Deane J in *Theophanous* in Australia and the minority judges in *Sullivan*.

As Barendt pointed out, however, *Derbyshire* ensured that the principle of freedom of expression was no longer merely a residuary freedom, the content of which was what remained after applying legal limitations and restrictions. It was now a principle of law which had to be taken into account. The importance of freedom of speech on matters of government and politics to the institution of representative government was declared in a striking manner.

This approach was confirmed to a large extent in *Reynolds v Times Newspapers Ltd.*[51] where the House of Lords examined the common law of defamation in respect of press statements about matters of public interest. Their Lordships, like the Court of Appeal earlier, made reference to the decisions of all the jurisdictions referred to above, as well as New Zealand, South Africa and India. The fact that the Human Rights Act 1998 was to come into operation in 2000 added to the relevance of Article 10 of the European Convention and the decisions of the European Court of Human Rights.

Despite the emphasis given by the European Court at various times and by the House of Lords in *Derbyshire* to the importance of free 'political' expression to democratic institutions, the Court rejected the view that that form of expression should be specially protected by 'generic privilege'. Although it was once again accepted that it was essential to a democratic system, it was thought 'unsound' to distinguish political discussion from discussion of other matters of public concern.

The leading judgment of Lord Nicholls accepted that, for purposes of the law of qualified privilege, the press had a duty to comment on political and other matters of public interest and that the public had a right to be informed. But this defence depended on certain conditions being satisfied. Generally the press had to act reasonably and fairly, which would depend on the circumstances of each case. Lord Nicholls set out ten matters to be taken into account, which were 'illustrations only'. They included the extent of public concern, the source of the information, the steps taken to verify it, whether comment was sought from the plaintiff and whether the

---

[48] ibid. 550.
[49] 'Libel and Freedom of Speech in English Law' [1993] PL 449 at 453.
[50] [1999] 3 WLR 1010. See p. 75 below (Beloff).
[51] ibid.

article contained the gist of the plaintiff's side of the story. In weighing up these factors the court should have regard to the fact that 'the press discharged vital functions as a bloodhound as well as a watchdog'.[52]

The relevance of whether the communication was in the area of 'political information' was not completely rejected. It was said that the court should be slow to conclude that a publication was not in the public interest 'especially when the information was in the field of political discussion'.[53] The general refusal to relate these new rules of qualified privilege specifically to political discussion is in marked contrast to the Australian approach. Of course, in Australia the constitutional principle is confined to such discussion because it is an implication derived from the constitutional requirement of representative government.

Having regard to the special importance attributed to communication on governmental matters by many of the courts referred to above, including the House of Lords itself, it is likely that among those matters of public interest covered by the new principle 'political' expression will be the area that is most prominent.

Lord Steyn's arguments for rejecting 'a generic qualified privilege' for this type of expression included that it was at variance with the jurisprudence of the European Court of Human Rights, which required a balancing exercise in the light of the facts of each case. It is not likely that that Court would object to greater latitude being given to an area of expression the importance of which the European Court has emphasized on several occasions. Whether an equal latitude should be given in certain circumstances to other subjects of public interest is a different question.

It is, however, possible that the British courts and the European Court would take a narrower view than in Australia of what constitutes 'political' discussion. For example, in examining the 'human rights jurisprudence', Lord Nicholls referred, inter alia, to the case of *Thorgeirson v Iceland*,[54] which concerned press reports of rumours of police brutality and a call for an independent investigation. The judgment said that case and some others did not involve political discussion.[55] That also seems to have been the view of the European Court, where they said that there was no warrant for distinguishing between political discussion and discussion on other matters of public concern.[56] That remark, however, was in reply to a submission[57] that the European Court had singled out political discussion for special protection; and that such discussion denoted 'direct or indirect participation by citizens in the decision-making process in a democratic society'.

In Australia it is likely that the communication in *Thorgeirson* would be regarded as within the constitutional area of protection. In *Lange*, for example, it was said that it covered communication about the affairs of the Executive, government departments

---

[52] ibid. 1027.
[53] ibid.
[54] (1992) 14 EHHR 843.
[55] *Reynolds* (n. 50 above) 1026.
[56] *Thorgeirson* (n. 54 above) 865, para. 64.
[57] ibid. 863–4, para. 61.

and many statutory authorities and public utilities.[58] In *Theophanous*, Mason CJ, Toohey and Gaudron JJ referred with approval to Barendt's view that 'political speech refers to all speech relevant to the development of public opinion on the whole range of issues which an intelligent citizen should think about'.[59]

It is likely also that a number of the factors listed by Lord Nicholls would be relevant to determining the issue of reasonable conduct under the Australian principles.

The coming into operation of the Human Rights Act 1998 will, of course, make Article 10 of the European Convention directly relevant. Section 3 would require the court in the situation in *Brind* to interpret the legislation in a way which is compatible with the Convention rights 'so far as it is possible to do so'. The decision might still be the same, but the question whether the language of the provision conferring the power was 'unambiguous' will no longer be conclusive.

5. CONCLUSION

There has been a remarkable unanimity of view, among the courts of the jurisdictions dealt with above, of the importance of freedom of expression or communication to the operation of democratic government. That has also been the case in respect of the courts of other countries not examined in this survey, such as India, New Zealand, Germany and South Africa. Whether the question is one of common law, statutory interpretation, constitutional rights or treaty provisions, the issues involved in determining what representative government requires and of balancing it with other social interests are essentially the same.

Even where the answers have differed there has been a lot of cross-fertilization. In England both the House of Lords and the Court of Appeal in *Henderson* extensively examined the law and decisions of other jurisdictions. Earlier, in *Derbyshire* the House of Lords accepted policies and values proclaimed in the United States. Similarly, in Australia, the positions in the United States, Canada, Britain and Europe were canvassed by the High Court. The same has occurred in New Zealand and South Africa. Although in Australia it has been the practice of the High Court for some years to turn to the law and legal decisions of other comparable countries and to international courts in respect of a variety of legal subjects, British courts, like those of the United States, tended to be more insular. It may be that these cases indicate a change to a more cosmopolitan judicial attitude.

Although the general issues have been much the same in each country the approaches have varied. Clearly social values have a great deal to do with that, in determining the communications that are worthy of protection, the essential elements of representative government, and balancing and adjusting freedom of expression with other pressing social interests. Much of the criticism of the United

---

[58] (1997) 189 CLR at 561.
[59] (1994) 182 CLR at 152, quoting from Barendt, *Freedom of Speech* (1987) 152.

States decisions includes statements to the effect that the American distrust of governmental regulation does not have its counterpart (at any rate to the same degree) in other western countries.

Whether the national cultural differences among the other countries I have dealt with are determinative of different judicial approaches and answers is more debatable. It is of course a mistake to think of each of these countries as having a uniform set of values. Judges and scholars within each country (including the United States) have come out with different viewpoints on the issues raised in this chapter.

With the coming into operation of the Human Rights Act 1998 in the United Kingdom, Australia will be the only major common law country without a statutory or constitutional 'bill of rights'. Nevertheless the High Court of Australia does have recourse to the constitutional decisions of other countries for the purposes of developing the common law. For constitutional purposes, however, freedom of communication rests, not on a general constitutional or statutory right, but on an implication arising from the provisions prescribing representative government. The guarantee in Australia, therefore, is based exclusively on the connection between that freedom and democratic institutions.

In the other countries and jurisdictions the courts are faced with a broader principle of rights; but the importance of the notion of 'political' expression is perhaps best manifested in the heavy weight accorded to its freedom when countervailing social interests are involved.

3

Freedom of Expression and Freedom of Religion: Some Thoughts on the Glenn Hoddle Case

SIR PATRICK ELIAS AND JASON COPPEL

1. THE *GLENN HODDLE* CASE

In an interview with *The Times* newspaper on 30 January 1999, at a time when he was employed by the Football Association (FA) as the manager of the England football team, Glenn Hoddle expressed his beliefs that people were reincarnated 'to learn and face some of the things you have done—good and bad'. He said: 'You and I have been physically given two hands and two legs and half-decent brains. Some people have not been born like that for a reason. The karma is working from another lifetime. I have nothing to hide about that. It is not only people with disabilities. What you sow, you have to reap.'[1]

Hoddle's comments—which were widely portrayed as an attack on disabled people—caused an immediate public outcry. The then Sports Minister Tony Banks said on the same day that Hoddle was 'from another world'. He continued 'I have listened carefully to Glenn Hoddle's views as expressed on the tape obtained by *The Observer*. They are totally unacceptable. If his theory is correct, he is in for real problems in the next life. He will probably be doomed to come back as Glenn Hoddle.' On 31 January, Margaret Hodge, then minister with responsibility for the disabled, called for Hoddle to step down, saying it was 'inappropriate' for him to hold the position of England coach.[2] On 1 February 1999, the Prime Minister, during an appearance on *This Morning with Richard and Judy*, said that it would be very difficult for Hoddle to stay in his job if he had been correctly reported. David Mellor, former Conservative cabinet minister and chairman of the Football Task Force said: 'Hoddle must either be made to go, or to see sense. At the very least he must be given an ultimatum to clean out his head or clear out his locker. Nothing less will do.'[3]

On the evening of 2 February, Hoddle was sacked by the FA for 'a serious error of judgment'. He subsequently apologized for causing 'misunderstanding and pain'.[4]

It is undeniable that Hoddle lost his high-profile and lucrative job as a result of expressing deeply-held religious views. He was penalized for exercising his freedom

---

[1] 'Hoddle's future in doubt after disabled slur', *The Guardian*, 30 January 1999.
[2] 'Explain yourself, FA tells Hoddle', *The Guardian*, 1 February 1999.
[3] 'He has got to be told to clean out his head or clear out his locker', *The Guardian*, 2 February 1999.
[4] 'England loses faith in Hoddle', *The Guardian*, 3 February 1999.

of expression and/or for manifesting his religious beliefs on the grounds that his views had upset the sensibilities of disabled people. His employer's reasoning was that Hoddle was the figurehead of an organization which had strived to promote disabled sport, and that it was inappropriate for him to make comments which were offensive to that important constituency.

Hoddle's case raises, therefore, important issues with regard to freedom of thought, conscience and religion under Article 9 and freedom of expression under Article 10 of the European Convention on Human Rights (ECHR). In which circumstances is it permissible, consistently with Article 9, to penalize individuals for manifesting their religious views? What degree of upset must be caused before interference with freedom of religion, or freedom of expression, is justified? To the extent that those disabled people who were offended by Hoddle had religious views which did not encompass reincarnation as punishment, what degree of affront to the religious views of others is necessary to justify a restriction upon freedom of expression? And, with regard to the justification put forward for Hoddle's dismissal, can an employee effectively contract-out of his fundamental rights by taking a particular job with particular responsibilities?

2. ECHR, ARTICLE 9

Freedom of religion, and of conscience, has a claim to being one of the most important freedoms of all. To be compelled to act contrary to one's conscience is a form of degradation; it demeans one's dignity and personal worth. Similarly, to be denied the right to practice one's religion would for many—we would suspect most—religious people be far more serious than the denial of political rights, such as the right to vote.

Under the European Convention on Human Rights, the protection given to conscience and religion is found in Article 9. In the *Kokkinakis* case the court recognized that for religious believers it protected something that was fundamental to their identity and their perception of life.[5] It is important to focus on the precise terms in which the provision is drafted.

1. Everyone has the right to freedom of thought, conscience and religion; this right includes freedom to change his religion or belief and freedom, either alone or in community with others and in public or private, to manifest his religion or belief, in worship, teaching, practice and observance.
2. Freedom to manifest one's religion or beliefs shall be subject only to such limitations as are prescribed by law and are necessary in a democratic society in the interests of public safety, for the protection of public order, health or morals, or for the protection of the rights and freedoms of others.

[5] (1994) 17 EHRR 397.

There are a number of concepts here that immediately cause difficulty. The concept of religion itself is one, although since non-religious beliefs are protected as well as religious ones, the need to define the concept has not proved to be a particularly pressing one. Broadly the approach of the Court has been to limit the protection to 'coherent views on fundamental problems'.[6] The concepts of 'worship, teaching, practice and observance' are also not without their problems. Does this cover prose-lytizing? This would more naturally seem to fall under Article 10, but in fact the European Commission of Human Rights has given a broad interpretation to these words. In *Hakanssøn v Sweden*, it held that trumpeting to people that fornication and alcoholism were against God's laws fell within the scope of Article 9, being a mani-festation of religion, and was, in principle, to be permitted.[7] Unfortunately, the applicant had expressed his views so loudly and in such a persistent manner that he had provoked the application of the exception under Article 9(2) whereby his free-dom of religion could be restricted for the protection of the rights of others. That decision should be contrasted with the decision in *Arrowsmith* where the Commis-sion held that although pacifism could properly be described as a principle of conscience or belief within Article 9, seeking to persuade soldiers to go absent with-out leave and to refuse to serve in Northern Ireland was not the actual expression of that belief but was rather an act motivated by that belief.[8] In short, you can express your beliefs with impunity but you may nevertheless fall outside the scope of Article 9 when you act upon them.[9]

3. THE RELATIONSHIP BETWEEN ARTICLES 9 AND 10

This paper is intended to explore an important interaction between Articles 9 and 10. The relationship between them operates at two levels. First, how far should the freedom of expression of others be restricted because it infringes my Article 9 rights? Second, to what extent should I modify the expression of my religious beliefs or the dictates of my conscience, because it might upset the susceptibilities of others? We shall deal with these two issues in turn.

3.1 Speech infringing Article 9

English law has protected the Christian religion by the law of blasphemy. This has not, however, protected that religion from criticism as such. In *R v Lemon*, Lord Scarman approved the following definition from Stephen's *Digest of the Criminal Law*:

---

[6] See, for example, *Campbell and Cosans v United Kingdom* (1982) 4 EHRR 293, para 36.
[7] (1983) 5 EHRR 297.
[8] *Arrowsmith v United Kingdom* (1980) 19 DR 5.
[9] This distinction has been relied upon in a number of cases. See Stavros, 'Freedom of Religion and Claims for Exemption from Generally Applicable Neutral Laws: Lessons from Across the Pond?' [1997] EHRLR 607.

Every publication is said to be blasphemous which contains any contemptuous, reviling, scurrilous or ludicrous matter relating to God, Jesus Christ, or the Bible, or the formularies of the Church of England as by law established. It is not blasphemous to speak or publish opinions hostile to the Christian religion, or to deny the existence of God, if the publication is couched in decent and temperate language. The test to be applied is as to the manner in which the doctrines are advocated and not as to the substance of the doctrines themselves.[10]

There has been considerable disquiet about this law. One criticism is that it applies only to protect the formal doctrines of the established Church and that it should be extended to all religions. In a society where a wide range of religious beliefs are practised, the current restriction is difficult to defend. However, attempts to spread it to protect other religions have failed.[11] Another quite different criticism challenges the justification for the law itself. It is said to be an unacceptable and unnecessary limitation on the right of free speech. On this view, the fact that speech causes offence ought not of itself to justify gagging the speaker, even where deeply held convictions are being lampooned or are made the subject of ridicule. The logic of this argument is that it is inappropriate to keep this law at all for any religion.

Article 9 does not, on its face, prohibit the kind of hostile comments which would amount to blasphemy in English law. There is no reason to suppose that comments or criticisms, scurrilous or otherwise, would of themselves adversely affect the ability to exercise Article 9 rights. Of course, they might do so because of the circumstances in which the verbal attacks were communicated. For example, demonstrations outside a church, synagogue or mosque in a manner that disrupted the services being carried on within might interfere with the freedom to manifest religious beliefs, such that the state may come under a positive obligation to intervene.[12]

However, the European Court of Human Rights in Strasbourg has extended the protection afforded by Article 9 so as to justify a prohibition upon certain speech which causes distress to the adherents of the religious faith in question. In *Otto-Preminger-Institut v Austria*,[13] the complainant wished to challenge the decision of the Austrian authorities which had confiscated copies of a film the day before it was due for its first screening. The film characterized the persons of God, Jesus and Mary in a manner which would no doubt have been offensive to many people. The authorities prevented it from being shown anywhere in Austria, and were held by a majority of the Court not to have infringed the right to freedom of expression under Article 10. The Court held that the film was liable to infringe 'the rights of others', such that a justification under Article 10(2) could be made out. The rights of others were, however, very loosely defined, so as to encompass a right not to be gratuitously offended. The Court stated:

[10] [1979] 1 All ER 898.
[11] See *R v Chief Metropolitan Stipendiary Magistrate, ex p Choudhury* [1991] 1 All ER 306.
[12] See, by analogy, *Plattform 'Ärzte für das Leben' v Austria* (1991) 13 EHRR 204.
[13] (1995) 19 EHRR 34.

However, as is borne out by the wording itself of Article 10 para. 2 (art. 10–2), whoever exercises the rights and freedoms enshrined in the first paragraph of that Article (art. 10–1) undertakes 'duties and responsibilities'. Amongst them—in the context of religious opinions and beliefs—may legitimately be included an obligation to avoid as far as possible expressions that are gratuitously offensive to others and thus an infringement of their rights, and which therefore do not contribute to any form of public debate capable of furthering progress in human affairs.[14]

The Court further stated that the justification for the restriction upon freedom of expression was the need 'to protect the right of citizens not to be insulted in their religious feelings by the public expression of views of other persons'.[15] In another passage it referred to their 'right to respect for their religious feelings', a right which is not expressed, and so can only be implicit, within Article 9.

The Court did recognize, however, that not every form of criticism will infringe that broadly-cast right:

Those who choose to exercise the freedom to manifest their religion, irrespective of whether they do so as members of a religious majority or a minority, cannot reasonably expect to be exempt from all criticism. They must tolerate and accept the denial by others of their religious beliefs and even the propagation by others of doctrines hostile to their faith. However, the manner in which religious beliefs and doctrines are opposed or denied is a matter which may engage the responsibility of the State, notably its responsibility to ensure the peaceful enjoyment of the right guaranteed under Article 9 to the holders of those beliefs and doctrines. Indeed, in extreme cases the effect of particular methods of opposing or denying religious beliefs can be such as to inhibit those who hold such beliefs from exercising their freedom to hold and express them.[16]

The Court also referred to its earlier decision in the *Kokkinakis* case,[17] when it had referred to the 'malicious violation of the spirit of tolerance' which it said was a feature of a democratic society.

The Court went on to find that even though the film would only be shown in cinemas which people would have to pay to enter, information about the nature of the film would be made available to potential viewers, and under seventeens would be excluded, the total ban was a proportionate response to the need to protect the susceptibilities of the offended group. In reaching this conclusion it gave significant weight to the local conditions prevailing in the Tyrolean region of Austria, where the film was due to be shown, and where the overwhelming majority of the population was Roman Catholic (although the measures taken by the authorities prevented the film from being shown even outside that region).

A major concern with the Court's approach, however, is that it would risk taking freedom of speech away from the satirists and caricaturists. It was not alleged in this case that the film inhibited anyone from holding their religious beliefs, even less from exercising them. It simply caused them offence, and it is difficult to understand

[14] ibid., para. 49. [15] ibid., para. 48. [16] ibid., para. 47.
[17] *Kokkinakis v Greece* (1994) 17 EHRR 397.

how the Court could have derived from the words of Article 9 a general right to have one's religious feelings respected. The danger of the Court's approach is that respect for religious feelings merges, in Article 9 at least, with respect for other deeply held beliefs, which then becomes difficult to distinguish from respect for the sensibilities of others generally. The outcome is an unjustifiably broad basis for restricting freedom of expression, to the detriment of those individuals, including Glenn Hoddle, whose views cause offence to others. In *Otto-Preminger-Institut*, the broad scope of the Court's unwarranted implication then enabled it to hold that the Austrian authorities had pursued a legitimate aim. Even then, however, it is difficult to see how it could be said that the total banning of the film (even outside the region where local conditions had justified its seizure) could constitute a proportionate response to the legitimate aim pursued.

The approach in the *Otto Preminger* case was then followed in *Wingrove v United Kingdom*.[18] A film entitled *Visions of Ecstasy* portrayed highly erotic scenes purporting to represent the visions of St Teresa of Avila, a sixteenth century Carmelite nun. The British Board of Film Censors refused to give it a certificate on the grounds that it was blasphemous. It was in fact made clear, however, that the same approach would have been adopted if other religions had been the subject of similar treatment. The film's director was advised that the decision could not be challenged effectively under English law, and sought a remedy before the European Court of Human Rights.

When the case came before the Court, Mr Wingrove contended that no justification could be advanced by the government under Article 10(2), for three reasons. First, he said that the restriction upon his freedom of expression was not 'prescribed by law' because the law of blasphemy was so ill-defined that it did not meet the test, adopted by the Court, of being formulated with sufficient clarity to enable persons to foresee to a degree that is reasonable in all the circumstances the consequences which a given action may entail. Secondly, it was alleged that the interference did not pursue a legitimate aim: the rights of others, asserted Mr Wingrove, could not properly extend to the disquiet some Christians may feel at the prospect that other people might see the film without being shocked. It was also argued that the aim pursued by the law of blasphemy was inherently illegitimate since it was discriminatory against other, non-Christian religions. Finally, it was contended that even if Article 9 rights were infringed, the banning of the video did not correspond to a pressing social need, and was not proportionate to the legitimate aims pursued.

All these arguments failed. The Court considered that although there was some inherent ambiguity in a law of the nature of blasphemy, and the authorities were given a degree of flexibility in determining whether or not the facts of any given case fell within the scope of the definition, nevertheless the definition was sufficiently well understood to pass the test of being 'prescribed by law'.[19] The Court followed the *Otto-Preminger* case in holding that the video represented a potential infringement of

---

[18] (1997) 24 EHRR 1.   [19] Para. 42–4.

Article 9 rights and could be restricted in the interests of protecting the rights of others not to be offended in their religious feelings. The Court did appear at least to raise the threshold for making out a 'legitimate aim' in this regard: 'substantial offence', or that others in society were 'seriously offended' was required. It refused, however, to consider the argument that the law of blasphemy was discriminatory and so failed to protect the Article 9 rights of non-Christians.[20] The Court explicitly recognized that state authorities would have a wider margin of appreciation when regulating freedom of expression in relation to matters which were liable to offend intimate personal convictions.[21]

The approach of the Court in *Wingrove* is reminiscent of the approach of the British courts to the blasphemy laws. There are, however, two significant distinctions. First, the protection afforded by Article 9 would extend to all religions. Secondly, whilst Article 9 may require that state action is taken in certain circumstances so as to protect religious sensitivities, Article 9 does not *require* that the state protect those sensitivities by making it a criminal offence to upset them. In the *Otto-Preminger-Institut* and *Wingrove* cases, the authorities had taken action and the complainant was the party seeking to assert the right to free speech. Would the position have been the same if the complainant had been a potential 'victim' complaining that the state had failed to take adequate steps to protect his Article 9 rights? It is very doubtful that it would: in Strasbourg at least, the state would have an equally broad discretion in deciding not to intervene and it is difficult to see that the facts of the two cases were sufficiently extreme as to require state action.

The latter issue arose in the case of *Choudhury v UK*, where it was alleged that the United Kingdom had failed to protect the Article 9 rights of Muslims in failing to prohibit the publication of Salman Rushdie's novel *The Satanic Verses* (this followed the failure to extend the law of blasphemy in the Divisional Court in the case referred to above).[22] The Commission rejected the application. It was not prepared to find that there was a positive duty for the state to provide a right to bring any specific form of proceedings against those who, by authorship or publication, offend the sensitivities of an individual or of a group of individuals. Moreover, since there was no such duty, it followed that it was not possible for the applicant to establish the breach of an Article 9 right, and accordingly an allegation that English law infringed the right to equality conferred by Article 14 also failed. Although this case predates *Otto-Preminger-Institut*, it is likely that it would be decided in the same way today.

3.2 Asserting Religious Views

We now turn to consider the position in which Glenn Hoddle found himself, where a person by expressing his religious beliefs or his principles of conscience causes distress to others. It is likely that the mere expression (or manifestation) of one's personal or religious beliefs would be protected by Article 9 but even if it is not in

[20] Para. 50.   [21] Para. 58.   [22] (1991) 12 HRLJ 172.

any particular case, such expression will fall under the protection of freedom of speech under Article 10. In most cases it is unlikely to matter whether Articles 9 or 10 are engaged, but exceptionally it could do so since the potential justifications for imposing restrictions under Article 10(2) are drafted in broader terms than the equivalent justifications under Article 9(2).

In our view, the Football Association would constitute a public authority within s. 6 of the Human Rights Act 1998, and so would come under an obligation to act compatibly with Convention rights. Although it is not an 'obvious public authority' to use the typology favoured by the Lord Chancellor,[23] it has public functions as the regulatory body for football, and the body in charge of the national team and so would fall within s. 6(3)(b) as a public authority by virtue of exercising one or more public functions. As such, the FA would escape the reach of Convention rights in its private acts (s. 6(5)). It is well-established that the employment decisions of public authorities fall, in principle, outside the realm of public law.[24] There is an interesting and important debate—to be had on another occasion—as to whether employment decisions are, by the same reasoning, private acts within s. 6(5) or, on the other hand, whether private acts are simply those which occur in the course of exercising private, that is, non-public, functions. Our view, in short, is that s. 6(5) would not assist the FA: the issues under s. 6(5) are not identical to those which arose under RSC Order 53 and Hoddle's dismissal was intimately related to the public functions of the FA.

On the assumption that this is correct, the dismissal of Hoddle in similar circumstances after 2 October 2000 would have raised a prima facie case of breach of s. 6(1) of the Act by infringement of Articles 9 and 10 of the European Convention on Human Rights. Hoddle had not interfered with the rights of others, not at least unless that concept is interpreted so broadly as to be meaningless. The disabled do not have the right under the Convention to have respect shown towards their disabilities. Despite the implications of *Otto-Preminger-Institut*, merely upsetting the sensitivities of a group, even a vulnerable minority group, should not of itself provide the basis for a limitation on the freedom of speech. Hoddle's words were spoken in the context of a newspaper interview which was probing him to find out about his private persona. It was not made in a scurrilous or malicious manner, nor was it intended to mock the disabled. Voltaire did not undertake to fight to the death to protect freedom of speech as long as no one was offended by it, and it would be a worthless freedom if that set its limits.

Whilst a future Glenn Hoddle might frame their claim as being for breach of s. 6(1), a claim could equally be brought for compensation for unfair dismissal, on the basis that an employer cannot be said to have acted 'reasonably' within s. 98 of the Employment Rights Act 1996 in circumstances where it has acted in breach of a Convention right. It would appear in fact that the domestic law of unfair dismissal

---

[23] *Hansard*, HL (series 5), vol. 583, cols. 796 and 811 (24 November 1997).
[24] For example, *R v East Berkshire HA, ex p Walsh* [1985] QB 152.

will require some adjustments before it is capable of responding adequately to the demands of protection of Convention rights. Thus far, the approach of the courts in freedom of expression cases has been merely to require Employment Tribunals to weigh up in a reasonable manner the conflicting demands of employee's freedom of expression and employer's commercial advancement.

In *Boychuk v H. J. Symons Holdings Ltd.*, for example, an audit clerk whose duties brought her into contact with members of the public was dismissed for persisting in wearing a white badge with the words 'Lesbians Ignite' on it in large red letters.[25] The Employment Appeal Tribunal held that although there are limits upon an employer's discretion to dismiss an employee because he will not accept an employer's standards in relation to attire, hair and behaviour, it is for the Employment Tribunal to strike a balance, according to the circumstances of the particular case, between the need of the employer to control the business for which he is responsible in the interests of the business and the reasonable freedom of the employee.[26] There is a marked contrast between that approach, and the requirements of Articles 9 and 10, which are cast in terms of a prima facie freedom on the part of the employee, which may be subject to derogation in narrowly defined circumstances. The correct approach involves not so much balancing one right against the other, but rather the employer establishing that the prima facie right of the employee has been restricted in a legitimate and proportionate manner.

4. CONTRACTING-OUT OF FREE SPEECH

The Hoddle saga raises another issue of major importance in the field of free speech. It is this: to what extent can an employee contract out of his Convention freedoms? Surprisingly, the Commission appears to have been willing to find that he can, both under Articles 9 and 10. In the *Ahmad* case, the complainant was a Muslim schoolteacher who wished to attend the mosque on a Friday afternoon whilst remaining on a full-time contract. His employers put him onto a part-time contract, excluding Fridays. He alleged that this infringed his rights under Article 9. In proceedings in the English Court of Appeal, Scarman LJ in a dissenting judgment expressed the strong view that his rights had indeed been infringed.[27] The Commission held that his case was not even admissible on the grounds that he had voluntarily accepted the job and could have retained his religious freedoms by resigning from it.[28] Similarly, in *Stedman*, the Commission held that the applicant's rights under Article 9 had not been infringed because her objection to a new contract obliging her to work on a Sunday could be cured by getting a different job.[29]

[25] [1977] IRLR 395.
[26] See also, in relation to hair, *Smith v Safeway plc.* [1996] ICR 868.
[27] *Ahmad v ILEA* [1978] QB 36.
[28] *Ahmad v UK* (1982) 4 EHRR 125.
[29] *Stedman v UK* (1997) 23 EHRR CD128.

The Commission has adopted a similar approach to Article 10. The leading case is *Rommelfanger v Germany*, which concerned the employee of a hospital run by the Catholic Church in Germany who had pro-abortion views.[30] Various specific provisions of his contract of employment presupposed that he would be guided by 'Christian principles' when performing his professional duties. He was dismissed for expressing his views in a collective letter to a magazine and, later, in a television interview. His claims for wrongful dismissal failed before the German courts; the Commission also rejected his complaint of breach of Article 10. It held that there had been no interference at all with his right to freedom of expression: provided that contractual restrictions upon freedom of expression are genuine and freely entered into, an individual cannot claim to be a victim of an interference with his freedom of expression when those contractual restrictions are enforced.[31]

The striking feature of these cases is that because there is deemed to be no interference at all with the rights protected by Articles 9(1) or 10(1), it does not become necessary for the employer to justify contractual restrictions under the Article 9(2) and 10(2) exceptions. The employer may well have been able to do so in both *Ahmad* and *Rommelfanger*, but did not have to as the relevant rights were simply not engaged. It remains to be seen whether the domestic courts will be content to excuse employers on that basis, or, taking advantage of their freedom to depart from Strasbourg case law where appropriate,[32] will prefer to require justification of restrictive contractual provisions.

Could the employers have relied upon a contractual restriction in the Hoddle case? There was no express restriction on Hoddle's freedom of speech. Arguably it could be said that the nature of the job was such that he was obliged not to upset potential English supporters or risk bringing some unpopularity upon the team or the Football Association. But if such vague terms are to provide a justification for limiting freedom of speech, then the potential restrictions on all employees would be very significant indeed. Moreover, they would be justified not because of the sensitivities of the minority group, some of whose members might have been upset by the remarks, but rather by the sensitivities of the employer concerned with his public image and commercial interests. This seems to be a feeble basis indeed for limiting free speech.

5. CONCLUSIONS

The Glenn Hoddle case gave rise to deeply polarized views as to the justification for his dismissal. Very few of the anti-Hoddle views were informed by any consideration

---

[30] (1989) 62 DR 151.
[31] See also *VRU v Holland* (1986) 46 DR 200.
[32] Human Rights Act 1998, s. 2(1).

of his fundamental rights to freedom of religion, and freedom of expression, which, quite apart from the European Convention on Human Rights, are said to be protected by the common law.[33] Looked at from a distance, and in the light of fundamental rights norms, Hoddle's case is, it is submitted, a regrettable example of trial—and conviction—by media. It can only be hoped that the Human Rights Act will provide a much-needed sense of perspective in similar cases in the future.

[33]   *R v Home Secretary ex p Moon* (1996) 8 Admin LR 477 (Art. 9); *Attorney-General v Guardian Newspapers (No. 2)* [1990] 1 AC 109 (Art. 10).

4

Politicians and the Press

MICHAEL J. BELOFF QC

1. INTRODUCTION

My purpose is to examine the extent to which the law does, and to the extent that it does to which it should, have special rules governing the relationship of politicians and the press. I should note, at the outset, that politicians and journalists are citizens: the law that applies to others, applies to them. My concern is to detect where the particular function of each has created *distinctive* rules or approaches. That relationship of politicians and the press, one of mutual fascination, is special because the role of each is vital in a democratic society, and the way in which the balance between their respective interests is struck is fundamental to its proper operation. The main areas selected for study will be; parliamentary privilege; libel law; protection of privacy; and the impact of the European Convention on Human Rights (ECHR) and the Human Rights Act 1998 (HRA) upon the foregoing.

2. THE PRIVILEGES OF PARLIAMENT

Parliamentary privilege is defined in *Erskine May*,[1] as

the sum of the peculiar rights enjoyed by each House collectively as a constituent part of the High Court of Parliament, and by Members of each House individually, without which they could not discharge their functions [and a] fundamental right necessary for the exercise of constitutional functions.

Members of Parliament certainly enjoy unusual powers, which intrinsically seem more appropriate to the judicial than to the legislative arm of government. Journalists (and others) are still in theory liable to sanctions for abusive contempts consisting of words or actions by any person which either House considers disrespectful, insulting or defamatory. As recently as 1957, the House of Commons contemplated using its penal powers in respect of an editor who had claimed in an article that members were evading petrol rationing but whose apology to the Committee of Privileges was assessed as inadequate. In practice, the House of Lords have long ceased to take notice of abusive contempts: and the Commons' decision in 1978 to require evidence of substantial interference before treating a matter as contempt has consis-

---

[1] 22nd edn., 1997, 65. Also 34 *Halsbury's Laws* (4th edn.,) para.1004.

tently reduced its scope. The Joint Committee on Parliamentary Privilege (JCCP) 1998–9[2] recommended that abusive contempt be abandoned as a separate head of contempt of Parliament.[3] They reasoned 'if the abuse is so sustained or of such a degree that it amounts to an improper interference with the House or its members, then it constitutes a contempt anyway'.

But in addition to this (blunt) sword, Members of Parliament have a shield. Article 9 of the Bill of Rights 1689 provides:

That the freedom of speech and debates or proceedings in Parliament ought not to be impeached or questioned in any court or place out of Parliament.[4]

In an Australian case[5] it was held, on the basis of an historical review of its origins, that Article 9 was enacted to give absolute protection to MPs only against legal actions launched by the Crown: it was no impediment to the right of 'every citizen to express publicly his *honest* opinion concerning the conduct of MPs: no matter to what extent that opinion may impeach or question that conduct'.

The modern—and more expansive—interpretation is that it immunizes members of both Houses from being subject to any penalty, civil or criminal, in any court or tribunal for what they have said in the course of proceedings in Parliament: it protects speech inside Parliament from being impeached or questioned outside Parliament.[6] Its rationale is that 'Freedom of speech is central to Parliament's role. Members must be able to speak and criticise without fear of penalty'.[7]

'Impeachment' is limited to cases where a Member of Parliament is sought to be made liable, either in criminal or civil proceedings, for what he has said in

---

[2]   Joint Committee on Parliamentary Privilege. HL Paper 43–1 (para.270). HC 214–1 (JCPP).

[3]   Summary at 24.

[4]   For the position in other jurisdictions see *The Speaker of the House of Assembly of Nova Scotia v Canadian Broadcasting Corporation* (1993) 100 DLR (4th) 212, at 224, 265–7, 270–2 (Canada); *Maha v Kipo* [1996] 2 LRC 328, at 331 b–c, f–g (Papua New Guinea); *Siale v Fotofili* [1987] LRC 240, at 243 a–b, 245 d–e (Tonga); *Parliamentary Privileges Act 1987*, s. 16(1)(2)(d); Basu *The Indian Constitution* 588/612; McGee *Parliamentary Practice in New Zealand* (1st edn.) 424 (2nd edn.) 471–2; Joseph, *Constitutional and Administrative Law in New Zealand* 375, 379; *USA Constitution Section 5*; Joubert, *Law of South Africa*, vol. 20, para. 8.

For civilian jurisdictions see *8th Report from European Community Committee of the House of Lords HL 105 of 1995–6*: Belgium *32*; Denmark *35*; France *35*, Germany *40/41*; Greece *43/44*; Ireland *45/46*; Portugal *48*; Spain *40*; The Netherlands *47*, apparently lacks such a concept.

[5]   *R v Murphy* (1986) 5 NSWR 18

[6]   Redlich, *The Procedure of the House of Commons* (1908) concludes (at 48): 'The statement in the Bill of Rights shows the limits within which the principle is to be applied: the claim made is not for absolute freedom of speech; speech is only to be independent of every authority except the private jurisdiction of Parliament over its own members. The autonomous jurisdiction of Parliament is the reverse side of the shield which protects the principle of freedom of speech, in the technical sense of the word. *The power of Parliament to judge the acts and speeches of its members is the starting point, a condition precedent for its complete and absolute liberation from the control of any exterior authority.*' [Emphasis in original] (see also JCPP, para.37).

[7]   JCPP, para. 12.

Parliament:[8] In addition, parties to litigation cannot bring into question anything said or done in the House by suggesting (whether by direct evidence, cross-examination, inference or submission), that the actions or words were inspired by improper motives or were untrue or misleading so as to embarrass a Member in relation to his parliamentary conduct, or to detract from the authority and dignity of the House.[9] For example, evidence of what a defendant said in the House of Commons may not be introduced to assist in proof of malice, in a libel action brought against him for words spoken outside Parliament.[10] The vitality of that principle was endorsed by the JCCP.[11] But not all commentators have accepted its virtue. Bernard Levin called it a 'mudslinger's charter'.[12]

This rule, designed to allow members of Parliament freedom to say what they will about whom they will (including the press), proved, in the event, to be a two-edged weapon. In *Prebble v Television New Zealand*[13] *(Prebble)* a former New Zealand minister brought a libel action over television criticism of his conduct in the House of Representatives. The Privy Council held that parliamentary privilege prevented the TV station from supporting its allegations of impropriety by reference to what had been said and done in the House, and, therefore, the action must be stayed. Lord Browne-Wilkinson noted that to allow the action to proceed would create 'a real danger that the media would be forced to abstain from the truthful disclosure of members' misbehaviour' which would constitute 'a most serious inroad into freedom of speech'.[14]

Ripples from the New Zealand action duly reached the white cliffs of Dover and echoed in the Strand. In 1994 Neil Hamilton MP was forced to resign his junior ministerial post because of the 'cash for questions scandal'. When he sued *The Guardian* in July 1995, for an allegation of corruption, the newspaper argued on the basis of *Prebble* that their inability to question what occurred in Parliament by calling evidence about his conduct and motives in tabling parliamentary questions and early day motions meant that a fair trial was impossible. That action too was duly stayed[15]

---

[8] See *Pepper v Hart* [1993] AC 593 at 638 B–D.

[9] Criticism in the press, however, does not amount to questioning in this sense.

[10] *Church of Scientology of California v Johnson-Smith* [1972] 1 QB 522 per Browne J.

[11] JCCP para. 40.

[12] *The Times*, 20 December 1990. A compendium of alleged abuse by trigger happy members is to be found in Munro, *Studies in Constitutional Law* (2nd edn., Butterworths, 1999) (Munro) 243–4 e.g. Ken Livingstone alleged that the murdered Airey Neave might have been involved in treason in Northern Ireland. Marshall, 'Impugning Parliamentary Immunity' [1994] PL 509 at 812 asks whether the right of citizens to criticize the behaviour of their elected representative truly exists if Article 9 means what it says.

[13] [1995] 1 AC 321. The South Australian Supreme Court, however, held that the privilege does not extend to present challenges to the truth or honesty of statements made in Parliament when the maker of the statement himself initiates the proceedings: *Wright and Advertiser Newspapers Ltd v Lewis* (1990) 53 SASR 416.

[14] [1995] 1 AC 321 at 338.

[15] *Hamilton and Greer v Hencke* (QBD, 21 July 1995). On this same ground, Owen J stayed a libel action brought by a Member of Parliament against a journalist, and the editor of *Today: Allason v Haines* The Times, 25 July 1995.

but (unsuccessfully) revived in August 1996, by virtue of a waiver of privilege by Mr Hamilton under s. 13 of the Defamation Act 1996[16] (which came into force on 4 September 1996).

The argument in favour of that provision was that MPs should be no worse off than ordinary members of the public who have been defamed, and that it was anomalous that a politician should be prevented from suing only where their conduct inside Parliament is in question, but at the same time free to sue over allegations about their conduct outside. Peter Tapsell MP said on the floor of the House that it saved MPs from persecution from what many people regard as an over-mighty press, 'that is owned, for the most part by foreigners'.[17]

The argument against that provision was that since Article 9 has the purpose of enabling Parliament as a whole to discharge its collective functions and to secure the independence of legislators,[18] and the privilege is essentially the privilege of the whole House,[19] it should therefore not be capable of being waived by one person. My own submission that s. 13 could not, against the historic constitutional back-cloth, be so interpreted was rejected by the House of Lords in *Hamilton v Al Fayed.*[20]

The *Prebble* dilemma remains. On the one hand, the press should be free to establish the truth of their criticism of politicians. Otherwise responsible politics will be diminished and irresponsible politics encouraged. On the other hand, politicians should be free to clear their names of false charges. Otherwise responsible journalism will be inhibited and irresponsible journalism encouraged.

The JCCP has therefore recommended that s. 13 be repealed and replaced by a power for each House to waive privilege so as to enable the Courts to decide a particular dispute.[21]

But should the law facilitate politicians suing critics of their Parliamentary

---

[16] 'Where the conduct of a person in or in relation to proceeding in Parliament is in issue in defamation proceedings, he may waive for the purpose of those proceedings, so far as concerns him, the protection of any enactment, or rule of law which prevents proceedings in Parliament being impeached or questioned in any court or place out of Parliament'.

[17] *Hansard*, HC (series 6) vol. 262, col. 58 (24 June 1996). O Tempora, O Murdoch!

[18] *Burdett v Abbott* (1811) 14 East 138, 104 ER 501; *Stockdale v Hansard* (1839) 9 Ad & E 1, 122 ER 1112.

[19] *Prebble* at 335. See further Bradley, 'The Courts in Conflict with Parliament' [1999] PL 384; Williams, ' "Only Flattery is Safe" Political Speech and the Defamation Act' [1996] MLR, May 1997, 388; Sharland and Loveland 'The Defamation Act 1996 and Political Libels' [1997] PL 113. The authors there suggest that the *Prebble* interpretation of Article 39 shows 'indifference to the electorate's interest in such litigation'. (Likewise s. 13 (itself insofar as it makes member's choice the criterion.)

[20] [2000] 2 WLR 609. It would no doubt constitute the offence of scandalizing the judiciary to suggest that their Lordship's decision was animated by a desire to add to the stock of human pleasure by permitting the libel action to proceed. In the event the libel action (won by Mr Al Fayed) provided endless press coverage in the last months of the millennium. It even became a TV play 'Justice in Wonderland' (BBC2 10pm, 4 March 2000). Mr Hamilton is, however, pressing an appeal.

[21] Report HC 43. HC 214, 1998–9. Leopold 'Analysis' [1999] PL 605 at 608–9 (see also Munro 240–3).

conduct[22] or should rather the law take the opposite direction? The question leads the inquirer on from the ancient precepts of parliamentary law to the modern principles of libel law.

3. LIBEL

3.1 General

'Politics are a good source of the raw material of libel actions.'[23] On the left, Harold Laski, Chairman of the Labour Party, sued the Newark Advertiser for suggesting that he preached revolutionary violence.[24] Three prominent Socialist politicians Aneurin Bevan, Richard Crossman and Morgan Phillips sued *The Spectator* over an article 'Death in Venice' which commented on their 'capacity to fill themselves like tanks with whisky and coffee'. It is popularly believed that the three lied their way to success.[25]

Bessie Braddock sued for the suggestion that she danced a jig on the floor of the House of Commons,[26] Michael Meacher for the allegation that he falsely claimed to be an agricultural labourer's son, *vulgariter* prolier than thou.[27] On the right Reggie Maudling sued over imputations of corruption in his relationship with architect John Poulson,[28] Lord Aldington for an allegation that he was responsible for handing over 75,000 Cossacks in Yugoslavia in 1945 to the Soviets,[29] Michael Ashcroft,

[22] A particular problem arises where the House has already ruled on a member's behaviour, and he then seeks to relitigate the issue in actions against the press who make the self-same accusations, see *Pickin v BRB* [1974] AC 765 per Lord Simon at 800; *Hamilton v Al Fayed* [2000] 2 WLR 609. If the recent proposals of the Neill Committee on Standards in Public Life, that MPs accused of misconduct should enjoy fair procedures and rights of appeal to an ad hoc Tribunal presided over by a retired judge, are accepted (*The Times*, 4 January 2000) waivers may well not be given to an 'convicted' MP.

[23] Bristow, *Judge for Yourself* (William Kimber, 1989) 41; Watkins, *A Slight Case of Libel* (Duckworth, 1990): Some case studies, 19–25; Hooper, *Public Scandal, Odium and Contempt* (Coronet Books, 1988); ch 8: (Libel and the Politicians). Loveland, 'Reforming libel law: The Public Law Dimension' [1997] ICLQ 561; Hooper, *Reputations Under Fire* (Little, Brown, 2000) ch. 15–18.

[24] 'The Laski Libel action' (Verbatim Report), *Daily Express* (1948); Krammick and Sherman, *Laski: A Life on the Left* (Hamish Hamilton, 1993) ch. 20; Hastings QC, *Cases in Court* (Heinmann, 1949) 55–72.

[25] The case is discussed in Morgan (ed.), *The Back Bench Diaries of Richard Crossman: Morgan* (Hamish Hamilton and Jonathan Cape, 1981) 628–33; Adamson, *Gilbert Beyfus: The Old Fox* (Frederick Muller, 1963) 236–48; Watkins (n. 23 above) 21–3; Hooper, (n. 23 above) 'Death in Venice' ch.10; Brivati, *Lord Goodman* [1999] RCB ch. 3 'The Venetian Blind'; Carter-Ruck, *Memoirs of a libel lawyer* (Weidenfeld & Nicholson, 1990) ch. 8.

Foot: *Aneurin Bevan*, vol.II (London Davis-Poynter, 1973) 536–8 vehemently disputes the charge.

[26] Carter-Ruck (n. 25 above) 'Bessie Braddock and the Transport Bill', ch. 15. See also Pimlott *Harold Wilson* (Harper Collins, 1993) 225–628 slag heap libels.

[27] Watkins (n. 23 above) passim. The case was a marvellous illustration of the impact of political correctness on the class system.

[28] Raphael, *My Learned Friends* (W. H. Allen, 1989). ch. 3.

[29] In November 1989 he was awarded £1.5 million. Mitchell 'The Cost of a Reputation: Aldington versus Tolstoy: the cases, course and consequence of the notorious libel case' (Topical Books, 1998).

Treasurer of the Conservative Party for allegations that he was involved in money laundering.[30]

The fin de siècle trinity of Archer[31] (consorting with a prostitute in Shepherds Market, London), Aitken[32] (accepting Arab hospitality, while a minister, at the Ritz in Paris) and Hamilton (taking brown envelopes from Mohammed Al Fayed all over the place) brought actions which entertained, if not edified.[33] Rupert Allason (alias Nigel West) sued everyone—usually with success.[34] Nor have the Liberals been entirely squeezed out. In *Wright v Gladstone*, the plaintiff was provoked into suing the sons of W. E. Gladstone because they had called him a liar for alleging that the GOM was a woman chaser. Both the defendants (and their father!) were acquitted. The Foreman added 'The jury wish to add that in their unanimous opinion, the evidence that has been placed before them has utterly vindicated the high moral character of the late W. E. Gladstone'.[35]

Would politicians be wise to develop a thicker skin? They are on the horns of a dilemma. Sue—and they add fuel to the fire. Refrain from suit and they do not dowse the sparks. It has been said that there is an unwritten rule that politicians do not (usually) bite the hand that (usually) feeds them. 'Political journalists . . . enjoy an unofficially privileged position in relation to the laws of libel . . . They occupy this protected place because of custom and practice'[36]. A partial immunity of the kind accorded, it may be, more to the court jester than the public watchdog. But as John Major said when explaining why he sued the *New Statesman* in 1993 for repetition of a rumour that he had had an affair with Claire Latimer, a Downing Street caterer: 'The Press, though they often complain about the laws of defamation, are quick to raise an eyebrow and note pointedly that someone has not sued'.[37]

---

[30]   The action against *The Times* was compromised in December 1999. Outsiders evaluated it as a no-score draw.

[31]   Archer was awarded £500,000. Alleged revelations against him about an effort to concoct an alibi prompted suggestions that the newspaper might claim the money back in 2000AD: Adoko, *The Libel case of the Century. The Jeffrey Archer Scandal* (London: Truth Publishers, P.O. Box 155, 1990). Raphael, (n. 28 above) ch. (1–4: Archer 1–41): Crick, *Jeffrey Archer: Stranger Than Fiction* (London: 4th Estate, 1999), ch. 20–1.

[32]   Aitken was impaled on the sword of truth. Harding, Leigh and Patrick, *Liar: The Fall of Jonathan Aitken* (London: 4th Estate, 1999), ch. 11–12.

[33]   Hamilton had early success. Carter-Ruck (n. 25 above) ch. 39: 'Maggie's Militant Tendency'. Raphael (n. 28 above) ch. 11: (Maggie's Militant Tendency).

[34]   He was profiled in his capacity as an indefatigable political plaintiff in the *Sunday Telegraph Magazine* 10 May 1999, 25–6.

[35]   Montgomery Hyde, *Norman Birkett* (Hamish Hamilton, 1964) 176–204. See also Montgomery Hyde, *Their Good Names* (Hamish Hamilton, 1970) ch. 10; Sparrow *The Great Defamers* (John Long, 1970) ch.19.

At a lesser level of political distinction, Jack Hayward, a Liberal Party Benefactor, was allegedly accused by the *Sunday Telegraph* of involvement in conspiracy to murder, Norman Scott, lover of Jeremy Thorpe. Hooper (note 23 above) ch.14.

[36]   Watkins (n. 23 above) 17–18.

[37]   John Major, *The Autobiography* (Harper Collins, 1999) 553–4.

3.2 Defamatory Imputations

The law of libel is obviously applicable to statements about politicians.[38] To accuse a politician of corruption, irresponsibility, disloyalty or incompetence is defamatory,[39] although it has been judicially suggested that criticism of public figures is subject to some kind of group discount.[40] In *Gorton v Australian Broadcasting Corporation*,[41] Fox J said:

The finding of a derogatory imputation is not the end of the matter: it must have been such as to affect adversely the reputation of the plaintiff. A person in public office expects to be, and is frequently, the subject of comment and criticism, and not a little of that comment or criticism is of a person's nature. Sometimes a slur is cast on his honesty or integrity. The television viewer recognises these things. The result is that criticisms and comments made of public figures are apt to have less impact than similar remarks made of others.

It has also been observed that

whether any particular words spoken of a politician are actionable may have to be judged in the light of his occupation—its environment of snap judgments and point-scoring and uncomfortably plain speaking including at times vehement discrimination—and the public's expectations with respect to it. For that reason, a criticism of occupational inconsistency is unlikely to be actionable if made of a politician though it may be if made of a university examiner.[42]

33. Capacity to Sue

When Derbyshire County Council sued *The Sunday Times* for a libel upon the council's so-called 'governing reputation', the newspaper argued that the common law right to free speech, buttressed by the European Convention on Human Rights (ECHR), would be violated if the council's claim were allowed to proceed. The House of Lords duly held that a local authority could not sue for attacks upon its corporate governing reputation because it is more important to uphold freedom of political speech to protect local or central government from criticism, whether or not warranted.[43]

---

[38] Gatley *on Libel and Slander* (9th edn., Sweet & Maxwell, 1998) ('Gatley') para. 2.33.
[39] Gatley (ibid.).   [40] Gatley (ibid.).
[41] (1973) 22 FLR 181 at 189.
[42] *Peterson v Advertiser Newspapers* (1995) 64 SASR 152, per Cox J. Any suggestions that this is an Antipodean eccentricity is belied by cases such as *Mutch v Robertson* 1981 SLJ 217: *Brooke v Lind* The Times, 26 March 1997.
[43] *Derbyshire County Council v Times Newspapers* [1993] AC 534 (*Derbyshire*). There were foreign precedents for this absolutist approach. In *City of Chicago v Tribune* 139 NE 86 (1923), the Supreme Court of Illinois held that the city could not maintain an action for libel. In *Die Spoorbond v South African Railways* [1946] AC 497 the Supreme Court of South Africa held that the South African Railways and Harbours, a governmental department of the Union of South Africa was not entitled to maintain such an action in respect of a publication alleged to have injured its reputation as the authority responsible for running the railways.

Lord Keith observed that to rule otherwise could have a 'chilling effect' on the exercise of free speech.[44] Subsequently, and on the same basis, French J. dismissed a libel action by British Coal against the National Union of Mineworkers on the footing that it was an 'arm of government'.[45] and Buckley J denied ability to sue to political parties.[46]

3.4 Fair Comment

It is well recognized that 'a man who chooses to enter the arena of politics must expect to suffer hard words at times'.[47] The public conduct of any person who holds or seeks public office or position of public trust is fit material for fair comment: it satisfies *one* of the three ingredients of the defence i.e. that the statement is made on a matter of public interest, although, elementarily, it must also be both comment and fair within the elastic meaning given to that adjective in libel law.[48] The private lives of politicians are also grist to the mill in so far as they tend to throw light on the politician's ability to perform his or her duties: 'if the policy of a government is to promote "family values", then it is submitted that the marital affairs of members of the government are of legitimate public interest'.[49] David Mellor, amongst many others, found this out to his cost. The boundary between fact and comment is blurred: a perceptive commentator has observed 'Politicians are regarded . . . as being closer to actors and performers than to businessmen and financiers',[50] in the sense that criticism of them will more readily be allotted to the category of opinion than factual assertion, thus enlarging the canvas upon which the journalist's pen (or word processor) can freely play.

3.5 Qualified Privilege

English libel law presumes the claimant to have an unblemished reputation. It also presumes in the claimant's favour that the words complained of are false.[51] It puts the burden on the defendant to prove the substantial truth of the publication. If the defendant attempts to make out the defence of justification, but without success, he exposes himself to the risk of increasing the damages. Furthermore, a strict liability rule applies: the defendant's state of mind is irrelevant in determining liability.[52]

---

[44] Derbyshire (n. 43 above) 548.
[45] QBD, 28 June 1996.
[46] *Goldsmith v Bhoyrul* [1998] QB 459. See Barendt, 'Libel and Freedom of Speech in English Law' [1993] PL 449); Loveland, 'The Constitutionalisation of Political Libels in the English Common Law?' [1998] PL 633.
[47] *Australian Consolidated Press v Uren* (1966) 117 CLR 185 at 210.
[48] Gatley (n. 38 above) para. 12.2.
[49] ibid. para. 12.2.
[50] Watkins (n. 23 above) 18.
[51] 'If the words are used which are defamatory and untrue, the law implies malice' *Reynolds v Sunday Times* [1999] 3 WLR 1010 *('Reynolds')* per Lord Hope at 1050.
[52] Where an alleged libel involves criticism of the conduct of government ministers or elected politicians, the civil law is more draconian in its effect upon freedom of political discussion by the media and

The defence of qualified privilege enables someone, without incurring legal liability, to make statements about another person which are defamatory and factually incorrect, or which cannot be proved by admissible evidence to be true. The basis of the privilege is the public interest in free speech. In a situation of qualified privilege, a person, stating what he believes to be the truth about another, is protected, provided that the statement is made honestly and without reckless disregard for truth.[53]

While Parliament has conferred qualified privilege for the fair and accurate reporting of various proceedings, to whomsoever they are published,[54] English law recognizes no general privilege to make defamatory statements to the world at large simply on the ground that they concern matter of public interest.[55] Thus a privilege for such publication has been the exception rather than the rule, even if it would be in the public interest for the public to know the information.

To have the benefit of the defence, the publisher must have a duty to make the statement and the recipient must also have an interest or duty in receiving it. Statements as to the conduct of candidates for public office may be privileged. 'It is contrary to public policy that electors should not have considerable latitude in discussing the qualifications of those who solicit their suffrages and so long as they do not speak maliciously they ought to be protected'.[56] But the lack of objectivity of political opponents is acknowledged: 'I need hardly say that there is no privilege known to law which allows persons engaged in politics to mis-state a fact about their opponents provided they say it honestly even if untruthfully.'[57] Outside that discrete area, the historic tendency of the common law of England and Wales has been to confine the defence to intimate situations.

In other jurisdictions Courts have taken a less severe line. As was observed in *Reynolds*[58] 'the solutions are not uniform . . . the chosen solutions have not lacked critics in their own countries'[59].

In *New York Times v Sullivan*[60] in 1964 the United States Supreme Court decided that Alabama libel law could not pass muster under the strong constitutional protection

---

citizen critics than is the common law crime of sedition which requires proof beyond reasonable doubt of a seditious intention.

[53] Gatley (n. 38 above) paras. 14.1–2.

[54] ibid. ch. 15; see Defamation Act 1996 amending the Defamation Act 1952.

[55] *Blackshaw v Lord* [1984] QB 1 (cf. *Webb v Times Publishing Co.* [1960] 2 QB 535) [discussed in Loveland 'Political Libels and Qualified Privilege—a British solution to a British Problem' [1997] PL 428] and Loveland 'Reforming Libel Law—the Public Law Dimension' [1997] EGLQ 560 at 577–80.

[56] *Bruce v Leiske* (1892) 219 R. 482 at 485. The limits of this privilege are unclear: Gatley (n. 38 above) paras. 14.32–14.33. In *Braddock v Bevins* [1948] 1 KB 880 allegedly libellous statements in an election address were held to be an occasion of qualified privilege. This was abolished by s. 10 of the Defamation Act 1952: Gatley (n. 38 above) para. 14.34.

[57] *Plummer v Chapman* [1962] 1 WLR 1469 per Diplock LJ at 1474.

[58] See Loveland for a discussion of the case in the Court of Appeal: 'Political Libels and Qualified Privilege: a British Solution to a British Problem' [1997] PL 428.

[59] [1999] 3 WLR 1010 per Lord Nicholls at 1021C.

[60] 376 US 254 (1964).

given to free speech by the First Amendment. 'Congress shall make no law . . . abridging the freedom of speech or of the press'.

Sullivan was an elected political commissioner who claimed that he had been libelled by statements about police action allegedly directed against students taking part in a civil rights demonstration. The Supreme Court ruled that as a public official he could not sue for a defamatory falsehood relating to his official conduct unless he proved with convincing clarity that the statement had been made in bad faith or with reckless disregard of whether it was true or false. The test was compendiously described as one of 'actual malice'.

Justice William Brennan observed that erroneous statement is inherent in free debate, and that it must be protected if free expression is to have the 'breathing space' it needs. A rule compelling the critic of official conduct to guarantee the truth of all his assertions leads to self-censorship. 'Under such a rule, would-be critics of official conduct may be debarred from voicing their criticism, even though it is believed to be true and even though it is in fact true, because of doubt whether it can be proved in court or fear of the expense of having to do so. The rule thus dampens the vigour and limits the variety of public debate'.[61] The doctrine applies to candidates for public office and to politicians in its full rigour.[62]

In India, the Supreme Court has followed *Sullivan*, holding that a public official cannot sue for such a libel unless he proves that the publication was made out of personal animosity or with reckless disregard for truth,[63] where malice is alleged. A defendant can defeat a claim of malice by proof that he acted after reasonable verification of the facts.[64]

In Australia, the High Court has widened common law qualified privilege for media publications relating to government or political matters in the widest sense, but it has required the media publisher to show that its conduct was reasonable.[65] The route to that conclusion took various twists and turns.

In *Australian Capital Television v The Commonwealth*[66] *(Australian Capital TV)* and *Nationwide News Party Ltd v Wills (Nationwide News)*,[67] a majority of the High Court of Australia distilled from the provisions of the Australian Federal Constitution, particularly from the concept of representative government that it found enshrined in it, an implied right to freedom of communication at least in relation to 'political discussion'. They therefore declared invalid an Act of the federal parliament

---

[61]   376 US 254 (1964) 279.

[62]   Gatley (n. 38 above) para. 14.84.

[63]   *Resogopal v State of Tamil Nadu* 1994 JT 1994 6 (SC) 524. Article 19 of the Indian Constitution guarantees free speech subject to 'reasonable restrictions'.

[64]   *Reynolds* (n. 51 above) at 1021.

[65]   *Theophanous v Herald and Weekly Times Ltd.* (1994) 68 ALJR 713; *Stephens v West Australian Newspapers Ltd.* (1994) 68 ALJR 765. See Trindade 'Political Discussion and the Law of Defamation' [1995] LQR 199. Loveland *'Sullivan v The New York Times* goes down under' [1996] PL 126; Lord Lester QC 'Defaming Politicians and Public Officials' [1995] PL 1; *Lange v Australian Broadcasting Corporation* [1997] 189 CLR 520.

[66]   [1992] 177 CLR 106.   [67]   [1992] 177 CLR.

which prohibited political advertising during election periods (*Australian Capital TV*) and another Act which prohibited criticism which might bring the Australian Industrial Relations Commission into disrepute (*Nationwide News*).

This reasoning was then transplanted to the discrete area of defamation law. In *Theophanous v Herald and Weekly Times,*[68] ('*Theophanous*'), the plaintiff, an Australian of Greek origin, was a member of the House of Representatives; the first defendant, published in its newspaper a month before an election to that body in letters written by the second defendant contained imputations that the plaintiff showed a bias towards Greeks as migrants and that he was an idiot.

In *Stephens v West Australian Newspapers Ltd,*[69] ('*Stephens*') the plaintiffs were members of the legislative council of Western Australia and they were also members of one of its standing committees. The defendant published in its newspaper three articles which claimed that in that capacity they had gone on an 'overseas junket of mammoth proportions at parliament's expense without the knowledge of parliament'.

Theophanous decided by a majority that the defamatory publication in question clearly fell within the concept of 'political discussion'. Even if it was false, it should be a protected publication since freedom of communication was to be implied in federal and state constitutions. However the burden was on the defendant to show that it was unaware of the falsity of the published material, it did not publish recklessly and took reasonable steps to check the accuracy of material.

What is the concept of 'political discussion'? It was said to include the 'discussion of conduct, policies or fitness of officers of government, political parties, public bodies, public officers and those seeking public office'. 'Discussion of political views and public conduct of persons who are engaged in activities have become the subject of political debate, e.g. trade union leaders' and 'political publications and addresses which are calculated to influence choices'. 'Criticism of the views, performance and capacity of a member of parliament and of the member's fitness for public office, particularly when an election is in the offing, is at the very centre of the freedom of political discussion'.[70]

While this analysis was constitution-specific (as indeed was the judgment in *Sullivan*), the High Court in *Theophanous* also expanded the defence of qualified privilege in relation to defamatory communications made in newspapers in the course of political discussion. Henceforth, the discussion of political matters in the newspapers was to be regarded as an occasion of qualified privilege:

---

[68] (1994) 68 ALJR 713.
[69] (1993–4) 182 CLR 211.
[70] (1993–4) 182 CLR 154 at 121, 123, 124 respectively. The majority decision in *Stephens* was to the same effect extended also to public discussion in the form of conduct and fitness of officers of the state legislature. For domestic discussion of what is 'political', see *R v Radio Authority, ex p Bull* [1998] QB 294. (Under the Broadcasting Act 1996 the Radio Authority can refuse permission to advertise to a body whose objects were mainly of 'a political nature' (not party political)); Amnesty International fell foul of this provision. See also *McGovern v AG* [1982] ch 321. (Amnesty International not entitled to charitable status because its objects were in part political.)

The public at large has an interest in the discussion of political matter such that each and every person has an interest, the kind contemplated at common law, in communicating his or her views on those matters and each and every person has an interest in receiving information on those matters.[71]

The High Court of Australia revisited the issue in *Lange v Australian Broadcasting Commission* ('*Lange*').[72] *Lange* laid down that the extended qualified privilege protected a communication made to the public on a government or political matter—even overseas matters. While malice defeats qualified privilege in limited circulation cases, a new test of reasonableness operates in mass circulation cases. The High Court considered that 'the reasonableness requirement was appropriate having regard to the greater damage done by mass dissemination compared with the limited publication normally involved on occasions of common law qualified privilege'.[73] *Lange* reasonableness went beyond the *Theophanous* reasonableness. The defendant had to show not only that it did not believe that imputation to be false, but that it had reasonable grounds for believing that it was true; not only that it took proper steps, so far as they were reasonably open, to verify the accuracy of the material); but also where practicable, to obtain a response.[74]

In *Lange v Atkinson*[75] (which concerned again criticism of the reproachable Mr Lange's behaviour as Prime Minister) the New Zealand Court of Appeal adapted the *Lange* defence from Australia to New Zealand but restricted it to statements about those 'elected or seeking election to Parliament' in New Zealand; it refused to incorporate into the extended defence of qualified privilege the requirement of reasonableness.[76] The Privy Council which heard the appeal, determined to refer the case back to the New Zealand Court of Appeal because 'there is a high element of judicial policy in the resolution of the issue' and 'the possibility of a difference between English and New Zealand Common Law has to be accepted, albeit not advocated'.[77]

In South Africa, the Supreme Court of Appeal has supported the Australian approach.[78] Press publication of defamatory statements of fact will not be regarded as unlawful if, upon consideration of all the circumstances, it is found to have been reasonable to publish the particular facts in a particular way and at the particular time. In considering the reasonableness of the publication account must be taken of

---

71 (1993–4) 182 CLR at 140. See generally on the Australian position. Gatley (note 38 above) para. 14.85.

72 *Lange v Australian Consolidated Press N.Z. Ltd.* (1997) 189 CLR 520.

73 (1997) 189 CLR 520 at 1021A.

74 The placing of the burden of proof upon the defendant of showing reasonable conduct further differentiates the Australian from the American law.

75 [1998] 3 NZLR 424.

76 This incurred the criticism of the New Zealand Law Commission (NZLC 3 September 1998).

77 *Reynolds* [1999] 3 WLR 1010 per Lord Cooke at 1044. 'In considering the decisions in other jurisdictions it is right to take into account that cultural differences played an important role' per Lord Steyn at 1031.

78 *Boyoshi v National Media Ltd* 1998 (4) SA 1196.

the nature, extent and tone of the allegations. Greater latitude is to be permitted when the discussion is political.

The Supreme Court of Canada rejected the *Sullivan* principle[79]—although they observed that issues involving the media and political comment on governmental policies such as had been an issue in *Theophanous* did not call for consideration on the facts.[80]

Just as in *Sullivan*, the fact that the plaintiff was a white segregationist, so in *Hill* the fact that the defendant was the Church of Scientology may have influenced the Court. Hard cases make bad law; atypical parties likewise.

3.6 Competing Interests?

Derbyshire did not decide what would happen if the individual politician, as distinct from the body of which he was a member, sued to vindicate his governmental reputation. Would English courts be prepared to confer special protection on 'political discussion' (the Australian device) or impose special restrictions on 'political plaintiffs'(the American device)?

In *Reynolds*,[81] the *Sunday Times* alleged that the Irish Taoiseach had deliberately lied to his Cabinet. The newspaper's case was that qualified privilege should extend to media publication to the public at large of information and opinions concerning government and political matters affecting the people of this country.

The House of Lords held that the press has a general duty to inform the public on political matters and that the public has a right to be so informed: and that the fact that newspapers are widely read by the public at large is no longer a ground for withholding of defence.[82]

But unlike the Antipodean, Indian and South African Commonwealth courts, the Law Lords declined to develop 'political information' as a generic category of information whose publication attracted qualified privilege irrespective of the circumstances. Lord Steyn was influenced by two matters, one pragmatic, one precedental, namely the fact that newspapers in England (unlike the United States) cannot be compelled to reveal their sources, and the Strasbourg jurisprudence.[83]

The Law Lords preferred the elasticity (critics would say uncertainty) of a different approach and enjoined consideration of all the circumstances of publication[84] which would enable the courts to give appropriate weight, in today's conditions, to the importance of freedom of expression by the media on all matters of public

---

[79] *Hill v Church of Scientology of Toronto* (1995) 126 DLR 4th 129] *('Hill')*. See above p. 40 (Zines).

[80] ibid. 196, para.137. See Huscroft 'Defamation, Damages and Freedom of Expression in Canada' (1996) 112 LQR 46.

[81] *Reynolds* [1999] 3 WLR 1010.

[82] Trindade, 'Defaming Politicians The English Approach' (1999) LQR (April) 175. On the Court of Appeal decision see Mullender, 'Defamation. Qualified Privilege and the ECHR' [1999] CLJ 15.

[83] [1999] 3 WLR 1010 at 1032–3.

[84] Listed (expressly but not exhaustively) by Lord Nicholls at 1022C–G

concern. Between politicians and the press, the scales were tilted in the latter's favour. Lord Nicholls said that 'The Court should be slow to conclude that a publication was not in the public interest, especially when the information is in the field of political discussion'.[85]

A new public interest defence, publication of information of public concern, may be relied upon provided that the newspaper or broadcaster has exercised its powers fairly and reasonably. But to have the benefit of the defence, reporters will have to show that their research has been careful and conscientious.

As Lord Nicholls observed: 'The common law does not seek to set a higher standard than that of responsible journalism, a standard the media themselves espouse'.[86] If that standard is not met, the media will have, as before, to satisfy the test of truth.

3.7 Damages

There was a period during the late eighties and early nineties when jury awards in the Court of England and Wales appeared to be generous to a fault: and, amongst others, politicians, such as Lords Aldington and Archer, were the beneficiaries. However, the Strasbourg Court gave impetus to a lowering of the tariff,[87] when in *Tolstoy v UK*[88] it quashed an award of £1.5 million made to Lord Aldington in respect of a defamatory pamphlet accusing him of war crimes on the ground, inter alia, that the award was 'disproportionate'.

There has as yet been no domestic ruling that the political context of an action has any peculiar relevance to the quantum of damages. But, the British Columbia Court of Appeal ruled that the guarantee of freedom of expression entrenched in the Constitution required that the Court exercise restraint in awarding damages for politically motivated defamation[89] although older jurisprudence had suggested that those who had taken on the burden of public life deserve more, rather than less, compensation, when their reputations are sullied by their opponents.[90]

4. PRIVACY

It is notorious that English law knows no tort of privacy,[91] nor has there been a

---

85 [1999] 3 WLR 1010 at 1027H.   86 ibid at 1025–6.
87 Gatley (n. 38 above) para. 9.2–9.3. See also Loveland, 'Reforming Libel Law. The Public Law Dimension' [1997] ICLQ 560 at 562–71.
88 (1995) 20 EHRR 422.
89 *Derrickson v Thomal* (1992) 10 CLLT 201 2d(1) 1.
90 It was subsequently doubted that this would apply in the case of civil servants denied the right of response: *Newson v Kexco Publishing Co.* (1995) 17 BCLR 3d 176. Leave to appeal to the SCC was refused (1992) 6 WWR viii.
91 Gatley (n. 38 above) ch. 21, section 2. Privacy is however protected in Art. 12 of UN Declaration of Human Rights and Art. 17 of the International Covenant on Civil and Political Rights as well as in Art. 8 of the European Convention on Human Rights.

uniform call for its introduction.[92] But in so far as there has been a movement in favour of such reform, the treatment of politicians has been significant in giving it impetus and, absent legislation, it appears possible that the courts would seize the initiative.[93]

Sir David Calcutt QC, a modern establishment fire-fighter, underwent a change of heart.[94] He gave a number of instances of, inter alia, politicians whose privacy had been invaded by press in ways which the Press Complaints Commission (PCC) had been powerless to prevent e.g. Clare Short MP, Virginia Bottomley MP, Paddy Ashdown MP, David Mellor MP, QC (the first two exposed as unmarried mothers: the second two as adulterers).[95]

Politicians have less rights to privacy than ordinary citizens, but they do not have none. The Canadian Supreme Court has said:[96]

It is generally recognised that certain aspects of the private life of a person who is engaged in a public activity or has acquired a certain notoriety can become matters of public interest. This is true, in particular, of artists and politicians . . .

A Research Working Paper for the Broadcasting Standards Commission (BSC)[97] tested public attitudes. Its conclusion was 'Politicians have low rights, but probably higher than film stars'.[98]

Quasi-law has reflected the same approach, as appears, for example, from:

* the BBC Code 'Privacy and the Gathering of Information':

1. General
Public figures are in a special position. The public should have facts that bear upon the ability or suitability of public figures to perform their duties! When the personal affairs of public figures become the proper subject of enquiry they do not forfeit all their rights to privacy.

* the ITC Programme Code:

2.1 General
. . . there will be occasions when the individual's right to privacy must be balanced against the public interest . . . Examples of how the public interest may be served include . . . (iv) exposing significant incompetence in public office. . . .

---

[92]   The Younger Report (Cmnd 5012 (1972), para. 659) and the Calcutt Report (Cmnd 1102 (1990) para. 12.5): both recommended that no general tort of invasion of privacy be introduced.
[93]   Lord Bingham of Cornhill LCJ, 'Should there be a law to protect the Rights of Personal Privacy?' [1996] EHRLR 450 at 461–2 (wrote at 462): 'But if, for whatever reason, legislation is not forthcoming, I think it almost inevitable that cases will arise in the Courts in which the need to give relief is obvious and pressing and when such cases do arise, I do not think the Courts will be found wanting.' See also Dame Mary Arden, 'The Future of the Law of Privacy' Kings College London, 26 November 1997.
[94]   Calcutt, *Review of Press Self-Regulation*, Cm. 2315 (1993) at xiii, para. 17.
[95]   ibid. at ch. 4.
[96]   *Les Editions Vice Versa v Aubty* (1998) 5 BHRC 437 at 443, para. 21.
[97]   Institute of Communication Studies: The University of Leeds. 'Regulating for Changing Values'.
[98]   ibid. 84.

2.9 Interviews without prior arrangement
Impromptu interviews with public figures . . . are a normal and unproblematic part of
news gathering . . .

• The BSC Code of Guidance June 1998 made under s. 107 of the Broadcasting
  Act 1996 targeted 'unjust or unfair treatment' or 'unwarranted infringement of
  privacy'.

Paragraph 14 of the BSC Code of Guidance states 'An infringement of privacy has
to be justified by an overriding public interest in disclosure of the information . . .
This would include . . . disclosing significant incompetence in public office.'

Paragraph 17 states: 'People in the public eye . . . because of the position they
hold . . . are in a special position. However, not all matters which interest the public
are in the public interest.'

The Broadcasting Standards Commission upheld a complaint of unwarranted
infringement of privacy made by Frank Field MP in respect of a BBC Watchdog
programme broadcast on 19 September 1996 which included an item concerning a
visit which members of the House of Commons made to Chile to find out about the
privatization of pensions there. The programme included footage of MPs filmed
without their permission at Heathrow Airport, on board the plane, in their hotel
lobby and in the street in Santiago, making it look as if it was 'something of a jaunt
at public expense . . .' even though the 'film revealed no wrongdoing, and there was
no reason to suppose that it would do so'.

The Press Complaints Commission case file shows a similar approach. Rupert
Allason MP complained that a report headlined 'Tory MP and his mistress' in the
Daily Mirror of 9 May 1996 constituted an invasion of his privacy in breach of
Clause 4 (Privacy) of the Code of Practice, and that he had been harassed by the
newspaper in breach of Clause 8 (Harassment). The newspaper relied on the MP's
portrayal of himself as a happily married family man. In its adjudication (March
1997) the Commission said:

As a matter of principle, the Commission strongly believed that the mere fact that a person is
a public figure did not in itself justify publication of intimate details of his or her private life
unless the story could be demonstrated to be in the public interest—although Members of
Parliament, as representatives of their constituents, clearly had to expect a greater degree of
public scrutiny. The Commission did not believe it could plausibly be argued that a Member
of Parliament had an absolute duty publicly to correct facts or impressions conveyed in interviews or an Election Address when they ceased to be accurate, especially when this might
occur some time after the election concerned, provided that the MP did not appear to be
continuing to foster that impression.

The Commission found that in the particular circumstances of this case, the newspaper had sufficient public interest justification under Clause 18(iii) for its intrusion
into the complainant's privacy, and therefore rejected the complaint under Clause 4
of the Code.

In another case Roger Gale MP complained that a report headlined 'Gun Shame of Tory MP's son' in *The Mirror* on 3 March 1997 contained an inaccurate account of an incident involving his fifteen-year-old son in breach of Clause 1 (Accuracy) of the Code of Practice. In its adjudication (May–June 1997) the Commission said:

However, one area of concern to the Commission is where the children of public figures feature in newspaper or magazine stories which would not be published or justified if they were children from ordinary families.

The Commission would like to reiterate that the mere fact of a family or other relationship to someone in the public eye does not *of itself* justify the publication of a story about them. Sometimes a family connection is central to a story which can be justified in the public interest; in other cases it merely provides illustration of a political or other point.

Where possible, stories about public figures which raise *issues* about, or involve, their children should be published without detail—including name—which might lead to the identification of the child. Where a story about the parents of the child is justified in the public interest, the vulnerable position of a child must be taken into consideration—and the child only identified in exceptional circumstances.

The most illustrious politician to complain was the Prime Minister, Tony Blair MP (and his wife) who submitted that articles and a leader in *The Mail on Sunday* on 24 January 1999 intruded into their daughter's privacy in breach of Clause 6 (Children).

The article, including one on the front page headlined 'Parents' Fury over Blairs in School Place Row' and an accompanying leader comment, concerned the decision by the Sacred Heart High School in Hammersmith to admit Kathryn Blair—the Prime Minister's daughter—while rejecting other local children. In its adjudication (August–September 1999) (upholding the complaint) the Commission said:

Clause 6 (Children) provides that young people should be free to complete their time at school without unnecessary intrusion, and that where material about the private life of a child is published, there must be justification other than the fame or position of his or her parents.

It is manifestly the role, and responsibility, of the press to scrutinise Government policies and the conduct of those responsible for them. The press should be entitled to relate such scrutiny to the children of politicians where their conduct in matters relating to their children has an impact on policy or gives rise to reasonable charges of hypocrisy. In appropriate cases this might provide the exceptional public interest justification required by the Code.[99]

The dividing line between what is in the public interest, and what is merely of interest to the public is easy to state, difficult to apply, but the National Heritage Committee[100] found itself able to distinguish between revelations of two of the predicaments of Norman Lamont, then Chancellor of the Exchequer: the financing

---

[99] In a more dramatic instance the same couple obtained what were perceived to be an ex parte injunction against the same newspaper on 4 March 2000 when intimate revelations of their family life from their ex-nanny appeared on the front page of the first edition.

[100] Fourth Report on Privacy and of Media Intrusion House of Commons 294–1 at para. 5. See also Lamont, *In Office* (Little Brown, 1999) 313–18.

of his legal advice by the taxpayer on the one hand, and his credit card transactions on the other, holding the former, acceptable, but not the latter. Were the common law to develop a privacy law autonomously or under Euro-influence, it would certainly need to grapple with similar distinctions.

5. THE EUROPEAN CONVENTION ON HUMAN RIGHTS

5.1 Freedom of Expression

Article 10 of the Convention guarantees the right to freedom of expression. It provides, so far as is relevant, as follows:

1. Everyone has the right to freedom of expression. This right shall include freedom to hold opinions and impart information and ideas without interference by public authority and regardless of frontiers . . .

2. The exercise of these freedoms, since it carries with it duties and responsibilities, may be subject to such formalities, conditions, restrictions or penalties as are prescribed by law and are necessary in a democratic society . . . for the protection of health or morals, for the protection of the regulation or rights of others, for preventing the disclosure of information received in confidence . . .

In *Lingens v Austria*[101] the publisher of a magazine printed two articles accusing the Austrian Chancellor of protecting former members of the Nazi SS for political reasons 'of the basest opportunism'.[102] He was convicted of criminal defamation and fined.

The Strasbourg Court decided that the Austrian courts had breached Lingen's right to free expression in breach of Article 10 of the Convention. It emphasized that freedom of the press:

affords the public one of the best means of discovering and forming an opinion of the ideas and attitudes of political leaders . . . Freedom of political debate is at the very core of the concept of a democratic society which prevails throughout the Convention . . . The limits of acceptable criticism are accordingly wider as regards a politician as such than as regards a private individual.[103]

It also draws a distinction, familiar to the common law between facts and value judgments: 'The existence of facts can be demonstrated, whereas the truth of value judgments is not susceptible of proof'.[104]

---

[101] (1986) 8 EHRR 407.
[102] See Loveland, 'Reforming Libel Law; the Public Law Dimension' [1997] ICLQ 164.
[103] (1986) 8 EHRR 407 at para. 42. See also *Castells v Spain* (1992) 14 EHRR 445 at para. 43; *Oberschlik v Austria* (1991) 19 EHRR at para. 60. They also stressed 'the demands of pluralism, tolerance and broadmindedness' (para. 41). In *Oberschlik v Austria* (1991) 19 EHRR 389 a journalist had suggested that for a politician to advocate welfare discrimination against immigrants reflected Nazi philosophy, and been convicted for so doing.
[104] (1988) 8 EHRR 407 at para. 46.

A politician, the Court held, inevitably and knowingly 'lays himself open to close scrutiny of his every word and deed by both journalists and the public at large, and he must consequently display a greater degree of tolerance'.[105] *Scienti* not *volenti* is the defence!

In *Castells v Spain*[106] where an opposition politician criticized the government in an article for failing to counter 'the ruthless hunting down of Basque dissidents', the Court drew a still nicer distinction between the degrees of criticism appropriate to various classes of persons: 'The limits of permissible criticism are wider with regard to the government than in relation to a private citizen, or even [sic] a politician', while noting (without expanding) that 'the freedom of political debate is undoubtedly not absolute in nature'.[107]

The Strasbourg Court has reflected both the American and Antipodean models. Sometimes emphasis is on identity of the object of the publication as a public figure, in others on the public interest content of the information. In *Incal v Turkey*,[108] the prosecution of the distributor of a leaflet accusing the Turkish Government of trying to drive Kurds out of Izmir by repressive policies for inciting hatred through racist words was held to be a disproportionate interference with the exercise of his right to freedom of expression, even if an interference in pursuit of a legitimate aim i.e. the prevention of disorder. The Court noted that speeches by opposition politicians were of great importance.[109] In *United Communist Party v Turkey*[110] where the Turkish Constitutional Court had dissolved a political party, the Court said 'there can be no democracy without pluralism. It is for that reason that freedom of expression as enshrined in Article 10 is applicable . . . The fact that their activities form part of a collective freedom of expression in itself entitles political parties to seek the protection of Article 10 . . . of the Convention'.[111] In Strasbourg as in the Strand, the press is given a particular level of protection.[112]

5.2 Privacy

Article 8 of the Convention guarantees the right to respect for the private life. It provides, so far as is relevant, as follows:

1. Everyone has the right to respect for his private and family life, his home and his correspondence.

---

[105]   ibid.   [106]   (1992) 14 EHRR 445.
[107]   In *Thorheir Thorgeirson v Iceland* Series A No. 239 (police brutality) the court said that there was no warrant for 'distinguishing between political discussion and discussion of other matters of public concern' (para. 46). This did not limit the special protection of Art. 10 to political discussion: but rather extended it more widely.
[108]   (1998) 29 EHRLR 449.
[109]   ibid.
[110]   (1998) 26 EHRR 449.
[111]   ibid. para. 42.
[112]   Tierney, 'Press Freedom and the Developing Jurisprudence of the ECHR' 1998 EHRLR 418; McBride 'Judges, Politicians and the Limits to Critical Comment' (1998) 23 EHRLR 76.

2. There shall be no interference by a public authority with the exercise of this right except such as is in accordance with the law and is necessary in a democratic society in the interests of . . . the economic well-being of the country, for the prevention of disorder or crime, for the protection of health or morals, or for the protection of the rights and freedoms of others.

'Article 8 has been used in a whole range of contexts; from phone tapping to the use of medical records in Court; from the rights of children whose parents are deported to the right to have records altered'.[113] Curiously intrusions by the press into private lives have been thinly, if at all, explored in the jurisprudence of the Convention organs.[114]

As to the general case law it appears that the protection of the privacy of the individual may require not only abstention from interference with the right, but positive action on the state's behalf for its effective implementation.[115]

However, as to the particular case law, in *Winer v UK*[116] it was specifically held that absence of a right of privacy in domestic law capable of being enforced against private individuals did not violate the applicant's rights under Article 8.

The rights set out in Article 10 and Article 8 are not absolute. The Convention requires a fair balance to be struck and maintained between conflicting rights, 'taking account of the importance which the Court of Human Rights has attached to freedom of the press to investigate political . . . matters in the public interest'[117] and any restriction upon them must satisfy the requirements of legal certainty, and be 'convincingly established by a compelling countervailing consideration, with the means employed being proportionate to the end sought to be achieved'.[118] Moreover 'The claim to respect for private life is automatically reduced to the extent that the individual himself brings his private life into contact with public life . . .'[119] Politicians who peep above the parapet risk press retaliation.

---

[113] Wadham and Mountfield, *Human Rights Act 1988* (Blackstone, 1999) at 40–3.

[114] See, e.g., Van Dijk and Van Hoof, *Theory and Practice of the ECHR* (3rd edn., Kluwer, 1999) 489–504 where it is not discussed; Feldman 'The Developing Scope of Article 8 of the European Convention on Human Rights' (1997) EHRLR (Issue 3) 265; Rabinder Singh, *The Future of Human Rights in the United Kingdom. Essays on Law and Practice* (Oxford: Hart Publishing, 1997) ch. 5.

But see *Earl Spencer v UK* App. Nos. 28851/95 and 28852/95 decision of 16th January 1998 which decided, interestingly, that the case was inadmissible because the Earl had not exhausted the domestic remedy provided by the law of confidence. Also in *Lingens* (1986) 8 EHRR 407 at para. 42, the Court said that the protection of the reputation of politicians could be protected under Art. 10(2) 'even when they are not acting in their private capacity' (see also para. 48) which suggests that the Convention *is* necessarily concerned with this aspect of the multi-faceted privacy right.

[115] Airey. Series A No. 32 (1979) 2 EHRR 305. In England, however, the HRA does not bind Parliament.

[116] 1986 Application No. 10871/84 48 DR 154.

[117] Mullender, 'Defamation. Qualified Privilege and the ECHR' [1999] CLJ 15.

[118] Singh, 'Privacy and the Media. The Impact of the Human Rights Bill' (see n. 114 above) at 21.

[119] *Bruggemann and Scheuten v Germany* Application No. 6959/75 at para. 55–6.

6. THE HUMAN RIGHTS ACT

When the HRA is brought fully into force, the English courts will be required to read and give effect to statutes, such as the Data Protection Acts, so far as possible, compatibly with Convention rights and to declare and to apply the common law compatibly with them also.[120]

But it was unnecessary to wait until 2 October 2000, to have *regard* to the relevance of Convention law in a common law context, since it is well established that English courts should, where possible, develop and apply the common law and equity in conformity with Convention rights, including the law protecting confidences and personal reputation.[121]

What will the impact of HRA be? English judges are certainly not constrained slavishly to follow Strasbourg jurisprudence.[122] All that can be said with a measure of confidence is that the coming into force of the HRA will be more relevant to privacy than to freedom of expression, given the identification of the common law with the Convention in the latter.[123]

7. IMPACT ON PRIVACY

There is a debate between academics, soluble only by the courts, as to whether or not the HRA creates private law claims rights in the same terms as Article 8 of the ECHR.[124] The better view is the judges will be able to fashion a right to privacy out of existing material; not to invent a new cause of action, although one judge has extra-curially doubted even that.[125] Public authorities, however, will certainly have to respect the right. For this purpose, BBC and Channel 4 may be public authorities: but not commercial channels. The PCC might also be liable under judicial review *qua* public authority for acting in a way incompatible with a complainant's Convention right of privacy.[126]

---

[120] *R. v DPP, ex p. Kebeline* [1999] 3 WLR 972, HL.

[121] See e.g. *Attorney-General v Guardian Newspapers (No.2)* [1990] AC 109; *Derbyshire* [1993] AC 534; *Reynolds* [1999] 3 WLR 1010.

[122] HRA, s. 3(1); Beloff, 'What Does it All Mean?' Lasok Memorial Lecture: (University of Exeter, 1998).

[123] See n. 117 above. The HRA, s. 12 protects press, as far as possible, from ex parte injunctions protecting privacy: regard has to be had, inter alia, to freedom of expression, and the public interest in publication.

[124] Hunt, ' "The Horizontal Effect" of the Human Rights Act' [1998] PL 423 takes one view, Wade ('Horizons of Horizontality' [2000] LQR 216 at 217) another. See also Singh (n. 114 above) at 23; Leigh, 'Horizontal Rights The Human Rights Act and Privacy: Lessons from the Commonwealth' [1999] ICLQ 57.

[125] Buxton LJ, 'The Human Rights Act and Private Law' (2000) LQR 116 at 48.

[126] Singh (n. 114 above) 79.

8. AUDIT

The case books are replete with sonorous descriptions of the importance of the press in a modern democracy, and the values of free expression. A classic statement is by Lord Steyn:

It is the lifeblood of democracy. The free flow of information and ideas informs political debate. It is a safety valve: people are more ready to accept decisions that go against them if they can in principle seek to influence them. It acts as a brake on the abuse of power by public officials. It facilitates the exposure of errors in the governance and administration of justice . . . of the country[127]

And there is no doubt that the developing case law is generally judged by commentators to be virtuous by the extent to which it lifts restraints from the press. There is, however, in my view, another side to the story, and one which I wish to articulate as an epilogue to my analysis of the status quo. For there is surely a difference between protecting the right of the press to express robust opinions about the political activities of politicians, and (subject as it may be to considerations of privacy) to tell the truth about them, and protecting the press from the consequence of publishing inaccuracies or telling lies.

Derbyshire in particular is unsatisfactory in a number of ways: both because of the questions that it left unanswered—what *is* an arm of government for this purpose?[128]—and because of the way in which it answered the questions posed to it. Although it purportedly borrowed from the reasoning of the American Supreme Court,[129] it gives a green light to the publication of falsehoods and licences malicious or reckless journalism in a way in which the Supreme Court, for all its tilting of the scales in favour of the press, did not. Balance does not enter into the *Derbyshire* equation at all. The tort of malicious falsehood, in theory available to politicians, provides no remedy since it will usually be impossible for them to establish economic loss; contrary to populist perception the profession of MP is not designed to generate profit—at any rate before retirement to the city or memorial authorship. The right of individuals to sue, held in *Derbyshire* to survive, will be vain where no individual is identified in the offending piece.[130] *Goldsmith* followed *Derbyshire* uncritically; but as has been aptly observed, 'parties do not govern . . . people do'.[131]

Nor does the *Sullivan* 'public figure' test provide a perfect solution. The majority of the High Court in *Theophanous* made it clear it was wary of introducing it to

[127] *R. v Secretary of State for the Home Department, ex p Simms* (1999) 3 WLR 328 at 337.
[128] The same kind of question arises in many contexts i.e. is a particular body amenable to judicial review? Is EC law directly effective against a particular body? Is a body a public authority for the purposes of s. 6 of the Human Rights Act 1998?
[129] *New York Times Co. v Sullivan* 376 US 254 (1964).
[130] [1993] AC 534 at 551. In any event that right is further inhibited by *Reynolds*.
[131] *Loveland* [1998] PL 633 at 633.

Australia since it 'tilts the balance unduly in favour of free speech against protecting an individual reputation'.[132]

In *Hill,* the Canadian Supreme Court stressed still more emphatically the need to balance a freedom of expression, which was *not* absolute, against the reputation of the individual.[133] They noted that *Sullivan* had increased burdens on the Court by requiring consideration of such open-textured questions: [who is a public figure? what is a matter of legitimate public concern?];[134] it had shifted focus away from key issue, [was statement false?], to subsidiary issue, [was the defendant negligent?];[135] it had necessitated inquiry into matters of media procedure;[136] it had increased cost of litigation;[137] above all it depreciated truth in public discourse.[138]

Still more devastatingly, in *Dun v Bradstreet Inc. and Greenmoss Builders Inc.*[139] two judges (including White J who was a member of the *Sullivan* Court) called for its reconsideration, saying that *Sullivan* polluted information about public officials and affairs, and destroyed personal reputations.[140] The Neill Committee report on practice and procedure in defamation[141] said 'standards of care and accuracy in the press are . . . not such as to give any confidence that the "Sullivan" defence would be treated responsibly'.[142]

There are indeed other principles to weigh against the two simple and attractive ideas, that democracy requires public debate and that people who enter public life must be prepared to put themselves in the firing line.[143]

Firstly, equality before the law should apply to politicians as much as anyone else. To divide the population into classes and attach different legal consequences to the membership of each is inherently discriminatory and requires at the very least powerful justification.

Secondly, the purpose of open debate is that it should lead to truth, not falsehood. If publication of untruths is too freely permitted by the law, policies will be deformed, cynicism increased and time needlessly spent as citizens turn wastefully, and even vainly, to other vehicles than the media for enlightenment.

Thirdly, personal autonomy and human dignity are critically involved. In *Silkin v Beaverbrook Newspapers*[144] Diplock J said 'Every man, *whether he is in public life* or not is entitled not to have lies told about him'. The right to reputation is a vital component of such overarching rights.

---

[132] (1994) 68 AJLR 713 at 724. *Sullivan* has been criticized for much the same reasons in Faulks, *Committee on Defamation* (London: HMSO, 1975), in the *Kirby Committee Report* (Australia Government Publishing Service, 1979) and in Keane *Final Report* (Dublin Law Commission 1991).

[133] (1995) 126 DLR (4th) 129 at 157–64 (paras. 107–22); 155–6 (paras. 100–7).

[134] ibid. at 166 (para. 127).   [135] ibid. 167 (para. 128).

[136] ibid. 166 (para. 129).   [137] ibid. 166 (para. 130).

[138] ibid. 166 (para. 131).   [139] 472 US 749 (1985).

[140] ibid. 767–9.   [141] Supreme Court Procedure Committee July 1991 paras. 164–5.

[142] ibid. See also Trindade 'Defamation in the Course of Political Discussion—The New Common Law Defence' [1998] LQR (January) 1; Loveland 'The Constitutionalisation of Political Libels in English Law' [1998] PL 633.

[143] S. Kentridge QC: 'Freedom of speech: Is it the Primary Right?'[1996] 45 ICLQ 253, 266–8 recapitulates many of the objections.   [144] [1958] 1 WLR 743 at 746.

There are surely some libels so gross and offensive that they should be publishable only on condition that they are proved to be true.[145]

And there are pragmatic considerations in play as well.

The power of the press is awesome. A powerful press is all too often an irresponsible press. Especially among the tabloids, in Lord Goodman's epigram 'Publish and damn someone else' is their watchword. The law should provide a check, not a spur to such licence.

Unbridled abuse can deter persons from entering public life. Cockburn CJ said 'The public have an equal interest in the maintenance of the public character of public men: and public affairs should not be conducted by men of honour . . . if we were to sanction attacks upon them, destructive of their honour and character and made without any foundation'.[146]

We should be careful in (rightly) protecting freedom to express vigorous opinion[147] but we acknowledge that the same tolerance is not automatically to be accorded to the promulgation of false facts.

The press have been drinking for so long in Last Chance Saloon, to use the phrase of David Mellor, subsequently, if coincidentally, one of the most notorious victims of press exposure, that they must be forgiven for having become intoxicated with their own power: which, as Baldwin pungently reminded us, they enjoy without responsibility—the prerogative of the harlot throughout the ages.

But I end with the reflection of the change of heart of a politician who ranks higher in history's lists than Baldwin. In 1787, before Thomas Jefferson entered government as Secretary of State, he expressed an 'unhesitating' preference for newspapers without government over government without newspapers. By 1807, after four years as Vice-President and six as President, he came round to the gloomier view that:

A man who never looks into a newspaper is better informed than he who reads them inasmuch as he who knows nothing is nearer to the truth than he whose mind is filled with falsehood and errors.

To which the press barons might reply, as did Mandy Rice Davies, 'well he would say that, wouldn't he?'

---

[145] Kentridge (n. 143 above) 267.

[146] *Campbell v Spottiswoode* (1863) 3 BS 769 at 777. At dinner at High Table in Trinity recently I discussed with two prominent politicians, Senator Gary Hart and Lord Lamont, both objects in their time of intense press interest, their attitude to libel laws. Senator Hart, with *Sullivan* in mind, said it was impossible in the USA for a politician to sue. Lord Lamont, considering the laws costs and delays, said that it was impracticable in the UK for one to do so.

[147] *Hector v Attorney-General of Antigua* [1990] 2 AC 312 at 318. Lord Bridge pointed out the need to expose those in government to criticism. Any attempt to style or fetter such criticism amounts to political censorship of the most insidious and objectionable kind.

5

The Protection of Political Discourse: Pragmatism or Incoherence?

CHRISTOPHER FORSYTH

It has been my great privilege to know Sir David Williams in several capacities. First, when I was a post-graduate student his lectures—always elegant, always insightful and with the deep scholarship enlivened by the personal touch—stimulated my interest in judicial review; and this has proved a life-long interest. Then he was the examiner of my PhD thesis and eased me through the ordeal of the oral examination and kindly overlooked its many flaws. Then as a colleague in the Law Faculty he has been helpful and understanding in all matters. When I was Junior Proctor and much involved with university ceremonial and administration we worked together in the Senate House a great deal; I hope that I served him well. In all these capacities he has been entirely consistent: always thoughtful, courteous, fair and efficient whatever the provocation—which was often considerable. Chaucer's words spring unbidden to mind as an apt description of our honorand: 'He was [and is] a verray parfit, gentil knyght.' I owe him a great deal and write the essay that follows as a tribute to him knowing all the while that it does not match the standard that he has set.

1. INTRODUCTION: THE CENTRAL INCONSISTENCY

There are two decisions of the House of Lords that will doubtless dominate for some time to come discussion of how the inevitable tension between the necessity, in a democracy, of free speech on matters of political moment and the protection of the reputation of those involved in the political process is to be resolved. They are *Derbyshire CC v Times Newspapers Ltd.*[1] and *Reynolds v Times Newspapers Ltd.*[2] Both will be discussed in more detail below, but for the present we may take the former as laying down that civil actions for defamation, brought by the institutions of central and local government, would amount to an undesirable fetter on the freedom to express that uninhibited criticism of government that is the hallmark of a democratic society and were thus contrary to the public interest. The latter case, on the other hand, lays down there is no genus of qualified privilege that protects the publication of political information. The creation of such a generic privilege would leave the reputation of those in public life insufficiently protected. Thus a politician could

---

[1]   [1993] 2 WLR 449, HL. See Loveland [1997] PL 428 and Barendt [1993] PL 449.
[2]   [1999] 3 WLR 1010, HL.

bring a defamation action in respect of allegations made against him in respect of his conduct while in government. The publishers of such allegations would be able to raise the defences of justification, fair comment and qualified privilege in the usual way—although the test of what was a privileged occasion was reformulated—but they would not be able to raise a special defence that protected political discourse at the expense of individual reputations.

The starting point of this essay is that there is a significant inconsistency between these two decisions. Government is not carried out by machines; it is carried out by persons, each with his or her own reputation. Everyone knows that individuals are in charge of public authorities. Much criticism of 'the Government' or 'the Council' therefore necessarily, or almost inevitably, has some impact on the reputation of the individuals in charge of the relevant institutions. Put more directly, the principle of group defamation,[3] which allows criticisms of a group to be transmuted in appropriate circumstances into criticisms of individuals, even if not mentioned by name, is the straightforward and relatively uncontroversial mechanism whereby criticisms of public authorities may be transmuted into criticism of the individuals who currently have stewardship of that public authority. And here is where the inconsistency comes to light: if free and vigorous criticism of public authorities is a necessary part of a democratic society how can free and vigorous criticism of the individuals in charge of those public authorities be avoided?

This inconsistency is at the heart of the leading decision of the United States Supreme Court, *New York Times Co. v Sullivan*.[4] That case, also to be discussed in more detail below, concerned criticism, inter alia, of police conduct in the treatment of civil rights demonstrators in Montgomery, Alabama. But no police officer was mentioned by name. The plaintiff was, however, an elected Commissioner of Public Affairs in Montgomery with responsibility for the local police. The Alabama Courts accepted that the average person knew that the police were under the control and direction of the relevant commissioner and thus the criticism of the police referred to him. But the Supreme Court disagreed sharply. Brennan J in the majority judgment said this:

For good reason 'no court of last resort in this country has ever held, or even suggested, that prosecutions for libel on government have any place in the American system of jurisprudence'.[5] The present proposition would side-step this obstacle by transmuting criticism of government, however impersonal it may seem on its face, into personal criticism, and hence potential libel of the official of which the government is composed. There is no legal alchemy by which a State may thus create the cause of action that would otherwise be denied for [such] a publication . . .

---

[3] Group defamation will be discussed below.
[4] 376 US 254 (1964).
[5] *City of Chicago v Tribune Co.* 307 Ill. 595 (1923) which essentially adopts the position in *Derbyshire*.

In other words, if it is necessary to allow that free criticism of public authority in order not to have 'a chilling effect' on freedom of expression, how can the individuals concerned remain free to sue, for their actions would have just as great, if not greater, 'chilling effect' on freedom of expression.[6]

Goldsmith v Bhoyrul[7] may serve as a local illustration of the inconsistency of the two principles. This was an action for damages for libel brought by the late Sir James Goldsmith and the Referendum Party (in form a company limited by guarantee) against certain journalists and the *Sunday Business*. The newspaper had published a report to the effect that 'Sir James Goldsmith has begun to pave the way for pulling the Referendum Party completely out of the General Election . . .'. Since the Referendum Party was campaigning on the basis that it would participate fully in the General Election in order to secure a referendum on the future relationship between the United Kingdom and Europe, it viewed this report as an allegation that it had lied to the electorate as to its true intentions.

An application was made by the respondent to strike out the claim made by the Referendum Party on the basis that the *Derbyshire* principle applied to political parties; and thus a political party could not maintain an action for libel. Buckley J, while recognising that 'great caution' should be applied, agreed that the Referendum Party could not sue. He said: [8]

it seems to me that the public interest in free speech and criticism in respect of those bodies putting themselves forward for office or to govern is also sufficiently strong to justify withholding the right to sue. Defamation actions or the threat of them would constitute a fetter on free speech at a time and on a topic when it is clearly in the public interest that there should be none . . .

The action by Sir James Goldsmith was allowed to continue.[9] But Sir James was in fact the founder of the Referendum Party which he had set up precisely in order to secure a referendum on the topic of Britain's future in Europe. On the issue of Britain in Europe there was really no difference between Sir James and the Referendum Party. If allowing the Referendum Party to sue would have a 'chilling effect' on free and vigorous debate on such matters, that very consequence must flow surely from allowing Sir James to sue.

This inconsistency between precluding public bodies from suing and permitting those in charge of those bodies to sue is seldom acknowledged. On the contrary the availability of the individual action is seen as in part justifying the restriction on the protection of reputation consequent upon denying the action to public bodies. Thus Lord Keith remarked in *Derbyshire*: 'A publication attacking the activities of the

---

[6] Essentially this same point was put to the Court of Appeal by Lord Lester in *Reynolds v Times Newspapers Ltd.* [1998] 3 WLR 862, 903–4 but not cogently answered.

[7] [1997] 4 All ER 268.

[8] ibid., at 270–1.

[9] There was a similar situation in *Derbyshire CC* itself for the council leader, Mr Bookbinder, was a plaintiff in that case and his statement of claim was 'for all practical purposes in identical terms [to that of the County Council]'.

authority will necessarily be an attack upon the body of councillors which represents the controlling party, or on the executives who carry on the day-to-day management of its affairs. If the individual reputations of any of these is wrongly impaired by the publication any of these can himself bring proceedings for defamation.'[10]

Now what is to be made of this inconsistency? Is it a sign of incoherence at the centre of the way in which the balance is struck between the protection of reputation and the freedom of political discourse? Or is it a sign of the pragmatic genius of the common law in producing a workable solution to an important problem by paying scant regard to the theoretical and analytical issues that may arise. This essay will use this inconsistency as a prism through which to view these issues often adopting a comparative perspective. We may begin with a fuller account of some of the leading decisions.

2. *DERBYSHIRE* AND *DIE SPOORBOND*

In *Derbyshire CC v Times Newspapers Ltd.*[11] the Times newspaper had questioned the propriety of certain investments made by the County Council for its superannuation fund. The sting of the alleged libel is summed up in the following headline—'Socialist tycoon's deals with Labour Chief', the tycoon being Mr Owen Oyston and the Labour Chief being the leader of the Council, Mr David Bookbinder. The Derbyshire County Council and its leader Mr Bookbinder instituted action for libel. It had been held in *Bognor Regis Urban District Council v Campion*[12] that local authorities did have a 'governing' reputation; and that reputation could be vindicated by a libel action. So in the narrowest terms the impact of the case was that the *Bognor Regis UDC* case was overruled. But the case is noteworthy for the unanimity of its reasoning—Lord Keith delivered the only speech—and the apparent ease with which he laid down that:

there [is] no public interest favouring the right of organs of government, whether central or local, to sue for libel, but that it is contrary to the public interest that they should have it. It is contrary to the public interest because to admit such action would place an undesirable fetter on freedom of speech.[13]

This conclusion was reached in reliance upon the reasoning of the similar decision of the Appellate Division of the Supreme Court of South Africa of *Die Spoorbond v South African Railways.*[14] Part of the dictum of Schreiner JA approved by the House of Lords was:

[10] [1993] 2 WLR 449, 459. Lord Keith also approved the remark made by Schreiner JA in *Die Spoorbond v South African Railways* [1946] AD 999, 1013 'if the criticism consists of defamatory utterances against individual servants of the state actions for defamation will lie at their suit'.
[11] [1993] 2 WLR 449. [12] [1972] 2 QB 169.
[13] [1993] 2 WLR 449 at 458D. [14] 1946 AD 999.

The normal means by which the Crown protects itself against attacks upon its management is political action and not litigation ... [But, exceptional cases aside,] any subject is free to express his opinion upon the management of the country's affairs without fear of legal consequences. I have no doubt that it would involve a serious interference with the free expression of opinion hitherto enjoyed in this country if the wealth of the state, derived from the state's subjects, could be used to launch against those subjects actions for defamation because they have, falsely and unfairly it may be, criticised or condemned the management of the country.

Die Spoorbond involved an employer suing a trade union, but the employer was the government department having charge of the railways in South Africa. The union had alleged, and this had been published in a newspaper, that the railways' administration had permitted trains to be run on important commuter lines in a dangerously overloaded condition and at dangerously high speeds; and thus it had daily endangered the lives of the travelling public. The government instituted a defamation action alleging that the article was false and defamatory and 'calculated to injure and did injure the plaintiff in the provision and carrying on by it of railways in the Union [of South Africa] and in its reputation as the authority controlling, managing and superintending such railways'.

Watermeyer CJ drew a sharp distinction between the reputation enjoyed by a trading or business corporation and the reputation of the Crown in relation to its trading and business activities—such as the running of railways. A business corporation existed solely for the purposes of carrying on that business but the Crown's 'main function is that of Government'.[15] As such the Crown's 'reputation or good name is not a frail thing connected with or attracted to the individuals who temporarily direct or manage some particular aspect of the many activities in which the Government engages. ... Its reputation is a far more robust and universal thing which seems to me to be invulnerable to attacks of this nature'.[16]

While both the House of Lords in *Derbyshire* and the Appellate Division in *Die Spoorbond* refer frequently to the importance of free speech, these decisions may, perhaps, be justified on broader public policy grounds than simply the protection of freedom of political discourse. Neither weighs the right to reputation against the right to free expression. Both treat the public authority as if it had no reputation protected by the law and thus there was nothing to put in the balance on the one side. In *Die Spoorbond* disapproval was expressed of the use of the state's wealth, derived from its subjects, to launch defamation actions against those subjects.[17] Could not some such principle, rather than freedom of expression as such, justify these decisions?

---

[15] [1946] AD 999, at 1009.

[16] *Die Spoorbond* thus deals with the attempt by central government to sue a subject for defamation while *Derbyshire* concerns a local government authority that sought to sue for libel. Lord Keith recognises this but remarks after quoting at length from Schreiner JA's judgment, that these 'observations may properly be regarded as no less applicable to a local authority than to a department of central government' ([1993] 2 WLR 449 at 459C). Schreiner JA, however, specifically left open the question of whether the principle applied to local government (at 1014).

[17] But note that ministers, civil servants and judges may bring state funded libel actions when they are attacked in the press (*The Times*, 22 February 2000).

3. *REYNOLDS*

Reynolds v Times Newspapers Ltd.[18] was a much more difficult decision than *Derbyshire*. The House of Lords was not unanimous—although their lordships did all agree on the most significant point, the non-existence of a generic defence protecting political discourse—and five speeches were delivered.

But let us start with the facts, stripped of some of their procedural complexities. Mr Albert Reynolds was the Taoiseach.[19] There was a political crisis in Ireland and he resigned. The *Sunday Times*, published in England, reported these events in an article published under the headline 'Why a fib too far proved fatal for the political career of Ireland's peacemaker and Mr Fixit.' The sting of the libel was that Mr Reynolds had deliberately misled the Dail and his cabinet colleagues through the suppression of vital information. The jury found at the original trial that the facts alleged were not true thus the defence of justification failed. And fair comment failed since the basic facts on which the comment rested were not true. Nor were the allegations a fair and accurate report of the proceedings in the Irish Parliament, so that species of qualified privilege also failed. The focus of the case thus fell upon whether, as the newspaper argued, there was a new category of privileged occasion: where political information[20] was communicated.

These arguments failed and the crucial conclusion reached by all the judges was that the common law should not develop a new category of qualified privilege whereby the publication of all political information would attract qualified privilege whatever the circumstances (other than where the plaintiff showed malice).[21] This would fail to provide adequate protection for the reputation of the individuals concerned. It would, moreover, be unsound in principle to distinguish political discussion from other matters of serious public concern. There was, however, some protection for political information embedded in the developed common law approach to privilege, viz., of considering whether there was a duty to publish the information to the intended recipients and whether they had an interest in receiving it.[22]

But there were important nuances of difference in the several reasons given by the judges to reject the generic defence. Lord Nicholls, with whom Lord Cooke and Lord Hobhouse expressly agreed, was primarily concerned that, because of the difficulties facing a plaintiff in proving malice by the publisher, the generic defence would mean that 'a newspaper, anxious to be first with a "scoop," would in practice be free to publish serious misstatements of fact based on the slenderest of materials.

---

[18] [1999] 3 WLR 1010, HL.   [19] Prime Minister.
[20] This was information, opinion and arguments concerning government and political matters that affect the people of the United Kingdom.
[21] The Court of Appeal had favoured a generic defence of qualified privilege in the context of political speech whose availability would depend upon the circumstances of the publication. See [1998] 3 WLR 862, 899–900.
[22] The reformulation of the defence of privilege will be discussed below.

Unless the paper chose later to withdraw the allegations, the politician thus defamed would have no means of clearing his name and the public would have no means of clearing his name, and the public would have no means of knowing where the truth lay'.[23] Moreover, 'it would be unsound in principle to distinguish political discussion from discussion of other matters of serious public concern'.[24] Lord Steyn was also impressed by the weakness of the plaintiff's position if he could only succeed by showing malice. He pointed out that in the US, the plaintiff was entitled to extensive pre-trial enquiry into the sources of the story and the editorial decision-making—but this was not the case locally.[25] Lord Hope's objections to a generic defence were rather different: he considered that a generic defence for political information was too ill defined and feared that the lack of clarity would be inappropriately exploited by the media.[26] For Lord Hobhouse the fact that there was no public interest in publishing misinformation was important. 'Misleading people and the purveying as facts statements which are not true is as destructive of democratic society and should form no part of such a society.'[27]

Thus if the newspaper had a defence it was to be found in the traditional common law approach to qualified privilege which was itself reformulated in several of the speeches and in the judgment of the Court of Appeal.[28] This reformulation will be discussed below.[29]

4. GROUP DEFAMATION: A RED HERRING?

The inconsistency which stimulated the writing of this essay may readily arise in circumstances in which no question of group defamation arises.[30] For instance, where the critical statement expressly refers both to the public authority and to the individual in charge of that authority—as was the case in both *Derbyshire* and *Goldsmith*—there is no difficulty over showing reference to the plaintiff authority or the individual plaintiff, although only the latter can sue. Thus the principle of group defamation is not a necessary condition for the creation of the inconsistency. None the less, the engine of group defamation can transmute criticism of an authority into criticisms of individuals and so raise the inconsistency in its acutest form.

This may be illustrated by a little known decision of the South African Appellate Division, *South African Associated Newspapers Ltd. v Estate Pelser*,[31] where group

---

[23] [1999] 3 WLR 1010 at 1024C.   [24] ibid., at 1027B.

[25] ibid., at 1032 referring to *Herbert v Lando* 441 US 153 (1979).

[26] ibid., at 1056.   [27] ibid., at 1059D.

[28] [1998]3 WLR 862 (Lord Bingham CJ and Hirst and Walker LJJ).   [29] At 97.

[30] The principle is simply that where a defendant's statement refers only to a class or group of persons and the plaintiff is not referred to by name, that statement may yet be understood as referring to the plaintiff. See *Knuffer v London Express Newspapers* [1944] AC 116 or *Aspro Travel Ltd v Owners Abroad Group* [1996] 1 WLR 132.

[31] 1975(4) SA 797 (A). Amid much comparative discussion no mention of this case was made in *Derbyshire* or *Reynolds*.

defamation allowed a Cabinet member to stifle criticism on a politically contentious matter. The facts were stark.[32] What had happened was that Kenneth Wilson (a white man) and Zacharia Makinitha (a black man) committed a murder and a robbery together. They were apprehended, tried and convicted on charges of murder and robbery. On the law as it then stood, the death sentence was the mandatory sentence for murder unless extenuating circumstances were shown. In the event the court found no extenuating circumstances; and both were sentenced to death. But Makinitha walked a lonely path to the gallows for the white man was reprieved.

The Director of the Centre for the Abolition of Capital Punishment (the late Professor Barend van Niekerk) was vehemently critical of this decision and his criticism was published by South African Associate Newspapers. The crucial words were:

One would have expected the Government to save the life of Makinitha, to avoid the obvious inference of discrimination; that they did not do so speaks volumes for their lack of concern for justice and the reputation of our law.

The Minister of Justice (P. C. Pelser) now instituted a defamation action against the newspapers and Professor Van Niekerk. This action was instituted in his personal capacity; had 'the Government' sued it would obviously have been met by *Die Spoorbond* defence.[33] Was Pelser, as the Minister of Justice, in fact referred to when criticism was made of 'the Government'? And, if he was referred to, should not *Die Spoorbond* principle be extended to ensure that criticism could be made freely of him.

The court found that since it was well known that decisions about the reprieve of a person sentenced to death were taken by the Cabinet it followed that the criticism of 'the Government' would be understood as referring to the individual Cabinet members that took the decision. The argument was, of course, pressed upon the Appellate Division that *Die Spoorbond* principle should be extended to deny Cabinet Ministers the right to sue as *Sullivan* suggests. But this was rejected by Wessels JA who said:

In this case . . . the court is only concerned with the personal right of a member of the [Cabinet] to sue for defamation in circumstances where it is alleged that defamatory matter was published with the intention[34] of injuring him personally. In my opinion counsel's submission [that *Die Spoorbond* principle be extended to Cabinet Ministers] was devoid of any real

---

[32] But the detailed facts show that there were rational grounds for distinguishing between the black man and the white man. Makinitha both carried and wielded the knife used to murder the victim (but Wilson did restrain the victim during the attack and sold the victim's watch). There was evidence of Wilson's disturbed upbringing, his mental retardation and other psychiatric problems and the fact that he was under the influence of alcohol and marijuana but no such evidence in regard to Makinitha. Makinitha's tally of previous convictions was more impressive including a long sentence for a robbery in which a knife was used to stab the victim.

[33] Discussed above, pp. 90–1. The government, using funds derived from the citizen, was almost certainly funding the litigation.

[34] In contrast with English law, the South African law of defamation, being founded upon the *actio injuriarum* of Roman Law, requires the intention to injure for liability. See below 100.

substance . . . The subject's undoubted right to express his opinion, freely, and without fear of legal consequences, upon the Government's management of the country's affairs would, in my opinion, remain unimpaired.[35]

This last sentence seems quite out of touch with reality: allowing Cabinet Ministers to sue for defamation when 'the Government' is criticised must amount to a far-reaching restriction on free political discussion. What is being stifled here is criticism of an important governmental decision. How can that not be an impairment of the right to express an 'opinion, freely, and without fear of legal consequences, upon the Government's management of the country's affairs'? And yet with the rejection of the generic defence in *Reynolds* the same position could in principle arise in English law.

To be sure there is no local example of criticism of a governmental decision in impersonal terms being used by a Cabinet Minister to found a libel action against a critic. And to be sure in many cases, as in South Africa,[36] justification, fair comment or privilege would provide a defence at trial.[37] But with no specific protection of political speech, criticism of governmental decisions or actions could be transmuted by group defamation into criticism of the individuals responsible who would be free to sue.

5. *NEW YORK TIMES CO. V SULLIVAN*: A GENERIC PRIVILEGE FOR POLITICAL SPEECH DEFEATED ONLY BY MALICE

The logical response to this inconsistency is to follow the path adopted by the Supreme Court of the United States in *New York Times Co. v Sullivan*.[38] So this is the moment to consider this influential case. It provides special protection for criticism of public authorities as well as public officials, save where the plaintiff shows that the criticism was motivated by malice. It thus recognizes the special value of political discourse in a free and democratic society even when the criticisms are shown to be false.

The case arose from an advertisement in the New York Times on the 29 March 1960 and its tale is a significant chapter in the history of the civil rights movement. The advertisement was inserted by the 'Committee to Defend Martin Luther King and the Struggle for Freedom in the South' and solicited financial contributions to support its work. It alleged the use of violence and illegal tactics by the authorities in the South to control the mass non-violent civil rights protests at the time. There were

[35] 1975(4) SA 797 (A) at 808A–B.
[36] These defences were not considered in *Estate Pelser*. The decision was concerned only with preliminary issues and the death of Pelser prevented the matter coming to trial.
[37] But a specific defence protecting political discourse, since it would be less expensive and time consuming and in principle more predictable, would be much more convenient for defendants.
[38] 376 US 254 (1964).

some factual errors.[39] No official was mentioned by name; and the suit of Sullivan, the elected Public Commissioner in Montgomery, Alabama was the first of several to reach the courts. The Alabama courts found for Sullivan but the Supreme Court reversed. After all, it had been held by the Supreme Court of Illinois as long ago as 1923 that:

every citizen has a right to criticise an inefficient or corrupt government without fear of civil as well as criminal prosecution. This absolute privilege is founded on the principle that it is advantageous for the public interest that the citizen should not be in any way fettered in his statements, and where the public service or due administration of justice is involved he shall have the right to speak his mind freely.[40]

City of Chicago v Tribune Co., from which these words come, although not a decision of the Supreme Court of the United States, is in effect the *Derbyshire* of the United States. The true significance of *Sullivan* is the point already adverted to: the insistence that the restriction on libel actions being brought by governmental bodies could not be side-stepped by permitting the public official in charge of the governmental body in question to sue—this, indeed, is the step that the House of Lords refused to take in *Reynolds*. But the vigour of the Supreme Court's vindication of the First Amendment right of free speech should be noted. Brennan J's opinion deserves to be quoted (and read) at length:

The general proposition that freedom of expression upon public questions is secured by the First Amendment has long been settled by our decisions . . . 'The maintenance of the opportunity for free political discussion to the end that government may be responsive to the will of the people and that changes may be obtained by lawful means, an opportunity essential to the security of the Republic, is a fundamental principle of our constitutional system.'[41] The First Amendment, said Judge Learned Hand, 'presupposes that right conclusions are more likely to be gathered out of a multitude of tongues, than through any kind of authoritative selection. To many this is, and always will be, folly; but we have staked upon it our all'.[42] Mr Justice Brandeis, in his concurring opinion in *Witney v California* 274 US 357, 375–376 . . . gave the principle its classic formulation:

Those who won our independence believed . . . that public discussion is a political duty; and that this should be a fundamental principle of the American government. They recognized the risks to which all human institutions are subject. But they knew that order cannot be secured merely through fear of punishment for its infraction; that it is hazardous to discourage thought, hope and imagination; that fear breeds repression; that repression breeds hate; that hate menaces stable government; that the path of safety lies in the opportunity to discuss freely supposed grievances and proposed remedies; and that the fitting

---

[39]   Factual error did not deprive the respondent of their defence. Brennan J at 272 said that 'erroneous statement is inevitable in free debate, and that it must be protected if the freedoms of expression are to have the "breathing space" that they need "to survive" '.

[40]   *City of Chicago v Tribune Co.* 139 NE 86 (1923). See Loveland in Loveland (ed.), *Importing the First Amendment* (Hart, 1998) 69–98.

[41]   *Stromberg v California* 283 US 359, 369 (1930).

[42]   *United States v Associated Press* 52 F Supp 362, 372 (1943).

remedy for evil counsels is good ones. Believing in the power of reason as applied through public discussion, they eschewed silence coerced through law . . . Recognizing the occasional tyrannies of governing majorities, they amended the Constitution so that free speech and assembly should be guaranteed.

Thus we consider this case against the background of a profound national commitment to the principles that debate on public issues should be uninhibited, robust and wide-open, and that it may well include vehement, caustic and sometimes unpleasantly sharp attacks on government and public officials . . . The present advertisement, as an expression of grievance and protest on one of the major public issues of our time, would seem clearly to qualify for the constitutional protection. . . .

The truth is that the principle that the common law's protection of free speech, even if not buttressed by special protection in a Bill of Rights, readily reaches as far ensuring that public authorities cannot sue for libel. But it has, thus far, not reached so far as to hold that individual officials whose reputations have been harmed in the criticism of such bodies are precluded from suing. The point here, and it is expressly made in *Sullivan*, is that the interest of the public in free speech outweighs—at least in the area of political discourse—the interest of the official in his reputation. The Supreme Court declared that the balance came down clearly on the side of freedom of speech and not on the protection of reputation.[43] The common law clearly strikes that balance elsewhere and leaves the inconsistency in place.

6. THE DIFFICULTIES WITH ADOPTING *SULLIVAN*

There are in fact weighty reasons why *Sullivan* has not been followed in the United Kingdom. Court of Appeal raised a particularly acute difficulty in *Reynolds*. 'If a businessman were said to have corrupted a serving politician, [a] "political speech" qualified privilege would, in the absence of malice, protect the publisher in a suit by the politician. But what of a suit by the businessman? If . . . the same privilege would apply to a suit by the businessman, it would seem unlikely that the privilege could be confined to political speech. . . .'[44] Indeed, post-*Sullivan* one of the most noteworthy developments in the United States has been the broadening of the concept of public officials to include celebrities and other public figures who 'occupy positions of such pervasive power and influence that they are deemed public figures for all purposes'.[45] Public officials, on the other hand, must have 'substantial responsibility . . . over the

---

[43] Relying upon *NAACP v Button* 371 US 405, 433 (1963) and *Sweeney v Patterson*, 76 DC 23, 24 (1942), where Judge Edgerton said: 'The interest of the public here outweighs the interests of appellant or any other individual. The protection of the public requires not merely discussion, but information. Political conduct and views which sometimes respectable people approve, and others condemn, are constantly imputed to Congressmen. Errors of fact . . . are inevitable . . . Whatever is added to the field of libel is taken from the field of free debate.'   [44] [1998] 3 WLR 862 at 910F.
[45] *Gertz v Welch* 418 US 323 (1974). Some plaintiffs, anxious to appear more important than perhaps they are, admit to being such persons: *Masson v New Yorker Magazine Inc.* 881 F 2d 1452 (1989).

conduct of governmental affairs' before the defence is available, thus junior officials can continue to vindicate their reputations.[46] Interesting as these examples are, they show that difficulties of definition are bound to arise as soon as individuals are put into a special category. But such difficulties of definition are surely not enough to deter the adoption of a *Sullivan* type defence if freedom of expression required this.

Furthermore, *Sullivan* must be seen against the procedural background of US law. And as we have seen, the House of Lords in *Reynolds* pointed out that in the United States the plaintiff was entitled to a pre-trial enquiry into the sources of the story and the editorial decision-making and so could the more readily establish malice—but this was not the case locally.[47] Moreover, the journalistic privilege to protect sources would also place the plaintiff at a disadvantage in defeating any generic defence that may be made available to defendants.[48] *Sullivan* also to many eyes strikes the balance between freedom of expression and the protection of reputation in the wrong way. It casts the focus on to the person. Some of this is inevitable since reference to the plaintiff is a crucial part of every defamation action and government is carried out by persons. But if free speech is what this is all about then the emphasis should not be upon the persons but upon the discourse.

These difficulties with *Sullivan*, though, surely only exemplify the deepest difficulty: the striking of the balance so firmly in favour of the protection of political speech. The United States may have 'staked its all' on the freest and most robust expressions of opinion in the belief that 'right conclusions are more likely to be gathered out of a multitude of tongues, than through any kind of authoritative selection'[49] but as *Reynolds* shows the common law has a deep mistrust of the press. Speaking of whether the professional ethics of journalists could be relied upon to ensure that a *Sullivan* defence—with proof of malice the only safeguard—would not be abused, Lord Nicholls said this: 'the sad reality is that the overall handling of these matters by the national press, with its own commercial interests to serve, does not always command general confidence'.[50] Lord Nicholls also remarked upon the power to cause harm and distress and the fact the press had, in general, no duty to take reasonable care.[51] Until the press does command that general confidence, the common law is unlikely to adopt a *Sullivan* defence.

---

[46]   *Rosenblatt v Baer* 383 US 75 (1966).

[47]   [1999] 3 WLR 1010 at 1032 referring to *Herbert v Lando* 441 US 153 (1979).

[48]   Contempt of Court Act 1981, s. 10 (disclosure of journalistic sources not to be ordered by court unless 'necessary in the interests of justice or national security or for the prevention of disorder or crime').

[49]   Although this argument is often attributed to Mill it is found first in Milton: 'Though all the winds of doctrine were let loose to play upon the earth, so Truth be in the field, we do injuriously by licensing and prohibiting to misdoubt her strength. Let her and Falsehood grapple; who ever knew Truth put to the worse, in free and open encounter' (*Areopagitica*). The difficulty with this is that in political discourse we are often not dealing with truth or falsehood but with questions of degree, opinion and interest (e.g. the level of taxation, or the organization of schools). But this too is addressed by Milton: 'but when complaints are freely heard, deeply considered, and speedily reformed, then is the utmost bound of civil liberty attained that wise men look forward' (ibid.).

[50]   [1999] 3 WLR 1010 at 1024.

[51]   ibid., at 1025 in reliance upon *Lange v Atkinson* [1998] 3 NZLR 424, 477.

7. STRIKING THE BALANCE ELSEWHERE: PROTECTING POLITICAL SPEECH PROVIDED THAT THE DEFENDANT ACTS REASONABLY

Although *Sullivan* has been followed outside the United States,[52] the predominant response to the question of the protection of political speech in many other jurisdictions has been to reject a *Sullivan* type defence but to protect the speech provided that the defendant is not at fault.[53] This generally takes the form of requiring that the defendant has acted reasonably. There is much to be said for such *via media*: the reputation of individuals is not left unprotected but political debate and discussion can take place in relative freedom. Each legal system, of course, approaches the issues from the standpoint of its own constitution and constitutional tradition and their own culture and law. Let us start with the tale in Australia.

Initially in *Theophanous v The Herald and Weekly Times*[54] the High Court of Australia accepted the defendant newspapers' argument that the implied protection of freedom of communication in relation to 'political discussion' contained in the Australian Constitution,[55] also protected the discussion of governmental and political matters and concerning members of the parliament in their official duties and their suitability for office.

Theophanous was, however, decided by a divided High Court (Mason CJ, Toohey, Gaudron and Deane JJ forming the majority with Brennan, Dawson and McHugh JJJ dissenting). Thus when there were significant changes in the personnel of the court in 1995–6, the scene was set for *Lange v Australian Broadcasting Corporation*[56] in which the *Theophanous* defence was reconsidered. The case concerned the broadcasting of a television documentary that alleged various improprieties against the plaintiff while he was a member of the New Zealand Parliament and later Prime Minister of New Zealand.[57] The High Court rejected the *Theophanous* defence: the implied protection of freedom of communication in relation to 'political discussion' contained in the Australian Constitution did 'not confer personal rights upon individuals'. All

---

[52] *Sullivan* type defences have been adopted in *Rajagopal (R.) v State of Tamil Nadu* (1994) 6 SCC 632, 650 (to succeed in a defamation action against a public official, plaintiff must show reckless disregard for truth) and *Lange v Atkinson* [1998] 3 NZLR 424, CA (qualified privilege, lost only when malice proved, protects statements, even if unreasonable, made about politicians). But this latter case went on appeal to the Privy Council which considered that the matter should be reheard by the New Zealand Court of Appeal in the light of *Reynolds*.

[53] For general discussion see Una Ni Raifeartaigh, 'Fault Issues and Libel Law—A Comparison between Irish, English and United States Law' (1991) 40 ICLQ 763.

[54] [1994] 3 LRC 369, (1994) 182 CLR 104 and to similar effect see *Stephens v West Australian Newspapers Ltd.* (1994) 182 CLR 211. Noted by F. A. Trinidade (1995) 111 LQR 199.

[55] This rests upon the two cases of *Nationwide News Pty. v Wills* (1992) 177 CLR 1, 108 ALR 681 and *Australian Capital Television Pty. Ltd. v Commonwealth* (1992) 177 CLR 106, 108 ALR 577 where the majority of the Australian High Court distilled from the constitutional establishment of representative government an implication of freedom of communication in order to give meaning to that concept of government.

[56] (1997) 189 CLR 520 noted by F. A. Trinidade (1998) 114 LQR 1.

[57] The High Court accepted that it did not matter that this was publication in Australia about political matters in New Zealand.

that the implied protection did was to 'preclude the curtailment of the protected freedom by the exercise of legislative or executive power'.[58] Thus the *Theophanous* defence 'is no longer available to an action in defamation in Australia even when the defamatory material is published in the course of a "political discussion" '.[59] In the jargon that the Human Rights Act 1998 has made current in the United Kingdom, the implied constitutional protection of free speech applied vertically not horizontally.

Thus the emphasis shifted to whether the common law defence of qualified privilege applied in these circumstances. The High Court expanded the common law defence of qualified privilege recognizing that the interest that individuals had in receiving and imparting information about political matters. However, the High Court recognized that the publication in most privileged occasions was limited but under the extended privilege it was broadcast. On such limited occasions mere honesty on the part of the publisher was required. 'As long as the publisher honestly and without malice uses the occasion for the purpose for which it is given, that person escapes liability even though the publication is false and defamatory.' [60] But with the unlimited publication of a broadcast the damage that can be caused by a publication which is false is so much greater than when it is published to a small number of persons that a requirement of reasonableness is imposed by the common law. The onus of showing reasonableness is cast upon the defendant and the crucial dictum in determining when a publication was reasonable is the following:

Whether the making of a publication was reasonable must depend upon all the circumstances of the case. But, as a general rule, a defendant's conduct in publishing material giving rise to a defamatory imputation will not be reasonable unless the defendant had reasonable grounds for believing that the imputation was true, took proper steps, so far as they were reasonably open, to verify the accuracy of the material and did not believe the imputation to be untrue. Furthermore, the defendant's conduct will not be reasonable unless the defendant has sought a response from the person defamed and published the response made (if any) except in cases where the seeking or publication of a response was not practicable or it was unnecessary to give the plaintiff an opportunity to respond.

Although there are many issues of definition and operation to be worked out[61] in practice, the movement towards a fault based approach to defamation when political criticism is broadcast is clear.

A similar tendency can be found in the South African law but based in a different and rather tangled legal and constitutional history. An important point is that Roman-Dutch law based the protection of reputation upon the *actio injuriarum* of Roman Law, founded in the Twelve Tables of 450BC. Unlike the common law the intention to insult (the *animus injuriandi*) is an essential element of the *actio injuriarum*. For

---

[58] (1997) 189 CLR 520 at 826 per Brennan CJ.
[59] Trinidade (1998) 4.
[60] (1997) 189 CLR 520 at 833.
[61] For instance, to establish the reasonableness of their publication the defendant will often need to disclose their sources.

much of the past century it has been a matter of acute debate whether the intent to injure was necessary where the press, with its great power, was the defendant. At first under the influence of English law, the courts tended to restrict the way in which a lack of *animus injuriandi* could be proved. The presumption of *animus injuriandi* that arose once the publication of defamatory words was shown could only be rebutted by proving one of the standard defences, not by showing the absence of *animus injuriandi* in general or in fact. A leading author wrote 'when jurists and judges say that *animus injuriandi* is part of the connotation of the wrong of defamation ... "it is only their fun" '.[62] However, the courts later re-established *animus injuriandi* with a vengeance insisting that mere intention was not enough, in addition there had to be knowledge of the unlawfulness of the publication.[63] Thus a genuine, even if unreasonable, belief that the occasion was privileged was just as good as an occasion that was in fact privileged. One commentator said that for a newspaper to be liable for defamation what was required was not only an intention to injure but the intention to 'be liable for it'.[64] But the law did not remain static; and after several false starts and reliance upon English law, strict liability became established for the media alone.[65]

The constitutional transformation of South Africa since 1992 has inevitably led to a reassessment of the protection of reputation. The leading case is *National Media Ltd. v Bogoshi*.[66] What had happened was that several articles allegedly defamatory of the plaintiff were published in the *City Press*, published by the respondent. The significance of this case is first of all it recognizes that there is no constitutional value in false statements of fact, but that erroneous statements of facts are inevitable in free debate.[67] The case also rejects the strict liability of the press and stresses instead the reasonableness of conduct of the respondent in assessing the lawfulness of the act in question. The onus is on the defendant to prove reasonableness.[68] The crucial dictum is:

Defendant's counsel, rightly in my view, accepted that there are compelling reasons for holding that the media should not be treated on the same footing as ordinary members of the public by permitting them to rely upon the absence of *animus injuriandi*, and that it would be appropriate to hold media defendants liable unless they were not negligent in the circumstances of the case.[69]

---

[62] McKerron, *The Law of Delict* (7th edn., 1971), 172.

[63] The trilogy of Appellate Division cases which established this were: *Jordaan v Van Biljon* 1962(1) SA 286 (A), *Craig v Voortrekkerpers* 1963(1) SA 149(A) and *Nydoo v Vengtas* 1965(1) SA 1 (A).

[64] Boberg, '*Animus injuriandi* and mistake' (1971) 88 SALJ 57, 69.

[65] *SAUK v O'Malley* 1977(3) SA 394 (A) and *Pakendorff en andere v De Flamingh* 1982(3) SA 146 (A).

[66] 1998(4) SA 1196(SCA). The case is curious in that neither the report of the Supreme Court of Appeal and of the court below (1996(3) SA 78(W)) reveals what was the substance of the alleged defamation. Other leading South African decisions on the same topic are: *Holomisa v Argus Newspapers Ltd.* 1996(2) SA 588 (W) and *Butelezi v South African Broadcasting Crp* [1998] 1 All SA 147 (D).

[67] 1998(4) SA 1196 (SCA), at 1209H relying on *Gertz v Robert Welch Inc.* 418 US 323 (1974).

[68] See ibid., Hefer JA at 1215I.

[69] *Bogoshi* at 1214 this conclusion is reached in reliance upon the dictum from *Lange* just cited.

We thus see in both South Africa and Australia a movement towards requiring that publication by the media should be subject to a requirement of reasonableness if the publication is to be privileged. What is fascinating about it is that while Australia approaches that position from the point of view of a background of strict liability for libel, South Africa approaches its very similar position from the background of an insistence on the intention to injure as a requirement for defamation.

8. STRIKING THE BALANCE IN ENGLAND: NON-GENERIC PRIVILEGE

As we have seen in *Reynolds* the House of Lords made it clear that the common law should not develop a new subject matter category of qualified privilege to protect political discourse. But the House of Lords also made it clear 'that qualified privilege was available in respect of political information upon application of the established common law test of whether there had been a duty to publish the material to the intended recipients and whether they had had an interest in receiving it'.[70] The question thus shifts to determining the contours of the non-generic defence where political discourse is in issue. The clearest guidance is to be found in the speech of Lord Nicholls where he summed up in these words:[71]

Depending upon the circumstances, the matters to be taken into account[72] include the following . . . 1. The seriousness of the allegation. The more serious the charge the more the public is misinformed and the individual harmed, if the allegation is not true. 2. The nature of the information, and the extent to which the subject matter is a matter of public concern. 3. The source of the information.[73] Some informants have no direct knowledge of the events. Some have their own axes to grind, or are being paid for their stories. 4. The steps taken to verify the information. 5. The status of the information. The allegations may have already been the subject of an investigation which commands respect. 6. The urgency of the matter. News is often a perishable commodity 7. Whether comment was sought from the plaintiff. He may have information others do not possess or have not disclosed. An approach to the plaintiff will not always be necessary. 8. Whether the article contained the gist of the plaintiff's side of the story. 9. The tone of the article. A newspaper can raise queries or call for an investigation. It need not adopt allegations as statements of fact. 10. The circumstances of the publication including the timing. This list is not exhaustive. The weight to be given to these and any other relevant factors will vary from case to case . . .

This dictum which will doubtless be much cited in court and much poured over late at night by libel readers forming a judgment about what can be published and what must be excluded from the next day's edition. However, it prompts two immediate comments. First, it appears very much as if a requirement of due care, or reason-

---

[70] [1999] 3 WLR 1010, at 1010 (headnote).

[71] ibid., at 1027.

[72] By the judge not the jury.

[73] An unwillingness to disclose its sources, however, will not in general weigh against the newspaper. See Lord Nicholls, [1999] 3 WRL 1010 at 1027.

ableness, is being secreted within the folds of the defence of privilege. Weighing seriousness, urgency, reliability of the information, whether the information has been checked and whether the plaintiff has been given an opportunity to respond all speaks of the imposition of the standard of reasonableness. This is little different from both *National Media Ltd v Bogoshi* and *Lange v Australian Broadcasting Corporation*. Notwithstanding the specific exclusion of the generic defence in *Reynolds* a considerable measure of convergence may be noted.

Secondly, it is clear that determining whether privilege will be available as a defence in any particular case requires consideration of the ten circumstances listed in the dictum. Thus the process whereby it is determined if the defence is available is non-mechanical. There is bound to be a greater measure of uncertainty than where a straightforward rule is to be applied—even making allowance for the inevitable uncertainty at the penumbra of the rule. But such a non-mechanical process whereby a balance is struck between the protection of reputation and the freedom of expression is more consistent with the jurisprudence of the European Court of Human Rights which 'in cases of competing rights and interests requires a balancing exercise in the light of the concrete facts of each case'.[74] Thus the application of a rule applicable to a particular category of case, such as those involving political speech, runs against the grain of the European approach.[75] The House of Lords has several times held that the common law's protection of free speech and that of Article 10 march together; and that on vital points there is no significant difference between them.[76] The rejection of the generic defence bears this out.

9. CONCLUSIONS

The preceding discussion has not brought to light a resolution of the inconsistency that first stimulated this essay. No resolution has been found for the conundrum that allows individuals to bring actions for libel in circumstances in which a public authority would be precluded from bringing action. If considerations of free speech preclude the public authority from bringing action, why do they not preclude the

---

[74] Per Lord Steyn at ibid. 1033 who was specifically influenced by this consideration amongst others to reject the generic defence.

[75] Space does not allow an account of the European jurisprudence here. But Article 10 clearly subjects the freedom 'to receive and impart information and ideas without interference by public authority' to limitations as 'are necessary in a democratic society . . . for the protection of the reputation or rights of others'. Thus a balancing process, well known in the European context, is clearly envisaged. The European jurisprudence is reviewed by Lord Nicholls (at 1026) who finds it in accord with the common law. It holds that the same principles apply to political discussion as to other matters of public concern (*Thorgeirson v Iceland* (1992) 14 EHRR 843) and recognizes the distinction between fact and opinion (*Lingens v Austria* (1986) 8 EHRR 407).

[76] *Attorney General v Guardian Newspapers Ltd. (No. 2)* [1990] 1 AC 109, 283–284; *Derbyshire* [1993] 2 WLR 449 at 551G and *Reynolds* [1999] 3 WLR 1010 at 1026. The Human Rights Act 1998 therefore may not have a great impact in this area. The significance of s. 12(1) is difficult to assess. See Lord Cooke in *Reynolds* at 1045.

individual. It may be that the view is taken that this conundrum is simply a reflection of the fact that with different plaintiffs the balance between the protection of reputation and the protection of free speech is inevitably struck in different places. But at the very least the conundrum shows how narrow is the protection afforded to free speech by *Derbyshire*. Notwithstanding the rhetoric about the 'chilling effect' on freedom of expression of defamation this decision does not carve out any significant area in which that 'chilling effect' is absent—almost invariably there will be an individual who will be able to sue.

It is clear, therefore, that *Derbyshire* and *Reynolds* represent the beginning not the end of English law's search for an appropriate balance to be struck between the two competing interests of protection of reputation and freedom of expression in the context of political speech. In England that balance is being struck in a different and more restrictive place to where it being struck in the United States. As pointed out above the lack of confidence in the press shown in *Reynolds* precludes the robust support for freedom of expression seen in the United States as essential to the proper functioning of democracy.[77] It may be that with us free speech is part of a moral birthright, essential for life as a free individual but not tied to any particular form of government.[78] This valuable insight does not, alas, help in the task of striking that balance.

But what is interesting is the way that in three societies—the United Kingdom, Australia and South Africa—with great similarities but also great differences between them have moved towards striking that balance in a similar place: publication in the press is protected provided that it was reasonable in the circumstances. Much, of course, is hidden behind the words used but there seems to be a common concept of fairness and reasonableness may well prove to be a workable solution.

---

[77]   See, for instance, the influential view of Alexander Meiklejohn that any restriction on expression of a criticism relevant to a political issue is a 'mutilation of the thinking process of the community against which the First Amendment . . . is directed. The principle of the freedom of speech springs from the necessities of the program of self-government' (*Free Speech* (1948) 26).

[78]   See Sir John Laws in Loveland (ed.), *Importing the First Amendment* (Hart, 1998), at 123.

6

Is the Privileged Position of Political Expression Justified?

IVAN HARE*

Expression which may be described as political is accorded a privileged legal status in most common law countries and under the European Convention of Human Rights. The aim of this piece is to question whether the manner in which this privilege has been formulated in some jurisdictions is desirable. The structure of the article is as follows. Part 1 provides a brief account of the extent to which United Kingdom law and the doctrine in a number of legal systems which are particularly relevant to domestic developments protect political speech. The remaining sections of the paper question this method. In Part 2 some of the difficulties of defining political speech and distinguishing it from other forms of expression are discussed. Part 3 addresses certain other characteristics of free speech analysis which may prove more revealing than a focus on the category of expression. Finally, Part 4 explains why it may be *more* legitimate to limit or regulate some forms of political speech than other forms of expressive activity. The aim throughout is not to argue against a high level of legal protection for political speech, but to advert to some of the dangers of resolving free speech issues by reference to *a priori* categorizations of types of expression.

1. LEGAL PROTECTION FOR POLITICAL SPEECH

English law accords a high level of protection to political speech. The terms of the Bill of Rights provide an absolute privilege for statements made in the course of proceedings in Parliament.[1] The courts have also recognized the need to protect the dissemination of information concerning legislative debates by extending qualified privilege to fair and accurate reports of parliamentary proceedings in newspapers.[2] A similar principle led the Court of Appeal to hold that an address delivered at a local election was entitled to qualified privilege.[3] More recently, English courts have held that, as a matter of common law, a democratically elected body may not sue in

---

* The author is grateful to Sir Kenneth Keith and Professor Peter Quint for their comments on an earlier draft.

[1] 'That the Freedome of Speech and Debates or Proceedings in Parlyament ought not to be impeached or questioned in any Court or Place out of Parlyament'. Bill of Rights 1689.

[2] *Wason v Walter* (1868) LR 4 QB 73.

[3] *Braddock v Bevins* [1948] 1 KB 580. This result was subsequently reversed by the Defamation Act 1952, s. 10.

defamation even if the allegations made against it were known to be false by the publisher.[4] This rule was considered essential to secure the political accountability of such bodies. At the level of individual comment, the Court of Appeal and House of Lords have accepted that the publication of political information to the public generally could fall within established heads of qualified privilege if there was a duty to publish the material to the intended recipients and the recipients had an interest in receiving it, taking account of all relevant circumstances surrounding the publication.[5]

Substantially because of the further efforts of former prime ministers, similar arguments have been canvassed in a number of other common law jurisdictions. Thus the High Court of Australia has recognized that qualified privilege may attach to statements concerning government and the political process provided that the disseminator of the information can prove that it was reasonable to publish it.[6] The Court of Appeal in New Zealand has held that statements about the conduct or suitability for office of those prospectively, currently or formerly elected to parliament may be protected by qualified privilege.[7] Likewise, the Supreme Court of Appeal in South Africa decided that it may be lawful to publish defamatory statements of fact as part of a discussion on political matters if it is considered reasonable to do so in the light of all the circumstances surrounding the publication.[8] Although the leading decision of the Supreme Court of Canada was held not to involve criticism of a public official, the Court affirmed the central importance of freedom of speech on matters of political concern.[9] In the Supreme Courts of the two largest common law jurisdictions, the protection of political speech has been carried to the point where a public official or public figure cannot succeed in a defamation action unless he can prove that the untrue allegation against him was made with actual malice, that is, with knowledge that it was untrue or with a reckless disregard for its truth or falsity.[10] At the supranational level, the European Court of Human Rights has

---

[4]   *Derbyshire CC v Times Newspapers Ltd* [1993] AC 534. This principle was applied to statements concerning a political party in *Goldsmith v Boyrul* [1998] QB 459 and to an 'arm of government' in *British Coal v National Union of Mineworkers* (QBD, 28 June 1996) (Lexis).

[5]   *Reynolds v Times Newspapers Ltd* [1998] 3 WLR 862, CA and [1999] 3 WLR 1010, HL on which see F. A. Trinidade, 'Defaming Politicians: The English Approach' (1999) 115 LQR 175. The House of Lords refused to develop a separate category of political information (see nn. 25 and 26 below and associated text).

[6]   *Lange v Australian Broadcasting Corporation* (1997) 189 CLR 520. This decision involved a reformulation of principles derived from the implied right to freedom of political discussion found to exist in *Nationwide News Pty. Ltd. v Wills* (1992) 177 CLR 1; *Australian Capital Television Pty. Ltd. v Commonwealth* (1992) 177 CLR 106; *Theophanous v Herald and Weekly Times Ltd.* (1994) 182 CLR 104 and *Stephens v West Australian Newspapers Ltd* (1994) 182 CLR 211. See also *Commonwealth v John Fairfax and Sons Ltd.* (1980) 147 CLR 39.

[7]   *Lange v Atkinson* [1998] 3 NZLR 424.

[8]   *National Media Ltd. v Bogoshi*, 1998 (4) SA 1196.

[9]   *Hill v Church of Scientology of Toronto* (1995) 126 DLR (4th) 129, 158–9 per Cory J. G. Huscroft, 'Defamation, Damages and Freedom of Expression in Canada' (1996) 112 LQR 46.

[10]   In the USA: *New York Times v Sullivan* 376 US 254 (1964); *Curtis Publishing Co. v Butts* 388 US 130 (1967) and *Gertz v Robert Welch, Inc.* 418 US 323 (1974) and in India: *Rajagopal(R) v State of Tamil Nadu* (1994) 6 SCC 632.

produced a line of doctrine which acknowledges the central importance of freedom of political expression to the interests protected by Article 10 of the Convention.[11]

As a result of these developments, and making allowances for differences of vocabulary, statements such as the following could have emerged from almost any one of the above courts.

Freedom of communication on matters of government and politics is an indispensable incident of that system of representative government which the Constitution creates.[12]

[A] profound national commitment to the principle that debate on public issues should be uninhibited, robust, and wide open, and that it may well include vehement, caustic, and sometimes unpleasantly sharp attacks on government and public officials.[13]

In a free and democratic society it is almost too obvious to need stating that those who hold office in government and who are responsible for public administration must always be open to criticism. Any attempt to stifle or fetter such criticism amounts to political censorship of the most insidious and objectionable kind.[14]

Freedom of public discussion of government (including the institutions and agencies of government) is not merely a desirable political privilege; it is inherent in the idea of a representative democracy.[15]

[A]t a pragmatic level, freedom to disseminate and receive information on political matters is essential to the proper functioning of the system of parliamentary democracy cherished in this country.[16]

[F]reedom of political debate is at the very core of the concept of a democratic society which prevails throughout the Convention . . . The limits of acceptable criticism are accordingly wider as regards a politician as such than as regards a private individual.[17]

It is difficult to imagine a guaranteed right more important to a democratic society than freedom of expression. Indeed a democracy cannot exist without that freedom to express new ideas and to put forward opinions about the functioning of public institutions. The concept of free and uninhibited speech permeates all truly democratic societies and institutions. The vital importance of the concept cannot be over-emphasized.[18]

Of course, this is not to deny that there are fundamental differences of approach within the different systems discussed above. Most strikingly, all of the above systems, with the exception of India, have explicitly rejected adoption of the actual malice standard from *New York Times v Sullivan*.[19] This diversity is not surprising. Although these jurisdictions share much by way of common legal heritage, there

---

[11] *Lingens v Austria* (1986) 8 EHRR 407; *Markt Intern v Germany* (1989) 12 EHRR 161; *Barfod v Denmark* (1989) 13 EHRR 493; *Castells v Spain* (1992) 14 EHRR 445; *Oberschlick v Austria* (1995) 19 EHRR 389.

[12] *Lange v Australian Broadcasting Corp* (n. 6 above) 559 per Brennan CJ

[13] *New York Times v Sullivan* (n. 10 above) 270, per Brennan J.

[14] *Hector v A-G of Antigua & Barbuda* [1990] 2 AC 312, 318, per Lord Bridge of Harwich

[15] *Nationwide News Pty. Ltd. v Wills* (n. 6 above) 48, per Brennan J.

[16] *Reynolds* (n. 5 above) 1022, per Lord Nicholls.

[17] *Lingens v Austria* (n. 11 above) para 42.

[18] *Edmonton Journal v Alberta (Attorney-General)* (1989) 64 DLR (4th) 577, 607, per Cory J.

[19] Note 13 above. The most thoughtful consideration and rejection of *Sullivan* is contained in the Canadian Supreme Court's decision in *Hill* (n. 9 above) 164–8, per Cory J.

remain highly significant differences of political culture and procedural and substantive doctrine. Indeed, the Privy Council in *Lange v Atkinson* recognized that 'striking a balance between freedom of expression and protection of reputation calls for a value judgment which depends upon local political and social conditions'. It therefore regarded its appellate role as limited and returned the substantive question to the New Zealand Court of Appeal for reconsideration in the light of *Reynolds*.[20] However, it remains plausible to argue that the major systems of the common law world have acknowledged that political speech is entitled to a high degree of protection, indeed in many cases, to a higher degree of protection than other forms of expression. The aim of the remainder of this paper is to challenge the method of dealing with political expression disputes through the *a priori* categorization of the speech by reference to its subject matter. The first part of this challenge is to describe the difficulties of defining political speech and distinguishing it from other sorts of expression.

2. DEFINING POLITICAL SPEECH

Certain forms of expression appear to fall clearly within the definition of political speech. For example, a report about the performance of a member of the legislature during a debate on a piece of proposed legislation is plainly a manifestation of political speech. Beyond such obvious illustrations, it becomes much more difficult to generalize. It is unsatisfactory to do so by reference to the intention of the speaker because such intention is difficult to verify and because many significant contributions to political debate are made by those, such as newspapers, with some commercial motivation in publication.[21] Equally, defining political speech by reference to the identity of the plaintiff may produce undesirable results. It is revealing that the United States Supreme Court in the years after *Sullivan* expanded the scope of the 'actual malice' rule from public officials to public figures.[22] Defining the scope of protected expression by reference to the status of the subject of the publication was also rejected by the Court of Appeal in *Gaddafi v Telegraph Group Ltd.* in the following terms:[23]

If a businessman were said to have corrupted a serving politician, [counsel for the publisher] Lord Lester's 'political speech' qualified privilege would, in the absence of malice, protect the publisher in a suit by the politician. But what of a suit by the businessman. If, as we under-

---

[20] *Lange v Atkinson* 28 October 1999 per Lord Nichol.
[21] Most famously, the allegedly libellous speech in *Sullivan* was contained in an advertisement. However, the Supreme Court held: 'The publication here was not a "commercial" advertisement . . . It conveyed information, expressed opinion, recited grievances, protested claimed abuses, and sought financial support on behalf of those whose existence and objectives are matters of the highest public interest and concern.' (n. 10 above) 266, per Brennan J.
[22] Note 10 above.
[23] CA, 28 October 1998 (Lexis), per Hirst L.J.

stood him to accept, the same privilege would apply in a suit by the businessman, it would seem unlikely that the privilege could be confined to political speech. But, if the privilege could be, and were so confined, we question whether the common convenience and welfare of society would be thereby served: there are, after all many matters which affect the public interest and the health of society much more profoundly than the small change of political controversy.

This uncertainty may be illustrated by reference to some of the free speech doctrine which was outlined in the previous section. One attempt to define political speech was that of the Court of Appeal of New Zealand in *Lange*:

We hold that the defence of qualified privilege applies to generally-published statements made about the actions and qualities of those currently or formerly elected to Parliament and those with immediate aspirations to be members, so far as those actions and qualities directly affect or affected their capacity (including their personal ability and willingness) to meet their public responsibilities.[24]

However, many would regard this as too narrow a definition of the type of expression which is essential to the functioning of the democratic process. For example, in the House of Lords in *Reynolds*, Lord Nicholls refused to create a new category of subject matter entitled to qualified privilege for political information partly because 'it would be unsound in principle to distinguish political discussion from other matters of serious public concern'.[25] This conclusion was also articulated by Lord Cooke of Thorndon:

It is doubtful whether the suggested new defence could sensibly be confined to political discussion. There are other public figures who exercise great practical power over the lives of people or great influence in the formation of public opinion or as role models. Such power or influence may indeed exceed that of most politicians. The rights and interests of citizens in democracies are not restricted to the casting of votes. Matters other than those pertaining to government and politics may be just as important in the community; and they may have as strong a claim to be free of restraints on freedom of speech.[26]

An example of this broader conception of the public interest is provided by the decision of the European Court of Human Rights in *Thorgeirson v Iceland*.[27] In this case, Thorgeirson was convicted of criminal defamation for two articles he had written concerning police brutality. In rejecting the argument that heightened scrutiny under the Convention applied only to speech involving political issues, the Court

---

[24] Note 7 above, 428, per Richardson, P., Henry, Keith and Blanchard J.J.

[25] Note 5 above, at 1027. This reflects the common law's traditional protection for fair comment on matters of public interest, with the concept of public interest receiving a very broad definition (see *London Artists Ltd v Littler* [1969] 2 QB 375, 391, per Lord Denning MR). See also s. 5 of the Contempt of Court Act 1981 and *Attorney-General v English* [1983] 1 AC 116. In *Rosenbloom v Metromedia Inc.* 403 US 29 (1971), the plurality of the US Supreme Court held that *Sullivan* should extend to 'all discussion and communication involving matters of public or general concern' (43–4), but this view was rejected by the majority of the Court in *Gertz* (n. 10 above).

[26] Note 5 above, at 1042.

[27] (1992) 14 EHRR 843.

stated that: '[t]here is no warrant in its case-law for distinguishing between political discussion and discussion of other matters of public concern'.[28]

These definitional disputes are mirrored in the theoretical writings on the subject. The most influential advocate of heightened protection for political speech under the First Amendment was Alexander Meiklejohn.[29] As initially formulated, Meiklejohn's definition of speech protected by the First Amendment was a very limited one:

The guarantee given by the First Amendment is not, then, assured to all speaking. It is assured only to speech which bears, directly or indirectly, upon issues with which the voters have to deal—only, therefore, to the consideration of matters of public interest.[30]

However, his later writings revealed that he accepted that it was impossible to define political expression so narrowly. Meiklejohn ultimately accepted that the First Amendment should protect education, philosophy, science, literature and art indeed all:

forms of thought and expression ... from which the voter derives ... the capacity for sane and objective judgment which, so far as possible, a ballot should express.[31]

Courts in the United Kingdom have grappled with the difficulty of defining what is 'political' in a number of areas of domestic law.[32] For example, as a matter of equity, a body will not be treated as fulfilling charitable purposes if its objects are political. *McGovern v Attorney-General*[33] concerned the question of whether a trust of Amnesty International was entitled to charitable status. The court decided that it was not because the main objects of the trust were in part political. Slade J provided the following definition:

---

[28]   (1992) 14 EHRR 843 para. 64.
[29]   This paper does not address the theoretical difficulties which may justify heightened protection for political speech upon which there is a vast literature in the US: H Kalven: 'The *New York Times Case*: A Note on "the Central Meaning of the First Amendment" ', (1964) Sup Ct Rev 191; W. J. Brennan: 'The Supreme Court and the Meiklejohn Interpretation of the First Amendment', (1965) 79 Harv L Rev 1; V. Blasi: 'The Checking Value of First Amendment Theory', [1977] Am B Found Res J 521; T. M. Scanlon: 'A Theory of Freedom of Expression', 1 Phil & Pub Aff 204 (1972); T Emerson, *The System of Freedom of Expression* (New York: Random House, 1970); C. E. Baker: 'Scope of the First Amendment Freedom of Speech' (1978) 25 UCLA L Rev 964 and *Human Liberty and Freedom of Speech* (Oxford, 1992) and F Schauer, *Free Speech–A Philosophical Enquiry* (Cambridge, 1982).
[30]   A.. Meiklejohn, *Political Freedom–The Constitutional Powers of the People* (New York: Harper: 1960), 79.
[31]   A Meiklejohn: 'The First Amendment Is an Absolute' (1961) Sup Ct Rev 245, 256. Some more modern advocates of the limited view of the First Amendment have criticized Meiklejohn for this more attenuated definition of political speech (R. H. Bork: 'Neutral Principles and Some First Amendment Problems' 47 Ind LJ 1 (1971)). Even Bork accepts in this piece 'the undeniable fact that there will be hard cases' in defining political speech (28). L. R. BeVier: 'The First Amendment and Political Speech: An Inquiry Into the Substance and Limits of Principle' 20 Stan LR 299 (1978). In *Theophanous*, (n. 6 above), 124, Mason CJ, Toohey and Gaudron JJ approved of Barendt's view that ' "political speech" refers to all speech relevant to the development of public opinion on the whole range of issues which an intelligent citizen should think about' (E Barendt, *Freedom of Speech* (Oxford, 1987) 152).
[32]   For an attempt to define 'political' in the context of the wearing of uniforms signifying association with a political organization in the Public Order Act 1936, s 1, see *O'Moran v DPP* [1975] QB 864.
[33]   [1982] Ch 321.

Trusts for political purposes . . . include . . . trusts of which a direct and principal purpose is either—(i) to further the interests of a particular political party, or (ii) to procure changes in the laws of this country, or (iii) to procure changes in the laws of a foreign country, or (iv) to procure a reversal of governmental policy or of particular decisions of governmental authorities in this country, or (v) to procure a reversal of governmental policy or of particular decisions of governmental authorities in a foreign country. This categorisation is not intended to be an exhaustive one.[34]

This definition is not confined to the field of trusts law as the decisions of the Divisional Court and the Court of Appeal in *R v Radio Authority, ex p Bull*[35] reveal. At issue was the interpretation of s 92(2)(a) of the Broadcasting Act 1990 which prohibits the inclusion in a licensed service of:

(i) any advertisement which is inserted by or on behalf of any body whose objects are wholly or mainly of a political nature, (ii) any advertisement which is directed towards any political end

The Radio Authority, the regulatory body for commercial radio, used this provision to prohibit an advertisement by Amnesty International which sought to draw attention to the plight of prisoners of conscience and the victims of genocide and torture on the ground that Amnesty was a body whose objects are wholly or mainly of a political nature. Amnesty unsuccessfully sought judicial review of the decision on the ground that the Authority had misinterpreted the provision. The Court of Appeal accepted the definition from *McGovern* and rejected the applicant's argument that promoting the observance of fundamental human rights could not be a political objective because it was required by international law. The Court went on to draw the following distinction:

To promote education on human rights, if it is an objective in itself . . . is a non-political objective. On the other hand if awareness of human rights in a particular country is promoted with the objective of bringing pressure to bear upon a government so that it will change its policy, the activity becomes political.[36]

The attempt to define what is political has also been considered in the context of the law on asylum and extradition. An applicant may seek to resist extradition or to seek asylum on the ground that their offence is political. One strand of the law on these subjects is that there must be a political struggle either in existence or contemplation between the government and one or more opposing factions within the state where the offence is committed and that the offence is an incident of this struggle. However, this definition did not prove entirely satisfactory as in *Re Kolczynski*[37] extradition was refused by the court in relation to a group of Polish sailors who had seized their vessel and sought refuge in an English port. There was no political

[34] ibid., at 340.
[35] [1995] 4 All ER 481, DC and [1997] 2 All ER 561, CA.
[36] ibid., at 572, per Lord Woolf MR.
[37] [1955] 1 QB 540.

disturbance in Poland at the time and the seamen were not supporters of any party which was at odds with any other. The court nevertheless held that the offence was of a political character because it involved measures taken to get away from a political ordering of society which was regarded as intolerable. On the other hand, an anarchist who had detonated a bomb in a café was refused the political exception because his anarchist philosophy was held to be opposed to all forms of government and politics.[38] Further difficulties arise when one comes to consider the remoteness of the crime from a political struggle and these were recently addressed in the following terms by Lord Mustill.

Take the case of an insurgent group which attacks an army post, as part of a campaign to overthrow the government by force. This would plainly be a political offence. . . . Change the case now so that the soldiers, lacking the weapons needed for the attack, steal them from an arsenal. Would not this in ordinary language be described as a political offence? . . . If one changes the case once more, so that instead of stealing arms directly the insurgents steal from a bank the money with which to buy them . . . I find it hard to see why the stealing of the money and its subsequent use to buy arms would not be a continuous causal chain of which all the links are political in nature; and if the logic is not clear I can foresee great difficulties in applying this criteria in practice.[39]

This passage reveals that the concerns expressed by Viscount Radcliffe almost half a century ago remain relevant:

What then is an offence of a political character? The courts, I am afraid, have been asking this question at intervals ever since it was first posed judicially in 1890 . . . and no definition has yet emerged or by now is ever likely to . . .

Generally speaking, the courts' reluctance to offer a definition has been due, I think, to the realisation that it is virtually impossible to find one that does not cover too wide a range.[40]

Further judicial recognition of the vagaries of the term 'political' emerges from *R v Barnett London BC, ex p Johnson*[41] in which judicial review was sought of the condition imposed on the organizers of a community festival that no political party or organization which sought to promote or oppose any political party or cause should be permitted to attend the festival. The Divisional Court held that the condition was open to such a variety of possible meanings as to be meaningless and that it was therefore unlawful.

These examples are not intended to provide an exhaustive description of the cases in which English courts have sought to define the term 'political' in the many contexts in which it has arisen, but to provide some indication of the variety of formulations which has been offered. This variety should make us hesitate before adopting a view of the importance of political expression which will inevitably lead to further litigation surrounding the definition of its organizing concept.

---

[38] *Re Meunier* [1894] 2 QB 415.
[39] *T v Secretary of State for the Home Department* [1996] 2 All ER 865, 881.
[40] *R v Governor of Brixton Prison, ex p Schtraks* [1964] AC 556, 589.
[41] (1990) 88 LGR 73.

3. OTHER ASPECTS OF FREE SPEECH ANALYSIS

The purpose of this section is to establish that free speech analysis requires a sensitivity to the context in which the speech occurs and to a range of factors which may be obscured if axiomatic importance is attached to the category into which the expression falls.

An example of the importance of context is provided by the recent decision of the House of Lords in *R v Secretary of State for the Home Department, ex p Simms*.[42] Simms was serving a life sentence for murder and sought judicial review of the Home Secretary's policy not to allow oral interviews with journalists unless the latter signed an undertaking not to publish any part of the interviews. The House of Lords held that the policy unlawfully interfered with a fundamental and basic right of the prisoner, that is, to seek through oral interviews to persuade a journalist to investigate the safety of the prisoner's conviction and to publicize his findings in an effort to gain access to justice for the prisoner. In the course of the leading speech, Lord Steyn stated:

The value of free speech in a particular case must be measured in specifics. . . . Given the purpose of a sentence of imprisonment, a prisoner can . . . not claim to join in a debate on the economy or on political issues by way of interviews with journalists. . . . But the free speech at stake in the present cases is qualitatively of a very different order. The prisoners are in prison because they are presumed to have been properly convicted. They wish to challenge the safety of their convictions. In principle it is not easy to conceive of a more important function which free speech might fulfil.[43]

In this context, then, speech concerning the safety of a prisoner's conviction is treated by the law as of greater significance than any contribution to debate on broader issues of public concern that the prisoner may wish to make.

Of the factors relevant to free speech analysis, one such is whether the speech constitutes a statement of fact or the advancement of an opinion. As the above examples show, English law has long distinguished between fact and opinion in the context of qualified privilege and this dichotomy was recently affirmed by the House of Lords.[44] This distinction has also been acknowledged by the Strasbourg Court:

In the Court's view, a careful distinction needs to be made between facts and value judgements. The existence of facts can be demonstrated, whereas the truth of value judgements is not susceptible to proof.[45]

Likewise, although it cannot be determinative of the definition of political expression, the identity of the subject matter of the speech may be extremely important. Some commentators have criticized the House of Lords in *Derbyshire* for failing to

[42] [1999] 3 All ER 400.
[43] ibid., 408.
[44] *Reynolds* (n. 5 above), 1023–4 per Lord Nicholls.
[45] *Lingens* (n. 11 above), para. 46 and *De Haes and Gijsels v Belgium* (1998) 25 EHRR 1.

apply its prohibition on defamation actions by elected bodies to cases brought by individual politicians.[46] This criticism ignores a number of relevant differences between the two situations. Most importantly, a case involving an individual politician requires the court to strike a balance between freedom of expression and the rights to reputation and privacy which are protected by most legal systems. There is no reason to strike this balance in a case involving a governmental body since it does not possess the uniquely human right to privacy[47] and its reputation is indistinguishable from its ability to perform its democratic function. A further distinction may be pertinent. A number of English cases makes the point that unless those in public life can protect their reputation in at least certain circumstances, some may be discouraged from embarking on such a career which would be to the detriment of the quality of those who serve the public interest.[48] Whatever one's view of the merits of this argument, it is clearly one which can have no application to criticism of governmental bodies whose continued existence is guaranteed by law.

A further factor which is relevant to free speech analysis is the medium by which the expression is communicated. Most developed legal systems accept that the right must be broadly defined to include a variety of forms of expressive conduct in addition to pure speech or writing. Nevertheless, such systems frequently draw distinctions between different modes of communication which may affect the extent to which it is legitimate for government to regulate. For example, the United States Supreme Court has acknowledged that '[e]ach medium of expression ... must be assessed for First Amendment purposes by standards suited to it, for each may present its own problems'.[49] Thus the broadcast media have traditionally been subject to a higher level of government intervention than the printed media in a number of systems.[50] The explanation for this lies partly in the original scarcity of available broadcast frequencies, but the revolution in cable and digital communications has not altered the fact that radio and television may be regarded as uniquely invasive forms of communication and so subject to a lower level of protection.[51]

The nature of the restriction is also crucial to free speech analysis. Traditionally, much of the hostility to the regulation of expression was directed towards governmental attempts to impose prior restraints.[52] The European Court of Human Rights expressed its general suspicion in *The Observer and The Guardian v United Kingdom*:

---

[46]   For example, I. Loveland, '*City of Chicago v Tribune Co*–in Contexts' in I. Loveland (ed), *Importing the First Amendment* (Hart Publishing, 1998) and 'The Constitutionalisation of Political Libels in English Common Law?' [1998] PL 633, and C. F. Forsyth, 'The Protection of Political Discourse: Pragmatism or Incoherence?' above, p. 870.

[47]   *Attorney-General v Jonathan Cape Ltd.* [1976] QB 752; cf *R v Broadcasting Standards Commission, ex p British Broadcasting Corp.* The Times, 12 April 2000.

[48]   e.g. *Campbell v Spottiswoode* (1863) 3 BS 769.

[49]   *Southeastern Promotions Ltd. v Conrad* 420 US 546, 557 (1975), per Blackmun J.

[50]   Article 10 of the ECHR states: 'This article shall not prevent States from requiring the licensing of broadcasting, television or cinema enterprises.'

[51]   *Sable Communications of California Inc. v Federal Communications Commission* 492 US 115 (1989) and *R v Radio Authority, ex p Bull* (n. 35 above).

[52]   *Bonnard v Perryman* [1891] 2 Ch 269; *Near v Minnesota* 283 US 697 (1931).

[T]he dangers inherent in prior restraint are such that they call for the most careful scrutiny on the part of the Court. This is especially so as far as the press is concerned, for news is a perishable commodity and to delay its publication, even for a short period, may well deprive it of all its value and interest.[53]

Courts are also sensitive to the nature of the sanction imposed after publication and will apply stricter scrutiny to a provision which imposes criminal sanctions than to one where the likely liability is only in damages.[54] In relation to civil liability and the potential chilling effect of large awards of damages, at least one court has even referred to the differential effect which awards of damages may have on distinct types of publisher: '[t]he chill factor is perhaps felt more keenly by the regional press, book publishers and broadcasters than the national press'.[55]

Another crucial distinction in advanced free speech doctrine is between restrictions which are content-neutral, those which are content-based and those which relate to the viewpoint of the speaker.[56] These terms require some explanation. A content-neutral restriction applies to speech whatever its subject-matter and will frequently be in the form of a restriction on the time, manner or place of an activity which is imposed for a purpose entirely unrelated to the suppression of the message conveyed by the speech.[57] Thus a content-neutral provision might prohibit the use of loudspeakers within 500 yards of a hospital. A content-based restriction would target a particular activity because of the content of the message. For example, a provision may seek to prohibit the use of offensive language or conduct.[58] Such a provision is directed at the suppression of a certain form of expression and is treated as highly suspect. Viewpoint-based regulation is a form of content restriction, but only affects statements which adopt one view on an issue. For example, a provision which prohibited the display of signs critical of a foreign government within 500 yards of that government's embassy would be viewpoint-based and subject to the most searching scrutiny.[59]

This section has not attempted to articulate all the factors which are likely to form part of any sophisticated attempt to analyse free speech cases,[60] but simply to argue that there are characteristics of expression and of the different types of speech regulation which may be more relevant to determining the level of protection to which the speech is entitled than an *a priori* categorization of the type of speech involved.[61]

---

[53] (1992) 14 EHRR 153, para. 60.

[54] *Lingens* (n. 11 above).

[55] *Reynolds* (n. 5 above), 1024, per Lord Nicholls. See Barendt *et al.*, *Libel and the Media: The Chilling Effect* (Oxford, 1997).

[56] D. Feldman: 'Content Neutrality' in I. Loveland (ed.), *Importing the First Amendment* (n. 46 above).

[57] G. R. Stone: 'Content-Neutral Restrictions' 54 U Chi L Rev 46 (1987).

[58] *Cohen v California* 403 US 15 (1971).

[59] Cf. *Boos v Barry* 485 US 312 (1988); *RAV v City of St Paul* 505 US 377, (1992).

[60] There is much doctrine in the United States on questions such as the captive audience and on the hostile audience problem.

[61] J. Fleming, 'Libel and Constitutional Free Speech' in P. Cane and J. Stapleton (eds.), *The Law of*

4. ARGUMENTS IN FAVOUR OF THE REGULATION OF POLITICAL EXPRESSION

The purpose of this section is to identify certain of the arguments in favour of some regulation of political expression by government. It should be stressed at the outset that this section does not attempt to dispute the importance of political expression, but simply to question whether it is appropriate to subject all forms of regulation to a heightened level of judicial scrutiny merely because they are aimed at, or may encompass, political speech. Indeed, a premise of this section is that political expression is so important to the proper functioning of government and the democratic process that it may be legitimate to regulate it to a greater degree than would be permissible with other forms of speech.

One of the disadvantages of the United States Supreme Court's approach to free speech is that the almost automatic association of political speech regulation with unconstitutionality distorts the manner in which the governmental process is carried out. Perhaps the most famous example of this is the decision in *Buckley v Valeo*[62] in which the Court struck down those parts of the Federal Election Campaign Act 1971 which sought to limit the amount of money which could be spent 'relative to a clearly identified candidate during a calendar year'.[63] The Court accepted that the Act was 'aimed in part at equalizing the relative ability of all voters to affect electoral outcomes by placing a ceiling on expenditures for political expression by citizens and groups'.[64] However, while upholding the restrictions placed on individual contributions, the Court held that the expenditure limits violated the First Amendment because they reduced the *quantity* of expression: by restricting the number of issues discussed, the depth of their exploration, and the size of the audience reached. The Court concluded that:

the concept that government may restrict the speech of some [in] order to enhance the relative voice of others is wholly foreign to the First Amendment, which was designed to secure the widest possible dissemination of information from diverse and antagonistic sources.[65]

This conception of free speech may lead to highly undesirable results. One such was revealed by the case of *First National Bank of Boston v Bellotti*.[66] Here the State of Massachusetts proposed a bill which would require the recycling of all bottles, but

---

Obligations–Essays for Patrick Atiyah (Oxford, 1991) and Lord Steyn in *Reynolds* (n. 5 above), 1032–3. There is a long-standing debate in the United States on the merits of categorization versus *ad hoc* balancing as a method of resolving First Amendment cases: L. B. Frantz: 'The First Amendment in the Balance' 71 Yale LJ 1424 (1962); W. Mendelson, 'On the Meaning of the First Amendment: Absolutes in the Balance', 50 Calif L Rev 821 (1962); L. B. Frantz, 'Is the First Amendment Law?–A Reply to Professor Mendelson 51 Calif L Rev 729 (1963) and F. Schauer: 'Categories and the First Amendment: A Play in Three Acts' 34 Vanderbilt Law Review 265 (1981).

[62] 424 US 1 (1976). See also *Rust v Sullivan* 111 SCt 1759 (1991).

[63] Section 608(e)(1).

[64] *Buckley v Valeo* (n. 62 above) at 17. See also *Australian Capital Television Pty. Ltd. v Commonwealth* (n. 6 above).

[65] ibid., 41.   [66] 435 US 765 (1978).

feared that corporations having a financial stake in the issue would drown out the voices of those who were in favour and thereby distort the nature of the debate. The State therefore proposed a limit on corporate expenditure. Although the State was able to show that the political committee which opposed the Bill had raised almost twenty times as much funding as those who favoured it, the Supreme Court invalidated the restriction:

> To be sure, corporate advertising may influence the outcome of the vote; this would be its purpose. But the fact that advocacy may persuade the electorate is hardly a reason to suppress it.[67]

Decisions such as these have led some commentators to argue that political speech in the United States has achieved the status of a shibboleth which the courts will defend against any attempt at regulation even where the regulation is proposed in an effort to further those interests which are said to give rise to the special status of political expression in the first place. Cass Sunstein states this fear in the following way:

> My special concern is that the First Amendment is sometimes used to undermine democracy. It is invoked as if it were a purposeless abstraction unrelated to democratic or indeed to any other public goals.[68]

Of course, it does not necessarily follow from privileging political expression that courts in other jurisdictions will follow the Supreme Court's method, but a focus on the category of the speech is more likely to lead to this approach than one which involves a higher degree of *ad hoc* balancing of interests as was advocated in the previous section.

The approach in the United Kingdom is clearly very different from that in the United States and there is a significant degree of regulation of free speech and politics in this country. The provisions which prohibit political advertising (except for party political broadcasts) on independent radio have already been mentioned. Likewise, restrictions on expenditure in order to secure the election of a particular candidate are a familiar part of United Kingdom law. For example, the Representation of the People Act 1983 limits the amount of money which unauthorised persons are permitted to spend on publications and other means of communication with a view to promoting or procuring the election of a particular candidate during the election period. Although an aspect of these restrictions was held to violate Article 10 of the European Convention on Human Rights in *Bowman v United Kingdom*,[69] it is important to remember that the Court did not question the legitimacy of imposing a limit.

---

[67] ibid., 790, per Powell J. See also *Citizens Against Rent Control v Berkeley* 102 SCt 434 (1981) and *FEC v National Conservative Political Action Committee* 105 SCt 1459 (1985); cf *Austin v Michigan Chamber of Commerce* 110 SCt 1391 (1990).
[68] C. Sunstein, *Democracy and the Problem of Free Speech* (New York: Free Press, 1993) 213. See also O. Fiss: 'Free Speech and Social Structure' 71 Iowa Law Rev 1405 (1986).
[69] (1998) 26 EHRR 1.

The Court finds it clear that the purpose of section 75 [of the Representation of the People Act] . . . is to contribute towards securing equality between candidates. It therefore concludes, as did the Commission, that the application of this law to Mrs. Bowman pursued the legitimate aim of protecting the rights of others, namely the candidates for election and the electorate in Halifax and, to the extent that the prosecution was intended to have a deterrent effect, elsewhere in the United Kingdom.[70]

Rather the Court's decision was merely that the level at which the restriction was set was disproportionately low in order to achieve the lawful purpose of ensuring that the political process was not dominated by wealthy supporters. The Court also referred to the relationship between Article 10 and Article 3 of Protocol 1 which protects the right to free elections. In most cases, the Court held that the two provisions are mutually reinforcing. However, it also noted that in the period preceding an election it may be legitimate to impose restrictions on freedom of speech which would not be appropriate at other times in order to secure the 'free expression of the opinion of the people in the choice of the legislature'.[71]

In other areas of public life, restrictions on political expression have also been upheld where they serve an important competing interest related to the functioning of government. For example, civil servants and local government employees may not engage in certain forms of political activity. Thus senior civil servants cannot participate in national political activities and may only take part in local political activities with the permission of their department or executive agency.[72] The definition of political activities includes standing for elected office in the United Kingdom or European Parliament, canvassing on behalf of a political party or candidate and expressing views in public whether orally or in writing on matters of national political controversy. Similar restrictions apply to 'politically restricted' local government employees including a prohibition on speaking publicly or publishing any material with the apparent intention of 'affecting public support for a political party'.[73] After the failure of a challenge to the vires of the regulations in domestic courts,[74] it was alleged that the regulations were in violation of Articles 10 and 11 and to Article 3 of Protocol 1 in Strasbourg. The Court rejected the challenge on all three grounds.[75]

---

[70]   ibid., para. 38. The decision of the Canadian Supreme Court in *Libman v Attorney-General of Quebec* (1997) 151 DLR (4th) 385 is to similar effect.

[71]   ibid., para. 43.

[72]   Civil Service Management Code (1996). See G. Morris, 'Political Activities of Public Servants and Freedom of Expression' in I. Loveland (ed.), *Importing the First Amendment* (n.46 above).

[73]   Local Government Officers (Political Restrictions) Regulations 1990, SI 1990/851 passed under the Local Government and Housing Act 1989.

[74]   *R v Secretary of State for the Environment, ex p NALGO* (1993) 5 Admin LR 785.

[75]   *Ahmed v United Kingdom* (2000) 29 EHRR 1. It should be noted that although the Court was unanimous in rejecting the claim based on Article 3 of Protocol 1, the result on Articles 10 and 11 was by a 6–3 majority. The Commission had held that there was a violation of Article 10 because the regulations were disproportionate to the aim pursued. However, even the Commission accepted that the aim of preserving an effective political democracy was a legitimate one (para 69). The Court upheld a ban on members of the armed forces or of the police joining political parties or engaging in political activities in *Rekvenyi v Hungary* (1999) 6 BHRC 555. See further *Wille v Lichtenstein* (Application No. 28396/95) 28 October 1999.

For present purposes, the most interesting part of the judgment is where the Court discusses the justifications for the restrictions. The Court accepted that it was a legitimate aim under the Convention to protect effective democracy, but was not satisfied that this was the only reason for the restrictions.

The Court observes that the local government system of the respondent State has long rested on a bond of trust between elected members and a permanent corps of local government officers who both advise them on policy and assume responsibility for the implementation of the policies adopted. That relationship of trust stems from the right of council members to expect that they are being assisted in their functions by officers who are politically neutral and whose loyalty is to the council as a whole. Members of the public also have a right to expect that the members whom they voted into office will discharge their mandate in accordance with the commitments they made during an electoral campaign and that the pursuit of that mandate will not founder on the political opposition of their members' own advisers; it is also to be noted that members of the public are equally entitled to expect that in their own dealings with local government departments they will be advised by politically neutral officers who are detached from the political fray.[76]

This final rationale was recently upheld by the Privy Council[77] in the following terms:

The preservation of the impartiality and neutrality of civil servants has long been recognised in democratic societies as of importance in the preservation of public confidence in the conduct of public affairs.[78]

A further justification for such restrictions was accepted by even the United States Supreme Court in a case concerning the validity of the law prohibiting federal employees from taking an 'active part in political management or in political campaigns'.[79] In upholding the Act, White J stated:

[I]t is in the best interests of the country, indeed essential, that federal service should depend upon meritorious performance rather than political service, and that the political influence of federal employees on others and on the electoral process should be limited.[80]

The argument of this section is not that all restrictions on political expression by civil servants are legitimate, merely that suitably phrased provisions which make adequate distinctions between those at different levels of the service and between different forms of expression may be justified as serving a number of legitimate governmental

---

[76]   ibid., para. 53.
[77]   *de Freitas v Permanent Secretary of the Ministry of Agriculture, Fisheries, Lands and Housing* [1999] 1 AC 69.
[78]   ibid., at 76, per Lord Clyde.
[79]   *United States Civil Service Commission v National Association of Letter Carriers, AFL-CIO* 413 US 548 (1973).
[80]   ibid., at 557. The Act has since been substantially amended. See further, *Government of the Republic of South Africa v Sunday Times Newspaper* [1995] 1 LRC 168 and *South African National Defence Force Union v Minister of Defence* (1996) 6 BHRC 574 and the Zimbabwean cases of *Nyambirai v National Social Security Authority* [1996] 1 LRC 64 and *Retrofit (Pvt) Ltd. v Posts and Telecommunications Corp* [1996] 4 LRC 489.

aims. In the Privy Council decision referred to above, an absolute prohibition on communication on matters of political controversy which applied irrespective of the level of civil service employment was held to violate the applicant's rights to freedom of expression and assembly.[81] This must be correct, but the acknowledgement by many leading constitutional courts of the legitimacy of restrictions on the political expression of some public servants is an important qualification to the assumption that political expression is sacrosanct.

More controversially, it may be argued that certain forms of speech which may be categorized as political serve to distort the democratic process by silencing and/or marginalizing those who are members of certain ethnic or other groups and inciting others to discriminate against them. For many, this argument is the strongest justification for provisions prohibiting incitement to racial hatred.[82] A rigid attachment to the overriding importance of political speech has made the prohibition of expressive conduct which is intended to intimidate racial and other minorities almost impossible in the United States.[83] Other jurisdictions have adopted what is arguably a more balanced view: one which acknowledges that incitement to racial hatred may cause identifiable harm to members of ethnic minority groups and materially affect their willingness to participate in the public life of the community in which they live.[84]

5. CONCLUSION

As stated in the introduction, the aim of this piece is not to challenge the view that political expression should be accorded a high level of protection as a matter of substantive law. Rather, the point is to question the most appropriate judicial method for realizing this aim. The conclusion is that it is not useful to attempt to resolve disputes about the scope of free speech by the use of methods of categorization which produce an *a priori* ordering of aspects of the public interest and private right. A system which involves a balancing of all relevant factors in a scale not

---

[81] This result is very similar to that reached by the Supreme Court of Canada in *Osborne v Canada (Treasury Board)* (1991) 82 DLR (4th) 321.

[82] Such as s. 18 of the Public Order Act 1986. See P. Leopold, 'Incitement to Hatred–The History of a Controversial Criminal Offence' [1977] PL 389; Wolffe, 'Values in Conflict: Incitement to Racial Hatred and the Public Order Act 1986' [1987] PL 85; W. Sadurski, 'On "Seeing Speech Through an Equality Lens" ' (1997) 16 OJLS 713; C. McCrudden, 'Freedom of Speech and Racial Equality' in P. Birks (ed.), *Pressing Problems in the Law Volume 1: Criminal Justice and Human Rights* (Oxford, 1995) and B. Hepple, 'Freedom of Expression and the Problem of Harassment' below, p. 177.

[83] *RAV v City of St Paul* (n. 59 above) and *Collin v Smith*, 578 F 2d 1197 (VII Circ 1978). Examples of the debate are M. Matsuda: 'Public Response to Racist Speech: Considering the Victim's Story' 87 Michigan L Rev 2358 (1988); C. R. Lawrence III, 'If He Hollers Let Him Go: Regulating Racist Speech on Campus' (1990) Duke LJ 431; F. S. Haiman, *'Speech Acts' and the First Amendment* (Southern Illinois University Press, 1993) and J. Weinstein, *Hate Speech, Pornography, and the Radical Attack on Free Speech Doctrine* (Westview, 1999).

[84] *Jersild v. Denmark* (1994) 19 EHRR 1; *Faurrisson v France Commission* No. 550/1993, UN Doc CCPR/C/58/D/550/1993 (1996); *R v Keegstra* 61 CCC (3d) 1 (1990) and *Ross v New Brunswick School District No. 15* [1996] 1 SCR 825.

distorted by prior weighting is to be preferred. It is sometimes argued that such methods are likely to produce uncertainty, but the examples of the difficulties of providing a satisfactory definition of political speech suggest that any attempt to use prior classification in order to achieve certainty will fail.

A final point is to suggest that the whole argument about political expression may have set off on the wrong foot in any event. It may be that the attempt to carve out a special category of political speech is merely misplaced and not misconceived. If it is the instrumental contribution of freedom of political expression to the democratic process which is thought worthy of special protection, would it not be more sensible to locate the protection of political expression in those provisions of fundamental rights documents which guarantee free elections and the citizens' right to participate in the democratic process? Freedom of political expression would then no longer occupy a privileged status within mainstream free speech doctrine: a position which may have the effect of undermining the level of protection afforded to other forms of speech. When analysed under the principal free speech provision (such as Article 10 of the European Convention) all expression would be presumptively entitled to the same level of protection, permitting the court to carry out the necessary act of balancing unencumbered by any prior assignment of value. Placing political expression firmly in the field of democratic rights would also enable the court to perceive, more easily than the United States Supreme Court has proved able to do, the circumstances in which unlimited freedom of political expression may actually conflict with the functioning of the democratic process.

The identification of freedom of political expression with representative democracy and responsible government is not a new idea. In *Lange*, the New Zealand Court of Appeal viewed freedom of political expression in the context of freedom of information legislation and the guarantee of the right to vote and to be a candidate in genuine periodic elections contained in the Bill of Rights Act 1990. Taken together, these rights contributed to the functioning of 'a democracy based on universal suffrage, with a government, which is responsible to Parliament and through it to the electorate'.[85] More strikingly, representative democracy was considered sufficiently fundamental to provide the occasion for the High Court of Australia to discover in the structure of the Australian Constitution a freedom of political expression which is explicit nowhere in the document itself.[86]

---

[85] Note 7 above at 462–4 per Richardson P, Henry, Keith and Blanchard JJ.
[86] Note 6 above.

7

Free Press and Fair Trial: Challenges and Change

A. T. H. SMITH

The implementation of the Human Rights Act 1998[1] affords an appropriate occasion to look afresh[2] at the law governing the complex interrelationship between free press and fair trial, particularly as it relates to the publication of prejudicial pre-trial material. United Kingdom[3] law regulating this area, the Contempt of Court Act 1981, was enacted under the spur of the European Convention of Human Rights, and as a result of the decision of the European Court of Human Rights in *Sunday Times v United Kingdom*.[4] That Act was intended to effect a 'permanent shift in the balance of public interest away from the protection of the administration of justice and in favour of freedom of speech'.[5] The purpose of this contribution to the celebration of the work of Sir David Williams[6] is to ask whether, in view of the fact that the free speech jurisprudence of the European Court is incorporated[7] into United Kingdom law at a stroke as the Act takes effect, and the fact that no other co-signatory to the Convention on Human Rights has a law comparable to contempt of court, a further shift might now be expected to occur? One of the challenges that the common law currently faces is as to its perception of the proper balance to be struck between free press and fair trial that is established by the Contempt of Court Act 1981 and the surviving common law.

---

[1] The Act comes into force on 2 October 2000.

[2] Previous recent studies include B. Naylor [1994] CLJ 492. D. Corker and M. Levi, 'Pre-Trial Publicity and its Treatment in the English Courts' [1996] Crim LR 622; C. Walker, 'Fundamental Rights, Fair Trials and the New Audio-Visual Sector' (1996) 59 MLR 517; for an American perspective, see Stephen J. Krause, 'Punishing the Press: Using Contempt of Court to Secure the Right to a Fair Trial' (1996) 76 Boston UL Rev. 537.

[3] Unusually, in the criminal law sphere, the law of Scotland was also included within the ambit of the Act.

[4] (1979) 2 EHRR 245.

[5] According to Lloyd LJ in *Attorney-General v Newspaper Publishing plc*. [1988] Ch 333, 382D-F. A similar shift has occurred in Canada, as a result of the enactment of the Canadian Charter of Rights and Freedoms: *Dagenais v Canadian Broadcasting Corp*. (1994) 120 DLR (4th) 12; but not in New Zealand, after the enactment of the Bill of Rights Act 1990; *Gisborne Herald Co. Ltd. v Solicitor-General* [1995] 3 NZLR 653.

[6] Sir David himself wrote several notes about the law of contempt of court in [1961] Crim LR 87, and again in (1969) 27 CLJ 9, [1975] CLJ 177, [1978] CLJ 196, [1980] CLJ 229 and [1990] CLJ. I am delighted to be afforded this opportunity to acknowledge publicly the wise advice and support that I have received from Sir David over many years.

[7] 'Incorporate', that is, to the extent that the United Kingdom courts are required by the Human Rights Act to 'take account of' it in the course of their deliberations: Human Rights Act 1998, s. 2(1).

The potentially destabilizing effect of the decision in the *Sunday Times* case was recognized by F. A. Mann, who warned at an early stage:[8]

It is important to realise that a far-reaching inroad into the traditional law of contempt of court has been made. In a potentially wide variety of cases the European Court may assume a revising function and impose continental standards or, perhaps one should say, abuses upon this country which, in the name of freedom of the press and discussion, are likely to lower English usages by the substitution of trial by media for trial by courts. It is a matter for legislative concern whether this country is prepared to assume the risk to which it is now exposed. If the answer is in the negative a change of English law so as to comply with the standards of the Strasbourg judgment, yet to avoid trial by newspaper is unlikely to prove workable.

Whether the law has proved to be 'workable' or unworkable is a matter of perception and judgment. It is certainly true that the application of the law in cases of allegedly prejudicial pre-trial publicity[9] can be a matter of acute difficulty, since, as Sir John Laws has put it extra-judicially:[10]

the court has to make a factual judgment about the future (always liable to be more subjective, or at least impressionistic, than a judgment based on evidence about the past) and to do so, as it were, in the eye of the free speech storm; and not just any judgment about the future, but one which as often as not requires the court to make an assessment of the thought-processes of a jury which will not be empanelled for weeks or even months to come.

It must also be acknowledged that the law has changed out of all recognition from that which preceded the 1981 Act, according to which mere pre-judgment of an issue in pending litigation might be treated as contempt irrespective of the intent of the alleged contemnor,[11] and where any blackening of a potential defendant's name or character would rapidly be visited with the most dire of consequences.

---

8 (1979) 95 LQR 348, 352.

9 The discussion in this paper is limited to contempts allegedly arising from pre-trial publicity. But I have argued elsewhere that the courts have, with the assistance of Parliament, been altogether readier to accept that the press has, for what might be termed 'constitutional' reasons, a role to play in the reporting of court proceedings and in the degree of protection that should be accorded to the protection of journalistic sources. See 'The Press, the Courts and the Constitution' (1999) 52 CLP 126. At least two other challenges to the existing law may be anticipated. The strict rule in s. 8 of the Contempt of Court Act 1981 protecting the secrecy of the jury room, and preventing any inquiry as to what occurred within or any revelation by a juror as to what occurred might well be challenged under the free speech provisions of Article 10. It may also be doubted whether the somewhat imprecise distinctions between civil and criminal contempts can survive intact. Where imprisonment is a real possible outcome of proceedings for failure to observe a court order, for example, it seems altogether likely that the 'autonomous' jurisprudence of the European Court would treat the proceedings as being criminal rather than civil in character, at least for the purposes of the procedural and other protections that are to be afforded the alleged contemnor. See *Christopher Newman (T/A Mantella Publishing) v Modern Bookbinders Ltd.* [2000] 2 All ER 814.

10 (2000) 116 LQR 157.

11 This was the effect of the decision of the House of Lords in *Attorney-General v Times Newspapers Ltd.* [1974] AC 273.

1. THE INTERNET[12]

A development to which the law may soon have to accommodate itself is the rapidly developing Internet, with its capacity to transmit information across borders almost instantaneously. When the Contempt of Court Act was passed, the technology barely existed. In the so-called 'information age', its use is no longer the preserve of a technologically adept few, but a household commonplace. Court orders that are effective in one jurisdiction, to prevent the identification of one of the parties (for example), can be ignored with effective impunity if the name is put on a site beyond the reach of the jurisdiction, but which is instantaneously accessible from within the jurisdiction. This became a real problem in Canada in the so-called Ken and Barbie case,[13] and in England, when the son of a prominent Cabinet Minister, who was embroiled in a drugs case, was identified in Scotland on a web site in breach of the English law forbidding the identification of minors charged with criminal offences.[14]

Another possible use of the World Wide Web was manifested recently in the course of a defamation action brought against Penguin Books by the author David Irving, who established his own web site on which to canvass the issues that were raised in the trial, and to pass judgment upon witnesses and the legal participants.[15] Since the trial of the action was by judge alone, it may be assumed that there was little risk of contempt by virtue of any prejudicial publicity that might have been generated by the production of the site. But it is quite possible that potential witnesses, for example, who are identified on the site (and, initially, with contact e-mail addresses given) might be intimidated by traffic generated by the existence of such a site. Even if the trial is non-jury, the potential that exists for harassing an opponent and his legal advisers that is presented by such an instantaneous publishing medium could greatly complicate the task confronting a litigant and his or her legal advisers.

It is not difficult to foresee developments here that might require control if the present law is to be effectively enforced. Newspaper articles written in foreign newspapers can be made available to a world-wide audience through a hypertext link. As

---

[12] See Alastair Bonnington, 'News Without Frontiers: Pre-Trial Prejudice and the Internet' in L. Edwards and C. Waelde (eds.), *Law and the Internet* (1997); C. Walker, 'Fundamental Rights, Fair Trials and the New Audio-Visual Sector' (1996) 59 MLR 517.

[13] The sensational Bernardo/Homolka litigation, involving the sexual abuse and killing of two teenage girls by a married couple, gave rise to attempts to control Internet reporting when the trial judge banned reporting of the trial of the husband. See Donald F. Theall, 'Canada, Censorship, and the Internet' in Klaus Petersen and Alan C. Hutchinson (eds.), *Censorship in Canada* (1998). Also available on CataLaw.com/logic/docs/dt-censor.html.

[14] See *The Times*, 24 December 1997.

[15] See http://www.fpp.co.uk. Clare Dyer, legal correspondent of *The Guardian* reported an incident in which the Lord Chancellor's Department 'has had a website closed down because material posted on it criticised the judges', asserting also that 'service providers have been quick to act on complaints since a high court ruling in March that they could be sued for defamation if they were alerted to offensive content but took no action', 8 November 1999. The decision in question was *Godfrey v Demon Internet Ltd.* [1999] 4 All ER 342.

the law stands, this practice could be stopped if the article in question falls foul of the contempt laws. But it is open to the easy jibe—why should the United Kingdom public be deprived of the opportunity of exercizing free speech rights that are available to citizens of other countries? There are sound answers to this question. Both the presumption of innocence and the right to a fair trial may be put in jeopardy if the evidence (especially contested and partially available evidence) is rehearsed (and, no doubt, speculated upon) in advance of the trial itself; the risk of contamination to the process of justice is perceived to be too great for the risk to be run. The freedom of the press to exercise its rights must be, not completely curtailed, but postponed.

2. MANIPULATION OF THE MEDIA BY PARTIES

Although it is difficult to document with any precision, there appears to be an increasing use of the media by parties to litigation. The detrimental effect of this was identified by The Lord Chancellor's Advisory Committee on Legal Education and Conduct, a body concerned with the standards to be observed by professional advisers. The Committee concluded:[16]

The law of contempt does not constitute an effective control on the media, the police or the defence, especially in the pre-trial stage of criminal proceedings, either with regard to prejudice to the outcome of judicial proceedings or to public recognition of the principle that the issues in criminal cases are to be determined exclusively by the courts . . . The court normally achieves effective control during the trial through co-operation with the media, although there remains a sense of unease about lapses from that norm . . . This control does not extend either to the pre-charge stage or, apparently, after conviction. . . .

So far as remarks made by professional lawyers are concerned, there are imposed considerable restraints upon public comment on pending court proceedings in which clients are involved, deriving from ethical obligations ultimately enforceable by disciplinary proceedings.[17] While recognizing the legitimate interests of the press and public in following court proceedings, Lord Woolf MR in *Hogdson v Imperial Tobacco Ltd*.[18] none the less emphasized that lawyers ought not to become engaged

---

[16] *Lawyers' Comments to the Media* (1997) 24. And see *Hodgson v Imperial Tobacco Ltd.* [1998] 1 WLR 1056, [1998] 2 All ER 673.

[17] The lawyer making out-of-court statements on behalf of a client enjoys qualified privilege in the law of defamation: *Regan v Taylor* [2000] EMLR 549.

[18] [1998] 1 WLR 1056, [1998] 2 All ER 673. Lord Woolf MR invoked the observations of Chief Justice Rehnquist in *Gentile v State Bar of Nevada* 500 1 US 1030, 111 SCR 2720 (1991) to the effect that 'extra-judicial statements by legal representatives can be especially unhelpful since they are likely to be received by the media as specially authoritative even if they are inaccurate'. The decision is discussed by A. Nicol Q.C. and Heather Rogers in 'Contempt of Court, Reporting Restrictions and Disclosure of Sources' in the *Yearbook of Media Law* (1999) at 387. See also *Shopfer v Switzerland*, 23 September 1998, not yet reported, discussed by Lord Lester of Herne Hill QC and Natalia Schiffrin in (1999) *Yearbook of European Media Law*.

in *commenting* about such proceedings to the press (as opposed to communicating facts). In truth, the law seems to be increasingly powerless to prevent it. A question appears to arise, therefore, as to whether or not the law ought to be strengthened in such a way as to prevent prejudicial pre-trial comment, and, if so, how this can be done consistently with the free speech requirements of the Convention.

A related development has been the involvement in litigation of publicity agents, such as Mr Max Clifford. He acted, for example, on behalf of the complainant in the prosecution of pop star Gary Glitter, securing the promise of a payment to a witness in the event of Mr Glitter's conviction.[19] He also offered his services in the case of the Norfolk farmer, Tony Martin, who is being prosecuted for the murder of an intruder.[20] Is it a coincidence, one wonders, that a letter from the firm of solicitors acting for Mr Martin appeared in the correspondence columns of *The Times*,[21] asking that the media should 'publicise such matters as are allowed by law in order that other people who have been in similar situations can write to us so that, where relevant, the fears and anxieties of families who face intruders at night in their own home can be seen, and that we may know whether similar incidents have arisen and what action those people have taken in order to protect themselves and their property'? The question of the extent to which it is permissible to use fatal force in defence of oneself in one's own home is, it is fair to say, a matter of public interest that ought to attract the protection of s. 5[22] of the Contempt of Court Act. But that is a rather different matter from a 'campaign' that is orchestrated to present a particular point of view about what is likely to be, one should imagine, a fairly central issue in the trial itself.

3. THE LAW OF CONTEMPT AS AN 'EFFECTIVE CONTROL'

It would appear that there are at least three reasons why the law of contempt may not be 'effective' in this context.[23] First, the doctrine of 'prior restraint' which inhibits the courts from banning speech in advance of its publication has been seen to be applicable in this context. In *Attorney-General v BBC*,[24] Lord Denning remarked that

---

[19] It has been reported that the Lord Chancellor has asked for a report from the trial judge, Butterfield J.: *The Times*, 12 November 1999.

[20] In the course of an article in *The Times*, 17 September 1999, 'How to win friends and influence people', Mr Clifford observes: 'For legal reasons, I can't go into detail about the case . . . My instincts told me that *The Daily Mail* and *The Mail on Sunday* would be the most effective newspapers for the campaign'. What 'campaign' is appropriate, in such a context? In April 2000, Martin was convicted of murder and sentenced to life imprisonment. An appeal has been lodged.

[21] On 13 October 1999.

[22] Section 5 is set out and discussed below, at pp. 129–30.

[23] Passing over, for the time being, the inevitably contested questions of the desirability of control, effective or otherwise, and how, in any event, we might measure the 'effectiveness' of any particular legal regime.

[24] [1981] AC 303, 311. See also *Schering v Falkman Chemicals* [1982] 1 QB 1.

the courts should not award [the Attorney-General] . . . an injunction except in a clear case where there would manifestly be a contempt of court for the publication to take place. The same reasoning applies here as in the cases where a party seeks to restrain the publication of a libel.

Once a trial has begun, the courts have power to prevent the publication of the proceedings in question, by virtue of s. 4(2) of the Act. But until a court is seised of a case, there may well be a judicial reluctance to interfere with the publication process.[25] Second, as a number of recent cases demonstrate, the strict liability threshold of 'substantial risk of serious prejudice'[26] that obtains when proceedings have become active,[27] is very high, and correspondingly difficult for the Attorney-General to demonstrate.

The third factor that may explain the increasing reluctance on the part of the courts to treat prejudicial pre-trial comment as contempt arises out of the greater acceptance that the law should not seek to be speaking with two voices—that if a trial has in fact been prejudiced by a pre-trial publication, then the author of the prejudice is prima facie guilty of contempt. Even more striking is the corollary—which the courts have also begun to accept—that if a newspaper *is* guilty of such a contempt in any particular situation, the convicted defendant's assertion that the trial was in consequence unfair and 'unsafe'[28] must be taken seriously, possibly even giving rise to the conclusion that the conviction was unsafe and therefore unsustainable.

3.1 When is a Risk 'Substantial'?

The Contempt of Court Bill first introduced in Parliament did not include the word 'substantial'; this was introduced as an opposition amendment. Lord Hailsham took the view that the inclusion of the word would make no difference to the outcome of any particular case,[29] and did not persist with his opposition to the amendment. Later Lord Diplock indicated his view that the words 'substantial risk' were 'intended to exclude a risk that is only remote'.[30] But in the most recent case in which this

---

[25]   But in *BBC Scotland, McDonald, Rodgers and Donald v United Kingdom* (1998) 25 EHRR CD 179, the Commission held inadmissible a complaint about the injunction granted to postpone transmission of a television programme relating to the treatment of prisoners in the course of a gaol riot when indictments alleging assault had been served on three of the prison officers. The Commission took the view that 'the interference corresponded to the "pressing social need" of ensuring a fair trial for the prison officers, and that it was "proportionate to the legitimate aim pursued" in that the broadcast was merely postponed. Moreover, the High Court gave "sufficient and relevant reasons" for its judgment'.

[26]   Considered more fully in Arlidge, Eady and Smith, *Contempt* (1999), ch. 4.

[27]   In criminal cases, proceedings become active for the purposes of 'the strict liability rule' when the suspected person is arrested or when a warrant is issued for his arrest, and in civil cases, when a case is set down for hearing.

[28]   The current test to be applied in deciding whether or not to allow an appeal under the Criminal Appeal Act 1968, s. 2(1) as amended by the Criminal Appeal Act 1995.

[29]   *Hansard,* HL (series 5) vol. 417, col. 143.

[30]   In *Attorney-General v English* [1983] AC 116, 142.

matter has been considered,[31] at least one member of the Divisional Court, Sedley LJ, appears to have found decisive the fact that, even though the risk in that case was undoubtedly one of serious prejudice to the course of justice, he could not be sure that the risk created by the publication was a substantial risk that a jury, properly directed to disregard its own sentiments and any media comment, would nevertheless have its own thoughts or value judgments reinforced by the article to a point where they influenced the verdict. The article in question, which compared the defendant's activities of using body parts for 'artistic' purposes to those of two convicted serial killers, Dennis Nilson and Jeffrey Dahmer would almost without question have been regarded as a serious contempt before the 1981 Act. In the same case, Collins J summarized the principles to be extracted from the earlier, post-Act decisions:[32]

the risk must be judged at the time the publication is made and must be more than remote. The potential prejudice must be serious, an ordinary English word which must be given its proper weight. The court must be sure that the risk exists before conviction. The nature of the published material and its presentation, the timing of the publication, the likelihood of its coming to the attention of jurors or potential jurors, the likely impact on the jury and the ability of the jury to abide by any individual judicial directions which seek to neutralise any prejudice are all relevant considerations in individual cases.

Unsuccessful applications to commit for contempt were initiated in *Attorney-General v Unger*.[33] Two articles had been published, in the *Manchester Evening News* and the *Daily Mail* respectively, referring to the fact that a home help had been stealing from her employer, and to the recording on video film of her taking money from the refrigerator in the kitchen, including two still pictures of the event itself, appropriately captioned. Proceedings were 'active'[34] at the time of publication, because she had been arrested and charged with two offences of theft. Simon Brown LJ commented that although his initial reaction had been that the publications constituted contempt of court, amounting as they did to the clearest possible statements that the accused was guilty, he was persuaded that this was 'a simplistic and no longer permissible view of the law'.

The court took the view that although the respondents had no business assuming that there would be no trial, the court was not satisfied to the required standard that there had arisen a substantial risk of serious prejudice. There would have been a significant 'fade factor' because of the interval before any jury trial and, unlike some other cases, there was no question of any inadmissible material having been

31 *Attorney-General v Guardian Newspapers Ltd.* [1999] EMLR 904.
32 Principally, *Attorney-General v Mirror Group Newspapers Ltd.* [1997] 1 All ER 456, discussed by the author at [1997] CLJ 467.
33 [1998] 1 Cr App R. 308, EMLR 280. See however, *Attorney-General v Birmingham Post and Mail Ltd.* [1998] 4 All ER 49, where it was held that the fact that a trial judge had stayed the proceedings and discharged the jury was not necessarily determinative of whether a contempt had been established, since the questions being considered in each case were not the same. Such a stay was highly likely to be a telling pointer on a contempt application.
34 Discussed in Arlidge, Eady and Smith, (n. 26 above) § 4–156 *et seq.*

published, such as previous convictions. He also focussed on the 'presumption that jurors will decide cases solely according to the evidence put before them and the directions they are given, a presumption central to the whole criminal process'.

Similar problems of proof may arise where the case is not yet active and the proceedings are governed by the common law. To begin with, it is not wholly clear what constitutes the *actus reus* of the contempt—whether there must still be a substantial risk, or whether something less will suffice, and whether any potential prejudice must be 'serious'.

For common law contempt by publication, in addition, it may be very difficult to establish the required *mens rea*, which seems to be nothing less than an intention to interfere with the administration of justice.[35] There is something of a mismatch here. The *actus reus* of contempt of court is the creation of a risk. But the *mens rea* is held to be not the intention to create the risk, but the actual intention to cause prejudice. Hence in a payment to witnesses type case, a newspaper can say with some plausibility that it had no intention to interfere with the administration of justice by offering to pay £25,000 to the witness in the event of a conviction. It seems probable that those responsible for the production of the newspaper knew perfectly well that they were creating a risk to the administration of justice by offering such a payment. The temptation to burnish evidence is in itself considerable. And the public perception that such evidence becomes untrustworthy as a result of such offers must itself amount to an interference with the process of justice. But an awareness on the part of the editor that all of this is so is insufficient to amount to an intention to interfere with the administration of justice.

3.2 Section 5—Discussing Public Affairs

The extent to which important public matters might be discussed notwithstanding that their ventilation might give rise to a risk of prejudice is addressed in s. 5 of the Contempt of Court Act 1981, which provides:

A publication made as or as part of a discussion in good faith of public affairs or other matters of general public interest is not to be treated as a contempt of court under the strict liability rule if the risk of impediment or prejudice to particular legal proceedings is merely incidental to the discussion.

Given the apparent centrality to the balance that it purports to strike as between free press and fair trial, the scope of the provision has caused the courts surprisingly little concern. But it must be appreciated that the section does not begin to apply until the Attorney-General has crossed the threshold for a strict liability contempt, and established that the discussion did indeed create a substantial risk of serious prejudice.[36] Further reflection suggests, however, that the provision is or might be more

---

[35] But see the discussion in Arlidge, Eady and Smith (n. 26 above) at § 5–121 *et seq.*
[36] The point was established in *Attorney-General v English* [1983] AC 116.

or less inherently unworkable. Can any conviction be 'safe' when the discussion surrounding it was such as to constitute a substantial risk of serious prejudice to the trial in question? Or, if a person's conviction is to stand notwithstanding that there was such a risk, the question might be posed: why should a defendant have to bear the burden of free speech interests of society, simply because his or her case happens to give rise to an issue of compelling social interest or importance? It might be possible to point here to a disjunction between, on the one hand, the risk of serious prejudice (which is sufficient for a finding of contempt) and the actual interference with the course of justice which affects the decision as to whether or not a conviction is safe or unsafe. And it may be, in any particular case, that steps have been taken at the trial itself to ensure that any risk created by the publicity does not materialize, or result in any actual prejudice, by such strategems as change of venue or by delaying the proceedings.

4. ABUSE OF PROCESS, UNSAFE CONVICTIONS AND THE LAW OF CONTEMPT

Historically, the common law has been quick to suppress or treat as contempt anything in the nature of prejudicial pre-trial comment. At least when it came to punishing newspapers for contempt, the spectre of trial by newspaper of the kind that flourished in the American media[37] was regarded as an unspeakable horror.[38] If the rights to a fair trial and freedom of speech were found to be in conflict, the proper course was to require the media to refrain from publishing until all possibility of risk of prejudice had passed.

But a rather different view tended to be taken when complaint was made by a convicted person that proceedings had been tainted by the adverse publicity of which the Attorney-General[39] had complained in the contempt proceedings. In that context, the courts manifested an altogether more robust willingness to trust to the ability on the part of members of the jury to adhere to their oaths to try the defendant only upon the evidence given before them in court. As Lawton J asserted in *R v Kray*[40]:

---

[37] M. R. Chesterman, 'O.J. and the Dingo: How Media Publicity for Criminal Jury Trials is Dealt With in Australia and America' (1997) 45 AJCL 109.

[38] A. L. Goodhart, 'Newspapers and Contempt of Court in England' (1935) 48 Harv LR 885; G. J. Webber, 'Trial by Newspaper' (1958) CLP 37; A. L. Goodhart (1964) 80 LQR 13; A. Boyle, 'Freedom of Expression as a Public Interest in English Law' [1982] PL 574; G. Marshall, 'Press Freedom and Free Speech Theory' [1992] PL 40.

[39] Proceedings for this species of contempt are almost invariably dealt with by way of reference to the Law Officers. The decision not to bring proceedings has been held to be immune from judicial review: *R v Taylor and Taylor* (1993) 98 Cr App R 361.

[40] (1969) 53 Cr App R 413. In *R v West* [1996] 2 Cr App R 374, a case where the applicant had been convicted of ten counts of murder in complicity with her husband who had committed suicide whilst in prison awaiting trial (and whose conduct had been the subject of an enormous amount of publicity that had an enormous potential for prejudice to the trial of his widow) the Court of Appeal took the

It is . . . a matter of human experience, and certainly a matter of experience of those who practice (sic) in the Criminal Courts, first, that the public's recollection is short, and, secondly, that the drama, if I may use that term, of a trial almost always has the effect of excluding from recollection that which went before.

A change of position began to manifest itself about ten years ago. In *R v Cullen, McCann and Shanahan*,[41] convictions for conspiracy to murder, and the consequent twenty-five year gaol sentences were quashed as a result of remarks by Lord Denning, and the Home Secretary, who had both made adverse remarks about the right to silence, even as it was being exercised by persons on trial. Newspaper coverage of the trial itself was held to be so prejudicial in *Taylor and Taylor*,[42] that convictions of murder were quashed because of the press coverage of the trial which led to such headlines as 'The Killer Mistress who was at Lover's Wedding', and 'Love Crazy Mistress Butchered Rival Wife Court Told'. Some of this was illustrated with a still from a video of the victim's wedding, showing one of the defendants kissing the groom (her lover), a peck on the cheek being turned into a passionate kiss by creative editing. The decision of the Attorney-General not to bring contempt proceedings was held to be not susceptible to the processes of judicial review.

Successful applications that trials should be halted for abuse of process were brought in *Attorney-General v ITN News Ltd*.[43] and *Attorney-General v MGN*.[44] In the latter case, the Attorney-General unsuccessfully brought proceedings against several newspapers, after a trial judge had halted a criminal trial on the grounds that prejudicial newspaper publicity had jeopardized the fairness of those proceedings. Notwithstanding that the trial had been halted, said the Divisional Court, the newspapers were not guilty of contempt of court. One Geoffrey Knights was being tried for wounding with intent. He was notorious for (inter alia) his 'tempestuous' relationship with the soap opera actress, Gillian Taylforth (herself no stranger to legal action, having failed in a much-publicized defamation action not long previously). Five newspapers produced in 'typical graphic tabloid style' articles dealing with the 'relationship', mentioning variously Knight's previous criminal record for violence, and giving an inaccurate account of the incident for which he was to stand trial several months later. One can say with some confidence that, had such material appeared before the decision of the European Court in 1979 in the *Sunday Times* case, English courts would have had no difficulty whatsoever in treating it as contempt. But the Divisional Court held that the application to commit the editor

---

view that although the press coverage had been adverse to the applicant it would be absurd if allegations of murder caused such shock that an accused could not be tried, and that provided that the judge warned the jury that they should act only on the evidence given in court, there was no reason to suppose that the trial was unfair. See also [1998] EHRLR 204, where the applicant's case that the conviction was unfair as a result of the hostile and unremittingly adverse pre-trial publicity was held by the Commission to have been lodged out of time and therefore inadmissible.

[41] (1990) 92 Cr App R 239.   [42] (1993) 98 Cr App R 361.
[43] [1995] 2 All ER 370.
[44] [1997] 1 All ER 456. See A. T. H. Smith [1997] CLJ 467.

of the newspaper for contempt of court must fail, since it could not be established, in the case of any of the respondents, that the threshold had been reached.

One area where the case breaks new ground is in the clear recognition that 'the court will look at each publication separately' to see whether or not the statutory test was satisfied, adding that 'the mere fact that, by reason of earlier publications, there is already some risk of prejudice does not prevent a finding that the latest publication has created a further risk'. But it is remarkably difficult to say of any particular publication, judged as it must be against the 'feeding frenzy' that the press can generate, that it has created a 'substantial risk of serious prejudice'. Dealing with each of the articles separately, the court concluded that none of them had reached the required standard, and the applications were dismissed. The result is that there has been published admittedly prejudicial material, but that no contempt has been committed. Schiemann LJ explained this by saying that:

A consequence of the need in contempt proceedings, in which respondents face imprisonment or a fine, to be sure and look at each publication separately and the need in trial proceedings to look at risk of prejudice created by the totality of publications can be that it is proper to stay proceedings on the ground of prejudice albeit that no individual is guilty of contempt. One may regret that situation or one may take the view that this is the best answer to a difficult problem.

Simon Brown LJ in *Unger*[45] referred to the two distinct lines of authority on the susceptibility of jurors, which had been considered by Schiemann LJ, and added his own comment on the point of principle:[46]

It seems to me important in these cases that the courts do not speak with two voices, one used to dismiss criminal appeals with the court roundly rejecting any suggestion that prejudice resulted from media publications, the other holding comparable publications to be in contempt, the courts on these occasions expressing grave doubts as to the jury's ability to forget or put aside what they have heard or read.

I am certainly not saying that in respect of one and the same publication there cannot be both a contempt (of the present, outcome, sort) and a safe conviction. Plainly there can, most obviously perhaps in cases where the trial has had to be moved or delayed to minimize the prejudice occasioned by some publication. But generally speaking it seems to me that unless a publication materially affects the course of trial in that kind of way, or requires directions from the court well beyond those ordinarily required and routinely given to juries to focus their attention on evidence called before them rather than whatever they may have heard or read outside court, or creates at the very least a seriously arguable ground for an appeal on the basis of prejudice, it is unlikely to be vulnerable to contempt proceedings under the strict liability rule.

It is the need to be seen to be speaking with only one voice that has promoted the readjustment between fair trial and free speech in favour of the latter that has been

---

[45] [1998] 1 Cr App R 308, EMLR 280, discussed above at n. 33.
[46] [1998] 1 Cr App R 308, 318E–F, [1998] EMLR 280, 291.

the moving spirit in this area of the law. As Lord Justice Simon Brown points out, steps can be taken to minimize or cancel out altogether the risk that the prejudice will result in actual injustice. What those steps might be will be discussed presently.

5. EUROPEAN FREE SPEECH JURISPRUDENCE

The United Kingdom's law of contempt of court has been found by the European Commission and Court to be in breach of the European Convention on a surprising number of occasions. In addition to the *Sunday Times* case itself, in *Harman v United Kingdom*[47] the Commission had held to be admissible as a breach of Article 10 the decision of the House of Lords that the disclosure of material to a journalist after that material had been read in open court was nevertheless a contempt, notwithstanding that the material had been made available initially through the process of discovery. In *Hodgson Woolf Productions and NUJ and Channel 4 v United Kingdom*,[48] the fact that there was no domestic mechanism through which aggrieved journalists could challenge the making of reporting postponement orders was held to give rise to an arguable breach of Article 10. Most recently, the decision of the House of Lords in *X Ltd. v Morgan-Grampian (Publishers) Ltd.*[49] that a journalist should be required to disclose his sources 'in the interests of justice' where this was required to trace the source of a leak of a secret draft corporate plan was held to give insufficient regard to the position of the press as the guardian of the public interest, in *Goodwin v United Kingdom*.[50]

The question needs to be asked as to why this series of reversals should have occurred. Two possibilities, at least, present themselves. In the first place, it could be traced to the difference of approach identified by the European Court itself in the *Sunday Times* case. According to the common law, the point to be struck between freedom of speech and information and the fairness of the trial was all a matter of 'balance'. But the European Court had taken an altogether different view of the nature of the decision making process, saying.[51]

Whilst emphasising that it is not its function to pronounce itself on an interpretation of English law adopted in the House of Lords, the court points out that it has to take a different approach. The court is faced not with a choice between two conflicting principles, but with a principle of freedom of expression that is subject to a number of exceptions which must be narrowly interpreted.

The balancing metaphor, so familiar to the common law, suggests that the scales are evenly weighted at the outset. What the Court is here pointing out is that it takes a different view. Although the 'rights of others' are to be taken into account (includ-

---

[47]   (1985) 7 EHRR 146.   [48]   (1987) 10 EHRR 503.
[49]   [1991] 1 AC 1.
[50]   (1996) 22 EHRR 123. See also *Fressoz and Roire v France* (Application No. 29183/95).
[51]   (1979) 2 EHRR 245, 281.

ing here the right to a fair trial, as guaranteed by Article 6) there is an ordering and set of priorities that places freedom of speech on a higher plane than it attains under the common law.

A second explanation of the record of the common law before the European Court is that the European Court has recognized the centrality and importance of press freedom to the democratic process far more wholeheartedly than have the courts of the common law.[52] The reverence for free speech, and in particular for political speech[53] is still accurately characterized by the Court's statement in *Handyside v United Kingdom*[54] in the much-cited passage:

Freedom of expression constitutes one of the essential foundations of . . . 'a democratic society' . . . , one of the basic conditions for its progress and for the development of every man . . . [It] is applicable not only to 'information' or 'ideals' that are favourably received or regarded as inoffensive or as a matter of indifference, but also those that offend, shock or disturb the State or any sector of the population. Such are the demands of that pluralism, tolerance and broad-mindedness without which there is no 'democratic society'.

The right to know what is being done in our names in the interests of justice is a vital part of that democratic process deserving therefore of a high degree of protection. Where the law of contempt strikes at the journalistic function, as in the case where a journalist might be required to reveal sources, the difference of view is striking and decisive. The point is, perhaps, most explicitly made by the European Court in the *Goodwin* decision.[55]

Protection of journalistic sources is one of the basic conditions for press freedom. . . . Without such protection, sources may be deterred from assisting the press in informing the public on matters of public interest. As a result the vital public-watchdog role of the press may be undermined and the ability of the press to provide accurate and reliable information may be adversely affected. Having regard to the importance of journalistic sources for press freedom in a democratic society and the potentially chilling effect an order of source disclosure has on the exercise of that freedom, such a measure cannot be compatible with the European Convention on Human Rights unless it is justified by an overriding requirement in the public interest.

In other words, where a restriction upon press freedom strikes at the function that the press might perform in a participatory democracy, the European Court will accord far less freedom of decision making to the national jurisdictions than it is prepared to allow where either blasphemy or the prohibitions upon racist speech are

---

[52] See A. T. H. Smith, 'The Press, The Courts and the Constitution' (1999) 52 CLP 126.
[53] Addressed in Ch. 6 of this work by Ivan Hare.
[54] [1976] 1 EHRR 737.
[55] (1996) 22 EHRR 123. See also *Roger Fressoz et Claude Roire v France* (Application No. 29183/95), where the Commission has taken the view that the punishment of a journalist for publishing material in breach of a duty of confidentiality was an unreasonable interference with the role of the journalist. In *Camelot Group plc v Centaur Communications* [1999] QB 124, the Court of Appeal insisted upon disclosure in the 'interests of justice' over the protest of protection of sources, purporting to distinguishing the *Goodwin* decision on the facts.

concerned.[56] How far this approach should be, or can be, translated into the domestic context is problematic. The margin of appreciation is not a doctrine that can be applied by the national courts. That slippery compromise seeks to respect national traditions whilst at the same time ensuring that a degree of universality in the protection of norms is achieved. The question therefore arises: could the fact that the majority of serious offences in this country are tried by a lay tribunal, the jury, give rise to an expectation that a body of law designed to protect the jury from adverse influences will be respected as being within the margins of tolerance permitted to a member state?

Some quite strong indications have recently been given that this may be permissible. The European Court has been prepared to act against conduct (prejudicial comment) which it believes to violate the presumption of innocence and the fairness of the trial. In *Worm v Austria*,[57] for example, the Court held that a conviction under s. 23 of the Austrian Media Act for exercising prohibited influence on criminal proceedings had not breached Article 10 of the Convention. The Austrian Court of Appeal had convicted the applicant and found that potential damage to the judicial proceedings was sufficient to sustain a conviction. Public figures, like any other defendants, are entitled to an impartial trial—the defendant had been a Vice Chancellor and Minister of Finance charged with tax evasion and fraud, and the journalist had written an article proclaiming a belief in guilt.

Similarly, in *Allenet de Ribemont v France*[58] where the French Minister of the Interior and a number of senior police officers held a press conference in which they named the applicant as one of the instigators of the murder of a French MP, the European Court held that the making of the statements violated the presumption of innocence protected by Article 6(2). The Court held in an action for compensation that the applicant was entitled to the sum of FF2M plus costs.

A third example that might be offered, much closer to home, is to be found in the decision of the Commission in *BBC Scotland v United Kingdom*[59] in which it was held that an injunction prohibiting the broadcasting of a report that might prejudice the outcome of an impending criminal trial was not in breach of Article 10 of the Convention.

6. FREE PRESS AND FAIR TRIAL: WHAT IS TO BE DONE?

On the supposition that the law as currently cast does not adequately protect the process of justice, in the sense that it neither protects the interests of free speech nor

---

[56] P. Mahoney, 'Universality versus Subsidiarity in the Strasbourg Case Law on Free Speech: Explaining Some Recent Judgments' [1997] EHRLR 364.

[57] (1997) 25 EHRR 454.

[58] (1995) 20 EHRR 557. See also the earlier case of *X v Austria* (1963) 11 D 31 where it was held that a virulent press campaign against an accused is capable of violating the right to a fair trial, especially where the trial was to be before a jury.

[59] (1998) 25 EHRR (CD) 179.

those of defendants at risk, a question arises as to how the balance is to be re-struck. In Canada, the need to re-examine this common law settlement arose from the fact that the adoption of the Canadian Charter of Rights and Freedoms had arguably altered the traditional balance as between free press and fair trial. In *Dagenais v Canadian Broadcasting Corp.*[60] the Supreme Court of Canada, by a majority adopted what might be seen as the United States/European approach to the protection of rights, and refused to forbid the transmission of a 'docudrama' that might have had some impact upon an impending trial. The Chief Justice rejected what he called the 'clash model' of rights exemplified in the common law. It was not so much a question of free press *or* fair trial, which required the courts to make a stark choice between the two when they came in to conflict. Rather, Lamer CJC said, where the right to a fair trial and publication came into conflict, since the Charter itself did not accord any priorities as between the competing rights, ways must be found by the courts to accommodate both to the maximum possible extent.

There are various devices of which the courts could avail themselves if it was thought appropriate to try and avoid or reduce the prejudicial impact that media communication, short of imposing outright ban. For example, in *Dagenais v Canadian Broadcasting Corp.*,[61] where the court was considering the possibility of enjoining the broadcast of a 'docudrama', Lamer CJC suggested a number of alternative measures:

Possibilities that readily come to mind, however, include adjourning trials, changing venues, sequestering jurors, allowing challenges for cause and *voir dires* during jury selection, and providing strong judicial direction to the jury.

All of these possibilities carry their own difficulties. Justice delayed is justice denied, and the right to a speedy trial is guaranteed by the European Convention. Change of venue is possible, but it can cause logistical difficulties for the prosecutor and defence alike, and is at odds with the common law assumption that the trial should ideally occur in the locations where the offence itself took place. Our treatment of juries has been a history of making their lives more comfortable, and in particular permitting them to depart to their homes even in the course of their deliberations. More recently,[62] the Court of Appeal reiterated its view that it would be wrong for the judge to permit juries to be questioned about their knowledge of the incident upon which they are about to be called to pass judgment.

---

[60] (1994) 120 DLR (4th) 12; see also *Phillips v Nova Scotia (Westray Inquiry)* (1995) 98 CCC (3d) 20. But see *Gisborne Herald Co. Ltd. v Solicitor-General* [1995] 3 NZLR 577, where the approach taken in *Dagenais* was considered but ultimately rejected.
[61] (1994) 94 CCC (3d) 289.
[62] *Andrews (Tracey)* [1999] Crim LR 156. By way of contrast P. Horwitz, 'Jury Selection After *Dagenais*: Prejudicial Pre-Trial Publicity' (1996) 42 CR 220.

7. A TENTATIVE CONCLUSION

At the outset of this inquiry, I had come to the somewhat gloomy conclusions that we are being drawn inexorably in the direction of trial by newspaper, and that the incorporation of the Convention by the Human Rights Act 1998 would hasten the process. There was, it seemed, a wholesale capitulation to the free-press rhetoric. F. A. Mann's predictions cited earlier seemed to be in the process of realization. Closer acquaintance with the jurisprudence of the European Court (here only sketched) leads me to the tentative conclusion that although political speech might enjoy an especially protected status under the European Convention, nevertheless the laws designed to preserve the fair trial rights of those particularly at risk in criminal trials are understood and respected to a higher degree than might be supposed. It may be that the law cannot be strengthened in ways that would satisfy critics such as the Lord Chancellor's Advisory Committee. And it may be that further thought must be given to some of the stratagems that might be employed to protect a defendant's right to a fair trial than the common law is currently prepared to concede. Had the jury been vetted in the unique circumstances of the trial of Rosemary West, for example, to explore the question whether the jurors could come to the task of deciding guilt or innocence in accordance with their oaths, one imagines that few would question the propriety of doing so. There is, in the common law of contempt of court, a unique contribution to be made to the civilized conduct of legal proceedings about which the United Kingdom should feel no need to be defensive; quite the contrary—the idea that rights should be determined by an impartial and dispassionate legal process is preserved and enhanced by a sensitively flexible law of contempt of court that may well serve as an exemplar to the European Court itself, and to other jurisdictions within the Council of Europe who are co-signatories to the European Convention on Human Rights.

8

Newsgathering as Protected Activity

DAVID A. SCHULZ*

1. INTRODUCTION

Twenty years ago *Mother Jones*, a popular magazine of the US counter-culture, had one of its reporters pose as a job applicant at a chemical factory. By engaging in covert photography while at the factory, the reporter documented the manufacture in the United States of illegal pesticides intended for the export market. The resulting exposé earned a National Magazine Award.[1] Today, it would more likely to earn a lawsuit.

In recent years, litigation over the techniques used to gather the news has become a growth industry in the United States. Such claims have been spurred on by the 1991 Supreme Court decision in *Cohen v Cowles Media Co.*[2] that rejected a newspaper's effort to assert a First Amendment defence against liability for a tort committed to obtain a news story. That case arose out of a promise of confidentiality made to Mr Cohen by a newspaper reporter in exchange for information about a political candidate. The promise was not kept and Cohen lost his political consultant's job as a result. In disallowing a First Amendment defence to Cohen's subsequent tort claim for 'promissory estoppel', the Supreme Court held that 'generally applicable' laws having only 'incidental effects' on the ability of the press to gather the news, do not offend the First Amendment.[3]

Ever since the *Cohen* ruling, an increasing flow of litigation has sought to impose liability on reporters for torts they allegedly have committed while seeking out the news—torts such as trespass, fraud, intrusion, and interference with contract. Yet, these same lawsuits seek to measure the damages caused by such newsgathering torts based upon the impact of the resulting adverse news report.[4]

---

* The author gratefully acknowledges the valuable assistance of Mark Weissman in the preparation of this article. An earlier version of this article was published by the Libel Defense Resource Center in 'The Media at the Millennium', *LDRC Bulletin* (December 1999) at 17.

[1] See Phillip Lawler, 'The Alternative Influence,' 16, 31 (1984).

[2] 501 US 663 (1991) (hereafter *'Cohen'*).

[3] 501 US at 669.

[4] E.g., *Shulman v Group W Prods. Inc.*, 18 Cal 4th 200, 26 Media L Rep 1737 (1998); (hereafter *'Shulman'*); *Desnick v America Broad. Cos.* 44 F 3d 1345, 23 Media L Rep 1161 (7th Cir 1995) (hereafter *'Desnick'*); *Medical Lab. Management Consultants v America Broad. Cos., Inc.* 30 F Supp. 2d 1182, 27 Media L Rep 1545 (D. Ariz 1998). Plaintiffs seek to recover damages resulting from the publication on the theory that the news report itself is a 'foreseeable' consequence of the original newsgathering tort. See, e.g., John J. Walsh *et al.*, 'Media Misbehavior and the Wages of Sin: The Constitutionality of Consequential Damages for Publication of Ill-Gotten Information,' 4 Wm & Mary Bill Rts. J 1111 (1996).

After the landmark ruling in *New York Times v Sullivan*[5] created a qualified constitutional privilege against certain libel claims, courts in the United States took an expansive view of the protection to be given to published news reports, even erroneous reports, in order to provide sufficient breathing space for the robust, wide-open exchanges intended by the First Amendment. The US Supreme Court, however, has yet to explore the extent to which this First Amendment protection of free speech and a free press[6] extends to the actions taken by journalists *before* publication, to protect their conduct in seeking out the news.

The absence of clear guidance from the Supreme Court on the scope of protection afforded to newsgathering activity under the First Amendment, combined with a misguided application by lower courts of the 'incidental impact' approach put forward in *Cohen*, has led to a confused and inconsistent body of case law and commentary disagreeing about the existence and extent of any First Amendment protection for the press when it seeks out the news. Some lower courts have construed *Cohen* to mean that no constitutional issue is raised when 'generally applicable,' non-publication tort claims are asserted against the press,[7] while other courts have recognized a First Amendment concern, yet have differed greatly on its proper scope and application.[8]

The chilling impact inevitably caused by the increase in litigation following *Cohen* suggests a need for a clear articulation of the scope of protection afforded to newsgathering by the First Amendment. Several approaches have been put forward in various contexts to address the constitutional concerns. One approach would avoid a constitutional conflict by construing narrowly the common law torts—trespass, deceit, intrusion and the like—so that they are not extended to impose liability for conduct these torts were never intended to regulate.[9] This approach was followed in *Desnick v American Broadcasting Co.*, where Judge Posner narrowly construed a number of tort claims advanced by the subject of a hidden camera investigation,

---

[5] 376 US 254 (1964).

[6] The First Amendment to the United States Constitution provides, in relevant part, that 'Congress shall make no law respecting an establishment of religion, or prohibiting the free exercise thereof; or abridging freedom of speech, or of the press. . . .'

[7] As used in this article, 'non-publication torts' refer to common law tort claims such as trespass, fraud, intrusion, infliction of emotional distress and the like, which do not require a publication or dissemination of information as an element of liability; 'publication torts' refer to tort claims such as defamation, false light and public disclosure of private facts, where liability at common law rests, in part, upon the dissemination of information.

[8] E.g., compare *Special Force Ministries v WCCO Television* 584 NW 2d 789, 793, 26 Media L Rep 2490 (Minn App 1998) (no First Amendment 'tension' holding press liable for fraud or trespass); *W.D.I.A. Corp. v McGraw-Hill, Inc.* 34 F Supp 2d 612, 624 (SD Ohio 1998) (rejecting any heightened scrutiny of claims against the press because law of fraud is 'generally applicable') with *Medical Lab. Management Consultants v America Broad. Cos.* 30 F Supp 2d 1182, 1186, 27 Media L Rep 1545 (D Ariz 1998) (news gathering tort claims require 'grappling with and finding a balance' between the fundamental rights of privacy and access to information of public interest); *Desnick* 44 F 3d at 1355 (production of the news entitled to 'all the safeguards' afforded to the broadcast of the news).

[9] See C. Foley and D. Schulz, 'Damage Considerations when the Press is Sued for Gathering the news', Libel & Newsgathering Litigation (PLI, 1998) at 129.

concluding that the common law torts did not create liability for the types of reporting challenged in that case.[10] Another approach, recently accepted by the Fourth Circuit in *Food Lion Inc. v Capital Cities/ABC Inc.*, addresses the constitutional concern primarily by limiting the measure of damages allowed in cases of newsgathering torts, prohibiting any recovery for reputational damage caused by the publication of a report if liability is asserted only upon the techniques used to gather the information.[11] Such approaches to protect legitimate, vigorous newsgathering activity may prove successful before the courts. This article, however, addresses a third approach: defining the nature of the constitutional protection that independently shields newsgathering activity.

This article first reviews the constitutional policies and judicial precedent that recognize newsgathering as a constitutionally protected activity, and demonstrates that the Supreme Court's holding in *Cohen* is not to the contrary. The article then reviews some of the approaches taken by the Supreme Court to resolve conflicts that have emerged with First Amendment rights in other contexts, and also describes the approaches that have been taken by media lawyers seeking to defend recent cases challenging newsgathering activity. The article finally outlines a set of legal principles drawn from this precedent that should guide the development of clear standards for the protection of newsgathering activity. A concise statement of the legal framework that will govern newsgathering torts is ultimately the best way to provide certainty and reduce the chilling impact generated by the current wave of litigation.

2. THE NATURE OF THE PROBLEM

From the widely-noted muzzling effect of the tobacco industry's dramatic threat of 'tortious interference' liability against CBS in 1995,[12] to the on-going barrage of litigation challenging the use of hidden cameras, the US press has faced a rising tide of litigation since the *Cohen* decision in 1991.[13] The variety of tort claims asserted, the

---

[10] 44 F 3d at 1352–3. See also, *Thomas v Pearl* 998 F 2d 447, 452 (7th Cir. 1993); *Medical Lab. Management Consultants v America Broad. Cos.* 30 F Supp 2d 1182, 1191, 27 Media L Rep 1545 (D Ariz 1998).

[11] *Food Lion Inc. v Capital Cities/ABC Inc.* 1999 WL 957738 (4th Cir 1999) (hereafter '*Food Lion*') (barring 'publication damages' for injury to reputation where no publication tort was alleged). See also, J. Borger, 'New Whines in Old Bottles: Taking Newsgathering Torts Off the Food Lion Shelf,' 34 Tort & Ins. LJ 61, 67 (1998) (urging the rejection of newsgathering tort claims altogether 'when the harm inflicted arises from the broadcast or publication rather than from the newsgathering activity'). See also A. Sims, 'Food for the Lions: Excessive Damages for Newsgathering Torts and the Limitations of Current First Amendment Doctrines', 78 BUL Rev 508 (1998) (urging that the focus 'should not be on limiting media liability for newsgathering torts, but rather on preventing the award of excessive damages').

[12] See, e.g., S. Baron *et al.*, 'Tortious Interference: The Limits of Common Law Liability for Newsgathering,' 4 Wm & Mary LJ 1027 (1996).

[13] See, e.g., *Wilson v Layne*—US—119 S Ct 1692 (1999); *Berger v Hanlon*—US—119 S Ct 1706 (1999); *Food Lion* 1999 WL 957738 (4th Cir 1999); *Sussman v American Broad. Cos.* No. 97–55410, 1999 WL 623475 (9th Cir 18 August 1999); *Deteresa v American Broad. Cos.* 121 F 3d 460, 25 Media L Rep 2038 (9th Cir 1997), *cert. denied*, 118 S Ct 1840 (1998); *Parker v Boyer* 93 F 3d 445, 24 Media L

aggressive tactics invoked to prevent investigative reports from being completed,[14] and the level of compensatory and punitive damages demanded after reports are disseminated, undoubtedly chills the vigorous pursuit of the news.[15] The spread of such chilling litigation makes the definition of the scope of newsgathering protection all the more urgent.

2.1 Newsgathering is a Constitutionally Protected Activity

A threshold question is whether the act of newsgathering itself is protected by the First Amendment. Since the Supreme Court's *Cohen* decision, some lower courts have found any constitutional analysis unnecessary in addressing traditional common law tort theories directed against the press. However, the constitutional significance of the newsgathering process has been recognized—directly and indirectly—by the Supreme Court, and the constitutional concerns cannot properly be disregarded when sanctions are to be imposed on investigative reporting activity. The protection of newsgathering is essential to realize fully the benefits of a system of free expression.

More than a quarter century ago, the Supreme Court observed that 'news gathering' is not without its 'First Amendment protection[s]', because 'without some protection for seeking out the news, freedom of the press could be eviscerated'.[16] Lower courts repeatedly have recognized that gathering the news is a necessary prerequisite to publishing it, so that a constitutional protection of newsgathering is essential to avoid media timidity and to preserve an unimpeded flow of information to the public.[17] As Judge Posner explained in *Desnick*, the reporting of the news:

Rep 2307 (8th Cir 1996); *Desnick* 44 F 3d 1345 (7th Cir. 1995); *Brooks v American Broad. Cos.* 932 F 2d 495, 18 Media L Rep 2121 (6th Cir 1991); *Peavy v Harman* 37 F Supp 2d 495 (ND Tex 1999); *Veilleux v National Broad. Co.* 8 F Supp 2d 23, 26 Media L Rep 1929 (D Me 1998); *W.D.I.A. Corp. v McGraw-Hill Inc.* 34 F Supp 2d. 612 (SD Ohio 1998); *Medical Lab. Management Consultants v American Broad. Cos.* 30 F Supp 1182, 27 Media L Rep 1545 (D Ariz 1998); *Ashcraft v Conoco*, No. 7:95-CV-187-BR, 1998 WL 404491, 26 Media L Rep 1620 (DNC 21 January 1998); *Reeves v Fox Television Network* 983 F Supp 703, 25 Media L Rep 2104 (ND Ohio 1997); *Barrett v Outlet Broad. Inc.* 22 F Supp 2d 726 (SD Ohio 1997); *Wolfson v Lewis*, 924 F Supp 1413, 24 Media L Rep 1609 (ED Pa 1996); *Aequitron Med. Inc. v CBS Inc.* No. 93 Civ 950, 1995 WL 406157, 24 Media L Rep 1025 (SDNY 10 July 1995); *Sanders v American Broad. Cos.* 20 Cal 4th 907, 27 Media L Rep 2025 (1999); *Shulman v Group W Prods. Inc.* 18 Cal 4th 200, 26 Media L Rep 1737 (1998); *SimTel Communications Inc. v National Broad. Co.* 71 Cal App 4th 1066, 27 Media L Rep 1865 (1999); *Marich v QRZ Media Inc.* 73 Cal App 4th 299, 27 Media L Rep 2036 (1999); *Special Force Ministries v WCCO Television* 584 NW 2d 789, 26 Media L Rep 2490 (Minn App 1998); *Dickerson v Raphael* 222 Mich App 185, 564 NW 2d 85 (1997); *KOVR-TV Inc. v Superior Court* 31 Cal App 4th 1023, 23 Media L Rep 1371 (Cal. App. 1995).

[14] See, e.g., 'Newsgathering Tactics on Trial' *Editor & Publisher* 18 December 1999 at 18 (describing a charity's recent efforts to halt publication of the results of a *Chicago Tribune* investigation into its practices by claiming illegal conduct by the investigative reporters).

[15] See, P. Lebel, 'The Constitutional Interest in Getting the News: Toward a First Amendment Protection from Tort Liability for Surreptitious Newsgathering,' 4 Wm & Mary Bill Rts J 1145, 1147 (1998); A. Sims, (n.11) at 526.

[16] *Branzburg v Hayes*, 408 US 665, 681 (1972).

[17] See, e.g., *FMC Corp. v Capital Cities/ABC Inc.* 915 F 2d 300, 18 Media L Rep 1195 (7th Cir 1990) (recognizing First Amendment protection for newsgathering); *Boddie v American Broad. Cos.* 881

is entitled to all the safeguards with which the Supreme Court has surrounded liability for defamation. And it is entitled to them regardless of the name of the tort, and, we add, regardless of whether the tort suit is aimed at the content of the broadcast *or the production of the broadcast.*[18]

The body of case law recognizing an affirmative right of public access to judicial proceedings also reflects the constitutional protection of newsgathering. The Supreme Court first upheld an enforceable constitutional right of access in *Richmond Newspapers Inc. v Virginia*, stating:

It is not crucial whether we describe this right to attend criminal trials to hear, see, and communicate observations concerning them as a 'right of access,' or a 'right to gather information,' for we have recognized that 'without some protection for seeking out the news, freedom of the press could be eviscerated.'[19]

In a concurring opinion, Justice Stevens underscored that *Richmond Newspapers* was 'a watershed case,' because 'for the first time, the Court unequivocally [held] that an arbitrary interference with access to important information is an abridgment of the freedoms of speech and of the press protected by the First Amendment.'[20] The Supreme Court's subsequent access decisions demonstrate the importance of ensuring that the press is not unreasonably restricted in its ability to act as a source of information for the public.[21]

Several policy considerations underlie the First Amendment's protection of newsgathering activity. In the constitutional scheme, the press serves to check governmental abuses of power, and provides the public with the important information necessary to self-governance. As Justice Stewart put it:

In setting up the three branches of the Federal Government, the Founders deliberately created an internally competitive system. . . . The primary purpose of the constitutional guarantee of

---

F 2d 267, 271, 16 Media L Rep 2038 (6th Cir 1989) (same); *von Bulow by Auersperg v von Bulow* 811 F 2d 136, 142, 13 Media L Rep 2041 (2d Cir 1987) (same); *Re Express-News Corp.* 695 F 2d 807, 808–9, 9 Media L Rep 1001 (5th Cir 1982) (same); *Riley v City of Chester* 612 F 2d 708, 713 (same); *Sanders v American Broad. Cos.* 60 Cal Rptr 2d 595, 597, 25 Media L Rep 1343 (Cal App 1997) (claims challenging newsgathering activity implicate First Amendment issues).

[18] 44 F 3d 1345, 1355, 23 Media L Rep 1161 (7th Cir 1995) (citations omitted, emphasis added). See also, *Allen v Combined Communications Corp.* 7 Media L Rep 2417, 2419 (Colo Dist Ct 1981) (First Amendment should protect all 'activities which are necessary for the publication of [a news story]'). Cf., *Zerilli v Evening News Association* 628 F 2d 217, 224, 6 Media L Rep 1530 (DC Cir 1980) (rejecting a § 1983 claim against the press due to the special factors presented in 'uncovering and publishing information' the press deems newsworthy).

[19] 448 US 555, 576 (1980) (citations omitted).

[20] ibid., at 582–3 (Stevens J concurring). In *First National Bank of Boston v Bellotti* 435 US 765, 783 (1978), the First Amendment 'goes beyond protection of the press and the self-expression of individuals to prohibit government from limiting the stock of information from which members of the public may draw.'

[21] See, e.g., *Press-Enter. Co. v Superior Court* 478 US 1, 13 (1982) (holding that right of access applies to preliminary hearings as they are conducted in California). See also, S. Baron *et al.,* 'Tortious Interference: The Limits of Common Law Liability for Newsgathering' 4 Wm & Mary Bill Rts J 1027 (1996).

a free press was a similar one: to create a fourth institution outside of the Government as an additional check on the three official branches.[22]

Justice Powell articulated a further function served by the press, acting as surrogate for the public:

No individual can obtain for himself the information needed for the intelligent discharge of his political responsibilities. For most citizens the prospect of personal familiarity with news-worthy events is hopelessly unrealistic. In seeking out the news, the press therefore acts as an agent of the public at large. It is the means by which the people receive that free flow of infor-mation and ideas essential to intelligent self-government.[23]

Like its role in checking against government abuse, the media's role as public informer advances the core purposes of free expression. Both of these roles require an ability vigorously to seek out the news.[24] The press, according to Justice Brennan, 'is not only protected when it speaks out, but when it performs all of the myriad tasks necessary for it to gather and disseminate the news'.[25]

Recent efforts to extend tort liability to punish the press for its newsgathering conduct, when the resulting truthful publications could not constitutionally be punished, serve to underscore the important interests at stake. In *Branzburg v Hayes*, a majority of the Court concluded that reporters were not entirely exempt 'from the normal duty of appearing before a grand jury', because the consequential burden on newsgathering was at best 'uncertain', and the weight of history demonstrated that requiring such testimony had 'not been a serious obstacle to either the development or retention of confidential news sources by the press'.[26] The same cannot be said when tort liability is imposed in novel ways that create significant obstacles to the development of the news. The impact of such liability is not 'uncertain', but rather is immediate and direct. And, the only 'weight of history' is a long history where such tort claims have not been asserted against the press.

Both Supreme Court precedent and the policy objectives of the First Amendment leave no doubt that aggressive and probing newsgathering activity is a key compo-nent of a free press, so that newsgathering activity may not be punished without a careful assessment of the implications of such punishment on our system of free expression.

2.2 'De-*Cohen*-izing' the First Amendment Analysis of Newsgathering

Notwithstanding the broad recognition of the constitutional importance of newsgath-ering, courts have long sought to sidestep any constitutional analysis by observing that

---

[22] Potter Stewart 'Or of the press,' 26 Hastings LJ 631 at 634 (1975).

[23] *Saxbe v Washington Post Co.* 417 US 843, 863 (1974) (Powell J dissenting).

[24] See Note, 'Press Passes and Trespasses: Newsgathering on Private Property' 84 Colum. L Rev 1298, 1321 (1984).

[25] William J. Brennan, Jr., 'Address' 32 Rutgers L Rev 173, 177 (1979).

[26] 408 US at 699.

there is no 'wall of immunity protecting newsmen from any liability for their conduct while gathering news'.[27] While the absence of 'immunity' may be true enough, this does not resolve the issue.

To say that there is no 'immunity' for torts committed in the course of gathering the news, is not to say that there is no constitutional protection at all for the gathering of the news. The same could be said of libel ('there is no immunity for damage to reputation caused from publishing the news'), but that does not deny the existence of constitutional limits on the scope of liability that may be imposed. In *New York Times v Sullivan*,[28] the Supreme Court found that the First Amendment does indeed restrict a law of general applicability, state common law of defamation. Again, in *Hustler Magazine Inc. v Falwell*,[29] the Supreme Court found a First Amendment limitation on the pursuit of a claim for the generally applicable tort of emotional distress, where liability was based upon the publication of a cartoon.

Plaintiffs alleging newsgathering torts have latched onto the Court's reference in *Cohen* to the propriety of 'generally applicable' laws having only 'incidental effects' on newsgathering, but they have done so without applying the Court's underlying analysis. Some lower courts have invoked this language to brush off any constitutional concerns altogether on the ground that common law torts are indeed 'generally applicable'.[30] The Supreme Court's rationale, however, is neither so simplistic nor so broad.

Cohen involved a claim for breach of promise brought by a source against a newspaper that reneged on a pledge of confidentiality. The critical limitation in *Cohen*—central to the Supreme Court's refusal to find any First Amendment defence to the claim for damages—is the Court's assessment that enforcing the common law of promissory estoppel against reporters would have only an 'incidental effect' on the ability of journalists to gather and report the news.[31] The Court analysed the likely impact of its holding in *Cohen* and concluded that enforcing the press promise at issue would possibly *enhance* the ability of journalists to gather information in the future, by reassuring sources that a reporter's pledge of confidentiality is indeed enforceable. In any event, Justice White concluded, holding reporters responsible for their promises of confidentiality would result in 'no more than . . . [an] incidental, and constitutionally insignificant' impact on newsgathering and reporting.[32] The

---

[27] *Galella v Onassis* 487 F 2d 986, 995, 1 Media L Rep 2425 (2d Cir 1973). Before *Cohen*, many courts had accepted that news organizations could be held liable for torts and crimes committed in the process of gathering the news. See, e.g., *Dietemann v Time Inc.* 449 F 2d 245, 1 Media L Rep 2417 (9th Cir 1971) (intrusion and emotional distress); *Stahl v State* 665 P 2d 839, 9 Media L Rep 1945 (Okla Crim App 1983) (trespass); *Le Mistral Inc. v Columbia Broad. Sys.* 61 AD 2d 491, 3 Media L Rep 1913 (NY App Div 1978) (trespass).

[28] 376 US 254 (1964).

[29] 485 US 46 (1988).

[30] E.g. *Special Force Ministries v WCCO Television* 584 NW 2d at 793; *W.D.I.A. Corp. v McGraw Hill, Inc.* 34 F Supp 2d at 624.

[31] *Cohen* 501 US at 671–2 (finding that if 'news organizations . . . have legal incentives not to disclose a confidential source's identity . . . [incentives are] no more than . . . incidental').

[32] ibid. at 672.

same can not be said about the impact of expanding the application of tort liability generally to newsgathering activity.

Cohen also is different from most of the newsgathering tort cases that have since been asserted because the restrictions violated by the press in *Cohen* were 'self-imposed', negotiated in advance between the reporter and his source.[33] The exact opposite is true when liability is imposed on newsgathering activity under theories of common law tort liability. This is especially so for common law torts such as intrusion, which require an after-the-fact assessment of a reporter's conduct to see if it was sufficiently 'outrageous' to be the basis of liability. The First Amendment does not permit such uncertainty when otherwise protected activities are involved.[34] Indeed, the chilling effect caused by the fear that liability will be imposed under such vague standards is one of the key factors that has led the Supreme Court to protect fully expression and activity, even when it is of doubtful social value.[35]

Moreover, tort claims asserted against the press can not be summarily accepted as 'generally applicable' when liability is asserted in novel ways against the press, liability that would never be asserted but for the subsequent publication of a news report. In *Cohen*, the Supreme Court specifically addressed this concern, analysing Minnesota law and concluding that the doctrine of promissory estoppel, as applied in Minnesota, 'does not target or single out the press' and 'would otherwise be enforced' against all citizens.[36] The same cannot be said when tort theories such as 'resumé fraud' are uniquely pursued against investigative reporters. In the *Food Lion* case, for example, a North Carolina jury assessed damages for false statements made by a reporter on a resumé, even though such resumé misrepresentations had never before led to an award of money damages upheld by any court in that state.[37]

Finally, *Cohen* is distinct from subsequent newsgathering tort cases for the further reason that the plaintiff did not seek to recover damages based upon loss of reputation or emotional distress. Rather, the damages sought were in the nature of breach of contract damages, and were measured by contract principles. The Supreme Court took this factor into account, too, in finding that Cohen's claim did not 'offend' the First Amendment.[38]

In short, there can be no serious dispute either that constitutional concerns are raised when newsgathering tort claims are asserted, or that these concerns may not properly be dismissed simply by characterizing a tort as 'generally applicable'. The

---

[33] ibid. at 671. The Court differentiated this situation from cases such as *The Florida Star v B.J.F.* 491 US 524 (1989) where the state sought to impose the terms of liability unilaterally on the press.

[34] See generally Norman Dorsen *et al., Emerson, Huber and Dorsen's Political and Civil Rights in the United States* (4th edn., 1976) 40–3.

[35] E.g., *Hustler Magazine Inc. v Falwell* 485 US 46, 52 (1988); *Smith v Goguen* 415 US 566 (1974).

[36] 501 US at 670, 672.

[37] The North Carolina jury found two ABC reporters to have engaged in fraud by misrepresenting who they were in order to obtain employment at Food Lion, and imposed money damages against ABC. The Court of Appeals subsequently threw out this fraud verdict on the grounds that plaintiff failed to show that any injury was caused by reasonable reliance on the false statements made by the reporters. *Food Lion* 1999 WL 957738.

[38] 501 US at 671.

precise extent of constitutional protection afforded to newsgathering remains to be determined by the courts.

3. APPROACHES TO A SOLUTION

3.1 Protecting First Amendment Interests in other Contexts

There is yet no settled framework for analysing the scope of constitutional protection of newsgathering in the United States, or for resolving conflicts between the First Amendment interest in newsgathering and other constitutionally protected interests. It is instructive, therefore, to review the Supreme Court's approach in other situations where First Amendment interests have conflicted with laws of general applicability. The following very brief discussion provides an overview that may inform the development of a legal structure for the analysis of newsgathering tort claims.

3.1.1 The Right to Petition

A conflict exists between the First Amendment and a law of general applicability when the act of petitioning the government (*i.e.*, filing a lawsuit or lobbying the legislature) is itself alleged to be an anti-competitive effort amounting to a violation of the antitrust laws. This conflict was presented to the Supreme Court in 1961 in *Eastern R.R. Presidents Conference v Noerr Motor Freight Inc.*,[39] where a group of trucking companies accused a railroad association, its members and their public relations firm of conspiring to promote the adoption of laws that would destroy the trucking business. The Court refused to permit the antitrust laws to impose liability based upon lobbying and litigation activity, even if the conduct was intended to drive a competitor out of business. The Court reasoned that the right to petition is closely related to freedom of speech and press, and that none of these rights can be abridged if government is to continue to reflect the will of the people.[40] The Supreme Court thus articulated a First Amendment privilege against antitrust liability based on lobbying activity or the filing of lawsuits against a competitor, allowing only a narrow 'sham' exception when the true purpose of an act was not to obtain governmental action but simply to inflict costs upon a competitor through the act of petitioning itself.[41] Courts subsequently have extended this approach to recognize a First Amendment privilege to petition the government that bars common law tort liability for interference with contractual relations, even outside of the antitrust context.[42]

---

[39] 365 US 127 (1961).

[40] 365 US at 137–38; see also *United Mine Workers of Am. v Pennington* 381 US 657 (1965).

[41] See 365 US at 144; see also *California Motor Transport Co. v Trucking Unlimited* 404 US 508 (1972). See generally Julian O. von Kalinowski *et al.*, Antitrust Laws and Trade Regulation (2dn edn., 1999) § 50.04[3].

[42] See, e.g., *Brownsville Golden Age Nursing Home Inc. v Wells* 839 F 2d 155, 159–60 (3d Cir. 1988); *Havoco of Am. Ltd. v Hollobow* 702 F 2d 643, 649–50 (7th Cir. 1983); *Sierra Club v Butz* 349 F Supp 934 (N.D. Cal. 1972).

3.1.2. *The Right of Free Speech*

The Supreme Court again defined a constitutional 'privilege' in order to resolve the conflict between the common law of libel and the right of free speech. In *New York Times v Sullivan*, the Court concluded that the First Amendment required the recognition of a privilege to comment upon the official conduct of public officials.[43] In an approach resembling the 'sham' exception adopted in *Noerr* just three years earlier, the Supreme Court defined the limits of this privilege by reference to the mental state of the defendant. A defamatory statement made knowing that it is false, or published in a manner so reckless as to be tantamount to a knowing falsehood, loses the privilege against liability that is otherwise provided by the First Amendment. Just as the First Amendment privilege in *Noerr* is lost if petitioning activity was intended only to inflict costs, the privilege in *Sullivan* is lost if the speech amounts to an intentional falsehood. Focusing on a defendant's mental state in the libel context allowed the Court to sidestep any analysis that required an assessment of the 'public interest' or 'newsworthiness' of particular speech in defining the scope of the privilege.

3.1.3 *The Right to Associate and Assemble*

Nearly twenty years later a different approach was taken by the Supreme Court to resolve a conflict between generally applicable tort liability and the rights of association and assembly presented in *National Association for the Advancement of Colored People v Claiborne Hardware Co.*[44] The case involved a consumer boycott of white merchants in Claiborne County, Mississippi, that was organized by a group of black activists. The boycott was intended to compel white business owners to support demands for racial justice that had been presented to civic and business leaders. Because some participants in the boycott used 'force, violence and threats' against other consumers, the Mississippi Supreme Court held the entire boycott tortious and awarded damages as well as injunctive relief.[45]

The Supreme Court reversed this outcome, holding that the non-violent elements of the boycott were protected by the First Amendment and therefore could not be the basis for a common law tort claim.[46] Rather than defining a 'privilege' limited only by its intentional misuse, the Court found that the appropriate 'constitutional inquiry' permitted a tort-based restriction of First Amendment activity only:

if it is within the constitutional power of the Government; if it furthers an important or substantial governmental interest; if the governmental interest is unrelated to the suppression of free expression; and if the incidental restriction on alleged First Amendment freedoms is no greater than is essential to the furtherance of that interest.[47]

---

[43] 376 US 254, 283 (1964).   [44] 458 US 886 (1982)   [45] 458 US at 894.

[46] The Court considered each element of the boycott separately and determined that each element—speech, assembly, association and petition for redress of grievances—was a 'form of speech or conduct that is ordinarily entitled to protection under the First and Fourteenth Amendments': 458 US at 907.

[47] 458 US at 912 n. 47. This balancing approach was first articulated in *United States v O'Brien* 391 US 367, 376–77 (1968) to assess the constitutionality of a statute punishing the destruction of a draft card as applied to someone who burned their card as an expression of opposition to the Vietnam War.

The Court recognized that States have a 'strong governmental interest in certain forms of economic regulation', and that such regulations may justify the imposition of incidental restrictions on the freedom of expression, citing specifically Congress' ability to prohibit secondary boycotts and picketing by labour unions.[48] The Court, however, also recognized that 'expression on public issues "has always rested on the highest rung of the hierarchy of First Amendment values" ', even though such expression 'may have a disruptive effect on local economic conditions'.[49] Because 'a major purpose of the boycott . . . was to influence government action' rather than to 'destroy legitimate competition', the Court concluded that the 'right of the States to regulate economic activity could not justify a complete prohibition against a nonviolent, politically motivated boycott designed to force governmental and economic change and to effectuate rights guaranteed by the Constitution itself.'[50]

Unfortunately, the Court failed to articulate how the application of this test in *Claiborne Hardware* compelled its conclusion that the First Amendment rights of the boycotters outweighed the governmental interest in regulating economic activity.[51] One commentator has suggested that 'the ground of decision could have been either that regulating the boycott was not "unrelated to the suppression of free expression", or that the regulation was "greater than [what was] essential to the furtherance of [the governmental] interest" ', but recognizes that the rationale is left 'unexplained'.[52] Another commentator reasons that the *Claiborne* Court must have 'reached the unstated conclusion that Mississippi's judicial prohibition of the boycott was related to the suppression of "free speech" ' because the opinion seems to incorporate a 'categorizing' approach.[53] Under the 'categorizing' approach, once the Court determines that a governmental interest is *not* unrelated to the suppression of free expression, it will deny constitutional protection only if the suppressed expression is 'fairly assignable' to one of a 'limited set of narrowly defined categories' of unprotected speech such as obscenity or 'fighting words'.[54] This 'may explain why the *Claiborne Hard-*

[48] ibid. at 912.

[49] ibid. at 913 (quoting *Carey v Brown* 447 US 455, 467 (1980)).

[50] ibid. at 914.

[51] Because the Court appeared to base its decision on the political motivation of the boycotters, several commentators have criticized the *Claiborne* court for failing to distinguish peaceful organized labour boycotts which, according to those commentators, may be equally motivated by desire to bring about political and social change, and yet explicitly receive no First Amendment protection under *Claiborne*. See Jeffrey F. Webb, 'Political Boycotts and Union Speech: A Critical First Amendment Analysis' 4 JL & Pol 579, 583 (1988); Gordon M. Orloff, Note, 'The Political Boycott: An Unprivileged Form of Expression' 1983 Duke LJ 1076 (1983); Note, 'Labor Picketing and Commercial Speech: Free Enterprise Values in the Doctrine of Free Speech' 91 Yale LJ 938 (1982).

[52] Jeffrey F. Webb (n. 48 above) at 582.

[53] See Barbara Ellen Cohen, Note, 'The Scope of First Amendment Protection for Political Boycotts: Means and Ends in First Amendment Analysis: NAACP v. Claiborne Hardware Co.' 1984 Wis L Rev 1273, 1286 (1984) (citing John Hart Ely, 'Flag Desecration: A Case Study in the Roles of Categorization and Balancing in First Amendment Analysis' 88 Harv LR 1482 (1975)).

[54] John Hart Ely, 'Flag Desecration: A Case Study in the Roles of Categorization and Balancing in First Amendment Analysis' 88 Harv LR 1482, 1491 (1975)

ware Court abruptly abandoned the balancing analysis suggested by its discussion of the governmental interest in regulating economic activity'.[55]

3.1.4 *The Right of Public Access to Judicial Proceedings*

In 1980 the Supreme Court recognized that the First Amendment protects a right of public access to judicial proceedings.[56] Over the next six years the Court defined the parameters of this right and the standards for determining its proper scope.[57] While the First Amendment right of access is not absolute, it may only be restricted

> by an overriding interest based on findings that closure is essential to preserve higher values and is narrowly tailored to serve that interest. The interest is to be articulated along with findings specific enough that a reviewing court can determine whether the closure order was properly entered.[58]

The requirement that closure be 'essential' to preserve some 'higher value' requires both the existence of a competing constitutional interest and the absence of alternatives to protect that interest other than a restriction on access.

This standard has been widely applied in many contexts to determine when the qualified right of access may be abridged.[59] Like the *Claiborne Hardware* approach, the access analysis follows a balancing approach, but one that imposes steep burdens on those seeking to limit the protected activity.

3.1.5 *Implications for Newsgathering*

Each of these various approaches might provide a basis for defining the scope of protection for newsgathering under the First Amendment, although each presents certain conceptual difficulties when measured against the underlying policies behind the constitutional protection of newsgathering. One commentator, for example, has attempted to articulate the recognition of a 'newsgathering privilege' as a model for newsgathering protection, at least in the context of claims for tortious interference brought against the press.[60] Such an approach would bar liability against a reporter for inducing a third party to breach a non-disclosure agreement, except when the reporter's purpose was not to gather information about a public figure on matters of public concern, but instead was intended solely to harm or to compete with the plaintiff.

---

[55] B. Cohen (n. 50 above) at 1286.

[56] *Richmond Newspapers Inc. v Virginia* 448 US 555 (1980).

[57] See *Globe Newspaper Co. v Superior Court* 457 US 596 (1982); *Press-Enter. Co. v Superior Court* 464 US 501 (1984); *Press-Enter. Co. v Superior Court* 478 US 1 (1986).

[58] *Press-Enter.* 464 US at 510.

[59] e.g., *United States v Amodeo* 71 F 3d 1044, 24 Media L Rep 1203 (2d Cir 1995) (access to judicial documents); *United States v Antar* 38 F 3d 1348, 22 Media L Rep 2417 (3d Cir 1994) (access to jurors); *Re New York Times Co*, 834 F 2d 1152, 14 Media L Rep 2013 (2d Cir 1987) (access to pretrial suppression wiretap-related documents).

[60] Mark J. Chasteen, 'In Search of a Smoking Gun: Tortious Interference with Non-Disclosure Agreements as an Obstacle to Newsgathering' 50 Fed Comm LJ 483 (1998).

A privilege approach seems defensible in the context of a claim for 'tortious inter-ference' asserted against a reporter for inducing the breach of a non-disclosure agree-ment, where the 'right' in conflict with newsgathering is the alleged right to keep important information from the public's knowledge. This is an objective beyond the scope of the tort's original concern with economic relationships, and an objective directly at odds with the public interest in access to information of legitimate public concern.[61] In these circumstances an exception to the privilege can be fashioned to protect the interest originally served by the tort—removing protection when the newsgathering activity is actually a 'sham' excuse for an intentional effort to inflict economic harm—in much the same way as the objectives of the First Amendment and the antitrust laws are reconciled in the *Noerr* analysis.

It is more difficult to articulate a 'newsgathering privilege,' however, where other types of tort liability are alleged, such as trespass, intrusion or fraud. In such cases, the 'right' asserted by a plaintiff cannot so readily be reconciled through an excep-tion based on 'bad faith' newsgathering. The suggestion that a reporter should have the right to enter private property at any time, so long as the entry is legitimately in the pursuit of news on a matter of public concern, does not adequately address the right protected by the trespass tort at common law.

None the less, one court has applied the 'privilege' approach to newsgathering, to reject a somewhat unusual 'intrusion' theory. In *Nicholson v McClatchy Newspapers*, a California appellate court recognized that:

> the news gathering component of the freedom of the press—the right to seek out informa-
> tion—is privileged at least to the extent it involves 'routine . . . reporting techniques' . . .
> [which] include asking persons questions, including those [persons] with confidential or
> restricted information.[62]

The plaintiffs in *McClatchy* sued for, among other things, intrusion arising out of a newspaper's investigation of a judicial candidate.[63] The allegedly offending conduct included actions such as 'soliciting, inquiring, requesting and persuading agents, employees and members of the [s]tate [b]ar to engage in the unauthorized and unlawful disclosure of information'.[64] The court found this conduct to be traditional newsgathering activity that is privileged under the First Amendment. 'For the same reason that "liability cannot be imposed on any theory for what has been determined to be a constitutionally protected publication", it cannot be imposed for constitu-tionally protected news gathering.'[65]

Applying the *Claiborne Hardware* approach to protect newsgathering would suggest a very different analysis. Under this approach a plaintiff would be required

---

[61] See S. Baron *et al.*, 'Tortious Interference: The Limits of Common Law Liability for Newsgather-ing,' 4 Wm & Mary Bill Rts J 1027 (1996).

[62] 177 Cal App 3d 509, 519, 12 Media L Rep 2009 (1986) (hereafter, '*McClatchy*') (quoting *Smith v Daily Mail Publishing Co.* 443 US 97, 103 (1979)).

[63] ibid. at 509–10.   [64] ibid. at 520.

[65] ibid. at 520–1 (quoting *Reader's Digest Association v Superior Court* 690 P 2d 610, 624 (Cal 1984)).

to demonstrate (1) a substantial interest furthered by the proposed imposition of tort liability on a journalist, (2) that was unrelated to the suppression of speech, and (3) limited to effect newsgathering no more than is essential to further that important interest.

Somewhat analogously, transporting the approach developed to define the qualified right of access into the analysis of newsgathering would ask the courts to protect newsgathering activity from tort liability unless it is demonstrated that (1) imposing liability is essential to preserve other 'higher values', (2) there is no alternative way to protect the conflicting value without restricting newsgathering activity, and (3) the imposition of liability is narrowly tailored to serve that interest.

Each of these approaches requires an express articulation of the competing interests, and would obligate the courts to minimize the impact on newsgathering activity imposed by the recognition of liability under a common law tort theory.

3.2 Current Approaches to the Protection of Newsgathering

Many of these concepts have been advanced by media lawyers in defence of the new spate of newsgathering tort claims. As noted, before *Cohen* there was little litigation attempting to impose liability on the media for non-publication torts, and hence few reported decisions defining the contours of constitutional protection for newsgathering. The issue occasionally was litigated in the context of trespass claims, leading one commentator to urge that a judicial balancing of interests is required in such cases:

> Courts considering newsgathering trespass cases should balance the benefits of granting access against the harms caused. . . . The press's newsgathering privilege . . . is strongest where its direct result is to check the potential for government abuse of power and to promote critical examination of the workings of government.[66]

This argument had occasional success in the few cases to address it.[67]

The defences advanced in the more recent spate of lawsuits necessarily reflect the unique facts and novel theories presented in each specific case. A review of three widely-followed cases demonstrates the types of constitutional arguments currently being advanced.

3.2.1 Shulman

The case of *Shulman v Group W Productions* arose out of a segment on a reality-based news programme documenting the rescue activities of a helicopter emergency service

---

[66] 'Press Passes and Trespasses: Newsgathering on Private Property' 84 Colum L Rev 1298, 1335 (1984).

[67] Cf. *People v Rewald* 65 Misc 2d 453, 318 NYS 2d 40 (Co Ct 1971) (balancing interests in a criminal trespass case against a reporter); *Stahl v State*, 665 P 2d 839 (Okla Crim App 1983) (same); *Allen v Combined Communications* 7 Media L Rep 2417 (Colo Dist Ct 1981) (balancing interests in a civil trespass case against a reporter); with *Anderson v. WROC–TV* 441 NY 2d 220 (Sup Ct 1981) (no constitutional defence to trespass claim against a reporter).

in Southern California. The plaintiffs, a mother and son, were passengers in a tragic accident on an interstate highway and had to be extracted from their overturned car. A cameraman accompanied a paramedic-flight nurse, who assisted in the rescue of the plaintiffs from the vehicle and accompanied them by helicopter to a hospital. The plaintiffs claimed that the subsequent broadcast of this rescue effort constituted a public disclosure of private facts, intrusion, intentional infliction of emotional distress and misappropriation. Their claims were all thrown out by the trial court.

On appeal, the defendant news organization asserted several constitutional defences to the various tort theories being advanced. First, it argued that failure to recognize a 'newsworthiness' defence to the public disclosure tort would be 'an error of constitutional significance', citing the Supreme Court precedent refusing to allow the punishment of truthful newsworthy information.[68] Second, the defendant argued that newsgathering conduct is constitutionally protected 'so long as (1) the information being gathered is about a matter of legitimate concern to the public and (2) the underlying conduct is lawful (*i.e.*, was undertaken without fraud, trespass, etc.).[69] The media defendant proposed this standard as 'the constitutional *minimum* for newsgathering activity', arguing that further analysis to define the scope of First Amendment protection for newsgathering would be required in cases where illegal activity had occurred.[70] The media defendant also argued that constitutional considerations required that any damages recoverable for the non-broadcast torts must exclude injury caused by the subsequent broadcast of its news report.

The California Supreme Court rejected the need for any independent constitutional analysis of the protection of newsgathering. It suggested instead that the newsgathering objective of the defendants was adequately taken into account in the analysis of the 'offensiveness' of the invasion of privacy required under the common law tort:

All the circumstances of an intrusion, including the motives or justification of the intruder, are pertinent to the offensiveness element. Motivation or justification becomes particularly important when the intrusion is by a member of the print or broadcast press in the pursuit of news material. . . . In deciding, therefore, whether a reporter's alleged intrusion into private matters (i.e., physical space, conversation or data) is 'offensive' and hence actionable as an invasion of privacy, courts must consider the extent to which the intrusion was, under the circumstances, justified by the legitimate motive of gathering the news. Information collecting techniques that may be highly offensive when done for socially unprotected reasons—for purposes of harassment, blackmail or prurient curiosity, for example—may not be offensive to a reasonable person when employed by journalists in pursuit of a socially or politically important story.[71]

---

[68] See *Cox Broad. Corp. v Cohn* 420 US 469, 496–7 (1975); *Oklahoma Publishing Co. v District Court* 430 US 308 (1977); *Smith v Daily Mail Publishing Co.* 443 US.97, 105–6 (1979); *Florida Star v B.J.F.* 491 US 524 (1989). Defendants also argued that California state law barred the punishment of the publication of truthful and newsworthy information unless a compelling interest was threatened, citing *Brisco v Reader's Digest Association*, 4 Cal 3d 529 (1971) and its progeny.
[69] *Shulman v Group W Productions Inc.*, Respondents' Brief on the Merits before the California Supreme Court (2 June 1997) at 35. [70] ibid.
[71] 74 Cal Rep 2d at 867 (footnote omitted).

Finding the common law adequately sensitive to the concerns of the press, the California court refused to articulate any distinct constitutional defence to the intrusion tort. Citing *Cohen*, the Court repeated that newsgathering activities enjoy 'no immunity or exemption from generally applicable laws'. The court acknowledged that generally applicable laws could conflict with the First Amendment if, as applied to the press, they resulted in 'a significant constriction of the flow of news to the public'.[72] However, it rejected the 'newsworthiness' of a story as an appropriate standard on which to base a constitutional privilege for newsgathering: 'the fact that a reporter may be seeking "newsworthy" material does not in itself privilege the investigatory activity'.[73] The California court found that the constitutional protection for newsgathering could bar liability against the press under a generally applicable tort, '[a]t most', in those cases where imposing tort liability would deprive the press 'of their "indispensable tools" '.[74]

The California court thus read into the common law tort an analysis of both 'the legitimate motive' of a reporter and the importance of a story, and it reversed the burdens adopted by the Supreme Court in defining the scope of constitutional protection in the petitioning and access contexts. Instead of requiring a demonstration by a plaintiff that the proposed restriction on First Amendment newsgathering activity is no broader than necessary to protect some 'higher value', the California court has said that any restriction on newsgathering activity is unobjectionable unless the press demonstrates that it would render newsgathering itself all but impossible.

3.2.2 Food Lion

In *Food Lion*, liability was imposed on a news organization by a jury under three distinct theories: fraud, trespass, and breach of duty by an employee to his employer. These claims arose out of the deception employed by two ABC reporters to obtain employment at a Food Lion grocery store in order to conduct a hidden camera investigation of the company's food handling procedures. The jury awarded plaintiffs a total of $1,402 in compensatory damages, but then tacked on to this award a whopping $5,545,750 to punish the defendants for their newsgathering techniques. The trial court ordered Food Lion to accept a remittitur of the punitive damage award to $315,000.

On appeal to the US Court of Appeals for the Fourth Circuit, the media defendants advanced two defences rooted in the First Amendment. Initially, they argued that, as a matter of constitutional principle, the press may not be singled out for punishment as the press. They claimed that this principle was violated because a common law action for fraud would never be extended by the state court to impose money damages for the type of 'resumé fraud' at issue in *Food Lion*, and because the types of speculative injury alleged by Food Lion are not generally awarded in tort claims brought against people other than the press.

---

[72] ibid. at 869, citing *Branzburg v Hayes* 408 US at 693.
[73] ibid. at 870.   [74] ibid.

The defendants also argued that the First Amendment protection of newsgathering mandates heightened scrutiny by the judiciary when tort claims are asserted against newsgathering activity.[75] ABC urged the Fourth Circuit to apply 'strict scrutiny' to Food Lion's claims because tort liability was imposed in a unique manner that singled out the press, or alternatively to apply 'intermediate scrutiny' because of the significant impact of the claims on expressive activity. If strict scrutiny applied, the plaintiff would have to establish a 'compelling governmental interest' to justify any restriction of newsgathering rights; under intermediate scrutiny a 'substantial governmental interest' would have to be demonstrated.[76] ABC asserted that neither level of scrutiny could be satisfied because there is no substantial state law interest in allowing private plaintiffs to recover damages for undercover reporting aimed at revealing information of public importance, at least when that undercover reporting 'neither caused nor threatened to cause any meaningful harm to anyone'.[77]

Citing *Cohen*, the Fourth Circuit rejected all of these constitutional arguments. After first throwing out the common law fraud claim because of plaintiff's failure to prove reasonable reliance on any of the misrepresentations made in the reporters' job applications,[78] the court held that neither of the remaining claims (trespass and breach of the duty of loyalty) singled out the press. Rather, '[e]ach applies to the daily transactions of the citizens of North and South Carolina'.

Without any explanation or analysis, the court stated its 'belie[f]' that applying these two torts against the press was unlikely to 'have more than an "incidental effect" on newsgathering'.[79] As did the California court in *Shulman*, the Fourth Circuit appeared to place the burden on the press to demonstrate that it could not function before any constitutional balancing of interests would be applied: 'We are convinced that the media can do its important job effectively without resort to the commission of run of the mill torts.'

While rejecting the constitutional defences to liability advanced by the media defendants, the Fourth Circuit firmly rejected Food Lion's claim that it should have been permitted to recover reputational damages caused by the broadcast, because such damage was proximately caused by the newsgathering torts. The court found

---

[75] The defendants claimed that the First Amendment requires either 'strict scrutiny' or 'intermediate scrutiny' of newsgathering torts. e.g., *Turner Broad. Sys. Inc. v FCC* 512 US 622, 640 (1994) (laws that single out the press always subject to heightened scrutiny); *Arkansas Writers' Project Inc. v Ragland* 481 US 221, 228 (1987) (requiring heightened scrutiny for laws with a 'disproportionate burden' on those engaged in First Amendment activity); *Minneapolis Star & Tribune Co. v Minnesota Commissioner of Revenue* 460 US 575, 582 (1983) (requiring strict scrutiny for law that singles out the press).

[76] See *Sable Communications v FCC* 492 US 115, 126 (1989) (strict scrutiny requires a 'compelling' interest); *United States v O'Brien* 391 US 367, 376 (1968) (intermediate scrutiny requires a 'substantial' interest).

[77] Brief for appellants, *Food Lion Inc. v Capital Cities/ABC Inc.* No. 97–2492 (9th Cir) at 41.

[78] Because punitive damages had been awarded only on the fraud claim, these damages fell with the dismissal of that claim. The jury had awarded compensatory damages of just one dollar each on the trespass and breach of duty claims, and the Fourth Circuit affirmed total damages only in the amount of $2.00.

[79] *Cohen* 501 US at 671–2.

that 'an overriding (and settled) First Amendment principle precludes the award of publication damages in this case'. The Fourth Circuit held that:

[w]hat Food Lion sought to do . . . was to recover defamation-type damages under non-reputational tort claims, without satisfying the stricter (First Amendment) standards of a defamation claim. We believe that such an end-run around First Amendment strictures is foreclosed by *Hustler [Magazine Inc. v Falwell]*.

3.2.3 W.D.I.A.

Fraud and breach of contract claims were asserted in *W.D.I.A. Corp. v McGraw-Hill Inc.*,[80] based upon the actions of a *Business Week* reporter collecting information for a story on the credit reporting industry. The article reported upon the ease with which detailed private credit information could be obtained through credit reporting companies. To 'test' the credit reporting system, the reporter contacted a number of bureaux, informed them (truthfully) that he was an editor at McGraw-Hill, but falsely indicated that he sought credit reports for the purpose of pre-employment screening, a permissible purpose under federal law. In completing the subscriber application, the reporter deliberately sought to 'raise red flags' to determine if the bureau was rigorously protecting the privacy interests of consumers. Two different federal identification numbers were provided, sections of the application were not completed and there were inconsistencies in the explanations provided for seeking access to the information. The bureau none the less authorized the reporter access to its database, where he was able to obtain credit reports on then-sitting Vice President Dan Quayle, among others.

Although the credit bureau that provided the reporter with access to the confidential data was not identified in the *Business Week* report, it subsequently sued for fraud and breach of contract. *W.D.I.A.* sought damages incurred in responding to subsequent governmental investigations allegedly prompted by the *Business Week* article, and $45 million in punitive damages. *Business Week* asserted a number of defences based on the common law, including the absence of proximate cause between the tortuous conduct alleged and the damages sought to be recovered, and the need to construe state tort law narrowly to avoid conflict with the constitutional protection for the publication of truthful information. *W.D.I.A.* also asserted that the First Amendment precludes recovery of reputational damages flowing from publication of information outside of a defamation claim.

As in *Food Lion*, the District Court rejected any First Amendment defence to liability under the 'incidental effects' approach in *Cohen*. The court recited the mantra that 'generally applicable laws do not offend the First Amendment just because their enforcement against the press has an incidental effect on news gathering'.[81] Then, describing fraud and breach of contract as 'generally applicable laws',

---

[80] 34 F Supp 2d 612 (D Ohio 1998).
[81] 501 US at 699.

the court brushed aside the need for any further First Amendment analysis. The court concluded that '[e]nforcement of the generally applicable laws against the press is not subject to stricter scrutiny than would be applied to enforcement against other persons or organizations'.[82] The court awarded *W.D.I.A.* about $3,800 for certain travel-related expenses incurred to mitigate damages in the immediate aftermath of the *Business Week* report, along with prejudgment interest, for a total award of about $7,500.

4. ARTICULATING THE SCOPE OF CONSTITUTIONAL PROTECTION

The defence of newsgathering tort cases suffers from the relative newness of the efforts to apply old tort theories to the newsgathering process, and from the absence yet of definitive guidance from the Supreme Court. These difficulties are magnified by the novel and rapidly evolving newsgathering technologies in use today. However, the rote invocation of the *Cohen* 'incidental effects' language, without analysis of the actual impact of tort liability on newsgathering, fails to acknowledge the significant constitutional issues that are presented. The various approaches taken by the Supreme Court to resolve First Amendment conflicts in other contexts, and the arguments being advanced in the recent newsgathering cases, suggest a number of factors that are relevant to a proper definition of the scope of constitutional protection for newsgathering:

4.1 Liability may not be Imposed for the Purpose of Suppressing the News

This requirement flows from the test articulated in *Claiborne Hardware*, and would prevent plaintiffs from pursuing litigation where the motive was solely to suppress information.

4.2 Liability Rules may not be Applied Uniquely against the Press

While the Justices of the Supreme Court have not agreed on whether the press clause has a separate and independent meaning in the First Amendment, at a minimum, it should require that unique liability not be imposed on bona fide newsgathering activity by the press, if such liability generally would not otherwise be imposed on other tortfeasors.

4.3 Liability for Newsgathering Activity should be Imposed only where such Liability is Essential to Advance a Compelling Governmental Interest

Whether this requirement is articulated as a 'qualified privilege' against liability, or as a judicial obligation to scrutinize strictly any claim for newsgathering liability, this

---

[82] 34 F Supp 2d 612, 624. The District Court declined to award punitive damages because the *Business Week* article served to inform Congress and the public 'about a matter of vital public interest and was done in such a way as to protect the identity of *W.D.I.A.* and the rights of the consumers.' ibid. at 628.

factor obligates litigants to (a) recognize directly the significant constitutional considerations in any newsgathering claim, (b) articulate the compelling state interest that justifies some restriction on newsgathering and (c) establish that the competing interest can only be protected through a limitation on newsgathering, and not through other means that would interfere less with the newsgathering process.

4.4 Liability for Newsgathering should be Narrowly Construed to Protect the Compelling Governmental Interest that has been Identified

Once a threshold determination has been made that a compelling interest can only be protected by restricting newsgathering, a showing should be required that the restriction on newsgathering is as narrow as possible.

In the newsgathering context these factors have important implications. First, an obligation to demonstrate a need to restrict newsgathering, and to show that the most narrow restriction is being applied, should require courts to construe common law tort liability narrowly to those situations that lie within the purpose of the tort. Trespass claims, for example, should be limited to the protection of property rights, in order to avoid unnecessary constitutional issues. Similarly, torts which at common law require some element of 'offensiveness', should require, as a matter of constitutional necessity, that the newsgathering purpose be considered in assessing offensiveness.

Difficult issues will continue to be presented by the tort of intrusion, which has evolved in some states into a tort to be free from press coverage. The California Supreme Court in *Sanders v American Broadcasting Cos.* essentially held that the tort of intrusion protects an individual's expectation not to be on television.[83] If courts indeed determine that such a privacy expectation exists, and is as constitutionally compelling as the interest in the newsgathering, the courts ultimately will be required to balance these competing interests. Analogies to the common law would then suggest that the balancing of interests may entail some assessment of the newsworthiness of the story being pursued and the offensiveness of the conduct undertaken to obtain the news, considerations that defendants unsuccessfully urged the court to take into account in *Shulman.*

A second implication is that torts that do not have any requirement of publication as an element of liability, should be limited to allowing recovery of non-publication damages only. This approach is consistent with the common law objective, and again, should be viewed as constitutionally compelled. An important contribution of the *Food Lion* litigation has been the express recognition of a constitutional limitation on the ability of plaintiffs to recover publication damages for non-publication torts—something the Ninth Circuit had rejected in *Dietemann.*[84] As the trial

---

[83]   20 Cal 4th 907, 27 Media L Rep 2025 (1999).
[84]   *Dietemann v Time Inc.* 449 F 2d 245, 1 Media L Rep 2417 (9th Cir 1971). Some cases since *Food Lion* have suggested that publication damages are beyond the scope of the tort of intrusion, although not reaching the constitutional issue. e.g. *Medical Lab. Management Consultants v American Broad. Cos. Inc.* 30 F Supp 2d at 1190 (and cases cited therein).

court held in barring Food Lion from recovering compensatory damages resulting from the ABC broadcast:

> To the extent that Food Lion's damages are reputational in nature, the Supreme Court's decision in *Hustler* prevents recovery. . . . Food Lion may recover only those damages resulting from ABC's alleged trespass, fraud, unfair and deceptive trade practices, as well as those from the other remaining claims. However, Food Lion may not recover any publication damages for injury to its reputation as a result of the Prime Time Live broadcast.[85]

Efforts to recover reputational injury and other publication damages through newsgathering torts raise constitutional issues all apart from the First Amendment protection of newsgathering itself. Allowing publication damages to be awarded as a result of a newsgathering tort would raise precisely the same speech-chilling concerns that led to the recognition of constitutional limits to liability for defamation. In *New York Times v Sullivan*, the Supreme Court stated that the First Amendment reflects 'a profound national commitment to the principle that debate on public issues should be uninhibited, robust and wide open. . . .'[86] Recognizing this constitutional commitment, the Court held in *Sullivan* that even the common law defence of truth was inadequate to allow defamation liability to be imposed by a public official because of the substantial chilling effect created through the mere threat of litigation. The very same chilling concerns are presented if a plaintiff can recover publication damages from the press by asserting a newsgathering tort, and then being exempt from meeting the constitutional standards that would apply to a defamation claim. Courts repeatedly have refused to allow plaintiffs to do such an end-run around the First Amendment by asserting that other tort liability has arisen out of a publication; the same analysis should apply when a publication is asserted to have been made possible by a newsgathering tort.[87]

5. CONCLUSION

The protection of newsgathering is an essential component of a system of free expression. It requires a careful analysis of the competing interests at stake whenever tort

---

[85] 887 F Supp at 823. Cf. *Allen v. Combined Communications* 7 Media L Rep 2417, 2420 (Colo Dist Ct 1981) (finding First Amendment requires additional burdens to state a trespass claim against a reporter).

[86] 376 US at 270.

[87] See e.g., *Hustler Magazine* 485 US at 56 (rejecting emotional distress cause of action arising out of a publication); *Moldea v New York Times Co.* 22 F 3d 310, 319, 22 Media L Rep 1673 (DC Cir 1994) (rejecting false light cause of action arising out of a publication); *Brown & Williamson Tobacco Corp. v Jacobson* 713 F 2d 262, 273, 9 Media L Rep 1936 (7th Cir 1983) (rejecting tortious interference cause of action); *Beverly Hills Foodland Inc. v United Food Commercial Workers Union* 39 F 3d 191, 196 (8th Cir. 1994) ('plaintiff may not avoid the protection afforded by the Constitution and federal labor law merely by the use of creative pleading'); *Aequitron Med. Inc. v CBS, Inc.* 964 F Supp 704, 710, 25 Media L Rep 1897 (S.D.N.Y. 1997) (tortious interference claim based on defamatory conduct must be 'governed by the "special rules" applicable to defamation cases').

liability is asserted against journalists engaged in gathering the news. The recognition of this fact by the courts will be essential to the development of a legal framework that can appropriately curtail the chilling effect created by the explosion of news-gathering litigation in the United States over the past decade.

9

Freedom of Assembly

ERIC BARENDT

1. INTRODUCTION

David Williams was one of the first legal scholars in this country to take a serious interest in civil liberties law. In *Keeping the Peace*,[1] published in 1967, he discussed the peace-keeping powers of the police and administrative authorities within the context of the freedom to hold meetings and to engage in lawful protest. Though the 1960s did see demonstrations on the streets, notably against the Vietnam war and apartheid, David Williams speculated whether the right of peaceful assembly was as important a freedom as it used to be in the nineteenth and early twentieth centuries. He referred to the other opportunities available for the communication of views and the expression of protest.[2] The correspondence columns of national and local newspapers, radio phone-in and current affairs programmes, and more recently Internet discussion groups and web sites provide platforms and fora to which many people enjoy relatively easy access. A vast amount of information is readily available and opinions are disseminated without any need to convene meetings or stage parades for their expression.

Despite these points, freedom of assembly remains a valued liberty. It is cherished by communities as diverse as the groups which took to the streets of London (very effectively) against the poll tax, gays campaigning for the repeal of discriminatory laws and practices, Orange Lodges claiming the right to use their traditional parade routes, and the demonstrators who attempted to protest (without much success) against the abuse of human rights in China to the face of President Jiang on his state visit to England. Recent street demonstrations in Seattle, and to a lesser extent London, have shown the strength of opposition to the impact of free trade and economic globalization. In all these cases there were plenty of other ways open to the marchers and protesters to express their views. Opponents of the poll tax could have written letters to the *Guardian*, while Ulster Protestants enjoy ample opportunities to air their views on radio and television. But there would be little support for the conclusion that freedom of assembly is valueless or that it is legitimate to restrict it, because of the existence of other means of communication.

English lawyers have often minimized, even denied, the significance of the freedom.

---

[1] *Keeping the Peace: the police and public order* (London: Hutchinson, 1967).
[2] ibid. 10.

For Dicey, it was nothing more than the exercise by a number of people of their individual freedoms to walk down the street in conversation with each other.[3] In *Duncan v Jones*, Lord Hewart CJ said that English law did not 'recognize any special right of public meeting for political or other purposes'.[4] According to Humphreys J, the case had nothing to do with the law of unlawful assembly, but merely concerned the scope of police powers to require demonstrators to move on if a breach of the peace was feared. However, recent decisions, or at least leading judgments, have taken a more sympathetic view of the assembly right.[5] Most notably, in *DPP v Jones* Lord Irvine LC and Lord Hutton formulated a broad common law right of public assembly. Lord Hutton was particularly clear. The right could be exercised on the highway, unless its exercise obstructed the movement of other users; otherwise the value of the freedom would be reduced.[6]

Moreover, the right of assembly, guaranteed by Article 11 of the European Convention on Human Rights (ECHR), is now part of English and Scots law. The limits on processions and static meetings imposed by the Public Order Act 1986, by the plethora of local and other special statutes regulating the use of open spaces, and by the exercise of police powers must all be interpreted and given effect subject to the Convention right; the courts must take account of rulings and decisions of the European Court and the (former) Human Rights Commission. So it will no longer be open to judges to adopt the negative approach of the Divisional Court in *Duncan v Jones*. They will be compelled in difficult cases to reflect on the meaning of the right of assembly, its scope and application, just as they will be called on to decide the extent to which the freedom of expression guaranteed by Article 10 of the ECHR covers, say, pornography and commercial advertising and to determine its impact on media regulation.

2. ASSEMBLY AND SPEECH

The right of assembly is certainly valued, but it is unclear why this is the case, given that there are so many other means of expression which do not give rise to the same difficulties and inconveniences for the general community as do street demonstrations. Moreover, the scope of the freedom is unclear. In particular, it is not obvious what legal rights it confers, or for that matter should confer, beyond those effectively protected by the right to freedom of expression. After all the latter right is not confined, at least in the view of the United States Supreme Court, to verbal speech and writing. Freedom of speech covers expressive conduct, such as the wearing of

---

[3] A. V. Dicey, *Introduction to the Study of the Law of the Constitution* (10th edn., London, 1961), 271–2.

[4] [1936] 1 KB 218, 222, QB.

[5] See, for example, Lord Denning MR in *Hubbard v Pitt* [1976] QB 142, 178–9, CA; Otten J in *Hirst and Agu v Chief Constable of West Yorkshire* (1987) 85 Cr App Rep 143, 151–2, DC.

[6] *DPP v Jones* [1999] 2 All ER 257, 293, HL.

arm-bands and flag-burning, and non-violent forms of protest such as sit-ins, pick-   γ
eting, and street parades and processions.

Indeed, in many US cases the right to freedom of assembly and the right to freedom of speech seem to be more or less interchangeable terms. In its first major ruling
on freedom of assembly, *De Jonge v Oregon*,[7] the Supreme Court held unconstitutional a statute which, as applied by the state courts, had made it an offence to participate in the conduct of a meeting of the Communist party, even though no speech
there advocated insurrection, violence or other unlawful activity. Chief Justice
Hughes referred to the right of peaceable assembly as a 'right cognate to those of free
speech and free press'; it was not compatible with the Constitution to make attendance at a public meeting 'for lawful discussion' a criminal offence. Arguably, this
case could have been decided simply on the basis of the free speech limb of the First
Amendment, without recourse to the related, but textually distinct, freedom of
assembly.

It is probably pertinent that in the US Constitution, it is the same clause—the
First Amendment—which guarantees freedom of the speech (and of the press) and
'the right of the people peaceably to assemble . . .' It equally protects 'the right to
petition the Government for a redress of grievances'.[8] It is therefore natural for
judges and writers to treat the two freedoms as if they were virtually synonymous,
freedom of assembly adding little, if anything, to a broad understanding of the right
to free speech. But the European Court and Commission of Human Rights have
experienced similar difficulties, despite the fact that the ECHR covers the two freedoms in separate provisions. In one recent case the Court considered the complaints,
arising from the arrest in the United Kingdom of a number of applicants engaged in
diverse forms of protest, under Article 10 (freedom of expression), adding that in its
view no separate issue was raised by the guarantee of freedom of assembly.[9] But an
application, challenging the refusal of a permit to hold a meeting in Trafalgar Square,
was treated as raising issues under Article 11; Articles 9 (freedom of thought and religion) and Article 10 were considered relevant to the interpretation of freedom of
assembly.[10]

The relationship of freedom of assembly and freedom of speech seems, therefore,
to be problematic, whether or not the two rights are covered by the same provision.
But it may be wrong to treat the former exclusively in terms of its close connection
with free speech. The two rights may overlap considerably, but freedom of assembly
may also justify the recognition of particular legal rights which might be difficult to
derive solely from a constitutional (or statutory) free speech provision. Freedom of
assembly may also rest on fundamental political rights and values other than those
which justify the special position of free speech. It is worth reflecting on these values,

---

[7] 90 US 353 (1937).
[8] For the significance of this right, see Part 3 below.
[9] *Steel v United Kingdom* (1999) 28 EHRR 603.
[10] *Rai, Allmond and 'Negotiate Now' v UK* (1995) 19 EHRR CD 93 (Europ HR Comm.)

for understanding them may, and perhaps should, influence the scope of the assembly right, just as the legal contours of freedom of speech are influenced by understanding the values and principles which support that freedom. If, for instance, we consider that the point of freedom of speech is to ensure that citizens have access to the information and views they need to make intelligent political choices, particularly at elections, then we will probably take a narrower view of its scope than we would if we considered the freedom an essential attribute of each individual's right to self-fulfilment and development. On the former perspective the right might be confined to political speech, while on the latter it would probably also cover literature and at least some forms of sexually explicit publication.

Quite apart from informing our understanding of its scope, teasing out the value of the right of assembly may have implications when the appropriateness of standard forms of restriction is assessed. For instance, it is common for legislation, or city regulations, to allow the police or local authority to re-route a procession or impose conditions, say, on the numbers of participants, on the ground that otherwise there would be significant disruption to community life. The authorities might fear that a procession along the proposed route would lead to an unacceptable traffic blockage or serious interference with normal commercial activity, shopping, and so on. They would argue that, from the perspective of freedom of speech, there could be little objection to the imposition of a condition that the procession, say, followed a different route from the one preferred by the organizers or that it was completed by, say, midday so as not to interfere with heavier afternoon shopping. After all, these restrictions on place and time would not, the police might argue, be imposed because of any dislike of the objects of the demonstration. Such conditions would not, therefore, amount to a contents-based restriction on speech, that is, a regulation which discriminates against a particular viewpoint, or type of speech, on the basis of its contents.

If freedom of assembly were little more than a special mode of exercising freedom of speech, there could perhaps be no constitutional objection to reasonable conditions of this sort, or for that matter, to the notice and permit requirements often imposed in this context. Moreover, it could be added that imposition of these requirements leave ample alternative means for the expression by the demonstrators of their views—writing to the newspapers, distributing pamphlets, or holding a meeting at another time and place. However, we will see in Part 4 of this essay that courts, particularly in the United States, have been generous in their treatment of meetings and processions, recognizing, for instance, that public authorities have a duty to make the streets and other public places available for their conduct. The argument that demonstrators could communicate their views in other ways has usually been dismissed, although it has been accepted in other contexts to support the dismissal of constitutional free speech claims. In summary, the distinctive treatment of meetings and processions suggests that the right to freedom of assembly rests, at least partly, on values other than those which lie at the basis of freedom of speech.

Another point should be made before offering some reflections on the value of freedom of assembly. The freedom is almost always asserted in the context of *political* protest, as the examples given in the opening pages of this essay show. The right is rarely, if ever, claimed in the context of other mass gatherings and events, such as the Notting Hill Carnival, concerts with enormous audiences ('Pavarotti in the Park'), the London Marathon, or for that matter those formal public events—Trooping the Colour or a state funeral—which attract vast crowds. These occasions may present the police and other authorities with problems of public order and the free movement of traffic as serious as those attending political demonstrations.[11] But they are usually not subject to the same legal regime of control as apply to political protest; for example, there is no obligation to give the police notice of a funeral or traditional civic procession under the public order legislation.[12] This is an important point. It suggests in the first place that English law may discriminate against political protest in relation to ceremonial demonstrations or popular entertainment although each category of event gives rise to similar difficulties. More generally, it highlights our imperfect grasp of the significance of freedom of assembly.

3. THE VALUE OF FREEDOM OF ASSEMBLY

David Williams himself argued that the value of freedom of assembly lies in its importance for people to whom other means of communication are unavailable or for whom these opportunities might be too expensive.[13] It is cheaper to take to the streets than it is to pay for advertising space in a newspaper on a public hoarding.[14] The freedom does indeed appear to be particularly valuable for minorities who feel that they are denied adequate time on the media or whose interests are imperfectly represented by political parties.[15] This point may explain why parades and meetings have, say, frequently been held by groups campaigning for the rights of gays and lesbians or against the Gulf War or NATO bombing of Serbia. It is less obviously applicable in the cases, say, of Loyalist parades in Ulster or of demonstrations for or against hunting with hounds, and other forms of protest which put across views frequently expressed in the press and on the broadcasting media.

Sometimes the free speech argument for the right of assembly is put in different terms. Public meetings and street processions enable participants to show the strength of their enthusiasm for a cause. It is important, it is said, for the public and

---

[11] See the discussion of policing of these events by P. A. J. Waddington, *Liberty and Order* (London: UCL Press, 1994) 43–50.

[12] Public Order Act 1986 (POA), s. 11(1), (2).

[13] *Keeping the Peace*, 10 and 130–1. For a recent treatment of the subject, see H. Fenwick, 'The Right to Protest, the Human Rights Act, and the Margin of Appreciation', (1999) 62 MLR 491.

[14] Political advertising on radio and television is forbidden by statute: Broadcasting Act 1990, s. 8(2)(a) (television) and s. 92(2)(a) (radio).

[15] Also see the judgment of the German Constitution Court in the leading *Brokdorf* case, involving a peaceful mass protest against the construction of a nuclear power station: 69 BVerfGE 315, 343 (1985).

for the government to appreciate the passion revealed by popular protest, because otherwise they might misjudge the practicability of a policy or legislative proposal. A recent instance of this phenomenon is the marches and meetings in Hyde Park of the Countryside Alliance to protest against a ban on fox hunting. Mass protest of this type brought out the depth of opposition to the recent Private Member's Bill much more effectively than would any letter writing campaign or succession of media interviews.

Another reason for tolerating mass protest is that it may act as a safety-valve; attempts to suppress meetings at which, say, anarchist views are expressed may make riots on the streets more, rather than less, likely.[16] The German Constitutional Court in the *Brokdorf* case, its leading ruling on freedom of assembly (*Versammlungsfreiheit*) has drawn attention to the value of mass demonstrations in providing early warnings to the authorities of popular disquiet.[17] This argument is strikingly similar to aspects of the classic case for freedom of speech made by Brandeis J in his concurring judgment in *Whitney v California*.[18]

> Those who won our independence . . . knew that order cannot be secured merely through fear of punishment for its infraction; that it is hazardous to discourage thought, hope and imagination; that fear breeds repression; that repression breeds hate; that hate menaces stable government; that the path of safety lies in the opportunity to discuss freely supposed grievances and proposed remedies; and that the fitting remedy for evil counsels is good ones.

Both this safety-valve argument and that deployed in the previous paragraph are broadly utilitarian; it is in the public interest to tolerate mass protest, either in order to appreciate the depth of popular feeling or to diffuse the dangers of disorder.[19] In contrast, the first argument for freedom of assembly focuses on fairness to minorities, or put another way, ensuring that their views may enter more easily into the 'market-place of ideas' than they would if access could only be obtained through the media.

However, while some of the traditional arguments for freedom of speech also support freedom of assembly, others apply less readily. In particular, it is hard to see what a street procession or mass demonstration contributes to the discovery of truth, the argument for liberty of discussion made by John Stuart Mill. Mill's argument from truth assumes that ideas will be exchanged and their merits openly debated, but these features are noticeably absent in protest activity. Indeed, meetings and street processions are frequently protected from counter-demonstrations, on the assumption that, instead of debate and dialogue, there is likely to be disorder and violence—the problem of the 'hostile audience'.[20]

---

[16] See the views of H. H. Asquith, Home Secretary, and A. J. Balfour on public meetings in Trafalgar Square in November 1893, discussed by Williams, *Keeping the Peace* 84.

[17] *Brokdorf* case 69 BVerfGE 315, 347 (1985).

[18] 274 US 357, 375–8 (1927).

[19] See G. Abernathy, *The Right of Assembly and Association*, (University of South Carolina Press, 1961) 5.

[20] For further discussion of the problems arising from the 'hostile audience', see Part 4 below.

Moreover, freedom of speech, at any rate in Anglo-American jurisprudence, is rarely concerned to ensure that political minorities have effective opportunities to communicate their views, the argument for the right to assembly made by Sir David Williams. The United States Supreme Court, for instance, has held incompatible with the First Amendment a right of reply to the press. It has also rejected the claim of an anti-Vietnam war group that freedom of speech requires recognition of a constitutional access right to communicate its views on television.[21] These are both situations where one might have expected the claims to have been upheld if freedom of speech implicitly conferred rights on minorities.

Equally, English law refuses to recognize legally enforceable rights of reply to personal attacks on the media. For the most part it treats freedom of speech as a liberty against state infringement; the freedom does not confer positive claim-rights of access to facilities for speech. The two best-known counter-examples are to be found, interestingly, in the context of public meetings. Candidates have a right to use schools and other public buildings for election meetings,[22] while the Education (No. 2) Act 1986 grants invited speakers a right to address audiences on university premises.[23]

These points suggest that freedom of assembly may be rooted in, or linked to, fundamental political values distinct from those which support freedom of speech. Historically there has been a close link, in both England and the United States, with the right to petition the Crown or government for the redress of grievances. The right of petition was given constitutional status in England through its incorporation in the Bill of Rights 1689,[24] while in the USA it is protected by the First Amendment together with freedom of speech and the right of peaceful assembly. In this country it was an important freedom in the eighteenth and early nineteenth centuries, largely because it enabled people without the vote to participate to some extent in political movements. Mass meetings were frequently accompanied by the presentation of petitions for parliamentary reform or against oppressive legislation.[25] With the decline in the effectiveness of petitioning by the middle of the nineteenth century, public meetings assumed greater importance.[26] Certainly, the second half of the nineteenth century may plausibly be regarded as a 'golden age' of public protest, albeit that demonstrations were much more peaceable in England than they were on the continent of Europe and in the United States.[27]

With the rise of political parties and the extension of the franchise to (virtually) all adults, the case for freedom of assembly must now be framed differently. It is no

[21] *CBS v FCC* 412 US 95 (1973).
[22] Representation of the People Act 1983, ss. 95–6.
[23] See E. M. Barendt, *Freedom of Speech* (Oxford University Press, 1987), 321–3.
[24] Article 5.
[25] See L. G. Mitchell, *Charles James Fox* (Penguin Books, 1997) 140, 145, 259, for the significance of petitioning in the 1790s.
[26] See R. Handley, 'Public Order, Petitioning and Freedom of Assembly' (1986) 7 *J. of Legal History* 123, 141.
[27] See the conclusions of D. C. Richter, *Riotous Victorians* (Ohio University Press, 1981) 163–6.

longer tenable to treat it as an alternative to the right to vote or stand for election, its role for many in the nineteenth century.[28] But it is still valuable as an essential feature of freedom of political activity and organization, vital to a liberal democracy. That seems to have been the perspective of the German Constitutional Court in the *Brokdorf* case. The Court regarded the right to demonstrate, guaranteed by Article 8 of the Basic Law, as an expression of direct popular sovereignty; it enables people, particularly minorities, to participate in the political process. Participation rights are not exhausted by membership of political parties, voting at elections and by the discharge of public, administrative responsibilities.[29] The Court also suggested that exercise of the right of assembly enables protesters to express their personalities by their physical presence, without the mediation or help of the mass media.

These suggestive remarks indicate why the exercise of the assembly right may be particularly important for groups unrepresented in the legislature (or under-represented owing to the electoral system) and which have few opportunities to influence the government through the press and broadcasting media. For example, opponents of motorway construction and genetically modified crops can claim with some plausibility that they can only contribute properly to public and political life by engaging in vigorous (and, it must be admitted, often disorderly) protest activity. Such activity gives them considerable media coverage and may persuade the authorities to reconsider their policies. Demonstrators such as eco-warriers feel in contrast that they have no chance of election to Parliament under the first-past-the-post system and little prospect of exercising any significant influence through membership of a major political party. Put most radically, the assembly right is valuable for active citizens who for reasons of temperament or principle are unwilling to participate in conventional party politics. Any free society should recognize such a right if it values widespread participation in political activity. Some constitutions, notably the German,[30] recognize the distinctive role of political parties, but none gives them a monopoly over such activity.

It is a reasonable surmise that modern democracies have ceased to take freedom of assembly very seriously, largely because political life has become dominated by the established parties and by the mass media. To make the case for it entirely in terms of the arguments conventionally used in support of freedom of speech and the press misses an important point. Meetings and demonstrations do almost invariably, whether explicitly or implicitly, express a particular point of view. But they also amount to an active engagement in the life of the community, challenging by their very form the exclusivity of conventional modes of civic activity: writing letters to newspapers, canvassing or raising money for political parties, standing for election,

---

[28]   But Austrian school-children justified their demonstration on the streets (and absence from class attendance) on 18 February 2000 with the argument that, in the absence of the right to vote, it was the only way to express their anger at the participation of the right-wing Freedom Party in the recently formed coalition government: *Independent* 19 February 2000, 13.

[29]   9 BVerfGE 315, 343–7 (1985).

[30]   Basic Law, art. 21.

and so on. The freedom has, therefore, as much in common with the freedom of association and the right to form free political parties, as it does with freedom of speech.

4. THE SCOPE OF FREEDOM OF ASSEMBLY

Inasmuch as there is an overlap with freedom of speech (or expression), freedom of assembly clearly covers rights to speak freely at meetings and to carry placards and shout slogans while processing lawfully along a highway. Furthermore, laws, regulations or police interference, which on their face or in application discriminate against a particular meeting, procession or other form of peaceable protest on the basis of the views expressed during the event would clearly be challengeable as an interference both with freedom of speech and freedom of assembly. In litigation of this type, the latter freedom adds little, if anything, to the scope of the former. The interesting question is whether freedom of assembly confers other legal rights, say, to hold a meeting on some types of public (or private) property or to choose the route of a procession.

The question is similar to one which has often been discussed in writing on the First Amendment: does the limb of the Amendment guaranteeing freedom of the press add anything to the freedom of speech clause, or does it merely apply to newspapers, magazines, and other print media the same rights conferred on all citizens to express themselves freely? One view is that freedom of speech and freedom of the press are more or less interchangeable concepts, another is that the latter gives the institutional media—broadcasters as well as the press—special rights, in particular editorial and organizational freedom and immunity from state regulation. Similar alternatives present themselves in the context of freedom of assembly.

If the values underlying this freedom are, as has been argued, of a broader character than those which justify freedom of speech, one might expect its scope to be correspondingly wider. Indeed, this does seem to be the case not only in the United States, but also in Germany and perhaps under the European Convention. In the United States the Supreme Court has often recognized a right to use streets, parks, and other public spaces or buildings to hold meetings or to demonstrate. The classic statement of its position is found in the judgment of Roberts J in *Hague v CIO*,[31] when the Court held incompatible with the First Amendment a city licensing system under which a trade union had been denied a permit to hold a meeting in a public park to explain the meaning of recent labour relations legislation. The passage is often considered to formulate a constitutional access right to hold meetings in public places:

---

[31] 307 US 496, 515–16 (1939).

The privilege of a citizen of the United States to use the streets and parks for the communication of views on national questions may be regulated in the interest of all; it is not absolute, but relative . . . but it must not, in the guise of regulation, be abridged and denied.

The precise scope of this principle, often referred to as the Roberts' Rules, is uncertain. In particular, it has not been authoritatively established whether a city or state could constitutionally prohibit in a non-discriminatory manner all meetings and street processions on the streets which amount to a serious interference with traffic or other aspect of normal community life. But leading judgments have formulated, for instance, constitutional rights to assemble peacefully on the grounds of a State House,[32] to protest and distribute leaflets against the Vietnam War in a bus terminal,[33] and to demonstrate on the pavements outside a high school (provided at least that the demonstration is not too noisy or disruptive).[34] Perhaps most radical was a Supreme Court decision upholding the right of five blacks to sit peacefully in a public library to protest against its segregation policy.[35] In his judgment for the Court majority, Fortas J held the First Amendment rights are not limited to verbal speech, but 'embrace appropriate types of action which certainly include the right . . . to protest by silent and reproachful presence, in a place where the protestants have every right to be, the unconstitutional segregation of public facilities'.

The recognition of a right to hold meetings on the streets, parks and other public fora could, admittedly, be explained simply in free speech terms. It might be said that, in some contexts, citizens have access or claim-rights to speak. Freedom of speech may sometimes amount to more than a Hohfeldian liberty. But the explanation is not entirely satisfactory. For in other circumstances the Supreme Court has rejected recognition of access rights. I have already referred to its denial of such rights in the context of the media, though there the position is complicated because, of course, the press editor or broadcaster denying the access right also claims, and claims successfully, a First Amendment free speech right. But the Supreme Court has dismissed claims under the First Amendment to use public property for speech in other contexts: to place political advertisements on city buses,[36] to compel a school authority to allow a non-recognized union postal facilities,[37] or to permit the use of lamp posts and other utility poles for election slogans.[38] Interestingly, the Court has often referred to the availability of other channels or means for communication as a justification for its rejection of constitutional claims to use public property for speech. In contrast, it has rarely taken this position in cases involving meetings and processions. In this way, freedom of assembly appears to be special, with a broader scope than the speech right considered independently from it.

32   *Edwards v South Carolina* 372 US 229 (1963).
33   *Wolin v Port of New York Authority* 392 F 2d 83 (2nd Cir. 1968) *cert. denied*, 393 US 940 (1968).
34   *Grayned v City of Rockford* 404 US 104 (1972).
35   *Brown v Louisiana* 383 US 131 (1966).
36   *Lehman v City of Shaker Heights* 418 US 298 (1974).
37   *Perry Education Assoc. v Perry Local Educators' Assoc.* 460 US 37 (1983).
38   *City of Los Angeles v Taxpayers for Vincent* 466 US 769 (1984).

The German Constitutional Court has emphasized that the freedom protects in the first place the right of demonstrators to choose the place, time, manner and content of the event. Moreover, it is incompatible with any official compulsion either to participate in, or to stay away from, a demonstration.[39] These rights are far from absolute, and may be circumscribed, as will be explained later, by procedural conditions or limited when necessary in the public interest. However, in principle they give freedom of assembly a specific organizational dimension, much as freedom of the press may confer on editors an institutional right to determine the content of their newspapers. Perhaps of more significance is the Constitutional Court's insistence that the authorities, in particular the police, have a duty to safeguard demonstrators against disruption,[40] an instance of the obligation to protect rights (*Schutzpflicht*) which characterizes the German approach to fundamental rights.[41] The European Court of Human Rights has adopted the same approach. In *Platform 'Ärtze für das Leben' v Austria*, it said:

Genuine, effective freedom of assembly cannot . . . be reduced to a mere duty on the part of the state not to interfere: a purely negative conception would not be compatible with the object and purpose of Article 11. Like Article 8, Article 11 sometimes requires positive measures to be taken, even in the sphere of relations between individuals, if need be. . . .

States, therefore, have a duty to protect demonstrators exercising freedom of assembly against disruption. This requirement contrasts sharply with the approach in decisions such as *O' Kelly v Harvey*,[42] *Duncan v Jones*[43] and *Piddington v Bates*,[44] where courts gave priority to public order, in effect conceding the speakers' opponents a veto on the holding of the meeting or picket.

One difficult issue is the extent to which freedom of assembly confers on the organizers of a march or meeting a right to choose a *particular* route or place. A precise location may be important to them, either because it is closely related to the object of the protest or because it provides them with a large audience. The former consideration may explain why the Supreme Court upheld the right of the blacks to sit-in in the library, the use of which had been denied them under official segregation policies.[45] It also influenced the decision that Martin Luther King had a right to organize a civil rights procession in a white suburb of Chicago, rather than be compelled to accept its routing in black areas.[46]

On the other hand, US courts have rejected rights to hold meetings and distribute

---

[39] *Brokdorf* 59 BVerfGE 313, 343 (1985).
[40] ibid. 355.
[41] For a discussion in English, see D. Grimm, 'Human Rights and Judicial Review in Germany' in D. M. Beatty (ed.) *Human Rights and Judicial Review* (Martinus Nijhoff, 1994) 267, 289–91.
[42] (1883) 15 Cox CC 435 (Ir CA).
[43] [1936] 1 KB 218, DC.
[44] [1960] 3 All ER 660, DC.
[45] *Brown v Louisiana* 383 US 131 (1966).
[46] *Dr. Martin Luther King v Chicago* 419 F Supp 667 (1976).

leaflets on prison grounds[47] and on an army base,[48] despite the connection in each case of the protest with the particular site. Equally, the Parades Commission in Ulster has frequently turned down applications from Orange Lodges to parade in Catholic areas, notwithstanding their claim that it is traditional to walk down a particular street. Further, the European Human Rights Commission rejected as inadmissible a claim that Article 11 of the ECHR conferred a right to hold a meeting in Trafalgar Square to urge the government to negotiate with the IRA; the Commission pointed out that there were plenty of other venues for such rallies.[49] In effect, the Commission upheld the absolute discretionary power of the responsible minister, now the Secretary of State for Culture, Media and Sport, to decide whether or not to permit a meeting to take place in the Square. Perhaps the most remarkable rules in English law in this context are the directions of the Metropolitan Police Commissioner to his force, in furtherance of annual Sessional Orders of the two Houses of Parliament, to disperse all assemblies likely to cause obstruction or disorder within the vicinity of Parliament.[50] These directions are strictly enforced, in effect preventing any mass protest which might inconvenience Members of Parliament.[51]

Clearly, therefore, organizers do not enjoy an absolute right to select the location of their assembly. An argument that the media would find it easier to cover a meeting in a particular square should not be decisive if it would cause significantly greater disruption there than it would in other places. Further, demonstrators' wishes should be of little account when their intention in routing a procession along a particular street is purely to antagonize or provoke local residents. But normally considerable weight should be given to their wishes. It was surely wrong, for instance, that protesters against the abuse by the Chinese government of human rights were not allowed to demonstrate to the face of President Jiang on his state visit; there was little reason to fear that their protests would provoke disorder. The reason is not primarily that freedom of speech entails a right to communicate ideas effectively or to a particular audience. We have seen that in many contexts courts, even in the United States, have rejected that perspective. Rather, it is a matter of respect for the autonomy of decision of those engaged in peaceful protest, a legitimate form of political activity.

---

[47] *Adderley v Florida* 385 US 39 (1966).
[48] *Greer v Spock* 424 US 828 (1976).
[49] *Rai, Allmond and 'Negotiate Now' v UK* (1995) 19 EHRR CD 93. The applicants were allowed to hold a meeting in Hyde Park.
[50] The directions are in law made under the Metropolitan Police Act 1839, s. 52.
[51] Waddington, *Liberty and Order*, 66–8, 121–2, 180–2. Strictly, the Sessional Orders, designed to protect the unimpeded access of MPs and peers to Parliament, are of no legal significance outside the Houses: *Papworth v Coventry* [1967] 1 WLR 663, 670, DC, per Winn LJ.

5. RESTRICTIONS ON FREEDOM OF ASSEMBLY

Many of the cases mentioned in the preceding section might equally have been covered in this part of the essay. One aspect of the common law approach to civil liberties has been that their scope has inevitably been discussed in terms of the extent of the limits imposed by statute and case law; meetings may only be held in so far as the law, properly applied by administrative authorities and the police, does not preclude them.[52] The most important general consequence of incorporation of the ECHR is that this approach is no longer tenable. Courts must now consider the scope of the right to freedom of peaceful assembly before they determine the legality of restraints imposed by public order (or other) legislation and the common law powers of the police to preserve the peace.

The imposition of restrictions on the time and place of meetings and processions to avoid disturbance to other aspects of community life has long been a feature of English law, as have the powers of the police to prevent disorder. The Public Order Act 1986 (POA) did, however, give the police wider powers than they enjoyed previously to give directions imposing conditions on the organizers of processions, including conditions on their route; the basis for exercising this power has been extended to enable directions to be given when the police fear serious damage to property, serious disruption to the community, or the deliberate intimidation of others, as well as serious public disorder.[53] For the first time directions may be imposed on the place, duration, and numbers attending static meetings of twenty or more people in public open spaces.[54] On the other hand, the scope of the police power to apply to a district council (or in London the Home Secretary) for an order banning all processions (or any class of processions) in the area for a period up to three months has not been significantly altered since 1936. The government did not implement its White Paper proposal for a power to ban a single march or procession.[55] This restraint constitutes a check on the freedom of the police and public authorities to discriminate against particular groups by banning their marches, while tolerating those of others which pose similar risks; on the other hand, the present law allows the application of a ban to peaceful and disorderly marches alike.

Perhaps the most important change made by the POA 1986 to this area of law was the introduction of a national compulsory notification requirement for processions, replacing obligations found in some (but not all) local statutes. Notice must be given six clear days before holding a procession demonstrating support or opposition to the views or conduct of any person or body. However, the requirement does not apply to 'commonly or customarily' held parades or to funeral processions. Nor does it apply where it is not 'reasonably practicable' to give any advance notice, an

---

[52] See *Duncan v Jones* [1936] 1 KB 218, DC.
[53] POA 1986, s. 12(1).
[54] ibid. s. 14.
[55] Home Office *Review of Public Order Law*, Cmnd. 9510 (1985) paras. 4.12–4.14.

exemption which allows for spontaneous protest.[56] The notice must identify the date and time of the march, its proposed route, and the organizer's name and address. Organizers commit an offence if they fail to give due notice or the march departs from the notified time and route.[57]

The arguments for a general notification requirement were well deployed in the Home Office papers preceding the legislation.[58] Notification enables the police to plan for possible disturbance and disruption to traffic. In practice, the route and other conditions, for example, with regard to stewarding are negotiated by the police and the organizers; the police in a sense facilitate marches by encouraging them to follow a standard route chosen in order to minimize disruption to normal commercial life.[59] The notice requirement should not be equated with a licensing system, under which the police or local authority have power to grant or refuse licences to protest, a clear prior restraint on freedom of speech and assembly. Surprisingly, mandatory permit systems have been approved in the United States, provided they confer only limited discretion on city officials to regulate the time, manner, and place of the procession for the convenience of the public. In its leading decision holding permit systems compatible with the First Amendment, the Supreme Court also upheld a statutory provision, requiring applicants to pay a fee, which varied according to the size of the demonstration and the likely cost of its policing.[60] The European Human Rights Commission has also ruled that normally the subjection of street processions to an authorization procedure does not interfere with freedom of assembly.[61]

Although not as significant a restraint on the exercise of freedom of assembly as a permit requirement, the notification provisions of the POA are in some respects problematic. First, they are clearly aimed at political marches. Funeral and customary processions are explicitly exempted from the notification requirement. So the provisions discriminate against political speech and protest, a contents-based distinction which is hard to justify in principle.[62] Secondly, the law requires advance notice of (some) processions but not of static meetings. The White Paper considered it would be impossible to define meetings of which the police might welcome advance

---

The German Constitutional Court has ruled that the constitutional right to freedom of assembly requires the exemption of spontaneous demonstrations (*Spontandemonstrationen*) from the general notice requirements imposed by the Assemblies Law of 15 November 1978, s. 14: 69 BVerfGE 315, 350–1 (1985); 85 BVerfGE 69, 74–5 (1991).

[57]   POA 1986, s. 12.

[58]   Green Paper, *Review of the Public Order Act 1936 and related legislation* (Cmnd. 7891, 1980) paras. 66–73, and White Paper, *Review of Public Order Law*, Cmnd. 9510 (1985) paras. 4.2–4.6.

[59]   See the conclusions of Waddington, *Liberty and Order*, 101–3.

[60]   *Cox v New Hampshire* 312 US 569 (1941). Proposals to charge the organizers of demonstrations for the costs of their policing have not been pursued in this country: see White Paper, *Review of Public Order Law*, paras. 6.16–6.18.

[61]   8191/78, *Rassemblement jurassien v Switzerland* 17 DR 93.

[62]   For a criticism of similar distinctions in US city ordinances, see C. E. Baker, *Human Liberty and Freedom of Speech* (New York: OUP, 1989), 163–5.

notice,[63] though this problem was apparently not insuperable for parades. These provisions run counter to the traditional principle that the law should treat processions more benignly than stationary meetings, since the former are prima facie a lawful exercise of the right of passage along the highway.[64] A third point is that the understandable exception for spontaneous demonstrations—instantaneous reactions to unexpected major events—arguably renders the six days' notification requirement incoherent. If the law can accommodate spontaneous demonstrations, why should it insist on six days' notice of other processions which may be planned only one or two days in advance?[65] The German Constitutional Court, by a majority, has held that the forty-eight hours' notice requirement in the *Versammlungsgesetz* (Assemblies Law) should be interpreted to require notice to be given immediately of meetings arranged only a few hours or one day in advance.[66]

An apparent oddity is the skeletal character of the notification requirement imposed by the POA; no indication need be given of the anticipated numbers or of the identity or political outlook of the participating groups, though one might expect these details to be crucial for police planning. But this information generally emerges in the course of negotiations between the organizers of the procession and the police. The point is that the notification requirement, as intended, provides the impetus for the police to bargain with the organizers. Arrangements are made for the march to take place smoothly, with the organizers and stewards assuming initial responsibility for good order. Typically, a number of conditions are agreed, rather than imposed by the police.[67]

Restraints imposed on the numbers of participants or on the duration and timing of public meetings or processions might at first glance seem acceptable. They may indeed be tolerable on conventional free speech principles. A prohibition on, say, demonstrations after 8.00 p.m. can be justified as a reasonable limit, in that it is imposed to preserve peace and quiet in the evening.[68] It leaves ample time and opportunity for the demonstrators' views to be expressed, either at meetings held earlier in the day or by other conventional means of communication. A limit on numbers is a sensible measure to reduce the risk of obstruction and inconvenience to drivers, shoppers, or people who just wish to walk in a park. It does not curtail the freedom of the *group* to meet and engage in peaceful protest, though it clearly inhibits the right of *individuals*, beyond the permitted numbers, to participate in the assembly. Equally, the prohibition on evening demonstrations prevents people who

---

63 *Review of Public Order Law*, para. 5.4.

64 For a classic expression of this view in English law, see A. L. Goodhart, 'Public Meetings and Processions' (1937) 6 CJJ 161. Also see R. Vorspan, 'Freedom of Assembly and the Right to Passage in Modern English Legal History' (1997) 34 *San Diego L Rev* 921, 978 *et seq.*

65 NUM marches to protest pit closures in October 1992 were held peacefully, though only four or five days' notice was given: see Waddington, *Liberty and Order* 70–5.

66 85 BVerfGE 69 (1991). Two dissenting judges would have held the application of the 48 hours notice requirement to such meetings unconstitutional.

67 Waddington, *Liberty and Order*, 75–9.

68 See *Abernathy v Conroy* 429 F 2d. 1170 (4th Cir 1970).

work until 8.00 p.m. from exercising their freedom of assembly.[69] If freedom of assembly is a right of individuals, as well as of groups and communities, restrictions of this character should be examined with care.

Traditionally English law in this area starts from the premise that it should effect a compromise between two competing rights, identified by Sir Leslie Scarman (as he then was) in a report written in 1974: freedom of assembly and a right to calm on the streets.[70] Indeed, the notification requirement was introduced to make it easier for the police to strike the appropriate balance. As already explained, they may impose conditions on the place, route, and duration of the assembly, or the numbers participating, in order to prevent disorder or minimize disruption. In effect, they are required to balance the competing rights. But in circumstances other than political protest, the law does not confer the same powers on the police, including, it should be emphasized, in the case of processions the ultimate power to apply for a total ban. Football matches, pop and other concerts (for example, Pavarotti in the Park), and New Year's Eve celebrations all create risks of disorder, traffic disruption, and disturbance of tranquillity, comparable to those often created by marches and other forms of political protest. Sometimes, as with recent 'anti-capitalist' demonstrations in the City of London, protests become violent and there is considerable property damage, and some personal injury. But crowds (and players) at football matches also behave violently on occasion, yet it is rarely suggested that matches may be banned, or played only on grounds where there is a minimal risk of such disorder.

If freedom of assembly is taken seriously, as the European Convention on Human Rights requires, in principle it is surely hard to justify the range of restrictions imposed by public order legislation. Of course, they make a lot of practical sense. They do enable the police to balance the two competing rights identified in the Scarman report. Their effect may be to facilitate marches, while reducing disruption to the rest of the community and minimizing the risk of disturbance from counter-demonstrators. But these ends could be achieved through the general criminal law and by the replacement of the obligatory notification requirement by a *voluntary* or *optional* procedure. Under the present law, the organizers of political (but not other) processions are compelled to submit to a negotiation process. The result is the taming and institutionalizing of protest.[71] This of course is acceptable to many, almost certainly the majority of the community. But it is hardly compatible with commitment to the right to freedom of peaceful assembly, particularly if the right is properly valued and understood as a mode of participation in political activity.

---

[69] See Baker, *Human Liberty and Freedom of Speech*, 182–90.
[70] See the Scarman Report on the Red Lion Square Disorders, Cmnd. 5919 (1974), para. 5.
[71] See the conclusions of Waddington, *Liberty and Order* ch. 8.

10

Freedom of Expression and the Problem of Harassment

BOB HEPPLE QC

1. INTRODUCTION

Freedom of expression is the dog that did not bark in the development of UK law on harassment. This is in sharp contrast to the United States where the battle over campus speech codes has spread to the workplace. In particular, the prohibition by Title VII of the Civil Rights Act 1964 of discriminatory harassment has been attacked as an unconstitutional infringement of freedom of speech guaranteed by the First Amendment.[1] The defenders of harassment law have argued that it is necessary to workplace equality and is consistent with the First Amendment.[2] Other commentators have taken a middle position and advocated some restrictions on the application of Title VII.[3]

This silent dog may soon bite in the United Kingdom as the incorporation by the Human Rights Act 1998 of Article 10 on the European Convention of Human Rights (ECHR) into domestic law forces government and the courts into an explicit reconciliation of the developing law against harassment with freedom of expression. Account will need to be taken of other Convention rights such as freedom from degrading treatment,[4] the right to respect for private life,[5] and freedom from discrimination in the exercise of Convention rights.[6] These values are relevant not only to discriminatory racial or sexual harassment, but also to legal constraints on other forms of harassment.

The *Oxford English Dictionary* meaning of 'harassment' includes 'to trouble, worry, distress with annoying labour, care, perplexity, importunity, misfortune etc.'. Yet the notion of 'freedom of expression' implies that what is annoying, disturbing, perplexing, even shocking to others must be protected. The presumption both at common law and under Article 10 of the ECHR is in favour of free expression, which is a 'foundational' value.[7] Sir David Williams has remarked that 'those who

---

[1] e.g., Kingsley R. Browne, 'Title VII as Censorship: Hostile-Environment Harassment and the First Amendment' (1991) 52 Ohio St. LJ 481.

[2] e.g., Cynthia L. Estlund, 'Freedom of Expression in the Workplace and the Problem of Discriminatory Harassment' (1997) 75 Texas LR 687.

[3] e.g. Nadine Strossen, 'The Tensions Between Regulating Workplace Harassment and the First Amendment: No Trump', (1995) 71 Chi-Kent LR 701.

[4] ECHR, Art. 3.   [5] ECHR, Art. 8.

[6] ECHR, Art. 14; and see the draft Protocol 12 (2000) which proposes to give a free-standing right to equality.

[7] D. Feldman, *Civil Liberties and Human Rights in England and Wales* (Oxford: Clarendon Press, 1993) 548.

express what others see as offensive and objectionable views, but are nevertheless within the limits of the law, are often defended on the "safety-valve" argument; and the corollary of that argument is that it is often inadvisable to sit on the safety valve'.[8] In the *Handyside* case[9] the European Court of Human Rights made it clear that Article 10 embraces not only information and ideas:

> that are favourably received or regarded as inoffensive but also . . . those that offend, shock, or disturb the state or any sector of the population. Such are the demands of that pluralism, tolerance and broadmindedness without which there is no 'democratic society'.

The law on harassment therefore needs to be closely scrutinized in order to ensure that expression is not being unjustifiably suppressed simply because words or conduct cause offence or are shocking and disturbing to others. There must be some other overriding consideration. Epithets such as 'political correctness' or 'censorship' hurled from one side, and 'racism' or 'sexism' from the other, do nothing to illuminate the choices which face judges and legislators when deciding whether or not to outlaw conduct and speech of this kind.

In the spirit of Lord Goff's remark in a related area that 'a crumb of analysis is worth a loaf of opinion' from academic writers,[10] this paper attempts to analyse the various forms of unlawful harassment and the justifications for the limits they impose on freedom of expression, taking account of comparative experience particularly in the United States, Canada and South Africa. First, the forms of expression which are legally constrained on grounds that the words or conduct amount to 'harassment' are examined. The offences of incitement to racial hatred and racially aggravated offences are included in this review, so that the similarities and differences between group hostility and harassment can be understood. Secondly, the extent to which these amount to 'expression' is analysed. Thirdly, the arguments for the restriction of these forms of expression are discussed in the light of the requirements of Article 10 (2) of the ECHR. Finally, some modest proposals are made for restructuring the law to take account of free expression arguments.

2. HARASSMENT AND HATE

2.1 Harassment as Disorderly Conduct

'Harassment' is the basis of criminal liability in certain public order offences. The heading of s. 5 of the Public Order Act 1986 is 'harassment, alarm or distress', but

---

[8]   D. G. T. Williams, 'The New Legal Framework' in B. Parekh and B. Hepple (eds.) *Racism and Freedom of Speech on the Campus* (London: Commission for Racial Equality, 1988) 8.

[9]   EHRR, A 24, para. 49 (1976).

[10] *Hunter v Canary Wharf Ltd* [1997] AC 673 at 694F.

as Professor A. T. H Smith points out, it is more accurately described as 'offensive conduct'.[11] The offence is wider than the old one, under the Public Order Act 1936, s. 5, of 'threatening, abusive or insulting behaviour' because there is no requirement of a breach of the peace. Instead the disorderly conduct must take place 'within the hearing or sight of a person likely to be caused harassment, alarm or distress thereby'. This is a significantly lower requirement than that of violence or the possibility of violence which is the basis of most public order offences. The offence complements s. 4 of the 1986 Act (fear or provocation of violence), and was considered necessary because of doubts whether the old offence covered a situation in which the victim (e.g. an elderly lady) was not likely to be provoked into violence. Moreover, unlike s. 4, the s. 5 conduct need not be 'towards another', and there is a defence that the defendant had no reason to believe that there was any person within hearing or sight who was likely to be caused harassment etc.[12]

What is harassment is a question of fact for magistrates, but Professor Smith tells us that 'mere annoyance or irritation caused by inconvenience is not sufficient' and that 'it would be an unusual use of language to say that a person was harassing another by a single act (such as a wolf whistle) since that term generally connotes an element of persistence'.[13] Moreover 'alarm or distress' connote something more than mere annoyance or upset. It is a defence that the conduct was reasonable.[14]

The more serious offence of 'intentional harassment, alarm or distress' in s. 4A of the 1986 Act was created by the Criminal Justice and Public Order Act 1994. It was aimed at racial harassment. but this was not mentioned in s. 4A so as to avoid the need for prosecutors to prove beyond reasonable doubt that the offence was racially motivated. So it could, in principle, cover intentional sexual harassment, harassment of gays and lesbians, and of disabled persons.

By virtue of s. 31 of the Crime and Disorder Act 1998, the courts are required to increase the sentence where the commission of the offence was 'racially aggravated'.[15] This includes offences under the Public Order Act 1986 and the Protection of Harassment Act 1997 (below). An offence is racially aggravated if, either at the time of committing the offence, or immediately before or after doing so, the offender demonstrates towards the victim of the offence hostility based on the victim's membership (or presumed membership) of a racial group, or the offence is motivated (wholly or partly) by hostility towards members of a racial group based on their membership of that group.[16]

---

[11] A. T. H. Smith, *Offences Against Public Order* (London: Sweet & Maxwell, 1987), para.7–01.
[12] Public Order Act 1986, s. 5(3)(a).
[13] Smith (n. 11 above) para. 7–07.
[14] Public Order Act 1986, s. 5(3)(c)
[15] Severe sentences are being imposed. In *R v Saunders*, Court of Criminal Appeal 17 December 1999, a sentence of 42 months was upheld for an assault occasioning actual bodily harm, accompanied by the words 'I don't like Pakis, fucking Pakis. Kick them out'. Lord Justice Rose VP said : 'The message has to be received and understood that racism is evil. It cannot co-exist with fairness and justice. It is incompatible with democratic civilisation.'
[16] Crime and Disorder Act 1998, s. 28(1).

2.2 Stalking and Related Wrongs

The Protection from Harassment Act 1997 was designed primarily to give the courts more effective powers to deal with stalkers, but the then Home Secretary (Mr Michael Howard MP) pointed out it is also apt to cover 'disruptive neighbours and those who target others because of the colour of their skin'.[17] The Act avoids the need to prove an intention to harass. It simply prohibits 'harassment'. This is committed where a course of conduct (which must involve conduct on at least two occasions and includes speech)[18] amounts to harassment of another, and the defendant knows or ought to know that it amounts to harassment.[19] This may constitute an arrestable offence, triable summarily.[20] It may also be a statutory tort. Damages may be awarded for (among other things) any anxiety caused by the harassment, and any financial loss caused by the harassment.[21] Some forms of stalking such as persistent telephone calls,[22] may arguably constitute a tort of harassment at common law, although such a development is rendered unnecessary by the 1997 Act.

2.3 Hate Speech

The link with public order is controversial in the case of so-called 'hate-speech'. Incitement to racial hatred has been regarded as a potentially dangerous form of expression distinguished from other kinds of threatening, abusive or insulting words. The Race Relations Act 1965, s. 6 required an intent to stir up hatred against any section of the public in Great Britain distinguished by colour, race, or ethnic or national origins. This was amended in 1976 and put into the context of public order legislation, and then further amended in the Public Order Act 1986, which brought together a range of racial hatred provisions in Part III. Strictly speaking, incitement to racial hatred is concerned with public order. As Sir David Williams pointed out in 1967,[23] this was 'the latest in a line of statutory crimes of incitement in English law' which did not require the test of a likelihood of disorder but which, nevertheless, belonged to the law of public order, merely relieving prosecutors of the need to prove a threat to the peace. He added that the restrictions it imposed on free speech had to be judged against the 'urgent contemporary problem' of easing the integration of the ethnic minority communities.

---

[17] *Hansard*, HC (series 6) vol. 287, col. 781 (17 December 1996).

[18] Protection from Harassment Act 1997, s. 7(3), (4).

[19] ibid., s. 1(1). The test is whether a reasonable person in possession of the same information would think that the course of conduct amounted to harassment of another: s. 1(2).

[20] ibid., s. 2.

[21] ibid., s. 3

[22] *Khorasandjian v Bush* [1993] Q.B.727, CA. Although the House of Lords held in *Hunter v Canary Wharf Ltd* [1997] AC 655, that this decision was wrong in holding that a person without an interest in land could sue in respect of private nuisance, the wider question whether there is a separate tort of harassment was not considered.

[23] David Williams, *Keeping the Peace: the police and public order* (London: Hutchinson,1967) 177.

In its current form, in s. 18 of the Public Order Act 1986, incitement of racial hatred goes beyond a public order offence, because people may be guilty if they use words or behaviour or display written material in private (except in a dwelling). This is the case even if there is no risk of a violent reaction because everyone agrees with the views expressed. There are related offences of publishing or distributing written material,[24] or giving a public performance of a play,[25] or distributing, showing or playing a recording,[26] intended or likely to stir up racial hatred.

These offences are to be distinguished from harassment, because of the requirement of 'hatred'. This is 'hatred against a group of persons in Great Britain defined by reference to colour, race, nationality (including citizenship), or ethnic or national origins.'[27] This is not further defined, but in effect means enmity or ill-will.[28] In recent years, there has been pressure from Muslim groups in Britain to extend the offence to incitement to religious hatred. In some cases, such as anti-semitic utterances, the incitement may be covered by the existing offences because the group, say Jews, are being targeted on ethnic rather than religious grounds. Indeed hate crimes directed against Muslims have been identified as a new form of cultural racism—they are usually targeted in terms of their perceived non-European culture.[29] But the United Kingdom is under an obligation by virtue of the International Covenant on Civil and Political Rights to prohibit incitement of religious hatred. Such incitement impedes the freedom of religion (also guaranteed by the ECHR, Article 9).

2.4 Peaceful Picketing

The link between public order and harassment is also tenuous when we come to consider some of the restrictions on peaceful picketing. In the nineteenth century, Parliament intervened to limit the range of vague criminal offences and civil wrongs which could be used against those who were regarded as 'harassers', particularly in the field of trade disputes, what would today be called industrial action. The judges had developed vague offences such as 'molestation' and 'obstruction' in order to restrain the freedom of expression of strike pickets and union organizers. There were differences of judicial opinion as to whether these covered only acts or threats of violence causing 'molestation' or 'obstruction',[30] or could embrace any conduct intended to 'coerce' the will of another.

Despite attempts in the Molestation of Workmen Act 1859 to permit peaceful persuasion of others to abstain from work, Baron Bramwell directed that phrases

---

[24] Public Order Act 1986, s. 19.

[25] ibid., s. 20

[26] ibid., s. 21. Broadcasting is also covered: s. 22, and possession of racially inflammatory material: s. 23.

[27] ibid., s. 17.

[28] Smith (n. 11 above), para. 9–06.

[29] T. Modood, in T. Modood and P. Werbner (eds.) *The Politics of Multiculturalism in the New Europe* (London, 1997) 4.

[30] See e.g., Rolfe B in *R v Selsby* (1847) 5 Cox CC at 497n.

such as 'Is he not dung?' and 'That's him', used by a picket against a non-striker, could constitute an offence if 'calculated to have a deterring effect on the minds of ordinary persons, by exposing them to have their motions watched, and to encounter black looks.'[31] The Criminal Law Amendment Act 1871 restricted the scope of 'molestation' and 'obstruction' but this did not prevent the courts from deciding that a threat that a lawful strike would take place if workers' demands were not met could constitute an improper molestation if the threat was an 'annoyance' sufficient to 'deter masters of ordinary nerve'.[32]

It was the Conspiracy and Protection of Property Act 1875 which marked the turning point. Offences such as 'threats', 'molestation' and 'obstruction' were dropped. A number of specific offences, first set out in the 1871 Act, were substantially re-enacted. An updated version of these offences, which are not limited to trade disputes, now appears in the Trade Union and Labour Relations (Consolidation) Act 1992 (TULRCA), s. 241. They include using violence or intimidation, persistently following a person about from place to place, hiding tools, clothes or other property, watching or besetting the house or other place where a person resides, works, or carries on business or happens to be, or following that person with two or more others in a disorderly manner in or through any street or road.

One crucial limitation is that it is only an offence if one of these acts is done 'wrongfully and without legal authority'. This requires the words or conduct at least to amount to a tort—for example private nuisance or possibly the emerging tort of harassment—before there can be criminal liability.[33] At present, a range of words and conduct, even short of actual or threatened violence or disorder, may constitute unlawful harassment at common law : for example peaceful picketing outside the home of a non-striker, or the hurling of abuse at persons going to work during a strike[34] and this may provide the necessary ingredient of wrongfulness.

Another limitation is that the act must be done with a view to 'compel' a person to do or abstain from doing something which the victim has a legal right to do or refrain from doing. So when anti-abortion demonstrators stood outside a clinic chanting abuse and displaying shocking pictures of aborted foetuses, but there was no evidence that anyone had been prevented from undergoing a termination of pregnancy, it was held there was no 'compulsion' and hence no offence.[35]

The 1875 Act also made it clear that attending at a place 'in order merely to obtain or communicate information' was not to be deemed watching and besetting. This was held, the following year, not to include peaceful 'persuasion' of others not to join a strike.[36] However, the Trade Disputes Act 1906, s. 2(1) established that

---

[31] *R v Druitt* (1867) 10 Cox CC 592.
[32] *R v Bunn* (1872) 12 Cox CC 316, per Brett J.
[33] If the decision in *Galt (Procurator Fiscal) v Philp* [1984] IRLR156, is right, a tort remains 'wrongful' even if protected by a trade disputes immunity, so picketing which involved an inducement of breach of contract could lead to an offence under s. 241.
[34] *Thomas v NUM* [1985] IRLR 136 at 149, 153.
[35] *DPP v Fidler* [1992] 1 WLR 91, DC.
[36] *R v Bauld* (1876) 13 Cox CC 282; upheld in *Lyons v Wilkins* [1899] 1 Ch. 255, CA.

peaceful picketing for the purposes of obtaining or communicating information or to persuade any person to work or abstain from working is lawful provided that this happens 'in contemplation or furtherance of a trade dispute'. This immunity has been limited by subsequent legislation, consolidated in TULRCA, s. 220, and has been restrictively interpreted by the courts. In particular, attendance in relatively large numbers has been sufficient for the courts to infer that the purpose went beyond the obtaining or imparting of information or peaceful persuasion.[37]

2.5 Discriminatory Harassment

The form of harassment which has excited most controversy in recent years is that based on less favourable treatment of a person on grounds of race,[38] sex or marital status,[39] or for a reason relating to his or her disability.[40] The anti-discrimination legislation in the United Kingdom does not specifically outlaw harassment on any of these grounds, in contrast to the recent Irish Equality Act and statutes in several other jurisdictions. The approach adopted by the draft directive under Article 13 of the EC Treaty is to deem harassment to be discrimination, but to define it as follows:

Harassment of a person related to any of the discriminatory grounds and areas [covered by the Directive] which has the purpose or effect of creating an intimidating, hostile, offensive or disturbing environment.

The present United Kingdom law on discriminatory harassment is a judicial gloss on the statutes.[41] It has been developed with the help of the European Commission Code of Practice on measures to combat sexual harassment[42] and the Equal Opportunities Commission (EOC) and Commission for Racial Equality (CRE) codes of practice on the elimination of discrimination and guidance issued by those Commissions on sexual and racial harassment.

The reliance on discrimination law has a number of curious results. The first of these is that there must be 'less favourable treatment'. This involves a comparative approach. So in *Stewart v Cleveland Guest (Engineering) Ltd.*[43] it was held that a woman could not complain of the display of pictures of nude women at the work-

---

[37] See the cases reviewed by S. Deakin and G. S. Morris, *Labour Law* (2nd edn., London: Butterworths, 1998) 928–9.

[38] Race Relations Act 1976, s. 1(1)(a).

[39] Sex Discrimination Act 1975, s. 1(1)(a).

[40] Disability Discrimination Act 1995, s. 5.

[41] The law on constructive unfair dismissal, and the law of contract, may also give protection where the conduct amounts to a breach of the duty of mutual trust and confidence: see generally, Deakin and Morris (n. 37 above) 330–5.

[42] Issued in accordance with the Resolution of the Council of Ministers [1990] OJ C157/3; on which see Commission of the European Communities, *How to Combat Sexual Harassment at Work* (Luxembourg, 1993).

[43] [1994] IRLR440. See also *Balgobin v London Borough of Tower Hamlets* [1987] IRLR 401 (requiring woman to continue to work with alleged harasser not less favourable treatment because man alleging homosexual advances would have been treated similarly).

place because a hypothetical man might also have complained so making the display gender neutral. This ignores the gist of the complaint about pornographic displays at the workplace, namely that they create a hostile working environment by undermining the dignity of women. If men also object this does not change the effect on women. Occasionally, the Employment Appeal Tribunal has been willing to accept that sexual harassment is sex discrimination *per se* without any need to make reference to how a man would have been treated in similar circumstances,[44] but so long as harassment remains tied to the concept of discrimination this difficulty will persist. Moreover, the exclusion from statutory protection of certain types of arbitrary discrimination, such as on grounds of sexual orientation, has left some vulnerable groups, such as gays and lesbians, unprotected.[45]

A second consequence of the reliance on the discrimination legislation is the need to show a 'detriment'. Although this has been broadly interpreted as going beyond so-called *quid pro quo* harassment (e.g. denying promotion to a woman who refused sexual favours),[46] abuse or an insult will not amount to a detriment unless 'a reasonable worker would or might take the view that he had thereby been disadvantaged in the circumstances in which he had thereafter to work'.[47] The conduct must be considered in relation to a particular victim: sexual innuendoes directed by A to B might be acceptable, but would not be if they came from C. It is the individual who must reasonably object to the conduct or speech in question.[48] Unlike the Protection from Harassment Act, however, there need not be a course of conduct: a 'detriment' on a single occasion is sufficient, provided it is serious.[49] If lewd conduct takes place in the sight or hearing of a woman, or racist jokes are told, it is the repetition of this behaviour after objection has been made, that shows that the conduct was directed against the complainant.[50]

These limitations on discriminatory harassment have led to proposals that harassment on specified prohibited grounds should be a separate wrong, or an aggravated form of a general wrong of bullying and harassment. A Private Member's Dignity at Work Bill, introduced in the House of Lords in 1996 by Lord Monkswell, proposed to confer the right to dignity at work on all employees and contract workers. It defined a breach of that right as any of the following: persistent or recurrent behaviour which is offensive, abusive or demeaning, verbal or physical; intimidation; persistent or recurrent behaviour which is malicious or insulting; penalties imposed

---

[44] e.g. *British Telecommunications plc v Williams* [1995] IRLR 668; *Strathclyde Regional Council v Porcelli* [1986] IRLR 134, Court of Session (harassment would not have happened had she been a man).
[45] *Smith v Gardner Merchant* [1996] IRLR 342.
[46] *Strathclyde Regional Council v Porcelli* [1986] IRLR 134
[47] *De Souza v Automobile Association* [1986] IRLR103, in which an instruction by a manager to 'get his typing done by the wog' was held to be a detriment, but the complainant failed on the ground that she had not shown that the manager intended her to overhear the remark or that he ought to have anticipated that it would be passed on to her.
[48] *Wileman v MinilecEngineering* [1988] IRLR 144.
[49] *Bracebridge Engineering Ltd v Darby* [1990] IRLR 3.
[50] e.g. *Johnstone v Fenton Barns (Scotland) Ltd.* Case S/1688/89, cited by C. Palmer, G. Moon and S. Cox, *Discrimination at Work* (3rd edn., London: Legal Action Group, 1997) 264.

without reasonable justification; or changes in duties and responsibilities to the employee's detriment and without reasonable justification. Remedies were provided through industrial tribunals. The Bill, supported by the Campaign against Bullying at Work, was said by its promoters to be needed in view of surveys which showed an alarming incidence of bullying at work.[51]

2.6 Analysis

This wide range of criminal and civil liability in which harassment or hostility towards a group is an ingredient displays several common features, and some significant differences.

First, all except discriminatory harassment can involve the commission of criminal offences. Stalking and peaceful picketing may also give rise to a tort. Discriminatory harassment may be a statutory tort or, in the employment context, a breach of contract.

Secondly, all of them prohibit some form of expression, whether by words or other conduct. But only in the cases of discriminatory harassment or incitement to racial hatred is a single act capable of giving rise to liability, and even in those cases some degree of persistence is likely to be needed to show that the conduct was directed against an individual (in the case of discrimination) or a group (in the case of hate speech).

Thirdly, liability is generally not dependent on proof of an intention to cause the harm in question. Conduct which is likely to have the effect is usually sufficient. The exceptions are the crime of intentional harassment etc. (s. 4A of the Public Order Act) and racially aggravated public order offences.

Fourthly, hostility towards a group is not a requirement except in the case of incitement to racial hatred and racially aggravated offences.

Fifthly, the unlawful conduct may occur in a private place (except a dwelling)[52] as well as a public one.

Finally, causing offence, annoyance or disturbance is generally not sufficient. The important exceptions are discriminatory harassment and peaceful picketing outside the area of trade disputes, or in trade disputes where the picketing is not simply informational or to persuade another to work or not to work.

---

[51] The Institute of Personnel Development survey conducted by the Harris Research Centre showed that one in eight people claimed to have been bullied at work over the previous five years; a survey by the University of Salford showed that 51% of their sample of 1,000 people had experienced bullying; and a survey by the MSF union said that 30% had been bullied: Lord Monkswell, *Hansard*, (series 5) vol. 576, col. 755, 4 December 1996. A survey for the TUC Women's Conference 1999 showed that many women are harassed or bullied for gender-related reasons.

[52] Employment for purposes of a private household is exempted by the Race Relations Act 1976, s. 4(3), but a corresponding exemption in the Sex Discrimination Act 1975, s. 6(3) was removed (following a decision of the European Court of Justice that this was contrary to EC equality law). The Disability Discrimination Act does not apply to certain small employers.

3. EXPRESSION

The first stage in any inquiry into the application of Article 10 of the ECHR is to ask whether the conduct in question is a form of 'expression'. Unlike the First Amendment to the United States Constitution, Article 10 is not limited to 'speech' and so embraces a wide range of conduct and action.

The main means of limiting freedom of expression in the ECHR is by way of justification under Article 10(2). The First Amendment, by contrast, contains no such textual limitation. This has led the United States Supreme Court to draw a bright line between protected and unprotected speech, the former enjoying near absolute protection, and the latter none. At one time fighting words, obscenity, defamation and commercial speech were considered to form 'no essential part of any exposition of ideas'[53] and so were unprotected. More recently, the Supreme Court has developed the law so as to protect some of these forms of conduct.

In *R.A.V. v City of St Paul*[54] a city ordinance prohibited the display of a symbol (such as, in this case, a burning cross) which 'one knows or has reason to know arouses anger, alarm or resentment in others on the basis of race, color, creed, religion or gender'. The Supreme Court accepted the state court's finding that the ordinance was restricted to fighting words, and so was 'unprotected speech'. Nevertheless, the majority of the Court held that by distinguishing among unprotected utterances on the basis of the viewpoints expressed, the ordinance was contrary to the First Amendment. Justice Scalia said:

Those who wish to use 'fighting words' in connection with other ideas—to express hostility, for example, on the basis of political affiliation, union membership or homosexuality are not covered. The First Amendment does not permit St Paul to impose special prohibitions on those speakers who express views on disfavoured subjects.[55]

The minority pointed out that this leads to the paradox that the ordinance was struck down for prohibiting not too much, but too little speech. But even the minority were willing to strike down the ordinance because it extended to behaviour which merely arouses anger, alarm, or resentment rather than being limited to conduct which inflicts injury or tends to incite immediate violence. The minority approach would permit sexist or racist speech which falls short of fighting words or incitement to violence. One may compare s. 16 of the South African Constitution which expressly excludes from the protection of freedom of expression not only 'incitement to immediate violence' but also 'advocacy of hatred that is based on race, ethnicity, gender, or religion, and that constitutes incitement to cause harm'.

Although the majority in *R.A.V.* distinguished Title VII of the Civil Rights Act on the grounds that this is concerned with discriminatory conduct and not speech, it

---

[53] *Chaplinsky v New Hampshire* 315 US 568 at 571–2, 62 S Ct 766 (1942).
[54] 563 US 377 (US); 112 S Ct 2538 (1992), and Cynthia J. Estlund, 'The Architecture of the First Amendment and the Case of Workplace Harassment' (1997) 72 Notre Dame LR 1361 at 1369 et seq.
[55] 112 S Ct 2538 at 2545.

has been pointed out[56] that 'much of what is part of a typical harassment complaint—that is most sexual innuendo, profanity, racist and sexist epithets, the display of non-obscene pornography, and the disparagement of women and minorities and their presence in the workplace, trade or profession' might now be protected speech.

The American case law is of limited relevance to the interpretation of Article 10 of the ECHR, because of the different structure of the First Amendment. However, it is indicative of the underlying values of free expression. Whether or not a particular form of harassment is 'expression' under the ECHR will depend on the approach taken by the court. One approach would be, like that in the *R.A.V.* case, content-neutral, eschewing any attempt to distinguish between different forms of expression. As long as the conduct has a communicative purpose it would fall within the ambit of Article 10(1). This would exclude violent conduct and also physical contact (e.g. unwelcome touching of a female employee). On the other hand, lewd or racist comments or jokes, disparaging remarks, and the display of nude pictures would constitute protected 'expression'. On this view, racist and anti-racist, sexist and anti-sexist speech and conduct are prima facie entitled to equal protection.

An alternative approach would be to examine the content of the expression in question to ask whether it furthers any of the values which underlie freedom of expression. This would involve the court in deciding whether or not certain communications were valueless or not. Feminists, such as Catherine MacKinnon, have argued that any words or pictures which convey the subordination of women or create a hostile environment for them contribute nothing of any value to political debate but offend another constitutional value, that of equality, and so should not be categorized as protected speech.[57] In Canada, however, a majority of the Supreme Court have held that hate propaganda is prima facie protected because freedom of expression covers all messages 'however unpopular, distasteful, or contrary to the mainstream', and this cannot be affected by competing rights such as equality, at the first stage of the analysis.[58]

The European Court of Human Rights has not yet had an opportunity to consider this issue directly, but the indications are that it would adopt a content-neutral approach at the first stage, leaving the evaluation of the expression in question to the second stage of the inquiry, under Article 10(2). This can be seen from *Jersild v Denmark*,[59] in which the Court held that the prosecution of a journalist for broadcasting a programme in which skinheads were heard using racially abusive language was a breach of Article 10. Significantly, the dissemination of racial abuse was treated as 'expression' in a content-neutral way. The Court was solely concerned with the issue under Article 10(2), whether the measures were 'necessary in a democratic society'(see below).

---

[56] Estlund (n. 54 above) 1371.
[57] Catherine MacKinnon, 'Pornography, Civil Rights and Speech' in Catherine Itzin (ed.), *Pornography: Women, Violence and Civil Liberties* (Oxford: Oxford University Press, 1992) 456.
[58] *R v Keegstra* [1990] 3 SCR697 at 727 (case of Holocaust-denial), see further below.
[59] ECtHR Series A 298 (1994).

One may, therefore, conclude that only violent conduct or unwanted physical contact is likely to be excluded from the scope of protection of Article 10(1).

4. JUSTIFICATION

4.1 Article 10(2)

Article 10(2) of the ECHR provides that:

The exercise of these freedoms, since it carries with it duties and responsibilities, may be subject to such formalities, conditions, restrictions or penalties as are prescribed by law and are necessary in a democratic society, in the interests of national security, territorial integrity or public safety, for the prevention of disorder or crime, for the protection of health or morals, for the protection of the reputation or rights of others, for preventing the disclosure of information received in confidence, or for maintaining the authority and impartiality of the judiciary.

The various restrictions or penalties on harassment analysed earlier are plainly 'prescribed by law'. Their aims relate in some cases to the 'prevention of disorder' and in all cases to the 'protection of the reputation and rights of others'. The question in issue is whether or not the restrictions are 'necessary' in a democratic society to achieve those aims.

To date, United Kingdom courts have not had to consider this limitation in the context of harassment. In a picketing case in 1993, where an injunction was sought to restrain the distribution of a leaflet urging consumers to boycott a product, Neill LJ raised the question of Article 10 of his own motion, but, in the event, it was unnecessary to deal with the point because of the finding that no tort had been committed.[60] In future, the starting point is likely to be the *Handyside* case[61] in which the needs of a pluralist, tolerant and broadminded democratic society are treated as paramount. The Court of Human Rights has also been influenced by the need of autonomous individuals to express their personality. The Court has been less influenced than the United States Supreme Court by the 'free market-place of ideas' approach, which regards free expression as the means by which truth is exposed.[62] The wording of Article 10(2) has led the Court to use the concept of proportionality rather than absolute rights for certain forms of expression.

In general, the 'margin of appreciation' allowed to national authorities by the Court of Human Rights has meant that the Court has been much influenced by a European wide consensus on the particular issue. Incitement to racial hatred is one

---

[60] *Middlebrook Mushrooms Ltd v T.G.W.U* [1993] ICR 612 at 620C.
[61] Above, n. 9
[62] See C. McCrudden, 'The Impact on Freedom of Speech'in B. S. Markesinis (ed.), The *Impact of the Human Rights Bill on English Law* (Oxford: Oxford University Press, 1998) 104–8; and generally, David Feldman, *Civil Liberties and Human Rights in England and Wales* 547–52.

on which there is such a consensus, but apart from the Member States of the European Union there is as yet no consensus on the extent to which some forms of sexual or racial harassment should be outlawed. So UK courts will have to decide these issues in the specific context of the values of pluralism, tolerance and broadmindedness in British society. They are likely to be influenced by the Court of Human Rights' insistence that 'necessary' implies the existence of a 'pressing social need', that the interference must be 'proportionate to the legitimate aim pursued', and that the reasons for the measure must be 'relevant and sufficient'.[63]

4.2 Disorderly Conduct and Stalking

The offence under s. 5 of the Public Order Act 1986 may be said to have the 'pressing social need' of preventing disorder and also protecting the rights of others, even though there is no requirement of an immediate threat of violence. The criminal offence is limited to those acts which are likely to cause harassment, alarm or distress, and exclude mere annoyance, irritation or inconvenience. In other words there are measurable effects on the physical or psychological health of a defined class of persons, namely those within hearing or sight of the conduct. It is submitted that this interference with expression is proportionate to the legitimate aims and would be a 'relevant and sufficient' reason for the measure. *A fortiori*, the more serious offence of intentional harassment etc. under s. 4A would pass the Article 10(2) test.

The criminal offence and civil wrong under the Protection of Harassment Act are also unproblematical, provided that 'harassment' is given a similar interpretation to that under the disorderly conduct offences, as the Home Secretary suggested would be the case.[64] Protection is given here to the reputation and rights of others. The critical ingredient, it is suggested, is that some physical or psychological harm or emotional distress is occasioned by the conduct in question.

4.3 Hate Speech

In the *Jersild* case (p. 187 above) the Court of Human Rights held that the conviction of the journalist was disproportionate to the legitimate objective of 'protecting the reputation and rights of others', given, inter alia, that the broadcast was by a responsible journalist in the context of a serious news programme. The medium and manner of communication are thus of great importance. The Court went out of its way to state that their decision was specific to this context, and that the skinheads' remarks 'were more than insulting to the targeted groups and did not enjoy the protection of Article 10'.[65] In other cases, as well, the Court has upheld measures to prevent incitement to

---

[63] *Ahmed v United Kingdom*, [1999] IRLR 188. Judgment of 2 September 1998, (ECtHR).
[64] *Hansard*, HC (series 6) vol. 287, col. 781 (17 December 1996).
[65] ECtHR Series A 298, para. 35.

racial or religious hatred or intolerance.[66] The need for such measures has been recognized in several international instruments.[67] There can be little doubt that the incitement to racial hatred provisions in Part III of the Public Order Act, and the sentencing powers in respect of racially aggravated offences will be regarded as justified in the United Kingdom, as would any extension to religious hatred.

While such measures would not pass muster under the First Amendment, laws of this kind are now widespread throughout Europe.[68] The German Constitution protects free speech, but the German Constitutional Court has held that denials of the Holocaust are not a legitimate exercise of this freedom. Ronald Dworkin argues that censorship of those fanatics who deny this monstrous crime against humanity is counter-productive and unnecessary. Instead the Holocaust-deniers should be refuted 'publicly, thoroughly and contemptuously'.[69] This argument, of course, presupposes that there is the possibility of free and open debate by rational persons. It is difficult to sustain this argument in a society where the means of access to the media is unequal, and the advocates of hate are in positions of power, while their victims are not. Spreading false news or historical lies is one thing, but spreading these in circumstances where they are intended or likely to stir racial hatred is another.[70]

If means and context are all-important to the prohibition of hate-speech, then it is legitimate for courts to draw a distinction between those situations in which the utterances relate to politics or public debate (e.g. the late Enoch Powell's notorious 'rivers of blood' speech), and those where racial epithets are hurled at others. While the former should enjoy protection in view of the underlying values of democracy and autonomy, the latter generally carry no adequate meaning. Another relevant factor, as contemplated in section 16 of the South African Constitution (above) is whether there is an incitement to cause harm. The Canadian Supreme Court has suggested that the harm in issue in the context of hate speech covers not only physical and psychological injury, but also social damage.[71] This may be compared with US cases which have regarded mental and emotional disturbance, or anger and distress, as insufficient to deprive speech of its constitutional protection.[72] It is submitted that the different structure of the First Amendment should lead UK courts to prefer the Canadian approach where, as under the ECHR, issues of legitimacy rather than prior classification as 'speech', are all-important.

---

[66]   e.g. *Otto-Preminger-Institut v Austria*, ECtHR Series A 295-A (1994)

[67]   See e.g. art. 20 of the International Covenant on Civil and Political Rights; art. 4 of the International Convention on the Elimination of all forms of Racial Discrimination.

[68]   For a survey see European Commission against Racism and Intolerance, *Legal Measures to Combat Racism and Intolerance in the Member States of the Council of Europe*, Report by the Swiss Institute of Comparative Law Lausanne (Strasbourg, Council of Europe, 1998).

[69]   Ronald Dworkin, *Freedom's Law* (Oxford: Oxford University Press, 1996) 223–6.

[70]   This is a distinction apparently accepted in Canada: compare *R v Keegstra* (n. 58 above), where the ban on wilful promotion of racial hatred was upheld, with *R v Zundel* [1992] 2 SCR 731, where a ban on the spread of false news was held to be overbroad.

[71]   *R v Keegstra* [1990] SCR 697.

[72]   *Collins v Smith* 578 F 2d 197 (1978).

4.4 Peaceful Picketing

Picketing involves expressive conduct and so falls prima facie under Article 10(1). So far as the criminal law is concerned (apart from the exercise of police powers to restrain breaches of the peace and to prevent obstruction) the main question mark hangs over the ambiguous requirement in s. 241 of the Trade Union and Labour Relations (Consolidation) Act that the conduct must be 'wrongful and without legal authority'. If, as noted earlier, the mere fact of peaceful picketing can be 'wrongful' because it constitutes the tort of harassment or private nuisance or an inducement of breach of contract even though protected by a trade disputes immunity, then these relatively minor civil wrongs can lead to conviction in a criminal court. Is this proportionate to the aim of protecting the rights of others? Questions of freedom of assembly, including demonstration, and association (Article 11 of the ECHR), also arise.

In the United Kingdom picketing has been regarded as protected speech on the ground that discussion of conditions in industry and the causes of labour disputes is indispensible to popular government.[73] The leading Canadian author argues that 'picketing is probably best regarded as commercial expression, since its main purpose is to encourage employees not to work and consumers not to buy'.[74] In the Canadian context, where both political and commercial expression are protected, the characterization does not matter much. But the indications are that commercial expression is not regarded by the Court of Human Rights as worthy of protection as political expression, or, at least, that Member States will be allowed a wider margin of appreciation in commercial cases.[75]

Courts in the United Kingdom may have to consider two particular questions. The first is whether the lack of protection for consumer picketing, where a tort is committed such as harassment, private nuisance or inducement of breach of contract, can be justified.[76] In view of the importance of free political activity to influence the conduct of consumers (e.g. to encourage ethical trading standards) it may be difficult to justify the absence of an immunity similar to that allowed in trade disputes.[77] The second question is whether the ban on some forms of secondary picketing[78] in trade disputes is justified. This kind of picketing involves putting pressure on a third party (e.g. a supplier of the employer in dispute) in order to influence the outcome of a dispute between the employer and its own employees. In the

---

[73] *Thornhill v Alabama* 310 U.S.88, 60 S Ct 736 (1940); cf. *International Brotherhood of Teamsters v Vogt* 354 US284, 77 S Ct 1166 (1957) where picketing was restrained when it prevented government from enforcing public policy.

[74] Hogg, *Constitutional Law of Canada* (4th edn., Toronto: Carswell, 1997) s. 40.8.

[75] See D. J. Harris, M. O'Boyle, C. Warbrick, *Law of the European Convention on Human Rights,* (London: Butterworths, 1995) 402–6.

[76] In *Middlebrook Mushrooms Ltd. v T.G.W.U.* (n. 60 above) the issue did not arise because on the facts there was no inducement to breach contracts.

[77] Trade Union and Labour Relations (Consolidation) Act 1992, s. 220.

[78] Ibid., s. 224(3).

United States[79] and in Canada[80] restrictions on this kind of industrial action have usually been regarded as legitimate in order to prevent the spread of action to so-called 'neutrals'. Although there is some doubt whether the restrictions are in conformity with ILO Conventions on the Freedom of Association, it seems unlikely that United Kingdom courts would reach a different conclusion from those in North America.

4.5 Discriminatory Harassment

As indicated earlier, the forms of conduct which may constitute discriminatory harassment range across a spectrum from rape and physical assault at one end, to racist and sexist jokes, offensive symbols and displays, and disparaging remarks at the other. The test, as proposed in the draft EC directive (above), is whether the conduct 'has the purpose or effect of creating an intimidating, hostile, offensive, or disturbing environment'. A similar test has been applied by the United States Supreme Court. To establish a violation of Title VII of the Civil Rights Act an employee must show that 'the workplace is permeated with discriminatory intimidation, ridicule and insult that is sufficiently severe or pervasive to alter the conditions of the victim's employment and create an abusive working environment.'[81] In both the United Kingdom and the United States liability is imposed on the employer for harassment by an employee in the course of employment, although the precise requirements for that vicarious and personal liability differ in detail.

There are at least three justifications for this interference with freedom of expression. The first is that a hostile working environment undermines the aim of equality (ECHR, Article 14). A great deal of empirical evidence exists to show that many women and members of ethnic minorities suffer harassment at work.[82] The argument is that this harassment helps to maintain sexual and racial segregation of the workforce by intimidating and alienating women and ethnic minorities. Certain workplaces or certain types of work are thus shut off from them. Another justification is based on the right to private life (ECHR, Article 8). Unwanted sexual conduct or innuendoes, homophobic ridicules and taunts, and similar conduct, strips away the identity and dignity of the individual 'by unceremoniously dragging the private sphere of intimate personal relationships into the public arena of the workplace'.[83] A third, and related justification is that harassment subjects the individual to 'degrading treatment' (ECHR, Article 3). This is particularly pertinent to racial discrimination, although

---

[79] e.g. *Giboney v Empire Storage and Ice Co* 336 US 490, 69 S Ct 684 (1949); *NLRB v Retail Store Employees Union* 447 US 607 ;100 S Ct 2372 (1980).

[80] *Retail, Wholesale and Department Store Union, Local 580 v Dolphin Delivery* (1986) 3 DLR (4th) 174, S Ct Can.

[81] *Harris v Forklift Systems Inc.* 510 US 17 (1993).

[82] See, Hazel Houghton-Jones, *Sexual Harassment* (London: Cavendish Publishing,1995); Sandra Fredman, *Women and the Law* (Oxford: Clarendon Press, 1997) 320–30.

[83] Fredman (n. 82 above) 320.

not necessarily limited to this. The dominant view seems to be that Article 3 of the ECHR is applicable even to single instances of direct and indirect discrimination.[84]

The question, therefore, is whether a particular prohibition on discriminatory harassment in a specific manner and place is proportionate to the legitimate aims of equality, the protection of private life and the dignity of the individual. The problem for the law, as Cynthia Estlund points out,[85] is that, in the case of workplace harassment, the employer may seek to minimize the risk of liability and damages by very broad prohibitions on any offensive speech or conduct, imposing censorship and subjecting employees alleged to be harassers to disciplinary sanctions. These may be disproportionate, or go beyond the bounds of unlawful harassment. On the university campus, it may lead to the banning of allegedly 'racist' speakers or attempts to prevent the circulation of views which a majority find distasteful, offensive or just plain ridiculous. Concern about this silencing of unpopular views on the campus, led to the enactment of s. 43 of the Education (No. 2) Act 1986 which requires education authorities to 'take such steps as are reasonably practicable to ensure that freedom of speech within the law is secured for members, students and employees of the establishment and for visiting speakers'.[86]

The workplace is different from the university campus in many ways. First, employees are economically dependent upon their employer, making them 'unwilling listeners'[87] or a captive audience, vulnerable to reprisals by the employer if they do not comply. Students, on the other hand, generally have the ability to walk away from or dispute offensive speech or conduct. Secondly, freedom of expression is central to the purpose of universities and other educational institutions. This is reflected in the statutory duty to ensure that the use of any premises of an educational body is not denied to an individual on any ground 'connected with the beliefs or views of that individual or any member of that body' or 'the policy and objectives of that body'.[88]

The workplace, on the other hand is still largely a private sphere in which the employer is generally able to lay down rules for the efficient management of the enterprise. Despite attempts to encourage 'social dialogue' between management and workers and their unions, particularly through the recognition of trade unions and EC-wide requirements for information and consultation of workers' representatives,[89] the workplace, unlike the academy, is not a place of public discourse. One of the central issues of modern employment law is the widening of workplace democracy, but it is misleading to pretend that the workplace can simply replicate political

---

[84] Harris *et.al.*, (n. 75 above) 82.

[85] Estlund (n. 2 above) at 698.

[86] See B. Parekh and B. Hepple (eds.) *Racism and Freedom of Speech on the Campus* (London: C.R.E.,1988).

[87] Estlund (n. 2 above) 716.

[88] Education (No. 2) Act 1986, s. 43(3).

[89] See Deakin and Morris (n. 37 above) 775–818 on information and consultation; and the recent Employment Relations Act 1999, introducing a statutory right to union recognition.

democracy. The disruptive employee, who undermines the mutual trust and confidence which is essential to the contract of employment, can be fairly dismissed (unless exercising protected rights such as those under the Public Interest Disclosure Act 1998, or to trade union membership or non-membership). The politician or professor who expresses morally unacceptable beliefs cannot be so easily restricted.

These considerations indicate that interference with freedom of expression may be easier to justify in the workplace than in the public sphere, including that of the academy. In particular, in the workplace the social damage—in the form of racial and gender segregation and stereotyping—caused by discriminatory harassment may be a factor which overrides freedom of expression. In the public sphere far more latitude is necessary in a democratic society.

5. PROPOSALS FOR REFORM

The general conclusion is that most of the present forms of unlawful harassment can be justified as 'necessary in a democratic society'. Some question marks, however, hang over the extension of hate speech prohibitions, peaceful picketing and discriminatory harassment.

5.1 Hate Speech

The Stephen Lawrence Inquiry Report recommended that consideration be given 'to allow prosecution of offences involving racist language or behaviour . . . where such conduct can be proved to have taken place otherwise than in a public place'.[90] No reasons were given for this recommendation. It appears to be based on the evidence, obtained by covert police surveillance, presented to the inquiry of disgusting racist language and behaviour used by some of the murder suspects in their own homes. Despite the natural repulsion against this kind of behaviour the recommendation is seriously flawed. Since s. 18 of the Public Order Act already covers private places, the recommendation seems to be that dwellings should also fall within the law. This would involve a substantial inroad on the right to private life, and also property rights, and so might prove to be incompatible with the ECHR. In practice, s. 18 has rarely been invoked (the Attorney-General's consent is needed) and it has been even rarer for prosecutions to succeed. Offences against harassment (which may be racially aggravated) are far more likely to result in the punishment of racists.

5.2 Peaceful Picketing

Section 241 of the Trade Union and Labour Relations (Consolidation) Act 1992

---

[90] Report of an Inquiry by Sir William MacPherson of Cluny, Cm. 4262–I (1999) 331, recommendation No. 39.

needs to be amended so as to make it clear that an act is not 'wrongful and without legal authority' if it is done in contemplation or furtherance of a trade dispute. This would have the effect of excluding this criminal offence in respect of picketing *per se*. Picketing could still be effectively controlled, from the point of view of public order, by the use of police powers.

The immunity from civil liability granted by s. 220 of the same Act, should be extended to consumer picketing. This would make the presence of pickets lawful (i.e. not a trespass to the highway, or harassment) provided it was confined to peacefully communicating or receiving information or persuading another to provide or not to provide or to purchase or not to purchase goods, facilities or services. This immunity should not be limited to trade disputes. This would have the effect of protecting freedom of expression through lawful demonstration. Mass picketing and violent picketing would remain unlawful.

5.3 Discriminatory Harassment

This civil wrong should be confined to the workplace, leaving other forms of harassment to be dealt with under the Protection from Harassment Act 1997, and special legislation such as that relating to the harassment of tenants. The enactment of employment-specific legislation would recognize the inequality of the employment relationship in which the (usually male white) manager is able to exert power over the (black or female) employee through harassing conduct.

One option would be to enact a statutory 'non-harassment' clause as a mandatory term of every contract of employment (like the equality clause for equal pay). This might be regarded as an example of the more general contractual duty of co-operation or mutual trust and confidence. The drawback is that this would not protect workseekers. Harassment and bullying should therefore be made a statutory employment tort either on a stand-alone basis or in combination with a contractual clause.

The major difference between the Protection from Harassment Act and the specific employment tort would be the wider definition of harassment and bullying in the workplace. In line with the EC draft directive and Code of Practice, the elements of the wrong would be:

(1) the act or other conduct is unwelcome to the person towards whom it is directed;
(2) it could reasonably be regarded as creating an intimidating, hostile, offensive or disturbing environment; and
(3) the victim has suffered or is likely to suffer some harm whether physical, psychological or emotional.

It may be objected that this last requirement is too restrictive of the class of people who can sue, but this is a tort or breach of contract which should not be actionable without an identifiable victim if freedom of discourse is to be maintained without unnecessary constraint. So far as tortious or contractual liability is concerned, the line should be drawn between those expressions which cause harm to individuals and those which do not. This does not preclude a wider obligation on employers to maintain a workplace which respects the dignity, privacy and right to equality of those who work there, that is to take active steps to prevent a hostile working environment. But this would be a public law duty spelt out in codes of practice, collective and workforce agreements, and monitored by trade unions and other representatives and the equality commissions, rather than an enforceable individual right.

It is a matter for consideration whether it should be necessary for the victim to prove that the unlawful harassment and bullying was on one or more of the prohibited grounds such as race, gender, religion, disability, sexual orientation etc., or whether (as in racially aggravated offences) these grounds should simply be a factor which would result in an award of aggravated damages. The argument for a general wrong of bullying and harassment is that it would avoid the need to prove the motivation of the harasser: the consequences of the harassment would be decisive. This would be an inclusive approach, protecting all employees (as Lord Monkswell's Bill proposed in 1996), but would recognize the special harm caused by harassment on the impermissible grounds.

11

Shoreham-by-Sea

LORD COOKE OF THORNDON

R v Chief Constable of Sussex, ex p International Trader's Ferry Ltd.[1] arose from an application for judicial review to quash the decision of the Chief Constable of Sussex to restrict special police protection for the applicant exporter's lorries at the port of Shoreham, against the activities of animal rights protesters, to two days a week or four a fortnight. The effect of his policy was to prevent the export of live calves to France from Shoreham except on those days. The application succeeded in the Divisional Court[2] on the ground of transgression by the Chief Constable of the principle of the free movement of goods, which is a fundamental principle of the EC Treaty. The Divisional Court decision was reversed by the Court of Appeal,[3] and the House of Lords affirmed the Court of Appeal.

In its earlier stages the case attracted some academic attention, because of its constitutional importance; in his speech Lord Slynn of Hadley referred[4] to 'a valuable analysis' by Catherine Barnard and Ivan Hare in the *Modern Law Review*.[5] I have not noticed, however, any academic commentary on the House of Lords decision, apart from some brief references. If in fact there has been little or none, the absence of a bark from the dog in the night may conceivably evidence a consensus that the ruling of the House reflects the opinion of rightthinking academic lawyers generally. Should that be so, one would not wish to disturb such an agreeable position; but there are points generated by the Shoreham case which may merit some discussion—even perforce with a brevity which may not seem to match the importance of some of them. In the light of the current vogue for festschrifts, however, brevity is not a vice.

The case has been destined for attention in the present festschrift since 9 June 1998, being its first day of argument in the House of Lords. The report in the Appeal Cases records the submission of P.M. Roth QC for the appellant company[6] that 'A person's right to do a lawful act cannot be diminished by another's threat to commit an unlawful act'. Naturally the list of authorities recorded as cited by counsel for this proposition begins with *Beatty v Gillbanks*.[7] It ends in the report with a reference[8] to 'Williams *The Law and Public Protest*'. This is an abbreviated version of what

---

[1]   [1999] 2 AC 418, [1999] 1 All ER 129.
[2]   [1996] QB 197, [1995] 4 All ER 364, Balcombe LJ and Popplewell J.
[3]   [1998] QB 477; [1997] 2 All ER 65, Kennedy, Millett and Swinton Thomas LJJ.
[4]   [1999] 2 AC at 434.   [5]   (1997) 60 MLR 394.
[6]   [1999] 2 AC at 421–2.   [7]   (1882) 9 QBD 308.
[8]   Cambridge-Tilburg Law Lectures, 1st series (1978) 27–39. A misspelling of the name of the lectures in the report has been corrected here.

counsel actually put, which was 'No less an authority than Sir David Williams has said that nearly a hundred years later *Beatty v Gillbanks* can still be regarded as one of the most important decisions ever made by an English court in the search for a balance between the competing demands of public order and individual rights.'

That way of introducing the quotation from Sir David was music to the ears of at least one of the recipient members of the Appellate Committee, although there is no reason to accuse Peter Roth of any knowledge of a particular friendship. Nor is there any obvious career link between Roth (St. Paul's School; New College, Oxford; Middle Temple) and Williams (Queen Elizabeth Grammar School; Emmanuel and Wolfson Colleges, Cambridge; Lincoln's Inn; earlier Nottingham University and Keble College, Oxford). Moreover the age gap is considerable. I think that the straightforward explanation must be the right one. Counsel was doing no more than reflecting truly the reputation that David Williams has gained as one of the most eminent writers since Dicey on civil liberties in English law—and, indeed, as more balanced in his views than Dicey chose to be. It may be suspected that Dicey was sometimes simplistic for the sake of emphasis. (Since the conference Roth QC has confirmed that he and Williams QC have never met.)

If *The Law and Public Protest*, like the other cases and writings cited for the company, was not enough to achieve allowance of the appeal in the Shoreham case, it nevertheless remains a valuable contribution to the field and is an excellent example of the work of David Williams. This is chiefly because of its balance and comprehensiveness. Its author recognized twenty-two years ago that there are limits to the principle in *Beatty v Gillbanks*, observing[9] prophetically that 'there are circumstances in which lawful activities may have to be restricted if other means of maintaining the peace are beyond the capacity of the police'. Insert 'financial' before 'capacity' and you have the Shoreham decision in a nutshell. He referred to statutory powers to regulate or ban processions, and acknowledged[10] that even at common law (partly because of the flexibility of the law of binding over to keep the peace) 'the courts are in practice rarely troubled by the direct application of *Beatty v Gillbanks*'. His most important point was and is that *Beatty v Gillbanks* continues to operate as a guideline to the police: it 'does genuinely reflect the attitude of a society and of its organised political forces'.[11]

The essay has one rather teasing feature. The Divisional Court which decided *Beatty v Gillbanks* consisted of Field and Cave JJ. The latter is recorded in the Queen's Bench Division report as simply concurring with the former. But the essay quotes[12] Cave J as saying: 'Am I forced to stay within doors because I know that a man intends to knock me down if I go out? And, if I do go out, am I guilty of provoking a breach of the peace?' That is a much easier question than the one which in fact arose in the case, for it omits any reference to joining in collective demonstrations. But no such observation is attributed to Cave J. in the only law report cited

---

[9] Note 8 above at p.32.   [10] ibid.   [11] ibid. at p.39.
[12] ibid. at p.29.

in the essay (9 QBD 308). Similarly the essay quotes[13] Field J as speaking of the 'lawful and laudable' activities of the Salvation Army; whereas that report contains no such commendatory phrase. It may be that the quotations are taken from a collateral or newspaper report and that this is apparent from other writings of the author—a thesis which I am unable to verify, writing as I do in a part of New Zealand free from law books. All this, however, may fairly be dismissed as a quibble.

Perhaps less of a quibble, but still not a criticism (since it deals with a matter not within the scope of the essay) is the following suggestion. *Beatty v Gillbanks* may have been wrongly decided and would have been better not reported; for, although the principle for which the case stands—that a person cannot be held to act unlawfully merely because his or her lawful conduct causes another to act unlawfully—is, in general, sound to the point of being obvious, it may not truly have answered the issue in that case.

Beatty v Gillbanks was a case stated by local justices on questions of law. The case stated is set out fully in the official report. The second main finding of fact made by the Weston-super-Mare justices was this:[14]

(b) These processions are formed at the hall of the Salvation Army, and after their formation proceed, headed by a musical band and flags and banners, through the aforesaid streets and places, collecting, *and for the purpose of collecting as they go*, a mob of persons with whom, attended by much shouting, singing, uproar and noise, they eventually return to the said hall, where a meeting is held.

I have supplied the italics. The case stated went on to mention the opposing organized band of persons, the Skeleton Army, and to make clear again that there was a mob in the habit of assembling in front of the Salvation Army in great numbers; some of whom, together with the Skeleton Army, assembled to dispute the passage of the Salvation Army through the streets, *some to encourage such passage*, with shouting, uproar and noise, to the great terror, disturbance, annoyance and inconvenience of the peaceable inhabitants of the town, and the endangering of the public peace.

In face of those findings the Salvation Army leaders may have been a little fortunate to avoid an inference that the disturbance of the peace was a natural consequence of their acts. Field J held[15] that 'the evidence set forth in the case does not support this contention; on the contrary it shews that the disturbances were caused by other people antagonistic to the appellants, and that no acts of violence were committed by them'. Conceivably the Divisional Court had access to some record or note of evidence not part of the case stated itself, but the judge did not say so; and on the findings of the justices some element of intentional provocation may well have been present.

At the beginning of the present millennium there might seem to be no profit in speculating on whether a case in the Divisional Court in the Victorian era was

[13] ibid.   [14] 9 QBD at 309.   [15] ibid. at 314.

correctly decided on its facts. Unfortunately, though, the problem presented by the facts of *Beatty v Gillbanks* is fairly typical and persistent. Assemblies, demonstrations and processions are as popular (to their organizers) modes of promoting causes as ever they were. Many of the participants are sincere believers in the cause in question, however controversial. Indeed, the existence of controversy is commonly the very *raison d'être* of the collective action. Yet, while the prevailing actuating motives may be innocent in the foregoing sense, that action almost inevitably hovers on the fringe of legality. The purpose of advertising (opponents might say flaunting) one's own allegiance, and converting others to it, can so easily be accompanied by a wish to denigrate adversary groups. The line between entirely inoffensive collective conduct and provocation may be fine. Who reads of another forthcoming sectarian march in Northern Ireland without a sense of foreboding?

In a democracy the rights of assembly, demonstration, procession and free speech are so valued that, save perhaps in the most extreme emergencies, anything in the nature of a total ban is anathema. It is not to be contemplated by the common law; and, as Sir David Williams stressed in his essay, the police normally exercise their statutory powers of control under the Public Order Act or otherwise with sensitivity and experienced discretion. To return to the example of Northern Ireland, I have no first-hand knowledge of the great, and apparently almost intractable, problems there. One must await with an open mind the findings of Lord Saville of Newdigate, Sir Edward Somers[16] and Chief Justice William Hoyt—as impartial a tribunal as one can imagine—in their inquiry into the events of Bloody Sunday 1972. It is dismaying, however, to read of statements from one quarter implying that the United Kingdom government can somehow ensure the findings it wants. But the point I am trying to make goes further than the issue of blame for some tragic killings. It is that the ultimate cause can be seen as a march which, illegality aside, may have been inherently a cause of trouble. Next to a resolution of the issue of the handing over of arms, it might be thought that the best evidence of genuine commitment to the peace process would be a *voluntary* abandonment by both sides of marches which, albeit often cherished as traditional, are all too likely to be in some degree inflammatory of conflicting opinions.

In practice the law in this area has to leave much to voluntary common sense or, when that does not operate, to findings as to the character of conduct which are addressed to the particular facts. This has been further illustrated since the Shoreham case by another decision of the House of Lords, *DPP v Jones*.[16a] *Jones* was decided in March 1999, *R v Chief Constable of Sussex* in November 1998, and there is no reference to the earlier case in the speeches in *Jones*. That is not surprising. Although in the same area of civil liberties, the two cases raise largely distinct issues. In the Shoreham case there was no doubt that, apart possibly from a few instances of retaliatory hostile reactions by lorry drivers, the company was carrying on a lawful trade; nor any doubt that by attempting to block the passage of the lorries and even on occasions to damage them (as by cutting brake cables) lawless elements among the

---

[16] Sadly, he has since resigned.   [16a] [1999] 2 All ER 257.

protesters were acting by no means peaceably. In *Jones*, on the other hand, protesters against the closure of Stonehenge to the public gathered on a highway verge near the monument carrying banners ('Never again', 'Stonehenge Campaign 10 years of Criminal Injustice', 'Free Stonehenge')[17] but without obstructing the highway, causing a nuisance or otherwise breaking the law—unless, as alleged by the prosecution, they were in breach of an order prohibiting trespassory assemblies in the vicinity of Stonehenge, made by the local council under the Public Order Act 1986 as amended in 1994. The Salisbury justices convicted the defendants, taking the view that such an assembly was not a lawful use of the highway and was therefore within the scope of the order. The Salisbury Crown Court (Judge MacLaren Webster QC and two justices) allowed an appeal, holding that there was not even a case to answer. In turn the Divisional Court (McCowan LJ and Collins J) allowed the prosecution's appeal, holding as had the original justices. In turn the House of Lords, by a majority of three (Lord Irvine of Lairg LC, Lord Clyde and Lord Hutton) to two (Lord Slynn of Hadley and Lord Hope) in effect approved the Crown Court's understanding of the law; so in the event the alleged trespassers won.

Apart from being an almost exquisite example of the uncertainty of the law in an elementary field, the main interest of *DPP v Jones* is that it establishes that the legitimate use of the highway is not confined to passing and repassing and activities incidental thereto. Provided that no obstruction or public nuisance is caused, and subject to statutory provision to the contrary, a peaceable assembly may be found to be a reasonable and therefore lawful use. If one may borrow the epithet attributed to Field J this is a salutary (and conscious) development of the common law, avowedly influenced (see especially the speech of the Lord Chancellor) by current conceptions of human rights. But it adds more fine lines.

As the reasoning in *DPP v Jones* would appear to extend to processions, the principle of *Beatty v Gillbanks* remains sound law, even if that case was a dubious application of the principle. It is *R v Chief Constable of Sussex* that has a greater potential impact on the principle. For the Shoreham case dispels any illusion that even a wholly innocent and lawful user of a highway has an absolute right to police protection against unlawful disturbance. Everything is relative: it is a matter of cost. Weston-super-Mare is not a large town. The population today is of the order of 70,000 or so and in 1882 was presumably much less. David Williams tells us in his essay that the clash which led the magistrates to issue a proclamation forbidding assemblies to the disturbance of the public peace in the public streets involved some 2,000 people. It is easy to imagine that the magistrates may not have had at their disposal a constabulary adequate to cope with disorder on such a scale. Although the Shoreham case did not decide that a lorry driver who disobeyed a police officer's

---

[17] Whereas the two latter legends were site specific, the first made the banner much more versatile. I am reminded of the sister of a colleague in New Zealand. A member of a religious order, she found it right from time to time to take part in public protests in support of any of a range of causes. These tended to multiply. In the interests of economy of preparation, she had a placard reading simply 'Shame!'.

instruction to turn back would have been guilty of obstructing the officer in the execution of his duty,[18] it may be difficult to resist that inference. Lord Slynn cites[19] a passage by Professor David Feldman which seems to support that view. If so, would not the Salvation Army marchers have faced a similar risk, notwithstanding Dicey's assertions[20] of the inefficacy of proclamations by officials?

Per contra there is an apparent implication of the Shoreham case from which civil libertarians may take satisfaction. This is that, at least upon application, the police owe to affected members of the public an enforceable legal duty (even possibly with the risk of damages[21]) to do what they reasonably can to protect lawful activities against unlawful interference of which they know or ought to know. The principle may not be limited to the free movement of goods. No judge held in the Shoreham case that the decision of the Chief Constable as to what police resources he was prepared to commit was simply nonjusticiable. On the contrary it may be at least implicit in the approach of the three courts throughout that case that the legality of his policy depended on its reasonableness.[22] What degree of judicial review the test of reasonableness here involves is a question with a European law dimension on which I abstain from embarking now.[23] The point is that there is such a test; and in the Shoreham case the review was quite intense.

A concluding reflection is that in this tract of common law the hard questions are once again, as in many other fields, not being answered by hard-and-fast rules. A use of the highway, as for an assembly or a procession, is lawful if in all the circumstances it is reasonable. A Chief Constable's decision on the extent of policing is lawful if in all the circumstances it is reasonable. As so often, it all reduces to a question of fact and degree. It might be thought that, taken together, *Beatty v Gillbanks* and the two recent House of Lords cases have settled the governing principles, or very largely so. But such is the difficulty and fascination of this branch of the law of civil liberties, and such the variety of facts, that academic lawyers may be expected to be still writing articles on the subject for the next hundred years and more. The contribution of David Williams in 1978 will still be a standard reference.

ADDENDA

Two readers have not seen my commitment to brevity as inhibiting them from suggesting additions. Naturally grateful, I respond as follows.

1. My brief paper mentions other writings of David Williams. It transpires that,

[18] See [1999] 2 AC at 435 per Lord Slynn and at 444 per Lord Hoffmann.
[19] ibid. at 435.
[20] See Williams (note 8 above) at 29.
[21] See [1999] 2 AC at 429 per Lord Slynn.
[22] That is not to say that the European Court of Justice will have jurisdiction to review the validity or proportionality of *all* police operations within a member state: see [1999] 1 AC at 450.
[23] The forthcoming festschrift for Lord Slynn, edited by Mads Andenas and to be published by Kluwer, is an appropriate context in which I attempt this subject.

some six years after the article cited to the House of Lords in the Shoreham case, he returned to the theme in 'The Principle of *Beatty v Gillbanks*: A Reappraisal', a contribution to a Canadian festschrift in honour of John LL. J. Edwards[24]. This is in effect a scholarly monograph on the case, with much information about the history of the Salvation Army, the temperance movement, the persons involved in the case (for example 'Captain' William Beatty or Beaty, evidently a leader of 'combative teetotalism' in Weston) and the judges and counsel. There is a remarkable range of sources, among which *The Western Mercury and Somersetshire Herald* of 1882 figures prominently. For those who seek a resumé of the case law and statutory provisions relevant to *Beatty v Gillbanks* up to 1985, this compendium must be essential reading. It is surely one of the author's finest pieces of research.

2. A recent Divisional Court decision including a review of *Beatty v Gillbanks* and cases old and comparatively new in that field is *Redmond-Bate v DPP*.[25] The appellant was one of a group of three women Christian fundamentalists who preached their religious beliefs from the steps of Wakefield Cathedral. Eventually they attracted a crowd of more than a hundred, some of whom were showing hostility. Fearing that the preaching might provoke violence, a police constable asked them to stop and on their refusal arrested them. The appellant was convicted by justices of obstructing a police officer in the execution of his duty. The conviction was affirmed in the Crown Court but quashed by the Divisional Court on a case stated on questions of law. On the facts the Divisional Court considered that, in the situation as perceived and recounted by him, the constable was not justified in apprehending a breach of the peace, much less a breach of the peace for which the three women would be responsible.

This is yet another possibly difficult case, nominally raising questions of law, but disposed of on the particular facts by a Divisional Court's view as to reasonableness. Nevertheless, some gloss may be added to the relevant law by Sedley LJ's formulation:[26]

It is only if otherwise lawful conduct gives rise to a reasonable apprehension that it will, by interfering with the rights or liberties of others, provoke violence which, though unlawful, would not be entirely unreasonable that a constable is empowered to take steps to prevent it.

Whether that formulation will survive the test of time remains to be seen. On a more rhetorical plane, however, survival is assured for Sedley LJ's memorable dictum:[27]

Free speech includes not only the inoffensive but the irritating, the contentious, the eccentric, the heretical, the unwelcome and the provocative provided it does not tend to provoke violence. Freedom only to speak inoffensively is not worth having.

I beg leave to close this brief incursion into the field with that ringing quotation.

---

[24] *Perspectives in Criminal Law* (Ontario: Canada Law Book Inc., 1985) 105.
[25] (1999) 7 BHRC 375, Sedley LJ and Collins J.
[26] ibid. 381.
[27] ibid. 382–3.

12

Freedom of Expression in the EU Legal Order and in EU Relations with Third Countries

DERRICK WYATT QC

1. INTRODUCTION

The process by which freedom of expression has entered the legal order of the European Union[1] and emerged as a value protected by the Union in its relations with third countries has been gradual, and explanation of the process as well as the result seems appropriate. The first stage in the process was the recognition by the Court of Justice of the European Communities of general principles of law binding upon the Community institutions in the performance of their tasks under the Treaties. A further stage was recognition that those general principles included human rights, as evidenced in particular by the European Court of Human Rights. The Court's case-law held that such principles were binding upon not only the Community institutions in the performance of their tasks under the Treaties, but also upon the Member States, when the latter implemented their Treaty obligations, and when they sought to rely upon express or implied derogations from the free movement provisions of the EC Treaty. Once an even indirect and evidentiary role for the European Convention on Human Rights was established, it was inevitable that freedom of expression would find its place in the legal order of the Community system, since Article 10 of the European Convention guaranteed freedom of expression. Freedom of expression was thus a general principle to be respected by the Community institutions and the Member States when they acted pursuant to Community obligations and in accordance with competences derived from Community law. Since the Community system from the outset bestowed extensive competences on the Community institutions as regards relations with third countries, it was also to be expected that the protection of human rights would find a place in the international trade relations of the Community. This was indeed to be the case, and provisions of the Treaties relating to Development Co-operation and the Common Foreign and Security Policy were in due course to incorporate references to human rights and fundamental freedoms and thereby, implicitly, to respect for freedom of expression.

---

[1] Much of the present paper is, strictly speaking, concerned with the legal order of the European Community, but in accordance with contemporary usage the present writer will refer to the law of the European Union when the generality of the context makes this appropriate.

2. GENERAL PRINCIPLES OF LAW AND HUMAN RIGHTS IN THE LEGAL ORDER OF THE
EUROPEAN UNION

2.1 General Principles

The EC Treaty has from the outset expressly laid down certain general legal principles, such as the duty of co-operation which binds both Member States and the Institutions in ensuring fulfilment of the obligations arising from the Treaty;[2] and the principle of non-discrimination on grounds of nationality.[3] Some general principles, such as proportionality, equality, and legitimate expectation, are wholly or mainly[4] the product of judicial development, though the principle of proportionality is now expressly recognized in the Treaty as a constitutional principle of the Community legal order. Fundamental rights travelled a similar road to proportionality; first recognized by the Court's case law, then endorsed by declarations of the Institutions, and finally written into the fundamental law of the European Union. General principles such as these have important legal effects. They place limits on the administrative and legislative competence of the Community institutions, and they govern the interpretation of provisions of Community law.[5]

The Court can hardly be said to have exceeded its jurisdiction by its recourse to the general principles of law. No Treaty regime, let alone the 'new legal order' of the Community, could be interpreted and applied in a legal vacuum. International tribunals have long been regarded as competent to draw upon the general principles of municipal law as a source of international law,[6] and the competence of the Court of Justice in the interpretation and application of Community law could surely have been intended to be no less. The Treaty might be said to imply as much. Article 220 EC (ex 164) provides that: 'The Court of Justice shall ensure that in the interpretation and application of this Treaty the law is observed.' While this formulation implies commitment to the rule of law, it has been argued that this implies a *corpus juris* outwith the express Treaty texts.[7] Other provisions are consistent with the proposition that the general principles of law constitute a source of Community law. Article 230 EC (ex 173) includes among the grounds of invalidity of Community

---

[2] Article 10 EC (ex 5).

[3] Article 12 EC (ex 6).

[4] The principle of proportionality was always recognized expressly in the Treaty in certain specific contexts, see e.g., Article 40(3) EC; now Article 34(2) (in the context of the common agricultural policy); the latter provision also provided that common organizations of the agricultural markets 'shall exclude any discrimination between producers or consumers within the Community'.

[5] Case 316/86 *Hauptzollamt Hamburg-Jonas v Krucken* [1988] ECR 2213, para. 22; Joined Cases 201 and 202/85 *Klensch* [1986] ECR 3466, para. 10; Joined Cases C-90/90 and C-91/90 *Neu and Others v Secrétaire d'état à l'Agriculture* [1991] ECR I-3617, para. 12.

[6] See Wyatt, 'New legal Order, or Old?' (1982) 7 ELRev 147 at 157. cf. Article 38 of the Statute of the International Court of Justice, which lists as a source of international law, 'the general principles of law recognized by civilized nations'.

[7] See Pescatore, 'Fundamental Rights and Freedoms in the System of the European Communities' [1970] AJIL 343 at 348.

acts infringement of 'any rule of law' relating to the Treaty's application, an expression wide enough to encompass the principles under consideration. Furthermore, Article 288(2) EC (ex 215(2)) provides that the non-contractual liability of the Community shall be determined 'in accordance with the general principles common to the laws of the Member States', which amounts to express recognition of the role of the general principles of Community law. In the sections of this chapter which follow, particular principles will be examined.

2.2 Human Rights and Fundamental Freedoms

Unlike the abortive Treaty for the establishment of a European Political Community, which provided explicitly for the application of Section I of the European Convention on Human Rights,[8] the EEC Treaty made no provision for the protection of human rights as such. Nevertheless, the Court of Justice soon made it clear that fundamental rights were implicitly recognized by Community law, and that they were capable of limiting the competence of the Community. Thus in *Stauder v City of Ulm*[9] the Court was asked by a German court whether a Commission Decision which conditioned the distribution of butter at reduced prices on the disclosure of the name of the recipient was compatible 'with the general principles of Community law in force'. The Court replied that on its true construction the Decision in question did not require the disclosure of the names of beneficiaries to retailers, and added that: 'Interpreted in this way the provision at issue contains nothing capable of prejudicing the fundamental rights . . . protected by the Court.'[10] The existence of fundamental rights as general principles of Community law was confirmed in the *Internationale Handelsgesellschaft* case, in which the Court stated:

In fact, respect for fundamental rights forms an integral part of the general principles of law protected by the Court of Justice. The protection of such rights, whilst inspired by the constitutional traditions common to the Member States, must be ensured within the framework of the structure and objectives of the Community.[11]

If *Stauder* confirmed the existence of fundamental rights in Community law, and *Internationale Handelsgesellschaft* identified their primary source as the national constitutional traditions of the Member States, *Nold v Commission* introduced a further source which was to prove of crucial importance: 'international treaties for the protection of human rights on which the Member States have collaborated or of which they are signatories'.[12] It was always clear that of the treaties referred to the European Convention on Human Rights was of special significance in this respect, and the Court has said as much in a consistent case-law.[13]

---

[8] One of the initiatives which predated the EEC Treaty but which failed to secure the support of all potential signatories.　　　　　　　　　　　　　　　　　[9] Case 29/69 [1969] ECR 419.
[10] ibid., para. 7.　　　　　　　　　　　　　　　[11] Case 11/70 [1970] ECR 1125 at para. 4.
[12] Case 4/73 [1974] ECR 491, para. 13.
[13] Case 222/84 *Johnston v Royal Ulster Constabulary* [1986] ECR 1651, para. 18; Case C-260/89

The Court's case law was endorsed by the Parliament, the Council and the Commission in their Joint Declaration of 5 April 1977.[14] Treaty endorsement came later. Article F(2) of the Treaty on European Union provided that the Union shall respect fundamental rights, as guaranteed by the European Convention and as they result from the constitutional traditions common to the Member States, as general principles of Community law. The latter provision appeared in Title I of the Union Treaty and under Article L it therefore did not fall within the jurisdiction of the Court of Justice. The Amsterdam amendments to the Treaty on European Union came into effect on 1 May 1999. Article 6(2) is in identical terms to Article F(2). In addition Article 46, which replaces Article L, provides that the Court's jurisdiction extends to 'Article 6(2) with regard to action of the institutions, insofar as the Court has jurisdiction under the Treaties establishing the European Communities and under this Treaty.'

The Court has referred to specific provisions of the European Convention on Human Rights (or its First Protocol) in a number of judgments. In *Hauer*[15] the Court held that the right to property is guaranteed in the Community legal order in accordance with the ideas common to the constitutions of the Member States, which are reflected in the First Protocol to the European Convention on Human Rights. However, the Court upheld a Community imposed restriction on the planting of vines as constituting a legitimate exception to the principle of a type recognized in the constitutional systems of the Member States.[16] The Court has denied that a guarantee afforded to the ownership of property can be extended to protect commercial interests, the uncertainties of which are part of the very essence of economic activity.[17] In *National Panasonic*[18] the Court relied upon an exception to the guarantee of respect for private and family life to be found in Article 8 of the European Convention on Human rights, in considering the scope of the investigative powers of the Commission under Regulation 17. In *Dow Benelux* the Court held that Article 8 of the Convention applied in Community law to protect the private dwellings of natural persons rather than the premises of undertakings. Nevertheless, investigative powers of the Commission were subject to the principle of proportionality.[19] In *Kirk* the Court, referring to Article 7 of the European Convention, which states that penal provisions shall not have retroactive effect, held that the retroactivity of a Community regulation could not have the effect of validating after the event national

---

Elliniki Radiophonia Tiléorassi AE (ERT) v Dimotiki Etairia Pliroforissis and others [1991] ECR I-2925, para. 41; Opinion 2/94 [1996] ECR I-1759, para. 33; Case C-299/95 *Kremzow v Austria* [1997] ECR I-2629, para. 14.

[14] [1997] OJ C 103/1.
[15] Case 44/79 [1979] ECR 3727.
[16] [1979] ECR 3727 at 3747.
[17] Case 4/73 *Nold* [1974] ECR 491; Joined Cases 154, etc./78, and 39, etc./79 *Valsabbia* [1980] ECR 907.
[18] Case 136/79 [1980] ECR 2033 at 2057.
[19] Case 85/87 [1989] ECR 3137 at paras. 28–30.

measures of a penal nature which imposed penalties for an act which was not punishable at the time it was committed.[20]

It is by this route that freedom of expression takes its place as a general principle of law, binding upon both the Community institutions, and the Member States, in all those circumstances in which they implement Community obligations, or exercise competences defined by Community law, for freedom of expression is guaranteed by Article 10 of the European Convention on Human Rights, as follows:

1. Everyone has the right to freedom of expression. This right shall include freedom to hold opinions and to receive and impart information and ideas without interference by public authority and regardless of frontiers. This article shall not prevent States from requiring the licensing of broadcasting, television or cinema enterprises.
2 . The exercise of these freedoms, since it carries with it duties and responsibilities, may be subject to such formalities, conditions, restrictions or penalties as are prescribed by law and are necessary in a democratic society, in the interests of national security, territorial integrity or public safety, for the prevention of disorder or crime, for the protection of health or morals, for the protection of the reputation or rights of others, for preventing the disclosure of information received in confidence, or for maintaining the authority and impartiality of the judiciary.

3. FREEDOM OF EXPRESSION AS A GENERAL PRINCIPLE WHICH BINDS THE MEMBER
STATES IN THE IMPLEMENTATION OF THEIR TREATY OBLIGATIONS

In the *Elliniki Radiophonia Tiléorassi* case[21], the questions referred to the European Court by the national court sought, inter alia, to ascertain whether a television monopoly held by a single company to which a Member State has granted exclusive rights for that purpose was consistent with the provisions of the Treaty guaranteeing the freedom to provide services between Member States and the right to freedom of expression guaranteed by Article 10 of the European Convention on Human Rights. The Court of Justice noted that the Treaty did not prohibit national measures which impeded the freedom to provide services provided that such measures could be justified on grounds of public policy, public security or public health, but emphasized that, in defining the scope left to Member States to derogate from the Treaty provisions on the freedom to provide services, account must be taken of the right to freedom of expression as a general principle of law. The Court stated:

41. With regard to Article 10 of the European Convention on Human Rights, referred to in the ninth and tenth questions, it must first be pointed out that, as the Court has consistently held, fundamental rights form an integral part of the general principles of law, the observance of which it ensures. For that purpose the Court draws inspiration from the constitutional traditions common to the Member States and from the guidelines supplied by international

---

[20]   Case 63/83 [1984] ECR 2689 at 2718.
[21]   Case C-260/89 *Elliniki Radiophonia Tiléorassi AE v Dimotiki Etairia Pliroforissis* [1991] ECR I-2925.

treaties for the protection of human rights on which the Member States have collaborated or of which they are signatories (see, in particular, the judgment in Case C-4/73 *Nold v Commission* [1974] ECR 491, paragraph 13). The European Convention on Human Rights has special significance in that respect (see in particular Case C-222/84 *Johnston v Chief Constable of the Royal Ulster Constabulary* [1986] ECR 1651, paragraph 18). It follows that, as the Court held in its judgment in Case C-5/88 *Wachauf v Federal Republic of Germany* [1989] ECR 2609, paragraph 19, the Community cannot accept measures which are incompatible with observance of the human rights thus recognized and guaranteed.

42. As the Court has held (see the judgment in Joined Cases C-60 and C-61/84 *Cinéthèque v Fédération Nationale des Cinémas Français* [1985] ECR 2605, paragraph 25, and the judgment in Case C-12/86 *Demirel v Stadt Schwaebisch Gmund* [1987] ECR 3719, paragraph 28), it has no power to examine the compatibility with the European Convention on Human Rights of national rules which do not fall within the scope of Community law. On the other hand, where such rules do fall within the scope of Community law, and reference is made to the Court for a preliminary ruling, it must provide all the criteria of interpretation needed by the national court to determine whether those rules are compatible with the fundamental rights the observance of which the Court ensures and which derive in particular from the European Convention on Human Rights.

43. In particular, where a Member State relies on the combined provisions of Articles 56 and 66 in order to justify rules which are likely to obstruct the exercise of the freedom to provide services, such justification, provided for by Community law, must be interpreted in the light of the general principles of law and in particular of fundamental rights. Thus the national rules in question can fall under the exceptions provided for by the combined provisions of Articles 56 and 66 only if they are compatible with the fundamental rights the observance of which is ensured by the Court.

44. It follows that in such a case it is for the national court, and if necessary, the Court of Justice to appraise the application of those provisions having regard to all the rules of Community law, including freedom of expression, as embodied in Article 10 of the European Convention on Human Rights, as a general principle of law the observance of which is ensured by the Court.

Defining the scope of express or implied exceptions to the provisions of the Treaty on the free movement of goods persons or services, in light of freedom of expression as a general principle of law, may face a national court with a complex and difficult task, as the *Familiapress* case[22] indicates. The national proceedings concerned the circulation in Austria of the weekly magazine 'Laura', which was published in Germany, and which contained crossword puzzles which gave readers a chance of winning prizes, which was contrary to the Austrian Law on Unfair Competition. The national court referred to the Court of Justice a question designed to establish whether Article 28 EC (ex 30) precluded 'application of legislation of Member State A prohibiting an undertaking established in Member State B from selling in Member State A a periodical produced in Member State B, where that periodical contains prize puzzle competitions or games which are lawfully organized in Member State B?'

---

[22] Case C-368/95 *Vereinigte Familiapress Zeitungsverlags- und vertriebs GmbH v Heinrich Bauer Verlag.* [1997] ECR I-3689.

The Court held that national rules such as those in issue in the proceedings before the referring court constituted in principle a measure having equivalent effect to a quantitative restriction within the meaning of Article 30 EC (now 28), but noted that the Austrian Government and the Commission had argued that the aim of the national legislation in question was to maintain press diversity, which was capable of constituting an overriding requirement in the general interest which might justify restrictions on the free movement of goods. The Austrian Government and the Commission also pointed to the very high degree of concentration of the press in Austria. The Austrian Government states that in the early 1990s the market share of the largest press group was 54.5% in Austria, as compared with only 34.7% in the United Kingdom and 23.9% in Germany. The Court stated:

18. Maintenance of press diversity may constitute an overriding requirement justifying a restriction on free movement of goods. Such diversity helps to safeguard freedom of expression, as protected by Article 10 of the European Convention on Human Rights and Fundamental Freedoms, which is one of the fundamental rights guaranteed by the Community legal order (see Case C-353/89 *Commission* v *Netherlands* [1991] ECR I-4069, paragraph 30, and Case C-148/91 *Vereiniging Veronica Omroep Organisatie v Commissariaat voor de Media* [1993] ECR I-487, paragraph 10).

26. A prohibition on selling publications which offer the chance to take part in prize games competitions may detract from freedom of expression. Article 10 of the European Convention for the Protection of Human Rights and Fundamental Freedoms does, however, permit derogations from that freedom for the purposes of maintaining press diversity, in so far as they are prescribed by law and are necessary in a democratic society (see the judgment of the European Court of Human Rights of 24 November 1993 in *Informationsverein Lentia and Others v Austria* Series A No. 276).

27. . . . it must therefore be determined whether a national prohibition such as that in issue in the main proceedings is proportionate to the aim of maintaining press diversity and whether that objective might not be attained by measures less restrictive of both intra-Community trade and freedom of expression.

28. To that end, it should be determined, first, whether newspapers which offer the chance of winning a prize in games, puzzles or competitions are in competition with those small press publishers who are deemed to be unable to offer comparable prizes and whom the contested legislation is intended to protect and, second, whether such a prospect of winning constitutes an incentive to purchase capable of bringing about a shift in demand.

29. It is for the national court to determine whether those conditions are satisfied on the basis of a study of the Austrian press market.

30. In carrying out that study, it will have to define the market for the product in question and to have regard to the market shares of individual publishers or press groups and the trend thereof.

31. Moreover, the national court will also have to assess the extent to which, from the consumer's standpoint, the product concerned can be replaced by papers which do not offer prizes, taking into account all the circumstances which may influence the decision to purchase, such as the presence of advertising on the title page referring to the chance of winning a prize, the likelihood of winning, the value of the prize or the extent to which winning depends on a test calling for a measure of ingenuity, skill or knowledge.

In a case such as this where the assessment is clearly one of considerable complexity, review by the national court should be confined to examining whether the national court has misdirected itself in law, or manifestly exceeded the bounds of its discretion.[23] The Court in *Familiapress* rejects application of an essentially *subjective* test, which it has allowed in a previous case,[24] and this is perhaps understandable, but it is less understandable and in the view of the present writer inappropriate to require the national court to undertake an investigation of the kind indicated in the foregoing paragraphs of the judgment of the Court of Justice and to invite the national court to substitute its own assessment for that of the Austrian legislature. That is not to criticize the recourse to considerations of freedom of expression and the maintenance of press diversity, but simply the intensity of review required of the national court.

4. FREEDOM OF EXPRESSION AS A CONSTRAINT ON COMMUNITY ACTION

4.1 Freedom of Expression and the Duty of Loyalty of Community Officials

Since the Community institutions are public authorities employing many thousands of officials, the problem of reconciling institutional loyalty with the right of officials to freedom of expression is far from theoretical. In *Traore*,[25] a case concerning journalists who the Court considered to be entitled to be established as officials of the Communities, the Court upheld the primacy in principle of freedom of expression over the duty of allegiance owed by officials to the Community, as follows:

16. Finally, it must be borne in mind that in any event the duty of allegiance to the Communities imposed on officials in the Staff Regulations cannot be interpreted in such a way as to conflict with freedom of expression, a fundamental right which the Court must ensure is respected in Community law, which is particularly important in cases, such as the present, concerning journalists whose primary duty is to write in complete independence of the views of either the ACP States or the Communities.

---

[23] An approach allowed by the Court in other contexts where national courts or the Community courts are called upon to review complex assessments, see Case C-120/97 *Upjohn Ltd v The Licensing Authority established by the Medicines Act 1968 and Others* [1999] 1 CMLR 825, at paras 33, 34, and see cases cited at para. 34.

[24] In Case C-275/92 *Schindler* [1994] ECR I-1039, paragraph 61, concerning freedom to provide services, the Court held that the special features of lotteries justify allowing national authorities a sufficient degree of latitude to determine what is required to protect the players and, more generally, in the light of the specific social and cultural features of each Member State, to maintain order in society, as regards the manner in which lotteries are operated, the size of the stakes and the allocation of the profits they yield. The Court therefore considered that it was for the national authorities to assess not only whether it is necessary to restrict the activities of lotteries but also whether they should be prohibited, provided that those restrictions are not discriminatory. See Case C-368/95 *Vereinigte Familiapress Zeitungsverlags- und vertriebs GmbH v Heinrich Bauer Verlag.* [1997] ECR I-3689, at paras. 20–4.

[25] Case C-100/88 *Augustin Oyowe and Amadou Traore v Commission of the European Communities* [1989] ECR I-4285.

Nevertheless, freedom of expression, pursuant to Article 10 of the European Convention on Human Rights 'since it carries with it duties and responsibilities, may be subject to such formalities, conditions, restrictions or penalties as are prescribed by law and are necessary in a democratic society, . . .'. Consistently with the reference in the second paragraph of Article 10 to restrictions necessary in a democratic society 'for the protection of the reputation or rights of others', the Court of Justice has held that the right of an official to express his opinions can under no circumstances be exercised by means of defamatory or insulting statements.[26] The European Court of Human Rights has upheld the right of civil servants to freedom of expression, but in the following qualified terms:

these principles apply also to civil servants. Although it is legitimate for a State to impose on civil servants, on account of their status, a duty of discretion, civil servants are individuals and, as such, qualify for the protection of Article 10 of the Convention. It therefore falls to the Court, having regard to the circumstances of each case, to determine whether a fair balance has been struck between the fundamental right of the individual to freedom of expression and the legitimate interest of a democratic State in ensuring that its civil service properly furthers the purposes enumerated in Article 10 § 2. In carrying out this review, the Court will bear in mind that whenever civil servants' right to freedom of expression is in issue the 'duties and responsibilities' referred to in Article 10 § 2 assume a special significance, which justifies leaving to the national authorities a certain margin of appreciation in determining whether the impugned interference is proportionate to the above aim (p. 26, § 53, and the *Ahmed and Others v the United Kingdom* judgment of 2 September 1998, Reports of Judgments and Decisions 1998–VI, p. 2378, § 56).[27]

The European Court of Human Rights has recognized that it is legitimate for a State to take proportionate steps to ensure that officials are seen to be politically neutral,[28] and this was a feature present in the much publicized judgment of the Court of First Instance of the European Communities in the *Connolly* case.[29] Mr Connolly was a senior Commission official responsible for a unit at the Directorate of Monetary Affairs, who published a book entitled: 'The Rotten Heart of Europe. The Dirty War for Europe's Money', during a period of leave which was granted in June 1995 for 'personal reasons'. Following his reinstatement at the Commission department in October 1995, Mr Connolly was the subject of disciplinary proceedings for the violation of the statutory obligations which are imposed on Community officials. Mr Connolly had not requested the necessary authorization to publish his work, the content of which, according to the Commission, was detrimental to his participation in the implementation of the Economic and Monetary Union as well as the image and reputation of the institution. Furthermore, it was considered that the overall

---

[26]   Case T-146/89 *Williams v Court of Auditors* [1991] ECR II-1293, para. 101; Case C-156/96 P *Williams v Court of Auditors* [1997] ECR I-239, at para. 10.

[27]   *Wille v Liechtenstein*, Judgment of 29 October 1999.

[28]   *Ahmed and Others v the United Kingdom*, Reports of Judgments and Decisions 1998–VI, 2378, para. 63.

[29]   Joined Cases T-34/96 and T-163/96 *Connolly v Commission* Judgment of 19 May 1999.

behaviour of Mr Connolly had undermined the authority of his post. On 16 January 1996, Mr Connolly was dismissed (without removal or reduction of his pension entitlement) following the opinion of the Disciplinary Board.

Mr Connolly brought an action to the Court of First Instance seeking the annulment of the opinion of the Disciplinary Board and the decision concerning his dismissal. In its analysis, the Court considered various aspects of the Statute governing the terms and conditions of service of officials of the European Communities and in particular its compatibility with an official's freedom of expression. The Court noted that it was contrary to the Statute for officials to accept remuneration from outside sources without prior authorization. This prohibition was justified by the need to guarantee their independence and loyalty. The Court confirmed that freedom of expression, which was guaranteed by the European Convention for the Protection of Human Rights, was a fundamental principle of Community law which must also apply to officials. The statutory provisions requiring an official to abstain from any measure, and in particular any public expression which could undermine the dignity of his post did not contravene the fundamental principle of freedom of expression. Furthermore, the need to obtain prior authorization for a publication, which was required only when the text in question is related to the activity of the Communities (including during periods of leave for personal reasons) did not contravene the official's freedom of expression. The Court noted that a decision refusing to allow publication was subject to judicial review. Furthermore, failure to secure prior authorization did not necessarily of itself lead to dismissal; the decision concerning Mr Connolly was primarily related to his behaviour, the controversial nature of his book and the nature of certain remarks which were considered to have damaged the reputation of several persons. This judgment seems in principle in line with the approach taken by the Court of Human Rights, which, as noted above, allows a certain margin appreciation to public authorities as regards the subject-matter in issue.

4.2 Freedom of Expression as a Constraint on the Law-making Powers of the Community Institutions

That freedom of expression may limit even the law-making competence of the Community institutions cannot be doubted in principle, though it is of course the case that by virtue of the subject matter of Community competences, restrictions on artistic or political expression are likely to be rare. That freedom of expression may in practice as well as in principle affect the scope of the law-making process is acknowledged in the preamble to European Parliament and Council Directive (EC) 98/43 on the approximation of the laws, regulations and administrative provisions of the Member States relating to the advertising and sponsorship of tobacco products.[30] The Directive contains wide-ranging prohibitions on the advertising and sponsorship of tobacco products. The ninth recital to the preamble states:

---

[30] [1998] OJ L213/9.

Whereas all forms of indirect advertising and sponsorship, and likewise free distribution, have the same effects as direct advertising, and whereas they should, *without prejudice to the fundamental principle of freedom of expression*, be regulated, including indirect forms of advertising which, while not mentioning the tobacco product directly, use brand names, trade marks, emblems or other distinctive features associated with tobacco products; whereas, however, Member States may defer application of these provisions to allow time for commercial practices to be adjusted and sponsorship of tobacco products to be replaced by other suitable forms of support; . . . (emphasis added).

Yet it is not at all clear that legislation regulating advertising is without prejudice to the fundamental principle of freedom of expression. The validity of the tobacco advertising directive has been challenged in the High Court and the question of validity referred to the Court of Justice of the European Communities.[31] One of the grounds of challenge is that the wide-ranging prohibition on the advertising of tobacco products infringes freedom of expression as a general principle of the Community legal order. The applicants argue that the Directive constitutes a prima facie infringement of Article 10(1) of the European Convention of Human Rights, since it inhibits the freedom of tobacco companies to inform the public about their goods, and to sponsor events which without that sponsorship might not take place at all. The applicants acknowledge that other forms of expression, including both artistic expression and the commercial and informational expression at issue in the current case, have not always been accorded the same degree of protection as accorded to political expression,[32] but emphasize that the right to receive and to impart commercial messages has been acknowledged as deserving a high degree of protection, and that this is particularly so when, as is invariably the case with tobacco advertising, such messages have a high informational content, specifically required by the competent authorities on the basis that it is in the public interest.[33] Furthermore, while Article 10(2) of the European Convention on Human Rights indicates that restrictions on freedom of expression may be justified if they are 'for the protection of health', the applicants argue, inter alia, that the directive in question has been adopted as an internal market measure having as its principal purpose the elimination of trade barriers and the removal of obstacles to competition as regards the cross-frontier provision of advertising media and services. The argument is developed that if the main purpose of the prohibition on advertising and sponsorship is developing the internal market, the restriction cannot properly be justified by reference to public health considerations. If, on the other hand, the main purpose of the directive is to protect public health, the directive would be ultra vires, since the Treaty base upon which the Directive was adopted authorizes only those Community measures which

---

[31] Case C-74/99 *R v Secretary of State for Trade and Industry, Secretary of State for Health, HM Attorney General, ex p Imperial Tobacco and others*, pending.

[32] *Casado Coca v Spain* A 285-A (1994), 18 EHRR 1 (commercial expression); *Markt Intern Verlag v FRG* A 165 (1989), 12 EHRR 161 (commercial expression); *Müller v Switzerland* A 133 (1988), 13 EHRR 212 (artistic expression).

[33] Case C-74/99 (n. 31 above) Opinion of Advocate General, para. 153.

have as their object 'the establishment and functioning of the internal market'.[34] It is unlikely that the Community will enact legislation governing the exercise of political speech, and it will no doubt be in the field of commercial speech that the issue of conflict between legislative regulation and freedom of expression will be addressed.

5. PROTECTING FREE SPEECH IN THIRD COUNTRIES THROUGH INTERNATIONAL TRADE RELATIONS

The position of human rights in general and freedom of expression in particular as general principles of the Community legal order has had repercussions in the economic and political relations between the Community and third countries. This has been facilitated by certain provisions of the Treaties relevant to external relations. Article 11 of the TEU (ex Article J.1) defines one of the objectives of the common foreign and security policy as being:

to develop and consolidate democracy and the rule of law, and respect for human rights and fundamental freedoms.

In a similar vein, Article 177(2) EC (ex 130u(2)) on development co-operation states:

Community policy in this area shall contribute to the general objective of developing and consolidating democracy and the rule of law, and to that of respecting human rights and fundamental freedoms.

The effects of imposing such obligations on the Community in its external relations is clearly demonstrated in the Treaty relations between the Community and the African Caribbean and Pacific States. In the Agreement amending the fourth ACP-EC Convention of Lomé signed in Mauritius on 4 November 1995 amended Article 5 contains the following statements on the safeguarding of human rights:

1. Cooperation shall be directed towards development centred on man, the main protagonist and beneficiary of development, which thus entails respect for and promotion of all human rights. Cooperation operations shall thus be conceived in accordance with this positive approach, where respect for human rights is recognised as a basic factor of real development and where cooperation is conceived as a contribution to the promotion of these rights. In this context development policy and cooperation shall be closely linked to respect for and enjoyment of fundamental human rights and to the recognition and application of democratic principles, the consolidation of the rule of law and good governance. The role and potential of initiatives taken by individuals and groups shall be recognised in order to achieve in practice real participation of the population in the development process in accordance with Article 13. In this context good governance shall be a particular aim of cooperation operations. Respect for human rights, democratic principles and the rule of law, which underpins relations

---

[34] The directive was adopted on the basis of Article 100a (now Article 95) EC.

between the ACP States and the Community and all provisions of the Convention, and governs the domestic and international policies of the Contracting Parties, shall constitute an essential element of this Convention.

2. The Contracting Parties therefore reiterate their deep attachment to human dignity and human rights, which are legitimate aspirations of individuals and peoples. The rights in question are all human rights, the various categories thereof being indivisible and interrelated, each having its own legitimacy: non-discriminatory treatment; fundamental human rights; civil and political rights; economic, social and cultural rights. Every individual shall have the right, in his own country or in a host country, to respect for his dignity and to protection by the law. ACP-EC cooperation shall help abolish the obstacles preventing individuals and peoples from actually enjoying to the full their economic, social political and cultural rights and this must be achieved through development which is essential to their dignity, their well-being and their self-fulfilment. The Contracting Parties hereby reaffirm their existing obligations and commitment in international law to strive to eliminate all forms of discrimination based on ethnic group, origin, race, nationality, colour, sex, language, religion or any other situation. This commitment applies more particularly to any situation in the ACP States or in the Community that may adversely affect the pursuit of the objectives of the Convention. The Member States (and/or, where appropriate, the Community itself) and the ACP States will continue to ensure, through the legal or administrative measures which they have or will have adopted, that migrant workers, students and other foreign nationals legally within their territory are not subjected to discrimination on the basis of racial, religious, cultural or social differences, notably in respect of housing, education, health care, other social services and employment.

The consequence of the above provisions is that the protection of human rights within the territory of the parties to the Lomé Convention becomes a matter of common concern. While the parties respect their respective constitutional arrangements, there can be no doubt that the protection of democratic processes and freedom of expression fall within the category of human rights referred to. This appears from the terms of the common position of 25 May 1998 defined by the Council on the basis of Article J.2 (see now Article 12) of the Treaty on European Union, concerning human rights, democratic principles, the rule of law and good governance in Africa,[35] Article 2 of which states, in relevant part:

The Union fully recognises the right of sovereign states to establish their own constitutional arrangements and to institute their own administrative structures according to their history, culture, tradition and social and ethnic composition. In this framework, the Union is committed to encourage and support the ongoing democratisation process in Africa on the basis of respect for the following principles:

(a) protection of human rights (civil and political, and social, economic and cultural);
(b) respect of basic democratic principles, including:
  —the right to choose and change leaders in free and fair elections,
  —separation of legislative, executive and judicial powers,
  —guarantees of freedom of expression, information, association and political organisation;

---

[35] 98/350 (CFSP) [1998] OJ L158/1.

(c) the rule of law, which permits citizens to defend their rights and which implies a legislative and judicial power giving full effect to human rights and fundamental freedoms and a fair, accessible and independent judicial system;

(d) good governance, including the transparent and accountable management of all a country's resources for the purposes of equitable and sustainable development. (emphasis added)

The consequences of the provisions of the Lomé Convention referred to above, in light of the foregoing common position, is that alleged infringements of freedom of expression by ACP countries becomes a matter of legitimate complaint within the constitutional framework of the European Union, as is indicated in the following resolution of the European Parliament on freedom of expression in Cameroon:[36]

A. whereas the journalist Pius Njawé, editor of the newspaper 'Le Messager', was arrested on 24 December 1997 following publication of an article reporting that Cameroon's President Paul Biya had had heart problems,

B. whereas a denial issued by the Presidency was published in a subsequent edition of the same newspaper,

C. whereas on *13 January 1998 Pius Njawé was sentenced to two years' imprisonment and a fine of CFA 500 000 for 'dissemination of inaccurate news',*

D. whereas at the same hearing a second journalist, Michel Michaut Moussala, was also sentenced to six months' imprisonment and a fine of CFA 1 million for an article, published in the 'Aurore Plus' weekly newspaper of which he is editor, criticizing the Director of the Cameroon Ports Authority, who is also a member of parliament belonging to the ruling party,

E. regretting that, despite the appeals made to the Cameroonian authorities by both political and civilian circles, no response has yet been received on the case of Pius Njawé,

F. *deploring the recent upsurge in violations of freedom of expression in the country,*

G. *whereas Cameroon is a signatory to the Lomé Convention, Article 5 of which stipulates that development aid is conditional upon respect for basic human rights and freedoms, one of the most prominent of which is freedom of expression,*

The European Parliament,

1. Deplores in the strongest terms the arrest and the heavy sentences meted out to Pius Njawé and Michel Michaut Moussala and calls for their immediate and unconditional release;

2. Calls on the Cameroonian Government to show all due respect for human rights and fundamental freedoms, and in particular freedom of expression;

3. *Calls on the Commission and the Council to ensure compliance with Article 5 of the Lomé Convention* and closely monitor the human rights situation in Cameroon;

4. Instructs its President to forward this resolution to the Commission, the Council, the Co-Presidents of the ACP-EU Joint Assembly and the Cameroonian Government. (emphasis added)

That the European Parliament should take it upon itself to address the human rights position in Cameroon in terms of an alleged violation of the rights of a named individual is worthy of remark. This approach is tantamount to a procedure for redress

---

[36] [1998] OJ C138/176.

of grievances, with a political response such as that indicated in paragraphs 3 and 4 above as the possible 'redress'. That the European Parliament should deal with individual grievances is not however inconsistent with the role expressly allocated to the Parliament by the EC Treaty. Indeed, Article 194 EC provides that any citizen of the Union, and any natural or legal person residing or having its registered office in a Member State, shall have the right to address, individually or in association with other citizens or persons, a petition to the European Parliament, on a matter which comes within the Community's field of activity, and which affects him, her or it directly. During the 1996/97 parliamentary year, the Committee examined some 600 petitions, mostly relating to social security, the environment, taxation, the free movement of persons and the recognition of qualifications.[37] The role of the European Parliament in addressing and seeking to redress the grievances of citizens of the Union may overlap with its role in reviewing alleged violations of human rights by third countries committed to human rights protection by their treaty relations with the European Community. In a Resolution on the arrest of the Italian citizen Dino Frisullo in Turkey, the European Parliament, pointing out that closer co-operation between the European Union and Turkey is conditional, 'first and foremost' upon full respect for human rights, noted that Dino Frisullo, was arrested on 21 March 1998 in Diyarkabir for taking part in celebrations to mark the Kurdish New Year, and for demonstrating in support of the fundamental rights of the Kurdish people. The resolution stated that 'the charge brought of "incitement to violence" is not warranted by Dino Frisullo's behaviour, which involved the exercise of the fundamental rights of freedom of assembly and freedom of expression', and, inter alia, called upon 'the Turkish Government to show respect for fundamental human rights, as required by the international conventions that Turkey has signed, and in particular to guarantee the rights of freedom of opinion and freedom of expression . . .'[38]

Provisions which in one way or another assert the Community's commitment to human rights in its external relations have become standard form in agreements with third countries. Thus in the Cooperation Agreement between the European

---

[37] General Report on the Activities of the European Communities (1997), section 3, para. 50.

[38] There is no 'human rights' clause in the Treaties and related instruments which establish the customs union between the EC and Turkey. The position of the EU as regards the significance of human rights in relations between the EU and Turkey was summarized as follows in the Commission's response to a question in the European Parliament: 'As regards relations between the EU and Turkey, the Luxembourg European Council on 12 and 13 December 1997, while confirming Turkey's eligibility for accession to the European Union, gave a reminder, in line with the Council's position stated at the meeting of the Association Council with Turkey held on 29 April 1997, that strengthening Turkey's links with the European Union also depended on that country's pursuit of the political and economic reforms on which it had embarked, including the alignment of human rights standards and practices on those in force in the European Union; respect for and protection of minorities; the establishment of satisfactory and stable relations between Greece and Turkey; the settlement of disputes, in particular by legal process, including the International Court of Justice; and support for negotiations under the aegis of the UN on a political settlement in Cyprus on the basis of the relevant UN Security Council Resolutions.' [1998] OJ C304/64.

Community and the Republic of India on partnership and development,[39] Article 1 states:

Respect for human rights and democratic principles is the basis for the cooperation between the Contracting Parties and for the provisions of this Agreement, and it constitutes an essential element of the Agreement.

The wording in the various agreements is not identical, but the essential aim is invariably the same, Thus in the Framework Cooperation Agreement between the European Economic Community and the Republics of Costa Rica, El Salvador, Guatemala, Honduras, Nicaragua and Panama,[40] Article 1 states:

Cooperation ties between the Community and Central America and this Agreement in its entirety shall be based on respect for democratic principles and human rights, which inspire the domestic and external policies of both the Community and Central America and which constitute an essential component of this Agreement.

Antagonism by the EU to human rights violations including unjustified interference with freedom of expression have characterized relations with certain of the States created within the space of the former Yugoslavia. Thus on 14 December 1998 the Council adopted a common position on the basis of Article J.2 of the TEU (now Article 12 of the TEU) on restrictive measures to be taken against persons in the Federal Republic of Yugoslavia acting against the independent media.[41] Article 1 of the common position reads as follows:

1. The persons listed in the Annex, who have been identified as being responsible for drafting, implementing, advocating or taking political advantage of the Serbian law on public information, shall be reported for the purpose of non-admission in the territories of the Member States.
2. Other senior FRY and Serbian representatives responsible for repressive action against the independent media shall be added to the list in the Annex should the FRY authorities fail to respond to the demands of the European Union. The Council shall update the list in the light of developments in the FRY.

The persons listed included the Deputy Prime Minister, the Serbian Information Minister, and the Serbian Minister for Justice.

As regards Croatia, the Commission indicated in a response, dated 13 March 1998, to a written question in the European Parliament. that it shared the concerns expressed by the questioner in relation to freedom of association and expression in Croatia, 'in particular as regards recent laws and restrictions on the activities of non-governmental organizations (NGOs) and independent media'. The Commission indicated that it has voiced its concern at various levels and on multiple occasions in contacts with the Croatian authorities. The Commission added:

---

[39] [1994] OJ L223/24.
[40] [1999] OJ L63/39.
[41] 98/725 (CFSP) [1998] OJ L345/1.

Respect for human rights is one of the conditions for the development of improved relations between Croatia and the Community. Indeed, freedom of expression and of association are specifically mentioned in the Council conclusions of 29 April 1997 which set out conditions for the development of bilateral relations with the countries covered by the Community's regional approach towards the countries of South Eastern Europe.

While it is impossible to undertake anything resembling a comprehensive survey of the practice of the Community institutions as regards third country relations in an essay such as this, the foregoing provides at least an indication of the significance which human rights in general, and freedom of expression in particular, have taken on in the context of the external relations of the EU. But it is worthy of note that the legal and political basis for the EU to address human rights violations in third countries results from the grant of extensive competence in external economic relations to the Community institutions, from the grant of significant competence to the EU in the field of Common Foreign and Security Policy, and from the undeniable fact that the EU comprises a trading partner of enormous importance in the world today.

PART II
Freedom of Information

13

The Relationship Between Freedom of Expression and Freedom of Information

THE HON SIR ANTHONY MASON AC KBE

1. INTRODUCTION

The purpose of this essay is to examine the relationship between freedom of expression and freedom of information. The two freedoms are often mentioned in the same breath, so to speak, as if they are so closely connected or intertwined that one (freedom of information) is part or counterpart of the other (freedom of expression).

International and European lawyers rather than traditional common lawyers have been astute to see that close connection. That is because guarantees of freedom in constitutions and international instruments expressly or impliedly include certain aspects of freedom of information in freedom of expression, that is the right to seek and impart, even the right to receive, information. As no such inclusion has arisen under the very limited common law conception of freedom of expression,[1] the common lawyer tends to see freedom of information as a statutory right of access to information. On the other hand, the growing realization that access to government held information is essential to effective freedom of expression in order to inform public discussion of major issues as a central element in modern representative government tends to bring the two freedoms into a very close relationship.

The impression that the two freedoms are closely interconnected is fostered by modern international instruments, such as the United Nations Covenant on Civil and Political Rights (ICCPR), the European Convention on Human Rights and Fundamental Freedoms (European Convention) and the American Convention on Human Rights (American Convention). Subject to some qualifications, the relevant articles of the Covenant and the two Conventions are expressed in somewhat similar terms. They all treat freedom of expression as including freedom of information.

2. 'FREEDOM OF EXPRESSION' AND 'FREEDOM OF INFORMATION' IN THE CONTEXT OF THE ICCPR AND THE EUROPEAN CONVENTION

This treatment raises a question as to what is meant by 'freedom of expression' and

---

[1] Note, however, *Reynolds v Times Newspapers Ltd.* [1999] 3 WLR 1010 at 1022, per Lord Nicholls of Birkenhead (where his Lordship referred to '[t]he high importance of the freedom to impart and receive information').

'freedom of information'. This question can be conveniently discussed, first, in the context of Article 19 of the ICCPR which is in significant respects similar to Article 10 of the European Convention.

2.1 The ICCPR

Article 19 of the ICCPR provides:

Freedom of Opinion, Expression and Information
1. Everyone shall have the right to hold opinions without interference.
2. Everyone shall have the right to freedom of expression; this right shall include freedom to seek, receive and impart information and ideas of all kinds, regardless of frontiers, either orally, in writing or in print, in the form of art, or through any other media of his choice.
3. The exercise of the rights provided for in paragraph 2 of this article carries with it special duties and responsibilities. It may therefore be subject to certain restrictions, but these shall only be such as are provided by law and are necessary:
    (a) For respect of the rights or reputations of others;
    (b) For the protection of national security or of public order (ordre public), or of public health or morals.

The concept of the right to freedom of expression, as it is formulated in paragraph 2 of Article 19, includes not only the right to impart information and ideas but also the right to seek and receive such information and ideas. (For the sake of convenience, I shall use the word 'information' in a sense inclusive of 'ideas', except when it becomes necessary to make a distinction between the two.) The restrictions which may be imposed upon the exercise of the right are limited by paragraph 3. The permitted restrictions are naturally appropriate to an exercise of the freedom which constitutes an imparting of information or ideas rather than a seeking or receipt of information. That is not to say that the permitted restrictions are inappropriate to a seeking or a receipt of information or ideas. But the permitted restrictions have more obvious application to a request for and the receipt of, rather than to the provision of, information.

The assumption which underlies the comments just made is that a request for information is as much an exercise of the right to freedom of expression as is a communication imparting information. It is not as easy to make a similar point about the receipt of information because the receipt of information may not involve any act of expression on the part of the receiver, apart from an antecedent request for information which is, of course, independently protected by paragraph 2. The provision of information to the receiver would, in most cases, constitute an exercise of the right of expression on the part of the provider. Accordingly, the protection of receipt on the part of the receiver will ensure that the provision of information which might not otherwise amount to an exercise of freedom of expression is not defeated by the imposition of impermissible restrictions on the receipt of information.

Apart from a possible implication arising from the protection of receipt of information, the provisions of Article 19 suggest that paragraph 2 imposes no obligation on government or government agencies to disclose information. In other words paragraph 2 is addressing a situation in which information is otherwise generally accessible. The paragraph does not purport in an explicit fashion to make information accessible which is not already accessible. The paragraph does not expressly impose an obligation to provide information or a right to obtain it.

One possible qualification to that general proposition is specific information relating to an individual, especially information held by an employer, a government or a government agency. The view has been expressed that:

> In the context of personal data and other specific information on a person, it is possible to assume that the individual concerned has a farther-reaching right to be informed of such data, in so far as this is not opposed by pressing interests of secrecy on the part of the State or a private data bank. It is, however, debatable whether the public mandate on the press and electronic media to inform the public truthfully of all events of interest implies a privileged right of journalists to seek information above and beyond that which is generally accessible.[2]

The negative aspect of the freedom certainly gives protection to the individual who seeks accessible information, from interference by the State, subject to the restrictions in paragraph 3.

Although paragraph 2 does not expressly impose any obligation on State agencies or private persons to make available information not otherwise accessible, it cannot be assumed that the interpretation of the article will stop short of recognizing such an obligation. The essentiality of freedom of expression and information to modern liberal democratic government, a matter to be discussed later, as well as the emergence of the modern information society, as indicated by the growing number of statutory enactments requiring disclosure of information, notably in the area of public administration, may lead to the implication in article 19 of such an obligation. The interpretation of the First Amendment to the United States Constitution may have a part to play here.

The difficulty in making such an implication is to frame it in a way that will protect legitimate government interests in confidentiality. But difficulty in framing an implication can be overcome by expressing the obligation to disclose in general terms subject to a reservation protecting compelling government interests in security and other matters.

It should be mentioned that, in the context of the ICCPR, information is to be given a broad meaning, extending not only to ideas, but also to opinion and comment.

The ICCPR, in protecting freedom of opinion from interference, unlike Article 10 of the European Convention,[3] does not limit the protection to protection against interference by 'public authority'.[4] The protection extends to interference by private parties.

---

[2] M. Nowak, 'Freedom of Opinion, Expression and Information', UN Covenant on Civil and Political Rights CCPR Commentary, 335–58.

[3] See the decision of the Austrian Constitutional Court on Art. 10 of the ECHR, 16 March 1987, Eu GRZ 237*f*.

[4] Contrast Art. 10(1) of the ECHR ('without interference by public authority').

As Manfred Nowak points out, every right of the individual with horizontal effects implies duties on other individuals.[5] Freedom of expression, as well as freedom to seek information, is capable of violating the rights of others, particularly the privacy of others. Nowak further points out that, as a consequence of the power to influence public opinion, the exercise of freedom of expression tends towards monopolization and concentration, thereby leading to a conflict with the freedom of expression and opinion of others.

The restriction on freedom of expression by reference to the 'reputations of others' is consistent with the protection of reputations of others as part of the protection of privacy in Article 17(1) of the ICCPR. By virtue of that provision, a State party to the ICCPR is bound to provide statutory protection against intentional infringement by untrue assertions[6] reflecting on honour and reputation.

Whatever the prospects of future development of paragraph 2 of Article 19 may be, the article clearly places freedom of information within the scope and framework of freedom of expression, subjecting the exercise of the right to freedom of information to the same limited restrictions as apply to freedom of expression and protecting both freedoms as negative liberties from statutory and other curtailments and encroachments.

2.2 The European Convention

Article 10 of the European Convention conceives freedom of expression as including both freedom of opinion and freedom to receive and impart information and ideas.[7] Although, unlike the ICCPR, Article 10(1) does not expressly protect the right actively to seek information, it seems that such a right may well be implied from the terms of the article.[8]

As with the ICCPR, the text of Article 10 seems to assume that the right to receive information relates to sources of information which are otherwise generally accessible. However, as has been pointed out by one commentator,[9] the Committee of Ministers of the Council of Europe takes a wider view. He notes that the 'Declaration on the

---

[5]   M. Nowak, 'Freedom of Opinion, Expression and Information', UN Covenant on Civil and Political Rights CCPR Commentary at 350.

[6]   M. Nowak, 'Freedom of Opinion, Expression and Information', UN Covenant on Civil and Political Rights CCPR Commentary at 353.

[7]   Article 10(1) ('Everyone has the right to freedom of expression. This right shall include freedom to hold opinions and to receive and impart information and ideas without interference by public authority . . .').

[8]   See Barendt, *Freedom of Speech*, 112, citing the Report of the Council of Europe on Activities in the Mass Media Field, DH/mm (83) 1, 5. See also J. E. S. Fawcett, *The Application of the European Convention on Human Rights*, 2nd edn. (Oxford: Clarendon Press, 1987) 262; G. Malinverni, 'Freedom of Information in the European Convention on Human Rights and in the International Covenant on Civil and Political Rights' (1983) 4 *Human Rights Law Journal* 443, 449.

[9]   P. Bayne, 'Freedom of Information and Political Free Speech' in T. Campbell and W. Sadurski (eds.), *Freedom of Communication* (Dartmouth, 1994) 207.

freedom of expression and information'[10] asserts that Article 10 states that the free-dom is 'a fundamental element' of the 'principles of genuine democracy, the rule of law and respect for human rights',[11] and that it is 'necessary for the social, economic, cultural and political development article of every human being'.[12] The Declaration goes on to support 'the pursuit of an open information policy in the media sector, including access to information, in order to enhance the individual's understanding of, and his ability to discuss freely political, social, economic and cultural matters'.[13] Elsewhere the Declaration sees an open information policy as serving the interest of the individual in expressing himself.[14] It would perhaps be going too far to see the Declaration as doing more than enunciating policies which are consistent with the general thrust of Article 10. At the same time, the Declaration identifies values which may influence future interpretation of the article.

2.3 The First Amendment to the United States Constitution

For present purposes, what is significant in the jurisprudence that has developed around the First Amendment's guarantee of free speech is the emergence of 'the right to know'. The right to know may be nothing more than a reflection of the right to speak, the right of the potential listener that the legislature and the government will not interfere with the liberty of the willing speaker.[15] But the right to know may include an individual's right to specific information or ideas free from interference, amounting, in the case of information which, by its nature or constitutional command, is open to the public, for example criminal trials,[16] to a positive obliga-tion to ensure that they are open to the public. This right falls well short of a require-ment that government open the conduct of all its business to the public.

It is well accepted that a right to know may not entail a correlative right in anyone to originate the communication.[17] So the protection of the right to know is mainly to be found in the restriction on the power of the State to prohibit the disclosure of information and ideas and to regulate expression by willing speakers by reference to content in a manner which unduly restricts the ultimate flow of information and ideas.[18]

---

[10] Adopted by the Council of Ministers on 29 April 1982. *Yearbook of the European Convention on Human Rights 1982* (Dordrecht: Martinus Nijhoff, 1986), Principal Dev 25–7.
[11] European Convention, Article 10, para. 1.
[12] ibid., para. 4.
[13] ibid., para. 8, II, c.
[14] ibid., para. 8, II, a.
[15] See Lawrence H. Tribe, *American Constitutional Law* (2nd edn., Foundation Press Inc., 1988) 944.
[16] ibid at 955 *et seq.*
[17] *Lamont v Postmaster General of the United States* 381 US 301 (1965).
[18] See the discussion in Lawrence H. Tribe, *American Constitutional Law* (2nd edn., The Foundation Press Inc., 1988) 954 *et seq.*

3. MODERN DEMOCRATIC GOVERNMENT AND THE INTERCONNECTION BETWEEN
FREEDOM OF EXPRESSION AND FREEDOM OF INFORMATION

Enough has already been said to convey the notion that the interconnection between freedom of expression and freedom of information derives much of its force from the circumstance that human rights and fundamental freedoms—and freedom of expression and freedom of information in particular—are seen as contributing in a major way to the efficacy of modern representative government. True it is that aspects of each freedom may be seen as manifestations of human rights jurisprudence that enable the individual to engage in self-expression and to give effect to the autonomy of the individual. But above all else, the enforcement of the two freedoms is seen as enhancing the notion of deliberative democracy or even participatory democracy. In that context, just as freedom of expression is considered to be an indispensable concomitant of modern democracy, so also is freedom of information. Freedom of expression, unsupported by freedom of information, is unlikely to play as effective a part in sustaining modern representative government as it would in situations where there is free access to information relating to the workings of government.

That is because it is of the essence of modern democratic government that the citizen is able to criticize government and contribute to its decision-making, whether policy-making or otherwise. Furthermore, there is a strong conviction that freedom of expression and freedom of information, recognized and implemented in jurisdictions which are not democratic, will ultimately lead to the introduction of democratic government. That conviction underlies the endeavours of the United States to develop international support for respect for human rights on the part of non-democratic regimes.

The interconnection between the two freedoms has become apparent as the rationale for freedom of information has been more persuasively articulated in the context of the individual's right of access to information. The rationale advanced to support the imposition on government of a statutory obligation to make information available is threefold. First, everyone 'has a right to know what information is held in government records about him personally'.[19] Secondly, government must be open to public scrutiny so as to be accountable and exposed to the judgment and evaluation of the citizens.[20] Thirdly, the provision of adequate information will lead to a higher level of public participation in the processes of policy-making and government.[21]

The second and third elements in the rationale for freedom of information correspond very closely with the arguments which assert that freedom of expression is an indispensable element in the efficacious working of modern representative government. The ability to criticize government and to participate effectively in government,

---

[19] 'Freedom of Information', *Report by the Australian Senate Standing Committee on Constitutional and Legal Affairs on the Freedom of Information Bill 1978, and aspects of the Archives Bill 1978*, para. 3.3.
[20] ibid., para. 3.4.
[21] ibid., para. 3.5.

if only indirectly by expressing one's views, depends upon the provision of adequate information about the workings of government and its decision-making processes. So much was explicitly recognized by Lord Simon of Glaisdale when he said:

The public interest in freedom of discussion . . . stems from the requirement that members of a democratic society should be sufficiently informed that they may influence intelligently the decisions which may affect themselves.[22]

Indeed, that is one of the benefits of proceedings by way of judicial review. These proceedings expose the decision-making process to public scrutiny and, on occasions, to justifiable criticism.

The relationship between government and citizen presented in the foregoing paragraphs, now largely accepted in modern liberal democracies, still has political opponents. They speak of the 'mandate' theory of government according to which an elected government enjoys a free hand to do what it thinks best, subject to the sanction of being voted out at the next election. On this view, the case for freedom of information is much weaker. Indeed, the proponents of this view would assert that efficiency in government will be promoted by drawing a veil of secrecy over the operations of government. This notion is both unacceptable and unsound.

4. THE COMMON LAW

Unfortunately the notion that the operations of government should be secret had a pervasive influence in the common law, particularly in relation to the doctrine of Crown privilege. The notion partly explains why freedom of information in contrast to freedom of expression is a relative latecomer on the scene.

Given that the close interconnection between the two freedoms has this contemporary association with modern liberal democracy, it is not surprising that the common law did not traditionally recognize such an interconnection. The absence of such a recognition is to be explained by the common law's treatment of the two freedoms. That treatment is, in turn, to be explained by the fact that the common law is judge-made law and is subordinate to statute. The doctrine of parliamentary sovereignty meant that the State through its legislative arm was, in theory, able to impose its will on the citizen. The acceptance of the doctrine precluded the judicial development of a concept of freedom which was immune from statutory abrogation.

4.1 Freedom of Expression

The concept of 'freedom of expression' as it has been recognized by the common law does not take the form of a positive or enforceable right. It is a negative liberty to communicate with others, or, as it has been put by Lord Browne-Wilkinson, 'an

---

[22] *Attorney-General v Times Newspapers Ltd.* [1974] AC 273 at 320.

immunity from interference by others'.[23] This means that a person may write or say what he pleases so long as he does not infringe any law or the rights of others. The freedom, unlike an entrenched right, however, is subject to statutory curtailment and may be restricted by judicial development of the common law as, for example, by any development of the law of defamation which affords greater protection to the reputation of the individual or of the law of privacy.

In the words of A. V. Dicey, 'it is essentially false' to say that:

> the right to the free expression of opinion, and especially that form of it which is known as the 'liberty of the press', are fundamental doctrines of the law of England . . . and . . . that our courts recognise the right of every man to say and write what he pleases, especially on social, political, or religious topics without fear of legal penalties.[24]

Nevertheless, Lord Goff of Chieveley was able to say that he could see 'no inconsistency between English law on this subject and Article 10 of the European Convention'.[25] His Lordship was referring to the content of free expression as it existed at common law, absent any relevant statutory restriction of the freedom.

Despite Dicey's statement, freedom of expression is and has been a value highly prized by the common law. It is so highly prized that, in the absence of a clear and unambiguous expression of intention, no statute will be construed as curtailing the freedom. The rule of construction applied by the common law to preserve freedom of expression is a particularly strong one and one that may require something more than general words to displace it.[26]

The high value placed by the common law on freedom of expression is illustrated by the law of defamation where the courts have had to resolve the tension between the twin policy goals of protection of the freedom and protection of reputation. The balance between the two has moved in more recent times in favour of the freedom, the high point of that freedom being the denial of a local authority's right to bring an action in defamation against a newspaper arising out of criticism of the authority.[27]

But that case did not deal with individual reputation and, in *Reynolds v Times Newspapers Ltd.*,[28] the House of Lords refused to reshape the common law of qualified privilege to cover a specific category of publication relating to political information, despite developments in other common law jurisdictions which allowed a greater latitude to publishers of such information under a wide-ranging defence of

---

[23]   *Wheeler v Leicester City Council* [1985] AC 1054 at 1065 per Browne-Wilkinson LJ.
[24]   *An Introduction to the Study of the Law of the Constitution* (10th edn., 1959) 239; quoted in *Nationwide News Pty. Ltd. v Wills* (1992) 177 CLR 1 at 48 per Brennan J.
[25]   *Attorney-General v Guardian Newspapers Ltd.* [1993]AC 534 at 551.
[26]   See *Re F (a minor)* (publication of information) [1977] Fam 58 at 99 per Scarman LJ; approved on appeal: *A-G v Leveller Magazine* [1979] AC 440 at 465 per Lord Edmund Davies; see also *Wheeler v Leicester City Council* [1985] AC 1054 at 1063–5 per Browne-Wilkinson LJ.
[27]   *Derbyshire County Council v Times Newspapers Ltd.* [1993] AC 534.
[28]   [1999] 3 WLR 1010 at 1027 per Lord Nicholls of Birkenhead.

qualified privilege.[29] The House of Lords did, however, recognize that the defence of qualified privilege involves a balancing of relevant factors and that, in arriving at that balance, the court could 'give appropriate weight, in today's conditions, to the importance of freedom of expression by the media on all matters of public concern'. The adoption of this balancing approach may result in an outcome which gives some latitude to publications relating to political information. Much will depend upon how the balance is reached in future cases.

4.2 Freedom of Information

The common law did not develop a concept of freedom of information, let alone formulate a body of jurisprudence based on such a concept. The expression 'freedom of information' is imprecise and uninstructive. The expression, in general, conveys that there is a right of access to information, notably government information and that it is freely available rather than closely restricted. This understanding derives, not from the common law, but from the impact of the United States Freedom of Information Act 1966[30] and similar statutes in other jurisdictions.[31] Freedom of Information legislation imposes an enforceable right to access to information.

Information, of its nature, is not freely available, unless the person who has it is either willing to make it available or is subject to some kind of enforceable duty to make it available. The common law—and for this purpose I include equity— imposed no general duty to make information available, except in particular situations where a right of access to information of a particular kind or documents might arise as a result of a specific contractual, equitable or other legal relationship. Where such a right existed, the courts would enforce it. Thus, the courts will enforce a councillor's right to see the public documents of a local authority by making an order for production, at least when there is a bona fide ground for seeing the document.[32]

Procedures in court proceedings, such as discovery, interrogatories, subpoenae and orders for production may also create an obligation to provide particular information or documents. But they fall far short of generating a general duty to provide information. Indeed, the common law denied a general right of access to government information.

The absence of such a right of access was in conformity with the culture of secrecy concerning the operations of government which thrived in the United Kingdom[33] and Australia, in sharp distinction to the United States where a stronger tradition of

---

[29] See *New York Times Co. v Sullivan* 376 US 254 (1964); see also *Lange v Australian Broadcasting Corp.* (1997) 189 CLR 520.

[30] 5 USC § 552 (1970 edn. and Supp V).

[31] See, for example, the Freedom of Information Act 1982 (Cth).

[32] *R v Southwold Corporation, ex p Wrightson* (1907) 97 LT 431 at 432 per Lord Alverstone; *R v Birmingham City Council, ex p O* [1983] 2 WLR 189.

[33] S. Brittain, *Steering the Economy: the Role of the Treasury*, (London: Penguin, 1971) 63. The Treasury has been influential in the United Kingdom and Australia in maintaining the culture of secrecy.

open government has prevailed,[34] a tradition which was partly but not entirely attributable to the First Amendment.

The old doctrine of Crown privilege provides a striking illustration of the common law's willingness to throw a protective cloak of secrecy over government decision-making processes and other activities. It was not until 1968 that the House of Lords made it clear in *Conway v Rimmer* [35] that, in considering an objection to production of documents on the ground of Crown privilege, the court must evaluate the respective public interests and determine on balance whether the public interest which calls for non-disclosure outweighs the public interest in the administration of justice that requires that the parties be given a fair trial on all the material evidence. Before then the courts exhibited a strong disposition to accept at face value affidavits claiming privilege by Ministers and heads of departments. *Conway v Rimmer* upheld the court's right to inspect the documents for the purpose of evaluating the claim and rejected the earlier view in relation to a claim for privilege covering a class of documents that privilege was necessary to encourage candour on the part of public servants in their advice to Ministers.[36]

The traditional view, based on the necessity for confidentiality of decision-making processes, especially at the highest level of policy-making, was reflected in the report dated January 1976 of the Committee of Privy Councillors on Ministerial Memoirs (the Radcliffe Committee). Paragraph 33 of the report stated:

33. . . . The constitutional doctrine which attributes to each member of a Government his share of collective responsibility for its actions and policies undertaken during the period of his membership is no more than an expression of this association in which individual attitudes and opinions are merged in the general resolution of the whole body. In our view such a system of working could not survive in practical terms unless the members were prepared to observe the confidentiality of all that has gone in the course of their deliberations.

Although this statement may be accepted as a justification for treating the general run of Cabinet discussions as confidential, at least while the issues are alive, the statement has an authoritarian ring to it. It contrasts sharply with the contemporary emphasis on openness and accountability of government. It reflected an attitude of mind which found expression in Sir Owen Dixon's assertion '[t]he counsels of the Crown are secret',[37] which must be treated as a statement of fact rather than a legal proposition.

It would be a mistake to conclude that freedom of information as such had no

---

[34] See *New York Times Co. v United States* 403 US 713 (1971) (where the Supreme Court refused an injunction to restrain publication in the interests of national security of the Pentagon papers, a series of papers on high level policy discussions and decisions relating to the Vietnam War, which had been taken from the Pentagon without authority).

[35] [1968] AC 910; see also *Alfred Crompton Amusement Machines Ltd. v Customs and Excise Commissioners (No. 2)* [1974] AC 405.

[36] Evidence to that effect was given and accepted in *Attorney-General v Jonathan Cape Ltd.* [1976] QB 752.

[37] *Australian Communist Party v The Commonwealth* (1951) 83 CLR 1 at 179.

place or part to play in the common law. True it is that freedom of information was not as highly prized a concept or value as freedom of expression. Freedom of information was not protected from statutory invasion by a strict rule of construction simply because the freedom was not considered to have the same importance as freedom of expression or other liberties, such as the liberty of the individual. And the common law—again I include equity—was prepared to enforce confidential obligations whether arising from contractual or other legal relationships.[38]

However, more recently, the general law (the law enunciated by the judges), has taken account of the importance of freedom of information in a number of ways. Thus, the courts, in setting the limits of the subject matter of copyright, have steadfastly refused to allow copyright to extend to the protection of ideas and information, insisting on the proposition that copyright protects expression and not the ideas or information which may be embodied in that expression. The distinction is by no means an easy one to maintain but it is important and its importance is that it recognizes that there is a paramount public interest in preserving public access to information and ideas in order to promote learning, knowledge, science and culture. In the well-known American case *Feist Publications Inc. v Rural Telephone Service Co.*,[39] the alphabetical listing of all telephone subscribers in a certain area was held not to involve the level of originality required for copyright protection, notwithstanding the commercial importance of the work and the effort, investment and organization that went into the work. *Feist Publications* reveals a tension between two propositions, namely that facts cannot be the subject of copyright, though compilation of facts can be. In that case, the element of selection was considered insufficient to amount to the element of originality which is required to sustain the existence of copyright.

The requirement of originality in order to support the existence of copyright seeks to provide a justification for the grant of the exclusive rights which copyright confers on the copyright owner. The grant of these exclusive rights precludes the dissemination of the subject of the copyright, subject to certain exceptions which are not relevant to this discussion. It is important therefore to limit the scope of the subject matter of copyright so that copyright protection does not amount to the suppression of ideas and information. Otherwise the protection would run counter to a guarantee of freedom of expression, such as the First Amendment to the United States Constitution.[40]

What I have just said about copyright concerns constitutional law and statutory interpretation rather than common law values. The courts, however, in dealing with the issues, are bringing to bear values which are now regarded as inherent in the common law. What is of even greater importance in the context of this essay is that access to information and ideas is not only seen as a public good but also as something that is protected by the First Amendment's guarantee of free speech. In other

---

[38] *Prince Albert v Strange* (1849) 1 H & T 1; *Argyll v Argyll* [1967] Ch 302; *Attorney-General v Guardian Newspapers Ltd. (No. 2)* [1990] 1 AC 109.
[39] 499 US 340 at 349 (1991).
[40] *Harper & Row Publishers Inc. v Nation Enterprises* 471 US 539 (1984).

words, the First Amendment's protection of free speech is seen as preserving and contributing to the free flow of information and ideas.

The common law itself did little to protect freedom of information, particularly government information.

The enforceability of obligations of confidence as between private parties, thought by many to be applicable to obligations of confidence owed by private persons to the Crown (or the State) is no longer fully applicable to obligations owed to the Crown. In the modern cases, a defence of so-called 'public interest immunity' has been recognized. The effect of the defence is that the obligation will give way to a superior public interest in the disclosure of the information.[41] This again is a comparatively recent development in the common law.

5. THE SOURCE OF RECENT DEVELOPMENTS IN THE LAW

The recent developments in common law doctrine are a reflection of a new appreciation of the importance of freedom of expression and freedom of information, most notably freedom of information, in modern liberal democratic government. As already mentioned, the recognition of that importance is illustrated by the treatment of freedom of information as an element in freedom of expression in Article 19 of the ICCPR and Article 10 of the European Convention on Human Rights and Fundamental Freedoms. And the Human Rights Act 1998 now requires that the English common law is to be developed and applied in a manner consistent with Article 10 and requires the courts to take into account the relevant decisions of the European Court of Human Rights.[42]

It is, however, a mistake to think that recognition of freedom of information as an indispensable element of good government is confined to the modern world. Aristotle considered that information was necessary if governments were to be held accountable. He dismissed the criticism that the public cannot understand information because they lack the necessary technical skills.[43] That criticism may have greater force in the modern world where technical complexity abounds. In the same vein as Aristotle, John Stuart Mill considered that a principal function of a representative assembly was 'to compel a full exposition and justification' from the government of all its actions.[44] James Madison wrote to the same effect.[45]

To the extent to which freedom of information provides openness and accountability, it brings advantages not offered by freedom of expression. Freedom of information

---

[41] *Attorney-General v Jonathan Cape Ltd.* [1976] QB 752; *Attorney-General v Guardian Newspapers Ltd. (No. 2)* [1990] 1 AC 1010; *Commonwealth v John Fairfax & Sons Ltd.* (1980) 147 CLR 39.

[42] Human Rights Act 1998, ss. 6 and 2.

[43] *The Politics*, tr. T. A. Sinclair, Book iii, ch ii, (London: Penguin, 1962) 124–5.

[44] J. S. Mill, *Representative Government*, (London: Everyman, 1964) 239.

[45] I. Brant, *James Madison: Commander in Chief 1812–1836*, vol. 6 (Indianapolis: Bobbs-Merrill, 1961) 450.

is seen as sustaining the characteristics of openness, transparency and accountability which are considered today as essential qualities of good representative government. There is, of course, a consequential linkage with political freedom of expression and the notion of a deliberative democracy but that does not detract from the fact that freedom of information has an independent value.

Freedom of expression is often taken to include freedom of opinion. Each of these two freedoms is dealt with separately in Article 19 of the ICCPR, as it is in Article 10 of the European Convention, though freedom of expression is expressed to include 'freedom to seek, receive and impart information'. The right to hold opinions is stated to be unqualified, that is, 'without interference'[46] whereas the exercise of the right to freedom of expression is qualified.[47]

Freedom of opinion and freedom of expression (including freedom of information) embrace two different historic conceptions of freedom, namely political (democratic) freedom of access 'to the State' and liberal freedom 'from the State', these conceptions corresponding to the broad notions of democracy and the rule of law.[48] Every individual has the freedom to form and hold opinions free from external indoctrination and to defend them without fear of repression. This is a fundamental characteristic of life in a free society which respects human dignity and the autonomy of the individual. This freedom is an element of individual privacy and is protected absolutely by the ICCPR and the European Convention against external interference.

Freedom of expression may also be considered as an element of individual privacy. The expression of one's views on any topic, be it important or trivial, is an exercise of the individual's autonomy and an essential characteristic of living in a society.

Beyond the area of strict privacy, however, freedom of expression is not given absolute protection. That is because the exercise of the right to the freedom can have a detrimental effect on the rights of others and the community. Most notably the right to the freedom may be exercised in a way that will interfere with the privacy of others. The freedom is therefore subject to certain limited restrictions, including respect for the rights or reputations of others, the protection of national security, public order, public health or morals.

Freedom of expression then may be seen as serving the private interests of the individual, enabling the citizen to lead his life as an autonomous individual in society. The freedom may also be seen as enabling the citizen to participate in the 'market place of ideas', to contribute to the formation of public opinion, to participate directly or indirectly in the political process and to oppose actions and policies which may be detrimental to his interests. In these ways, the freedom is both a civil and political right.

[46]   ICCPR, Art. 19(1); European Convention, Art. 10(1).
[47]   ICCPR, Art. 19(3); European Convention, Art. 10(3).
[48]   M. Nowak, 'Freedom of Opinion, Expression and Information', UN Covenant on Civil and Political Rights CCPR Commentary, 335–58.

Freedom of information, on the other hand, is a narrower concept. In contradistinction to the ICCPR concept of freedom of expression, it is viewed primarily as a right of access to information held by government and public authorities, whether the information relates to the individual or the workings of government. In other words, it is seen as a right of access arising from a duty imposed upon the State and public authorities to make information available.

6. CONCLUDING COMMENT

There is an intersection between freedom of expression and freedom of information in that the former includes freedom to seek, receive and impart information. That intersection may extend, as it does in the United States, to the inclusion of a 'right to know', though the boundaries of that concept remain blurred. An individual's right to know may extend to the provision of specific information about the individual held by government and public authorities. In time, that may extend to information about an individual by corporations. Such an extension would conform to the present trend of applying human rights standards to non-government entities. It is possible that extension may be based on human rights other than freedom of information and freedom of expression.

For the future, there will be a greater intersection between freedom of information and privacy as the capacity of information technology threatens the privacy and autonomy of the individual through the collection and storage of data, the exploitation of personal information for a variety of purposes and surveillance.[49] Developments in that area may perhaps prove to be more important than developments relating to the established connection between freedom of information and expression in the area of public law.

But even in that area there is an overwhelming case for extending the obligations of government and public authorities to make comprehensive disclosure of their actions and decision-making processes, without the need for any antecedent application for the provision of information. In this respect, it is disconcerting to note that, in some jurisdictions, freedom of information statutes have received a restrictive rather than a liberal interpretation.

---

[49] See, for example, *Case of Klass and Others*, ECHR Series A, No. 28, 1978.

14

Information as a Human Right

STEPHEN SEDLEY

'Oh God, they have deceived me': George III on his deathbed.

We are accustomed to finding that we have been lied to. To insure ourselves against such deceptions we repeat the mantra that we don't believe everything we read in the newspapers. There have been, and must still be, parts of the world where the reputation of the press is such that people don't believe anything they read in their newspapers: I recall that in Czechoslovakia in the 1960s nobody believed that United States aircraft were dropping cluster-bombs and napalm on Vietnam because the official newspaper, piquantly named *Pravda* (Truth), reported daily that they were. Because our experience in the United Kingdom is less uniformly bad, we tend to give initial credence to what we are told. Yet repeated revelations over recent years that people in whom the public put its trust have been lying not only to the media but to Parliament and the courts have shaken our confidence in our own scepticism.

We need anchorage in some version of reality to keep us from going wholly adrift; but whatever version of reality we choose involves a certain act of faith, or at least of trust. Whom are we to believe? Freedom of expression, a right for which people have literally gone to the stake, has only a distorted bearing on this question because it has to do not with your right to know but with my right to tell you what I think you ought to know. Its triumph in the age of the Enlightenment had and still has a curiously economistic relationship with the right of others to know. Milton, defending the freedom to print without official licence, had argued that 'bad books . . . to a discreet and judicious reader serve in many respects to discover, to confute, to forewarn, and to illustrate.' He commended John Selden's learning because it proved:

not only by great authorities brought together, but by exquisite reasons and theorems almost mathematically demonstrative, that all opinions, yea errors, known, read, and collated, are of main service and assistance toward the speedy attainment of what is truest. . . . For who knows not that truth is strong, next to the Almighty? She needs no policies, nor stratagems, nor licensings to make her victorious; those are the shifts and the defences that error uses against her power.[1]

Here, well over a century before Adam Smith gave it political and legal respectability,[2] was the theory of the marketplace of ideas in which the true, commended by its

---

[1] *Areopagitica* (1644).
[2] See P. S. Atiyah *The Rise and Fall of Freedom of Contract*, ch. 11; Douglas Hay, 'The State and the Market in 1800', *Past and Present*, vol. 162.

manifest virtue, would drive out the false. In the mouth of Justice Holmes, echoing John Stuart Mill, it became part of the jurisprudence of the First Amendment: 'The best test of truth is the power of the thought to get itself accepted in the competition of the market.'[3] Among countless citations of it, Holmes's dictum is the third of four reasons given by Lord Steyn in a significant recent decision on prisoners' rights[4] for placing a high value upon freedom of speech. The first is that freedom of speech is important for its own sake: this I take to mean that it is important to everyone to be able to speak their mind; and so it is, though it is also important for the speaker to consider what harm it can sometimes do. The second is that it promotes self-fulfilment—an aspect, perhaps, of the first reason. The last is that 'freedom of speech is the lifeblood of a democracy'. The physiological metaphor is an apt one because, as Lord Steyn goes on to point out, free speech enables opinion and fact to be carried round the body politic in the hope, if not the expectation, that they will be heeded by others.

But all these reasons lie on what economists would call the supply side. None of them engages with the needs of the recipient of whatever is to be communicated; nor with the situation of others to whom the information or opinion may relate; nor—importantly to this essay—with the situation of those who desire information and cannot get it, or who need information which they do not know exists, or whose lives and possibilities are blighted by silence or by lies. Do they have anything worth calling a right to information?

One of the reasons why it is necessary to ask the question is that history should by now have exploded any serious belief in the marketplace of ideas. We know that truth does not necessarily drive out falsehood: as often as not the reverse happens. To take two random historical examples, Admiral Byng's court martial and execution were engineered and sealed by a mendacious pamphlet campaign orchestrated by the wretched Duke of Newcastle to divert attention from the strategic ineptitude of his own administration; while in France Marie-Antoinette's reputation was irredeemably mired from the moment of her marriage to the Dauphin by a huge and apparently spontaneous literature accusing her on no real evidence of every sexual deviation imaginable.[5] In such a marketplace the truth, even where it is known (as it certainly was in Byng's case and largely was in Dreyfus's), doesn't stand a chance. We know that, as in any real marketplace, the huckster's megaphone can drown the voices of honest traders, the snake-oil merchant prospers while the market gardener goes home empty-handed. In one of the few real-life markets which enjoy near-perfect competition, the used car salesman is a byword for mendacity. It was the century of mass-communication—our century—which was the century of mass-murder driven

---

3 *Abraham v US,* 250 US 616, 630 (1919).
4 *R v Home Secretary, ex p Simms and O'Brien* [1999] 3 WLR 328.
5 Byng, for whom not only Voltaire and Richelieu but his opponent de la Galissonière interceded, is at least now acknowledged to have been shot *pour encourager les autres.* Poor Marie-Antoinette remains indelibly credited with having said of the starving populace '*Qu'ils mangent de la brioche*'—an old cant phrase quoted by Rousseau, *Confessions* (1740), fifteen years before she was born.

by lie-machines. If the victory of truth were ineluctable, only that would be true which triumphed and all that triumphed would be true.

Nor does the fact that we now know these things prove that truth sooner or later prevails: only that it prevails often enough to make it a certainty that just as commonly lies prevail. So does the fact that we have to criminalize people in a variety of contexts for lying—lying about others, lying about merchandise, lying about a company's prospects, lying to secure some benefit for themselves, lying to a court. We do not believe our own cliché that the truth will out, and we would be fools if we did. It is our good fortune to live in a society where there are means—mostly journalistic, sometimes forensic, very occasionally parliamentary—of outing it; but untruths may logically be carried, knowingly or not, by the same vehicles.

Even if the fictional marketplace of ideas is subtracted from the justifications of the right of free speech, the right remains a necessary condition of life in a democracy and—one may add—of the functioning of the rule of law. But is it a sufficient condition? If we stop imagining that an epistemological Darwinism can be depended upon to expel the false and enthrone the true, what assurance remains that a general right of free expression will not permit the triumph of falsehood? Is it necessary therefore to complement free expression, in the toolkit of human rights, by a right to information?[6]

We have come some way over the past half-century towards recognizing information as more than a discretionary gift on the part of those who hold it. Governments pay constant tribute to its importance, and the present government is in the throes of legislating to give the public an enforceable right of access to much official information. The content and ambit of the legislation are heavily contested, and I write at a moment when the final form of the legislation is still unclear. But it is important to appreciate why government is so perennially cautious about opening its cupboards and filing cabinets. It is not the product of some Freudian hangup afflicting permanent secretaries, nor of mere nervousness or embarrassment on the part of ministers. (New Zealand not long ago acquired a respectable freedom of information statute[7] by handing the job over to a committee composed largely of senior civil servants, which broke the deadlock which had paralysed the politicians.) It is because the want of access to government information is a necessary condition of the ability of ministers to feed their versions of fact through lobby journalists to the public[8].

Information is after all not a holy grail; not even a fixed quantity. News is news

---

[6] I say complement where others would say balance or qualify; but these are differences of attitude rather than of principle.

[7] Official Information Act 1982.

[8] During the 1970s I had to see a Minister about a matter affecting lives abroad. The Minister began by demanding the assurance of everyone present that the meeting would be completely confidential. Next morning an account of my role in the meeting (sufficiently imaginative to result in a substantial libel settlement) appeared in one of the daily broadsheets. Mystified how the press even knew of the meeting, I rang the two others who, along with a senior civil servant, had been present and asked if either of them had spoken to a journalist. Neither had—but one of them, a veteran MP, roared with laughter at my bafflement. 'How do you think government in this country is run?' he said.

only when it has been acquired, reported, selected, written up, sub-edited and captioned. Medium and message may not be the same thing, but they are synergistic and commonly indistinguishable: the newsreader's tone can by itself give a wholly unintended slant to the written text. But I propose to avoid the philosophy of truth-telling in favour of an assumption—which I will not defend—that there is in the world a fund of things which are worth knowing either instrumentally or for their own sake but to which only a few have immediate access. That they may be contentious or even falsifiable does not make them, for my purpose, any the less facts: indeed it is irresistibly tempting to define facts—as someone once defined news —as anything someone doesn't want you to know. Such facts tend to be held by research establishments, by large enterprises, by governments and (by design or by accident) by the army of information seekers and traders who travel with them like pilot fish.

This congeries of fact-holders possesses complicated mechanisms, cultural, ethical or rule-based, for controlling the outflow of information without impeding a maximal inflow. The mechanisms are almost always self-interested, driven not by any acknowledged right in others to know what the organization knows but by what it suits the organization that others should know—or, what is not the same thing, should be told. The pilot fish (parliamentary lobby journalists are a good example) are part of it, for their future nourishment depends on their present trustworthiness. But for everyone in the organization the rules are backed by sanctions, often career-threatening, because all organizations know that there is a widespread tendency to leak. Some leaking is done, no doubt, from motives more base than those underlying the secrecy. Some will be done out of true high-mindedness. But it is all done at risk, for it has always been a corollary of the dependence of power on knowledge that power will denounce knowledge which it is unable to control. [9]

The law has come slowly and partially to reverse the risk in selected situations. The tort of breach of confidence has from its infancy been answerable by the exposure of iniquity;[10] but a right to information calls in question the very notion of property in knowledge on which it is founded.[11] Much more recently Parliament has

---

[9]   Thus Milton, fulminating against the licensing of books, recalled his visit to Italy in 1638-9: 'There it was that I found and visited the famous Galileo, grown old a prisoner of the Inquisition, for thinking in astronomy otherwise than the Franciscan and Dominican licensers thought.' (*Areopagitica*, 1644). But the church had earlier reached an uneasy compromise with Galileo. The Jesuit Cardinal Bellarmine had warned the clergy that there were forms of mathematical proof to which dogma might finally have to yield, and the liberalizing moment of Barberini's election to the papacy afforded a few vital years of toleration before Galileo was made in 1632 to recant. (Relevantly to my theme, it was not until over a century after his death (by Barretti in 1757) that the celebrated rejoinder *'Eppur si muove'* was ascribed to him.) If factuality is negotiable, the important thing for Milton's argument was not that Copernican science would inexorably supersede the anthropocentric universe but that it was entitled to the opportunity of doing so.

[10]   *Gartside v Outram* (1856) 26 LJCh 113 (taking the tort's infancy to date from *Prince Albert v Strange* (1849) 2 DeG & Sm 652, 1 Mac & G 25: but see the earlier cases noted at 8 (1) *Halsbury's Laws* (4th edn.) 401, n.1)

[11]   Intellectual property as a human right is subject to lawful control of its use 'in the general interest' (ECHR, Protocol 1, Art. 1).

legislated to protect whistle-blowers from victimization.[12] These are acknowledgements that there is information which others, perhaps the whole world, have a right to know: but they are expressed not in terms of the rights of humanity but of wrongs by which fact-holders may forfeit their own rights. If, however, beyond the law of trade and state secrets, facts are to be regarded not as commodities capable of appropriation and hoarding but as part of the shared necessities of human life, the law still falls short. Its premise remains the proprietorial one, and from it flow countless daily distortions and lacunae in things people want or need to know for entirely legitimate purposes.

We know that our newly acquired human rights instrument, the European Convention, contains no express right to information. Nor do any of the other international or constitutional instruments of which I am aware. Even the most recent and most meticulously liberal, that of South Africa, dropped an enforceable right of reply from its original draft.[13] In the United States, legislative attempts to secure a legal right of reply have been struck down under the First Amendment[14]—logically enough, since the necessary premise of the prohibition on the abridgement of free speech is the possession of it, and ex hypothesi those who need a right of reply don't possess it. There remains in general no way in the developed world of making the media carry the other side of an argument if they don't want to; nor of preventing the dissemination by them of disinformation; nor of stopping them from imposing selective information blackouts.[15]

But the European Court of Human Rights has had from time to time to think about the provision of information by states as a secondary right or obligation derived from the tabulated rights in the Convention. In 1998,[16] it had to consider the rights of people living downwind of a toxic chemical plant near Manfredonia. The Court, in contrast to the Commission, would not accept that the ignorance in which local people had been kept infringed Article 10 of the Convention which begins:

Everyone has the right to freedom of expression. This right shall include freedom to

---

[12] Public Interest Disclosure Act 1998.

[13] viz: 'There shall be freedom of thought, speech, expression and opinion, including a free press which shall respect the right to reply.' The final part has now been limited to regulation of state-funded or state-controlled media to reflect diversity of opinion. But there is a constitutional right of access to official information.

[14] e.g. *Miami Herald v Tornillo* 418 US 241 (1974).

[15] Even to begin to illustrate these propositions would fill the space allocated to this paper, but I know of no journalist who would seriously contest them, at least in relation to others. The press—even the quality press—is particularly sensitive to criticism of itself (critiques, if reported, tend to have the word 'outburst' in the headline). I once, and only once, gave an interview to a legal journalist about whether judges were out of touch. The sole omission from the published account of it was my remark that the average journalist asks more damn-fool questions in a day than the average judge asks in a year.

[16] *Guerra v Italy* (1998) 26 EHRR 357.

hold opinions and to receive and impart information and ideas without interference by public authority . . .

The reason, a narrow one, was that the EEC mechanism for accident readiness and public information was in place in Italy; it was just that it had not worked: the case was therefore not one where government was actively obstructing the flow of information. The Commission, however, by a slender majority, had taken a much firmer line. It held: 'The current state of European law . . . confirms that public information is now an essential tool for protecting public wellbeing and health in situations of danger to the environment.' It cited a 1996 resolution of the Parliamentary Assembly of the Council of Europe to the effect that in relation to nuclear energy and related matters: 'public access to clear and full information . . . must be viewed as a basic human right.' This the Commission took to be evidence of a developing body of European opinion in favour of the recognition of a fundamental right to information in relation to environmental and personal hazards. Article 10, it concluded, placed on states an obligation not simply to make such information accessible but to publish it.

Such a right, if recognized, cannot be treated as parasitic on the tabulated Convention rights. It is, if anything, an implicit prior right by which violation of or respect for other rights can be known. This is possibly why the Court went the other way on Article 10. Its reasoning, however, was terse and narrow: it came to no more than that this was not a case of active suppression of information by the state and so differed from the decisions on press freedom—I will come to them in a moment— in which the Court had recognized the 'right' of the public to be informed as a corollary of the right of free expression. The dissenting members of the Commission, the United Kingdom's member among them, had put it better, if conservatively: a positive obligation to inform would distort the language of Article 10 and would go beyond any decision of the Court. The second of these reasons, while true, is an example of Professor Cornford's axiom that nothing should be done for the first time.[17] The first is a respectable strict constructionist's view of the Convention, but it perhaps takes too little account of the Court's own view of the Convention, in other cases, as a 'living instrument' capable of growth with changing circumstances.

The payoff for the inhabitants of Manfredonia was that the Court went on to hold that Article 8, requiring respect for private and family life, did carry a right to information where, as here, the information was relevant to the enjoyment of the right. Its reasoning, particularly in view of its decision on Article 10, was pretty laconic: the applicants were denied

essential information that would have enabled them to assess the risks they and their families might run if they continued to live at Manfredonia, a town particularly exposed to danger in the event of an accident at the factory.

---

[17] F. M. Cornford, *Microcosmographia Academica* (1908) ch. VII.

Guerra was thus a positive but short step towards a right to information. It was followed, however, in *McGinley and Egan v UK*,[18] by a stronger assertion of the right, this time in favour of servicemen who had been exposed to nuclear test explosions. The claim failed on its facts, but the Court was prepared to enunciate a positive obligation on the state in these terms:

Where a government engages in hazardous activities such as those in issue in the present case, which might have hidden adverse consequences on the health of those involved in such activities, respect for private and family life under Article 8 requires that an effective and accessible procedure be established which enables such persons to seek all relevant and appropriate information.

There is something odd about discovering a right to information in the entrails of Article 8, which says nothing about information, and refusing to discern it in Article 10 which explicitly integrates 'freedom . . . to receive . . . information and ideas without interference by public authority' in the right of free expression. Yet in its recent jurisprudence the Court has stayed with its early decisions that the words I have quoted are included in Article 10 not to accord any right to information but simply to stop governments interfering with 'information that others wish or may be willing to impart'.[19] It is not idle to wonder why, in that case, the framers bothered to put them there at all.

The dominance of the fact-holder in Convention jurisprudence is reinforced by the strong body of Court decisions on press freedom. This is so even where the rhetoric of the court picks up that of the press: 'Not only does the press have the task of imparting . . . information and ideas [on matters of public interest]: the public also has a right to receive them.'[20] Nothing in the Court's jurisprudence so far has carried the right to information under Article 10 beyond an echo of the right of the media to convey their messages. And here there are perhaps the beginnings of a contrast with the English law of defamation. In a recent recasting of the law of qualified privilege[21] Lord Nicholls dropped the old formula of a duty to report coupled with a public interest in knowing, in favour of a single test—'whether the public was entitled to know the particular information'. This finally cuts out the mealy-mouthed plea that it was purely out of a sense of duty that the defendant published its allegations. It places in the centre of the frame what I would regard as the constitutional issue of a right to information.

Even so, all reportage involves selection and presentation, and no Ministry of Truth will ever, one hopes, come to exercise control over these. Journalists can legitimately defend their presentation and choice of data as the way they give the public

---

[18] (1998) 27 EHRR 1.

[19] *Leander v Sweden* (1987) 9 EHRR 433, para. 74; and see *Gaskin v UK* (1989) 12 EHRR 36, though the Court was careful, as always, to tie the proposition to the facts of the particular case.

[20] *Observer and Guardian v UK* (1991) 14 EHRR 153, para. 59; reiterated in *Thorgeirson v Iceland* (1992) 14 EHRR 843, para. 63.

[21] *Reynolds v Times Newspapers Ltd* [1999] 3 WLR 1010.

what it wants, which is not bald or endless facts but information that readers find interesting. This, at least, is the immovable object encountered by the otherwise irre-sistible force of the fact that in a society where less than one tenth of reported crime is violent, the proportion of violent to other crime reported in the press ranges from 18–22 per cent in the broadsheets to 30–35 per cent in the mid-range press and 50–60 per cent in the red-top tabloids. If readers were to find that nine tenths of their paper's crime reports loyally reflected run-of-the-mill frauds and motoring offences, they would switch to another paper.

But where does this end? The public—82 per cent of it—believes that judges systematically under-sentence. Yet a clear majority of the same sample, given the facts of a real-life case, turns out to favour a sentence lighter than that imposed by the trial judge and standardized by the Court of Appeal.[22] There is only one possible source of the disinformation responsible for this paradox. But who is to speak for the right of the public not to be deceived by the press, and where is the rights instrument which will give legitimacy to the claim? The issue is not only a moral one. Ignorance and misinformation create a fear of crime which distorts people's lives. The belief that criminals are simply let off by the courts disinclines some people to report crime or to press charges. It inclines others to take the law into their own hands. And in their turn politicians, rather than challenging the myths, have responded to them as if they were the reality: the history of criminal justice legislation since the liberaliz-ing moment of the Criminal Justice Act 1991, quite consciously spurred on by a segment of the press, has been an almost continuous escalation of punitive responses to crime.

Where then may we look, outside Article 8 of the Convention, for a nascent right to information? The patriation of the Convention by the Human Rights Act 1998 is not, it is worth reiterating, the landing of aliens bent upon abducting members of the UK judiciary and returning them to the bench programmed to speak in a strange idiom. It is an organic enlargement of our system, much of which is already open to such change; and it's therefore appropriate to look within our own law for doctrines which will require and may even welcome adaptation to the Convention's standards.

I will take a single example, the doctrine of informed consent to medical inter-vention. Because it is an artefact entirely of the common law, no problem of resistant statutory provision affects it: it will have to become Convention-compliant. Both because the common law has always prioritized the physical autonomy of the indi-vidual and because more recently the availability of recourse to Strasbourg has sharp-ened awareness of the issues and the pitfalls, the courts have been circumspect about

---

[22] M. Hough and J. Roberts, *Attitudes to Punishment: findings from the British Crime Survey* (Home Office Research Study 179, 1998). The sample was a large one, 8000, and the result confirmed that of a survey of jurors—i.e. members of the public who, uniquely, knew all the facts of the case—conducted for the Royal Commission on Criminal Justice (Report 1993: Research Study No. 19, *The Crown Court study*): most of these considered the sentences passed on defendants they had convicted to be about right or on the high side. That no reader of the press would ever guess that it was so trenchantly argued in an address to the Society of Editors by Lord Justice Judge (see UK Press Gazette (16 July 1999) 19)— with what effect remains to be seen.

permitting medical or psychiatric intervention against the will of the patient;[23] less so, for good reason, against that of an adult who purports to speak for the patient.[24] But refusal, like consent, presumes knowledge, and it is the patient's right to know which remains a fraught issue. The House of Lords, given the opportunity in the mid-1980s to recast the law for our era,[25] opted by a majority for a standard of information which left in the doctor's hands the critical question of how much the patient should know, and the Court of Appeal[26] thereafter leaned towards the most conservative of the four majority speeches as representing the law: so long as the doctor acts in a way of which at least some responsible colleagues would approve, his or her judgment of what the patient ought to know will not be negligent.

The case for not requiring more of doctors, at least when it comes to treatment, is a not inconsiderable one which has held the ring for almost half a century.[27] It has probably played a major part in preventing the development of defensive medicine in this country. But in relation to the initial decision to undergo or to decline treatment its role is far less obvious: indeed the two can be regarded as antithetical. For the very decision to undergo treatment involves a submission to the risk of failure or accident or misjudgment, all falling short of negligence. If the patient is also to be denied a fully informed choice about whether to assume these risks, it can be cogently said that the 'disequilibrium of power between doctor and patient'[28] has become a slippery slope.

It was the pioneering voice of human rights in the United Kingdom, that of Lord Scarman, which spoke out in *Sidaway* against medical paternalism and in favour of personal autonomy. 'The doctor's duty,' he reasoned, 'arises from his patient's rights'; so that included in the doctor's duty of care was 'a proper respect for his patient's rights' of which 'the duty to warn' was part. Drawing on recent Canadian law, he proposed that a risk should be regarded by the law as significant enough to warn the patient of it if a reasonable person in the patient's—not the doctor's—position would think it so; unless clinical judgment indicated that the warning itself would do disproportionate harm to the patient.

Behind the difference of view we can now see far more clearly than we did in the mid-1980s the chasm between the common law's focus on doctors' duties as the fulcrum of liability and the Convention's concern with affirmative rights. It may well be that the courts will be asked to revisit the issue of informed consent to medical intervention in the light of the Human Rights Act. If they are to do so, it is to be expected that they will be invited to look again at the case law of other common law

---

[23] In contrast to the earlier record of the European Court of Human Rights, which in *Neilson v Denmark* (1988) 11 EHRR 175 sanctioned the power of a parent to have a refractory child placed in a psychiatric institution without engaging any responsibility on the part of the state.

[24] See generally Markesinis and Deakin, *Tort Law* (4th edn.) pp. 249–57.

[25] *Sidaway v Bethlem Royal Hospital Governors* [1985] AC 871.

[26] *Gold v Haringey Health Authority* [1987] 2 All ER 888.

[27] *Bolam v Friern Hospital Management Committee* [1957] 2 All ER 118.

[28] The phrase is that of Professor Ian Kennedy, to whose chapter, 'Patients, doctors and human rights', in R.Blackburn and J.Taylor (eds.), *Human Rights for the 1990s*, I am indebted.

countries, both those with and those without rights instruments.[29] They will certainly be asked to think afresh about the issue in the light of Article 8 of the Convention, since respect for private life is plainly engaged and because most medical treatment, being furnished by the state, is unaffected by the problem of horizontality. But one hopes too that thought will be given to the wider principles of human dignity and autonomy which underlie the entirety of human rights instruments. Neither concept is uncomplicated: each takes on a different aspect depending, for example, on whether the individual is regarded as a free agent or as a member of a community.[30] But both have something to say about the balance of power between doctor and patient and therefore about the measure of the latter's undoubted right to information about his or her own chances.

And in recent years, as the prospect of a rights instrument has come closer, the law has quietly moved forward on this front. In 1997,[31] reasserting the received test of medical competence, Lord Browne-Wilkinson set on one side the question of disclosure of risk; and a year later[32] in the Court of Appeal Lord Woolf, drawing the threads together, held:

it seems to me to be the law . . . that if there is a significant risk which would affect the judgment of a reasonable patient, then in the normal course it is the responsibility of a doctor to inform the patient of that significant risk . . .

Thus information may be coming to feature not as a parasitic requirement of another tabulated right but as a prior requisite if other rights are to have value and substance. It was in the case[33] which in 1929 finally enabled the courts of this country to put behind them a deeply embarrassing body of decisions which denied women the status of persons in the democratic process that Lord Sankey LC, in the Privy Council, described the Canadian constitution as a living tree, capable of growth within its natural limits. The metaphor has been adopted by the Canadian Supreme Court in its development of the Charter of Rights and Freedoms and echoed by the Strasbourg court in its description of the Convention as a 'living instrument'.[34] In the field of information and human rights, at least, the space and season for growth — and for the accompanying shedding of dead wood—are palpably there.

---

[29] e.g. *Rogers v Whittaker* (1992) 67 ALJR 47.

[30] See generally David Feldman, 'Human Dignity as a Legal Value' [1999] PL 682 and [2000] PL 61. Perhaps the sharpest example of the conflict is the French Conseil d'État's decision that it was lawful for municipalities to ban dwarf-throwing contests, notwithstanding the wishes of the participants, because the spectacle in which they took part was an affront to their own dignity: CE, ass. 27 October 1995.

[31] *Bolitho v City and Hackney Health Authority* [1997] AC 232, 243.

[32] *Pearce v United Bristol Healthcare NHS Trust* [1999] PIQR P53.

[33] *Edwards v A-G for Canada* [1930] AC 124.

[34] *Tyrer v UK* (1978) 2 EHRR 1, 10.

15

Freedom of Information: The New Proposals

STEPHANIE PALMER

> Sweeping assertions of executive secrecy ought not to be tolerated in a democratic country. . . .
>
> D. Williams *Not in the Public Interest* (1965)

The Labour Party's first term in office has been characterized by a commitment to modernize British politics through radical constitutional change. One of the key elements of this bold initiative is to alter the relationship between the state and the citizen. There are a number of important features of this agenda including the Human Rights Act 1998, devolution, reform of the House of Lords and the proposed freedom of information legislation. The Lord Chancellor has promised that the government 'will govern with a new spirit of openness . . . [in] partnership with the people'.[1]

This paper critically analyses the recently unveiled proposals to implement freedom of information legislation in England and Wales.[2] In particular, it analyses whether these changes will effect a major shift in the relationship between the governed and the government and transform the culture of secrecy so prevalent in the United Kingdom.

1. INTRODUCTION

In 1997, the government quickly acted on its election promise to introduce freedom of information (FOI) by publishing a White Paper outlining its proposals for a Freedom of Information Act and inviting public comment.[3] It was acknowledged in this White Paper that:

Unnecessary secrecy in government leads to arrogance in governance and defective decision-making. The perception of excessive secrecy has become a corrosive influence in the decline of public confidence in government. Moreover, the climate of public opinion has changed: people expect greater openness and accountability from government than they used to.[4]

---

[1] Lord Irvine of Lairg, 'Constitutional Reform and a Bill of Rights' [1997] EHRLR 483.
[2] FOI is a devolved power and the Scottish government has introduced its own Freedom of Information Bill.
[3] Your Right to Know (Cm. 3818) (hereafter referred to as White Paper).
[4] White Paper, para. 1.1.

This statement is a clear reaction to the ethos of secrecy that has been a hallmark of the Westminster style of government. The traditional position in the United Kingdom is that all official information is secret unless governments choose to disclose it. Openness and transparency have been alien concepts in British government administration as the priority has been to protect official information. Stringent secrecy laws and no general statutory right of access to government-held information have permitted governments the freedom to regulate the public dissemination of information. The government controls the form in which information is released as well as the timing of any release. This authoritarian position aroused suspicions that governments could, and indeed would, elevate their interests over all others. These suspicions seemed confirmed by the inquiry into the arms to Iraq affair and the collapse of the *Matrix Churchill* trial. Sir Richard Scott's Report on the affair commented upon the 'consistent undervaluing by government of the public interest that full information should be available to Parliament'[5] which had contributed to a lack of governmental accountability.

The secrecy ethos of British governments has also been buttressed by the criminal law through the Official Secrets Act. The Official Secrets Act 1911 protected all government information regardless of its public interest or its importance. This 'blanket ban' on the release of all unauthorized official information made it impossible to argue directly for FOI legislation: a necessary prerequisite was the repeal of the notorious s. 2 of the Official Secrets Act 1911. As David Williams so elegantly stated in 1965:

Our knowledge of the workings of the central government nowadays is to a very large degree controlled by the Official Secrets Acts. Outsiders cannot look in. Insiders can look out, but they dare not speak out. Solemn and stern reminders of the terms of the Official Secrets Acts have engendered a general attitude of caution.[6]

Although reformed in 1989, the specified categories of information protected by the criminal law are still broad and there is no provision for a public interest defence.[7] Civil servants remain subject to disciplinary proceedings for any disclosures of information violating internal civil service rules and instructions.

In the United Kingdom there has been a trend, albeit hesitant, towards less secrecy in government.[8] We have come a long way since the 1976 'Croham Directive', instructing heads of departments to publish 'as much as possible of the factual and analytical material used as the background to major policy studies' but which remained secret until leaked some years later. In 1993 the previous Conservative

---

[5] Report of the Inquiry into the Export of Defence Equipment and Dual-Use Goods to Iraq and Related Prosecutions HC 115 (1995–6) vols.1–V at para. D1.165.

[6] David Williams, *Not in the Public Interest* (London: Hutchinson, 1965) 208.

[7] See S. Palmer, 'Tightening Secrecy Law: The Official Secrets Act 1989' [1990] PL 243.

[8] During the 1980s and 1990s some progress had been made in establishing a right of access to certain categories of information. See for example Local Government (Access to Information) Act 1985, Environmental Information Regulations 1992, the Data Protection Acts 1984 and 1998.

government published a White Paper on Open Government.[9] It proposed the introduction of a Code of Practice on Access to Government Information.[10] This non-statutory Code came into force in April 1994 and is still in operation at this date. One result of the introduction of the Code was that it raised expectations of greater openness in the public sector. The Code requires government departments to respond to requests for information but it does not make the disclosure of official information obligatory. It also contained wide class-based exemptions. The Parliamentary Commissioner for Administration has been given a role in investigating complaints that departments have not complied with the Code,[11] yet there have been few complaints to the Commissioner concerning breaches of the Code. The reason for the paucity of complaints can probably be explained by the fact that there is no direct access to the Commissioner: individuals have to proceed through their Member of Parliament. Overall these modest changes have not reversed the established atmosphere of secrecy in government. It is clear that a far more radical approach would be required in order to achieve a truly open system of government.

In December 1997, the newly elected Labour government published a White Paper that set out proposals for the introduction of a Freedom of Information legislation. These proposals seemed to signal the intention of the government to effect a fundamental change to the administrative culture in the United Kingdom. The scope of the proposed Bill was to have an impressively wide application. The White Paper stated that it would cover not only government departments but, amongst others, privatized utilities, quangos, local bodies, Universities and Public Service broadcasters. Services performed for public authorities under contract would also be subject to the new FOI Act. According to these proposals, exemptions should be limited to the following seven areas: national security; defence and international relations; law enforcement; personal privacy; commercial confidentiality; the safety of the individual, the public or the environment; information supplied in confidence; and the integrity of the decision-making and policy advice processes in government. The test for disclosure was based on an assessment of harm that disclosure might cause, and the need to safeguard the public interest.[12] In order to guarantee that decisions on disclosure would be based on a presumption of openness, the appropriate test for most categories of information was a substantial harm test. Of particular significance was the White Paper's total rejection of a ministerial veto or conclusive certificates mechanism. It was proposed that FOI legislation should be enforced by an Information Commissioner who would have the power to order disclosure of records and information. In addition the new legislation was to be accompanied by a policy of 'active' disclosure.

In spite of some flaws, the White Paper proposals were largely welcomed[13] but

---

[9] Cm. 2290 (1993).   [10] Ibid., 32.   [11] Ibid., clause 11.
[12] White Paper, para. 3.4.
[13] See P. Birkinshaw, 'An "all singin' and all dancin' " affair: the new Labour government's proposals for freedom of information' [1998] PL 176; R. Hazell, *Commentary on the Freedom of Information White*

after the first year in office and a number of embarrassing disclosures, the government developed cold feet. Justice Michael Kirby has identified 'seven deadly sins of FOI'. The first was 'strangled at birth'. He reports an Australian politician as saying 'that it was imperative for any government proposing a FOI law to get the legislation enacted within the first year of office, lest the skeletons accumulating in the governmental cupboard thereafter render the prospect of enforceable rights of access to information too politically uncongenial to press on with'.[14] Unfortunately, the first sin has been committed. In July 1998, responsibility for Freedom of Information was moved from the Cabinet Office to the Home Office after the sacking of the minister responsible for its publication and amidst rumours that the White Paper proposals would be severely watered down.

In May 1999, the government published a draft Freedom of Information Bill[15] for further consultation and for pre-legislative scrutiny by the House of Commons Select Committee on Public Administration[16] and the House of Lords Delegated Powers and Deregulation Committee.[17] This disappointing Bill abandoned many of the principles contained in the 1998 White Paper. Although providing a right to information, the draft Bill contained numerous devices ensuring that secrecy could be maintained by a government determined to do so.

Subsequently, in November 1999 the government finally presented its long-awaited Freedom of Information Bill to Parliament. Although the Home Secretary responded to some of the criticisms of the draft Bill,[18] the Bill currently before Parliament has emerged as a 'pale shadow' of the proposals outlined in the White Paper. Any initial optimism that new FOI legislation would sweep aside the atmosphere of secrecy and radically alter the administrative culture in the United Kingdom has faded. In contrast, the new Scottish Executive has published proposals for an FOI Act in Scotland that rejects many of the key elements of the Bill before Westminster. In particular, its proposals concerning the publication of policy advice and the power of the Scottish Commissioner to order disclosure differ from the draft Bill

---

Paper (The Constitution Unit, 1998) and S. Palmer, 'Freedom of Information—Principles and Problems: A Comparative Analysis of the Australian and Proposed UK Systems' in *Constitutional Reform in the United Kingdom: Practice and Principles* (The University of Cambridge Centre for Public Law) (Oxford: Hart Publishing, 1998) 147.

[14] Justice Michael Kirby, 'Freedom of Information: The Seven Deadly Sins' [1998] EHRLR 245, 249.

[15] Freedom of Information: Consultation on Draft Legislation, Cm. 4355 (1999).

[16] House of Commons, Public Administration Select Committee, Third Report session 1998–9, 'Freedom of Information Draft Bill', HC 570, July 1999.

[17] 'Report from the Select Committee Appointed to Consider the Draft Freedom of Information Bill' session 1998–99, HL 97, July 1999.

[18] The Home Secretary made some important concessions in the second draft Bill. For example, the time for responding to requests was reduced to twenty working days; the remarkable 'jigsaw' exemption which allowed information to be withheld if it could be harmful in combination with other information was abandoned as was the right of the authorities to insist on knowing why an applicant wanted information or to disclose information on condition it was not given to a journalist.

before Westminster.[19] It seems necessary to canvass once again the reasons why access to information is important. Whether openness in government can be converted from hollow rhetoric to vibrant reality depends in large measure on the extent to which the reforms are grounded in democratic principle. The next section will outline the arguments justifying openness in government. These grounds are not self-contained and tend to overlap each other. The final section will assess whether the government's proposed Bill can ensure the effective enjoyment of the citizen's right to know.

2. PRINCIPLES OF FREEDOM OF INFORMATION

Open government is a vital characteristic of a democratic society.[20] A number of related justifications flow from the recognition of this democratic mandate. The United Kingdom is a democratic society and people now expect to be fully informed about the government's actions, policies and decisions. Without information, individuals are unable to exercise their rights and responsibilities effectively. There is also an accompanying expectation by citizens to be able to participate in and perhaps even to influence government policy-making. Government consultation with the community has been enormously increased by the availability and sophistication of information technology. Indeed the increased consultation has raised expectations of openness and greater transparency in the bureaucracy. Electing a parliamentary representative every few years seems an insufficient involvement with the business of government. Although the issue has been hardly touched upon by politicians, the possibilities of democracy in the world today have changed. The merits of participatory democracy could be re-examined now that the technical feasibility is closer at hand.[21] Such ideas cannot be entertained unless sufficient information is available.

Access to information must be a prerequisite to the proper and effective functioning of a healthy democratic society. In our political system the Executive is not sufficiently responsible to Parliament. The political reality is that the Executive has significant control over Parliament. Without openness, the principle of responsible government is undermined. The work of select committees, the efficacy of parliamentary questions, the effectiveness of opposition parties and pressure groups all depend on the availability and accessibility of information. Power is at the heart of secrecy in government and power and information are inextricably linked.[22] The

---

[19] See 'An Open Scotland. Freedom of Information: A Consultation'. This document was laid before the Scottish Parliament by the Scottish Ministers in November 1999.

[20] Open government and freedom of information are not synonymous concepts. Freedom of information requires governments to disclose information requested by interested parties whereas open government suggests more transparency but not necessarily any right to enforce it.

[21] See D. Held, *Models of Democracy* (2nd edn., Cambridge: Polity, 1996) 327.

[22] See E. W. Thomas, 'Secrecy and Open Government' in P. D. Finn (ed.), *Essays on Law and Government: Principles and Values* (Sydney, Australia: The Law Book Company, 1995).

Executive has possession of a vast amount of information and is in a position to authorize selective disclosure in a manner and at a time convenient for the government. Partial disclosure may distort accountability.

The constitutional conventions of individual and collective ministerial responsibility are frequently used to legitimate the maintenance of government secrecy, by 'enforcing an internal governmental discipline in the control of information'.[23] The traditional theory of Ministerial responsibility has led to the practice whereby Ministers decide for themselves what information should or should not be disclosed to Parliament. Yet the reality is that the doctrine has been eroded to the point where it has been described as deserving 'the status of a legal fiction'.[24] Ministers frequently use their power to 'leak' information or give non-attributable briefings to journalists when it is politically expedient. The manipulation of information is inevitable. It is an inadequate means of securing official information. A right to freedom of information may not prohibit leaks in the future but it may make it possible to obtain a complete picture.

FOI legislation is a potentially important tool to redress the imbalance in power. It also enables more effective supervision of the Executive within Parliament. In Australia, the opposition parties have made extensive use of the access to information provisions under the Freedom of Information Act 1982. On the one hand, the theory assumes that the potential exposure to criticism should enhance the government's performance. On the other, the threat of increased criticism makes a strong freedom of information legislation an unattractive prospect for governments. Yet one of the fundamental purposes of FOI legislation should be to strike a balance between competing public interests of openness and secrecy: neither are absolute values. In order for freedom of information legislation to satisfy the democratic mandate, the unfettered discretion accorded to governments to control the release of information must be subordinated to wider public interest considerations. These ideas have received judicial recognition in freedom of expression decisions such as *Derbyshire C.C. v Times Newspapers Ltd.*,[25] which stressed the importance of uninhibited criticism of government bodies as an important part of the democratic process; and in *Spycatcher (No. 2)*,[26] where Lord Keith cited with approval from the Australian High Court: 'It is unacceptable, in our democratic society that there should be a restraint on the publication of information relating to government when the only vice of that information is that it enables the public to discuss, review and criticize government action.'[27]

The political culture in the United Kingdom has not encouraged any idea of 'participatory democracy' which could have lent legitimacy to claims by individuals

[23]　C. Turpin, *British Government and the Constitution* (4th edn.) (London: Butterworths, 1999) 523.
[24]　D. Feldman, 'Public Law Values in the House of Lords' (1990) 106 LQR 246, 254.
[25]　[1993] 2 WLR 449.
[26]　*Attorney-General v Guardian Newspapers Ltd. (No. 2)* [1990] 1 AC 109.
[27]　Ibid, citing from *Commonwealth of Australia v John Fairfax and Sons Ltd.* (1980) 147 CLR 39, at 52 per Mason J.

and groups for access to government-held information. Indeed it is widely assumed that government information is the property of the government, even though this valuable resource is created and maintained at the taxpayers' expense. This traditional view was 'discerned' by Nevil Johnson in a Note issued by the Head of the Civil Service in 1985 that 'in some sense all information gained in the course of duty is the private property of the Government of the day and, therefore, to be disclosed only if its disclosure is regarded as desirable and duly authorised.'[28] This view is at odds with the role of government in a mature democracy. The Queensland Information Commissioner has summarized the position:

The information which public officials, both elected and appointed, acquire or generate in office is not acquired or generated for their own benefit, but for purposes related to the legitimate discharge of their duties of office, and ultimately for the service of the public for whose benefit the institutions of government exist, and who ultimately (through one kind of impost or another) fund the institutions of government and the salaries of officials.[29]

Lord Lester has also commented, during his evidence to the Commons Select Committee on Public Administration that, apart from some necessary exceptions,

information about political and government activity obtained by public officials in the course of their duty is not, or should not properly be regarded as *government* property, however much it is clothed in Crown or parliamentary copyright, or protected by official secrets legislation, or by the law protecting confidential information and personal privacy, or by the law of contract. Ultimately, information about political and governmental activity belongs to the people whose interests Ministers and civil servants are elected or appointed to serve.[30]

A further justification put forward for increased openness in government and FOI legislation focuses on the public's needs as consumers.[31] Information on consumer and environmental issues provides citizens with the opportunity to make informed decisions as well as contribute to the public debate.[32]

Finally, every citizen should have a right to know what information is held about themselves in government records. A vast amount of information is stored by government. The Franks Committee in 1972 observed that: 'The government possesses some information, at least, about every citizen and every firm in the land, in some

---

[28] Memorandum to the Treasury and Civil Service Committee, Seventh Report, HC 92-II (1985–86), 172 cited in C. Turpin (n. 23 above) 523.

[29] *Re Eccleston and Dept. of Family Services and Aboriginal and Islander Affairs* (1993) 1 QAR 60, 73. Cited in Australian Law Reform Commission Report No 77, para. 4.9. Note also the influence of the High Court 'free speech' cases and the value placed on ensuring the proper working of representative democracy. See *Australian Capital Television Pty. Ltd. v Commonwealth* (1992) 177 CLR 106 and *Nationwide News Pty. Ltd. v Wills* (1992) 177 CLR 1.

[30] Evidence to the House of Commons, Public Administration Select Committee (29 June 1999).

[31] See D. Oliver, *Government in the United Kingdom: The Search for Accountability, Effectiveness and Citizenship* (Milton Keynes: Open University Press, 1991) 169; Thomas (n. 22 above) 196.

[32] The government has specifically recognized the role of people as citizens and consumers in the White Paper, 'Modernising Government' Cm. 4310 (1999).

cases it possesses a very considerable amount of such information.'[33] There is a natural and healthy desire by citizens to know what information the government holds about individuals and, if necessary, to check and correct inaccurate data. In this sense issues of privacy and FOI should not be viewed as totally separate developments. The Data Protection Act 1998 was passed to give effect to the EC Data Protection Directive[34] and, amongst other things, provides for individuals to seek access to personal information about themselves if the information is held in computerized or certain structured files. The FOI Bill proposes to extend these rights, in some circumstances, to information held in unstructured files[35] and contains a limited right for third parties to obtain personal information where access is consistent with the principles set out in the Data Protection Act 1998.

Openness in government is viewed as a democratic right but freedom of information can also be regarded as part of the general right of freedom of expression. Article 10 of the European Convention on Human Rights guarantees the right to receive and impart information. There is, however, no express guarantee for the right of access to information in the European Convention on Human Rights (ECHR).[36] Article 10 of the ECHR provides for a right to 'receive information' which has been held to be limited to receiving information 'that others wish or may be willing to impart'[37]. More recently, the European Court of Human Rights has developed a limited right of access to information by way of a positive obligation under Article 8 (respect for private and family life). In the case of *Gaskin v UK*,[38] the Court found that in some circumstances an obligation on the government to impart information may arise. The United Kingdom was found to have violated the principle of proportionality in Article 8 because it failed to provide for an independent authority to decide on the issue of disclosure. The UK procedures were unsuccessfully challenged in *McGinley and E. E. v UK*.[39] The case concerned two servicemen who were exposed to nuclear bomb tests in the Pacific forty years ago and have been denied access to their medical records. The European Court found no violation of either Article 6 or Article 8. Nevertheless, the Court stated:

Where a Government engages in hazardous activities, such as those in issue in the present case, which might have hidden adverse consequences on the health of those involved in such activities, respect for private and family life under Article 8 requires that an effective and accessible procedure be established which enables such persons to seek all relevant and appropriate information.[40]

---

[33] *Report of the Departmental Committee on s. 2 of the Official Secrets Act 1911*, under the Chairmanship of Lord Franks, Cmnd. 5104, para. 192 (1972).

[34] Council Directive (EC) 95/46 OJ L281/31.   [35] FOI Bill, s. 68.

[36] See G. Malinverni, 'Freedom of Information in the European Convention on Human Rights and in the International Covenant on Civil and Political Rights' (1983) 4 Human Rights Law Journal 443–60.

[37] *Leander v Sweden* (1987) Series A No. 116, 29, para.74.

[38] (1990) 12 EHRR 36. See also *Guerra v Italy* (1998) 26 EHRR 357.

[39] (1998) 27 EHRR 1   [40] ibid. 45.

The Human Rights Act will underpin the access provisions for individuals who are seeking information about themselves but will not directly provide equivalent support for the other aspects of FOI legislation. It is crucial therefore that the legislation reflects the constitutional arguments and democratic principles outlined above by providing an FOI system that can achieve a real cultural shift in public administration. The release of information under an FOI law is not an end in itself. Administrative systems of 'active' voluntary disclosure as envisaged in the White Paper, close monitoring of the operation of FOI, the giving of reasons for administrative decisions and the oversight of an independent decision-maker who has the power to stand up to government are essential. The FOI law is an important ingredient in reasserting the principle of accountable government. But open government should be understood as an important constitutional principle in its own right. Individuals already have access to information relating to their affairs in the hands of government through the Data Protection Act. A true test of whether the new legislation underpins the constitutional principles of openness and accountability lies with providing greater public scrutiny of the process of government, including the making and developing of policy. As the Bill is in the process of passing through Parliament, the next section will focus on the central issues in the FOI Bill.

3. SOME FEATURES OF THE PROPOSED FREEDOM OF INFORMATION BILL

According to the Home Secretary, Mr Jack Straw, the proposed FOI Bill 'lays down for the first time in our constitutional history that the public have a right to know about the work of Government and all other public authorities'.[41] In the White Paper the government acknowledged that it is in the best position to champion the cause of open government and to challenge the entrenched secrecy culture that has been an established feature of the administration of the UK government. It is still not clear to what extent the draft Bill will achieve these objectives.

The government has decided not to include a 'purpose clause' in the draft Bill.[42] The advantage of including the objective in the legislation itself is that it is likely to encourage an interpretation of the law that is consistent with its democratic purpose by establishing a clear presumption in favour of disclosure. These provisions are in evidence in other FOI legislation: in Australia, New Zealand and Ireland.[43] In New Zealand, for example, 'the Ombudsmen have stressed time and time again that the Act must receive such fair large and liberal interpretation as will best attain the

[41] *Hansard,* HC (series 6) vol. 340, col. 714 (7 December 1999) and see also White Paper, para. 7.6.

[42] See e.g. the views of the Data Protection Registrar, Elizabeth French, given in her evidence to the House of Commons Select Committee on Public Administration (28 June 1999) paras. 2.4. to 2.6. The Scottish Executive has signalled that the Scottish Bill may contain a 'purpose clause'.

[43] See the Australian Federal Freedom of Information Act 1982, s. 3; New Zealand Official Information Act 1982, ss. 4 and 5. The purpose of the Irish Act is set out in the long title of the Freedom of Information Act 1997.

objects of the Act set out in sections 4 and 5'.[44] Experience from Australia suggests that it is essential that the object of the legislation should include the underlying principle of the Act.[45] The section setting out the objectives of the Australian FOI Act has led to some interpretative difficulties: it was possible to conclude that the right of access provided by the Act was an end in itself, whereas an object clause which explained the broader public interest to be served by enabling access to government documents would encourage an interpretation favourable to disclosure.[46] It is to be hoped that the government will reconsider their position on this issue.[47]

The Bill has some good points. First, a statutory right of access to information, as opposed to a Code, has a major psychological as well as legal effect. Second, the legislation will be fully retrospective which will avoid any problems with an 'access gap': documents created fewer than thirty years ago but before 1999. Third, it covers a wide range of organizations at all levels of government. The schedule of public authorities includes such diverse bodies as the Advisory Committee on Hazardous Substances, the Law Commission, the Parole Board and the Zoos Forum. Fourth, it provides for free access to the Information Commissioner and an appeal to a Tribunal. Finally, there are strict limits on the response times. The Home Secretary took the advice of the Select Committees and reduced the response time from forty to twenty working days following the date of receipt.[48] The government has also promised to repeal the numerous secrecy clauses in other statutes.[49]

In order to assess whether the proposed Bill satisfies the essential constitutional principles vital for an effective FOI, a number of criteria must be satisfied. First, the current Bill creates an enforceable public right of access to official information.[50] The efficacy of this right could be undermined if there are extensive exceptions from the general principle of openness. Lessons from other countries that have introduced FOI legislation indicate that the sharpest debates concern the exemptions. To what extent will the exceptions to the FOI principle endanger the likelihood of achieving greater transparency? Second, do the proposals provide for effective independent scrutiny? Finally, does the draft Bill encourage a system of 'active disclosure'?

---

[44] Eagles, Taggart and Liddell, *Freedom of Information in New Zealand* (Auckland; OUP, 1992) 4.

[45] Australian Law Reform Commission, Report No. 77, Administrative Review Council, Report No. 40, *Open Government: a review of the federal Freedom of Information Act 1982* (hereafter referred to as the ALRC). Section 3 of the Australian Freedom of Information Act states that the object of the legislation is 'to extend as far as possible the right of the Australian community to access information in the possession of the Government of the Commonwealth'.

[46] ALRC, paras. 4.4–4.6.

[47] See also the comments of Dr Clark, *Hansard*, HC (series 6) vol. 340, col. 741 (7 December 1999).

[48] FOI Bill, clause 9.

[49] *Hansard*, HC (series 6) vol. 340, col. 738 (7 December 1999).

[50] There is no directly enforceable right of public access through the courts eg no claim for breach of statutory duty. Part IV provides for enforcement through the Commissioner.

3.1 The exemptions

Clause 1 of the Bill provides for a general right of access to information held by public authorities.[51] Part II of the Bill sets out the circumstances where a public authority is under no duty to provide access. Exemptions to the right of access are features of all FOI legislation. The purpose of the exemption provisions is to balance the objective of providing access to government information against legitimate claims for protection.[52] Inevitably, a tension exists between the principle of a right to know and any claim a government is permitted to make to resist disclosure of a document or information. The scope of exemptions in FOI legislation and the degree of independent supervision are crucial. If the exemptions are too extensive, they make a mockery of such legislation.

In the White Paper, the government proposed that 'the test for disclosure [of exempt material] under FOI should be based on an assessment of the harm that disclosure might cause, and the need to safeguard the public interest'.[53] In order to guarantee that decisions on disclosure would be based on a presumption of openness, the appropriate test for most categories of information should be a *substantial* harm test.[54] This set a high hurdle for the public authority to establish. This formulation suggested that it would be necessary to demonstrate that substantial harm would flow from the release rather than merely could do so. Only a limited number of interests were to be protected by the harm test and disclosure was to be assessed on a 'contents basis' rather than a 'class basis'.[55] The seven exemptions in the White Paper, in contrast to the fifteen set out in the 1994 Code of Practice, were: national security, defence and international relations, law enforcement, personal privacy, commercial confidentiality, the safety of the individual, the public and the environment, information supplied in confidence and decision-making and policy advice.

The Bill departs from the White Paper suggestions. The number of exemptions has increased from seven to over twenty. In addition, the Secretary of State has the power to exempt further information at short notice after weighing up competing public interests.[56] In those areas dealing with a harm exemption, the Bill has adopted the far weaker test of 'prejudice' or 'is likely to prejudice'.[57] The two Select Committees recommended that the appropriate test should be 'substantially prejudice' for at least some exemptions.[58] During the parliamentary debates, the Home Secretary cited with approval the views of the Confederation of British Industry:

---

[51] Definition of public authorities, see clauses 2–5.
[52] See discussion in ALRC (above n. 45), para. 8.1.
[53] White Paper, para. 3.4.
[54] White Paper, para. 3.7.
[55] The reference to contents and class-based exemptions is borrowing terminology from public interest immunity claims.
[56] FOI Bill, clause 43.
[57] See clauses 24–7, 29, 31, 41.
[58] HC 570, para. 71; HL 97, para. 25.

We believe the test for disclosing information should be one of simple harm and not substantial harm . . . Any attempt to limit the ability to withhold information to that which may cause substantial harm to a business may prevent the voluntary disclosure of information to Government. Without proper assurances, we do not consider that the Government's approach will achieve the objective of two-way openness and trust.[59]

The Home Secretary went on to state that the test referred to a probability of harm and not a possibility.[60] The same point was made in the Consultation Document where it was stated that 'the prejudice must be real, actual or "of substance".'[61] If this is what the government intends then they should qualify the word prejudice by either 'serious' or 'substantial'.[62]

Again in stark contrast to the White Paper proposals,[63] the Bill introduces blanket or 'class' exemptions that would permit all information within a particular class to be withheld, regardless of any harm. These class-based exemptions are highly controversial and entirely out of tune with recent developments in public interest immunity claims.[64] These exemptions apply to all information relating to the formulation or development of government policy, all ministerial communications, the obtaining of advice from law officers, information about ministers' private offices, information about various security bodies, information obtained in confidence from other governments and international bodies, information held by the police or regulators in connection with investigations into offences, including those in which all the proceedings have ended, court records including the final report of any tribunal or statutory inquiry, information subject to parliamentary privilege, information about honours, information accepted by a public authority in confidence, information subject to legal professional privilege, information about trade secrets, information whose disclosure is prohibited by statute or Community obligations, and information which is reasonably accessible to the public already.

Some of these broad categories of class exemptions can only be described as astonishing. A highly controversial issue in most FOI legislation is whether decision-making and policy advice should be disclosed. Such information will be of great interest to the media, opposition MPs and pressure groups, as well as individuals. Achieving greater transparency in government requires more of this type of information to be released but this is precisely the sort of material that most governments seek to keep confidential. Premature disclosure of policy advice could genuinely interfere with the government's ability to develop policy. Nevertheless, some internal discussion could be disclosed without harm and would be consistent with the open government principle. Considered assessments of a publicly announced policy are

[59] *Hansard,* HC (series 6) vol. 340, col.725 (7 December 1999).
[60] ibid. col. 717.
[61] Cm. 4355, para. 36.
[62] See evidence of Lord Lester to the House of Commons Select Committee, see n. 30 above.
[63] White Paper, para. 3.8.
[64] See *R v Chief Constable of the West Midlands Police Force, ex p Wiley* [1995] 1 AC 274. See also M. Supperstone, 'A New Approach to Public Interest Immunity?' [1997] PL 211.

highly unlikely to be harmful to policy development. The decision of the government to release the minutes of the monthly meetings between the Chancellor of the Exchequer and the Governor of the Bank of England, just six weeks after the meeting had taken place, has not been detrimental to the decision-making process.[65]

The White Paper sensibly distinguished between decision-making and policy advice on the one hand, and factual and background material on the other. It suggested that the latter should be made publicly available.[66] Under the Bill, a class exemption covers information relating to 'the formulation or development of government policy' without any reference to the distinction outlined in the White Paper, 'ministerial communications' or 'the operation of any Ministerial private office'.[67] The effect of this clause is that even routine communications such as a Minister's letter to colleagues reminding them that new regulations are about to come into force would be exempt and subject to no test of harm.[68] This clause is even wider when read together with the exemption applying to disclosures of information that would 'in the reasonable opinion' of the authority prejudice the convention of collective ministerial responsibility, inhibit 'the free and frank provision of advice', or the exchange of views for the purposes of deliberation, or otherwise prejudice 'the effective conduct of public affairs'.[69] The government's background paper confirms that the subjective harm test (the reasonable opinion of a Minister) will prevent the Commissioner challenging these decisions unless irrational.[70] Policy information, including purely factual material and scientific advice, is very well insulated against disclosure under this FOI Bill. There is a countervailing duty on Ministers to consider the public interest. Clause 13, as amended, imposes a duty to disclose information, including policy-related material, if the balance of public interest is in favour of disclosure.[71]

The distinction is short-sighted. Increased transparency in decision-making could even be beneficial for governments. For example, background material could show a policy decision was made for objective reasons and not for short-term political advantage. Knowledge that analysis may be exposed to outside scrutiny could even improve the quality of advice. This material could be protected adequately by a harm test. Maurice Frankel, of the Campaign for Freedom of Information, has concluded that the Bill on this point is even more limited than the Code introduced by John Major. The reversal of the White Paper approach is deeply disappointing and the current proposals frustrate the underlying principles and central aims of FOI.

A further surprising class exemption covers information held by the police,

---

[65] Campaign for Freedom of Information, *Key Issues* (1997) 6. Compare the decision of *Burmah Oil Co v Bank of England* [1980] AC 1090.

[66] White Paper, para. 3.13. [67] FOI Bill, clause 33.

[68] Campaign for Freedom of Information, Briefing for Second Reading (December 1999) 14.

[69] FOI Bill, clause 34(2).

[70] Home Office, 'FOI. Preparation of Draft Legislation. Background Material' (1999) 12.

[71] FOI Bill, clauses 13(4) and (5) but see clause 52. See discussion below.

prosecuting authorities and a wide range of regulatory bodies.[72] This includes investigations by both the police and regulatory bodies, including Trading Standards Officers to Health and Safety Executive Inspectors. The exemption applies to information which has 'at any time been held' for the purpose of an investigation which could have led to proceedings for an offence, or was held by a prosecuting authority in connection with potential proceedings.[73] In a response to the recommendations of the Public Administration Select Committee Report on the Freedom of Information Draft Bill, the government argued that this exemption was necessary 'to preserve the judicial process and to ensure that the criminal courts remain the sole forum for determining guilt'.[74] Yet clause 29 already permits information to be withheld in circumstances where it might 'prejudice the administration of justice' or 'the prevention or detection of a crime'.[75] The potential effect of this exemption is to provide protection for any evidence of wrongdoing, incompetence or default. Miscarriages of justice could be shielded from scrutiny, unless leave for judicial review is granted. Has the government already forgotten the questions raised by the Macpherson Report into the Stephen Lawrence murder inquiry? In fact, the Macpherson Report proposed: 'That a FOI Act should apply to all areas of policing, both operational and administrative, subject only to the "substantial harm" test for withholding disclosure.'[76]

The Bill provides a very broad definition for the exemption concerning trade secrets, and information whose 'disclosure would, or would be likely to, prejudice the commercial interests of any person (including the public authority holding it)'.[77] All overseas legislation contains similar clauses designed to protect individuals and companies against disclosure that would result in material financial loss, prejudice the outcome of contract negotiations or place them at a competitive disadvantage.[78] This clause in the Bill is unusual compared to other FOI legislation in one respect. The Bill imposes no statutory duty to notify or consult the individual or body who supplied the commercial information, before disclosing it. This notification procedure overseas is known as a 'reverse FOI procedure'. In Australia, for example, the reverse procedure gives companies an opportunity to be notified, to make representations and to appeal to the Administrative Appeals tribunal.[79] It is to be hoped that a right to appeal to the Commissioner will be included in future reforms.

---

[72]   FOI Bill, clause 28(1).

[73]   This class exemption has been narrowed in that investigations which could not lead to proceedings for an offence are no longer subject to the class exemption.

[74]   Government response to the Public Administration Select Committee on the FOI Draft Bill, 22 October 1999.

[75]   See FOI Bill, clause 29(1)(a)–(c) and (g).

[76]   The Stephen Lawrence Inquiry: Report of an Inquiry by Sir W. Macpherson, Cm. 4262 (1999), Recommendation 9.

[77]   FOI Bill, clause 41.

[78]   See e.g. Freedom of Information Act 1982 (Australia), s. 43 and Freedom of Information Act 1997 (Ireland), s. 27.

[79]   Freedom of Information Act 1982 (Australia) s. 27(1). Complaints can also be made to the Ombudsman (ibid., s. 57).

The Bill also provides for 'public interest disclosures' for information falling under nearly all of the exemptions.[80] This key provision was strengthened during the Bill's passage through the Commons.[81] In Australia, New Zealand and Ireland, an overriding public interest test applies to most of the exemption provisions: the effect of the public interest test is to deter public authorities from automatically withholding requested information because it falls within an exemption. As a consequence, public authorities must engage in a balancing exercise to weigh up the effects of disclosure in each individual case. Initially, the Bill differed quite dramatically from the overseas public interest test as it relied on voluntary disclosure without a public interest override. Where it appears to the authority that, in all the circumstances of the case, the public interest in disclosing the information outweighs the public interest in maintaining the exemption in question the public authority shall communicate the information to the applicant.[82] Disclosure through the public interest test provides the only opportunity for access to an enormous amount of material held by authorities, especially the class exemptions.[83]

The public interest amendment is an important concession. Where harm-based exemptions are involved, information whose disclosure could lead to prejudice might still be disclosed on the grounds of overriding public interest. Even where an exemption applies, an authority must disclose information where the public interest in disclosure outweighs the public interest in maintaining the exemption. Access on public interest grounds is the only means to seek the disclosure of class exemption information. This is unsatisfactory. These broad exemptions include all information falling within the class, regardless of harm. Surely the application of a harm test would make more sense and have the advantage of being a relatively simple test. In contrast, the new arrangement is quite complex as it involves identifying and balancing public interests. Arguably the weighing of these competing interests would be easier with a purpose clause. There is some scope here for effective scrutiny and enforcement by the Commissioner as she has the power to order disclosure in the public interest. In relation to exempt information, the Commissioner's power is subject to a ministerial veto.[84]

3.2 Independent Scrutiny and Enforcement

An effective and independent system of enforcement of the public right to access is

---

[80] FOI Bill, clause 13(1)(a) lists the few exceptions.
[81] Hansard, HC. vol. 347, cols. 916–35 (4 April 2000).
[82] FOI Bill, clause 13(4)(b).
[83] The concept of public interest has been developed in breach of confidence actions. See *Lion Laboratories Ltd. v Evans* [1984] 2 All ER 417. There is a statutory public interest test in the Data Protection Act 1998, s. 32(1). The Open Government Code also requires authorities to disclose exempt information in the public interest, in particular where it would assist public understanding of an issue, improve transparency and accountability of government or where disclosure may expose wrongdoing, a risk to public health, safety or the environment. See the official guidance on the code.
[84] See discussion below.

essential if a freedom of information system is to operate effectively. The White Paper had given a key role to the Information Commissioner to investigate complaints that a public authority has failed to comply with the requirements of the Act either by refusing to disclose information, or by imposing excessive charges for information. It also suggested that the Commissioner should have the power to order disclosure of records and information but he or she could not enforce this directly: an order for contempt would have to be sought from the High Court.[85]

The role of Information Commissioner is given a prominent place in the Bill. This is advantageous as the Commissioner has expertise in the field and it avoids overburdening the courts. The Commissioner will perform twin roles in relation to data protection and freedom of information thereby avoiding conflict between the two agencies. Nevertheless, there are still tensions as the dual roles could emphasize differing public interest values.

Some rather worrying clauses concerning the role of the Commissioner have been reconsidered. For example, the proposal to make it a criminal offence for the Commissioner to release detailed information on the handling of complaints against government departments. The Home Secretary has also abandoned the clause that the Commissioner may be denied access to information where it would lead to self-incrimination by a public authority.

The critical factor is the Commissioner's powers of independent scrutiny and enforcement. Without this feature in an FOI system, there will be minimal public confidence in its operation. Any person may apply to the Commissioner for a decision concerning a request for information.[86] If the Commissioner is satisfied that a public authority has not complied with any of the requirements relating to access to information held by public authorities, she may serve 'an enforcement notice'.[87] It sets out the steps which, in the Commissioner's opinion, should be taken to rectify the situation. If a public authority fails to comply with the notice, the Bill provides that the Commissioner may certify this failure to the High Court.[88]

As mentioned above, the Commissioner has power to order the disclosure of nearly all information on public interest grounds but her decision could be over-ridden by a ministerial veto under clause 52. This clause provides that a public authority does not have to comply with an enforcement notice issued by the Commissioner concerning public interest disclosure if the 'accountable person' for that authority certifies within twenty days that 'he has on reasonable grounds, formed the opinion that the authority did not fail to comply with section 13 in relation to that request.' The 'accountable person' will usually be a Minister of the Crown.[89]

In 1997, the government explicitly rejected the introduction of a Ministerial veto.

---

[85]   The government has announced that the present Data Protection Registrar, Elizabeth France, will hold the post of Commissioner.   [86]   FOI Bill, clause 49.
[87]   FOI Bill, clause 51.   [88]   FOI Bill, clause 53(1) and (3).
[89]   FOI Bill clause 52(4). The government has announced that it will further restrict the Executive override..

The White paper stated: 'We have considered this possibility, but decided against it, believing that a government veto would undermine the authority of the Information Commissioner and erode public confidence in the Act'[90] The existence and scope of the executive override strikes at the heart of FOI legislation as it maintains ministerial control over disclosure. The fear is that this power could be abused to protect ministers and public authorities from embarrassment. Even if an authority has been negligent or complacent it may avoid scrutiny. The only remaining option would be to seek judicial review. The ministerial veto power is a critical weakness at the heart of the Bill.

3.3 Active disclosure and good administrative practice

Part III of the Bill requires the Secretary of State to issue a code of practice providing guidance to public authorities on administrative matters concerned with the discharge of their functions under the legislation.[91] The code will include critical elements concerning the practical functioning of the new FOI regime. Robert Hazell observes that relegating key elements to codes of practice is a negative signal to public servants. 'Even if the legal effect is essentially the same, the political effect is different. Civil servants are very astute in reading political messages; the messages in the draft bill will not encourage them to be more open.'[92] The inclusion of a purpose clause would encourage civil servants to be more innovative and risk taking.[93]

The Bill also places a duty on the Commissioner to promote good practice and public authorities' compliance with the Bill.[94] Where an authority's practice as required by the Code is not followed, the Commissioner may give the authority a practice recommendation.[95] This recommendation will set out the steps necessary to achieve conformity. If a public authority fails to comply, the Bill provides that the Commissioner may certify this failure to the High Court. After inquiries, the High Court may 'deal with the authority as if it had committed a contempt of court.'[96] The Commissioner is also under an obligation to disseminate information to the public about FOI.[97] Public authorities are required to adopt and maintain a scheme relating to the publication of information by the authority that is to be approved by the Commissioner.[98] In adopting or reviewing such a scheme, a public authority shall have regard to the public interest in access to information and in the publication of reasons for decisions made by the authority.[99] The success of these schemes is crucial in order for FOI legislation to achieve its objectives.

If information is to be refused, clause 15 requires an authority to advise the applicant on why the exemption applies.[100] There is no duty to tell the dissatisfied

---

[90] White Paper, para. 5.18.   [91] FOI Bill, clause 44.
[92] R. Hazell, Commentary on Draft Freedom of Information Bill (The Constitution Unit) (1999) 23.
[93] ibid.   [94] FOI Bill, clause 46.
[95] FOI Bill, clause 47.   [96] FOI Bill, clause 53(3).   [97] FOI Bill, clause 46(2).
[98] FOI Bill, clause 17.   [99] FOI Bill, clause 17(3)(a) and (b).
[100] FOI Bill, clause 15(1).

applicant that he or she can appeal to the Commissioner. It is highly unsatisfactory that there is no statutory duty to advise or help applicants. Where an authority refuses information pursuant to clause 13 (discretionary disclosures) reasons must be given for the decision.[101] There is no obligation to provide reasons if 'the statement would involve the disclosure of information which would itself be exempt information.'[102] This 'opt out' should be used sparingly as good administrative practice requires the giving of reasons.

4. CONCLUSION

The government's FOI Bill will not ensure that the culture and practices of secrecy in government and other public authorities are set aside for good. The right of access is eroded by the wide exemptions, especially in the areas of policy advice, information from investigations and commercial information. The public interest test provides the only opportunity to assess exempt information but the existence of a ministerial veto makes it possible to conceal harmless information. The Commissioner has been given insufficient powers of enforcement. A strong commitment to openness would give the independent Commissioner a public interest override and the power to order disclosure with few exceptions. These proposals hardly signify a new relationship between the state and its citizens. It is likely that some features of the Bill will be changed or amended during its passage through Parliament.[103] It seems highly unlikely, however, that the government will agree to give any further powers to the Information Commissioner.

This Bill, in its current form, is a deeply disappointing document. It falls short of the commitment made in the government's own White Paper which aimed to reverse the culture and practices of secrecy in government. It has ignored many of the good practices and pitfalls that are evident in the freedom of information legislation of overseas countries with a similar political system to the United Kingdom. Although providing a right to information, the Bill contains devices ensuring that secrecy can be maintained by a government or public authority determined to do so. The structure of the Bill is likely to encourage judicial review applications. Freedom of information is a democratic imperative and this Bill may be just another step on the long road toward establishing a genuinely open government.

---

[101]   FOI Bill, clause 15(3).   [102]   FOI Bill, clause 15(4).

[103]   The government are proposing only limited amendments to the Bill to be moved in Committee in the House of Lords. These include removing statistical information from the class exemption for information about the formulation of government policy. The definition of 'the accountable person' who can exercise the veto under clause 52 is limited to Cabinet Ministers.

16

Confidentiality

RICHARD SCOTT

There are two basic principles that underlie, or ought to underlie, the law of confidentiality. The first is that private individuals are entitled to protection against the disclosure without consent of confidential information about themselves and their activities unless there is a sufficient public interest reason why the information should be disclosed. The second principle is that government, including local authorities and other emanations of government, such as the National Health Service, the Court Service, the Prison Service etc., are not entitled to protection from disclosure of information about themselves and their activities unless there is a sufficient public interest requiring the protection of the information from disclosure. I regard each of these two principles as self-evidently necessary in a mature democracy. I regard them also as representing the law, properly understood.

As to the first principle, the need that private information about private individuals should not be disclosed without their consent seems to me to be obvious. There is, sad to say, Court of Appeal authority for the view that English law does not recognize an independent right of privacy. The authority is *Kaye v Robertson*.[1] It is, of course, the case, that some well-established torts provide some degree of protection to privacy. The law of trespass protects against intrusion on to private property. But it has its limitations: see *Bernstein v Sky Views Ltd.*,[2] in which an action in trespass to prevent an aircraft flying over the plaintiff's property and taking unauthorized photographs failed. The law of nuisance provides some protection but it, too, has limitations: see *Hunter v Canary Wharf Ltd.*,[3] in which it was held that only a person with an interest in land could sue. The law of contract can provide protection but that, of course, requires there to be a contract. Sometimes a contract can be implied, but often that is impossible.

However, the protection given by courts of equity to confidential information has shown itself capable of providing protection against certain types of invasion of privacy: see *Stephens v Avery*,[4] in which, Sir Nicolas Browne-Wilkinson V-C expressed the view that equity would intervene to protect confidential information if the disclosure of the information would in the circumstances be unconscionable.

None the less, in *Kaye v Robertson* the Court of Appeal, without, it must be said, having been referred to any of the cases under which protection had been given to confidential information, held that English law did not recognize a right to privacy

---

[1] [1991] FSR 62.   [2] [1978] QB 479.
[3] [1997] AC 655.   [4] [1988] Ch 419.

or provide, otherwise than via some established tort, a remedy for the invasion of privacy. Bingham LJ noted that 'It is this invasion of his privacy which underlies the plaintiff's complaint' but held that 'it [i.e. the invasion of privacy] alone, however gross, does not entitle him to relief in English law'. And Leggatt LJ, after noting that 'the right to privacy, or "the right to be let alone", has gained acceptance in most jurisdictions in the United States' said that 'This right has so long been disregarded here that it can be recognised now only by the legislature'.

I believe this decision to have been wrong. It did not take into account the long line of cases in which the protection given by the courts to confidential information had become, in effect, a protection against the unwarranted invasion of privacy.

One of the earliest cases was *Prince Albert v Strange*[5] in which an injunction was granted restraining the public exhibition of etchings which had been made by the Prince Consort. The grant of the injunction was expressed to be based on breach of trust, breach of contract, property rights in the etchings, as well as breach of confidence. *Argyll v Argyll*[6] provides a clearer example of protection given to privacy. The Duchess of Argyll was granted an injunction restraining the disclosure in a national newspaper of intimate marital secrets. The decision, by Ungoed-Thomas J, to grant the injunction represented a recognition of the right of the Duchess to have her private life kept private. The decision has been commented on in a number of subsequent cases but its correctness has not, to my knowledge, been called into question.

Stephens v Avery was a case in which a remedy was sought after information had been disclosed about a private relationship. The plaintiff and the first defendant had been friends. In the course of the friendship the first defendant became aware of a lesbian relationship between the plaintiff and another woman. The first defendant supplied details of this to the newspaper defendant. The newspaper published the story. The plaintiff claimed damages for breach of confidence. The Vice-Chancellor, Sir Nicolas Browne-Wilkinson, declined to strike the action out. He held, in line with *Argyll v Argyll*, that private information relating to sexual conduct of an individual was capable of being protected by the law of confidence.

In both *Argyll v Argyll* and in *Stephens v Avery* confidential information had been disclosed, in one way or another, by the plaintiff to the defendant. But the injunction granted in *Argyll* was not limited to information communicated by the Duchess to the Duke. It covered all private information about the Duchess acquired by the Duke from their marital relationship. This would have included information obtained by the Duke from observation of the Duchess, or, simply, from sharing the same bed. *Argyll v Argyll* established, therefore, that it is not a necessary pre-condition of protection against the disclosure of confidential information that the information should have been specifically disclosed by a confider. Suppose the Duke had kept private memoirs. Could the Duchess have obtained an injunction restraining him from continuing to do so? Plainly not. Could she have obtained an injunction restraining him from making public the contents of his memoirs? Plainly, yes. So

---

[5] (1849) 1 Mac & G 25.　　[6] [1967] Ch 302.

what would have been the position if the Duke's private memoirs had been stolen, and the newspaper had acquired them from the thief? Would a newspaper which had purchased the information from a thief be in a more favourable position than a newspaper which had purchased the information from the confidant? It is surely inconceivable that that, in law, could be so. What system of jurisprudence would regard as tortious the disclosure of the material by the Duke but would permit the disclosure of the material by someone who had stolen it from the Duke?

The same point can be made regarding a case like *Stephens v Avery*. If details of the lesbian affair had been confided to the defendant in a letter from the plaintiff, the publication of that letter might, consistently with the views expressed by the Vice-Chancellor, constitute a tortious breach of confidence. How could a thief, who had stolen the letter from the defendant, be in a better position?

There is, indeed, some authority for the conclusion that a thief would not be in any better position then the confidant. *Francome v Mirror Group Newspaper*[7] is the case. The plaintiff, John Francome, was the champion National Hunt jockey. Unidentified persons bugged his home telephone and taped his private telephone conversations. The *Mirror* acquired the tapes. The plaintiff sued for an injunction to restrain publication. The conversations eavesdropped upon had been obviously private conversations. So the injunction was sought on the ground that the Mirror was bound by the confidential character of the conversations. The Court of Appeal upheld the grant of an interlocutory injunction restraining the newspaper until trial of the action from publishing any article based on the contents of the taped telephone conversations. This case does not constitute as strong an authority as it would have done had the same order been made at trial. It does, however, recognize that those who carry out the illegal recording of private telephone conversations may come under the same obligation to respect the confidential nature of the conversations as the parties to the conversations. The court recognized that John Francome was entitled, prima facie, to have the privacy of his private telephone conversations protected. The contrary view that had earlier been expressed by Sir Robert Megarry, Vice-Chancellor, in *Malone v Metropolitan Police Commissioner*[8] should, in my opinion, no longer be regarded as good law.

It is, I suggest, now established that private conversations, whether surreptitiously recorded by a party to the conversations, or misappropriated by the theft of some written record, or obtained by the unauthorized tapping of a telephone, will be protected against unwarranted disclosure. So, too, would intimate family or personal details known to members of the family be protected against unwarranted disclosure. The cases to which I have referred seem to me to establish that that is so. And there is, in my opinion, no sensible reason in principle or in practice for distinguishing between the eavesdropper who overhears private conversations, the 'Peeping Tom' who spies through the bedroom curtains, or the intrusive photographer with his long range telephoto lens. Each of these is, in one way or another, coming into possession

---

[7] [1984] 1 WLR 892.   [8] [1979] Ch 334.

of private information. The misuse of that information can be restrained by injunction (e.g. *Argyll v Argyll, Francome v Daily Mirror*) or, if disclosure has already occurred, be remedied by an award of damages (*Stephens v Avery*).

But *Kaye v Robertson* stands in the way. The plaintiff was a well-known actor, suing by his next friend. He had been involved in a car accident and had suffered serious injuries to his head and brain. He was in intensive care in hospital. A journalist obtained unauthorized access to his hospital bed and took photographs of him, including photographs of the scars on his head. The journalist had not been able to obtain an effective consent from the plaintiff for the taking of these photographs. So the journalist was in no better position than if the photographs had been taken surreptitiously with a zoom lens from across the street. The judge at first instance granted an injunction to restrain the publication of the photographs. The Court of Appeal discharged the injunction, expressing regret that English law did not provide a remedy for the invasion of privacy that had taken place. But no mention was made of the confidential information cases. If a family friend or relation had, with Mr Kaye's consent, taken the photographs for the purpose of a family album, the friend could surely have been restrained from sending copies of the photographs to the national press. A newspaper, which had purchased the photographs from the friend or relation would, since the private character of the photographs would have been obvious, be unlikely to be in any stronger position. *Argyll v Argyll* would be a clear authority in point. If the photographs of Mr Kaye's head had been taken by a doctor for the purpose of use in a teaching hospital or in a learned journal, the doctor would surely be restrained from general publication. Here, too, a newspaper purchaser from the doctor would be unlikely to be in any stronger position. The doctor might have been able to justify publication in a medical journal or for teaching purposes, provided he avoided identifying Mr Kaye as the subject, but could not possibly justify publication in a national newspaper. All of this seems to me clear law and in accordance with authority (see e.g. *W. v Edgell*).[9]

So why did the Court of Appeal treat the trespassing photographer as having more extensive rights to the photographs he had taken than would have been the case had a friend or doctor taken the photographs? The reason is that the Court of Appeal was not referred to the breach of confidence cases. The question whether a person who, through wrongdoing, comes into possession of confidential information can be in a better position than a person who acquires the information with the consent of the confider was discussed by Dunn J in *Franklin v Gliddins*.[10] The defendant in the case had stolen a cutting from a nectarine tree that the plaintiff had grown in his orchard by careful and selective grafting. The judge referred to the English cases on breach of confidential information, including *Prince Albert v Strange* and *Argyll v Argyll*, and said this:

---

[9] [1990] Ch 359.   [10] [1997] Queensland Reports 72.

I find myself quite unable to accept that a thief who steals a trade secret knowing it to be a trade secret with the intention of using it in commercial competition with its owner to the detriment of the latter and so uses it, is less unconscionable than a traitorous servant. The thief is unconscionable because he plans to use and does use his own wrong conduct to better his position in competition with the owner, and also to place himself in a better position than that of a person who deals consensually with the owner.[11]

The same approach could, in my opinion, have been used in *Kaye v Robertson*. But whether *Kaye v Robertson* was rightly or wrongly decided, the obstacle that it appeared to have placed in the path of the development of rights of privacy in English law can, I think, now be side-stepped. The route around the obstacle is Article 8 of the Human Rights Convention. On 2 October 2000 the Human Rights Act 1998 will come into effect. Under s. 1(2) of the Act the Convention rights, including the rights under Article 8, become part of English domestic law.

Article 8 provides as follows:

(1) Everyone has the right to respect for his private and family life, his home and his correspondence.
(2) There shall be no interference by a public authority with the exercise of this right except such as is in accordance with the law and is necessary in a democratic society in the interests of national security, public safety or the economic well-being of the country, for the prevention of disorder or crime, for the protection of health or morals, or for the protection of the rights and freedom of others.

Article 8(1) would, I suggest, be broken by the disclosure of marital secrets (*Argyll v Argyll*) or by the disclosure of details of private relationships (*Stephens v Avery*), or by the publication of unauthorized photographs of an individual in his home or other private place taken from a hovering helicopter or an aircraft (*Bernstein v Sky Views Ltd.*), or indeed a spy satellite, or taken by a trespassing intruder (*Kaye v Robertson*) or by someone using a zoom lens, or by the publication by an eavesdropper of details of private and confidential conversations (*Francome v Daily Mirror*).

Article 8(2) refers to 'interference by a public authority'. It is state interference with the privacy of individuals that is the primary target of Article 8 (see *Kroon v Netherlands*[12]). It is, however, well arguable that not only should the state refrain from interference with private life but it also should provide an effective system for the protection of privacy against interference by others (see *Stjerna v Finland*[13]). And 'public authority' in Article 8(2) would, as defined, include the courts of law. So, it is, at the least, highly arguable that if, in the future, a *Kaye v Robertson* or *Bernstein v Sky Views Ltd.* or *Stephens v Avery* or *Francome v Daily Mirror* situation should arise, the courts will have a duty, unless the case can be brought with one or other of the Article 8(2) exceptions, to provide a remedy against the invasion of privacy that will have taken place.

---

[11] [1997] Queensland Reports 72 at 80.   [12] (1994) 19 EHRR 263.
[13] (1994) 24 EHRR.

Accordingly, whatever may be the state of the law today, which depends on the view taken of *Kaye v Robertson* as a compelling authority, the courts of this country can, as from 2 October 2000, continue the process of developing a law of privacy in accordance with the first principle expressed at the beginning of this essay—a process interrupted, only temporarily I hope, by *Kaye v Robertson*.

Let me turn to the second principle. The question whether confidential information belonging to government should be protected on the same basis and by application of the same principles as apply to confidential information belonging to private individuals has been debated in a number of cases. One of the clearest statements of the issue was made by Mason J, in the High Court of Australia in *Commonwealth of Australia v Fairfax & Sons. Ltd.*[14] Mason J declined to grant an interlocutory injunction restraining publication of previous unpublished communications between the Australian and Indonesian Governments. He said this:[15]

> the plaintiff must show, not only that the information is confidential in quality and that it was imparted so as to import an obligation of confidence, but also that there will be an unauthorised use of that information to the detriment of the party communicating it (*Coco v A. N. Clark (Engineers) Ltd.* [1969] R.P.C. 41, 47). The question then, when the executive government seeks the protection given by equity, is: What detriment does it need to show? The equitable principle has been fashioned to protect the personal, private and proprietary interests of the citizen, not to protect the very different interests of the executive government. It acts, or is supposed to act, not according to standards of private interest, but in the public interest. This is not to say that equity will not protect information in the hands of the government, but it is to say that when equity protects government information it will look at the matter through different spectacles. It may be a sufficient detriment to the citizen that disclosure of information about his affairs will expose his actions to public discussion and criticism. But it can scarcely be a relevant detriment to the government that publication of material concerning its actions will expose it to public discussion and criticism. It is unacceptable in our democratic society that there should be a restraint on the publication of information relating to government when the only vice of that information is that it enables the public to discuss, review and criticise government action. Accordingly the court will determine the government's claim to confidentiality by reference to the public interest. Unless disclosure is likely to injure the public interest it will not be protected.

A similar approach to the protection from disclosure of confidential information belonging to government had, earlier, been enunciated by Lord Widgery CJ in *Attorney-General v Jonathan Cape Ltd.*[16] and was approved in the *Spycatcher* litigation.[17]

It is, in my opinion, now established as the legally correct approach. Moreover, it corresponds with constitutional principle. Ministers are accountable for what they do as Ministers and for what is done in the departments of which they are in charge. At the heart of the principle of accountability lies the obligation of Ministers to give

---

[14] (1980) 147 CLR 39.   [15] (1980) 147 CLR 39 at 50–7.
[16] [1976] QB 752 at 770–1.
[17] [1990] 1 AC 109, at first instance (at 151–152), in the Court of Appeal (at 203 and 218) and in the House of Lords (at 257–258, 270 and 283).

information about the activities of their departments and about the actions and omissions of their civil servants. Sometimes the public interest will require that information be withheld. Information about the operations and personnel of the security and intelligence agencies is an example. But unless there is an acceptable public interest reason for withholding information, the constitutional principle of accountability requires that if information about government or its activities is sought the information should be disclosed. A public interest reason for withholding the information may justify a refusal to disclose it; the confidential character of the information cannot by itself do so.

It seems to me that, in principle, there should no protection given against the disclosure of confidential information that the government, if asked to do so, ought to disclose. If there is no sufficient public interest to justify the withholding of the information from the public, how can there be a sufficient public interest to restrain the public disclosure of the information? The simplicity of this proposition is, however, somewhat undermined by a combination of s. 1 of the Official Secrets Act 1989 and the judgment of the Court of Appeal in *Attorney-General v Blake*.[18]

Under s. 1 of the Official Secrets Act 1989 a member of the security or intelligence services is guilty of a criminal offence if without lawful authority he discloses information relating to security or intelligence which he has acquired by virtue of his position as a member of those services. The offence is committed whether or not the disclosure is damaging to the public interest (compare ss. 2, 3 and 4).

Attorney-General v Blake raised the question whether any, and if so what, civil remedy could be given to the Crown where information had been disclosed in breach of s. 1 of the Official Secrets Act 1989 but where the information was not said to be confidential and the disclosure was not said to be damaging to the public interest. The case arose out of the unauthorized disclosure by Blake of information he had acquired while a member of the Secret Intelligence Service. The information was contained in Blake's autobiography which Jonathan Cape Ltd. was about to publish. Blake was due to be paid royalties by the publishers. The Court of Appeal accepted that a private law remedy was not available to the Crown but held that the Crown was entitled to a remedy in aid of the criminal law. The Court of Appeal held, in short, that since Blake was guilty of a serious criminal offence, i.e. a breach of s. 1 of the Official Secrets Act 1989, from which he stood to derive financial benefits, the Attorney-General was entitled to intervene and grant an injunction in aid of the criminal law. In some cases an injunction can be sought restraining the commission of conduct which, if committed, would constitute a criminal offence (see e.g. *Attorney-General v Chaudry*).[19] But Blake had already committed the criminal offence. Alternatively, held the Court of Appeal, the court can grant an injunction restraining the wrongdoer from receiving financial benefit from his wrongdoing. So an injunction was granted restraining Blake from receiving any royalties from the publishers. What the House of Lords will make of this novel form of relief remains

---

[18] [1998] Ch 439.   [19] [1971] 1 WLR 1614.

to be seen. As it stands, however, the case is authority for the proposition that, if the disclosure of government information would be a criminal offence e.g. under the Official Secrets Act 1989, the disclosure can be restrained by an injunction granted in aid of the criminal law notwithstanding that the information is not confidential and that its disclosure is not alleged to be damaging to the public interest.

Subject, however, to the *Attorney-General v Blake* exception, the proposition that government is not entitled to protection of its information from disclosure unless the disclosure would be damaging to the public interest remains, in my opinion, valid.

There is, of course, scope for dispute in any particular case as to whether a sufficiently strong public interest justifying the protection from disclosure of government information can be shown. Similarly, or conversely, where disclosure of private information is in question, there will often be scope for dispute as to whether a sufficient public interest reason for disclosure can be shown. The answer in any particular case will depend on the facts of that case. In the government information cases it will depend upon the balance to be struck between the public interest reasons in favour of protection of the information from disclosure and the countervailing interest of the public in receiving information about government and its activities. In the private information cases the balance to be struck will be between the right of the individual to have his privacy respected (Article 8(1)) and the Article 8(2) reasons put forward to justify the disclosure of the information. How the balance is struck will determine how the law develops. What is important, however, is that the law should now be allowed to develop on the basis of the two basic principles with which I began this essay. It should not subsequently be necessary to have to argue for the acceptance of either.

17

The Public Interest Disclosure Act 1998

YVONNE CRIPPS

1. INTRODUCTION

Disclosures made by public and private sector workers acting in the public interest may be crucially important in protecting the public from a range of hazards including injury, risk to life, fraud, financial malpractice and environmental damage. Those who make such disclosures deserve legal protection.

Even jurisdictions in which there is wide-ranging freedom of information legislation will benefit from occasional disclosures by public-spirited individuals who focus initial attention on matters of which the public ought to be aware. Damaging or potentially damaging activities that would otherwise escape detection, may, at a relatively early stage, come to the notice of workers who may or may not have the courage to speak out. Notorious examples of such situations include the Piper Alpha disaster,[1] the Clapham Junction train collision,[2] the foundering of the Herald of Free Enterprise,[3] the arms to Iraq affair[4] and the collapse of the Bank of Credit and Commerce International (BCCI).[5]

When an individual is public-spirited, concern for workmates or the wider public may dictate that information about crimes or other types of wrongdoing is passed to appropriate recipients despite the employment risks that are associated with such disclosures. These risks may extend to loss of livelihood and ostracization by other employers and, if protective legislation is to be effective, they should be taken into account, alongside the need to balance the public interest in disclosure with the legitimate interests of employers.

The Public Interest Disclosure Bill was preceded by two Bills similarly inspired by the belief that our legal system should not abandon workers who disclose information in the public interest. The two earlier Bills, introduced by Tony Wright, MP, and Don Touhig, MP, failed for lack of parliamentary time. They were intended to

---

[1] See the report of Lord Cullen, *Public Inquiry into the Piper Alpha Disaster*, Cm. 1310 (November 1990).

[2] See Sir Anthony Hidden's *Investigation into the Clapham Junction Railway Accident*, Cm. 820 (November 1989).

[3] See the Report of the Sheen Inquiry, Department of Transport (HMSO, Ct. No. 8074, 1987).

[4] Sir Richard Scott, V-C, emphasized the significance of the disclosures made by an employee of Matrix Churchill. See *Report of the Inquiry into the Export of Defence Equipment and Dual-Use Goods to Iraq and Related Prosecutions* (HMSO, 15 February 1996) 1271.

[5] See Lord Bingham's *Inquiry into the Supervision of the Bank of Credit and Commerce International*, Cm. 198 (October 1992).

protect public-spirited workers from unforgiving employers and they reflected what was then the virtual absence from British and EC[6] employment law of protections for such workers.[7]

Those who introduced and drafted the Public Interest Disclosure Bill, as in the case of the earlier Bills, benefited greatly from the advice and campaigning zeal of Public Concern at Work, a charity founded and directed by Guy Dehn to give support and assistance to workers who have disclosed, or wish to disclose, information in the public interest.[8] The Bill was introduced by Richard Shepherd, MP, as a Private Member's Bill and led through the House of Lords by Lord Borrie, QC, the then Chairman of Public Concern at Work. It received all-party support and passed rapidly into law, with no second reading debate, as a result of considerable parliamentary consensus on the need for the Bill and on its precise terms. Careful drafting also led to support from both employer and employee organizations. The Public Interest Disclosure Act 1998 (PIDA) came into force on 2 July 1999.

Judges, enjoying the freedom of the common law, have identified a public interest defence to the action for breach of confidence[9] and a similar defence exists, inter alia, in relation to actions for breach of copyright.[10] These defences, sensitively expounded in various contexts, remain intact after the implementation of PIDA. Workers who contemplate making public interest disclosures will probably fear victimization by their employers more than they fear an action for breach of confidence, whether or not they are aware of the niceties of the common law defences. Thus, prior to the passage of PIDA, a chilling effect on disclosure is likely to have resulted from lack of employment protection. Some workers will be sufficiently concerned and brave to speak out whatever the consequences,[11] but many who, prior to PIDA, sought advice from their union or an advisory service while deciding whether or not to make a disclosure will have experienced more of a frost than a chill. It is to be hoped and expected that the legislation will improve that situation or that it will at least provide some assistance for those who feel that they must speak out. Of course no statute, not even the Public Interest Disclosure Act, can offer complete

---

[6] Note, however, Article 8 of Council Directive (EEC) 89/391 (OJ L183/1) in relation to the victimization of employees who make disclosures about health and safety in the workplace. See also ss. 44 and 100 of the Employment Rights Act 1996 and Y. Cripps, *The Legal Implications of Disclosure in the Public Interest* (2nd edn., Sweet & Maxwell, 1994) ch. 11A.

[7] cf. the position in the United States and Australia and note, for example, the Whistleblower Protection Act 1989, 5 USC 2320, the Whistleblowers Protection Act 1993 (South Australia), the Whistleblowers Protection Act 1994 (Queensland) and the Public Interest Disclosure Act 1994 (Australian Capital Territory). See D. Lewis, K. Schroder and S. Homewood, 'A Short Guide to the Public Interest Disclosure Act 1998' (Centre for Research in Industrial and Commercial Law, Middlesex University).

[8] The Campaign for Freedom of Information, directed by Maurice Frankel, also played a very important role in the formulation of the legislation.

[9] Y. Cripps, *The Legal Implications of Disclosure in the Public Interest*, (n. 6 above), ch. 2.

[10] ibid., ch. 4.

[11] Note the possibility of defamation actions, although a worker acting in the public interest and making an accurate disclosure would be able to rely on the defence of justification. See Y. Cripps, *The Legal Implications of Disclosure in the Public Interest*, (n. 6 above) chapter 6.

protection. PIDA does not, for example, protect against victimization by other employers and indeed it is difficult, although not entirely impossible,[12] for any legislation to protect against ostracization of that kind or in certain circumstances against co-workers' fear of guilt by association.[13] The legislation is, however, greatly to be welcomed for the way in which it protects workers in a manner which takes account of the legitimate interests of employers. It encourages workers to make their disclosures, where possible, within the relevant organization and to regard disclosure in the first instance to a wider audience as a course to be avoided if a more measured response might avail. In this context it is important to remember that disclosure within the workplace will not only be less damaging for employers but also for workers, not least in terms of their subsequent appeal to other employers. PIDA, with its emphasis on qualities of honesty and reasonableness, should, even if only to a limited extent, enhance that appeal and match admiration for the genuinely public spirited with real, even if not impossibly comprehensive, protection.

Rather than creating a single statutory defence for all workers who disclose information in what they reasonably believe to be the public interest, the Act sacrifices simplicity for refinement by means of a complex regime of 'protected' and 'qualifying' disclosures. This is achieved by inserting new provisions, inter alia, into the Employment Rights Act 1996 (ERA). These provisions are designed to safeguard, from reprisal by employers, 'workers' who make a 'qualifying disclosure'. The extent to which qualifying disclosures are 'protected' will depend on the circumstances in which the disclosure is made and, in particular, on the nature of the recipient of the disclosure. Thus under the new statutory regime, public interest disclosures within the workplace are, in general, easier to protect than those made, for example, directly to the news media. The Act places a premium on responsible disclosure and on seeking to have matters of concern rectified, where possible, within the workplace. The spectre of disclosure to a wider audience in situations where there are inadequate workplace mechanisms for disclosure may also foster in the workplace the creation of an atmosphere and procedures conducive to internal disclosure about wrongdoing, dangerous practices and other forms of malpractice.

Where the legislation requires good faith or reasonable belief, the onus of proof is placed on the worker making the disclosure. The employer is not required to prove malice, bad faith or unreasonableness, although it might be argued that this will deter public-spirited workers from raising important concerns if they seek preliminary advice from unions or others advising on the Act. It is also to be hoped that the emphasis in the legislation on disclosure in accordance with employers' workplace procedures will not handicap workers who shun flawed or inadequate workplace disclosure mechanisms.

---

[12] See the Whistleblowers Protection Act 1993 (South Australia).
[13] J. Gobert and M. Punch, 'Whistleblowers, the Public Interest, and the Public Interest Disclosure Act 1998'(2000) 63 MLR 25.

2. THE DEFINITION OF A WORKER

One of the many virtues of the new legislation is that workers are very broadly defined in s. 43K of the ERA.[14] For the purposes of the Public Interest Disclosure Act, they include certain agency workers and third-party contractors if their work is essentially under the control of their alleged employer. Such contractors come within the definition of a worker even if they do not perform the work personally. Medical and dental personnel[15] working under legislation governing the National Health Service and individuals working under training contracts are also covered by PIDA, as are most employees of the Crown.[16] Disclosures by others who are self-employed, volunteers, members of the security services,[17] and the police service[18] are not protected by the legislation.

It is especially lamentable that the police have been excluded from the protection of the legislation, particularly when the quashing of unsound convictions obtained by police officers using unlawful means is far from unknown. The exclusion is all the more striking when it is remembered that actual or likely miscarriages of justice are expressly defined as qualifying disclosures in s. 43B(1)(c) of PIDA and that senior police officers consulted during the consultative phase of the legislation expressed a preference for the inclusion of police officers within the Act. Both the Association of Chief Police Officers and the Police Complaints Authority criticized the proposed exclusion of police officers and this led to 'an absolute commitment' by the government,[19] not yet honoured, to confer equivalent protection on police officers by regulation. The Minister also told the Standing Committee that the Home Office would begin a review of various regulations governing the police once the Bill was enacted and that if existing police regulations could not provide equivalent protection then other measures would be implemented.[20] The Chief Police Officers who criticized the Bill were doubtless motivated by a belief not only in justice for accused persons but also by a desire ultimately to protect the reputation of their forces by reassuring

---

[14]   This section extends the definitions of 'worker' and 'employee' contained in s. 230 of the ERA. The definition of a worker in s. 230(3) appears sufficiently broad to cover non-executive directors. Note, by analogy in relation to the narrower term 'employee', the case of *Secretary of State for Trade and Industry v Bottrill* [1999] IRLR 326, CA. By virtue of s. 12 of PIDA workers whose contracts ordinarily require them to work outside Great Britain are not protected. The ERA, s. 43K(2) extends the definition of an employer.

[15]   Those providing ophthalmic or pharmaceutical services under National Health Service legislation are also included.

[16]   See s. 191(2)(aa) of the ERA in relation to Pt. IVA of the ERA. By virtue of ss. 193(2)(bb) and (bc) of the ERA, Pt. IVA and section 47B of the ERA do not apply to certain employees of the Crown who handle information concerning national security.

[17]   ERA, s. 193(4). The armed services are not covered as they were not included in the Employment Rights Act 1996. See also s. 11 of PIDA.

[18]   ERA, s. 200(1). Civilian staff in the police service may, however, claim protection.

[19]   See *Hansard*, HC (series 6), vol. 310, cols. 1143–4.

[20]   Parliamentary Debates, HC Standing Committee D, 11 March 1998, cols. 16–17 and G. Dehn's annotations of PIDA in Current Law Statutes, Public Interest Disclosure Act 1998, 23–5.

the public that disclosure of unlawful practices would be encouraged so that any problems could be speedily addressed.

3. THE SUBJECT MATTER OF DISCLOSURES

Section 43A of the ERA defines a 'protected disclosure' as a 'qualifying disclosure' made by a worker in accordance with any of s. 43C to 43H of the ERA, while s. 43B(1)[21] defines a 'qualifying disclosure' as any disclosure which, in the reasonable belief of the worker making the disclosure, tends to show one or more of the following which need not necessarily be related to the worker's employment:

(a) that a criminal offence has been committed, is being committed, or is likely to be committed,

(b) that a person has failed, is failing, or is likely to fail to comply with a legal obligation,

(c) that a miscarriage of justice has occurred, is occurring, or is likely to occur,

(d) that the health or safety of any individual has been, is being, or is likely to be endangered,

(e) that the environment has been, is being, or is likely to be damaged,

(f) that information tending to show any matter falling within any one of the preceding paragraphs has been, is being or is likely to be, deliberately concealed.

Section 43B(3) excludes from the definition of a qualifying disclosure a disclosure that would in itself constitute an offence, for example, a breach of the Official Secrets Act 1989. As Professor Sir David Williams QC pointed out in his seminal work on official secrecy,[22] the broad sweep of official secrets legislation may capture information which the public has an interest in receiving, and that view is as correct today in relation to the 1989 statute as it was with regard to the Act of 1911.[23] Section 43B(3) is thus arguably over-broad, especially in view of the fact that PIDA also requires reasonableness[24] on the part of the person making a disclosure and a disclosure that might pose a genuine risk to national security is not likely to be regarded as reasonable. And who, on what standard of proof,[25] and at what point in proceedings, will determine

---

[21] For the purposes of s. 43B(1) it does not matter whether the relevant failure takes place in the United Kingdom or elsewhere and whether the law applying to it is that of the United Kingdom or another country or territory. See s. 43B(2) of the ERA.

[22] D. G. T. Williams, *Not in the Public Interest: The Problem of Security in Democracy* (1965).

[23] The public interest defence applied in Clive Ponting's case (*R v Ponting* [1985] Crim LR 318) may, however, assist an accused to avoid conviction under the Official Secrets Act and the very existence of the Public Interest Disclosure Act should enhance the likelihood of success with that defence when the disclosure is made in a public spirited way.

[24] See below.

[25] With regard to the likely standard of proof, see G. Dehn (n. 20 above) 23–8 and the views expressed in favour of the criminal standard by Lord Nolan (*Hansard*, HL (series 5) vol. 590, col. 614 (5 June 1998)) and Lord Borrie (*Hansard*, HL (series 5) vol. 590, cols. 616–17 (5 June 1998)) during the House of Lords debate on the Public Interest Disclosure Bill. See also *Re a Solicitor* [1992] 2 All ER 335.

whether an offence has been committed? We can predict that the employment tribunals charged with the task of hearing cases under PIDA will not feel confident dealing with such issues.

4. THE RECIPIENTS OF DISCLOSURES

Once it is established that a disclosure 'qualifies', it is necessary to ascertain that the disclosure is 'protected' by virtue of being in accordance with any of s. 43C to 43H.[26] These sections focus largely on the recipient of the disclosure and transform a qualifying disclosure into a protected one if a disclosure by a worker:

(1) is made in good faith to the employer of the person who makes the disclosure, or, in situations where the disclosure relates to the conduct of another person (or to a matter for which another person has legal responsibility), to that other person;[27] or

(2) is made in the course of obtaining legal advice;[28] or

(3) is made in good faith to a Minister of the Crown if the worker's employer is appointed under any enactment by a Minister of the Crown or if the employer is a body any of whose members are so appointed;[29] or

(4) is made in good faith to a person prescribed by an Order made by the Secretary of State[30] and the worker reasonably believes that the disclosure relates to matters within the remit of the person prescribed and that the information disclosed and any allegation contained in it are substantially true;[31] or

(5) is made in good faith by a worker who does not act for personal gain and who reasonably believes that the information disclosed and any allegation contained in it are substantially true and in all the circumstances of the case it is reasonable for the worker to make the disclosure; provided that

    (a) at the time of making the disclosure the worker reasonably believes that he will be subject to a detriment by his employer if he makes a disclosure to his employer or to one of the persons specified in an Order by the Secretary of State, or

---

[26] By virtue of s. 43L(3), a disclosure of information may be protected even though the recipient of the information is already aware of it.   [27] ERA, s. 43C.

[28] ERA, s. 43D. ERA, s. 43B(4) provides that 'a disclosure of information in respect of which a claim to legal professional privilege . . . could be maintained in legal proceedings is not a qualifying disclosure if it is made by a person to whom the information had been disclosed in the course of obtaining legal advice'. This is designed to prevent legal advisers who are privy to workers' disclosures from repeating them and then claiming that they have made a protected disclosure.

[29] ERA, s. 43E.

[30] In an Order of 2 July 1999, thirty-eight individuals and regulatory bodies and their remits were specified by the Secretary of State. They include the Chief Executive of the Criminal Cases Review Commission, the Comptroller and Auditor General of the National Audit Office, the Director of the Serious Fraud Office, the Health and Safety Executive, the Environment Agency, the Financial Services Authority and local authorities responsible for enforcing consumer protection legislation.

[31] ERA, s. 43F.

(b) in a case where no person is prescribed by Order in relation to the relevant failure, the worker reasonably believes that it is likely that evidence relating to the relevant failure will be concealed or destroyed if he makes a disclosure to his employer, or

(c) the worker has previously made a disclosure of substantially the same information either to his employer or to a prescribed person.[32]

If any of these conditions (a), (b) or (c) are met then the worker makes a protected disclosure even though the recipient of the disclosure is not the worker's employer or a person specified in an Order. Thus, for example, a disclosure to the news media could be protected under this provision.[33]

Disclosures to persons other than employers and prescribed persons or bodies will also be protected if the failure which is disclosed is 'of an exceptionally serious nature',[34] provided that the disclosure is made in good faith by a worker who does not act for personal gain and who reasonably believes that the information disclosed and any allegation contained in it are substantially true and that in all the circumstances of the case it is reasonable for the worker to make the disclosure.

5. REASONABLENESS

By virtue of ERA, ss. 43B, 43C, 43F, 43G and 43H, reasonable belief on the part of a worker making a disclosure is a prerequisite for protection. But it is only in ss. 43G(3) and 43H(2) that guidance is given on determining whether it was reasonable for a worker to make a disclosure.

Section 43H(2) informs us that in determining whether disclosures regarding 'exceptionally serious' failures are reasonable, particular regard will be had to the identity of the person to whom the disclosure is made.

Where reasonableness is required in s. 43G, (that is, in situations involving disclosure to persons *other than*: employers, other persons responsible for relevant failures, Ministers of the Crown, legal advisers and persons prescribed by virtue of the new legislation), reasonableness is to be measured in accordance with s. 43G(3). The determinants of reasonableness include the identity of the person to whom the disclosure is made;[35] the seriousness of the relevant failure; whether the relevant failure is continuing or is likely to occur in the future; and whether the disclosure is made in breach of a duty of confidentiality owed by the employer to any other person.

---

[32] ERA, s. 43G(4) states that a subsequent disclosure may be regarded as a disclosure of substantially the same information as a previous disclosure even though the subsequent disclosure extends to information about action taken or not taken by any person as a result of the previous disclosure.

[33] ERA, s. 43G. [34] ERA, s. 43H.

[35] See Y. Cripps, *The Legal Implications of Disclosure in the Public Interest* (n. 6 above) ch. 2B(5) in relation to the importance of the identity of the recipient of information in the context of an action for breach of confidence.

If the facts reveal that a previous disclosure of substantially the same information has been made, an assessment of reasonableness will then include an examination of any action taken as a result of the previous disclosure as well as any action which might reasonably be expected to have been taken. If the disclosure of substantially the same information on the previous occasion was to the worker's employer, the investigation of reasonableness will also extend to the question whether on the previous occasion the worker used any disclosure procedure made available by his employer.

Section 43G(3)(d) is the only provision in the new legislation to address the question whether the disclosure involves a breach of confidence and it is notable that the legislators, in bringing breach of confidence into s. 43(G)(3) in terms of the assessment of the reasonableness of a disclosure, were concerned solely with duties of confidence owed by the employer to third parties and not with any duty of confidence owed by the worker to the employer. It is in any event important to appreciate that obligations of confidence arguably do not attach in the first place to information relating to wrongdoing[36] and logic dictates that this point applies to obligations of confidence owed by employers to others in just the same way that it applies to obligations of confidence owed by workers to employers.[37]

6. DISCLOSURE FOR REWARD

The effect of s. 43G(1)(c) is that in situations in which a disclosure is made to persons other than employers—that is to other persons responsible for relevant failures; Ministers of the Crown; legal advisers; and persons prescribed by virtue of the new legislation—the disclosure will not be protected under PIDA if it is made for 'purposes of personal gain'. Section 43H(1)(c) prescribes that disclosures regarding 'exceptionally serious' failures will not be protected if they are made for 'purposes of personal gain'.

Sections 43G and 43H are limited in scope and it would appear from construction of the wider provisions of the Act that workers are entitled to benefit from disclosures that they make 'in-house' as long as those disclosures do not relate to 'exceptionally serious matters'. Section 43L(2) specifically provides that in determining whether a person makes a disclosure for purposes of personal gain, any reward payable by or under any enactment will be disregarded. This latter provision tends to draw attention to a contrast between the new British legislation and statutes on public interest disclosure in, inter alia, the United States and Australia. In those jurisdictions it is not uncommon to find statutory provision for financial rewards for public-spirited employees who disclose information in the public interest. Such

---

[36] See Y. Cripps, *The Legal Implications of Disclosure in the Public Interest*, 25–6.

[37] Note also that the standards set out in PIDA may come to influence judges deciding whether to allow workers a public interest defence in the context of actions for breach of confidence.

rewards are not linked to any compensation for unfair dismissal or other workplace retaliation.

The choice of the phrase 'personal gain' is interesting in that it appears to be broader than 'financial gain'. Given that disclosures by workers to *employers* are not constrained by reference to personal gain unless the disclosures relate to exceptionally serious matters, the breadth of the phrase 'personal gain' as opposed to 'financial gain', will, by inference, be beneficial to employees who disclose 'in-house'. Those who disclose to persons who are not employers might well have been grateful for the narrower phrase 'financial gain', although, sadly, it is in any case unlikely that benefits other than financial ones will accrue to those who make even the most public-spirited disclosures. Financial benefits are only likely to occur in Britain in some cases of disclosure to the news media. The legislative denial of protection in cases in which there is personal gain for disclosures made outside the workplace is presumably at least partly designed to remove an incentive for choosing to make a disclosure to a damagingly wide audience instead of first attempting to draw attention 'in-house' to matters of concern. But it is unfortunate that, as a result of s. 43H of PIDA, personal gain will disqualify from employment protection under PIDA those workers who act reasonably and in good faith in believing that they are disclosing, whether 'in-house' or not, information about *exceptionally serious matters*. This can be contrasted with the operation of the common law public interest defence to the action for breach of confidence. In that context, gain received in respect of public interest disclosures to the media, whether of exceptionally serious matters or not, does not automatically preclude common law protection from actions for breach of confidence. The emphasis is placed more on the question whether the public has an interest in receiving the information disclosed than on the motive or gain of the person making the disclosure.[38] It might be thought that in the employment context a focus on the motive of the worker disclosing information is more appropriate than it is in relation to a public interest defence to an action for breach of confidence, but s. 43H in any event requires good faith and reasonableness in addition to the absence of personal gain.

7. NON-DISCLOSURE CLAUSES

Echoing concerns expressed by Lord Nolan in his first report, *Standards in Public Life*,[39] s. 43J of PIDA renders certain 'gagging clauses' void. Any provision in any agreement between employer and worker will be void in so far as it purports to preclude the worker from making a *protected* disclosure and from instituting or continuing any proceedings under the Employment Rights Act or any proceedings for breach of contract. Section 43J is thus sufficiently broad to extend to gagging

---

[38] See *Initial Services Ltd. v Putterill* [1968] 1 QB 396 and Y. Cripps, *The Legal Implications of Disclosure in the Public Interest* (n. 6 above) ch. 2B(3).

[39] Cm. 2850–1 (May 1995).

clauses contained in contracts relating to the settlement of disputes being heard by employment tribunals. Prior to the implementation of PIDA, it was not unknown for employers to include in such settlement agreements clauses attempting to prevent workers from disclosing their concerns even to official regulators.[40]

Unfortunately there is a danger that in certain situations s. 43J might be interpreted as diminishing common law protections for workers. It is arguable that such protections exist in terms of indications by judges in various cases that they would regard clauses prohibiting disclosure as invalid in so far as they might be interpreted as prohibiting disclosures that are in the public interest.[41] Section 43J of the ERA declares void only those agreements that preclude the worker from making a 'protected disclosure'. It is to be hoped that in cases where the worker has made a public-spirited disclosure but has not met the conditions imposed in the new legislation, s. 43J will not be interpreted as impliedly indicating that a gagging clause may still function to prevent, for example, a disclosure about serious mismanagement if the disclosure does not reveal unlawful behaviour.

8. USING THE PUBLIC INTEREST DISCLOSURE ACT TO PROTECT WORKERS AGAINST REPRISALS

By virtue of the newly added s. 103A and 105(6A) of the ERA, an employee's dismissal or selection for redundancy will automatically be regarded as unfair if the reason or a principal reason for the dismissal was that the employee made a 'protected disclosure'.[42] But this provision will be of no avail to workers who are not employees.[43] Such workers are likely to resort to s. 47B of the ERA which gives them a right not to be subjected to any detriment for making a protected disclosure.[44] Section 47B(1) includes in the meaning of detriment 'any act, or any deliberate failure to act' by an employer on the ground that the worker 'has made' a protected disclosure.[45] Thus a failure to treat the worker as other similar workers are treated, for example by

[40] See G. Dehn (n. 20 above) 23–16. See also *Re a Company's Application* [1989] 3 WLR 265. Auditors and others are under legislative duties to disclose matters of concern. See Y. Cripps, 'New Statutory Duties of Disclosure for Auditors in the Regulated Financial Sector'[1996] LQR 667. Note also the European Union Money Laundering Directive 1991 and the Money Laundering Regulations 1993, SI 1993, No. 1933.

[41] See Y. Cripps, *The Legal Implications of Disclosure in the Public Interest* (n. 6 above) 37–41

[42] Section 103A is inserted by s. 5 of PIDA. There is no upper age limit and no requirement for a qualifying period of service in relation to s. 103A. See ERA, s. 108 and 109. Note also that s. 16 of PIDA amends s. 237 of the Trade Union and Labour Relations (Consolidation) Act 1992 to allow employees taking part in unofficial industrial action and who are dismissed for making protected disclosures to claim that they have been unfairly dismissed.

[43] For example, those working on work contracts as opposed to contracts of employment. The ERA, s. 48(1A) entitles a worker to complain to an employment tribunal. See also ss. 205(1) and 205(1A) of the ERA.

[44] cf. s. 146 of the Trade Union and Labour Relations (Consolidation) Act 1992.

[45] In general, section 47B(2) excludes from section 47B(1) a worker who is an employee complaining of dismissal.

failing to give a pay increase, might be regarded as a detriment for the purposes of the section. Although s. 47B(1) refers to a worker who 'has made' a protected disclosure, this should not be interpreted as excluding detriments incurred in the lead up to a disclosure. If, for example, a worker disclosed to a co-worker an intention to disclose to an employer information that would amount to a protected disclosure under the Act and the worker was, in consequence, subjected to a detriment by the employer then s. 47B(1) should operate. Perhaps the provision also extends to employers who fail to protect from detriments by third parties workers making protected disclosures. The Act does not, however, create a tort of victimization which would cast the third party as a defendant.[46] Nor, unlike race,[47] sex[48] and disability[49] discrimination legislation and the Trade Union and Labour Relations (Consolidation) Act 1992,[50] does it protect against stigmatization in the form of third party employers refusing to employ.

There are in any event questions of onus and causation. By virtue of s. 48(2) of the ERA, once the worker has established a detriment under s. 47B, the employer must effectively show that the detriment was not imposed on the ground of the worker having made a protected disclosure.

9. REMEDIES

Section 37 of the Employment Relations Act 1999 raises, from £12,000 to £50,000, the compensation ceiling in most cases of unfair dismissal. Under PIDA, however, there is now no upper limit on compensation when an employee is dismissed principally for making a protected disclosure. This important change was introduced[51] in recognition of the fact that employees who are contemplating public interest disclosures that may lead to their dismissal may well be deterred by advice that even if they were to win a claim for unfair dismissal they would only receive a maximum of £50,000 in lieu of their lost livelihood and in the face of the stigma which accompanies dismissal and may prevent them from obtaining employment in the future. Compensation for retaliatory employer actions that fall short of dismissal is also

[46] cf. the Whistleblowers Protection Act 1993 (South Australia); the Whistleblowers Protection Act 1994 (Queensland); and the Public Interest Disclosure Act 1994 (Australian Capital Territory) and see D. Lewis, K. Schroder and S. Homewood, 'A Short Guide to the Public Interest Disclosure Act 1998', Centre for Research in Industrial and Commercial Law, Middlesex University) 10. With regard to the activities of employers prejudicing employees' employment prospects, see *Mahmud and Malik v Bank of Credit and Commerce International SA* [1997] 3 WLR 95 and Y. Cripps, 'The Consequences of Disclosure in the Public Interest' in C. Forsyth and I. Hare (eds.) *The Golden Metwand and the Crooked Cord: Essays in Honour of Sir William Wade QC* (Oxford University Press, 1998).

[47] Race Relations Act 1976, s. 4.

[48] Sex Discrimination Act 1975, s. 6.

[49] Disability Discrimination Act 1995, s. 4(5). Note also s. 55 of the Disability Discrimination Act 1995 in relation to victimization.

[50] See s. 137.

[51] See the Public Interest Disclosure (Compensation) Order 1999, SI 1999/1548, 2 July 1999.

unlimited but may well involve smaller sums than compensation for dismissal, depending on the severity of the retaliation.

Reinstatement or re-engagement are also available as remedies in the normal way if employees are dismissed[52] but the Public Interest Disclosure Act also provides for interim relief[53] in the form of an order obliging the employer to reinstate or continue the employee's employment pending a full hearing if it seems likely that the hearing will establish that the employee was dismissed for making a protected disclosure. Especially in the absence of an interim continuation or reinstatement order, but perhaps inevitably in any event, the employer is likely to argue that the employment relationship has irrevocably broken down.

Even if the disclosure of an employee turns out not to be covered by PIDA, he might still attempt to bring a claim in the ordinary way for unfair dismissal under the ERA 1996 or an action for breach of contract for wrongful dismissal.[54] His chances of success under pre-existing law would, however, be extremely limited.[55]

10. PRE-EXISTING LEGISLATIVE EMPLOYMENT PROTECTION

Section 94 of the Employment Rights Act 1996 gives employees the right not to be unfairly dismissed and s. 98 of the Act places the onus on employers to justify their principal reason for dismissal within the terms set out in the section. In that sense, the employee's task might appear easier here than under PIDA because the latter places much of the onus on the worker, for example to show that he acted reasonably, in good faith and with reasonable belief in the accuracy of his disclosure. First appearances would, however, be deceptive because a body of case law lies behind the seemingly open-ended s. 98.

Section 98(1)(b), refers not only to the specific justifiable reasons for dismissal enumerated within s. 98(2) but also and in the alternative to 'some other substantial reason of a kind such as to justify the dismissal of an employee holding the position which the employee held'. Employees who have argued that dismissal for the reason that they disclosed information in the public interest to an audience outside the workplace did not represent dismissal for a 'substantial reason of a kind such as to justify dismissal' have not succeeded[56] under the direct statutory precursors of ss. 94 and 98.[57] Yet the possibility of success with such a claim should not be entirely

---

[52]   See Y. Cripps, *The Legal Implications of Disclosure in the Public Interest* (n. 6 above) Ch. 11F with regard to difficulties surrounding the reinstatement or re-engagement of employees who are dismissed as a result of making or attempting to make public interest disclosures.

[53]   See s. 9 of the Public Interest Disclosure Act and ss. 128(1)(b) and 129(1) of the ERA.

[54]   See Y. Cripps, *The Legal Implications of Disclosure in the Public Interest* (n. 6 above) Ch. 12. Note also the possibility that public sector employees may make an application for judicial review once other remedies have been exhausted.   [55]   ibid., Ch. 11 and Ch.12.

[56]   See, for example, *Thornely* v *Aircraft Research Association Ltd.* (EAT, 669/76, May 11 1977).

[57]   Employment Protection (Consolidation) Act 1978 ss. 54 and 57 and, before that, para. 6 of Sch. 1 of the Trade Union and Labour Relations Act 1974.

ignored. There are cases[58] in which tribunals have upheld the contention that dismissals on account of public interest disclosures to audiences *within* the workplace were unfair within the terms of the statutory precursors of s. 94 and 98 of the ERA. Workers will, however, have a better chance of success under PIDA and if they fail the tests set out in the new provisions, tribunals are unlikely to assist them under the old.

11. CONCLUSION

The Public Interest Disclosure Act considerably enhances the protections available for workers who disclose information in the public interest and may thereby create an atmosphere conducive to such disclosures. It represents a distinct advance for freedom of information and freedom of expression in the United Kingdom.

Questions may be raised about whether it was wise to set out in the new legislation an exhaustive list of subject matters appropriate for disclosure. As Salmon LJ observed in *Initial Services Ltd.* v *Putterill*[59] in relation to an earlier case,[60] '[w]hat was iniquity in 1856 may be too narrow or perhaps too wide for 1967'. And even at the time the Act was passed, not long after the collapse of BCCI and Barings, it was perhaps surprising that a category of disclosure relating to gross mismanagement was not included in the all-important list.

The legislation imposes no specific duty on employers and other recipients of information to rectify matters disclosed[61] but the Act is drafted in such a way as to facilitate disclosure to a wider audience in the event that no remedial action is taken with regard to relevant disclosures. It thus reduces the likelihood of unresponsiveness to workers' concerns.

The effect of the Human Rights Act 1998 on disclosure in the public interest has been very ably addressed by others in this volume[62] but it cannot be overemphasized that the Human Rights Act, with its guarantee of freedom of expression, will have a major part to play, along with the Public Interest Disclosure Act, in protecting workers from public, and potentially private, sector employers who retaliate against them for disclosing or attempting to disclose information which the public has an interest in receiving. This, too, will appropriately depend on liberal interpretation and a protective spirit on the part of the judiciary.

---

[58] See Y. Cripps (note 6 above) ch. 11C.

[59] [1968] 1 QB 396.

[60] *Gartside v Outram* (1856) 26 LJCh 113.

[61] Lord Nolan has recommended that organizations, particularly those operating in the public sector, should have in place a set of policies and procedures governing disclosures of information about matters of concern. See Committee on Standards in Public Life, Second Report, Cm. 3270-1, (May 1996) 21.

[62] See also L. Vickers, 'Whistleblowing in the Public Sector and ECHR' [1997] PL 594.

18

Linkage Between Access to Information and Judicial Review

CLIVE LEWIS

1. INTRODUCTION

This paper considers the extent to which the substantive principles of public law and more particularly the process of and procedure of judicial review encourages or requires openness and transparency on the part of decision-makers. Openness can involve two separate issues: namely, the giving of reasons for why a particular decision has been reached and also the disclosure of documents or other primary material used in a decision-making process. A number of theoretical and practical justifications have been advanced for the giving of reasons, including improving the quality of decision-making and the rights of the individual concerned. These reasons have been well canvassed in the literature.[1] From the point of a court engaged in judicial review, however, the most pressing justification is the need to know why a particular decision has been taken. Absent some indication of the reasoning underlying a decision, the courts will, in practice, have difficulty in identifying whether or not the decision is flawed by some reviewable error.

The common law imposes relatively few obligations on public bodies to explain the reasoning underlying their decisions. Similarly, in terms of the procedure for judicial review, there is little specific obligation placed upon a public body to disclose documents or provide reasons for its decision. The courts have on the whole, however, been able, by a variety of means, to cajole or encourage administrative decision-makers to provide sufficient information as to the reasons underlying decisions to enable the court to carry out the task of ensuring that, on the information available, the public body acted lawfully in the sense that its decision is based on a correct interpretation of the law and having regard to the principles of rationality and relevance. Certainly, once a court has been persuaded to grant permission to apply for judicial review, the dynamic of judicial review usually does force public bodies to offer an explanation of the decision-making process. The courts, therefore, will usually have some means of ensuring that they are able to perform the task of resolving disputes in the public law field between the individual and a public body. A different question, more relevant to access to documents and primary material, is whether the courts are simply too ready to rely upon

---

[1] See De Smith, Woolf and Jowell, *Judicial Review of Adminstrative* Action (5th edn. §§9-040–9.044; dicta of Sedley J in *R v Institute for Higher Education, ex p Institute of Dental Surgery* [1994] 1 WLR 242.

written evidence from respondents and too reluctant to order disclosure of the primary material concerning the taking of a decision.

The substantive principles of public law have imposed even fewer obligations to disclose the documents and primary information used in the decision-making process. The rules of procedure do not impose any specific obligation in relation to disclosure of documents in judicial review. The courts have the power to make specific orders for disclosure of documents but, in practice, they have adopted a self-limiting approach to this jurisdiction. This restrictive approach is said to be based, at least in part, upon the particular nature of the judicial review jurisdiction. The cases frequently reiterate that judicial review is not a fact-finding process but is supervisory and limited to correcting errors of law as appear from the material available. This description of the jurisdiction, and the self-imposed limitations that flow from this view, rather than the absence of formal legal rules, appears to be the principal practical restriction on insisting on greater openness and transparency via the judicial review process. Substantive principles of public law rarely impose obligations of disclosure in relation to information, with the exception of the rules of natural justice. This may require a decision-maker to disclose particular documents to a person who will be affected by a decision prior to taking the decision, as happened most recently in the *Pinochet* case.[2]

2. ENCOURAGING THE GIVING OF REASONS

2.1 Substantive Principles

The substantive common law principles of public law are directed towards ensuring the lawfulness of a particular decision. The courts act to ensure that the decision-maker has correctly interpreted the relevant law, has observed relevant procedural obligations and has observed the principles of rationality and relevancy in reaching a decision. The common law rules are not, in general, geared towards ensuring access to information as a goal in itself.

The development of a wide-ranging obligation to provide reasons for decisions would, of course, mark a major step towards insistence on transparency in decision-making. Such a rule could easily have been justified by reference to the view of the courts' role of ensuring that a public body has acted lawfully in the context of resolving disputes in the public law field. Unless the courts know the reasons for a particular decision, they will not be in a position to determine whether the public body has acted lawfully. That logic is followed by the European Court of Justice in the European context. The European Court of Justice has emphasized that the role of the national court is to ensure full and effective protection of rights derived from Euro-

---

[2]   *R v Secretary of State for the Home Department, ex p Amnesty International* (15 February 2000).

pean Union law. The Court has interpreted that principle as requiring national authorities to give reasons for decisions refusing to recognize a claim based on European law rights. Unless the reasons are given, the national court cannot determine whether the decision is compatible with European Union law. Thus the national authorities had to give their reasons for rejecting a claim that a person was entitled under Articles 39 and 43 (ex Articles 48 and 59) of the EC Treaty to practise as a lawyer.[3] In the context of the European Union's own administrative decisions, Article 253 of the EC Treaty requires that reasons be given. The European Court has again confirmed that the basic reason for this requirement is the need for interested parties to protect their rights and to enable the Court of Justice to exercise its power to review the lawfulness of a decision.[4]

The English common law has, however, not followed that logic. It still does not recognize any general duty to give reasons for administrative decisions. The fact that an absence of reasons may prevent the court from identifying a reviewable error is not of itself a ground for imposing an obligation to give reasons.[5] The courts are, however, clearly alive to the risk that an unreasoned decision may be an unlawful one. Doubtless for that very reason, the courts have developed a variety of principles or techniques to ensure that sufficient information is obtained about the decision-making process as to enable the judicial review jurisdiction not to be stifled.

First, the courts have recognized certain situations where reasons will be required and the situations where such a duty is imposed are likely to increase. Fairness may require that reasons for a decision be given. That may arise because of the nature of a particular decision which may require the giving of reasons for a particular type of decision. Alternatively a particular decision may appear to be so unusual or aberrant that fairness may require the giving of reasons. The best-known example of the former is *Ex p Doody*[6] where the House of Lords held that the Home Secretary was required to give reasons to a prisoner sentenced to life when departing from the view of the judge as to the appropriate time to be served in prison. The best-known example of the latter category is probably *ex p. Cunningham*[7] where the Court of Appeal found a decision awarding compensation to a dismissed civil servant to be so aberrant on its face that reasons were required for the decision. Another category of cases calling for reasons or explanation arises when a decision-maker is expected to act in accordance with guidance. He may depart from the guidance but will normally have to give reasons for departing. The indication at present is that the courts are prepared to apply these principles relatively robustly if they consider it necessary to ensure that they have the means to supervise a decision which is either of real importance to the

---

[3] Case C-340/89 *Vlassopoulou v Ministerium für Justiz Bunders and Europaangelegenheithen Baden-Württemberg* [1991] I-ECR 2357.

[4] See, e.g. Case T-105/95 *World Wildlife Fund v Commission* [1997] ECR II-313.

[5] See *Ex p Institute of Dental Surgery* (n. 1 above) at 258.

[6] *R v Secretary of State for the Home Department, ex p Doody* [1994] 1 AC 534.

[7] *R v Civil Service Appeal Board, ex p Cunningham* [1991] 4 All ER 310.

individual concerned or which appears on its face to be sufficiently odd as to require explanation.[8]

Secondly, a variant on the need to give reasons arises from the ability of the courts in certain circumstances to draw adverse inferences from the absence of reasons for a particular decision. Where all the known facts and circumstances appear to point to one decision, and the decision-maker has, without any explanation reached the opposite conclusion, a court may infer that there was no valid reason for the decision.[9] In practice, the courts have been reluctant to draw such an inference from the absence of reasons. Often, there will be material in existence which could justify the decision or the courts have been prepared to assume the existence of a reason. In other cases, the courts have been reluctant to make the inference and appear to be ready to assume that there must be a reason for the decision. This approach has not, in practice, been used as a means of encouraging a silent decision-maker to explain his actions.

In addition, there may well be a statutory duty to give reasons. Such duties have been imposed in a variety of fields from housing to education. Decision-makers must provide adequate reasons when statute obliges them to do so; failure to do so will inevitably prompt a judicial review application.

Finally, in practice, there will be many situations where some explanation or reason for a particular decision will be available (whether legally required or not) or it will be possible to glean, at least prima facie, what motivated the decision-maker to act as he did. The general run of cases before the courts do not start off with a complete and absolute refusal on the part of a public body to offer any explanations for its actions. The rare reported occasions of that happening tend to be situations where, as a matter of principle, the decision-making was seeking to justify as a general rule the absence of any obligation to give reasons, usually, but not invariably, because the type of decision is one in which the decision-maker considers that reasons cannot or should not as a general rule be given.[10]

2.2 Procedural Considerations

An applicant will, of course, need permission to apply for judicial review. To obtain that, he must establish that it is arguable that the decision is invalid. Once permission has been granted, there is no specific obligation as a matter of the rules of procedure to file evidence, simply an obligation to do so within fifty-six days if the respondent chooses to do so. There is no automatic obligation to disclose any documents. There is not even a requirement that the respondent file anything resembling

---

[8] See, e.g., the judgment Lord Woolf MR in *R v Secretary of State for the Home Department, ex p Al Fayed* [1997] 1 All ER 228; he would have imposed a duty to give reasons had it not been for an express statutory prohibition on doing so. Even, the court held that the (different) obligation to give an indication of the likely grounds for a decision to enable the individual to make representations applied.

[9] *R v Secretary of State for Trade and Industry, ex p Lonrho* [1989] 1 WLR 525.

[10] See, e.g., *Ex p Cunningham* (n. 7 above).

a defence or statement as to the grounds upon which the respondent contests the applicant's application.

The practical reality is, however, different. Once permission has been granted, a respondent will have little practical choice and will invariably file an affidavit or witness statement offering some explanation of the decision-making process and explaining why the applicant's case is unfounded. In *R v Lancashire CC, ex p Huddleston*, Sir John Donaldson MR went so far as to hold that there was a duty on the respondent to make 'full and fair disclosure'. Purchas LJ approached the matter more circumspectly, indicating that when permission had been granted, public bodies 'should set out fully what they did and why, *so far as is necessary, fully and fairly to meet the challenge*'. Although described as a duty, the reality is that the principle reflects the expectations of the court as to what a responsible public body should do, once it is clear that the courts consider that there is a challenge to its actions which merits further argument. There are no specific sanctions that can be visited for a breach of this 'duty' or expectation; however, as Purchas LJ observed, the courts do have power by way of ordering disclosure or even cross-examination, to obtain information and may also simply decide that the applicant has made out a case and, as no satisfactory answer has been forthcoming, relief should be granted. Lord Woolf MR has also indicated that a failure to provide frank disclosure to the court will 'usually' be reason for the court ordering discovery.[11]

Once permission has been granted a public body will usually accept the practical necessity of filing evidence dealing with the decision. There may be a variety of reasons prompting such an attitude. It may simply be a reflection on the part of the public body that unless it offers an explanation, it runs the risk that the courts might regard its decision-making process as flawed. It may be that the application is based on only partial information or knowledge and the public body by giving its version of events will be able to see off the challenge. It may reflect acceptance of the view espoused by Sir John Donaldson MR that the modern approach to judicial review involves a partnership between the courts and the public body to ensure that the decisions that are taken are lawful ones. There may be an element of all three motives.

Even before permission has been granted, there are procedural means available which may result in pressure being placed upon a public body to justify its action. First, the applicant is now encouraged to send a letter before applying for permission setting out the basis of his complaint and inviting the respondent to review its decision. This is usually thought of as an additional protection for the putative respondent; he may review an unlawful decision or he may be able to demonstrate convincingly that the applicant's claim is misconceived. A claim indicating, for example, that certain considerations had been ignored may well be dealt with by a simple explanation that the considerations were taken into account but were

---

[11] In *Ex p Fayed* (n. 8 above) at 239d.

outweighed by other matters. The letter before action may, however, assist an applicant in establishing that some arguable error may have occurred. A carefully drafted letter, explaining the applicant's view of the law or the relevant considerations in his case may elicit a response where none had previously been provided and that response may, or may not, indicate a potentially reviewable error has been made. Similarly, an applicant may be in a forensically stronger position if he appears to be the recipient of an unusual or aberrant decision (whether or not sufficient to call for the giving of reasons), has asked for an explanation and none has been offered.

Secondly, applications are made without notice to the respondent and are usually dealt with on the papers (although it may be made orally). It is open to the court to adjourn a without notice application (whether made on the papers or orally) to open court and to invite the putative respondent to attend and make representations. This can have the practical effect of converting the *Huddleston* post-permission 'obligation' to offer an explanation into a pre-permission 'obligation'. Such a course of action will frequently mean in practice that a judge is troubled by some aspect of the decision-making process as it appears from the application papers. Unless a respondent is able and willing to offer some explanation which indicates that the application is, in fact, unarguable, permission is likely to be granted.

2.3 Criticism of the Existing Position

The common law, with resort to its usual pragmatic blend of principle and procedure has largely ensured that the courts can, at least, ensure that they are in a position to exercise their supervisory control, at least where someone is adamant on testing the decision. The primary criticism is one of principle. The law currently presents an unhappy patchwork. There is no clear obligation to provide reasons and no real principled justification for the absence of such an obligation. The circumstances when a legal obligation to explain a decision are by no means clear. Frequently the law has to rely on the implied 'sanction' of granting permission and forcing a public body to a full judicial review if no adequate explanation is given beforehand or of ordering disclosure or inferring illegality and granting a remedy if no adequate explanation is offered by the respondent for a decision. There remains, of course, a risk (the extent of which is not capable of quantification) that unlawful decisions might be reached which, because of the absence of reasons which reveal the potential unlawfulness, remain undetected and unchallenged. At present, however, the prospect of persuading a court to grant permission for judicial review on the basis that an unreasoned decision is unlawful, or that there is a duty to give reasons (in the particular circumstances of the case), together with the need for full explanation thereafter, appears, on the whole, to offer sufficient means for the courts to perform their supervisory role of controlling the legality of decision-making.

3. SUPPLEMENTATION OF WRITTEN REASONS

The courts have also had to consider the quite different question of when a respondent may rely upon written evidence supplementing the reasons for a decision. The concern here is not so much ensuring that the court has material available to exercise its supervisory jurisdiction but rather that a decision taken for one set of reasons which is legally flawed is not made the subject of an *ex post facto* rationalization by the giving of fresh reasons in an attempt to shore up the validity of the original decision.

The position is this. Where the decision was originally accompanied by reasons, the courts will receive evidence to elucidate or confirm the reasons given.[12] The courts will not permit a respondent to rely upon written evidence which seeks to assert that the real reasons for the decision were wholly different from the reasons given at the time[13] or to show that the decision-maker meant something different from what was unambiguously said in a reasoned decision letter.[14] Where, therefore, an authority sent a decision letter stating that a person was intentionally homeless and that there was no evidence to confirm his story that he had left his original home because of intimidation, they could not thereafter rely upon an affidavit giving entirely different reasons, namely that the authority had accepted his story but still considered he was intentionally homeless.[15] There may be other situations where the reasons are simply a short, possibly inadequate, summary of the reasons for the decision. Here the court may allow the respondent to rely upon written evidence setting out the full reasoning process. The courts will, however, be alert to ensure that the written evidence does indeed reflect the reasons existing at the time of the decision and are not an *ex post facto* rationalization of the decision. Thus, in one case, a child was permanently excluded from school and the reason given was simply that that was a reasonable course of action in the circumstances. Although that statement of reasons was inadequate, the courts allowed the respondent to rely upon affidavit evidence setting out the reasons as there was no suggestion that the affidavit did not in fact record the contemporaneous reasons and there had been no change of position and the affidavit evidence was not offering an *ex post facto* rationalization.[16] Where no reasons at all were given for the original decision, written evidence explaining the decision is to be encouraged.[17]

---

[12] *R v Westminster City Council, ex p.Ermakov* [1996] 2 All ER 303 at 315g–316h.
[13] ibid.
[14] *Re C and P* [1992] COD 29. There are also a small number of tribunals such as arbitration awards and immigration tribunals where, it seems, no evidence can be adduced to expand upon the reasons and situations where, unusually, the mere inadequacy of reason is a ground for quashing, where reasons cannot be adduced by written evidence.
[15] *R v Westminster City Council, ex p Ermakov* [1996] 2 All ER 303.
[16] *R v Northamptonshire CC, ex p W.* [1998] COD 110.
[17] *Re C. and P.* [1992] COD 29. This is in accordance with the obligation on the public body to make full and frank disclosure as discussed below once permission for judicial review has been granted. See also *R v Secretary of State for the Home Department, ex p Peries* [1998] COD 150.

4.1 Procedural Obligations

The second obvious link between judicial review and access to information concerns the rules on disclosure of documents (formerly, the process of discovery). A major limiting factor needs to be recognized at the outset. The rules of disclosure are designed to ensure that documents are disclosed in the context of the particular substantive application with which the court is dealing to enable the court to resolve that application. The process of disclosure cannot be used as a means of obtaining documents for some purpose unconnected with the disposal of the particular case before the court in which the application for disclosure is made.[18] So, for example, a court which quashed a decision and remitted the matter back to the decision-maker for reconsideration could not order the disclosure of documents for the purpose of enabling the individual to use those documents as part of the process of reconsideration by that decision-maker.[19]

Disclosure of documents remains important for two principal reasons. First, there is the question of whether the contemporaneous documentation reveals any flaw relating to the decision, which is unknown to the applicant and has not been referred to in any affidavit or witness statement filed on the part of the respondent. The second concerns the extent to which the reasons given in an affidavit accurately reflect the reasons for the decisions.

Disclosure of documents has never been automatic in judicial review applications. Relevant documents, including the contemporaneous documentation surrounding the taking of the decision, will not therefore automatically be disclosed to an applicant who has obtained permission to apply for judicial review.

The court has a discretion to order disclosure. The attitude of the courts in the judicial review jurisdiction to disclosure is restrictive and it is rare for the courts to order disclosure. They have only rarely been prepared to do so and then only when disclosure was really necessary to enable them to deal with the judicial review application.[20] Two areas of concern have, in particular, attracted concern. First, the courts have consistently discouraged any application that they consider to be a fishing expedition, that is applications for disclosure made in the hope that something might emerge which might form the basis of a claim for judicial review. Secondly, the courts have consistently held that they will not allow an application for disclosure in order to go behind an affidavit or witness statement unless there is material outside that contained in the affidavit or witness statement which suggests that it is in some way inaccurate, incomplete or misleading.

---

[18] *R v Secretary of State for Education and Science, ex p G.* The Times, 1 July 1989.
[19] ibid.
[20] See generally Lewis, *Judicial Remedies in Public Law* (2nd edn., 2000) paras. 9-100—9-107.

A number of objections can legitimately be made of the present practice in relation to disclosure in judicial review. First, it is not easy to see the objection to disclosure of relevant contemporaneous documentation dealing with the decision under challenge. In this situation, the applicant will already have surmounted the hurdle of establishing that there is an arguable error of law. The respondent will know that the decision is under challenge and may be quashed. It is difficult to see why the relevant contemporaneous material should not be routinely disclosed. If that material discloses that there was some further error, unknown at that stage to the applicant, which invalidates the decision, it is difficult to see what public interest merits non-disclosure of that material. Furthermore, as the Law Commission noted, the evidence relating to the decision will usually be in the hands of the respondent. It appears in those circumstances unduly restrictive to limit disclosure to situations where the applicant has material indicating that the affidavit or witness statement is inaccurate, incomplete or misleading. Such an approach places undue reliance on the decision-maker and requires too great a degree of self-policing to encourage sufficient confidence in the process of judicial scrutiny.

A second objection concerns the unduly limited approach taken to disputes of fact in judicial review. It is correct that many challenges will not involve questions of disputed fact. They will either involve questions of statutory construction or will involve undisputed fact or facts that appear clearly from the contemporaneous record. There are a number of cases where facts are in dispute. These will include, most significantly, disputes over what factors a decision-maker did or did not take into account when reaching a decision. In such circumstances, the contemporaneous documentation indicating what actually happened during the decision-making process ought generally, and subject to concerns of confidentiality and public interest immunity, to be disclosed, not least because that is likely to be the best evidence of what actually happened.

4.2 Substantive Principles

The substantive principles of the common law are not, in general, concerned with access to documents or primary material. There are, of course, exceptions to that position. Most notably, a body may be required to observe the principles of natural justice before taking a decision. That common law obligation normally arises where a public body is taking a decision which will affect significant rights or interests of an individual. The principles of natural justice or procedural fairness require that the individual who is the potential recipient of an adverse decision is informed of the case against him. That may, in certain cases, require simply disclosure of the gist of the case against the individual so that he may be able to deal with the allegations made. In other cases, natural justice will require the disclosure to the individual of reports or other material which will be supplied to and used by the decision-maker so that the individual may make representations upon that material. Judicial review will be available to quash a final decision based upon material which was not disclosed to the individual.[21] In appropriate cases, the courts may intervene and quash a refusal to disclose relevant material even before the substantive decision is taken.[22] This obligation is likely to apply only in the cases of individuals who are the recipient of the decision and where that decision is one having a significant effect on important rights such as the right to liberty. More recently, however, the court in the *Pinochet* case[23] has ruled that the Home Secretary had to disclose the medical reports on Senator Pinochet's fitness to stand trial to states seeking his extradition. Challenges to general or normative decisions or challenges by public interest pressure groups to particular decisions are unlikely to generate an obligation to ensure access to documents. The disclosure of documentation is, generally, one aspect (albeit an important aspect) of a particular principle of public law, namely the obligation to observe natural justice. The obligation is directed at ensuring that the individual has sufficient information before a particular decision is taken affecting that individual. It does not itself impose an obligation to provide an explanation of why the final decision was taken[24] except in the limited circumstances discussed above where the courts consider that fairness, exceptionally, requires the provision of reasons.

5. CONCLUSION

Judicial review has relatively limited potential for ensuring access to information. The substantive law governing the provision of reasons is, in principle, the most promising means of ensuring some degree of openness and some means of abstracting information from decision-makers. The role of the law in requiring reasons would have an easy justification in terms of enabling the courts to carry out their task of ensuring that decisions are not unlawful. The common law has not, so far, followed the logic of that justification, unlike the principles developed by the European Court of Justice. Despite this theoretical lacuna in the armoury of public law, the courts have on the whole managed to ensure sufficient information is provided to ensure scrutiny of decisions. This is partly by incrementally increasing the situations where the giving of reasons is required and partly by the 'risks' attached to not giving reasons. So far as disclosure of primary information is concerned, judicial review is not likely ever to be an adequate means of ensuring a free flow of information. First, disclosure in judicial review will and can realistically only ever be directed towards ensuring that documentation is disclosed for the purposes of dealing with the particular application before the court. It can, realistically, have no wider mandate. Secondly, the procedural rules and more importantly the attitude of the courts give little hope of using judicial review as a means of access to documentation.

---

[21]   *R v Parole Board ex p. Wilson* [1992] QB 740; *R v Secretary of State for the Home Department, ex p Hickey (No. 2)* [1995] 1 WLR 734.
[22]   *R v Secretary of State for the Home Department, ex p Hickey (No. 2)* (n. 21 above).
[23]   See n. 2 above.
[24]   *R v Secretary of State for the Home Department, ex p Al Fayed* (n. 8 above).

19

Information and Privacy

DAVID FELDMAN

Sir David Williams has influenced public law for many years. From an early stage in his career, he took the subject seriously enough to subject it to rigorous analysis. This convinced many that the law of civil liberties was more than a more or less random collection of interferences with freedoms. His scholarly yet accessible works were concerned with principles without losing sight of the social and political setting which gives meaning to statutes and judgments. Sir David set a generation on the way to the realization that the Diceyan view of legal liberalism, namely that anything is permitted which is not forbidden, was an absence of principle masquerading as a principle. The international law of human rights has now come to be accepted as a normative framework for evaluating and developing municipal law. A concern to maintain a principled approach to the law while being sensitive to social needs is one of the hallmarks of international human rights law. It is in that spirit that this essay seeks to examine the range of norms which govern the relationship between information and privacy, maintaining privacy under the pressure of data processing and data sharing, in international and municipal law.

1. THE VARIETIES OF NORMS FOR PROTECTING RIGHTS OVER INFORMATION

Personal information is important. In the electronic age, those who control information about my health, wealth, ambitions and weaknesses can manipulate, if not control, my life. More information about more people is more readily accessible than ever before, and the growth will not abate. Where the data subject consents to the way in which it is proposed to deal with information about him or her, no serious problem arises. This essay therefore deals only with situations in which the data subject has not consented to the way in which the information is dealt with.

Norms governing the collection, storage and use of information are of many kinds and operate at different levels, some international, some national, and some local. There are also norms which are designed for particular spheres of activity, such as medicine or criminal investigation. The form of the norms varies. At each level and in each sphere, some are 'soft law' or 'quasi-legislation', intended to be influential without giving rise to legal rights, obligations or remedies. Julia Black has pointed out that rules have other dimensions besides those of content or substance. These include their permissive or mandatory character, their legal status, and their structure. The last of these dimensions, structure, itself has four elements: the level of inclusiveness; the level of precision; the level of complexity; and the level of clarity which the rule achieves. In the context of rules to govern regulatory regimes for commerce and industry, Black argues that the choice of a type of rule (i.e. the character, status and structure of rules used by the regulator) is often not made with full regard to the strategic value of a specific type of rule in the context in question.[1] The same seems to be true of the rules governing the interface between privacy and freedom of information, at both international and national levels, as the structure of norms in national and international law demonstrates.

First at international level there is soft law. Such norms are encouraged by the fact that mandatory rule-making is constrained by the proprieties of international relations between sovereign states. Recommendations of the Committee of Ministers of the Council of Europe are of this kind, establishing agreed guidelines for the development of good practice by each State Party. Other types of soft law are intended to be more prescriptive, yet working through administrative rather than legal channels. For example, when the Cabinet Office published *Open Government: Code of Practice on Access to Government Information*[2] it was clearly meant to prescribe how governmental bodies should respond to requests for information. It is and was sufficiently detailed to allow it to be used in this way, and to permit the Parliamentary Commissioner for Administration to adjudicate on complaints about non-disclosure under it. The Cabinet Office even considered it worthwhile to publish guidance on the interpretation of the Code,[3] which would hardly have happened had the Code been regarded as merely advisory.

Alongside this soft law, there is an increasing amount of 'real law', with legislation or common law conferring legal rights and imposing legal duties, enforced by statutory bodies with remedies available from courts or tribunals. At the international level, there is (for example) a structure of legal rights and obligations under the International Covenant on Civil and Political Rights, Articles 17 and 19, and the European Convention on Human Rights (ECHR), Articles 8 and 10. In European Union law, there is the Data Protection Directive, and in the near future there may also be an EU Charter of Human Rights to spell out the rights to which the Maastricht and Amsterdam Treaties have committed the institutions and Member States of the EU (although it is possible that any Charter will take the form of soft rather than real law). In municipal law, we have the Data Protection Acts 1984 and 1998, the law of breach of confidence, and a Government-sponsored Freedom of Information Bill which was introduced to the House of Commons on 18 November 1999 and at the time of writing is under consideration there.

These norms are underpinned by different sets of values and protect different types of interests, reflecting the varied functions of the bodies which produce them. The Council of Europe is concerned to protect individual rights but also to facilitate

---

[1] J. M. Black, ' "Which Arrow?": rule type and regulatory policy' [1995] PL 95–118.

[2] Cabinet Office, 1994.

[3] *Open Government: Code of Practice on Access to Government Information: Guidance on Interpretation* (2nd edn., Cabinet Office, 1997).

cross-border data flows. The Commission of the European Union has mainly economic concerns, and favours openness in access to government-held information partly because of the way that can improve opportunities for economic growth and employment, particularly but not exclusively in the area of information technology. Transparency of government action in relation to public procurement is also seen as crucial to achieve a genuine internal market within the EU.[4] On the other hand, the EU Data Protection Directive is expressly concerned with the right to privacy, as are the rights arising under Article 8 of the European Convention on Human Rights. In the United Kingdom, the public interest in access to government-held information is seen mainly from the point of view of enhancing democracy, but may also significantly enhance or interfere with personal privacy and business and governmental efficacy. These interests inevitably give rise to tensions, if not actual conflicts, between the norms governing information.

Ideally, within any system of law there should be a reasonably coherent approach to the law of information to ensure that these tensions or conflicts can be approached by reference to general principles which have been agreed either for the purpose of all disputes about access to information or for the purpose of disputes relating to a particular sector of government or a particular type of information. However, in practice only limited agreement has been achieved. The law of information is a patchwork which has built up in a fairly disorganized way. The principal movement towards convergence and coherence of norms stems from international institutions. At national and local levels, the picture is of confusion, to which forthcoming developments may bring a modicum of order.

The norms governing the control of personal information overlap untidily with those governing freedom of information. In the House of Commons, this point was noted by the Select Committee on Public Administration when it examined the Government's White Paper on freedom of information[5] in 1998. The Committee generally welcomed the proposals, but in its Report[6] expressed concern about the lack of a satisfactory way of dealing with the overlap between freedom of information and the protection of rights to respect for private and family life. At the international level, these privacy rights give rise to a range of obligations. In particular, they impose duties on the State not only in respect of the way in which information is acquired, but also in relation to safeguarding, processing and giving data subjects[7]

---

[4] See for instance European Commission, *Public Sector Information: A Key Resource for Europe. Green Paper on Public Sector Information in the Information Society* (COM(1998)585) 5. For discussion of the commercial factors favouring freedom of information, see the essay by Richard Thomas in this volume (Ch. 23).

[5] *Your Right to Know: the Government's Proposals for a Freedom of Information Act*, Cm. 3818 (December 1997).

[6] *Your Right to Know: the Government's Proposals for a Freedom of Information Act*, HC 398 of 1997–98, at paras. 10–20.

[7] By 'data subject' here is meant not only, as in Data Protection Act 1998, s. 1(1), any individual who is the subject of personal data, but any person or organization who or which is the subject of data of a sensitive nature, whether personally, commercially, or otherwise.

access to it. The rules and principles which afford security for information in the hands of public authorities are formulated at different levels of government, and have various degrees of legal force. At the international level, there is a great deal of soft law stemming from the Council of Europe. Next, there is a legal right to respect for private and family life under Article 8 of the European Convention on Human Rights which imposes both negative and positive obligations on States as a matter of international law, enforceable through the machinery of the European Court of Human Rights. In the European Community's legal order, the Data Protection Directive (EC) 95/46[8] laid down requirements for Member States to adopt data-protection legislation at the national level in order to protect privacy in relation to both computerized and manual files. There are also strict rules governing confidentiality at the Community level, which (among other effects) make public-interest 'whistle-blowing' hazardous. The principles provided in the Directive apply also to initiatives to share data through police co-operation under the auspices of the Schengen *acquis* and the Interpol Convention.

At national level, the United Kingdom Parliament passed the Data Protection Act 1984 to impose obligations on people who hold and process personal information using computers, and to establish a regulatory mechanism (registration with and supervision by the Data Protection Registrar and the application of Data Protection Principles) for such activities. This was an early response to the growing power of computer-based information systems, which has grown exponentially since then. Legislation (primary and subordinate) gave rise to limited extensions of the rights of data subjects to certain types of information held in paper files, which were implemented in respect of certain information held by social services departments of local authorities, some medical records, and medical reports.[9] When the government came to draft legislation to give effect to the EC Data Protection Directive, it took the opportunity to harmonize the treatment of computerized and manual records across a wide range of fields. While the Data Protection Directive applies only in relation to matters within the purview of the EC, the Data Protection Act 1998 extends the operation of revised Data Protection Principles across most systems for holding and using personal information (although there are some exemptions relating to manual records until 24 October 2007), and similarly extends the regulatory jurisdiction of the Data Protection Commissioner (as she is known under the 1998 Act). Although the Data Protection Act 1998 (unlike the Data Protection Directive) does not refer to 'privacy' as a fundamental value underpinning the legislation, the Act will have to be interpreted having proper regard to the right to respect for private and family life under Article 8 of the European Convention on Human Rights, by reason of the interpretative obligation under Human Rights Act 1998, s. 3, and (in the case of matters within the purview of EU law) the EU Treaties. Article 8 rights also restrict

[8] [1995] OJ L281/31.
[9] Access to Personal Files Act 1987; Access to Personal Files (Social Services) Regulations 1989, SI 1989/206; Access to Personal Files (Housing) Regulations 1989, SI 1989/503; Access to Medical Reports Act 1988; Access to Health Records Act 1990.

the legislative competence of the Scottish Parliament, the Northern Ireland Assembly and the Welsh Assembly,[10] and the legislative and administrative competence of all public authorities.[11]

The Data Protection Act 1998 was enacted before the Freedom of Information Bill was drafted because of the historical accident that the United Kingdom was required under EC law to implement the Data Protection Directive by 24 October 1998. Because the legislation governing data protection was already in place, the Freedom of Information Bill had to be drafted to fit into the legal landscape already shaped by the data protection legislation. This partly explains the restricted nature of the right to freedom of information, already noted by most commentators. Not only do privacy interests thus receive a certain primacy over freedom of information interests in the structure of the legislation, but the regulation of the statutory freedom of information regime is to be put in the hands of the Data Protection Commissioner and the Data Protection Tribunal, who are to be re-titled the Information Commissioner and the Information Tribunal for this purpose. Apart from the additional workload for those bodies and the cost of establishing and running the Office of the Commissioner (estimated, probably very conservatively, by the Government at £6.5 million per year[12]), there may be a tension between the Commissioner's well-established responsibility for data protection and the new responsibility for freedom of information, although if the Commissioner can resolve this it offers hope of a more coherent approach to the regulation of information.

In addition to legislation and soft law formulated specifically to protect privacy interests in information, there is a body of common law which deals directly with restricting information in order to preserve confidentiality, particularly but not exclusively in relation to personal or business information.[13] The reach of the equitable doctrine of breach of confidence has been extended from the protection of genuinely personal information not previously disclosed by the person who is its subject, to sensitive business information, until it is now capable of covering also information about state agencies[14] and information held by public authorities which people have disclosed to them (voluntarily or under compulsion) for particular purposes.[15] Furthermore, the ability of public authorities to deny people access to certain kinds of information for the purposes of litigation is enhanced by the doctrine of public interest immunity. This came under exhaustive scrutiny in the

---

[10] Scotland Act 1998, ss. 29(2), 57; Northern Ireland Act 1998, ss. 6, 24; Government of Wales Act 1998, s. 107.

[11] Human Rights Act 1998, s. 6(1).

[12] *Freedom of Information Bill Explanatory Notes*, House of Commons Bill 5-EN, 18 November 1999, para. 280.

[13] See the essay by Sir Richard Scott in this volume (Ch. 16).

[14] See for example *Attorney-General v Jonathan Cape Ltd.* [1976] QB 752; *Attorney-General v Guardian Newspapers Ltd.* [1990] 1 AC 109, HL.

[15] *Taylor v Serious Fraud Office* [1999] 2 AC 177, HL.

light of the Arms to Iraq affair and the report of the Scott Inquiry,[16] after which it was announced that Government Ministers would make claims to public interest immunity only if the Minister believed that the disclosure of a particular document 'will cause real damage or harm to the public interest'.[17]

Thus the law of information is now an area in which international and municipal law, soft law and hard law, public law and private law, statute and common law, and access to information and privacy, interact. It is also a field in which the law is dynamic. To understand how the norms governing access to information are likely to interact over the next few years, it is useful to examine the influence of these different kinds and fields of law, starting at the international level and working down.

2. THE INTERNATIONAL PLANE

In international law, such pressure as there has been for freedom of governmental information has come either from the commercial lobby (as mentioned above) or, with more general significance in terms of public interests, from states concerned about the potential impact of environmental changes resulting from the industrial, energy-producing or military activities of other states.[18] At United Nations level, the emphasis has generally been on protecting privacy.[19] The General Assembly reacted to the increasing power of data-processing technology very early.[20] The Secretary General delivered a report in 1976 which suggested a possible framework for legislation to protect privacy against technological invasion,[21] and another one entitled *Points for Possible Inclusion in Draft International Standards for the Protection of the Rights of the Individual against Threats arising from the Use of Computerised Personal Data Systems.*[22] These reports in turn led to the adoption by the General Assembly in 1995 of *Guidelines for the Regulation of Computerized Personal Files,*[23] and also influenced the development of standards within the OECD[24] and European institutions.

---

[16] Sir Richard Scott, *Return to an Address of the Honourable the House of Commons dated 15th February 1996 for the report of the Inquiry into the export of Defence Equipment and Dual-use Goods to Iraq and Related Prosecutions* (London: HMSO, 1996).

[17] *Hansard*, HC (series 6), vol. 287, col. 949 (18 December 1996). Sir Nicholas Lyell A-G. The 'real damage' test is intended to equate to 'substantial harm': see Sir Nicholas Lyell at col. 951.

[18] On the importance of duties to provide information under environmental treaties, see the essay by Sir Kenneth Keith in this volume (Ch. 21).

[19] In relation to the setting of international standards, I am deeply indebted to James Michael, *Privacy and Human Rights* (Paris and Aldershot: UNESCO and Dartmouth Press, 1994), ch. 2, and to Jeremy McBride, 'Specific European and International Standards relevant to the Disclosure of Crime Prevention Data', an unpublished paper presented at a JUSTICE seminar on *Disclosure of Crime Prevention Data and the Rights to Respect for Private Life*, 25 January 2000.

[20] See General Assembly Resolution 2450 of 1968 and Declaration 3348 of 1975.

[21] E/CN.4/1116.   [22] E/CN.4/1233.

[23] Resolution 45/95.

[24] OECD, *Guidelines governing the Protection of Privacy and Transborder Data Flows of Personal Data* (1980).

Within Europe, the approach to regulating access to information has been influenced by the need to facilitate cross-border information flow, both between private entities and between public enterprises, and also to some extent between public and private enterprises.[25] In order to achieve this, it has been necessary to ensure that data subjects enjoy similar standards of protection in all European states, in order that less assurance of protection in country B than in country A should not inhibit the transmission of information from A to B. Consistent standards of protection for individual privacy against unauthorized use of personal data is a necessary condition for a genuinely free flow of information between states, individuals and enterprises. As Jeremy McBride points out,[26] this led to a treaty, the Council of Europe Convention for the Protection of Individuals with regard to the Automatic Processing of Personal Data (1981). It was also the catalyst for two Resolutions of the Committee of Ministers of the Council of Europe, No. (73)22 on the Protection of Individuals vis-à-vis Electronic Data Banks in the Private Sector, and No. (74)29 on Protection of Individuals vis-à-vis Electronic Data Banks in the Public Sector. In addition, the Committee of Ministers adopted no less than a dozen Recommendations, relating to the storage, transmission and processing of personal data, between 1981 and 1999.[27]

Of those instruments, only the Council of Europe Convention gives rise to legal obligations (in international rather than municipal law) on the contracting states. As McBride observes,[28] although the form of the instruments is very varied:

the principles shaping them are remarkably uniform, being concerned to ensure that data is fairly and lawfully collected and processed, that it is stored, used and disclosed only for legitimate purposes, that it is adequate, relevant and not excessive for those purposes, that it is accurate and that it is kept secure and for no longer than is necessary. Furthermore the data subject should have access to the data and be able to have it erased, rectified, completed or amended in so far as any of the applicable standards are not being observed by the data

---

[25] In particular contexts, special treaties or legal regimes have been introduced to require that the flow of information and ideas is not hindered. See for example the European Convention on Transfrontier Television, 1990, and the EC Directive (EEC) 89/552, adopted by the Council of Ministers on 20 June 1997, [1997] OJ L202, on which see Eric Barendt, *Broadcasting Law* (Oxford: Clarendon Press, 1993) and Perry Keller, 'The New Television without Frontiers Directive' (1997/98) 2 Yearbook of Media and Entertainment Law 177–95.

[26] See n. 19 above, at 2.

[27] McBride (n. 19 above), 2, provides the following list: Regulations for Automated Medical Data Banks (R(81)1); Protection of Personal Data used for Scientific Research and Statistics (R(83)10); Protection of Personal Data used for the Purposes of Direct Marketing (R(85)20); Protection of Personal Data used for Social Security Purposes (R(86)1); Regulating the Use of Personal Data in the Police Sector (R(87)15); Protection of Personal Data used for Employment Purposes (R(89)2); Protection of Personal Data used for Payment and other Related Operations (R(90)19); Communication to Third Parties of Personal Data held by Public Bodies (R(91)10); Protection of Personal Data in the Area of Telecommunication Services, with particular reference to Telephone Services (R(95)4); Protection of Medical Data (R(97)5); Protection of Personal Data Collected and Processed for Statistical Purposes (R(97)18); and Protection of Privacy on the Internet (R(99)5). McBride also notes that 'the Council of Europe has (with the Commission of the European Communities and the International Chamber of Commerce) also devised a *Model Contract to ensure equivalent Data Protection in the context of transborder dataflows with explanatory memorandum* (1989)'.

[28] McBride (n. 19 above) 2.

controller. The differences between the various instruments essentially concern the degree of elaboration, particularly as regards their application to specific contexts.

On the other hand, McBride points out, the principles are generally not supported by strong enforcement mechanisms. Even the Council of Europe Convention only establishes a Consultative Committee to make proposals. There is no requirement for State Parties to report to the Committee on compliance with the standards, much less any enforcement or adjudicative mechanism. This, he suggests, was perhaps because of 'a perception by the member States of the 1981 Convention as a technical instrument rather than a human rights guarantee'.[29]

However, there are two European provisions which do have some enforceability. Perhaps because of increasing recognition that the storage, use and disclosure of personal information is capable of interfering with the right to respect for privacy, European Union Directive (EC) 95/46 on the Protection of Individuals with regard to the Processing of Personal Data and on the Free Movement of Personal Data[30] required Member States to give effect in national law to the principles set out in the Directive by 24 October 1998 (although, as noted earlier, representations from the United Kingdom resulted in a staged introduction of the regulatory regime for manually processed records). The Directive was conceived at least partly as a measure to protect the human right to privacy. It expressly refers to the other international instrument which gives rise to enforceable rights to information privacy in international law, Article 8 of the European Convention on Human Rights (1950), which states:

1. Everyone has the right to respect for his private and family life, his home and his correspondence.
2. There shall be no interference by a public authority with the exercise of this right except such as is in accordance with the law and is necessary in a democratic society in the interests of national security, public safety or the economic well-being of the country, for the prevention of disorder or crime, for the protection of health or morals, or for the protection of the rights and freedoms of others.

When the ECHR was drafted, it would probably not have been thought that the guarantee of a right to respect for private and family life would have brought with it rights in respect of information. Not only was the technology of data processing then in its infancy, but the historical context out of which the Convention grew would have suggested a limited application for the right. As Judge Sir Gerald Fitzmaurice wrote in his dissenting opinion in *Marckx v Belgium*,[31] one of the early cases on Article 8 in the context of the Belgian law governing the legitimacy of children, the motivation behind Article 8 stemmed from:

the whole gamut of fascist and communist inquisitorial practices such as had scarcely been

---

[29] McBride (n. 19 above) 3.
[30] See n. 8 above.
[31] ECtHR, Series A, No. 31 at 42 (Judgment of 13 June 1979).

known, at least in Western Europe, since the eras of religious intolerance and oppression, until (ideology replacing religion) they became prevalent again in many countries between the two world wars and subsequently. . . . [I]t was for the avoidance of these horrors, tyrannies and vexations that 'private and family life . . . home and . . . correspondence' were to be respected—not for the regulation of the civil status of babies.

The same might have been said, *mutatis mutandis*, about data protection. The Article was to ensure that individuals 'were no longer to be subjected to the four o'clock in the morning rat-a-tat on the door; to domestic intrusions, searches and questionings'[32] rather than to secure particular standards of information storage.

Yet the Commission and Court have treated the ECHR as a dynamic instrument to be interpreted in the light of developing social conditions. Article 8 has been the subject of particularly vigorous and dynamic interpretation. In a long series of judgments, the Court has brought such matters as sexuality, names, civil status, official recognition of gender reassignment, the duties of public authorities towards members of extended families when making child welfare decisions, telephone interception, environmental pollution in residential areas, searches of business premises, and other matters of moral and physical integrity, within the scope of Article 8.[33] One of the fields which the Court has regarded as affecting the right to respect for private and family life, home and correspondence is control over information. The Court has referred to the 1981 Convention and the Council of Europe Committee of Ministers Recommendation R(89)14 on *The Ethical Issues of HIV Infection in the Health Care and Social Settings* when interpreting Article 8 in relation to personal information,[34] implying that the 1981 Convention is regarded as giving an indication of the standards which must be met in order to afford a level of protection in this context which is adequate to amount to respect for private and family life under Article 8. As McBride suggests, the Court, which is currently the only European forum for deciding authoritatively on the standards of protection for personal data which are required by the right to respect for private and family life, home and correspondence, is in effect harmonizing the principles of data protection found fairly consistently in the various international instruments, and is converting them into human-rights requirements in a way which gives them some legal teeth.[35] In this way the Court is conferring a degree of enforceability on standards which were originally contained in norms intended by their drafters and ratifiers to be unenforceable, and to which they might not have agreed had they expected them to be enforced against them.

The Court, in other words, seems to be sifting and giving legal force to the

---

[32] ibid. per Judge Sir Gerald Fitzmaurice.

[33] See Keir Starmer, *European Human Rights Law: The Human Rights Act 1998 and the European Convention on Human Rights* (London: Legal Action Group, 1999) 125–9, 417–29, 477–91, 517–52; Stephen Grosz, Jack Beatson QC and Peter Duffy QC, *Human Rights: the 1998 Act and the European Convention* (London: Sweet & Maxwell, 1999) 265–91.

[34] *Z. v Finland*, RJD 1997–I, 323, at para. 95 (Judgment of 25 February 1997).

[35] McBride (n. 19 above) 3–4.

principles outlined in other instruments which either impose no legal duties on states or, lacking enforcement machinery, contain rules of imperfect obligation. This is particularly significant in the United Kingdom, as courts, tribunals and regulators prepare to deal with both the Data Protection Act 1998 and the Human Rights Act 1998. It is possible to identify the main elements of the Court's interpretation of Article 8 in relation to personal information.

First, the Court has taken a generous view of the scope of the right to respect in relation to personal information. The State interferes with interests protected by Article 8(1) whenever a public authority obtains, holds, processes or disseminates information about one's private or family life, home or correspondence. In principle, the Court has held, Article 8(1) requires the State to ensure that the manner in which information is acquired, the way it is stored, the way it is processed, the steps taken to ensure its accuracy, the period for which it is kept, the information given to the data subject about the data held, any disclosure of the data, and the purposes for which the information is obtained, stored, processed and disclosed, are all justifiable under Article 8(2). In *Rotaru v Romania*, a Grand Chamber of the European Court of Human Rights held by sixteen votes to one that the collection and holding by a State agency of information about aspects of the applicant's life fell within the scope of protection for 'private life' within the meaning of Article 8(1). This was so even though the information purported to be about the applicant's political activities, not least because 'some of the information has been declared false and is likely to injure the applicant's reputation'. The Romanian Secret Service had violated Article 8 both by holding the information and by refusing to allow the applicant to refute it, and also by releasing it with the erroneous claim that it related to the applicant when it actually related to someone else of the same name. The Court held unanimously that the legal regime governing the holding of information gave insufficient legal foundation for the holding of the information to be in accordance with the law, within the meaning of Article 8(2). The Court found violations of Article 8 and 13. Six judges expressly, and one impliedly, went further (obiter) in separate concurring opinions, deciding that the holding of information about someone's political activity as a youth for a period of over 50 years could not be said to be for any of the legitimate purposes under Article 8(2). This suggests a growing willingness to subject to careful scrutiny a State's assertion about the purpose for which information was held, reducing the scope of the margin of appreciation in this area.[36] Thus photographing a person at a police station without his or her consent is an interference with private life which requires justification,[37] as is the retention of the photograph (at least if the photograph is stored in a form and a file which will allow the subject to be identified for the purpose of an authority's public functions).[38] The same applies to the taking,

[36] ECtHR, App. No. 28341/95, Judgment of 4 May 2000, especially at paras. 43, 44 and 46 of the judgment.

[37] *Murray and others v United Kingdom* (1995) 19 EHRR 193 (ECtHR).

[38] Compare *Friedl v Austria*, ECtHR Series A, No. 305-B, where the Commission held (on a point which was not considered by the Court) that photographs of the applicant at a public demonstration, in

retention, use and disclosure of records of fingerprints, DNA samples, medical tests, and police interviews relating to a person's private (for example sexual) life.[39] We will return to justifications under Article 8(2) shortly. For the moment, it is enough to note that possession of information about private and family life always requires justification, even if the data controller does nothing with it.[40]

Article 8 also gives rise to certain positive obligations on the State, which must take action to ensure that private and family life, home and correspondence are adequately protected. These obligations may include providing evidence to people when it affects their private and family lives. For example, in *Gaskin v United Kingdom*[41] the social services department in Liverpool had refused to disclose to a man who had formerly been a child in the local authority's care information held on his file about the reasons for decisions taken about him while in care. The Court held that the information which the applicant was seeking was essential to his understanding of his early life, so that refusing the information prima facie interfered with his right to respect for his private and family life. Not only was there an obligation to disclose the information unless non-disclosure could be justified under Article 8(2); the State had also had, and had failed to discharge, a positive obligation, flowing from the right to respect for private life, to ensure that demands for such information would be evaluated on their merits by an independent decision-maker in the light of the principles in Article 8. As a matter of human rights law, it was not open to the local authority to have a blanket policy of refusing to disclose reports on file without the consent of the people who had prepared them, even if the reports were considered to be confidential as between the reporter and the authority. The interests in disclosure of each report had to be balanced on a case by case basis, in the light of the Article 8 criteria, reaching an objectively justifiable conclusion. In a similar way, the State was held in *McGinley and Egan v United Kingdom*[42] to have violated the rights of servicemen who had been made to witness tests of nuclear devices without adequate protection when it refused to disclose information about the levels of radioactivity which had affected them.

Rights to information do not lie solely in the hands of data subjects. Sometimes a person's life may be incidentally but closely affected by information about someone or

---

which the applicant was not identified, and which were kept on an administrative file but not on a system allowing for data processing or use in criminal records, did not interfere with the applicant's right under Article 8(1). It would have been more satisfactory, in the light of the Court's case law, to hold that the holding of the photograph interfered with Article 8(1), but was justifiable under Article 8(2).

[39] *McVeigh, O'Neill and Evans v United Kingdom* (1981) 5 EHRR 71 (ECtHR); *Z. v Finland*, RJD 1997-I, 323, (1997) 25 EHRR 371 (Judgment of 25 February 1997) (ECtHR); *Lustig-Prean v United Kingdom* (1999) 7 BHRC 65 (ECtHR).

[40] *Leander v Sweden* (1987) 9 EHRR 433 (ECtHR); *Hilton v United Kingdom* (1988) 57 DR 108, ECommnHR.

[41] (1989) 12 EHRR 36 (ECtHR).

[42] (1999) 27 EHRR 1 (ECtHR).

something else. The Court held in *Guerra v Italy*[43] that the State had interfered with the rights to respect for private life and the home of people living in an area which, to the knowledge of the competent authorities, had been subject to pollution with arsenic, where the State had not taken steps to inform the residents and enable them to take remedial or evasive action. This case did not involve a duty to disclose to one person information of a personal kind relating to someone else. However, if it is established that people may have a right to receive information from the State about substantial threats to their welfare of which State agencies are aware, it might involve disclosing personal information about someone who is known to represent a threat to identifiable people, or people in a known area. For example, in *T.V. v Finland*[44] the Commission held that it had been permissible to disclose a prisoner's HIV+ status to the prison staff responsible for his custody so that they might take precautions against infection, thus protecting their rights. In that case the complaint had come from the prisoner that there had been an improper disclosure of medical information, and it was held to have been justifiable to make the disclosure. However, suppose that the prison staff had been kept in ignorance of the prisoner's HIV+ status. It might have been possible for them to argue that the failure to warn them had put them in danger, because it had deprived them of an effective opportunity to protect themselves against the risk of infection. In such a case, the State might have been held to have interfered with their right to respect for their private life, by reason of the failure to pass to them the information about T.V.'s medical condition.

Thus Article 8 may sometimes give rise to rights which conflict with a person's interest in maintaining the confidentiality of personal information. Other rights which may give rise to conflict with a data subject's Article 8 rights include the right to a fair trial and the right to life. In all such cases any interference with Article 8 rights must be justified within the terms of Article 8(2). The same applies, of course, *a fortiori* where a data subject's right to protection for personal information is interfered with to advance a public interest rather than another person's Convention right. What criteria govern the justifiability of such an interference?

As is well known, under Article 8(2) the interference must be assessed against the following tests. First, was the interference 'in accordance with the law'? Secondly, was it for one of the legitimate aims listed in Article 8(2)? Thirdly, was the interference 'necessary in a democratic society' for that purpose? In relation to the first and third questions, the Court has given special and autonomous meanings to the terms 'in accordance with the law' and 'necessary in a democratic society'. It is important to remember that each stage of the collection, storage, handling and disposal or dissemination of information represents a separate interference with the right under Article 8(1), and each of these interferences must be separately assessed against the Article 8(2) criteria.

The expression 'in accordance with the law' has been interpreted as embodying

---

[43] (1998) 26 EHRR 357 (ECtHR).
[44] 76A DR 140 at 150–1 (1994) (ECommnHR).

four requirements. First, the interference must not have been unlawful under municipal law. Secondly, the interference must be securely authorized by positive municipal law. Thus in *Malone v United Kingdom*[45] and *Halford v United Kingdom*[46] the Court held that alleged interceptions of telephone calls were incapable of being justified under Article 8(2) when there was no legal regime for authorizing and regulating the interceptions in question, despite the interceptions not having been unlawful in English law. In the *Malone* case, the interception had taken place before the Interception of Communications Act 1985 was passed. (Indeed, the Act was passed in order to bring municipal law into line with the requirements of the ECHR as enunciated in the *Malone* judgment.) In the *Halford* case, the interceptions fell outside the scope of the 1985 Act, as the Act applies only to calls over a public telephone network while Alison Halford's calls had been intercepted on an internal telephone network at her place of work. At present, intrusive surveillance by the police which does not involve entry to premises or interception of communications, and the use of informers, are not regulated by law, but only by Home Office guidance and police force orders. Any interference with the right to respect for private life which they cause therefore appears to be unjustifiable under Article 8, although the position will be considerably improved if the Regulation of Investigatory Powers Bill, presented to the House of Commons on 9 February 2000, becomes law.[47]

Thirdly, the rule authorizing the interference in municipal law must be sufficiently accessible to those affected by it and sufficiently clear to enable people to foresee with sufficient certainty the circumstances in which they are liable to be subjected to an interference with their right. The common law may be adequately clear and accessible, and substantive legal standards may sometimes be complemented by administrative rules providing for procedures to be followed, if adequately publicized. However, where the substance of a rule is contained only in administrative directions which have no legal force, or in the case-law of courts in systems which do not accord binding force to judicial decisions as precedents, the interference authorized by the rule will not be in accordance with the law or prescribed by law.[48] Fourthly, any discretion given to a public authority must be defined, and the manner of its exercise delimited, with sufficient clarity and respect for the rule of law to protect people adequately against arbitrary interference.[49] For example, it is not enough for a law on interception of communications to provide protection from interception for a privacy-related interest (such as legal professional privilege) if it does not provide a procedure which is independent of

---

[45] Series A, No. 82, (1984) 7 EHRR 14.
[46] RJD 1997-III, No. 39 (1997) 24 EHRR 523 (Judgment of 25 June 1997).
[47] HC Bill 64 of 1999–2000. See especially clauses 25–45.
[48] See further *Huvig v France* (1990) 12 EHRR 527; *Kruslin v France* (1990) 12 EHRR 547; *Kopp v Switzerland* (1999) 27 EHRR 91; *Valenzuela Contreras v Spain* (1999) 28 EHRR 483 and see *Amann v Switzerland*, App. No. 27798/95, Judgment of 16 February 2000, showing that these are demanding requirements.
[49] *Malone v United Kingdom*, (n. 45 above) at para. 68 of the judgment.

the executive and of investigators for assessing whether a particular communication is legally privileged.[50]

When we come to the next test under Article 8(2), we find that the paragraph provides an exhaustive list of the purposes for which the State may interfere with the rights. They are fairly broadly drafted, but the Court may look for evidence that the interference was actually undertaken for the purpose which the State claims, and may also conclude that a particular act or omission was not reasonably capable of advancing a particular purpose. For instance, in *Z. v Finland*,[51] the investigation file in a case of rape and attempted manslaughter was subject to a ten-year delay on publication because of the confidentiality of medical details referred to in it. The applicant alleged that publication violated her Article 8 rights, and that a delay of thirty years should have been imposed. The Commission and the Court accepted that the publication of the judgment would advance the protection of the rights and freedoms of others, specifically the right of members of the public to have access to the case material. The Court recognized that there is a public interest in the transparency of court proceedings in order to maintain public confidence in the courts, and that the right of the public to have access to the case material was a legitimate aim. The Commission had also decided that public access to the material was aimed at the prevention of crime. However, the Court differed on this point, adopting a more literal reading of the term 'prevention of crime' than had the Commission. The Court also doubted whether the Commission had been correct to decide that the publication of the applicant's full name as well as her medical condition pursued any of the legitimate aims under Article 8(2), although it was not necessary finally to decide the point.[52]

This makes it clear that the Court is prepared to look critically at claims by States to have been pursuing a legitimate purpose in interfering with a right. It is likely that the level of scrutiny will vary somewhat according to the purpose in question. It may be more difficult for the Court to assess a State's claim to have been acting in pursuit of national security (which involves consideration of information which the State may be unable safely to reveal) or the protection of morals (which the Court has frequently held are variable and localized and in respect of which national authorities are better placed than the Court to form authoritative views) than a claim to have been pursuing public safety, the economic well-being of the country, the prevention of disorder or crime, the protection of health, or the protection of the rights and freedoms of others.

It is not enough that the making of the relevant rule was prompted by a real desire to advance a legitimate purpose. As the approach taken by the Court in *Z. v Finland*, above, shows, there must also have been an objectively verifiable likelihood that each decision, act or omission made under the rule was objectively calculated to advance

---

[50] *Kopp v Switzerland* (n. 48 above).
[51] RJD 1997-I, 323, (1997) 25 EHRR 371 (Judgment of 25 February 1997).
[52] ibid. at para. 78 of the judgment.

that purpose. In every case the State must be ready to establish to the Court's satisfaction that, at the time of the rule, decision, act or omission which interferes with a Convention right, there was reasonably believed to be a real causal nexus between the interference and one of the legitimate purposes under the Convention. It is important to bear this point in mind in relation to the holding and disclosure of personal information, where a long series of acts or failures to act may impact in different ways at different times on interests protected by Article 8(1).

The last test under Article 8(2) is that the interference to be justified must be shown to be 'necessary in a democratic society' for one of the legitimate purposes. As interpreted by the Court, this imposes a number of requirements to be met before an interference which is in accordance with the law and pursues a legitimate purpose can be said to be justified.

While for practical reasons 'necessary' is not treated as meaning that the interference must have been the only possible way of pursuing the legitimate purpose, it is far from being an empty term. Taken as a whole, 'necessary in a democratic society' means that the interference with the right must be a response to a pressing social need, and must be a proportionate response. Furthermore, the Court's model of democracy does not entail mere majority rule. The idea of democratic society entails respect for the democratic values of pluralism, tolerance and broad-mindedness and protection against arbitrary invasion of citizens' rights. In a democracy which respects Convention rights, minorities must be adequately protected against unfair treatment and the abuse by the majority of a dominant position.[53] Proportionality is assessed mainly by asking whether the interference with the right is more extensive than is justified by the legitimate aim. This involves balancing the seriousness of the interference against the seriousness of the threat to the interests which are protected within the purposes for which it is legitimate to interfere with the right. Part of that balancing exercise requires the Court to consider whether the extent of the interference is greater than is reasonably necessary to achieve the legitimate aim, and whether there are adequate safeguards against arbitrariness and unjustified interference.

Several factors affect the way in which the Court views the collection, storage and use of information under this criterion. These include:

(a) the nature of the material disclosed. The Court regards some categories of information as particularly sensitive or intimate in terms of privacy, so that its management requires special care and its disclosure requires specially compelling reasons. Such categories include information about a person's health, such as his or her HIV status,[54] and information about an individual's sexual orientation and activity;[55]

---

[53] *Handyside v United Kingdom* (1976) 1 EHRR 737 at para. 49 of the judgment; *Chassagnou v France*, Judgment of 29 April 1999 at para. 112.

[54] *Z. v Finland* (n. 51 above).

[55] *Lustig-Prean v United Kingdom*, ECtHR (Judgment of 27 September 1999).

(b) the range of people who have access to the material, and the nature of their interests in it. The decision of the Commission in *T.V. v Finland*,[56] mentioned earlier,
offers an example: it was held that the State could justify disclosing the prisoner's
HIV+ status to the prison staff responsible for his custody so that they might
take precautions against infection, thus protecting their rights;

(c) the gravity of the threat or the social importance of the purpose for which the
disclosure is contemplated, judged according to the particular facts of the case;

(d) the gravity of the impact on the data subject of the disclosure. Thus it requires
particular care where information is used in a way which might threaten the data
subject's employment prospects;[57]

(e) the steps taken to protect the identity and other details relating to, and the
privacy-related interests of, the data subject. For example, in *M.S. v Sweden*[58] the
Court decided that disclosing medical records to a Social Insurance Office which
required them to assess the applicant's application for compensation for a back
injury was supported by relevant and sufficient reasons and was not disproportionate, because the records were obtained only when the applicant had sought
a benefit, they were necessary in order to assess her legal entitlement to the benefit, and the Social Insurance Office was under a legal duty to maintain their
confidentiality; and

(f) the fairness and sufficiency of the procedure for deciding whether and to what
extent retention, processing and disclosure of information are justified, ensuring
that the data subject's interests are fully considered.

The judgment of the Court in *Z. v Finland*[59] provides a good example of the operation of these considerations. In the course of criminal proceedings against the applicant's husband for attempted manslaughter, the criminal courts had to decide
whether he knew or should have known that he had been HIV+ at the time when he
had allegedly raped several women. The applicant, his wife, was known to be HIV+,
and the courts considered it relevant to establish when she had discovered this. The
prosecutor had ordered the seizure of medical records relating to her, and the court
of first instance had ordered her medical advisers to give evidence. On convicting her
husband of some of the charges, the court had ordered that the case materials (which
included the medical records) should not be made available to the public for ten
years. Under statute, a period of non-disclosure for up to forty years could have been
ordered. The Helsinki Court of Appeal convicted the husband on two extra charges,
referring in its judgment to the applicant's health records, and then faxed its judgment to the press. Details were published in newspapers.

The applicant complained of violations of her right to respect for private and
family life. On the question whether the interference with the applicant's right to
respect for private and family life had been necessary in a democratic society for

---

[56] 76A DR 140 at 150–1 (1994).   [57] *Leander v Sweden* (n. 40 above).
[58] (1997) 3 BHRC 248 (ECtHR).
[59] RJD 1997-I, 323, (1997) 25 EHRR 371 (Judgment of 25 February 1997).

crime prevention, the European Court of Human Rights treated each stage of the process as requiring separate consideration. The majority of the Court (Judge De Meyer dissenting on this point) also decided that the municipal courts had been entitled to require the medical advisers to give evidence, because Finnish law allowed such evidence to be given without the patient's consent in only very limited circumstances, and in this there had been a strong public interest in prosecuting the husband for all his alleged offences, to which the evidence of the advisers about the applicant was relevant as showing when he was likely to have known or suspected his own HIV status. The evidence had been given in camera, and the city court had ordered that the case file should be kept confidential. The interference had been supported by 'relevant and sufficient reasons which corresponded to an overriding requirement in the interest of the legitimate aim pursued', and was not disproportionate.[60] The same considerations applied to the seizure of the applicant's medical records and their inclusion in the investigation file.[61]

On the other hand, the Court did not consider that the order to keep the medical data confidential for only ten years had given adequate weight to the applicant's interests. 'The further interference which she would suffer if the medical information were to be made accessible to the public after ten years is not supported by reasons which could be considered sufficient to override her interest in the data remaining confidential for a longer period.' Public access after ten years would be a disproportionate interference with her Article 8 right. There was thus a violation of Article 8 under this head.[62] This made it inevitable that the Court would hold that the publication of the Court of Appeal's judgment containing details of the applicant's identity and medical condition was unsupported by cogent reasons, and accordingly violated Article 8.[63]

This points to a number of general principles. First, the more intimate information is, the more carefully the Court will scrutinize the reasons for compelling disclosure to or retention by a public authority. Secondly, the greater the effect of disclosure on the data subject's private, family and social life and employment, the more compelling will be the reasons required to justify compelled disclosure, and the stronger will be the safeguards required for the security of the information. Thirdly, the stronger the public interest in maintaining confidentiality, the more compelling will be the public-interest reasons required to justify overriding them. Fourthly, the State's obligations under Article 8 do not cease at the time of disclosure to the State. Use or disclosure of the information by a public authority, or allowing public access generally, represents a further interference with the data subject's rights under Article 8. The State must therefore have in place a procedure compelling the relevant public authority carefully to consider, on a case-by-case basis, whether the public interest in allowing further use or disclosure of the information is sufficiently compelling to justify overriding the interest in maintaining confidentiality according

---

[60] Judgment of the Court at para. 104. [61] ibid., para. 108.
[62] ibid., para. 112. [63] ibid., para. 113.

to the principles developed under Article 8(2). Part of that procedure should include an opportunity for review by an independent, and preferably judicial, body, and must allow the interests of the data subject to be put adequately before each decision-maker. The relevant substantive rules must be clearly set out, and any discretion clearly delimited, in accessible positive law, and any procedural directions of an administrative kind must be accessible to those who are likely to be affected. Finally, the procedures must be adequate to ensure that the exercise of legal powers to interfere with Article 8 rights, introduced to the law for a legitimate purpose, are not in practice used in any case for another purpose.[64]

3. THE NATIONAL PLANE

Within the United Kingdom, there has been as great a mixture of norms governing the control of private information as in the international sphere, and the purposes of these norms have been as varied. There has been a good deal of soft law: the guidelines and Code of Practice already mentioned have been supplemented by guidance and codes of practice promulgated by organizations and bodies representing particular professions such as the Press Complaints Commission, the Governors of the BBC, the Independent Television Commission, the Broadcasting Standards Commission, and the British Medical Association (BMA).[65] On the 'real law' front, the data protection principles under the Data Protection Acts 1984 and 1998 bind all data controllers who are within the Acts' purview. The principles broadly reflect the consensus which has emerged at international level about the principles to be applied, but are given teeth by the work of the Data Protection Commissioner and the Tribunal. For example, the legal obligations on data controllers only begin with registration. There is then a statutory obligation to ensure that all activity in relation to the data complies with the data protection principles. Under the first principle, a set of conditions is laid down for any data processing, and an additional set of requirements must be met if the data to be processed are personal. The principles under the Data Protection Act 1998 meet the obligations imposed by international and European law, and, in case of doubt, will be interpreted in the light of the Data Protection Directive and in such a manner as to comply so far as possible with the Convention rights under the Human Rights Act 1998.

Alongside the statutory data protection principles, but not identical to them, are legal restrictions on the handling and sharing of information deriving from other areas of law. One such field is breach of confidence. This deals only with disclosure

---

[64] See ECHR, Art. 18.

[65] See British Medical Association, *Confidentiality and Disclosure of Health Information*, accessible on the BMA's website at http://web.bma.org.uk/public/pubother.nsf/webdocsvw/confidentiality and Peter Moodie and Moira Wright, 'Confidentiality, codes and courts: an examination of the significance of professional guidelines on medical ethics in determining the legal rights of confidentiality' (2000) 29 *Anglo-American Law Review* 39–66.

of information, not with its storage or processing, but applies to sensitive information about business and sometimes government as well as that which is strictly private in the personal sense. Common law duties of confidence have been developed to a point at which one can say that, in principle, all information obtained by a public authority for the purpose of its public functions is held subject to a prima facie obligation not to disclose it to anyone else. The duty of non-disclosure can be overridden by a recognized public interest in disclosure, but that public interest must be weighty on the facts of the case, and the disclosure must be to an appropriate person or body.[66]

However, the structure of the law on breach of confidence is different from that which is applied in Strasbourg under Article 8 of the ECHR. Unlike Article 8(2), the common law of breach of confidence does not exhaustively delimit the public interests for which duties of confidence can be overridden. Nor does the common law apply a test equivalent to that of necessity in a democratic society: there is no 'pressing social need' requirement, and the test of proportionality is usually applied in a somewhat impressionistic way. Although the tests under Article 8(2) involve the exercise of judgment, the European Court of Human Rights typically sets out all the interests (public and private) favouring the enforcement of the right to privacy and favouring interfering with it, and gives an indication of the weight which it attaches to each on the facts of the case and the reasons for those weights. English courts rarely approach decisions about the public interest in restraining or permitting a breach of confidence as systematically as that.

Besides potentially reaching results at common law which are incompatible with the requirements of Article 8 of the ECHR,[67] the law of breach of confidence has two other drawbacks as a protection for private information. First, because the balancing of the public interest against the duty of confidence is approached unscientifically, those who hold confidential information can have relatively little confidence that the law will support their decision if they decide to disclose information, unless a court has sanctioned the disclosure first. This can lead to defensive non-disclosure in cases when disclosure might be justified by powerful public interests. Secondly, and conversely, the lack of clarity and predictability in this area of law means that some holders of personal information may misunderstand their obligations and succumb to pressure to release information which should have been withheld. Although the uncertainty probably does not reach the level at which the decision could be said to be not in accordance with the law for the purposes of Article 8, it reduces the value of the doctrine as a protection for personal information.

Further difficulties are produced by the fact that the standards which the law of breach of confidence imposes are not the same as those in the Data Protection Act

---

[66] *Taylor v Serious Fraud Office* [1999] 2 AC 177, HL. See the essay by Sir Richard Scott in this volume (Ch. 16).

[67] See e.g. *Observer and Guardian v United Kingdom* ECtHR Series A, No. 216, (Judgment of 26 November 1991).

1998. The Act has been drafted in order to meet the European standards, especially those contained in the Data Protection Directive but also those in the 1981 Convention and the ECHR. The law of breach of confidence overlaps awkwardly with the provisions of the 1998 Act, which are much more explicit than the common law in respect of the standards to be applied and the process of reasoning to be followed, particularly when deciding where the public interest lies.

As if this were not enough, there are further layers of law shortly to be introduced by the Human Rights Act 1998 and, if and when it is passed and comes into force, the Freedom of Information Bill. The Bill should cause relatively few problems in relation to personal information, both because it is drafted to fit in with the Data Protection Act 1998 (with a few amendments to the latter) and because of the exemption given in it to preserve privacy by clauses 38 and 39 of the Bill.[68] The primacy of privacy should ensure that the Bill will have little effect on personal information. The Human Rights Act 1998 is a different matter. It imports Article 8 into municipal law, making it unlawful for public authorities to act in a manner incompatible with a Convention right unless the incompatibility is unavoidably demanded by primary legislation which cannot be interpreted to allow compatibility. Although the duty under s. 3 of the Act, to interpret legislation so far as possible to avoid incompatibility with Convention rights, does not apply to the common law, courts and tribunals are public authorities within the meaning of the Act. It may follow that the courts dealing with common law breach of confidence claims will have to fashion their approach to the claim, and to the grant of any remedy, to ensure that the result is compatible with Article 8 of the Convention. That might often be fairly simple to achieve: it could simply involve adopting an approach to the balance between the core right and any countervailing public-interest considerations which matches the step-by-step process required by Article 8(2). This would have the dual advantages of providing a more principled and systematic basis for reasoning towards such judgments than is currently available, and ensuring that the law of breach of confidence develops principles which are similar to those underlying the Data Protection Act 1998 (based as it is on European standards), thus securing consistency of standards between the common law and statute.

On the other hand, there could be additional difficulties rather than greater simplicity if the courts take a different line on Article 8 from that developed in Strasbourg. Such a divergence might occur, for instance, if the courts adopt a more restrictive interpretation of the rights under the Article, or a more extensive interpretation of the legitimate grounds for interfering with them, than the Strasbourg organs have done. This is possible, because s. 2 of the Human Rights Act 1998 requires that the Strasbourg jurisprudence must be taken into account, but not necessarily followed, by municipal courts and tribunals. It is to be hoped that judges will interpret Convention rights at least as generously as have the Strasbourg organs, not least because failing to do so will defeat one of the purposes of the Act by forcing litigants to have recourse to Strasbourg in order to vindicate their rights.

---

[68] For a commentary on the Bill, see the essay by Stephanie Palmer in Ch. 15 of this volume.

Another possible cause of divergence between the United Kingdom and Strasbourg in respect of Article 8 rights, and one more likely to present real problems for the judges, is the strong possibility of a clash between the Article 8 rights of data subjects and the Article 10 rights of the press to freedom of expression, including the right to receive and impart information and ideas. Any collision between rights will require careful handling, ensuring that any restriction of either right to accommodate the other will be justifiable under the terms of the Article which confers the right which is limited. Some rights are entirely unqualified. For example, a clash between the right to be free of torture or inhuman or degrading treatment or punishment under Article 3 and any other right which is capable of qualification will have to be resolved in favour of the Article 3 right. However, the right to freedom of expression is a qualified right. Although the European Court of Human Rights has given considerable weight to the importance of the press to a democratic polity, particularly in contributing to public information on political matters, Article 10(2) refers to the 'duties and responsibilities' which a right to freedom of expression carries with it as justifying the State in interfering with the right for the purposes specified in that paragraph. Like an interference with rights under Article 8, any interference with freedom of expression must be 'prescribed by law' (which, like 'in accordance with the law' in Article 8(2), is a translation of '*prévue par la loi*' in the French text, and given the same meaning by the Court) and 'necessary in a demo-cratic society' for one of the legitimate aims exhaustively listed there. In principle, this gives a good deal of leeway to courts and tribunals to balance Article 10 rights and Article 8 rights in the event of a conflict in the light of the particular circumstances.

This flexibility may be limited by s. 12 so far as remedies, rather than substantive law, are concerned. The section applies where 'a court is considering whether to grant any relief which, if granted, might affect the exercise of the Convention right to freedom of expression'.[69] In other words, it comes into play only after a court has decided, in non-criminal proceedings,[70] that unlawful action is threatened or has occurred, and is considering relief, whether interlocutory or final. The section then restricts the availability of ex parte relief and interim orders restraining publication.[71] In relation to proceedings for breach of confidence and defamation, the effect of this is that no pre-trial order will be made restraining publication 'unless the court is satisfied that the applicant is likely to establish that publication should not be allowed'.[72] While this will often produce the same results as would be reached at common law, there may be subtle (or not so subtle) differences. For example, in actions for breach of confidence the courts currently start from the position that it is proper to restrain publication pending trial, as otherwise the subject matter of the action (the confidentiality of the information) will be destroyed.[73] Under s. 12, this principle will apply only where the applicant can satisfy the court that he or she is

---

[69] Human Rights Act 1998, s. 12(1).   [70] See Human Rights Act 1998, s. 12(5).
[71] Human Rights Act 1998, s. 12(2), (3).   [72] ibid., s. 12(3).
[73] *Attorney-General v Guardian Newspapers Ltd.* [1987] 1 WLR 1248, HL (the first *Spycatcher* case).

likely to establish a claim to a final injunction at trial. In assessing the degree of likelihood of this happening in a case where the respondent claims, or it appears to the
court, that the case concerns journalistic, literary or artistic material or conduct relating to it, s. 12(4) requires the court to

have particular regard . . . to—
(a) the extent to which—
    (i) the material has, or is about to, become available to the public; or
    (ii) it is, or would be, in the public interest for the material to be published;
(b) any relevant privacy code.

This appears to indicate that it will not generally be proper to grant an interim
injunction restraining publication in the press where the information is already, or is
likely to come, into the public domain, as in the *Spycatcher* case, and the journalist
has not breached the privacy provisions of any Code of Practice which applies, such
as those issued by the Press Complaints Commission, the Broadcasting Standards
Commission, the Independent Television Commission, and the Governors of the
BBC.

As well as the specific provisions governing orders restraining publication before
trial, s. 12(4) of the Act provides that, whenever a court is considering granting any
relief (other than in criminal proceedings) which might affect the exercise of a right
under Article 10 whether or not it involves journalistic, literary or artistic material,
the court 'must have particular regard to the importance of the Convention right to
freedom of expression . . .'. In cases concerning the disclosure of personal information, this could mean that in any clash between rights under Article 8 and rights
under Article 10 greater weight should be given to the latter. However, such an interpretation could make it impossible for the court to provide adequate protection for
a person's right to respect for private life. On Strasbourg principles, it would be unacceptable to adopt an interpretation which always gave greater weight to rights under
Article 10 than to other rights. As noted earlier, the Court requires that any interference with a right under Article 8(1) should be assessed in the light of the facts of
the particular case to see whether it can be justified under the terms of Article 8(2),
just as any interference with a right under Article 10(1) must be justifiable on a case
by case basis under Article 10(2). If s. 12 were to be interpreted as preventing a court
from carrying out that careful analysis of the various rights and interests in the light
of the facts of the particular case, it would violate the rights of data subjects under
Article 8. But the terms of s. 12(4) are by no means unequivocal, and the overriding
interpretative obligation under s. 3 of the Act is to read and give effect to all legislation, including the Act itself, '[s]o far as it is possible to do so . . . in a way which is
compatible with the Convention rights'. It seems to follow that the importance of
the right to freedom of expression to which the court must have particular regard
under s. 12 cannot be regarded as outweighing other rights in cases where that would
result in an incompatibility with Convention rights. If this means that s. 12 has a
restricted effect, that is probably consistent with the intention of its drafters: the

government rejected an amendment which would have had the effect that Article 10 would always have trumped Article 8.[74]

Cutting across this mixture of standards for protecting personal information comes a raft of rules which are designed to maximize the sharing of information for a range of purposes including child welfare, crime prevention and the detection of welfare fraud. The idea that child welfare decision-making should take account of information known to health workers and police as well as social services departments led to an emphasis on joint working and information sharing in the Children Act 1989, ss. 17 and 47 in respect of information about a person's record of committing sexual abuse.[75] This has been extended to other areas. The powers of the police to share information with civil litigants were considered in *Marcel v Commissioner of Police of the Metropolis*,[76] where it was held that the police owed a duty to use information which comes into their possession in the course of an investigation only for the purposes of their own functions, unless an overriding public interest (such as that in child protection) justified disclosure. Other organizations with statutory powers or duties to collect personal information, such as tax authorities, are bound by statutory duties of non-disclosure. Evidence gathered by some other bodies, such as the Department of Trade or the Serious Fraud Office, under coercive powers has been passed on to facilitate criminal investigations by other authorities, and has even been admitted in evidence at criminal trials, although this was held to violate rights under Article 6[77] and has accordingly been significantly restricted by the Youth Justice and Criminal Evidence Act 1999, ss. 58 and 59 and Sch. 3.

The overriding concern of the present government, however, has been to facilitate the investigation of crime, if necessary at the expense of the right to personal privacy. For example, the realization that police bugging and burgling operations were both unlawful in municipal law and in violation of Article 8 of the ECHR led to their being put on a statutory footing in Part III of the Police Act 1997. In the face of worries that releasing information was likely to be ultra vires public bodies, duties of non-disclosure were relaxed. The Social Security Administration (Fraud) Act 1997, ss. 1 and 2 allowed tax authorities and various other public bodies to release information to investigators of suspected social security fraud. The Crime and Disorder Act 1998, s. 115, conferred a wide-ranging power to disclose information where the disclosure is 'necessary or expedient' for the purposes of the Act (mainly crime-prevention and investigation) on 'any person' as long as the disclosure was made to the police, a local authority, a probation committee, or a health authority. These dispensations from duties of confidentiality are less extensive than they appear, since the data controllers remain subject to the Data Protection Acts 1984 and 1998 (where they apply), and to the rights of data subjects under Article 8 of the ECHR

---

[74] *Hansard*, HC (series 6) vol. 315, cols. 542–3 (2 July 1998).
[75] On the extent of the duty of disclosure, see *Re L (Sexual Abuse: Disclosure)* [1999] 1 WLR 299, CA.
[76] [1992] Ch 225, CA.
[77] *Saunders v United Kingdom*, (1996) 23 EHRR 313 (Judgment of 17 December 1996) (ECtHR).

by virtue of the Human Rights Act 1998 (when it comes into force). Apart from this, the data controller generally has a discretion rather than a duty to disclose (save in relation to crimes such as espionage, drug trafficking and terrorism, and under the Money Laundering Regulations 1993), and should weigh up the competing interests before making a disclosure. It has been said that it will generally be desirable to inform the data subject that a disclosure is contemplated, so that he or she may make representations and challenge the decision, unless there are pressing reasons for not giving warning.[78] In making disclosure decisions, public authorities are subject both to the Human Rights Act 1998 and to the general principles of judicial review, as *R v Chief Constable of North Wales, ex p AB and CD*[79] makes clear, but the court will not make the decision which lies properly with the public authority.[80] However, public law is an unsatisfactory way of protecting rights under Article 8 of the ECHR: as *Ex p AB and CD* made clear, the court in judicial review proceedings does not start from a presumption that an interference with an Article 8(1) right is illegitimate and in need of powerful justification,[81] although this may change when the Human Rights Act 1998 comes into force. A person who is the subject of information held by private people, companies and organizations is more strongly protected by the Data Protection Principles, but not by public law.[82]

The limited effect of s. 115 of the Crime and Disorder Act 1998 on accepted legal principles has not stopped the police in some areas from seeking to obtain astonishingly wide categories of material. Anecdotal evidence includes requests for the names of all those using a needle exchange service, which could have undermined years of work building the confidence of addicts in the service, and requests for the names of all those whose medical or educational records are 'flagged' to indicate suspicions of abuse, regardless of any assessment of the reliability of the evidence supporting the suspicion. In these cases, disclosure was refused, but there is no way of knowing whether similar requests are being complied with in other parts of the country. There are particular problems surrounding the control of information under data sharing arrangements which the Crime and Disorder Act 1998 encourages or requires. For example, to what extent can the organization co-operating with a local authority in a Youth Offending Team properly have access to databases controlled by the other partners, such as the Police National Computer, health records, or education records? Who is responsible under the Data Protection Act as the data controller in respect of

---

[78] *Woolgar v Chief Constable of Sussex Police* [2000] 1 WLR 25 at 37, CA, per Kennedy LJ.

[79] [1999] QB 396, DC and CA. On the government's proposals for taking steps to protect the public against released paedophiles, see *Hansard*, HL (series 5) vol. 589, col. 479 (5 May 1998).

[80] *Woolgar v Chief Constable of Sussex Police* [2000] 1 WLR 25, CA.

[81] See Rabinder Singh, *The Future of Human Rights in the United Kingdom* (Oxford: Hart Publishing, 1997), ch. 5.

[82] The protection of public law may not greatly assist the data subject. Courts have sometimes shown themselves willing to give a very extensive reading to a body's *vires* and, as usual, a restricted reach to the principle of *Wednesbury* unreasonableness, in order to validate a disclosure of personal information which seems at first sight to be bizarre. See *R. v Brentwood Borough Council, ex p Peck* The Times, 18 December 1997, DC, on a local authority's discretion to hand over CCTV footage of a man attempting suicide to a broadcasting company.

the information which is shared between members of a Youth Offending Team? What are the duties of members of the Team in relation to information which they have gained from their Team partners when they are engaged in investigative activities which lie outside the scope of the Team?

The Home Office has issued guidance on the use of s. 115,[83] but takes the view that each of the forty-three police forces in the country should be left to work out its own procedures for operating the section. Some consistency might be guaranteed by a Code of Practice with statutory authority, like those issued under the Police and Criminal Evidence Act 1984, to govern all disclosure requests, but at present it is difficult if not impossible even to gain a national picture of practices in this area. As a result, the operation of s. 115 probably does not comply with Article 8 of the ECHR. Disclosure of personal information pursuant to the section is an interference with the right to respect for private life, and the use of guidance rather than law to regulate the resulting discretion probably means that the interference is not in accordance with the law as that term is understood for Article 8 purposes. Even if it is in accordance with the law, the possibility that disclosure may be made where it is thought to be merely 'expedient' rather than 'necessary' opens the door to disclosures which cannot be said to be 'necessary in a democratic society' for the prevention of crime, although once the Human Rights Act 1998 is in force the word 'expedient' will have to be interpreted, if possible, in a way that avoids incompatibility with Article 8 and other Convention rights.

4. CONCLUSION

A mix of standards, legal and quasi-legal, contributes to the determination of cases where it is necessary to balance the right to confidentiality of personal information against third parties' rights to have access to it and public interests in disclosure. The substance of these rules or principles is pulled in different directions by competing policy objectives. At the international level, these standards are being harmonized by common acceptance of certain data protection principles and a growing recognition that protecting personal information is a human-rights issue, not merely a matter of good administration. At national level, the Data Protection Act 1998 is influenced by the international and EU standards and is compatible with them. On the other hand, the law of breach of confidence offers only uncertain protection, and a growing number of statutory provisions permit sensitive personal information to be disclosed, leaving it to the data controller to assess the weight of competing rights and interests with little guidance except the general standards derived from international instruments and the Data Protection Principles under the Data Protection Acts 1984 and 1998.

---

[83] See the Home Office website at http://www.homeoffice.gov.uk/cdact/index.htm for the guidance.

But substance is not the only significant quality of rules, as Julia Black has pointed out.[84] The evidence seems to suggest that types of norms which make up the inter-woven rules of law and principles for regulation governing the balance between privacy and freedom of information are not chosen with a sufficient level of strategic, or even tactical, awareness of their respective strengths and weaknesses. Add to this a significant degree of inconsistency between the substance of some of the rules and principles and the result is that important rights and interests receive inadequate legal protection.

The Human Rights Act 1998 and the Data Protection Act 1998 are likely to require public authorities to reflect ever more carefully on the way in which interests and rights are balanced against each other, on a case by case basis and by reference to principled criteria derived directly or indirectly from international standards. Is it too much to hope that, in time, it may be possible to draft legislation which formulates principles at a certain level of generality to govern the whole field of acquisition of, access to, and management, processing and disclosure of personal information, backed by a series of Codes of Practice issued under statutory authority on the application of the principles to discrete areas of activity? The enterprise of producing an holistic approach to the legal protection of information privacy would make an excellent long-term project for the Law Commission, and would gladden the hearts of many a civil libertarian. In the meantime, those who have to operate under the existing norms will continue to face the problem of reconciling their multiple objectives, levels of enforceability and (where available) methods of enforcement.

---

[84]   J. M. Black, ' "Which Arrow?": rule type and regulatory policy' [1995] PL 95–118.

20

Information, Privacy, and Technology: Citizens, Clients, or Consumers?

ALFRED C. AMAN, JR.

Introduction

In his classic book, *Not in the Public Interest*, Professor Sir David Williams states: 'It is desirable that as far as possible the workings of the central government should either be subject to publicity or subject to some form of independent scrutiny. Sweeping assertions of executive secrecy ought not to be tolerated in a democratic country.'[1] He concludes that 'secrecy and security have to be balanced against the legitimate demands for an informed public opinion which is, when all is said and done, the essential element in a country which claims to be democratic.'[2] These words are as important and wise today as they were in 1965. Indeed, the emphasis on democracy, an informed public opinion and the public interest embody values and an approach towards governance that, in this era of globalization, is more important than ever before. Freedom of Information legislation is intended to further these values and to make the status and role of citizen meaningful.[3]

In this essay, I shall explore the themes of democracy and an informed citizenry in the context of the Freedom of Information Act in the United States as well as other legislation designed to shed light on government. I shall argue that the values of democracy, openness and an informed citizenry that such legislation seeks to further can no longer be assured if the Act focuses only on the government or on entities deemed state actors. Though there are many reforms advocated for the Freedom of Information Act (FOIA) in the United States, many of which are needed and plausible,[4] this paper will focus on the question that I believe today to be the most fundamental: should the Freedom of Information Act be extended to cover private entities and if so, which ones? I will argue that in a variety of contexts today, the needs of an informed citizenry and a vibrant democracy can no longer be met by focusing only on the state. Certain information held by private entities also may be 'not in the public interest'.

---

[1] David Williams, *Not in the Public Interest* (London: Hutchinson, 1965) 215.

[2] ibid., at 216.

[3] See generally, Alfred Aman and William Mayton, in *Administrative Law* (ch. 17) 'Citizens' access to governmentally held information', (West Group Publishing. 1993) 614–67.

[4] See, e.g., Charles J. Wichman III, Note, 'Ridding FOIA of Those "Unanticipated Consequences": Repaving a Necessary Road to Freedom', 47 Duke LJ 1213, 1247–54 (1998) (herein after cited as 'Unanticipated Consequences').

A significant aspect of the social, economic, and legal impact of global processes today is that the roles of public and private entities are changing, and that the question of what is public and what is private is also changing, often crossing or blurring lines that were formerly clear.[5] For example, responsibilities such as prisons, snow and garbage removal, or the determination of welfare eligibility were once undertaken primarily in the public sector. Today, these and other seemingly public functions often are contracted out to the private sector;[6] however, as Judge Patricia Wald has recently observed:

> The privatization train is not reserved for criminals. State and local governments have contracted with private operations to take care of the most vulnerable, dependent, and disempowered members of society—children, the unemployed, the physically and mentally disabled—whose servicing for most of the 20th century has been quintessentially a 'public' responsibility.[7]

The shift from the state to the private sector does not necessarily lessen the public's need for information about how these institutions work, if democratic governance is to be furthered. But the traditional relationship of citizen to the state may, in fact, be altered. When the private sector is involved in managing prisons, or other public functions, for example, the role of citizen converges with that of client. But the nature of this kind of client relationship usually cannot and should not be captured solely in market terms. Clearly, there is a role for citizens to play here, too. There remains a public component to the performance of such duties, one that a narrow conception of markets and the need to generate profits is likely to ignore. In certain contexts, the market must be made more accountable and the FOIA can and should play such a role, even when private entities are involved.[8]

Closely related to the impact of global market processes on new alignments of the public and the private is the impact of technology. Technologies such as the Internet are global by definition. Information can be shared instantaneously around the world. Moreover, computer technology makes the collection and dissemination and analysis of data easier than ever before. Technology also can make it easier and cheaper for the government to share its information with its citizens. But information that is collected for one purpose can be used or sold for other purposes.[9] This

---

[5] See Alfred C. Aman Jr., 'The Globalizing State: A Future Oriented Perspective on the Public/Private Distinction, Federalism, and Democracy', 31 Vand J Trans'l Law 769, 799, 816–819 (1998) (arguing that the metaphor of the 'citizen-as-customer' assumes too bright a line between what government does and who government is) (herein after cited as 'The Globalizing State').

[6] Aman (n. 5 above) at 831–7.

[7] Hon. Patricia M. Wald, 70 Temple L Rev 1085, 1098 (1997).

[8] See generally, Cass R. Sunstein, 'Informational Regulation and Informational Standing: Akins and Beyond', 147 U Pa L Rev 613, (1999); ([T]here can be little doubt that a number of statutes in the last forty years were designed to ensure disclosure of information, and that mandatory disclosure is an increasingly pervasive and important regulatory tool. Indeed, informational regulation, or regulation through disclosure, has become one of the most striking developments in the last generation of American law.)

[9] See, e.g., *Reno v Condon*, No. 98-1464, 2000 US Lexis 503 (2000) (holding that federal legislation limiting states' ability to sell personal information garnered from state department of motor vehicles' driver's licence databases is a proper exercise of congressional authority under the Commerce Clause).

can mean profits in the private sector, not to speak of revenue for the public sector that is derived from sources other than taxes.[10] These possibilities raise new questions: Are there now new privacy concerns on the part of citizens resulting from new technologies that need to be protected? To what extent should citizens be protected when they engage in behaviour that characterizes consumers in general? In the contracting-out situations mentioned above, citizens become, in effect, clients, but are there also citizenship concerns when only consumers are involved? When is the use of personal information supplied in a commercial or a public context, and then sold for use in other contexts, neither 'in the private nor the public interest'?

When it comes to individual and collective privacy concerns, the use or sale of personal information, usually freely given in a commercial transaction, may create the need for protecting citizens as consumers, at least in some contexts. And some of these contexts go beyond just profit-making opportunities, and may involve a kind of profiling designed to influence the political process and voting behaviour. In fact,

the fundamental concern about privacy in cyberspace is about the ways in which the collection, processing, and use of personal information in the computer-network environment contribute to a loss of individual power and autonomy.[11]

Put another way, access to this information is access to a certain kind of power—the power to influence and persuade or manipulate based on sophisticated profiting techniques.

The roles of consumer and client differ in such contexts. When citizens are clients they are, in effect, part of a contract for carrying out a public function. In other words, they are like third-party beneficiaries to the contracts entered into by the government and the private sector. As consumers, however, citizens undertake certain transactions for themselves alone. Citizens as clients may need information from the government and the private sector, but as consumers, they may need to prevent personal information from being used privately in ways of which they are unaware, or would not likely authorize if they knew.

Thus, in approaching these information issues in these various contexts, this essay shall distinguish between and among the roles of citizen, client and consumer. Citizens need certain kinds of information to exercise their democratic rights effectively; however, at some point, citizens as consumers also may have certain negative rights against the collection and dissemination of personal information that pertains only to them as consumers or to individuals like them. Similarly, there also are contexts in which citizens as clients need information from the private sector.

To explore these issues, Part 1 of this essay first will briefly set forth an overview of the Freedom of Information Act and some other information statutes as they have developed in the United States, noting, in particular, the relationship of the individual to the government. FOIA legislation allows us to focus on the role of individuals

---

[10] ibid. at 5–6.
[11] Oscar H. Gandy, Jr., 'Legitimate Business Interest: No End in Sight? An Inquiry into the Status of Privacy in Cyberspace' (1996) U Chi Legal F 77.

as citizens, and their consequent need for information to be effective citizens. It assumes a rather bright line between what is public and private and approaches issues involving information as primarily a governmental issue; that is, it usually focuses on the question of when information held by the government should be made public.

In some respects, the real-world basis of this bright line distinction between the government and the private sector is fast becoming a part of the past. Accordingly, in Part 2, I will argue that an approach that focuses only on the nature of the actor involved is no longer sufficient for determining whether certain information should or should not be public. Indeed, global processes and a variety of public/private partnerships now challenge the public/private distinction. Not to recognize this fact can undercut substantially the central purposes of FOIA legislation. Part 2 makes some modest suggestions for reconceptualizing the 'public interest' and the role of information in seemingly private contexts serving public functions.

Part 3 then examines the role of the individual as consumer and the citizen's relationship to private entities that seek to profit from information freely given in one context, but then used for other purposes. I specifically look at various individual privacy claims, noting that three forms of remedies—technological market approaches, voluntary regulatory approaches, and regulatory solutions—are available. The paper concludes with a discussion of market approaches to regulation in general, noting that the market should be viewed, in many contexts, as a regulatory tool. In this, I take issue with those who regard the market as a separate system wholly apart from the public sector. The market is, nowadays, integral to the demands of an informed citizen and a vibrant democracy and we must devise ways of ensuring it is accountable. The regulation of the future not only raises the question of citizens' trust or distrust of government and the private sector—but also rearranges those terms in relation to specific needs and goals. This essay concludes that public/private disputes in the context of FOIA and privacy legislation should be resolved by placing more emphasis on the legitimate privacy expectations of individuals and the needs of an informed citizenry, and less on the public or private identities of the actors involved.

1. FOIA—AN OVERVIEW[12]

In the late 1960s and throughout the 1970s, Congress passed a number of legislative Acts aimed at increasing the openness with which various parts of the national government carried out its regulatory responsibilities. The most important of these was the Freedom of Information Act (FOIA), passed in 1966.[13] FOIA and its subsequent amendments establish a liberal disclosure policy regarding public access to

---

[12]   This section draws heavily on a slightly revised version of sections 17.1–17.2 in Alfred Aman and William Mayton, *Administrative Law*, (n. 3 above) 614–24.

[13]   Pub. L. No. 89-487, 80 Stat 250 (1966) (codified as amended at 5 USCA § 552).

information obtained, generated and held by the government.[14] 'Any person' is entitled to request and receive identifiable records held by an agency, unless the records in question fall within one of the Act's nine exemptions.[15] Other limitations as set forth by the statute are that the request be made of 'an agency' and that the information sought be definable as 'agency records'. These two limitations, as we shall see below, are particularly important when public functions are contracted out to the private sector. They are also important in the more common (and less dramatic) instance of a government agency engaging a private entity for research on a one-time or even a somewhat regular basis.

Disclosure is the norm of the FOIA. A requester's motives or her relation to the information she seeks to acquire are irrelevant.[16] An agency's refusal to disclose requested information is subject to *de novo* judicial review and the government has the burden of proving that the information it seeks to withhold is, in fact, exempt from disclosure.[17] Indeed, this kind of access is seen as crucial to the individual's role of citizen in society. Of course, the Act assumes that information is sought from an agency—essentially, a state actor.

The FOIA is not the only form of information-based legislation designed to enhance citizens' ability to participate in governmental affairs. In 1972, Congress passed the Federal Advisory Committee Act (FACA)[18] designed to ensure greater openness with regard to the various boards of experts and advisers upon which agencies sometimes rely for advice. The FACA attempts to ensure that the use of such private advisory bodies did not result in private solutions for public matters. Thus, the Act provides, among other things, that advisory board meetings be noticed and take place in public. It also attempts to ensure that there be a wide cross-section of interests represented on such Boards. This Act anticipates the need to ensure that notwithstanding their private nature that certain actors who are influential in the decision-making process not be withheld from public view.

The FACA was the forerunner of the government in the Sunshine Act passed by Congress in 1976.[19] Just as the Freedom of Information Act established a norm of openness for agency deliberations, this Act requires that most meetings of multi-member government commissions be noticed in advance and held in public. The title of the Act is derived from a statement by Justice Brandeis and it reflects the basic premises of this Act: 'Publicity is justly commended as a remedy for social and industrial disease. Sunlight is said to be the best disinfectant and electric light the most efficient policeman.'[20]

---

[14] The Act was amended significantly in 1974, Pub. L. No. 93-502, 88 Stat. 1561; in 1976, Pub. L. No. 94-409, 90 Stat 1241; and in 1986, Pub. L. No. 99-570, 100 Stat 3207 (1986).

[15] 5 USCA § 552(a)(3).

[16] 5 USCA § 552(a)(4)(B).

[17] ibid.

[18] Pub. L. No. 92-463, 5 USCA App.I.

[19] Pub. L. No. 94-409, 390 Stat 1241 (1976) (codified as amended at 5 USCA § 552(b)).

[20] L. Brandeis, *Other People's Money* 62 (National Home Library Foundation edn., 1933).

Congress passed the Federal Privacy Act in 1974.[21] Unlike the FOIA, the FACA and the Sunshine Act, the Privacy Act is more directly concerned with individuals, but individuals in their capacity as citizens. The basic premise of this Act is that the federal government's ability to use sophisticated information technology, such as computer data banks, greatly magnifies the potential for the harm that can result to individual privacy interests. The Act thus sets limits on the ability of government to use information obtained from its citizens. To enforce these limits, the Act relies on openness to ameliorate potential harms. It enables individuals to determine what records pertaining to them are being collected, maintained and used by federal agencies. It seeks to prevent the use of records obtained for one purpose to later be used for an entirely different purpose, without individual consent. And it also seeks to enable individuals to gain access to information pertaining to them and to correct or amend those records if they are wrong.[22] As we shall see below, it is precisely these kinds of problems that computer technology exacerbates, raising the question of whether and how statutory protections should be provided for consumers vis-à-vis the private sector.

The common assumption underlying the FOIA, Privacy and the Government in the Sunshine Act is that open government leads to better government. Open government is in accord with the basic principles of democracy and the need for citizens to know how their government, in fact, functions. This enables the citizenry to make proper evaluations of the wisdom of governmental uses of power. It also, however, is in accord with a healthy sense of distrust of governmental power as well and the need to control agency discretion to ensure that the law is administered properly. In this sense, open government and the publicity that goes along with it provides not only valuable information but a means of effectively constraining government and thus protecting citizens from any potential abuses of governmental power.[23] To be sure,

---

[21]   Pub. L. No. 93-579, 88 Stat 1896 (1974) (codified as amended at 5 USCA § 552(a)).

[22]   ibid. § 2(a).

[23]   Potential abuses of private power that could influence governmental power also weighs heavily on the minds of many citizens. At least one author finds evidence of the growing importance of the 'right to know' emerging from certain United States Supreme Court holdings that address citizens' attempts to garner information from private lobbying groups and government agencies. See Mall Pollack, 'The Right to Know?: Delimiting Database Protection at the Juncture of the Commerce Clause, the Intellectual Property Clause and the First Amendment', 17 Cardozo Arts & Ent. LJ 47, n. 105 (1999). One of the cases which Professor Pollack cites is *Federal Election Commission v Akins* 524 US 11 (1998). In Akins, the respondents, voters with views opposed to those of the American Israel Public Affairs Committee (AIPAC), filed a complaint with the petitioner Federal Election Commission (FEC). The complaint asked the FEC to order the AIPAC to make public information about its members, contributions and expenditures pursuant to the Federal Election Campaign Act of 1971 (FECA). The Act imposes extensive record keeping and disclosure requirements on 'political committees' 2 USC § 431 *et seq*. The FEC found that the AIPAC was not a political committee. The Court concluded that the respondents, as voters, had prudential and constitutional standing to petition for a declaration that the FEC unlawfully dismissed their complaint.: 524 US at 26. The Court concluded that 'the informational injury at issue here, directly related to voting, the most basic of political rights, is sufficiently concrete and specific such that the fact that it is widely shared does not deprive Congress of constitutional power to authorize its vindication in federal courts': ibid. at 24–5. After settling the standing issue, however, the Court refused to reach the issue of whether the AIPAC was a 'political committee' under the FECA. Professor Sunstein calls Akins

there are often other important interests at stake that militate in favour of governmental confidentiality, such as when national security interests or the trade secrets of a corporation are at stake. Most of the above statutes thus provide for a number of exemptions to their basic goals of openness and disclosure. Balancing these various policy interests and goals has given rise to a good deal of litigation and case law, especially under the Freedom of Information Act.

Despite its persistent critics,[24] the FOIA is now endemic to the modern concept of citizens' access to information in the United States. With its nine exemptions, the Act attempts to achieve a rational balancing of the public's interest in information against the government's interest in effective and efficient operation; however, by requiring *de novo* judicial review and placing the burden of proving exemption status on the agency, citizen access to information has been greatly facilitated. This is in accord with the basic purposes of the Act. The FOIA springs from the popular distrust of governments, and from Congress's adversarial relationship with the Executive. In essence, the FOIA is an attempt to regulate the regulators:

There is no obligation in the Constitution compelling the American people to trust their government. And where a segment of the state enjoys no popular mandate for its actions, it should be willing to disclose the information responsibly, not only to enhance public knowledge of its activities, but also to cultivate a degree of trust (or to dispel distrust).[25]

The FOIA can thus be viewed as a remarkable democratic achievement. Its self-appointed guardians—citizens—and the investigative press, can point to hundreds of public interest stories made possible by FOIA requests. FOIA disclosures brought to life the Army's secret investigation of the My Lai massacre, improper Internal Revenue Service monitoring of political dissidents, the Bay of Pigs debacle, and the Air Force's payment of defense contractors' lobbying costs, CIA mind control experiments, and FBI smear campaigns—among other things. Indeed, the mere existence of a judicially-enforced FOIA has encouraged many agencies voluntarily to release information on a regular basis.

Critics of the FOIA, however, assert that the democratic intentions of the Act have not been realized. They claim that in practice the Act has been abused by private interests, spawning unintended side effects. For example, the Drug Enforcement Administration claims that 60 per cent of the FOIA requests it receives are from imprisoned or known drug traffickers. Some critics contend that the FOIA's users are often organized crime figures and convicts who seek disclosure of law enforcement investigations. Regulated industries note that competitors routinely use FOIA

'by far the most important pronouncement on the general issue of standing to obtain information'. See Sunstein, (n. 7 above), at 616.

[24] The remainder of this section draws heavily from Alfred Aman and William Mayton, *Administrative Law* (n. 3 above) 665–7.

[25] 'Press Notices on Disclosures made Pursuant to the Federal FOIA, 1972–1980' compiled by Harold C. Relyea and Suzanne Cavanagh, reprinted in Tom Rigley and Harold C. Relyea (eds.), *Freedom of Information Trends in the Information Age* 144 App. (1983) (prepared for and published in *FOI Act Hearings of House Subcomm. on Govt. Information and Individual Rights*, 14, 15, and 16 July 1981).

requests to attempt to gain access to marketable trade secrets. Government lawyers complain of being surprised and swamped by redundant FOIA 'discovery' requests. Due to a lack of centralized FOIA oversight, disparate agency compliance procedures, and unrealistic deadlines, some agencies face request backlogs that will take years to fulfill. Judicial oversight of the FOIA has proven to be slow, costly, and inefficient: despite elaborate indexing requirements for withheld materials and provisions for in camera inspection of allegedly exempt documents, the courts have been frustrated by agency intransigence and the unenviable task of evaluating and balancing asserted national security or law enforcement interests against the public's statutory right to know. Recently, many courts have had to recognize that the Act is often used for purposes it was not designed to further. The 'core doctrine' judicial approach has attempted to narrow the scope of the Act.[26]

Other critics question the unforeseen and spiralling costs of the Act caused by the breadth of the FOIA's mandate, its ad hoc administration, and indirect costs that make accurate analysis impossible. There is little question that taxpayers are footing a sizeable bill. By most estimates, the government now spends $100–200 million annually complying with FOIA requests. Amendments to the Act have focused on this problem in particular. In 1986, for example, Congress passed the Freedom of Information Reform Act which significantly increased administrative agencies' abilities to charge requesters for the costs of processing requests. In 1996, Congress addressed broader issues having to do not only with the cost of the Act, but computer technology as well. The Electronic Freedom of Information Act (E-FOIA) Amendments of 1996[27] attempt to bring the FOIA into the electronic age and, arguably, use technology in ways that might ultimately lower the costs of the Act. For example, the Act creates so-called electronic reading rooms by placing certain agency records on-line, thereby promoting access to government information by way of the Internet. The E-FOIA also has provisions likely to increase costs—such as those providing for expedited review as well as requiring that information be provided in the format requested by the person making the claim.

Cost, delay, access, balancing the needs of citizens' access to information with justifiable governmental reasons for maintaining confidentiality, as well as the unintended consequences and uses of this Act are the components of the typical regulatory discourse that surrounds it. By and large, these costs would seem to justify the benefits provided by open government. There are, undoubtedly, important reforms yet to come,[28] but—as already suggested above—the most important aspect of the future of the FOIA involves the future of the state and its relationship to the private sector. The changing role of what I have called elsewhere the 'globalizing state'[29] now

---

[26]   See Fred Cate *et. al.* 'The Right to Privacy and the Public's Right to Know: The Central Purpose of the Freedom of Information Act', Admin L Rev 41 (1994).
[27]   Electronic Freedom of Information Act of 1996, Pub. L. No. 104-231, 110 Stat. 3048 (codified as amended at 5 USC 552 (1999)).
[28]   See, e.g., 'Unanticipated Consequences', 47 Duke LJ (n. 4 above).
[29]   See Alfred Aman, 'The Globalizing State' (n. 5 above) at 812–16.

places the needs and the role of citizens in a new light. Privatization, deregulation, contracting out and various combinations of public and private power, often transnational in nature, have raised more fundamental questions not only for the FOIA, but regulatory legislation in general. There often seems to be a convergence of roles when individuals relate to the government, not just as citizens, but clients and consumers as well. I propose that these changes place more emphasis on the notion of 'interest', and less on public versus private. Interest needs to be defined in terms of legitimating governance through transparency and advancing democratic values and participation. When citizens are clients or consumers, or both, what is 'not in the public interest', may not be in the private interest either. These issues are, to a large extent, greatly affected by how the public/private distinction plays out in the context of FOIA litigation, which Part 2 will now discuss.

2. FOIA, PRIVATIZATION AND THE PUBLIC/PRIVATE DISTINCTION

An important change in US administrative law over the past twenty years or so has been the increasing reliance on the market to reach results that traditionally were mandated more directly by command-control regulations.[30] Such approaches often have taken the form of using market mechanisms as a regulatory means of reaching statutory goals. Various aspects of environmental regulation have pioneered these approaches.[31]

Privatization can, however, take many forms. In the United States, it rarely means the selling off of public assets, since the government rarely has owned such entities as electric utilities or telephone companies. Governments have, however, regulated them. Privatization is thus often used as a synonym for deregulation or the replacement of command-control regulation with less intrusive forms of market regulation. Whatever form privatization takes, it usually results in blurring stereotypical distinctions between 'public' and 'private'.[32]

More significantly, privatization also refers to an increasingly popular approach used by federal, state, and municipal governments to cut costs: contracting out duties and responsibilities once performed by governmental entities to the lowest, private sector bidder. Such an approach may cut costs, but it can have a serious effect on the flow of information to the public if the public/private divide is treated formalistically. When private companies take over prisons, aspects of welfare screening, education, or city services such as snow or garbage removal, records created through the performance of

---

[30] See generally, Alfred Aman, *Administrative Law in a Global Era* (Cornell University Press, 1992).
[31] ibid. 108–25.
[32] A Public and private cost is one such area that is converging. For example, as the cost of public higher education increases, more public universities have involved themselves in private fund-raising, and begun to raise their prices to where the difference between the cost of public and private education is narrowing. See Richard A. Matasar, 'Private Publics, Public Privates: An Essay on Convergence in Higher Education' 10 U Fla JL & Pub Pol'y 5, 11 (1998).

a public duty that clearly would have been subject to the FOIA if done by a governmental agency can now become private records, solely by virtue of the contractor's non-governmental status. As one report recently noted:

Without predictable judicial or legislative standards, the public risks being shut out of the privatization process. Without public awareness, public oversight of the operation of privatized governmental operations will be inadequate. It is clear that public access often suffers once governmental operations are turned over to private entities. Private enterprises serve managers, owners and shareholders, not taxpayers. According to fundamental democratic principles, governmental services conducted by private operators should be just as accountable as services provided by public agencies. The public and the press must be able to scrutinize the activities of private actors performing governmental services, just as the public and the press already scrutinize public activities under public records statutes.[33]

Revising the FOIA to take into account the role of the market and various forms of deregulation and privatization today is necessary if the broad citizenship goals of this Act are to remain within reach. When citizens are clients, they do not necessarily lose their need for information, though the essential nature of a private enterprise makes it, initially at least, focused more on profits and the stockholders than on providing information to taxpayers. At a minimum, the statute should be amended to include all private entities to whom public functions have been contracted. Clearly, these are instances in which the mere label of 'private' can result in cutting off information that clearly would 'not be in the public interest'.

A mix of public and private is common in various FOIA contexts, but the resolution of these issues now takes on a greater importance, given the trend toward greater use of the private sector to carry out public responsibilities. Not all mixtures of the public and the private need be nor should be dealt with categorically. The public/private distinction can create the kind of discretion that courts need to differentiate between FOIA requests that further the goals of the statute and those that seek only to advance private, litigation strategies. As courts and commentators have grappled with this problem they have unfortunately, but not unexpectedly, been very state-centered in their approach to these issues. This is due to the fact that the FOIA legislation itself speaks only in terms of 'agencies' and 'agency records'. By definition, agencies are governmental in nature, and the analysis inevitably proceeds by asking

---

[33] Matthew D. Bunker and Charles N. Davis, *Privatized Government Functions and Freedom of Information: Public Accountability in an Age of Private Governance* (paper on file with author) 25. The contexts in which this issue arises are legion. See generally Julie Barker Pape, 'Physician Data Bank: The Public's Right to know Versus the Physician's Right to Privacy' 66 Fordham L Rev 975 (1997) (noting the conflict between a physicians' right to privacy versus the public's right to know physician information contained in the National Practitioner's Database, mandated by the Health Care Quality Information Act); Christina N. Smith, 'The Limits of Privatization: Privacy in the Context of Tax Collection' 47 Case W Res JIL 627 (1997) (asking whether tax payer information culled by private tax collectors should be subject to disclosure under the FOIA); and Mary L. Saenz Gutierrez, 'Oklahoma's New Adoption Code and Disclosure of Identifying Information' 34 Tulsa LJ 133 (1998) (asking whether birth and health records possessed by adoption agencies should be available to adoptees in search of their biological parents or relevant health and diagnostic information.

such questions as the extent to which the government controls the day-to-day operations of the private entity involved or, alternatively, whether the private entity is
engaged in activities that are governmental in nature.

The first approach is clearly reflected in the leading case dealing with the issue of
what is an agency for purposes of the FOIA, *Forsham* v *Harris*.[34] That case dealt with
a common FOIA problem—the applicability of the statute to private entities such as
universities or individual professors who have been commissioned by the federal
government to undertake certain research. Specifically, in *Forsham* the FOIA peti-
tioners sought the release of the raw data on which the commissioned research was
based. It was possessed by private physicians and scientists who undertook this
research pursuant to federal grants from the National Institute of Arthritis, Metabo-
lism, and Digestive Diseases (NIAMDD). The Supreme Court held that this private
research firm was not an 'agency', nor were the raw data 'agency records'.[35]
NIAMDD supervised the grantees, it had access to and permanent custody of some
of the documents, but it did not exercise these rights, nor did it take charge of the
day-to-day operations of the programme.[36] Private grantees which were not
controlled by the federal government were not agencies for purposes of the Act.
Federal funding and supervision alone were not enough to trigger the Act.[37]

This case was consistent with the Court's earlier decision in *United States v
Orleans*[38] where, in the context of the Federal Tort Claims Act, the Court dealt with
a federally-funded community action agency. Though this agency was completely
funded by the government, it was independently operated and not subject to control
by the government. Thus, the court concluded, it was not an agency for purposes of
the Act.

These cases and their narrow, government control approach to the question of
what is an agency do not bode well for issues arising in a contracting out situation.
Firms to which government business is contracted out usually retain their independence. Indeed, the primary purpose of contracting out in the first place is to take
advantage of the market-oriented and market-based decision-making such firms
make possible. This is one of the key areas from which, it is hoped, efficiencies will
result.

Agency records are defined contextually. The Supreme Court requires 'some relationship between an "agency" [and a] "record" requested'.[39] Generally, courts require
that the government agency involved must 'either create or obtain' the material
sought.[40] Moreover, the agency involved must have control over these records when
the request is sought.[41]

These tests may be reasonable in light of the statutory language involved, but the
state-centred nature of their focus does not address directly or adequately the central
value questions at issue. Under what circumstances should information be available

---

[34] 445 US 169 (1980).   [35] ibid. at 170.   [36] ibid. at 180.
[37] ibid.   [38] 425 US 118 (1976).
[39] 445 US at 182.   [40] ibid.
[41] See *United States DOJ v Tax Analysts*, 492 US 136, 145 (1989).

to the public regardless of the public or private character of the entities involved, and regardless of the relationship a private entity has to the government or the governmental quality of the tasks it performs? It is the nature of the information that is essential and not the nature of the entity that holds it.

Most proposals dealing with judicial interpretation of the statute also are usually state-centred. A common approach is to argue by analogy and seek to determine whether the activity undertaken by the private entity involved is, in fact, a 'public function'. The public function approach can be seen as an extension of the United States Supreme Court's state action concept, where entities performing functions for the government are deemed state actors for constitutional purposes. Arguably, if these entities can be termed 'state actors' under the Constitution, they should be subject to access as governmental agencies under the FOIA.[42] This approach is a step in the right direction and could result in the extension of the FOIA for those cases that are, in effect, public in nature. 'If the state delegates a function that affects the public welfare and makes the need for accountability high, it can be argued that the entity is performing a public function and should be a state actor for all purposes, including FOIA.'[43] Rather than leave such determination to judicial interpretations of what is an 'agency' or 'agency record', the FOIA should be amended explicitly to apply to private entities that carry out public functions or to whom such functions specifically have been contracted out. Such an approach more explicitly recognizes that the public/private divide is less important than the nature of the information sought. Focusing on the primary purposes of FOIA should be the goal.[44]

---

[42]   See M. Bunker and C. Davis, 'Privatized Government Functions and Freedom of Information' (n. 33 above) 18–22.

[43]   See Craig D. Fesier, 'Privatization and the Freedom of Information Act: An Analysis of Public Access to Private Entities Under Federal Law', 52 Fed. Comm LJ 21, 60–1 (1999).

[44]   This is not to argue that there may not be, in some circumstances, a need for the public/private distinction, especially when litigants sell information more to discredit individuals than advance democracy. For example, Tobacco giant R. J. Reynolds used Georgia's open record laws to try to compel a Georgia researcher to release the names of children who had participated in a study that measured the popularity of Joe Camel with children. The state amended the law before the researcher released the names. See Aaron Zitner, 'U.S. Curtails Research-Disclosure Law', Boston Globe, 14 October 1999 at A13. The possibility that the tactics used by R. J. Reynolds could be employed under the FOIA increased when Senator Richard Shelby (Republican, Alabama) inserted a provision in the Omnibus Appropriations Bill for fiscal year 1999 (P.L. 105–277), that required the White House Office of Management and Budget (OMB) to revise Circular A-110, which governs federal grants to hospitals, universities, and non-profit organizations. The provision requires that all grant-receiving agencies divulge all their data upon request under the FOIA. Apparently, Senator Shelby inserted the provision after the Environmental Protection Agency refused his request to produce data that were used to develop new Clean Air Act regulations. The data belonged to the private universities that had conducted the research upon which the regulations were based. See David Applegate, 'Political Scene', Geotimes, August 1999 (visited 19 January 2000) <http://www.agiweb.org/ geotimes/aug99/scene.html>. In response, Representative George E. Brown, Jr. (Democrat, California) introduced H.R. 88, which would amend the provision: Congressional Record, 7 January 1999, E32 (comments of Rep. Brown). The fear is that the OMB's revision endangers 'a whole range of public–private partnerships which facilitate the commercialization of new products and technologies and provide a mechanism for holding down the increasing cost of research and development for individual firms and industries.' Letter to F. James Charney, Policy Analyst, Office of Management and Budget, April 2, 1999 (visited 20 January 2000) <http://www.house.gov/ science_democrats/archive/gbona110.htm>.

3. NOT IN THE PRIVATE INTEREST—CITIZENS AS CONSUMERS

Quite apart from the information that citizens may need, either from the government or from private entities, to enable them to exercise their democratic rights effectively, there are a variety of new privacy issues that arise today, largely because of computer technology. Technology and computer-generated databases raise threats to democracy as well as provide the means to advance it.[45] The sheer quantity of information now available in electronic form today has increased access to that information in contrast to limited access in the past.[46] Also, technology has altered the public's perception that its personal data are as secure in electronic form as the data once were, or that the public's 'zone of privacy' is as expansive as it once was.[47] Moreover, emerging technology may alter the very concept of what constitutes a 'reasonable expectation of privacy'.[48]

The ability to collect, sell and combine information freely given by consumers in numerous contexts to obtain profiles of individuals as well as groups, raises a number of privacy issues. Are there rights of citizens that prevent any and all information about them personally or in the aggregate from being commodified? And given that information is a commodity, perhaps the *sine qua non* of a globalizing economy that feeds on data the way the industrial revolution fed on coal, should consumers who are identified with their profiles also retain a property interest in them?[49] This question is particularly relevant, given that consumer profiles from the private sector are sometimes sold to government agencies,[50] the private sector, or

---

[45] See 'Symposium on Cyberspace', 5 Indiana Journal of Global Legal Studies 415 *et seq.* (1998).

[46] See Frederick Schauer, 'Internet Privacy and the Public–Private Distinction', 38 Jurimetrics J. 555, 557 (1998).

[47] ibid. at 559–60.

[48] ibid. at 561–2.

[49] The founders of the United States viewed the security of property holdings 'a matter not just of private self-interest but of general *political* concern' that implicated the guarantee of 'one's independence and competence as a participant in public affairs': Frank I. Michelman, 'Possession vs. Distribution in the Constitutional Idea of Property' 72 Iowa Law Rev 1319, 1329 (1987). Security of property 'was thought necessary to ensure the authenticity and reliability of one's politically expressed judgment regarding what course of policy would best conduce to the rights and other interests of the governed' (ibid.). The person for whom such security became doubtful or contingent 'would too likely act in public councils either as the tool of his patron or as the tool of his own particular, immediate, and possibly delusive material interest' (ibid.). Such actions would run counter to the interests of 'national prosperity or common liberty' (ibid.). A person acting thus was viewed, not as 'independent,' but as 'corrupt' (ibid.).

[50] In the early 1980s, the Selective Service System used a mailing list compiled by Farrell's Ice Cream Parlor Restaurant chain to inform young men that they were liable for draft registration. Farrell's asked customers to fill out birthday cards in order to receive free ice-cream. The cards included the names, addresses, and birthdays of the customers. The cards notified customers that the information would be shared with 'appropriate' groups, such as the National Geographic. In 1983, the New Jersey list broker that distributed Farrell's list sold the list to the Selective Service. The Selective Service used the list to mail approximately 3,000 draft registration warnings each month to young men who were about to turn eighteen. David Burnham, 'Selective Service to Stop Use of Birthday List', *NY Times*, 4 August 1984, at section 1, p. 5.

even political candidates[51] in order to influence citizen choice or behaviour. In this section, I will very briefly analyse two dimensions of consumer data. The first dimension is economic. The second dimension is frequently overlooked in favour of the first, i.e., the intangible rights of consumers implicated by their consumer data. Then I will survey three possible solutions to the problems of privacy and consumer data: voluntary industry self-regulation, a market or technological approach, and traditional government regulation.

3.1 The transaction and opportunity costs of gathering consumer data

The growing effectiveness with which consumer data are culled, collated, and sold 'suggests that transaction costs may decrease leading to more efficient markets and increased consumer satisfaction', as well as 'an increased quality of life'.[52] The transaction costs of computerized exchanges of data themselves stem almost exclusively from the electronic architecture of the Internet. As Professor Lessig notes, '[C]omputer code is law.'[53] The World Wide Web evolved out of a decentralized network of computers developed by the US military in the 1960s to guard against a missile attack taking out the military's computer network by targeting one key computer site. The system that was developed allowed different computer hardware and software configurations to communicate with one another. The result was that no computer could recognize whether the same person or a different person had just logged on to the network, or had been logged on, at any given moment. Therefore, the same web page needed to be transmitted each time the same client requested it, which increased transaction costs.

The solution to this cost problem is the so-called 'cookie', a text file that stores information on the client's side, and which reduces transaction costs (analogous to the way pizza delivery companies now store customer data on computers and use caller ID so that a customer does not have to spend time giving out his or her name, address, and phone number each time a pizza is ordered). In the case of cookies, the consumer information is stored on the consumer's computer hard drive and accessed by the merchant's server whenever the consumer logs on to the merchant's web page.[54] However, storing such data may incur an opportunity cost inasmuch as

---

[51] A. Michael Froomkin, 'Flood Control on the Information Ocean: Living with Anonymity, Digital Cash, and Distributed Databases', 15 J.L & Com 395, n. 315 (1996) (recounting author's own experience with a political campaign where consumer profiles were purchased to assist in targeted ad and speech campaigns).

[52] ibid. at 481: 'Some very consumer-friendly technologies, notably intelligent agents, use the consumer's behavior to anticipate her desires and select information that may be of particular interest.'

[53] Quoted in Letter from Deborah Pierce, Staff Attorney, Electronic Frontier Foundation, to Secretary, Federal Trade Commission, 18 October 1999 (Visited 14 November 1999) <http://www.ftc.gov/bcp/profiling/comments/pierce3.htm>.

[54] Cookies have an optional feature such that they can contain expiration dates, after which time a server can no longer read the cookie. Or, cookies can contain no expiration date to start with, and so will become unreadable once the client concludes his or her session. Netscape's version 3.0 browser for the first time gave users the option of receiving warnings and declining cookies. See *Federal Trade Commission,*

knowledge that their personal data are being harvested may deter consumers from taking advantages offered by new communications technology, such as reading information on line, if consumers know their reading habits are going to be profiled.[55] The question, then, is how much information about consumers' patterns and choices can the private sector extract before chilling consumers' use of the Internet in certain ways?

3.2 Intangible right to an intangible commodity?

A recent Louis Harris/Alan Westin survey of consumer attitudes toward privacy reveals that more than 80 per cent of US adults believe they have lost control over how companies collect and use consumers' personal information.[56] More than 75 per cent of consumers want, among other rights, to be informed of what kind of personal information companies are collecting, how it will be used, and the chance to see the information and verify its accuracy.[57] ' "How much do they know and how do they use that knowledge?" Senator Patrick Leahy (D-VT) asked in 1989, reflecting the growing anxiety about private industry's ability to amass enormous databases of personal consumer information. Addressing the Direct Marketing Association at its annual Government Affairs conference in 1989, Sen. Leahy told assembled marketers that "[y]ou have the power to sway people, the power to influence events, especially in a free and open society like ours. You have the power also to obliterate privacy" . . .'. Richard A. Barton, 'Privacy: The Gathering Storm' 10 Folio: The Magazine for Magazine Management 18, 128 (1989). More than 90 per cent of Internet users and those engaged in electronic commerce want to know what kind of personal information businesses are collecting, and how they are using it[58]—yet few web sites provide a contact who can tell consumers what consumer data the web site is holding, or even the data practices of the company.[59]

Some commentators have suggested that the consumer should retain a private

---

Public Workshop on Consumer Privacy on the Global Information Infrastructure(4 June 1996) 12–13 (Visited 13 November 1999) <http://www.ftc.gov/bcp/privacy/wkshp96/pw960604.pdf>. In an *amicus* brief filed on behalf of the Federal Communications Commission's (FCC) petition for rehearing in *U.S. West, Inc. v FCC* (10th Cir 98–9518), *amici* argued that '[c]itizens have a legitimate expectation of privacy with respect to sensitive personal information such as who they call on a telephone, and a carrier's right to communicate information about products and services does not include the right to build detailed profiles based on personal information obtained through private telephone calls'. See nn. 87, 107, at 70–5 (remarks by Paul Harter, Public Policy Counsel, Netscape Comm. Corp.).

[55] Letter from Deborah Pierce, Staff Attorney, Electronic Frontier Foundation, to FTC, October 18, 1999 (visited 14 November 1999) <http://www.ftc.gov/bcp/profiling/comments/pierce2.htm>.

[56] Alan F. Westin, '*Privacy for Consumers*', *Washington Times*, 26 January 1999 at A19.

[57] ibid.

[58] *Internet Privacy: Hearing on S. 809 Before the Subcomm. on Communication of the Senate Committee on Commerce, Science and Transportation* (hereinafter 'Internet Privacy'), 106th Congress (1999) (statement of Deirdre Mulligan, Center for Democracy and Technology).

[59] ibid. (statement of Christine Varney, Hogan and Hartson).

property right in personal data:[60] 'After all, if marketers want this information so badly, maybe they should go ahead and pay us for it.'[61] The absence of choice argues for the creation of a consumer property right in her own consumer data in order to confer that choice upon her. Consumers would be hard pressed to function in this technological era if they insisted on transacting solely with cash—businesses such as airlines have made it exceedingly difficult to purchase items, e.g., airline tickets in advance, with cash. Moreover, discounts are frequently not extended to cash trans-actions. Since personal information is disclosed automatically when purchasing with a credit card, the consumer is left with no choice but to disclose the information:[62] '[I]ndividuals have lost control over their identities.'[63]

[T]he older conception of privacy is that in order to protect yourself you have to retreat from society. . . . [C]ritical to enhancing privacy is allowing people to step forward and participate fully while not having the cost of that participation be the loss of control over their personal information. This is not only critical to protect their privacy, but also to enhancing other crit-ical democratic values such as free speech, the right to receive information. [P]eople will be wary about taking risks and deterred from taking those risks, about exploring new ideas and communicating with others and receiving information, if they are concerned that the infor-mation about those explorations and about those communications is revealed to others.[64]

---

[60] While creating a property interest in one's consumer data is a possibility, it is improbable. The California Supreme Court has held that a person does not retain an ownership interest in his excised genetic information. See *Moore v. Regents of Univ. of Calif.* 51 Cal 3d 120, 271, Cal Rptr 146, 155–6 (Cal. 1990) (cert denied, 499 US 936 (1991)). See also *Miles Inc. v Scripps Clinic & Research Foundation*, 810 F Supp 1091, 1096–8 (US Dist 1993). The court's discussion in *Miles* of the policy implications of *Moore* could apply analogously to the personal profiling of consumers; the court noted that the policy implica-tions in *Moore* had the potential to extend into non-medical contexts. For example, consumers who have notice of the commercial use of their consumer data may have little claim to conversion of that data, which further implies that consumers have the right to give informed consent with regards to the use of personal data. Likewise, businesses could have a fiduciary duty to solicit informed consent from consumers. On the other hand, such a system could stifle entrepreneurship inasmuch as a business could be liable for tracking down the pedigree of every bit of consumer data it acquires. This in turn could give rise to consumer data title insurance companies, which would further increase transaction costs. See also Froomkin (n. 51 above) at 492:

> So long as the courts refuse to rewrite or ignore contracts of adhesion, and as long as in each individ-ual transaction the cost of not providing the information is disproportionate to the loss (which is a function of the cumulation of the transactions, not any single transaction), a property rights approach appears unlikely to have much real influence on database creation.

It seems unlikely that a state court would hold that a person retains an ownership interest in excised consumer information.

[61] Dennise Caruso, '*New Microsoft Network Will Offer a Wealth of Privacy*', *NY Times*, 24 July 1995, at D5. It would be a mistake to flatly characterize all entrepreneurs as rabid, privacy violators with an eye only on the bottom line. Consumers' ability to access and control their personal data lies at the heart of contemporary ethical debates within the marketing industry. See Gene R. Laczniak, 'Marketing Ethics: Onward Toward Great Expectations', 12 J Pub Pol'y & Mktg 1, 91 (1993).

[62] See generally David J. Klein, 'Keeping Business out of the Bedroom: Protecting Personal Privacy Interests from the Retail World', 15 J Marshall J Computer & Info L 391 (1997).

[63] ibid.

[64] See Federal Trade Commission, n. 54 above, (speech by Janlori Goldman, Deputy Director, Center for Democracy and Technology).

In addition to lack of voluntariness of the disclosure of consumer data, there is also a risk that consumers will suffer *de facto* discrimination in the form of 'electronic red lining',[65] which impairs consumers' ability to gather information about goods or services.[66] Because any enterprising person or business can read a consumer's personal information literally as if it were an open electronic book, individuals and groups are more vulnerable to being targeted, stereotyped, and segregated,[67] particularly given the frequent, even gross inaccuracies contained in some consumer profiles.[68]

The collection of information about an individual's use of networked information informs and enhances the operation of a discriminatory technology that depends on the reliable assignment of individuals to groups. . . . The administrative use of knowledge regarding such groups contributes to the establishment and maintenance of a kind of categorical vulnerability where people assigned to, or identified with, such groups become the victims of discrimination. This vulnerability represents a challenge to the egalitarian ideals underlying contemporary and traditional understandings of both polity and market.[69]

Companies ' "prejudge the future behavior of consumers, leading some of these firms to ignore certain types of people, and thereby limit such persons' access to information about goods and services" '.[70] When consumer profiling is combined with 'geodemographic clustering techniques', telephone calls from low-income neighbourhoods could potentially be identified by their telephone exchange, and so steered away from the product or service being offered by being dumped into a queue, put on hold, or given a recorded message to suggest the unavailability of the desired good or service.[71] 'This type of "electronic redlining" could also occur online as profiling becomes more sophisticated.'[72] Moreover, given the complexity of statistical predictive models, '[i]t seems

---

[65] See Pierce (n. 55 above). In the text 'Data Privacy Law', the author notes that some direct marketing firms advertise their lists based on how ethnic the last names sound, and guarantee the ability to target all the 'Wongs and Garcias' out there. Assuming that the 'Wongs and Garcias' prefer certain goods and services over others is to assume they don't prefer certain goods and services they may in fact desire. Hence, the flow of goods and services to certain discrete and insular groups could erroneously be redirected away from them in what would amount to de facto economic discrimination. The issue is made more complex by situations such as the merger of AOL, which purports not to sell subscriber personal data, with Abacus, the largest catalogue database firm in the United States, see *Internet Privacy* (n. 58 above) (remarks of Marc Rotenberg, Electronic Freedom Foundation), and the ability of private companies to 'marry' personal consumer information with publicly available records to make highly accurate and detailed profiles of customers. Christine Varney, *Morning Edition* (National Public Radio broadcast, 11 June 1997). See also John McChesney, *Morning Edition* (National Public Radio broadcast, 10 June 1997) (reporting on selling of public records to private 'look-up companies').

[66] See Pierce (n. 55 above).

[67] Richard A. Spinello, 'The End of Privacy: Companies That Collect Information for a Specific Purpose Can Resell or Reuse It for Other Purposes With Impunity' 176 America 1, 9 (1997).

[68] See Joel R. Reidenberg, 'Setting Standards for Fair Information Practice in the U.S. Private Sector', 80 Iowa Law Rev 497 at 534 (n. 200 above).

[69] See Gandy (n. 11 above) at 79.

[70] ibid. quoting Roger Clarke, 'Profiling: A Hidden Challenge to the Regulation of Data Surveillance', 4 JL & Info Sci 2 (1993).

[71] ibid.

[72] See Pierce (n. 55 above).

unlikely that individuals would be able to contest the accuracy of individual components of such models, and then prevail in a claim of discrimination'.[73] Arguably, consumers have just as strong an interest in the free flow of goods as they do in the workings of their government. Access to information would help to assure that the flow of goods was not being arbitrarily restricted to some portions of the market.

3.3 Industry Self-Regulation

Most of the literature has focused on gaining access to records in the context of a governmental setting; however, there has been another thread weaving itself in the dialogue—access to and control of private consumer information in private sector databases. For example, early concerns about the burgeoning ability to computerize personal data resulted in an advisory committee of the US Department of Health, Education and Welfare (HEW) recommending that a federal code of 'fair information practices' be promulgated to encompass public *and* private computerized databases.[74] The code provided that no data systems would be maintained in secret, that individuals should have access to the information and be advised as to how it would be used, that information collected for one purpose would not be used for another purpose, that individuals must have a way to correct erroneous information, and that organizations collecting data must assure its accuracy and fair use.[75] Similar principles were incorporated into guidelines issued by the Organization for Economic Cooperation and Development in 1980.[76] These early recommendations remain today's core concepts of 'choice and access', the twin 'well-accepted fair information practices for all organizations in the computer age'.[77]

US Federal Trade Commission officials, when discussing consumer privacy, use

---

[73] See Gandy (n. 11 above) at 120–1.

[74] See Susan E. Gindin, 'Lost and Found in Cyberspace: Information Privacy in the Age of the Internet', 34 San Diego LR 1153, 1219 (1997).

[75] ibid. at 1219.

[76] ibid.

[77] Westin (n. 56 above) at A19. Representative Edward J. Markey (D-MA), in testimony during the Senate Banking Committee Hearing on Financial Privacy, asserted that 'consumers should have a right to know when personal information is being collected about them, and get access to such information for review or correction'. *Financial Privacy: Hearing on S. 187 Before the Senate Committee on Banking, Housing, and Urban Affairs*, 106th Congress (1999) (statement of Rep. Edward J. Markey (D-MA)). Marc Rotenberg, Director of the Electronic Privacy Information Center, has said that a good privacy policy 'should explain how and why personal information is being collected, how it will be used, and whether the individual can get access to the personal information. We think this is critical.' Marc Rotenberg, Remarks at News Conference on Consumer Privacy (9 June 1997), available in Lexis, FDCH Political Transcripts. On the other hand, others advocate only control without access. America On Line's (AOL) deputy director of law and public policy, and senior legal counsel, told the House Banking and Financial Services Committee Subcommittee on Financial Institutions and consumer Credit that AOL believed consumers have a right to know what information was being collected, how it would be used, and what choices consumers had in disclosing the information, yet never mentioned the consumer's rights to know exactly what the information was, or whether consumers should have a right to correct erroneous information. See *Internet Privacy* (n. 58 above) (remarks of Jill A. Lesser, Vice President Domestic Public Policy, America Online); but see remarks of Christine Varney, Hogan & Hartson: '[C]onsumers have a right to

terms like 'substantive fair information principles', which include '[n]otice, consent, access and security',[78] and have shown some concern about the effects of inaccurate consumer information.[79] The Georgetown Internet Privacy Policy Survey (GIPPS) analysed commercial web sites to find to what extent Web sites offered consumers 'notice,[80] choice,[81] access,[82] or security',[83] as well as 'contact information a consumer could use to ask a question about the site's information practices or to complain to the company or another organization about privacy'.[84] Of the sites surveyed, less than 14 per cent contained all five elements: notice, choice, access, security, and contact information.[85] The findings prompted FTC Chairman Robert Pitofsky to express the Commission's concern over industry practices and consumer privacy; however, he reiterated the Commission's desire to let the market supply a solution to the problem through innovations such as privacy seals of approval.[86] Others are more specific. Gandy, for example, has called for the following five-part approach:

(1) Collection of consumer data for expressly limited purposes,[87] and no collection of data from third parties.
(2) Informing consumers about how data is collected and how it will be used.
(3) The ability to access and correct information, with the data gatherer assuming responsibility for the accuracy of the information.
(4) Assuring that data are not used for any but the stated purpose.
(5) Informed consent from consumers prior to gathering data.[88]

---

see the data that is held about them is accurate and . . . one mechanism for checking accuracy is access' (ibid.).

[78] See *Internet Privacy* (n. 58 above) (remarks of FTC Commissioner Sheila Anthony).

[79] See Bob Edwards, *Morning Edition* (National Public Radio broadcast, 11 June 1997).

[80] 'Notice . . . was defined to include statements about what information is collected, how the information is collected, how the information collected will be used, whether the information will be reused or disclosed to third parties, and whether the site said anything about its use or non-use of Cookies.' Mary J. Culnan, *Georgetown Internet Privacy Policy Survey: Report to the Federal Trade Commission* 9 (1999) (hereinafter GIPPS) (visited 13 November 1999) <http://www.msb.edu/faculty/culnanm/GIPPS/mmrpt.PDF>.

[81] 'Choice . . . was defined to include statements regarding choice offered about being contacted again by the same organization and choice about having non-aggregate personal information collected by the Web site disclosed to third parties.' (ibid.).

[82] 'Access . . . was defined to include allowing consumers to review or ask questions about the information the site has collected and whether the sites disclosed how inaccuracies in personal information the site had collected were handled.' See Culnan (n. 80 above). See also Mary J. Culnan, *Privacy and the Top 100 Web Sites: Report to the Federal Trade Commission* (1999) (visited 13 November 1999) <http://www.msb.edu/faculty/culnanm/GIPPS/oparpt.PDF> (assessing notice, choice, access, security, and contact information for the top 100 commercial Web sites).

[83] 'Security . . . was defined to include protecting information during transmission and during subsequent storage.' See GIPPS (n. 80 above).

[84] ibid.   [85] ibid.

[86] See *Internet Privacy* (n. 58 above) (remarks of FTC Chairman Robert Pitofsky).

[87] See also Spiros Simitis, 'Reviewing Privacy in an Information Society', 135 U Pa L Rev 707, 740–1 (arguing that data collectors should have an identifiable specific purpose for the data, and not collect data merely for anticipated future use).

[88] See Gandy (n. 11 above) at 136–7.

3.4 Technological, Market Solutions

The United States government favours voluntary compliance with industry standards. Even those who favour such an approach, however, confess that so far, the voluntary approach has not yielded satisfactory results. They advocate more entrepreneurship in adapting technology to the needs of consumers and data protection. A world of possibilities lies implicit in the particular computer code being used. Sophisticated methods have been devised to protect consumer privacy. For example, cryptographers have invented a method to transmit value over the Internet with digital tokens that are the equivalent of cash. Such an approach avoids the 'audit trail' left by a credit card purchase; however, the technology nevertheless makes it possible that the record of digital cash purchases could be aggregated, and the consumer's spending habits thus profiled.

If consumers use a traceable payments mechanism for the purchase of information as well as goods, the potential for consumer profiles grows larger still. [E]very newspaper article accessed, every online catalog perused, every political debate sampled, will leave an information residue. These data can be collected to form a highly detailed profile of the consumer-citizen. The existence of such detailed dossiers on spending and intellectual preferences would be unprecedented.[89]

The so-called 'blinded coin' is one solution to the problem of data trails. A bank issues a digital coin (analogous to a regular traveller's cheque) affixed with a unique random serial number of which the bank keeps no record. The bank sells the digital coin to the consumer. The consumer multiplies the bank's random serial number by her own large random number, thus 'blinding' the coin. The consumer transmits the coin back to the bank, which signs the coin with its privacy key. The bank only knows the customer has purchased a coin of a certain denomination. When the consumer gets her blinded coin back from the bank, she mathematically restores the coin's true serial number by removing the blinded number. The consumer now has a digital coin with a valid bank serial number, and the bank's privacy signature. The bank does not know which real serial number is attached to a particular consumer's coin, only that a coin with that serial number is in circulation. The consumer can spend the coin without her identity being disclosable to the bank.[90] A variation on this model would require a third-party trustee, rather than the bank, to keep a record of which customers purchased what digital coin. Yet another variation would require multiple trustees, all of whom must agree before consumer data are released.[91] The trick now is how to keep the consumer from making digital copies of her digital coin.[92]

---

[89] See Froomkin (n. 51 above) at 453–4.
[90] ibid. at 460–2: 'On October 23, 1995, Mark Twain Bank of St. Louis, Missouri became the world's first financial institution to issue blinded digital coins backed by value.'
[91] ibid. at 461.   [92] ibid. at 462.

Outside the realm of banking, P3P—the Privacy Preferences Project—'will enable Web sites to express their privacy practices and users to exercise preferences over those practices' (internal quotes omitted).[93] A further possibility is software that creates pseudo identities for users when they browse the Internet.[94] Yet another possibility is the power of consumer backlash. In January 1999, Intel came under fire for programming its Pentium III chips to transmit automatically a unique identifier for a web site that a user visited: 'The company said the technology would help online retailers eliminate fraud by verifying a customer's identity.' After consumer privacy groups attacked the computer chip manufacturer, it shipped its Pentium III chips with the option of activating the feature or leaving it turned off.[95]

3.5 Regulation

Still other commentators argue for government intervention, advocating that the government codify certain voluntary standards into law.[96] 'The regulation of the treatment of personal information would secure participation by citizens in the communications process. Moreover, in commercial speech cases, courts are willing to uphold regulations if the government can regulate the underlying economic activity.'[97] Simitis adds that '[d]espite their different approaches to the problem, statutes, drafts, administrative procedures, court decisions, and reports of control agencies now offer a solid basis for identifying at least four essentials of an efficient processing regulation'. These four essentials include recognizing the unique nature of data processing, limiting the use of data to the expressed purpose for which it was collected, continuous updating of data regulations, and 'an independent authority to enforce data regulations'.[98] Gindin proposes 'fair information practice guidelines' that include federal guarantees of individual control over the collection and distribution of personal information, which would include the right to access and correct one's personal data.[99]

Lawmakers have begun to respond to such proposals by drafting legislation that would allow consumers access to their personal information from business entities.

---

[93]   See Pierce (n. 55 above).
[94]   ibid.
[95]   See Teena Massingill, 'Your Right to Privacy of Personal Data is Up for Grabs, Experts Say', *Contra Costa Times* 29 August 1999, available in EBSCO.
[96]   See generally David J. Klein, 'Keeping Business out of the Bedroom: Protecting Personal Privacy Interests from the Retail World', 15 J Marshall J Computer & Info L 391 (1997).
[97]   See Reidenberg (n. 68 above) at 540 (citing to *Posadas de P.R. Assocs. v Tourism Co. of P.R.* 478 US 328 (1986) (holding that government power to regulate gambling gives it the power to regulate gambling advertisement)).
[98]   See Simitis (n. 87 above) at 737–8. Although such a regulatory agency would likely be challenged in the courts, the Supreme Court has held that 'neither incorporated nor unincorporated associations can plead an unqualified right to conduct their affairs in secret'. See also *California Bankers Association v Secretary of the Treasury*, 416 US 21, 65 (1974). The Court added that a law enforcement interest could legitimately allow the government to require a bank to profile its customers (ibid. at 66–7).
[99]   Gindin (n. 74 above) at 1155, 1222.

In the 106th Congress, S.809, sponsored by Senator Conrad Burns (R-Mont.), would require Internet sites to give consumers the opportunity to look at information that had been collected about them, as well as limit disclosure of the information.[100] The Federal Trade Commission, however, which favours a voluntary free market approach, voted 3–1 not to endorse the Bill.[101] Others have argued that conflicts between state and federal personal privacy laws could be resolved by applying a 'quasi-FOIA standard to state law concerning consumer-business transactions'.[102] Yet another suggestion is for states to broaden the scope of the Restatement 2nd of Torts' privacy standard of appropriation to FOIA exemption six.[103] The reason is that without customer profiles, companies would be unable to realize the economic gain of reselling the profiles. At bare minimum, these scholars argue, states should require businesses to give consumers an opt-out opportunity.[104]

Such reasoning helps to bolster an argument that purely private entities, or private entities that contract with the government, should be subject to some sort of FOIA-like law, especially if the issue is one of control and voluntariness on the part of the consumer who must of necessity divulge personal information to such businesses.[105] Others are less confident in the state's ability to regulate private data acquisition:

As U.S. lawyers we are most accustomed to thinking about the problems of data creation, dissemination, and access in certain delimited categories such as the First Amendment, intellectual property rules, the torts of invasion of privacy and defamation, and perhaps in the ambit of a few narrowly defined statutes such as the Privacy Act or the Fair Credit Reporting Act. These categories are valuable, but are collectively inadequate to the regulatory and social challenges posed by the information production, collection, and processing booms now under way.[106]

Simitis also notes the drawbacks of legislation inasmuch as legislation typically has failed to anticipate future technological exigencies.[107]

The emphasis must shift to a context-bound allocation of information embodied in a complex system of both specific and substantive regulations. Yet, no matter how precise the rules, they nevertheless remain provisional measures because of the incessant advances in technology. Regulations on the collection and retrieval of personal data thus present a classic case of sunset legislation.[108]

[100] 'Give Surfers Some Privacy', *The Tennessean* 23 August 1999 at 10A.
[101] ibid.
[102] See generally David J. Klein, 'Keeping Business out of the Bedroom: Protecting Personal Privacy Interests from the Retail World', 15 J Marshall J Computer & Info L 391 (1997).
[103] ibid.   [104] ibid.
[105] See generally John Hagel III and Marc Singer, *Net Worth* (1999). The authors argue that emerging technologies that give consumers more power over what information they disclose, at least on the Internet, afford an entrepreneurial opportunity for 'infomediaires', third-party data brokers to whom consumers would turn over their own electronic records of personal consumption habits to be compiled, collated, then peddled to businesses who see such information. The consumer would then reap the financial benefit of selling his or her personal data, and the infomediary would collect a commission or fee.
[106] See Froomkin (n. 51 above) at 399.
[107] See Simitis (n. 87 above) at 741–2.
[108] ibid. at 742.

The existence of such laws would allow prosecutors aggressively to pursue violators. For example, in June 1999, Minnesota sued US Bancorp, which has 1,023 affiliated banks and branches, for allegedly peddling customer account data to a telemarketing firm without customers' permission. US Bancorp settled the lawsuit in July 1999 for $3 million without admitting any wrongdoing. Bank of America, Wells Fargo and Union Bank, which control nearly 60 per cent of the California market, admitted to having 'sold or traded personal or financial information about their customers with outside vendors or telemarketers'.[109] Presumably, such acts on the parts of banks would come under the exacting scrutiny of states' Attorney General.

4. CONCLUSION

The flow of information to the government and, especially, the private sector, now raises questions whether some of this information is either in the public or the private interest. Resolving such issues, such as when information given in one context can be used or sold for use in another, or when the FOIA should be extended to private entities will have important ramifications for United States FOIA and privacy laws. How these questions are resolved is, I believe, paradigmatic of larger regulatory concerns as well. Issues involving the market and instances in which accountability may be required over and above that provided by usual market processes are closely related to issues involving regulation in general and the future role the state will play in an increasingly global political economy. Information-based regulation will, I believe, be an important ingredient of any new regulatory paradigm likely to emerge in the future. Thus, analysing the public/private aspects of FOIA and privacy legislation in general against a backdrop of changing conceptions of the public and the private can provide new ways of bringing accountability and democracy to the market and to some of the new public/private partnerships now being created.

As we have seen, one important rationale for the Freedom of Information Act is the ability of citizens to obtain the information necessary to further an informed public and a vibrant democracy. Another driving force for this legislation, however, is citizens' distrust of government and government officials. The two rationales are, of course, closely related in that citizens have a right to information that will enable them to make informed judgments about both the direction of public policy and the competency of those making these decisions. But the element of distrust can be over-extended especially when market issues are involved. Regulating the regulators—as if any affirmative governmental action is likely to be bad by definition—can result in favouring market approaches over regulatory approaches for reasons that have little to do with the fundamental democracy values that FOIA legislation intends to

---

[109] See Teena Massingill, 'Your Right to Privacy of Personal Data is Up for Grabs, Experts Say', *Contra Costa Times*, 29 August 1999, available in EBSCO.

further.[110] Moreover, an either/or debate between regulation or the market can prevent the development of a new regulatory paradigm by overemphasizing the divide between the public and the private or regulation and the market. The end result is that the market, conceived of in traditional terms, may be preferred when, in fact, the true regulatory challenge is how best to make the market accountable and transparent, given the global aspects of the technologies involved and the difficulty of regulating directly the multiple contexts in which privacy concerns now arise. Democratizing the market and extending to it some of the transparency we seek from government is one of the main challenges we now face. In the future, we must ask not only what is 'not in the public interest' but, also, what is 'not just in the private interest'.

---

[110] 'The central harm of lying or hiding the truth is the manipulation of others' choices, i.e., the refusal to allow them to act as agents worthy of Kantian respect.' Pollack, (n. 23 above) at 74.

21

Freedom of Information and International Law

K. J. KEITH

Thirty-five years ago a fellow of Keble College, Oxford, set out to try to lessen or even subvert one passion of British civil servants—their 'passion for secrecy'. The book which resulted, *Not in the Public Interest—the Problem of Security in Democracy*,[1] is a masterpiece of description, analysis and prescription.[2]

The description comes from a wide range of sources which soon became familiar to the writer's growing band of admiring readers: parliamentary proceedings, official reports of commissions, committees and privy councillors, newspaper reports, books and articles (running far beyond the familiar, at least to this lawyer), as well as the statute books and law reports.

The analysis begins on the first page of the Introduction and goes directly to the advantages and disadvantages of the extensive 'veil of secrecy drawn over much of the working of central government'. The veil is so extensive, on one view, that

it defeats its own purpose. For an undiscriminating rejection of independent scrutiny and an inflexible aversion to publicity are likely as not to perpetuate inefficiency in several areas of government and they are scarcely calculated to attract the confidence and approval of the majority of the people. But others argue that, apart from considerations of security proper, the machinery of government would become too slow and too cumbersome and often too inefficient were it to be operated in a full blaze of publicity.[3]

The Introduction ends by identifying the ultimate danger of executive secrecy in a much governed country:

* I am very grateful for comments on earlier drafts of this paper by David Baragwanath, Treasa Dunworth, Nicola Grant (and also for her outstanding research assistance), Bryce Harland, Rodney Harrison, Paul Hunt, Catherine Iorns, Jocelyn Keith, John McGrath, Janet McLean, Geoffrey Palmer and Michael Taggart. I have also taken account of the other papers and discussions at the Conference.

The Feldman, Mason and Sedley papers address one aspect of my title: the extent to which a right of access to information can be drawn out of international guarantees of freedom of expression and of the right to respect for privacy and family. Some of the United Nations material in Part 3 of the paper might be used, especially in the environmental area, to support particular rights of access as well as rights to be informed.

[1] London: Hutchinson, 1965.

[2] The quality of the book was recognized at once by the reviews which consistently with the author's approach appeared in a wide range of publications: e.g. Lord Chorley (1966) 29 Mod LR 469 ('his numerous criticisms are both judicious and temperate'); (1965) 216 *Economist* 347 (24 July) (along with reviews of books on Curzon and Proust); (1965) 249 *Punch* 288 (25 August); and (1965) *Times Literary Supplement* 747 (2 September).

[3] n.1 above 9.

it denies the knowledge essential for an informed public opinion and . . . it inhibits effective scrutiny and criticism of the government and the administration.[4]

The prescription appears in the conclusion: the operation of the Official Secrets Acts had to be severely confined; the proposed Ombudsman had to have access to the internal minutes of government in support of the power of publicity, the ultimate sanction of that parliamentary office; and the judges had to adopt a bolder approach to matters hidden under the cloak of Crown privilege (as public interest immunity was then called), to better exercise their function of standing between citizens and the executive.

Secrecy and security have to be balanced against the legitimate demands for an informed public operation which is, when all is said and done, the essential element in a country which claims to be democratic.[5]

Some of these proposals have been acted on, if belatedly.

This tribute to that author, Sir David Williams, takes up some of the categories of information with which he was concerned—especially information relating to foreign, defence and security matters—and considers them in terms of international law as well as national law.

Within its wide scope, this paper is selective and exploratory, indicating matters which call for much fuller research. It begins with a brief account of the deferential attitudes often adopted by legislatures and courts to foreign, defence and security matters, and also to Cabinet proceedings, while also recording some significant qualifications to, and changes in, those attitudes. That deference appears in relation to both substantive areas of law and the release of official information. The second part summarizes the reasons given nationally for changing to a more open approach to the release of official information. Those reasons are taken up in the international context in the third part of the paper which also calls attention to some of the many requirements of open processes and disclosure of information increasingly imposed by international law.[6] The paper concludes by suggesting some consequences for national constitutional, legal and educational practices and attitudes.

---

[4] n.1 above 11.
[5] ibid. 207–16.
[6] While Professor Fred Aman's paper (Ch. 20) is about the movement of national public power into private hands (or the application of public law controls over some private power) mine is about the movement of such power into international hands (or the application of public law to or the exercise of equivalent controls over those hands). A third movement is to local hands as with devolution. The movement, allocation or exercise of powers into or by private hands should not mean that public law controls are excluded. The international obligations of states, considered in the third part of this paper, help identify the areas where those controls should apply. Thus the fact that telephone services are provided by private companies does not take them outside the regime of the International Telecommunications Union.

1. INTERNATIONAL RELATIONS, DEFENCE AND NATIONAL SECURITY: LEGISLATORS AND JUDGES DEFER

National legislatures and courts have routinely treated information (along with other substantive issues), relating to foreign, defence or security matters as distinct from information (and other issues) relating to 'domestic' or 'home' affairs.[7] So the criminal law imposes the heaviest penalties on those engaged in spying for the benefit of foreign, especially enemy, powers; such a law was recently invoked by the English Court of Appeal to provide a civil remedy, possibly including future income from the sale of George Blake's book.[8] The law setting up or recognizing intelligence services frequently gives them extensive and unusual powers to gather foreign sourced information and confers on them matching protections from legal remedies and other official scrutiny. So far as substantive matters are concerned, immigration legislation may confer broad powers of deportation on Ministers for undefined reasons of national security and the Crown under legislative authority might also invoke such reasons to control the use of intellectual property.

Courts similarly may invoke broad concepts of 'act of state' and the like to avoid addressing what are characterized as international or diplomatic or prerogative or political questions.[9] The New Zealand Court of Appeal in a recent decision, *Choudry v Attorney-General*,[10] referred to the areas of national security, defence and international relations in this way:

Both Courts and legislatures have at times seen those areas as non justiciable, or as barely justiciable, or as requiring judicial deference to Ministerial exercises of discretion. Those positions have been seen in court rulings relating to governmental decisions and processes, for instance:

---

[7] See e.g. Thomas M. Franck, *Political Questions: Judicial Answers. Does the Rule of Law Apply to Foreign Affairs?* (1992), H. P. Lee, Hanks and Mariboto, *In the Name of National Security The Legal Dimensions* (1995), Laurence Lustgarten and Ian Leigh, *In from the Cold: National Security and Parliamentary Democracy* (Oxford: Clarendon, 1994), and more generally on the prerogative, Paul Craig, 'Prerogative, Precedent and Power' in Christopher Forsyth and Ivan Hare (eds.) *The Golden Metwand and the Crooked Cord: Essays on Public Law in Honour of Sir William Wade* (Oxford: Clarendon, 1998) 65.

[8] *Attorney-General* v. *Blake* [1998] 1 All ER 853.

[9] See e.g. *Buttes Gas and Gas Oil Company v Hammer* [1982] AC 889, *CCSU v Minister for Civil Services* (the *GCHQ case*) [1985] AC 374 and the *Duke of York* case (1460) conveniently reproduced and discussed in Weston, 'Political Questions' (1925) 38 Harv LR 296, 302–3 and *Seville v Elizade* (1940) 112 F 2d 29 and the discussions in the books cited in n.7 above. Lustgarten and Leigh 'document a striking pattern of judicial self-abrogation in cases involving issues of national security', 353.

[10] [1999] 3 NZLR 399. This litigation was the subject of two judgments of the Court. In the first the Court (a) held that the Security Intelligence Service had no power to enter premises in exercise of its power to intercept communications (a ruling reversed by legislation) and (b) suggested that the Prime Minister consider submitting a more detailed certificate justifying the claim of public interest immunity. Some precision in the drafting of the certificate was required so the Court could effectively discharge its responsibility of deciding whether matters of security outweighed the need for disclosure; *Choudry v Attorney-General* [1999] 2 NZLR 582 (discussed in the last part of the paper). In the second case, from which the following passages are extracted, the Court divided with the majority accepting that the revised certificate met the required standard without the need for judicial inspection of the documents; Thomas J, dissenting, would have inspected those documents which were still withheld (some having been released between the two hearings).

- determining foreign and defence policy: thus the House of Lords ruled that there can be no challenge in court to the exercise by the Crown of its exclusive discretion concerning the disposition and armament of armed forces; that is true also of treaties and alliances for mutual defence, *Chandler v DPP* [1964] AC 763, 790–791, 796, 800, 813; and indeed for the making of treaties in general, eg *R v Foreign Secretary, ex parte Rees Mogg* [1994] QB 552, 569–570
- characterising certain goods as urgently required for requisition in connection with the defence of the realm, the prosecution of the war, or other matters involving national security. 'Those who are responsible for the national security must be the sole judges of what the national security requires. It would obviously be undesirable that such matters should be made the subject of evidence in a Court of law or otherwise discussed in public,' *The Zamora* [1916] 2 AC 77, 107 (PC) (although see the actual result in that case)
- supporting the Court's inherent jurisdiction to protect the names of witnesses who are employed by the Security Intelligence Service, *Taylor v Attorney-General* [1975] 2 NZLR 675
- denying or severely limiting natural justice to immigrants or to state employees or the right of unions to be consulted, eg *R v Home Secretary ex parte Hosenball* [1997] 3 All ER 452; *Chiarelli v Canada (Minister of Justice)* (1992) 90 DLR (4th) 289, 310–313 (SCC); *CCSU v Minister for Civil Service (the GCHQ case)* [1985] AC 374; in the last, Lord Fraser (402) quoted the two sentences quoted above from *The Zamora* and Lord Diplock said flatly that national security 'is par excellence a non-justiciable question. The judicial process is totally inept to deal with the sort of problems which it involves'.[11]

But, the Court continued, courts do not of course always abstain or defer. In recent decades they have applied wider powers of review. Thus:

- the Supreme Court of Canada has held that the prerogative power relating to defence may be subject to a challenge under the Charter of Rights, *Operation Dismantle v The Queen* [1985] 1 SCR 441 (although the particular challenge failed)
- courts in several jurisdictions have rejected challenges, based on claimed threats to Britain's national security, to the release of the *Spycatcher* (*The Spycatcher* Cases [1989] 2 FSR; compare *Attorney-General v Turnaround Distribution Ltd* [1989] 1 FSR 169 (Simon Brown J)); as did the United States Supreme Court in respect of *The Pentagon Papers* (*New York Times Co v United States* (1971) 403 US 713)
- a New Zealand naval officer was held entitled to natural justice in respect of decisions affecting his grading notwithstanding arguments of national security (*Bradley v Attorney-General* [1988] 2 NZLR 454).[12]

Both this deferential attitude and movements from it also appear in cases about access to information and freedom of information legislation. For instance in leading Commonwealth cases of the 1960s and, indeed, later in which the courts reasserted their power to examine Ministerial claims to withhold information sought

---

[11] [1999] 3 NZLR 403–4. Sir Stephen Sedley in the course of the Conference referred to the verdict of the jury in *R v Ponting* [1985] Crim LR 318, comparing it to the Penn and Mead juries and inferentially raising the question of the significance of the *Chandler* ruling in the light of that verdict and the expert evidence called in support of the defence.
[12] ibid. 404.

in the course of litigation, judges routinely recognized that certain categories of information essentially remained protected. Within those categories were:

• defence matters or military secrets of the kind involved in the otherwise overruled or massively distinguished *Duncan v Cammell Laird*[13]—plans of a submarine, sought during World War II:

The flame of individual rights and justice must burn more palely when it is ringed by the more dramatic light of bombed buildings;[14]

• national security;[15]
• despatches from ambassadors abroad;[16] and
• Cabinet papers.[17]

The final category did not long survive in a number of parts of the common law world including the United States,[18] Australia,[19] New Zealand,[20] and Canada.[21] In addition, a more general change of attitude began to occur in the litigation context as the balancing exercise in *Conway v Rimmer*, coupled with greater insight by judges into what was mere governmental convenience as opposed to public interest, led to recognition that public interest immunity claims were frequently being made on grounds that did not outweigh the legitimate interests of litigants in full disclosure.

The change in attitude with respect to Cabinet papers is of significance because the reasons for the change have wider application. Those reasons recognize the very wide and at times widening area of government activity. In particular if there is to be equality before the law of parties to litigation in those many areas, any procedural advantage of the Crown as litigant should be removed or reduced to the greatest extent possible. Another more general reason was the move towards open government in the 1960s and later, with steps being taken

• by Parliaments, especially in the Ombudsman legislation; in legislation requiring open procedures of hearings and consultation and reasons for decisions and establishing appeal rights; and in legislation and practice enhancing controls over the making of subordinate legislation. In his recent outstanding contribution, *Secrecy*[22], American politician and scholar Daniel Patrick Moynihan uses the

---

[13] [1942] AC 624.

[14] Lord Pearce in *Conway v Rimmer* [1968] AC at 982; see also e.g. Lord Reid at 951 referring to *United States v Reynolds* 345 US 1, 9–10 (1953).

[15] E.g. Cooke J in *Environmental Defence Society v South Pacific Aluminium Ltd (No. 2)* [1981] 1 NZLR 153, 156.   [16] Lord Morris in *Conway v Rimmer* [1968] AC at 973.

[17] E.g. Lord Reid in *Conway v Rimmer* [1968] AC at 952.

[18] *United States v Nixon* 418 US 683 (1974).

[19] *Sankey v Whitlam* (1978) 142 CLR 1.

[20] *Environmental Defence Society v South Pacific Aluminium Co. Ltd.* [1981] 1 NZLR 146; *Fletcher Timber Ltd. v Attorney-General* [1984] 1 NZLR 290; *Brightwell v Accident Compensation Corporation* [1985] 1 NZLR 132.

[21] *Carey v Ontario* (1986) 35 DLR (4th) 161 (SCC) (applying Woodhouse P's judgment in *Fletcher Timber*); see also *Attorney-General v Jonathan Cape Ltd.* [1976] QB 752 and *Burmah Oil Co v Bank of England* [1980] AC 1090.

[22] (New Haven: Yale, 1998) 226–7.

Federal Administration Procedure Act 1946 with its similar requirements of openness as the basis for his proposed reform in respect of information relating to national security and foreign affairs;

- by Courts in reasserting the principles of natural justice, notably in *Ridge v Baldwin*;[23] and

- by administrative means (for instance, in the introduction of codes of practice, in effect granting broad approval for the release of information, with a resulting reduction in the impact of the Official Secrets Acts enacted at Westminster and continuing to apply in the former Empire).[24]

The change in respect of Cabinet papers was also significant because of its emphasis on examining the detail of the claim to secrecy. It reflected the move away from 'class claims', where the status of the material was seen as determinative, to claims based on the content of the material. A blanket reference to 'Cabinet proceedings' was no longer good enough; rather, particular public interests and the threat to them had to be identified and substantiated.

By the 1980s, the statute book in several jurisdictions included freedom of information Acts. Some judges have been willing to draw on that legislation in stating and developing the law of public interest immunity. So Woodhouse P in the New Zealand Court of Appeal referred to 'the contemporary movement towards open government in New Zealand has found statutory expression in the Official Information Act 1982 which states as the first of its purposes expressed in its long title that it is "an Act to make information more freely available" ';[25] Richardson J quoted this passage from the *Report of the Committee on Official Information, Towards More Open Government*:

New Zealand is a small country. The Government has a pervasive involvement in our everyday national life. This involvement is not only felt, but is also sought, by New Zealanders, who have tended to view successive Governments as their agents, and have expected them to act as such. The Government is a principal agency in deploying the resources required to undertake many large scale projects, and there is considerable pressure for it to sustain its role as a major developer, particularly as an alternative to overseas ownership and control. No less striking is the extent to which Government is involved in economic direction, regulation, and intervention. Along with the impact of the State budget and expenditures, there are important controls on, for example, wages, prices, the use of labour, transport, banking, and overseas investment. Our social support systems also rely heavily on central government. History and circumstances give New Zealanders special reason for wanting to know what their Government is doing and why.[26]

---

[23] [1964] AC 40.

[24] I have considered these matters more fully in a New Zealand context in a tribute to Sir Guy Powles who, as New Zealand's first Ombudsman, helped popularize that office throughout the common law world, 'Open Government in New Zealand' (1987) 17 VUWLR 333.

[25] *Fletcher Timber* (n. 20 above) 296.

[26] ibid. 302; see also McMullin J at 305–6; and in *Brightwell* (n. 20 above) Cooke J at 139, Richardson J at 146 and McMullin J at 152.

The next part considers more fully the purposes and reasons stated in and underlying the New Zealand Official Information Act. For the moment, it is enough to note the judicial emphasis on the broad movement towards greater openness, and on the value of particular provisions of freedom of information and other legislation even when they are not directly in point in the particular case. Such arguments in the courts, in a sense returning to the old doctrine of 'the equity of the statute', have not, however, always been successful, as appears from the difference between the New South Wales Court of Appeal and the High Court of Australia in *Public Service Board v Osmond*.[27] But whatever the judicial attitude, the legislative developments continue to be valuable at the policy level in identifying broader movements towards more open government.

2. THE CASE FOR MORE OPEN GOVERNMENT IS RECOGNIZED NATIONALLY

Legislation in a number of countries, official and unofficial proposals and scholarly writing over the last three decades have established or at least clarified the reasons for open government and demonstrate varying approaches to the protection of interests of the state, including its interests in international relations, defence and security.[28]

The open government principle is a reversal of the earlier principle incorporated in Official Secrets Acts which forbad release unless release was authorized for good reason. The principle now is that official information is to be made available unless one of the good reasons set out in the new legislation for withholding it is established.

That principle is based on both particular and general interests of those seeking information. The particular interest of the individual may, for instance, lead to a correction of the information or to a challenge to the use being made of it (sometimes through data protection or privacy legislation); the release may facilitate some action by the individuals to protect their rights and interests; or the information may be relevant to decisions being made by state agencies concerning that individual, for instance in a criminal prosecution or in civil or administrative proceedings. The next part of this paper provides a number of examples of the recognition of analogous particular interests being recognized in the international community.

The more general interest is the interest of the individual as a citizen. The New Zealand Official Information Act 1982, in a provision which drew on Scandinavian

---

[27] (1986) 159 CLR 656; see the contributions by Justice Michael Kirby and Michael Taggart in Michael Taggart (ed.), *Judicial Review of Administrative Action in the 1980s: Problems and Prospects* (Auckland: Oxford University Press, 1986) 36, 53; and David Kelly 'The Osmond Case: Common Law and Statute Law' (1986) 60 ALJ 513.

[28] See Part 2 of Stephanie Palmer's essay for a fuller discussion of the reasons in the particular context of the United Kingdom Bill. The New Zealand legislation is discussed in detail in Ian Eagles, Michael Taggart and Grant Liddell, *Freedom of Information in New Zealand* (Auckland: Oxford University Press, 1992).

and United States legislation, legislative proposals in Australia and Canada and much scholarship, attempted to catch the essence of this more general purpose in this way:

The purposes of this Act are, consistently with the principle of the Executive Government's responsibility to Parliament,—
(a) To increase progressively the availability of official information to the people of New Zealand in order—
   (i) To enable their more effective participation in the making and administration of laws and policies; and
   (ii) To promote the accountability of Ministers of the Crown and officials,—
   and thereby to enhance respect for the law and to promote the good government of New Zealand . . .[29]

The Report on which the legislation was based explained those purposes:

The case for more openness in government is compelling. It rests on the democratic principles of encouraging participation in public affairs and ensuring the accountability of those in office; . . . A no less important consideration is that the Government requires public understanding and support to get its policies carried out. This can come only from an informed public. . . . There is in addition a special feature of the New Zealand setting for these arguments to which we wish to draw attention. [That 'special feature' is elaborated in the paragraph quoted by Richardson J in *Fletcher Timber* set out in Part 1 of this chapter.]

The Report then considered those three matters:

Participation . . . the principle that a better informed public is better able to play the part required of it in the democratic system—and to judge policies and electoral platforms.
Accountability . . . access of citizens to official information is an essential factor in making sure that politicians and administrators are accountable for their actions. Secrecy is an impediment to accountability . . .
Effective government
Notwithstanding the need for participation and accountability, the Government's essential task is still to govern. If it is to do this effectively it has to win votes and secure public support. . . . Better information flows would in these circumstances help towards more flexible development of policy.
  As the major force in national activity the Government needs to have its aims broadly supported, its decisions understood and accepted. It is not to be expected that every one of these decisions will be popular; but the Government depends ultimately on public cooperation with the changes its decisions impose upon people.[30]

All those elements—participation, accountability and enhancing respect for the law and better government—are critical for the processes of the international community. The fraught beginning or, rather, non-beginning of the latest World Trade Organisation round of trade liberalization negotiations provide an example, if a

[29] Official Information Act 1982, s. 4.
[30] Committee on Official Information, *Towards More Open Government*, General Report (Wellington: Government Printer, 1980), 14–16.

negative one. The *Economist*[31] contrasts the relative success of the World Bank in dealing with external critics. 'Now the NGOs [after earlier conflict] are surprisingly quiet about the World Bank. The reason is that the Bank has made a huge effort to co-opt them'. But while the 'new World Bank is more transparent, . . . it is also more beholden to a new set of special interests'—raising a further set of questions about international governance. Are the non-governmental organizations (NGOs) the first step towards 'international civil society' or do they represent a dangerous shift of power to unelected and unaccountable special interest groups? The relative recent success of the World Bank, involving as it does greater openness, has been carefully documented in relation to policies affecting indigenous peoples which call for their informed participation in development projects.[32]

The third purpose of the New Zealand Act is negative. It places a restraint on the purposes supporting general and particular access. That purpose is 'to protect official information to the extent consistent with the public interest and the preservation of personal privacy'.[33]

The Act elaborates that purpose by stating good reasons for withholding information. The statement of those reasons in the areas of international relations, defence and national security highlights special characteristics that those areas may have and suggests related limits that might apply to obligations of openness imposed by international law.

At least four questions arise for the international law maker as well as for the national one:

(1) How is the interest to be defined? Some of the interests are substantive—(state) security, (national) defence, international or foreign relations or policy—and others are procedural—the entrusting of information in confidence by other governments and by international organizations. The latter interest reflects the fact that much of the information can be sensitive not because of its content but rather for the need to protect sources.

(2) Is a test of damage or prejudice or consequence in the particular circumstances to be made out or is it enough if the information falls within a category (e.g. information authorized under executive criteria to be kept secret in the interest of national defence or foreign policy; information provided in confidence by a foreign government; or information about tax matters provided by a foreign tax administration)? And if a test of consequence is included, how is it to be drafted—making available the information would (be likely to) (might) prejudice, endanger, damage (seriously) . . .; or withholding is necessary to protect the stated interests? While everything cannot be decided by the wording, it can give a very clear direction.

---

[31] 11 December 1999. For another contemporary commentary see Michael Byers 'Woken up in Seattle' *London Review of Books*, vol. 22 no. 1, (6 January 2000) 16.

[32] Benedict Kingsbury, 'Operational Policies of International Institutions as part of the Law-Making Process: The World Bank and Indigenous Peoples' in Guy S Goodwin—Gill and Stefan Tolmin (eds.), *The Reality of International Law: Essays in honour of Ian Brownlie* (Oxford: Clarendon, 1999) 323.

[33] Official Information Act 1982, s. 4(c).

(3) Even if the test for withholding is made out, can release nevertheless be required on the basis that the public interest in openness is greater?

(4) Who has the power to decide whether the good reason for withholding has been established? Even if the general answer is an independent body, such as a court, tribunal or Ombudsman, the executive may have selective powers of veto to protect, for example, national security.[34]

To anticipate some of the later discussion and to return to David Williams's book, those questions suggest that simply to assert 'the Defence of the Realm' may not, indeed should not, be good enough. More discriminating reasoning should be required if information is to be withheld. As with substantive claims of non-justiciability, one starting point is to distinguish between the constitutional limits on judicial power (for instance that certain matters of policy are for elected and accountable politicians to decide) and practical limits on the ability of the Judges to assess the government's claim in the context of litigation.[35]

I now turn to some of the international practice and relate it to the broader movement towards more open government.

3. AND ALSO INTERNATIONALLY

A related movement has been seen in the evolution of the lawmaking and governance functions of the international community over the last century. One image of those functions is a confined one, limited to matters of war and peace or at least to matters which are said not to be of any general public or professional interest, carried out secretly by princes in exercise of their unfettered prerogatives—and as a consequence to be taught as an extra subject at the end of the law degree and as an optional subject at that.

Because of their special and limited character, those international functions are not thought to be subject to the familiar democratic, legislative and judicial processes which apply routinely to other functions of the State or at least not subject to the same extent.

But does that limited image reflect reality? A few facts, reviewed in this part of the paper, show that it does not. That gap between the image and the reality has serious consequences for governmental processes as suggested in the final part of this paper.

3.1 'Open Covenants . . .'

The centennial commemorations, within the last year, of the first Hague Peace Conference, have helped highlight that major new beginning in multilateral diplomacy: the

---

[34] The New Zealand Law Commission has recently considered aspects of these questions in its *Review of the Official Information Act 1982* (NZLC R 40, 1997) ch. 7.
[35] See the valuable decision in chs. 6, 7 and 12 of Lustgarten and Leigh (n. 7 above).

1899 Conference, as compared for instance with the 1815 Congress of Vienna, prepared general rules to govern future matters of major importance (disarmament, the law of armed conflict and the peaceful settlement of international disputes) rather than resolving major political questions, especially those arising from a just concluded European war; the participating states were there on an equal footing, signing the relevant documents in alphabetical order for instance, rather than being ranked; and the press (and through it various bodies which would now be called NGOs) were present and received regular briefings.[36] While those three features were not completely unprecedented (the first Geneva Conference for the protection of war victims in 1863 provides an earlier, limited example), the 1899 Conference may properly be seen as the first step in the process of continuing multilateral diplomacy within an ever widening reach of subject matter. The non-governmental element had been emphasized as early as 1873 by the creation of the Institut de Droit International and the International Law Association—both recognizing that the making of international law was something too important to be left to governments. Special interest bodies were also proliferating, some such as the British and Foreign Anti-Slavery Society having been established earlier in the century. In the course of the following century, the official components of that process were to become institutionalized in the League of Nations and the United Nations and many other associated bodies.

After the United States entered the Great War and in the context of a growing demand for the abolition of secret diplomacy, President Woodrow Wilson, in the first of the Fourteen Points promulgated on 8 January 1918, stated that in future there were to be

Open covenants of peace, openly arrived at, after which there shall be no private international understandings of any kind but diplomacy shall proceed always frankly and in the public view.[37]

One participant in the Versailles Conference which soon followed criticized Wilson's failure, as he saw it, to recognize the essential distinction between policy which was a legitimate subject for popular control and negotiation which was not:

Less than a year after making this pronouncement, President Wilson was himself called upon to negotiate one of the most important covenants that have ever been concluded, namely the Treaty of Versailles. That treaty was certainly an open covenant since its terms were published before they were submitted to the approval of the sovereign authority in the several signatory States. Yet with equal certainty it was not 'openly arrived at'. In fact few negotiations in history have been so secret, or indeed so occult.

Not only were Germany and her allies excluded from any part in the discussion; not only were all the minor Powers kept in the dark regarding the several stages of the negotiations; not only were the press accorded no information beyond the most meagre of official bulletins; but

---

[36] e.g. Arthur Eyffinger, *The 1899 Hague Peace Conference 'The Parliament of Man, the Federation of the World'* (The Hague: Kluwer, 1999).
[37] Arthur S Link (ed.), *The Papers of Woodrow Wilson* vol 45, 534.

in the end President Wilson shut himself up in his own study with Lloyd George and Clemenceau, while an American marine with fixed bayonet marched up and down in order to prevent the intrusion of all experts, diplomatists or plenipotentiaries, including even the President's own colleagues on the American Delegation.

I am not contending for the moment that such secrecy was not inevitable, I am merely pointing out that it was unparalleled. It proves that the highest apostle of 'open diplomacy' found, when it came to practice, that open negotiation was totally unworkable. And it shows how false was the position into which President Wilson (a gifted and in many ways a noble man) had placed himself, by having failed, in January 1918, to foresee that there was all the difference in the world between 'open covenants' and 'openly arrived at'—between policy and negotiation.[38]

This criticism may be unfair, for President Wilson had explained as early as March 1918 in a letter to his Secretary of State that:

When I pronounced for open diplomacy, I meant not that there should be no private discussion of delicate matters, but that no secret agreements of any sort should be entered into and that all international relations, when fixed, should be open, above board, and explicit.[39]

The negotiating stage—'openly arrived at'—is touched on again in the final part of this paper. The first part of the First Point—that covenants are to be open—was given concrete expression in Article 18 of the Covenant of the League of Nations which also set out a sanction for breach:

Every treaty or international engagement entered into hereafter by any Member of the League shall be forthwith registered with the Secretariat and shall as soon as possible be published by it. No such treaty or international engagement shall be binding until so registered.[40]

Article 102 of the Charter of the United Nations is now the governing provision:

1. Every treaty and every international agreement entered into by any Member of the United Nations after the present Charter comes into force shall as soon as possible be registered with the Secretariat and published by it.
2. No party to any such treaty or international agreement which has not been registered in accordance with the provisions of paragraph 1 of this Article may invoke that treaty or agreement before any organ of the United Nations.[41]

3.2 The Wide and Increasing Scope of International Regulation

Among the practical consequences of those international obligations of openness are the 1,700 volumes of League of Nations and United Nations Treaty Series and the

---

[38] Harold Nicolson, *Diplomacy* (2nd edn., London: Oxford, 1950), 83–4.
[39] *The Papers of Woodrow Wilson*, vol 46, 606; that letter was read into the Congressional Record; see also vol 51, 495; and note that 'openly arrived at' was added to the text and at a later stage of the drafting of the Fourteen Points, vol 45, 511.
[40] See Manley Hudson, 'The Registration and Publication of Treaties' (1925) 19 AJIL 273 and 'The Registration of Treaties' (1930) 24 AJIL 752.
[41] See Palitha Kohona, 'The United Nations Treaty Collection on the Internet' (1998) 92 AJIL 140.

40,000 treaties (now registered at the rate of about two each day) that they publish. Professor Clive Parry provided an invaluable 200 volume complement covering the period from the Treaties of Westphalia of 1648 to the beginnings of those volumes. With national treaty series, they document the ever widening scope of the subject matter of international regulation. Writing just before the end of the Second World War, a distinguished British diplomat put the point generally in one short sentence: every branch of human activity in one form or another could now come within the purview of diplomacy.[42] To be somewhat more specific, a recent publication by the New Zealand Law Commission[43] helps provide this non-exhaustive description of the subject matter of treaties:

war and peace, such as the United Nations Charter, treaties of alliance, the Geneva and Hague Conventions relating to warfare and the protection of the victims of armed conflict, armistices, treaties of peace, the Statute of the International Court of Justice, the Hague Convention establishing the Permanent Court of Arbitration, regional and bilateral treaties for the resolution of disputes, the Vienna Conventions on Diplomatic and Consular Relations;

disarmament and arms control, such as the Nuclear Test Ban Treaties, the Non-proliferation Treaty, the Convention on the Comprehensive Prohibition of Chemical Weapons, the Ottawa Convention on Land Mines, the Statute of the International Atomic Energy Agency, and regional arms control measures, for instance in Africa, Latin America, the South Pacific and Antarctica;

international trade, including the World Trade Organisation (WTO) agreements, regional economic agreements (as in Europe and North and South America), and a great number of bilateral agreements such as the Australia New Zealand Closer Economic Relations Trade Agreement (CER);

international commercial transactions, concerning both the relationship between states (eg, customs facilitation, common nomenclature for tariffs) and private commercial transactions (including treaties regulating carriage by land, sea and air, the international sale of goods and international commercial arbitration);

international communications, for example by sea and by air, where many multilateral and bilateral treaties regulate traffic rights, safety and liability; international telecommunications; the recognition of qualifications, for example in respect of piloting ships and aircraft and driving motor vehicles;

the law of international spaces, particularly the long-established law of the sea, the relatively new law of the air, and the much newer law of outer space; and the law relating to specific areas such as Antarctica, international canals, and areas of particular international concern;

the law relating to the environment, which is a matter of relatively recent general concern and includes treaties relating to the protection of whales and other marine life, oil pollution, the ozone layer, wetlands, and methods of warfare threatening environmental destruction—some specific examples being the Framework Convention on Climate Change and the Convention on Biological Diversity (concluded at the United Nations Conference on the Environment and Development in 1992), and the Basel Convention on the Control of Trans-boundary Movements of Hazardous Wastes and their Disposal;

---

[42] Victor Wellesley, *Fetters of Diplomacy* (London: Hutchinson, 1944) 7.
[43] *A New Zealand Guide to International Law and its Sources* (NZLC R 34 1996), para. 24.

human rights and related matters, including the general instruments drawn up by the United Nations (international covenants on economic, social and cultural rights and on civil and political rights), and on more particular matters (eg, genocide, terrorism, slavery, refugees, prostitution, the political rights of women, discrimination on grounds of race and sex), and the regional instruments especially in Europe and the Americas;

labour conditions and relations, particularly the 150 or more conventions drawn up by the International Labour Organisation since 1919; and

other areas of international and economic and social cooperation, such as the gathering and dissemination of information (health and other statistics, and the work of the World Meteorological Organisation), and combating crimes with international ramifications (eg, slavery, drug trafficking, international hostage-taking, and hijacking of aircraft and ships).

That description shows up the falsity of the image (or caricature) given of the scope of international law at the beginning of this part. International law plainly has an extensive impact on many areas of activity which might, on the basis of the image, be thought to be subject only to national law. The description highlights questions about the ways in which the international community, individual states, their citizens and other interested bodies do or do not participate in, contribute to, or influence the agenda setting, the drafting and negotiation of the texts, their adoption and their implementation, including their implementation in national law. Those questions are considered in the last part of the paper.

3.3 Obligations of Disclosure

The remainder of this part considers aspects of the information and openness obligations imposed by international law. States are increasingly obliged to notify or to provide information about actions they are proposing or taking, or about matters about which they know. The obligations may also be imposed on international organizations, one notable instance among many being the World Weather Watch, provided by the World Meteorological Organisation. These obligations may have legal as well as practical consequences, as appears for instance from the controversial judgment of the International Court in the *Nicaragua* case.[44]

Sometimes the obligations, while still being procedural, will be more extensive, for example also to consult or to seek agreement or to be subject to inspection. Sometimes they will be accompanied by substantive obligations, for example to take action against a source of transboundary pollution of which it has given notice.

The obligations cover vast ranges of activity as appears from just a few examples taken from the New Zealand Law Commission's categories. Parties to armed conflicts are obliged to establish systems for informing their enemies of the prisoners of war and civilian interneees they are holding and for facilitating exchanges of messages. They are obliged to disseminate information about international humanitarian law to

[44] *Military and Paramilitary Activities in and against Nicaragua (Nicaragua v USA)* [1984] ICJ Reps 392, discussed by M Reisman, 'Dissemination of information by international organisations . . .' (1987) 17 VUWLR 53.

their populations and especially to the armed forces. Disarmament treaties increasingly include extensive reporting obligations and inspection powers. International trade agreements require exchanges of information, for instance about tariffs and other controls on trade. And double taxation agreements essentially depend for their effectiveness on the sharing of information about taxpayers between tax administrations.

Information must be shared in support of the complex body of regulation governing international communications. Scientific and research findings are required to be widely disseminated under some of the treaties affecting international spaces such as Antarctica. Information obligations are to be found throughout the law relating to the environment and human rights, including labour rights. International economic and social co-operation, including co-operation in the suppression of crime with international consequences, requires extensive information exchanges, as well as general publications, for instance of statistical material, on a worldwide, comparative basis.

The following brief survey highlights relevant aspects of human rights conventions and environmental treaties. Human rights treaties often require the parties to inform the depository or other relevant international body of the steps they have taken to implement the treaty in their domestic law. That obligation may arise only at the outset or, as with international labour conventions and with the major recent human rights treaties, it may be recurring. Given the diffuse, general interest of other parties in compliance with such treaties, this reporting can be equated to the general interest purpose for freedom of information legislation: to return to the wording of the New Zealand Official Information Act, it is designed to promote the accountability of the parties and as a result to enhance respect by them for the law in question. That purpose is also supported by monitoring committees which consider the reports and question representatives of the state parties. The power has further informational elements and values since NGOs—international as well as national—increasingly take opportunities to participate in the preparation of the national report and in its examination by the monitoring committee in particular by preparing 'shadow reports'. In the next round of reporting, monitoring committees, NGOs and governments will be able to build on that experience, with the purpose of seeking greater compliance with the obligations. That process can be enhanced by appropriate publicity being given to the observations and recommendations of the monitoring committee. The New Zealand Ministry of Foreign Affairs and Trade, for instance, regularly publishes the government's exchanges with the committees and the committees' conclusions.

The environmental treaties, by contrast, more commonly engage the particular interests of affected states, although given the interdependence of many aspects of worldwide environmental systems, the common heritage of humanity will sometimes also be engaged. The Rio Declaration on Environment and Development (1992) states the duties at a level of generality in respect of natural disasters and proposed or actual (human) activities:

Principle 18
States shall immediately notify other States of any natural disasters or other emergencies that are likely to produce sudden harmful effects on the environment of those States. Every effort shall be made by the international community to help States so afflicted.

Principle 19
States shall provide prior and timely notification and relevant information to potentially affected States on activities that may have a significant adverse transboundary environmental effect and shall consult with those States at an early stage and in good faith.

The Declaration also addresses the national situation in a way which extends beyond the directly affected individual to the generally concerned citizen:

Principle 10
Environmental issues are best handled with the participation of all concerned citizens, at the relevant level. At the national level, each individual shall have appropriate access to information concerning the environment that is held by public authorities, including information on hazardous materials and activities in their communities, and the opportunity to participate in decision-making processes. States shall facilitate and encourage public awareness and participation by making information widely available. Effective access to judicial and administrative proceedings, including redress and remedy, shall be provided.

That principle has been taken up, for instance, within Europe by the Convention on Access to Information, Public Participation in Decision Making and Access to Justice in Environmental Matters of 25 June 1998.[45] States parties are to guarantee to every person those three matters in accordance with the terms of the convention.

Many of those obligations to inform arise from the particular threatening situation, although some of the national planning processes, including those contemplated in that European Convention, will be on a regular, periodic basis, as with many of the human rights treaties mentioned earlier.

Those treaties also point to a further variable: obligations which are additional to the reporting or informing obligation, such as the obligation to respond to questions from the monitoring committee and to consider in good faith any recommendations or suggestions the committee makes. Further obligations are also a common feature of environmental treaties as appears from work being done at present by the United Nations International Law Commission (ILC) on international liability for injurious consequences arising out of acts not prohibited by international law, a topic initially developed for the Commission by my late colleague, Professor R. Q. Quentin-Baxter.[46]

In that broader context that Commission has prepared draft provisions based on many of those treaties as well as on principle, judicial decisions and state practice, in an endeavour to state and develop the law applying to activities not prohibited by international law which risk causing significant transboundary harm through their

---

[45]   38 ILM 517.
[46]   See in particular his third report including his schematic outline (1982) *Yearbook of the ILC*, vol II, part 1, 51.

physical consequences.[47] The Commission's draft begins with the basic obligation of states to take all appropriate measures to prevent, or to minimize the risk of, significant transboundary harm.[48] That obligation is supported by obligations to co-operate in preventing or minimizing the risk of significant transboundary harm[49] and, when deciding to authorize an activity, to make an impact assessment: the decision is to be based on an evaluation of the possible transboundary harm caused by that activity.[50] Such an obligation to undertake an impact assessment was invoked by New Zealand when it returned to the International Court in 1995 in an attempt to prevent France from undertaking underground nuclear testing in the South Pacific. The Court did not however reach the substance of the matter.[51]

The public and any state likely to be affected are also to be provided with relevant information about the activity, the risk and likely harm. Their views are to be sought.[52] The various processes can lead to substantive obligations as appears from these draft provisions:

Article 11. Consultations on preventive measures
1. The States concerned shall enter into consultations, at the request of any of them, with a view to achieving acceptable solutions regarding measures to be adopted in order to prevent, or to minimize the risk of, significant transboundary harm.
2. States shall seek solutions based on an equitable balance of interests in the light of article 12 [which sets out relevant factors and circumstances].
3. If the consultations referred to in paragraph 1 fail to produce an agreed solution, the State of origin shall nevertheless take into account the interests of States likely to be affected in case it decides to authorize the activity to be pursued, without prejudice to the rights of any State likely to be affected.

A state can also initiate the process if it has not been informed and has reasonable grounds to believe that an activity planned or carried out in the territory or otherwise under the jurisdiction or control of another State may have a risk of causing significant transboundary harm. The States have a continuing obligation to exchange information:

Article 14. Exchange of information
While the activity is being carried out, the States concerned shall exchange in a timely manner all available information relevant to preventing, or minimizing the risk of, significant transboundary harm.

3.4 Reasons for International Openness

Such provisions for open procedures have a range of purposes which can, as already

---

[47] 1998 ILC Report, ch. 4. [48] Article 3.
[49] Article 4. [50] Article 8.
[51] *New Zealand at the International Court of Justice: French Nuclear Testing in the Pacific* (Wellington: New Zealand Ministry of Foreign Affairs and Trade, 1996), 182–9 (also arguing that there was no national security exception to the obligation to undertake the assessment).
[52] Articles 9 and 10.

indicated, be related to those which underlie national freedom of information legislation.

At the outset is the broad proposition that knowledge is power. Kofi Annan, the UN Secretary-General, in speaking to the World Bank in 1997, stressed the challenge of making information available to all, an outcome greatly facilitated by the information revolution:

All of us—the United Nations, the World Bank, governments, the private sector, members of civil society—must form a global partnership for information.

We must do so wherever and whenever we can, above all, because this new revolution leaves us no choice. Development, peace and democracy are no longer the exclusive responsibility of governments, global organizations or intergovernmental bodies.

The great democratizing power of information has given us all the chance to effect change and alleviate poverty in ways we cannot even imagine today. . . . With information on our side, with knowledge a potential for all, the path to poverty can be reversed.

Knowledge is power. Information is liberating. Education is the premise of progress, in every society, in every family. . . .

For democracy to take root, it needs institutions, respect for the law, integrity of the armed forces and free and regular elections. In all these areas, the United Nations has been working to implement lasting democracy, and we have been doing so by spreading information and encouraging knowledge.

Why? Because an educated electorate is a powerful electorate. Because an informed citizenry is the greatest defender of freedom. Because an enlightened government is a democratizing government.

The quantity and quality of available information is changing dramatically every day in every country in the world. Citizens are gaining greater and greater access to information, too. And, perhaps most importantly, the spread of information is making accountability and transparency facts of life for any free government.

The consent of the governed—the condition for any free society—must be an informed, enlightened consent. The challenge now, for us, is to make information available to all.[53]

The UNESCO Constitution had earlier captured a negative side of the proposition in its recognition that ignorance of each other's ways and lives has been a common cause, throughout the history of mankind, of that suspicion and mistrust between the peoples of the world through which their differences have all too often broken into war. 'Wars,' the Constitution declares, 'begin in the minds of men' and accordingly 'it is in the minds of men that the defences of peace must be constructed'. Daniel Patrick Moynihan has recently brilliantly documented how the American system of governmental secrecy developed over the last century 'blighted prudent policy making. The documents that he unearthed [in the course of a Senate inquiry] prove dramatically how secrecy changed the history of the Cold War and changed it more lamentably than we expected. . . . Secrecy is a losing proposition. It is, as Senator Moynihan has told us, for losers'.[54]

---

[53] Press release SG/SM/6268.
[54] Richard Gid Powers in the Introduction to *Secrecy* (n. 22 above).

Some of the more specific reasons for openness also respond to the general interests of the world community rather than to the interests of particular states. That is true for instance of human rights reporting and monitoring provisions. As noted, their purpose is to help ensure compliance with the treaties in question. Such reporting obligations may also be supported, as with disarmament and arms control treaties and the Geneva Conventions for the protection of war victims, by powers of visit, inspection and reporting which may or may not be public, sometimes with the prospect of sanctions.

A more particular purpose is prevention, or at least mitigation, of damage, injury and disaster. That appears not only in many of the environmental treaties, such as those concluded after the Torrey Canyon maritime disaster and the Chernobyl nuclear power plant meltdown, but also in agreements relating to troop movements, and the US–USSR hotline agreement. As those examples show, the obligation may arise from matters falling within the direct control of states or merely subject to their jurisdiction.

Under at least one convention a central purpose is to correct false information. According to the 1952 Convention on the International Right of Correction:

The Contracting States

Desiring to implement the right of their peoples to be fully and reliably informed,
Desiring to improve understanding between their peoples through the free flow of information and opinion,
Desiring thereby to protect mankind from the scourge of war, to prevent the recurrence of aggression from any source, and to combat all propaganda which is either designed or likely to provoke or encourage any threat to peace, breach of the peace, or act of aggression,
Considering the danger to the maintenance of friendly relations between peoples and to the preservation of peace, arising from the publication of inaccurate reports . . .
Considering, however, that it is not at present practicable to institute, on the international level, a procedure for verifying the accuracy of a report which might lead to the imposition of penalties for the publication of false or distorted reports,
Considering, moreover, that to prevent the publication of reports of this nature or to reduce their pernicious effects, it is above all necessary to promote a wide circulation of news and to heighten the sense of responsibility of those regularly engaged in the dissemination of news.

The Convention accordingly attempts to establish a means for States to secure commensurate publicity for their corrections to the challenged reports.[55]

The centrality of information for the proper functioning of the international system is highlighted by the recent critical reports prepared by and for the UN on its operations in Srebrenica[56] and Rwanda.[57] In the latter case the Independent Inquiry team recommended among other things that:

---

[55] Hilding Eek's *Freedom of Information as a Project of International Legislation* (1953) provides interesting background to a still incomplete process.
[56] 15 November 1999, A/54/549
[57] 16 December 1999.

The early warning capacity of the United Nations needs to be improved, through better cooperation with outside actors including NGOs and academics, as well as within the Secretariat.
. . .

An effective flow of information needs to be ensured within the UN system.

Further improvements should be made in the flow of information to the Security Council.

The flow of information on human rights issues should be improved.

The preparation and publication of that report, along with the full acceptance of its recommendations and of institutional and personal responsibility by Kofi Annan, the Secretary-General of the United Nations, themselves contribute to better understanding and enhance the prospect for the future of prevention and effective responses, given of course that the major powers and through them the Security Council demonstrate the necessary commitment. On releasing the Rwanda report, the Secretary-General said this:

Both Reports—my own on Srebrenica, and that of the independent Inquiry on Rwanda—reflect a profound determination to present the truth about these calamities. Of all my aims as Secretary-General, there is none to which I feel more deeply committed than that of enabling the United Nations never again to fail in protecting a civilian population from genocide or mass slaughter.

3.5 Limits on Disclosure Obligations: National Security and Confidentiality

The discussion so far is about the obligations of disclosure and the reasons for them. But, to return to the qualifying or negative purpose of the New Zealand Official Information Act, the treaty material also places limits on the obligations to disclose, to protect various state interests especially in the area of national security. So the ILC draft on liability provides that

Article 15. National security and industrial secrets
Data and information vital to the national security of the State of origin or to the protection of industrial secrets may be withheld, but the State of origin shall cooperate in good faith with the other States concerned in providing as much information as can be provided under the circumstances.

That provision is modelled on the provision in the Convention on the Law on the Non-Navigational Uses of Watercourses, although that protective provision does not extend beyond national defence and security to industrial secrets, thereby avoiding the danger of commercial reasons being misused to protect information. On their face both exceptions are objective in the sense that the State does not conclusively decide that the exception applies. By contrast, it might appear, provisions of the General Agreement on Tariffs and Trade (GATT) and related instruments enable states to withhold information simply on their assessment of their security interests. The GATT provisions read as follows:

Security Exceptions

Nothing in this Agreement shall be construed

(a) to require any contracting party to furnish any information the disclosure of which it considers contrary to its essential security interests; or

(b) to prevent any contracting party from taking any action which it considers necessary for the protection of its essential security interests
    (i)   relating to fissionable materials or the materials from which they are derived;
    (ii) relating to the traffic in arms, ammunition and implements of war and such traffic in other goods and materials as is carried on directly for the purpose of supplying a military establishment;
    (iii) taken in time of war or other emergency in international relations; or

(c) to prevent any contracting party from taking any action in pursuance of its obligations under the United Nations Charter for the maintenance of international peace and security.[58]

The detail of para. (b) of the provision, distinguishing as it does between different security interests, suggests that the contracting party does not have complete freedom. A recent study based on the wording and history of the provision and the practice relating to it reached this balanced conclusion:

In principle, the competence of the WTO Dispute Settlement Body, the panels and the Appellate Body to hear and pass judgment on cases of nullification or impairment is neither directly nor indirectly limited by the invocation of the national security exception of Article XXI of GATT 1994 by the defendant state party. Nevertheless, history, function, state practice and the text of the provision strongly suggest that parts of the legal requirements set out are essentially subjective concepts to be defined *in concreto*, in most instances by the defendant party. In particular, the concept of national security, or 'essential security interests,' is a function of contemporary sovereignty, and as such demands individualization, or individual definition, by the state concerned before its concepts of 'emergency' and 'necessity.' WTO members, in other words, reserve a certain definitional prerogative to themselves. Any panel dealing with such issues will have to defer to the government concerned in that regard.

Nevertheless, the reach of this prerogative is limited by the concepts themselves. They are broad and in need of further definition but are clearly not unlimited. To establish these limits is an interpretative task and as such is subject to panel and Appellate Body review. That review is imperative is amply demonstrated by the obvious danger of abuse, as well as the essentially rule-based approach underlying the WTO in general, and the 'new' dispute settlement mechanism in particular. The world trading system's policies of security and predictability (DSU Art. 3) demand that some controls be placed on such discretion.[59]

---

[58] Article XXI of GATT; there are similar provisions in the General Agreement on Trade in Services, Art. XIV bis and Agreement on Trade Related Aspects of Intellectual Property Rights, Art. 73. The Chemical Weapons Convention provides for inspection by and the provision of extensive information by States Parties to the Secretariat. An Annex to the Convention on the Prohibition of Confidential Information gives the power to classify information to the State in issue. Among David Williams's many contributions is a discussion of who should decide disputes about access to information; 'Official Secrecy in the Courts' in P. R. Glazebrook (ed.), *Reshaping the Criminal Law: Essays in Honour of Glanville Williams* (London: Stevens, 1978) 154, 167, 172–3.

[59] Hannes Schloemann and Stefan Ohloff 'Constitutionalisation and dispute settlement in the WTO: National security as an issue of competence' (1999) 93 AJIL 424, 450; see also Antonio Perez 'WTO and UN Law: Institutional Comity in National Security' (1998) 23 Yale JIL 301.

The power to withhold information, conferred in para. (a), is not stated within the same constraints and the authors' opinion is that the wording 'leaves little room for third party interpretive efforts'. The wording 'leaves vast discretion . . . Although "consideration" must be exercised in good faith, showing that a government acted in bad faith is next to impossible in practice, where the information to be disclosed is known only by the member concerned'.[60] The provision is also not subject to any balancing or limiting factor. By contrast the power conferred by the 1998 European Environmental Convention, mentioned earlier, to withhold information on the ground that disclosure would adversely affect international relations, national defence or public security, is subject to this direction:

The . . . grounds for refusal shall be interpreted in a restrictive way, taking into account the public interest served by disclosure and taking into account whether the information requested relates to emissions into the environment.[61]

The issue arising under the provisions is like that presented by the 'self judging' defence and domestic jurisdiction reservations to acceptances of the jurisdiction of the International Court. On the one side is the apparent commitment to the international rule of law and submission to third party adjudication but on the other is asserted the sovereign claim to declare a matter political or non-justiciable. The latter interest or instinct is still very strong.[62]

A similar caution is also frequently to be observed in the protection accorded internationally (as nationally) to information provided in confidence. The practice of the International Committee of the Red Cross (ICRC) provides a notable example. It calculates, on the basis of over 130 years of experience, that it can more effectively pursue its vital humanitarian mission, which depends on state co-operation for access, by communicating only with the parties to the conflict and governments affected. It is only in the most extreme cases that it speaks out on particular atrocities, seeing publicity as very much a last resort—but as nevertheless available to it.[63]

---

[60]   ibid. 445.   [61]   See n. 45 above, Art. 4(4).

[62]   e.g. Shabtai Rosenne, *The Law and Practice of the International Court 1920–1996* (The Hague: Nijhoff, 1997) ch. 12.

[63]   e.g. Caroline Moorehead, *Dunant's Dream: War, Switzerland and the History of the Red Cross* (London: Harper Collins, 1998) and *International Review of the Red Cross*, No. 221, March–April 1981. The special, perhaps unique position of ICRC employees has been recognized by a ruling of a trial chamber of the International Criminal Tribunal for former Yugoslavia given on 27 July 1999 and released on 1 October 1999. The chamber ruled that customary international law provides the ICRC with an absolute right to non-disclosure of information relating to the work of the ICRC in the possession of one of its employees; consequently no issue arises about balancing its confidentiality interest against the interest of justice. The chamber reached that conclusion on the basis of the principle derived from the mandate entrusted to the ICRC under the Geneva Conventions (with 188 States parties) and Additional Protocols; and in particular it focused on the three fundamental principles of impartiality, neutrality and independence. The right to non-disclosure of information relating to the ICRC's activities in the possession of its employees in judicial proceedings is necessary for the effective discharge by the ICRC of its mandate; *Prosecutor v Blagoje Simic and others* Case No IT-95-9-PT, 27 July 1999; Judge David Hunt in a separate opinion did not on his view of the facts have to reach the issue whether the protection was absolute. See also the ICTY Press Release, 8 October 1999, *International Review of the Red Cross*, No. 836, December 1999, 945.

The reasoning in the ICRC case can be replicated, if with variations, in many other areas. Thus the worldwide chemical industry may well not have been willing to accept the Chemical Weapons Convention with its extensive requirements of disclosure to, and wide inspection powers by the Secretariat without extensive protections of confidential information including trade secrets. The information is made available only to allow for the testing of compliance. These two instances highlight that information might be disclosed only to the relevant international body or to other states directly affected, or to the public at large. A further variable is that the obligation may be positive, requiring notification, or negative, permitting access, in either case on a restricted basis (to those directly affected) or generally (including the public at large). The choices between those variables are of course critical in the elaboration of information regimes.

This small sample of international practice and agreements again highlights the need for care in responding to broad claims to secrecy in respect of international and related matters. Blanket claims cannot be sustained.

4. CONSEQUENCES FOR NATIONAL INSTITUTIONS

This overview suggests consequences for attitudes commonly taken by national institutions towards international relations, defence and security, for national constitutional systems, and for the legal profession and legal education.

First, while legislatures and courts continue to treat international relations, defence and national security as areas with special characteristics, some signs are appearing of a more careful discriminating approach. Those signs recognize that some of the claims to unfettered executive power or to uncontrolled protection of information may be extravagant and indeed dangerous. Some of the information may be able to be made public without any disadvantage and indeed often with real advantage.

I refer again to Senator Moynihan's *Secrecy*. It is a sustained compelling argument, supported by a wealth of detail, that secrecy has had disastrous consequences for United States foreign policy and in particular for its (and the world's) relationships with Russia:

What if we had better calculated the forces of ethnicity so that we could have avoided going directly from the 'end' of the Cold War to a new Balkan War, leaving little attention and far fewer resources for the shattered Soviet empire?

There it rests, with the one remaining large and positive possibility. Openness. East and West paid hideous costs for keeping matters of state closed to the people whom the states embodied.[64]

He proposes that:

---

[64] n. 22 above, 226.

In order for a culture of openness to develop within government, the present culture of secrecy must be restrained by statute. Let law determine behavior, as it did in the case of the Administrative Procedure Act. A statute defining and limiting secrecy will not put an end to over-classification and needless classification, but it will help.[65]

He quoted George Kennan to support the proposition that a huge proportion of classifying is futile anyway:

It is my conviction, based on some 70 years of experience, first as a government official and then in the past 45 years as an historian, that the need by our government for *secret* intelligence about affairs elsewhere in the world has been vastly overrated. I would say that something upwards of 95% of what we need to know about foreign countries could be very well obtained by careful and competent study of perfectly legitimate sources of information open and available to us in the rich library and archival holdings of this country.' As for the remaining 5%, we could easily and nonsecretively, find most of that in similar sources abroad.[66]

A critical aspect of the operation of freedom of information regimes is education, especially of the public sector, emphasizing the Moynihan lesson that openness will often produce better decisions;[67] at the least, those who have had the opportunity to participate have less reason to complain.

A recent examination by the New Zealand Court of Appeal of legislative choices made by the New Zealand Parliament helps indicate possible lines of decision. The Court did that when suggesting that the Prime Minister, as Minister in charge of the Security Intelligence Service, consider submitting a more particular certificate in support of a claim to withhold certain Service documents. The statute book:

(a) uses 'security' or 'national security' alone or along with defence
   • for the purposes of defining criminal offences
   • to justify the refusal of the disclosure of information to the public
   • to justify the refusal of the disclosure of information to, and cooperation with, foreign law enforcement agencies
   • to allow state use of intellectual and industrial property
   • to support state exemption from resource management and building consents requirements
   • as a ground for deportation
(b) distinguishes between local and foreign aspects of security, for instance in security intelligence service legislation
(c) distinguishes between process and substantive aspects of security
(d) defines 'security' narrowly or widely, for instance by including or not terrorism, and making wide reference to international or economic wellbeing

---

[65] n. 22 above, 226.
[66] ibid. 227.
[67] The New Zealand Law Commission has stated its conclusion that the assumption that policy advice will eventually be released under the Official Information Act has improved the quality and transparency of the advice (n. 34 above) para. E18. The mindset of Wellington Ministers and officials appears to be sharply different from those in Whitehall, at least so far as the latter can be assessed from the Freedom of Information Bill currently (March 2000) before Parliament in Westminster.

(e) sometimes confers apparently conclusive power on Ministers to prevent independent examination of an issue including release of information

It was obvious that not all risks to national security called for equal treatment.[68]

The lessons learned in the working of national freedom of information regimes, notably the frequent disclosure of Cabinet papers following the assessment of particular and competing interests, are capable of being applied more widely. And, to anticipate the next comment, an unduly deferential attitude, when taken with the huge globalizing forces sweeping the world, will remove regular open democratic and parliamentary processes from areas of activity where they once played a full role.

The second comment relates to the fact that much law is now being made elsewhere and not, in the first instance at least, through national lawmaking bodies. That fact is now more widely recognized, indeed to the extent of sometimes being stigmatized as involving 'a democratic deficit'—a criticism which may fail to have regard to the fact that Ministers who negotiate international commitments or who are responsible for that process are elected and democratically accountable. Important steps have been and continue to be made in the United Kingdom (building on the steps first taken in 1924), Australia and New Zealand to address this matter, notably through enhanced parliamentary participation in the acceptance of treaties.[69] But, as extensive commentary and reform proposals indicate, those changes relate to only one phase of the treaty making process and further reform is called for. The recent reforms relate to the stage of the acceptance of treaties. They do not include the earlier stages of agenda setting and negotiation—the 'openly arrived at' stage of Woodrow Wilson's first point—nor all of the later stages of implementation.

So far as agenda setting and negotiation are concerned, we begin with the prerogative of the executive to conduct foreign and defence policy. In law, as noted at the outset, those powers were essentially not subject to judicial control and were indifferently, if at all, subject to parliamentary scrutiny. But Parliaments have increasingly claimed control, or at least a role, especially in respect of the disposition of the armed forces abroad in situations of armed conflict, as well as in treaty making. Interested groups and individuals are now also much more involved, greatly helped by new technology. So, recently, NGOs have had critical roles in:

- agenda setting, for instance, in getting the banning of anti-personnel land mines on to the international agenda and taking the proposed Multilateral Agreement on Investment off it;
- the actual negotiation, for example, of the Rome Statute on the International Criminal Court; and
- the implementation of the international texts, such as in the follow-up work on that Statute and national reporting to monitoring committees set up under human rights treaties.

---

[68] *Choudry v Attorney-General* [1999] 2 NZLR 582, 594–5. See further n. 10 above.

[69] See e.g. New Zealand Law Commission, *The Treaty Making Process: Reform and the Role of Parliament* (NZLC R 45 1997) especially appendix A.

Improvements can also be observed in respect of the statutory implementation of treaty provisions, with some signs that parliamentary drafters are more willing, when it is appropriate, to leave the treaty text to speak for itself as part of national law.

Finally, the globalizing forces present us with a real challenge as lawyers in practice, in the law schools and on the bench. Do they not require a new understanding of law and legal systems in which state systems have a sharply different role? When we moved from official *secrets* legislation to *freedom* of information legislation, 'the Queen's papers became the people's'.[70] Well over a century ago Professor F. W. Maitland told us that about half the cases reported in the Queen's Bench reports had to do with rules of administrative law,[71] but, as Sir David Williams has reminded us, it was more than half a century later that the indefatigable Sir William Wade got the message through to the wider legal profession, in England at least.[72] The proper recognition of the place of international law and its processes in our national systems may require an even bigger change of mindset, along the lines indicated by Tolstoy in the final paragraph of *War and Peace*. Given his great affection for our part of the world, Sir David might prefer this image from a great New Zealand poet, Allen Curnow:

> Simply by sailing in a new direction
> You could enlarge the world.[73]

---

[70] *Lange v Atkinson* [1998] 3 NZLR 424, 463; see similarly Sir Stephen Sedley's reference to the proprietorial premise of much law bearing on information, and Lord Lester's evidence, quoted by Stephanie Palmer, that official information is not or should not be regarded as government property; ultimately that information belongs to the people whose interests Ministers and civil servants are elected or appointed to serve.

[71] F. W. Maitland, *The Constitutional History of England* (lectures delivered in 1888) (Cambridge, 1908) 505.

[72] 'Sir William Wade' in Christopher Forsyth and Ivan Hare (eds.) (n. 7 above) 1, e.g. the reference to the excitement of the pioneer at 13.

[73] *Landfall in Unknown Seas* (1943).

22

Freedom of Information in Commercial Disputes

MALCOLM CLARKE

1. INTRODUCTION

A current assumption of commerce and of commercial law is that decisions are more likely to be 'good' decisions if reached by persons fully and freely informed. This is widely accepted not only as regards persons making contracts but also those who must help to resolve disputes between contracting parties later. This paper concerns information and the settlement of contractual disputes. Once the facts are clear, they must be tested against the contract. This paper considers mainly the task of working out what the contract means, and some obstacles to the free availability of the information needed. The relevant information is primarily found in the relevant contract terms but it is not free unless it can be understood.[1] Transparency of content is of particular importance when contracts are in standard form because market efficiency depends on easy and accurate product comparison. In the case of insurance, for example,

product disclosure is about the contract, coverage and exclusions. A policyholder or adviser needs to know exactly what risks are covered and what risks are excluded from the coverage. . . . Lack of information in this area may cause serious trouble to policyholders but also impose huge costs to society in some instances (liability claims). Policyholders need also to know about the premium and any additional charges such as agents commissions in order to make comparisons and effectively 'shop around' in the market.[2]

What is true of insurance contracts is no less true of standard form contracts in other areas. What is true for contracting parties and their advisers is no less true for the tribunal which may have to resolve disputes at a later stage. As Lord Mustill said in a recently published lecture,[3] it is 'no good concluding a tight contract if it is written down in words which are contradictory, ambiguous, incomplete, or incomprehensible. It is no good having an agreement which is well conceived and reduced to writing, if the dispute resolution procedures cannot be relied on . . . The fact that the whole process from negotiation to judgment, award or settlement, is a continuum of risk management has already been recognized in some industries where dispute resolution is an integral and properly thought-out element of the contractual scheme as

---

[1] Beatson, *Anson's Law of Contract* (27th edn., Oxford: OUP 1998) 159 *et seq.*

[2] K. Kruni, 'Information Disclosure in a Competitive Insurance Market—The Government Role', Geneva Papers on Risk and Insurance, 23 (No. 87, April 1998) 224–46, 233.

[3] Lord Mustill, 'Convergence and Divergence in Marine Insurance Law' (2000) 31 JMLC 1–14, 13.

a whole'. In the ideal world of minimal transaction costs, contracts are clear and concise. They require no further explanation or special knowledge to be understood and applied. However, if this world exists, English law has not yet found it. Lord Justice Staughton once remarked that, over forty years as a barrister and a judge, 'something like 90 per cent of cases on contract law that I met were concerned with interpretation'.[4]

2. FREEDOM OF ACCESS: FINDING CONTRACT TERMS

As a preliminary requirement, the terms of the contract in their entirety must be accessible. If not so at the time of contracting, the rule of contract law is that they are not part of the contract anyway. The basic rule of contract law is that a person contracting on the standard terms of the other party is bound by those terms although, in actuality, that person is sometimes quite unaware of their very existence still less their content.[5] It is a rule designed to reduce transaction costs. It rests on a presumption that people know or should know that the terms exist and that, if they want to read them, they can obtain them. Such products are regarded like the confections of the cafeteria—it is cheaper to say 'take it or leave it' but, if you want it, 'come and get it' than to take a customer's order and serve it. However, the law does little to ensure that terms are easy to find or to read.

In a famous railway case the court assumed, as it would of people today, that Mrs Thompson knew that railway companies have contract terms. The particular term, however, could be found only by following the instruction on her ticket to see the company's timetable, where the term was printed on page 552. The Court of Appeal held that she was bound by the term even though she was illiterate.[6] That was in 1929. If the Mrs Thompson of today, contemplating a Christmas shopping trip to Calais and wishing perhaps to see if the 'information explosion' has changed anything, tried to get a copy of Eurorail conditions, she would find that, although the law has changed in her favour, in practice they are just as hard to get.

As to the law, the 1929 decision was described as the 'high-water mark' of the common law rule of constructive notice.[7] The Mrs Thompson of today can turn to the Unfair Terms in Consumer Contracts Regulations 1999. The Office of Fair Trading has published a list of categories of terms that might be regarded as unfair.[8] Heading the list of unfair terms is the category of 'hidden terms', terms with which the person has no real opportunity of becoming acquainted before the conclusion of

---

[4] 'Interpretation of Maritime Contracts' (1995) 26 JMLC 259–71, 260.
[5] *British Crane Hire Corp. Ltd. v Ipswich Plant Hire Ltd.* [1975] QB 303, CA.; *Circle Freight Int. Ltd. v Medeast Gulf Exports Ltd.* [1988] 2 Lloyd's Rep. 427, CA.
[6] *Thompson v LM.S. Ry. Co.* [1930] 1 KB 41.
[7] G. C. Cheshire, C. H. S. Fifoot, M. P. Furmston, *Cheshire & Fifoot's Law of Contract* (6th edn., London; Butterworths, 1964) 110.
[8] Office of Fair Trading, *Unfair Contract Terms*, Bulletin No. 4 (December 1997) 11.

the contract'.[9] It seems likely that the term of 1929 would be struck out of the modern consumer contract on that ground.

If, however, Mrs Thompson were not a consumer but a business person going to a meeting in Paris, she would find that the law still allows lawyers to bury their treasure in small print. Winn J once said of a document before the court that it 'conforms to customary mercantile practice' in that it could be read only 'by eyes with an acuity unlikely to be enjoyed by any individual possessing sufficient maturity of mind to understand it' and was 'verbose, tautologous and obscure'. Moreover, he was concerned with a condition in that document which could be found only 'at a stage somewhat beyond the middle of the Sabbath day's journey' which the reader of the document had to perform'.[10] It was a commercial case and he applied it nonetheless. That was in 1959 but in practice today things are not much better. An indefensible practice in a world of word processors and websites is that of the updating of documents by reference to other documents or by supplements with a gaggle of gobbetts and amendments. A common example, which affects consumers and people in business alike, is that of the annual renewal of insurance policies by a sheet or two of paper listing the amendments and which leaves the insured to piece them all together. Little better is the practice of incorporation by reference.

3. FREEDOM OF COMPREHENSION: PLAIN ENGLISH

Once one has gathered together all the terms of the contract, the next step is to seek to make sense of the jigsaw. In recent years there has been a movement for contracts to be in 'plain English'. This is the modern medium for Mondeo man, the stereotype who has replaced the man once found in the street or on the Clapham omnibus but who now prefers to be seen in his car talking in plain terms on his mobile phone. Plain English is for Mondeo man on the assumption that (when he is not driving his car or talking on his phone) he has the time and interest to read his contracts. The movement is for transparency at the contracting stage but, of course, if used then, it will also be the medium at the dispute stage. The 'plain English' movement has been driven largely by dislike of people such as lawyers and civil servants, and of the language they use. The sentiments are not new. It was St Luke who wrote: 'Woe unto you, lawyers! for ye have taken away the key of knowledge: ye entered not in yourselves, and them that were entering in ye hindered.'[11] Today, there is scepticism about so-called experts, and a movement for demystification which, as regards documents, is manifested in the movement for 'plain' English. Unfortunately, plain English, like Mondeo man himself, is something of a fantasy, which leaves such

---

[9] This is a reference to the Unfair Terms in Consumer Contracts Regs. 1994, SI 1994/3159, Sch. 3, para. 1(I).

[10] *Derby Cables Ltd. v Frederick Oldridge Ltd.* [1959] 2 Lloyd's Rep 140, 149, 150.

[11] St. Luke, xi: 52.

people as believe in it in a fool's paradise as long as no dispute arises but which may well leave them in the dark when it does.

One of the first problems is a lack of agreement about whose English is plain English. Was it George Bernard Shaw who spoke of the United Kingdom and the United States as two nations divided by a common language? No doubt he would have agreed with the Office of Fair Trading, which recently condemned[12] the use of American English in contracts as not being plain and intelligible, as required by the Unfair Terms in Consumer Contracts Regulations 1999.[13] But what would they have made of the English spoken and written in Scotland and Wales or, for that matter, Yorkshire and Cornwall and the modern BBC? Let us suppose, however, for argument's sake, that plain English is located in Essex, further problems for the cause of plainness are inherent in the nature of the words themselves.

First, the meaning of words changes. One of the virtues of a living language is adaptability: Essex English changes not only with the place but also the time. It has not been calcified by any *Académie Anglaise* in London, Oxford or anywhere else. Even the OED will soon be on line. Moreover, one publisher of dictionaries no longer purports to produce a definitive written work but has joined a university department to create a database of the use of English, which has well over 200 million entries and changes all the time. The plain meaning, it has been suggested,[14] is 'incapable of responding without lag to a world that changes faster than language'.[15] Moreover, some words, such as 'building' and 'goods', have a fringe of meaning, a penumbra of uncertainty, that defies precise definition.

Second, words mean different things to different people. The user of plain English must allow for the emotive power of words. Even at the same place and the same time, such as Essex 2000, words may mean slightly different things to different people on account of the purely personal associations or desires which those people bring to the words. Like Alice in Wonderland, people in Essex are likely to think that words mean (or should mean) what they want them to mean. For example, in spite of serious efforts by the insurance industry to make its policies more transparent, of the 3,444 cases closed by the Insurance Ombudsman Bureau in 1998, 52 per cent[16] concerned coverage disputes. People from Land's End to John O' Groats find it hard to accept that *their* insurance does not cover *their* loss; and that what is plain to them is not plain to others.

As was once observed (in China rather than Essex) 'he who knows does not speak, he who speaks does not know'. However, if to be entirely plain is plainly impossible, it is no more possible in practice for people, like certain orders of monks, to live in

---

[12] Office of Fair Trading, *Unfair Contract Terms*, Bulletin No. 5 (October 1998) 41.

[13] S.I 1994/3159, reg. 3(2).

[14] F. Schauer, 'Statutory Construction and the Coordinating Function of Plain Meaning' 1990 Sup Ct Rev 231–56, 252.

[15] For example, in *Re NRG Victory Reinsurance Ltd.* [1995] 1 All ER 533 the court applied an 'ordinary' meaning of 'insurance' which differed from that in the dictionary.

[16] Insurance Ombudsman Bureau, Annual Report 1999, 24.

silence. Ground rules must be agreed. Contracts must be composed. Clarity should be sought. In practice, fortunately, it is often possible to be plain enough for the purpose in hand by using the language most suited to the intended readership. However, the contemporary faith in plain English, it is submitted, does not provide anything like salvation. There is no English, old or new, that will be sufficiently understood by everybody; and if plain English in the vernacular sense, whether of pub or club, is employed for any but the simplest contracts, it will scarcely be understood by anybody once subjected to the scrutiny of a court.

4. FREEDOM OF COMPREHENSION: PLAIN PRECEDENT

4.1 The Role of Precedent

When people want to give precise instructions to computers, they do not use words in plain English or plain American, whether that of Silicon Valley or Silicon Fen. They use special languages. This is not to suggest for contracts the language of mathematics. As Glanville Williams once observed, Euclidean geometry 'starts from notions of points and lines which, having no size, are not objects of sense; thus the figures constructed from these notions are not objects of sense either',[17] at least, not for laymen. Nonetheless, for precise and predictable communication, technical language is unavoidable in some degree and in the life of the law that language is largely the language of precedent. If a word or phrase acquires a meaning by precedent which it does not bear in plain English, that, surely, is justifiable in the interests of certainty. Lawyers who draft contracts, as well as judges who interpret them, know what it means even if others do not.[18] Some disputes, at least, will be avoided and others expeditiously settled if those concerned can rely on that.

Like any traveller in a foreign land, the Essex man who comes to the world of contracts must not expect signs in Essex English. If he does not understand what he reads, he must get a dictionary or an interpreter—a book or a legal adviser. When it comes to commercial contracts and perhaps also consumer contracts, this still seems to be the best accommodation of certainty and comprehension. This has been acknowledged, for example, by the Banking Code.[19] Article 1.1 provides that subscribers to the Code will 'give you information on our services and products in plain language'. However, it continues: 'and offer help if there is any aspect which you do not understand'. At the end is a definition section which begins with the caution: 'These definitions explain the meaning of words and terms used in the Code. They are not precise legal or technical definitions.' Again, the Insurance Law of New York (s. 142) requires that policies use words with common and everyday

---

[17] G. L. Williams, 'Language and the Law' (1945) 61 LQR 293–303, 300.
[18] *Newbury v Turngiant* (1991) 63 P & CR 458, 478 per Staughton LJ, CA.
[19] 1998 edition, in effect from 31 March 1999.

meanings to facilitate readability and to aid the insured or policyholder in under-standing' the cover, *wherever practicable*. My submission is that something of this order is the best we can expect.

4.2 The Limits of Precedent

For the legal meaning of a word or phrase the search for precedent often begins with an established textbook and, if nothing comes quickly to hand, and then the searcher turns to a database, the virtual library. There the search may start in the local juris-diction but, if desired, spread as far afield, for example, as unprinted decisions of courts in Australia. And why not? Prima facie lawyers in the common law world speak the same language and the word 'widget' means the same in one place as it does in another. But does it? There are at least two phenomena that suggest that this cannot be assumed.

One arises even within a single jurisdiction when a lawyer from one branch of the law comes, perhaps as judge, to another branch and finds a word which looks famil-iar but in reality means something else. A well known example is 'warranty' which means one thing in a sales contract and another in an insurance policy. Arguably, another example is 'appropriation' in civil law and criminal law. The meaning in criminal law was muddied in *Gomez*[20] by judges who, having spent most of their legal lives in other branches of the law, did not fully appreciate the significance of the distinction between theft and criminal deception.

The other, which can be regarded as a more general instance of the first, stems from globalization of legal services and hence of drafting: the possibility that a docu-ment drafted by a lawyer of one jurisdiction will be available for use by a lawyer, perhaps of the same firm, in another. This may well occur in areas of commercial law, such as transport and insurance, which, in practice, have few boundaries.

For example, the storm in the Channel which the English courts would regard as a 'peril of the seas' sufficient to exonerate a sea carrier for cargo damage might look, to the courts of New York, like no more than a storm in an English teacup and anything but sufficient to excuse.[21] Again, one might have thought that a 'riot' in London would be a 'riot' in New York and vice versa. However, in one case,[22] a large aircraft was quietly hijacked in the air by a small group of terrorists, two on the aircraft and the rest on the ground. The English insurer argued before the court in New York that this was a riot and that, therefore, the loss of the aircraft was excluded from the insurance cover. Having politely expressed 'deference' on matters of insurance law to

---

[20]   *R v Gomez* [1993] AC 442.

[21]   M. A. Clarke, 'A Way with Words: Some Obstacles to Uniform Transport Law', ULR 1998, 351–69, 352 *et seq*. Australian law is still closer to the English view: *Great China Metal Industries Co. v Malaysian Shipping Corp.* (1998) 72 ALJR 1592, HCA. Ping-fat, 'Perils of the sea in marine cargo claims:an Australian perspective', (1999) 18 Trading Law 184–97. Concerning divergent interpretation of 'wilful misconduct': see Clarke 361 *et seq*.

[22]   *Pan American World Airways Inc. v Aetna Casualty & Surety Co.* [1974] 1 Lloyd's Rep 207, SDNY, 1973.

the 'ancestral authorities on the old mysteries', the court dismissed the argument. The 'notion of a flying riot in geographic instalments cannot be squeezed into the ancient formula'.[23] Riot, said the court, cannot be 'conducted by mail, by telephone, or as in the present case, by radio'.[24] The court preferred what it saw as the common sense and popular idea of riot, which connoted some degree of tumult. In English common law there is precedent for a quiet riot of only three people.[25] English law has been changed by statute[26] and now requires twelve people for a riot. Although, obviously, tumult is more likely with the statutory dozen than the common law trio, it is still likely that in English law a quiet riot by a disciplined rugby team is possible; but that a court in New York would still be unimpressed.

5. FREEDOM OF COMPREHENSION: A PLAIN BACKGROUND

In practice the quest for the meaning of a single word or short phrase often begins with the dictionary. The limits of dictionaries are well known,[27] not least that the dictionary meaning may be out of date. Steyn LJ, as he then was, once said that dictionaries 'never solve concrete problems of construction. The meaning of words cannot be ascertained divorced from their context'.[28] But what is that? Clearly, it includes the rest of the document: a succession of circles—the phrase, the sentence, the paragraph, the part of the contract, the whole of the contract. However, he also said that 'part of the contextual scene is the purpose of the provision'.[29] To get a clear picture of that the court must look beyond the contractual document, but how far? Perhaps the past dealings of the parities, the market in which they deal.[30] At this point the reader of a document, especially the court, must face problems of uncertainty and cost brought to a head by Lord Hoffmann's 'school' of interpretation which finds the true meaning of a contractual document by the study of the 'matrix' or 'background' of the contract.

According to traditional teaching on interpretation, the search for meaning of a word or phrase takes the court outward from one circle (sentence, paragraph and so on) to another, until it meets a barrier on the outskirts of the document in the form of the parol evidence rule. Traditionally, if a court wants to go outside the document, it has to take one of three routes. The first is marked 'technical': that, although the words appear clear they have a technical meaning that is not apparent without seeking

---

[23] ibid. at 232 per Frankel, DJ.
[24] *Pan American World Airways Inc. v Aetna Casualty & Surety Co.* [1975] 1 Lloyd's Rep 77, 99 per Hays, J. (US CA, 2 Cir).
[25] *Motor Union Ins. Co. Ltd. v Boggan* (1923) 130 L.T. 588, HL.
[26] By the Public Order Act 1936, s. 1.
[27] See n. 14 above.
[28] In *Arbuthnot v Fagan* (CA, 30 July 1993), quoted by Mance J in *Charter Reinsurance Co. Ltd. v Fagan* [1997] AC 313, 326.
[29] ibid.
[30] M. A. Clarke, *The Law of Insurance Contracts* (London: LLP, 2000) ch. 15–3.

extrinsic evidence.[31] The second is marked 'ambiguity': that the words are not clear when read in the context of the document alone and the ambiguity must be resolved by taking a wider view.[32] The third is marked 'absurdity': that a literal reading of the words in the context of the document alone gives a meaning that is not just unreasonable but unworkable or absurd; and that that meaning should be avoided by taking a wider view that makes more sense.[33] The wider view takes in the purpose of the contract and, more than that, it takes some account of the background in which such contracts are constructed.

This is well illustrated by the 1997 decision of the Court of Appeal in *Adams v British Airways plc*.[34] The plaintiffs, junior British Airways (BA) pilots, had contracts of employment with terms about their seniority over 'new entrants'. Then BA merged with another airline, British Caledonian (B. Cal.), and pilots from B. Cal. were not treated as 'new entrants', as the plaintiffs said they should have been, but ranked above the plaintiffs. Indeed, Sir Thomas Bingham MR, agreed that a 'literal reading of the language of the plaintiffs' contracts yields the construction for which the plaintiffs contended and which the judge upheld'.[35] However, the other members of the Court of Appeal agreed with his reason for allowing the appeal. As regards construction of the contract of employment, the 'starting point is that the parties meant what they said and said what they meant'; but a contract today must 'be construed in its factual setting as known to the parties at the time. Where the meaning of an agreement is clear beyond argument, the factual setting will have little or no bearing on construction; but to construe an agreement in its factual setting is a proper, because a common sense, approach to construction, and it is not necessary to find an agreement ambiguous before following it'.[36]

In the particular case, common sense suggested a wider view. He observed that it may have been that the parties to the agreement did not direct their minds to the possibility of a large-scale merger of airline operations such as occurred, but it was 'permissible to ask whether the parities can reasonably be supposed to have intended the agreement to apply in such an event'. He concluded that it would have been 'very surprising if BA had intended to bind itself so as to be obliged to choose between accepting consequences which were foreseeably absurd and giving its pilots a right of veto redeemable, if at all, only at a potentially high price'.[37]

In short, in 1997 the law was that a court must apply the terms of the contract as they were written, unless they were ambiguous or their consequences were manifestly absurd. Only then was the court entitled to look outside the contract itself to the setting in which it was concluded.

---

[31] K. Lewison, *The Interpretation of Contracts* (2nd edn., London: Sweet & Maxwell, 1997) ch. 4.09.
[32] Lewison (n. 31 above) ch. 7.05.   [33] Clarke (n. 30 above) ch. 15–4.
[34] [1996] IRLR 574.   [35] ibid. 577.
[36] ibid.
[37] ibid. Among the consequences would have been that senior captains from B. Cal. would have had to serve under junior pilots from BA on routes and in aircraft which the former knew better than the latter.

5.1 Breaking Bounds: The *Investors'* Case

The traditional barrier was broken in 1997 by Lord Hoffmann in the *Investors* case.[38] He referred to 'the fundamental change which has overtaken this branch of the law, particularly as a result of the speeches of Lord Wilberforce' and concluded that, in the search for what the parties meant, almost all 'the old intellectual baggage of "legal" interpretation has been discarded'.[39] Instead, he said, the 'meaning of a document . . . is what the parties using those words against the relevant background would reasonably have been understood to mean. The background may not merely enable the reasonable man to choose between the possible meanings of words which are ambiguous but even . . . to conclude that the parties must, for whatever reason, have used the wrong words or syntax'.[40] The background was what 'was famously referred to by Lord Wilberforce as "the matrix of fact", but', continued Lord Hoffmann, 'this phrase is, if anything, an understated description of what the background may include. *Subject to the requirement that it should have been reasonably available to the parties . . . it includes absolutely anything* which would have affected the way in which the language of the document would have been understood by a reasonable man'.[41] Not surprisingly, these statements have been read as allowing the court out into the wider world beyond the document itself to consider extrinsic evidence of the entire background from the start. The corollary is that the court is no longer required to justify excursions through the barrier and out of the context of the document on the traditional and limited grounds.

All this is more of a novelty than Lord Hoffman would have us believe. Sir Christopher Staughton has shown[42] that the speeches of Lord Wilberforce[43] do not fully support Lord Hoffmann's conclusion. Indeed, in an earlier case but one which post-dates the relevant speeches of Lord Wilberforce, Lord Hoffmann himself denied that 'business common sense' might authorize the court to 'rewrite the language which the parties have used'.[44] It remains to be seen to what extent the words of Lord Hoffmann will be given the literal effect which, it seems, he is ready to deny to the contract wording of others. A leading commentator has suggested that, although in *Investors* Lord Hoffmann spoke of 'fundamental change', the 'difference between the traditional approach and the modern approach is more a difference of emphasis, albeit a very important difference of emphasis'.[45] However, if the difference is

---

[38] *Investors Compensation Scheme Ltd. v West Bromwich B.S.* [1998] 1 WLR 896, HL. Some courts, however, have taken the view that nothing has changed, e.g., *NLA Group v Bowers* [1999] 1 Lloyd's Rep 109, 112 per Timothy Walker J, concerning the interpretation of a Lloyd's slip policy.
[39] *Investors* (n. 38 above) 912.
[40] ibid. 913, with reference to *Antaios C.N. S.A. v Salen Rederierna A.B.* [1985] AC 191, 201 per Lord Diplock. Lord Goff, Lord Hope and Lord Clyde agreed with Lord Hoffmann.
[41] ibid. 912 (italics supplied).   [42] [1999] CLJ 303–13, 307.
[43] Notably *Prenn v Simmonds* [1971] 1 WLR 1381, 1385, HL.
[44] *Co-operative Wholesale Society v National Westminster Bank plc* [1995] 1 EGLR 97, 99.
[45] Morgan 'The Construction of Leases and Other Documents' (1999) 3 L & T Rev 88, 89. See also *NLA Group v Bowers* [1999] 1 Lloyd's Rep 109, 112 per Timothy Walker J.

anything much more than a difference of emphasis, English law would have reached the surprising position of allowing the courts more scope for 'creative interpretation'[46] than permitted to courts in the USA. On the one hand, courts there have recently been more cautious in application of the doctrine of reasonable expectations.[47] On the other hand, apart from that doctrine, courts in the USA still insist that they must apply the ordinary and literal meaning of words unless there is ambiguity.[48]

Decisions reported in England since *Investors* provide little hard evidence of fundamental change. In *Ham v Somak Travel*,[49] for example, people on holiday sustained injuries in an accident to a hot air balloon due to the negligence of the balloon operator. The holiday company discharged liability to the victims and sought indemnity under liability insurance in which, however, there was an exclusion in respect of 'injury . . . arising out of the . . . use of (a) craft designed to travel in or through air space . . . (b) motor vehicles' for which no specific indemnity was provided by the policy. There was a specific indemnity for certain motor vehicles but that was all. According to the traditional rules of interpretation the exclusion applied. However, reference to background of the kind advocated by Lord Hoffmann suggested otherwise. The Court of Appeal held that the exclusion was clear and should apply.

More recently, in *MDIS v Swinbank*, however, the Court of Appeal took a very small step out into the wider world of Lord Hoffmann to seek 'the meaning which the document would convey to a reasonable person having all the background knowledge' of the parties at the time of contract.[50] In the operative clause of a liability policy the insurer undertook to 'indemnify the Assured . . . against any claim for which the Assured may become legally liable . . . *alleging*: (a) Neglect Error or Omission'.[51] The policy also excluded claims 'resulting from' inter alia fraud by employees which the insured could reasonably have discovered. The insured settled a claim which alleged negligence but made no mention of fraud, although fraud had occurred. Dissenting, Peter Gibson LJ put a literal interpretation on the policy,[52] and concluded that the insurer should pay. The majority, however, read the words in the background of legal precedent and held otherwise.

---

[46] This was what it was called by Lord Lloyd dissenting in *Investors* (n. 38 above) at 904.

[47] See *Longaberger Co. v US Fidelity Co.*, 31 F Supp 2d 594 (SD Ohio, 1998). Doctrine rejected in England for non-consumer cases in *Smit Tak Offshore Services Ltd. v Youell* [1992] 1 Lloyd's Rep. 154, CA.

[48] See e.g. *S. W. Energy Corp. v Continental*, 974 P 2d 1239 (Utah, 1999). Of course, as ambiguity is tested there not by the lawyer's reading but that of the ordinary man, courts are more likely to find ambiguity.

[49] (CA, 4 February 1998). See also *Kirkaldy & Sons Ltd. v Walker* [1999] Lloyd's Rep IR 410, 416 per Longmore J. Cf *Kumar v AGF* [1999] Lloyd's Rep IR 147, 152 per Thomas J. Further, doubts have been expressed whether judges are or can practicably be placed in a position to make an informed judgment: M.A. Clarke 'Policies and Perceptions of Insurance' (Oxford, 1998) 242 *et seq.*

[50] [1999] Lloyd's Rep IR 516, 521, CA.   [51] Emphasis added.

[52] [1999] Lloyd's Rep IR 516 at 526, insisting that it was no accident that the exception referred to the result of discoverable fraud while the operative clause merely required an allegation.

The *MDIS* case is not a significant application of the Hoffmann 'school'. First, the background was all too apparent to the court, for it was 'well known amongst insurance lawyers and indeed brokers for many years and would have been likely to have been in the back of the minds of those negotiating this contract'.[53] Second, the actual decision was driven by an element of public policy, namely, transparency in litigation. The decision avoids a result whereby, when the claim settled alleges no more than neglect, the insurers must pay even though, given the opportunity to do so in court, they can prove that the proximate cause of the liability was something excluded by the policy. It discourages the well informed third party claimant to be 'economical with the truth'[54] by making a selective presentation of the facts to ensure that the insurance pays.

5.2 The Cost of Freedom

The particular background of legal precedent[55] in *MDIS* was but a CD-ROM away from the judges. Anyway, the substance of it was indeed well known to them, as was the tailoring of claims to match the insurance cover. That was also true of the particular background information in *Investors* itself and other such recent cases.[56] In *Kingscroft v Nissan (No. 2)*,[57] however, the hearing lasted from 14 April to 28 May 1999 and the court spent an appreciable part of that time looking at the background to reinsurance transactions although, the case being complex in other respects too, it is difficult to know exactly how much.

Kingscroft illustrates one of the difficulties about the *Investors* approach. As Sir Christopher Staughton observed of *Investors*, it is 'hard to imagine a ruling more calculated to perpetuate the vast cost of commercial litigation'.[58] The same point had been made before in *Dellborg*[59] by Saville LJ, as he then was, a decision of the Court of Appeal which regrettably has not been reported in printed form. Having acknowledged that 'nowadays agreements are not interpreted in a vacuum, but having regard to what the cases have described as the aim or purpose of the agreement and its surrounding circumstances', Saville LJ, with whom Thorpe and Judge LJJ agreed, referred to the traditional rule and continued:

However, where the words used have an unambiguous and sensible meaning as a matter of ordinary language, I see serious objections in an approach which would permit the surrounding circumstances to alter that meaning. Firstly . . . [this] would do nothing but add to the costs and delays of litigation and indeed arbitration, much of which is concerned with interpreting agreements. Secondly, the position of third parties (which would include assignees of contractual

---

[53] ibid. 422 per Clarke LJ

[54] For judicial statements that one must look behind the face of the claim, see Clarke (n. 30 above) 17–4E.

[55] It was mainly the judgment of Devlin J, as he then was, in *West Wake Price & Co. v Ching* [1957] 1 WLR 45, 53–4. [56] e.g. *Kumar v AGF* [1999] Lloyd's Rep IR 147.

[57] [1999] Lloyd's Rep IR 603. [58] ibid.

[59] *National Bank of Sharjah v Dellborg* (CA, 9 July 1997).

rights) does not seem to have been considered at all. They are unlikely in the nature of things to be aware of the surrounding circumstances. Where the words of the agreement have only one meaning, and that meaning is not self evidently nonsensical, is the third party justified in taking that to be the agreement that was made, or unable to rely on the words used without examining (which it is likely to be difficult or impossible for third parties to do) all the surrounding circumstances? If the former is the case, the law would have to treat the agreement as meaning one thing to the parties and another to third parties, hardly a satisfactory state of affairs. If the latter is the case, then unless third parties can discover all the surrounding circumstances and are satisfied that they make no difference, they cannot safely proceed to act on the basis of what the agreement actually says. This again would seem to be highly unsatisfactory.

As any researcher knows, a lot of time and hence money can be spent on a line of inquiry before it becomes clear that it is not worth going on; and, once a researcher is well on the way there is always an innate reluctance to stop. In an era of abundant information the line may be long and costly. Even if the court backs off any inquiry, the possibility of inquiry creates uncertainty and that alone has a cost. As Lord Lloyd, dissenting in the *Investors* case, said: 'Purposive interpretation of a contract is a useful tool where the purpose can be identified with reasonable certainty. But creative interpretation is another thing altogether.'[60]

5.3 Information Reasonably Available

5.3.1 *The Cost of Research*

Lord Hoffmann might well point out in reply that he did qualify his enthusiasm for background information with the 'requirement' that the matrix of fact 'should have been reasonably available to the parties'.[61]

What is 'reasonably available to the parties' is very much a relative matter of means. The means are principally a matter of money and technology. What is 'reasonably available' to litigants with a large fighting fund may not be 'reasonably available' to others. Indeed, the Civil Procedure Rules[62] (CPR) state that the handling of a case is to be proportionate to the financial position of the parties. Background is sometimes effectively out of the reach of litigants who cannot find it or cannot afford it, sometimes both of them. Speaking mainly of the shipping industry, Sturley has claimed that even 'in a sophisticated commercial transaction, parties often make decisions without the benefit of information that is readily available but too expensive to gather'.[63]

---

[60] See n. 38 above at 904. cf also earlier statements such as that of Bankes LJ in *Farr v Motor Traders Mutual Insurance Society* [1920] 3 KB 669, 673, CA; and the caution advocated by McMeel: [1998] LMCLQ 382.

[61] See Sir Christopher Staughton, 'How Do the Courts Interpret Commercial Contracts?' [1999] CLJ 303–13, 307.

[62] Part 1.1(2) (C).

[63] Michael F. Sturley, 'Changing Liability Rules and Marine Insurance' (1993) 24 JMLC 119–49, 125.

Many illustrations can be made. One, of increasing importance today, concerns statutes enacting international conventions. The records of the legislative history (*travaux préparatoires*) may throw light on interpretation but some *travaux* are simply too far away, buried in the basements of foreign places.[64] Particular points of history may be closer to hand but inaccessible in point of time—submerged in material of such volume that it takes too long to find them. However, the information 'explosion' and the means of access, such as the Internet, search 'engines' and the like, are in a state of constant development. *Travaux* which once could be reached only by tramping across Europe can now be called up on screen at the touch of a button. None the less, both common sense and fairness combine to suggest that Sir Christopher Staughton was also right when he said that 'nothing is relevant to the interpretation of a contract, unless it is known, or at least capable of being known, to both parties *when the contract was made*'.[65]

Even in a world of unlimited means, however, a line would have to be drawn somewhere. People have neither unlimited time or patience. Sir Edward Scrutton once said that it is 'no good taking so long over a case that all the original persons have died, and the lawyers have got all the estate'.[66] People generally, as well as the parties to a particular dispute, need to know where they 'stand'. As far as fairness allows, disputes should be settled quickly as well as cheaply. The secret is to know not only when to start but also when to stop.

5.3.2 The Perception of the Court

What is 'reasonably available' to the parties depends not only on the parties but on the perception of the court, which is charged to manage the conduct of litigation and thus to authorize, or not, any inquiry into background. It depends, therefore, on the knowledge and awareness of the particular judge about what information might be out there and whether it is 'worth' trying to get it; and whether he considers it 'worth it', depends on the judge's sense of the importance of the case and thus of the inquiry to the parties and perhaps also to society at large. Baker reminds us that in the long vacation around 1698 Holt CJ 'had all the eminent merchants in London with him at his chambers at Serjeant's Inn'[67] to advise him about promissory notes, and continues:

The judges should strive, as he undoubtedly did, to keep abreast of current commercial opinion before attempting to improve or refine the principles of mercantile jurisprudence, and should ensure as far as possible that the law fulfils reasonable expectations. When they have an opportunity to develop or perfect the law, they should also bear in mind the convenience

---

[64] For example, the *travaux* of the CMR convention on the international carriage of goods by road are to be found only in the library of the United Nations in Geneva.

[65] Rt. Hon. Lord Justice Staughton, 'Interpretation of Maritime Contracts', (1995) 26 JMLC 259–71, 263. See also A. Brandi-Dohrn, 'Auslegung internationalen Einheitsprivatrecht' TranspR 1996, 45–57, 51 *et seq.*

[66] 'The Work of the Commercial Courts' [1921] CLJ 6–20, 9, 14.

[67] *Mutford v Walcot* (1700) 1 Ld Raym 574, 575.

of international harmonization and pay due regard to considered opinions from other jurisdictions. But, in the end, English mercantile law must be the responsibility of the judges and
not the City.[68]

Theirs is a difficult responsibility. As regards interpretation of contracts, and whether
to research the background, the responsibility is one that judges should not have to
shoulder unless really necessary. That was the position before Lord Hoffmann incited
them to throw off the 'old intellectual baggage of "legal" interpretation' and to shoulder the new responsibility that inevitably comes with the new freedom. This is a
responsibility which, no doubt, they will meet in most cases but one for which, none
the less, they have not been fully trained. Judges neither are nor pretend to be omni-
scient.

An illustration, if one is needed, is found in the rule of law, that disputes over
restraint of trade are resolved according to the 'interests of the parties'. The rule
works well enough in most cases because the parties can put argument to the court
about those interests, with which they are familiar, and any differences are justiciable.[69] Occasionally, however, restraint decisions have turned not on the parties'
interests but on what the court perceived to be the interests of the public at large. In
a case in 1967, the House dealt with tied garages and spoke with the confidence and
conviction that came, to a degree at least, from the having the benefit of a recent
report on the matter by the Monopolies Commission.[70] In a later case about
restraints in the record industry, however, the court also took a view on the public
interest but did not have any such advantage. Lacking the relevant data, a court led
by no less a judge than Lord Diplock reached what was probably the wrong decision.[71]

5.3.3 The Role of the Judge

In cases like that, what should the court have done? Conducted its own research?
Probably, not. In an essay in honour of a distinguished and faithful supporter of the
Welsh Rugby XV, that is not, one might say, the judges' 'put in'. Judges are more
referee than scrum-half. English judges (shorthand of course for judges from other
parts of the United Kingdom too) are mostly drawn from successful barristers who,
as such, have developed an astonishing ability to absorb new information, to master
a brief. Even so, the volume of information available now is such that the 'information overload' might be overwhelming, even for persons of such ability. Lacking the
research assistants (clerks) available to justices of the United States' Supreme Court,

---

[68] J. H. Baker, 'The Law Merchant as a Source of English Law', in W. J. Swadling and G. H. Jones,
'The Search for Principle: Essays in Honour of Lord Goff of Chieveley' (Oxford, 2000) 79–96, 96.

[69] It has been argued elsewhere that a 'good' rule of law is one which encourages the 'right' person
to seek out the information relevant to the regulated activity: M. A. Clarke, 'Mistakes of Value: Allocation of the Risk of Ignorance in English Law' in *Festschrift für Erwin Deutsch* (Cologne, 1999) 111–29.

[70] *Esso Petroleum Co. Ltd. v Harper's Garage (Stourport) Ltd.* [1968] AC 269.

[71] M. J. Trebilcock, 'The Doctrine of Inequality of Bargaining Power: Post-Benthamite Economics
in the House of Lords' (1976) 26 U Toronto LJ 359–85, concerning *Schroeder Music Publishing Co. Ltd.
v Macaulay* [1974] 1 WLR 1308, HL.

English judges cannot really be expected to do more than read a few law reports and, dare one hope, the occasional academic work. Lord Mansfield developed English commercial law from his own knowledge of practice and custom, much of it acquired by his own personal and professional contact with merchants and under-writers. Something of this tradition survives. In a jurisdiction where most judges once practised at the Bar, there is still a sentiment that judges know what business people want, without having to ask.[72] They have dealt with these people as clients and learned their ways. But, even if that is true of the mysteries of commerce and finance, a wider range of expertise may sometimes be required of the court today. Ideally, judges might be sent on courses or given sabbatical leave for further study. In the world as it is, however, perhaps such spare time as they get might be best spent relaxing on the golf course. Then they might turn to what is a fundamental feature of education of every kind, learning to know where and how to look. Today, that means first and foremost learning about information technology. If the judge knows how to surf the catalogue of the virtual library, and identify the background issues that matter, at least the judge will then be better placed to commission and control the research of others, notably but not only, counsel. He is a wise man who knows what he does not know, but he is a wiser man who knows where to find it.

Traditionally, the judge reaches a decision on the basis of the argument and accumulated wisdom of counsel. However, counsel can scarcely be expected to undertake research on, for example, the economic background of a case, if there is little chance that the results will be given due consideration by the court.[73] So, if research of any kind is to come through counsel the initiative must come first from the judge. To a degree this was true in the past but is more so now under the CPR. In the idiom of the ivory tower, the role of the judge has become like that of a head of department who manages research[74]—research by counsel and, in appropriate cases, by others.

5.3.4 *The Role of Experts*

Apart from the research of counsel personally and what can be trawled from the net, the judge may well wish to seek the knowledge of experts. In the recent past experts have come to be seen as a significant source of delay and expense. They are some-times necessary none the less and the work of Lord Woolf led to Part 35 of the CPR, which deals with the employment of experts to assist the court. No party may call an expert, or put in evidence an expert's report without the permission of the court.[75] The court may give directions concerning the work undertaken by experts, and limit

---

[72] Staughton, 'Good Faith and Fairness in Commercial Contract Law' (1994) 7 JCL 193–6, 194.

[73] Further, some have questioned whether members of the Bar are best qualified to undertake or to commission extra-legal research: P. Birks, 'Adjudication and Interpretation in the Common Law: A Century of Change' (1994) 14 LS 156–79, 170; B. S. Markesinis, 'A Matter of Style' (1994) 110 LQR 607–28, 622.

[74] A role described in the USA more prosaically as that of 'gatekeeper': *Daubert v Merrell Dow Pharmaceuticals, Inc.* 509 US 579 (1993), applied in *Kumho Tire Co. Ltd. v Patrick Carmichael*, 526 US 380 (1999).

[75] CPR, Part 35.4 (1).

in advance their fees and expenses.[76] Moreover, each expert will have to set out the substance of all material instructions received, with evident consequences for the recovery of costs if the expert wanders from his brief. A significant feature of Part 35 is that the court may ask for a single expert to co-ordinate and present to the court the view of experts in the relevant field. This will be usual in Fast Track cases and, moreover, evidence will generally be given in a written report rather than orally in court. In all this the initiative and the responsibility remains with the judge as 'head of research'.[77]

In the USA it is common for amicus briefs, some of high quality, to be put before the Supreme Court at the initiative and expense not of the Court but of outside bodies concerned about the decision. Such briefs for the English courts have been proposed, for example, by the International Group of P. & I. Clubs on matters of marine insurance.[78] Another suggestion is that briefs might be submitted by the Financial Law Panel on matters affecting wholesale financial markets and services in the United Kingdom. In Germany there is an encouraging precedent for procedures of this kind, whereby certain research institutes, financed by the state, are expected to help the courts on, for example, issues of foreign and comparative law. Whether there will be developments of this kind is England, insofar as the initiative comes from outsiders, seems unlikely on grounds of time and thus cost. More likely, is that expertise of this kind will sometimes be commissioned by the court.

5.4 Assessment and Evaluation

Even so, it is one thing that the right research is commissioned and put before the court, it is another to have it assessed, evaluated and brought to bear on the case. All that still has to be done mainly by lawyers, judges or counsel or both. Even information that is available and affordable may still be indigestible. To return to the example of the restraint of trade cases,[79] they often require the balancing of 'a mass of conflicting economic, social and other interests which a court of law might be ill-adapted to achieve'.[80] Indeed, some years before the *Investors* decision,[81] it was Lord Hoffmann himself, as a puisne judge, who expressed such caution in a case about the liability of auditors whose accounts were relied on by the bidder in a take-over. He

---

[76]   CPR, Part 35.8 (4).

[77]   Solicitors now face the same problem as the judge. How can they assess the strength of their client's case, especially in technical matters, without the assistance of an expert at a prior stage, in order to know whether to seek a court approved expert in the first place and, if approved, to instruct the joint expert properly? The cost of so doing may be lost. Contingent fee arrangements with (expert) witnesses are not allowed by the Law Society's Guide to Professional Conduct (August 1999) 21.11. See Scott, 'Single Joint Experts' 143 Sol J 30 July 1999, Supplement, 26. See also Harmer, 'Experts—Thinking Aloud' [1999] JPIL 253. For the contention that the Law Society's Guidance is an infringement of Art. 6 of the Human Rights Convention, see Underwood, 'Conditional Fees', Sol J, 29 October 1999, 1000.

[78]   D. R. O'May, 'Marine Insurance Law: Can the Lawyers be Trusted?' [1987] LMCLQ 29–42, 36.

[79]   *Mutford* (n. 69 above).

[80]   Ungoed-Thomas J. in *Texaco Ltd. v Mulberry Filling Station Ltd.* [1972] 1 WLR 814, 827.

[81]   Above, note 38.

referred to the 'wider utilitarian calculations' that might have a bearing on the decision and continued:

For example, some might think that efficiency of the economy requires that company management should be subject to the discipline of take-overs and that take-overs should therefore be encouraged by reducing the risk that a bidder relying on published financial statements will find that he has been misled. For this purpose it may be necessary to bankrupt a few accountants to encourage the others. On the other hand, if the decision in *Caparo's* case[82] had gone the other way, firms of accountants below a certain size may have been deterred by insurance costs from competing for the audit work of public limited companies potentially liable to take-over bids. This would have driven such companies into the hands of the largest firms. Such speculative thoughts, while occasionally entertained by judges, tend to be left unarticulated and with good reason: the courts are ill-equipped to evaluate them in any convincing fashion. If the wider economic effects of a decision are contrary to the public interest, the legislature must correct it.[83]

Twenty or more years earlier, Lord Simon pointed out that the 'training and qualification of a judge is to elucidate the problem immediately before him, so that its features stand out in stereoscopic clarity. [But] the very qualifications for the judicial process thus impose limitations on its use. This is why judicial advance should be gradual. 'I am not trained to see the distant scene: one step is enough for me' should be the motto on the wall opposite the judge's desk. It is, I concede, a less spectacular method of progression than somersaults and cartwheels; but it is the one best suited to the capacity and resources of a judge. We are likely to perform better the duties society imposes on us if we recognise our limitations'.[84]

None the less judges have to decide cases. We 'do not have trial by expert in this country; we have trial by Judge'.[85] It is the judges who must reach a decision on the basis of the information presented to them. This may be difficult. In complex medical or scientific cases 'particularly where there is no general agreement in the relevant scientific community, the judge may well be faced with the assessment of the validity of conflicting scientific or medical theses in an area involving advanced scientific concepts or complex technical issues, sometimes at the cutting edge of modern research. This may well be the case if there is litigation about GM foods, where knowledge and research are in their early stages, raising questions of causation'.[86] In this

---

[82]   *Caparo Industries plc v Dickman* [1990] 2 AC 605.

[83]   *Morgan Crucible Co. plc v Hill Samuel & Co. Ltd.* [1991] Ch. 295, 303. He also said (ibid.): 'I am conscious of the fact that courts do not have the information on which to form anything more than a broad view of the economic consequences of their decisions. For this reason they are more concerned with what appears to be fair and reasonable' than with wider issues. Into its concern with the former, the court could bring certain 'economic realities', however, these appear to amount to little more than commercial common sense.

[84]   *Miliangos v George Frank (Textiles) Ltd.* [1976] AC 443, 481–2.

[85]   *Liddell v Middleton* [1996] PIQR 36, 44 per Stuart-Smith LJ, CA. Concerning the proper role of the expert, see *The Ikerian Reefer* [1993] 2 Lloyd's Rep. 68, 81–2 per Cresswell J; and Baker, quoted at n. 68 above.

[86]   Williams and Melville [1999] JPIL 183, 187.

situation, unless the judge possesses the scientific knowledge or training to reach a decision, it is most important that the expert should be independent and frank.

If, however, there is more than one expert and their evidence conflicts, the 'temptation for the judge without scientific background may be to look at the expert witnesses in the same way that lay witnesses would be looked at so that the one who gave evidence "best" will be accepted without regard to such things as his status and reputation in the scientific community in which he works'.[87] In this situation it has been suggested[88] that the court should use its power[89] to appoint assessors. Indeed this may be desirable at an early stage, if the right kind of expert is to be commissioned. This might be at the first case management conference where the court has to decide what that evidence, if any, is to be.

The judges have to do the best they can with the information that they have got. It is for the judges to see that they have got what they can of what society can afford. To enable judges to fulfil this difficult role it is perhaps for society to see that the judge is, in Lord Hoffmann's words, 'better equipped to speculate'.

6. FREEDOM OF AMMUNITION: FIGHTING IN THE DARK

Finally, this paper focuses on information problems of a different kind in a particular context, insurance. Much has been written about the information asymmetry which is said to impede efficient insurance cover, unless there is an effective rule of disclosure of relevant information at the time of contract. This part of the paper is concerned less with that than with the availability of information at the time of insurance claims and disputes.

6.1 Agents

Before claiming at all, either in the sense of requesting the insurer to pay or, if the insurer refuses, bringing proceedings, the insured may well wish to be sure that he has a leg to stand on in the claims department or the court. Sometimes the information lies with the broker who arranged the cover. The law requires insurance brokers, like other agents, to be in a position to give an account to their principal of what they have done. A particular contract of agency may require more.[90] Clearly, an insurance broker must be able to account to the client not only for the content of the policy but also the circumstances in which it was issued—not only at the time of

---

[87] ibid. 188. This danger must have been reduced in some degree by Part 35, r.7 of the CPR whereby, if the parties have not agreed a joint nomination, the court can turn to the appropriate professional body for a nomination.

[88] ibid. 190.

[89] An old power now exercised under s. 70 of the Supreme Court Act 1981 (CPR Part 35, r.15).

[90] *Yasuda Fire and Marine Ins. Co. Ltd. v Orion Marine Ins. Underwriting Agency Ltd.* [1995] 3 All ER 211, 219 per Colman J; affirmed on other issues: [1998] Lloyd's Rep IR 343, CA. See also the A.B.I. Code of Practice for General Business (Principle E).

issue but, if necessary, years later when the client wants the insurer to respond. When a contract of agency comes to an end, the primary duties of the agent come to an end but the duty to hold and, on reasonable request, to produce relevant information, a duty that arises independently of contract,[91] continues, even though the cumulative burden across the broker's client base may be considerable. The rule of law is clear, sensible and not unduly burdensome. Once brokers were bound to keep, almost literally, miles of files. Today, however, for the broker with a modern record and retrieval system the client's file is but a disk or two away from his desk. The brokers who survive the changes current in the insurance industry should be able to provide the necessary information on reasonable request.

6.2 Claims against an Insurer by the Insured

In England, it 'is an essential condition of the policy of insurance that the underwriters shall be treated with good faith, not merely in reference to the inception of the risk, but in the steps taken to carry out the contract'.[92] Insurance law connects at this point with the rest of contract law through the general rule of co-operation: when it 'appears that both parties have agreed that something shall be done, which cannot be effectually done unless both parties concur in doing it, the construction of the contract is that each agrees to do all that is necessary to be done on his part for the carrying out of that thing, though there may be no express words to that effect'.[93] The duty of good faith in insurance contracts continues throughout the contractual relationship at a level appropriate to the moment.[94]

The main manifestation of the duty of good faith is the duty of disclosure by the insured to the insurer,[95] both most prominent and most demanding at the time of contract formation. This is an unusual rule born of particular times and circumstances which no longer prevail. The time was the middle of the eighteenth century and the midwife was Lord Mansfield.[96] It was a time when, as it seemed to those concerned, the world was larger than today and matters affecting the risk were more distant in both time and space. As Lord Mustill observed in a recent lecture, a

---

[91] *Yasuda* (n. 90 above) 220 *et seq.*

[92] *Boulton v Houlder Bros. & Co.* [1904] 1 KB 784, 791–2 per Mathew LJ, CA. See also *Orakpo v Barclays Insurance Services* [1995] LRLR 443, 451 per Hoffmann LJ, CA; and *New Hampshire Ins. Co. v M.G.N. Ltd.* [1997] LRLR 24, 61 per Staughton LJ, CA.

[93] *Mackay v Dick* (1881) 6 App Cas 251, 263 per Lord Blackburn. See also *Southern Foundries Ltd. v Shirlaw* [1940] AC 701, 717 per Lord Atkin.

[94] *Manifest Shipping Co Ltd v Uni-Polaris Shipping Co. Ltd., The Star Sea* [1997] 1 Lloyd's Rep 360, 370, per Leggatt LJ, CA. M. A. Clarke, 'Good Faith and Good Seamanship', [1998] LMCLQ 465.The insurers appealed to the House of Lords; however, such is the current pressure of cases, the hearing is unlikely to be before the end of the year 2000.

[95] The duty of good faith is mutual: *Banque Financière* case [1990] 1 QB 665, CA. For example, if the insurer is aware that goods lost have been undervalued by the claimant, the indemnity insurer is obliged to draw that to the attention at the time of claim: see the Insurance Ombudsman, *Annual Report 1994*, 34. However, in practice, disputes mostly turn on whether the insured has sufficiently disclosed to the insurer.

[96] *Carter v Boehm* (1766) 3 Burr 1905.

student of marine insurance law looking back across the centuries would recognize that 'the world within which insurance was written was now different beyond recognition', and that after inventions and innovations early in the nineteenth century, the 'world abruptly shrank, with the increased speed and reliability of communications and transport'.[97] Today, in spite of the Global Positioning System (GPS) and global information networks, a case can still be made for the duty of good faith in the law of marine insurance. However, a rule suitable for the insurance of a ship on the other side of the ocean is not necessarily the right rule for insurance on the office block the other side of the street. This is why, in the United States, by the end of the last century the Mansfield rule was limited largely to marine risks. This is why the Mansfield rule has been dropped or modified in most other common law countries. It remains in full force only in England. The rule has been much debated[98] and for that reason should be mentioned, albeit only in passing, in a paper, which is more concerned with the availability of information when claims arise.

The duty of disclosure bites not only at the time of contract but whenever thereafter the insured has to supply information to enable the insurer to make a decision.[99] Obviously, this includes the insurer's response to a claim by the insured, who must, said Lord Ellenborough long ago, make 'full disclosure of the circumstances of the case'.[100] The strictness of the duty of disclosure varies according to the phase in the relationship. It is strictest when the insured first makes the contract. It extends to all material information, whether or not the applicant was aware of its materiality and, in some cases, whether or not he had the information at all.[101] When the insured makes a claim, however, misrepresentation or non-disclosure do not defeat a claim, unless there is fraud.[102] Before the insurer has 'taken a person on', i.e. undertaken to carry the risk, including the risk presented by the person in question (the moral hazard), the rule of disclosure is strict. Once the insurer has taken that person on, however, the law presumes that the insurer has agreed to bear the risk that the insured will be careless not only in relation to the insured subject-matter but also that he might be careless, if and when he makes a claim. Only fraud, in the common law sense, defeats a claim altogether.

When making a claim, the duty of co-operation as much as the duty of disclosure requires the claimant insured to supply information in his possession about the circumstances of the loss on reasonable request. But for how long? In *The Star Sea*,[103] a decision of the Court of Appeal, Leggatt LJ stated that the 'mere fact of rejection of the claim by underwriters would not in our judgment bring the duty to an end'. Rejection may be but the first move in the process of negotiation and compromise.

97   Mustill (n. 3 above) 3.
98   See Clarke (above note 49) 96 ff.
99   *The Litsion Pride* [1985] 1 Lloyd's Rep. 437, 511 per Hirst J. See also *Commercial Union Assurance Co. v Niger Co. Ltd.* (1922) 13 Ll L Rep 75, 82 per Lord Sumner, HL.
100   *Shepherd v Chewter* (1808) 1 Camp 274, 275.
101   See Clarke (n. 30 above) 23–8.
102   *The Star Sea* (n. 94 above).
103   ibid.

If so, it is well settled, not just for insurance contracts but for all kinds of contract, that parties to a compromise of claim owe a good faith duty of disclosure.[104]

None the less, if a claim is disputed, the duty must end sooner rather than later. In *The Star Sea* disclosure was sought by the insurer after the claim had been made in order to assist the insurers in their defence in court. The insurer did not get it. Once the claim has been rejected by the insurer and the claimant has gone to court, the game has changed and so has the relationship. Co-operation in good faith has become conflict at arms' length. The rules of the game, if it can still be called a game, are different. The insurance duty of disclosure has been 'supplanted by the procedural regime of the Rules of the Supreme Court, by which alone for purposes of the action the obligations of the parties as to discovery were governed'.[105] Once battle has been joined, there is 'no reason why adversaries should be under a duty to provide ammunition for each other',[106] except as provided in the Rules of War.

6.3 Claims against an Insurer by a Third Party

Finally, let us flag a bizarre obstacle to getting information, an obstacle of considerable practical importance, that arises from the courts' interpretation of the Third Parties (Rights Against Insurers) Act 1930. Under the Act, if A is liable to B, A is bankrupt but has liability insurance, in certain circumstances B has a direct right of action against A's insurer. B cannot recover, however, until he has gone to the expense of 'establishing' the liability of A.[107] Clearly, before he does this, B would very much like to know the extent of A's cover and whether A's insurer is likely to pay up in the end.

Under s. 2 of the Act, A is obliged, at the request of B, to give information that includes the address of A's insurer. If A can be found at all and the information supplied 'discloses reasonable ground for supposing' that B does get rights under the Act, the insurer is obliged to tell B whether indeed there is cover. If so, the insurer must inform B about the terms of the cover, and allow B to inspect and copy 'all contracts of insurance, receipts for premiums, and other relevant documents'. However, s. 2(1) states that none of these duties impinge unless the purpose of B's inquiry is to ascertain whether any rights *have* been transferred to B. The courts have put a literal interpretation on s. 2 and held that rights, including the right to information, are transferred only when liability is established.[108] The courts have put the cart before the horse and B, now bereft of both cart and horse, can test the thickness of the ice only by walking on it.

---

[104] G. H. Treitel, *The Law of Contract* (10th edn., Sweet & Maxwell, 2000) 84.

[105] [1995] 1 Lloyd's Rep. 651, 667 per Tuckey J in the court below in that case, an opinion adopted by Leggatt LJ ([1997] 1 Lloyd's Rep 360, CA).

[106] ibid., per Leggatt LJ.

[107] See Clarke (n. 30 above) 5–8C.

[108] *Nigel Upchurch Associates v The Aldridge Estates Investment Co Ltd.* [1993] 1 Lloyd's Rep. 535; confirmed by *Woolwich Building Society v Taylor* [1995] 1 BCLC 132. See also *Burns v Shuttlehurst Ltd.* [1999] 2 All ER 27, CA.

The courts' interpretation is not compelling and, clearly, is out of line with the purpose of the Act.[109] The resulting rule is in stark contrast with rulings in the United States, where it has been held, for example, that, if an insurer is aware of the possibility of a claim under a (liability) policy by a person not party to the contract (and thus perhaps not aware of its terms), the insurer must notify that person of relevant terms.[110] Moreover, in Australia the relevant law seems to be moving in the American direction.[111] Meanwhile in the United Kingdom a joint consultation paper of the Law Commission and the Scottish Law Commission has been published suggesting that policy information should be more readily available.[112] The Commission plans to consider reforms of the 1930 Act in a report to be published later this year.

In conclusion, I am happy to say that David, as a colleague, has always been available, fair and forthright, something undoubtedly sought by English justice in commercial affairs but less than perfectly achieved.

[109] Sir Jonathan Mance, 'Insolvency at Sea' [1995] LMCLQ 34, 42. See also Clarke (n. 30 above) 5–8F2.
[110] Concerning a term requiring notice or suit within a certain time: *Union Automobile Indemnity Co. v Shields*, 79 F 3d 39 (7 Cir 1996). See further K. D. Syverud, 'On the Demand for Liability Insurance', 72 Texas L R 1629–53, 1634 *et seq* (1994).
[111] See the decision of the New South Wales Court of Appeal in *Kelly v Murphy* (1993) 11 ACLC 1, 230; and of the High Court of Australia in *Gerah Imports Pty. Ltd. v The Duke Group Ltd.* (1994) 68 ALJR 196.
[112] Law Commission Consultation Paper No. 152 (1998) ch. 13.

23

Freedom of Information: The Implications for Business

RICHARD THOMAS

1. THE BENEFITS OF ACCESS

Whitehall's notorious 'Culture of Secrecy' has been in significant decline for at least ten years, but sharp reminders of the traditional Civil Service mind-set are still to be found. A few years ago the Department of Trade and Industry published advice for the business community entitled: 'Protecting Business Information—Understanding the Risks'.[1] Under the main heading of 'The Threat', the sub-heading on the third page alarmingly groups together:

Pressure groups, saboteurs and terrorist organisations

But the DTI is absolutely right to identify the importance of information to the business community. We are constantly told that we live in the Information Society—sometimes elevated to the Knowledge Society or even the Intelligence Society. Today, as the opening paragraph of the DTI paper correctly states: 'Business is driven by information. It is your most valuable asset.'

It is widely thought that Freedom of Information is supported by campaigners, the media and academics, and must be opposed by business. This is completely mistaken. Provided that their own genuine secrets remain secret, businesses—as corporate citizens, in the same way as individual citizens—have a very strong interest in ensuring maximum access to information held by the government and public authorities. Very few businesses get far without encountering the activities—positive and negative—of government, regulators and other parts of the public sector. Proposals and decisions for the public sector present both opportunities and threats. Either way, businesses have a strong need to know about governmental activity.

In fact, as sophisticated companies know, a treasure trove of reports, surveys, statistics, analyses, opinions and recommendations has been amassed by the various organs of government over the past decades. Information relating to such matters as market intelligence, customer needs, personnel issues, public procurement, registers, and existing government policy can all be useful. Government contractors have a particular interest in understanding government's needs. Published information—including that obtained through Parliamentary Questions—is only the tip of the

---

[1] Information Security Policy Group, DTI. URN 96/938.

iceberg. But many businesses are ignorant about just how much information is held by the government which could help them commercially. They assume a culture of secrecy and are not aware of the extent to which a more open environment has developed over the past ten to fifteen years. A great deal of information can be obtained by a simple written or telephoned request, which occasionally needs to be reinforced by reference to the Open Government Code.

But there remains a great deal of information which is not freely available and frustrations can often develop when, for example:

- inefficiencies or delays occur when obtaining supposedly publicly available information;
- a department will neither confirm, nor deny, the existence of information which it may hold;
- a document is placed in the House of Commons Library, which severely restricts, but does not totally prevent, access;
- a company wants to know more about (and perhaps correct) information held about itself;
- a department acknowledges that information exists, but refuses to disclose it.

Examples where Clifford Chance or its clients have encountered problems in accessing information include:

- internal guidance used by regulatory authorities;
- rules dealing with corporate hospitality;
- decisions of tribunals associated with financial regulators;
- details of licences issued by a regulatory authority;
- reasons for decisions on mergers and other competition issues;
- factual responses to governmental criticism of private pension providers;
- details of prospective public sector contracts;
- current and historical guidance on the announcement of contract awards during election periods;
- formal ministerial correspondence relating to the powers of a state-owned company;
- framework documents relating to the future of Next Steps Agencies;
- details of corporate criminal convictions.

2. THE RIGHT TO INFORMATION

Commenting on the 1997 White Paper on Freedom of Information, the Clifford Chance Briefing stated:

The government hopes to bring about a sea-change in attitude, and alter the future conduct of government itself. A presumption of openness will come to replace the 'tradition of secrecy', engendering a whole new relationship between business and government.

It is difficult now to sustain that statement. The Bill marks a clear departure from the White Paper. There will be a right to information, and this is welcome insofar as it goes. But the rights and duties proposed by the draft Bill are cast in a sea of qualifications, restrictions and exemptions to such an extent that it is doubtful whether the legislation will by itself achieve any significant cultural change. Many of these qualifications, restrictions and exemptions are individually understandable and (perhaps with some refinement) justifiable. But there is no central theme of greater openness.

The Bill's long title states simply that it is to 'make provision for the disclosure of information . . .'. This is only slightly less neutral in purpose and in effect than the draft long title, replacing the word 'about' with 'for'. Given the inevitable attention in the Bill to the detail of the exemptions and other restrictions and their elasticity—there is a real risk that, as the legislation is implemented and enforced with legal advice based on the wording of the statute alone, emphasis is likely to be placed on finding reasons to block disclosure. This would run counter to the government's declared intention that:

[The right of access to information] . . . will radically transform the relationship between Government and citizens . . . [and] . . . Legislation is an essential step towards greater openness in the public sector. (Consultation Paper, paras. 2 and 4)

Legislation is not sufficient to achieve the desired change of culture, but it does play an important symbolic and substantive role.

Absent from the Bill (except in specific contexts) is any clear endorsement of the principles of greater openness and transparency. Considerable support has been given for a firm 'purpose clause' along the lines of: 'The purpose of this Act is to facilitate public access to information held by public authorities.'

Although purpose clauses are not widely used, there are examples in such varied fields as child welfare, transport, arbitration, regulation of legal services and legal aid. A recent example is s. 37(1) of the Crime and Disorder Act 1998, a Home Office measure, which states that: 'It shall be the principal aim of the youth justice system to prevent offending by children and young persons.'

A House of Lords debate on purposes clauses (21 January 1998) indicated strong back-bench support for their use and concluded with a statement from Lord McIntosh on behalf of the government:

we believe . . . that there are circumstances where they are appropriate. They are used from time to time where they are required and are intended to have legal effect.[2]

A purpose clause for the Freedom of Information Bill would have both legal and symbolic effect. It would fall squarely within the category of purpose clauses which, in the Lords debate, the Minister identified as appropriate:

guiding principles according to which the rules set out in the legislation are to be interpreted

---

[2] *Hansard*, HL (series 5) vol. 584, col. 1601 (21 January 1998).

and understood. In this case a legal effect is intended: the statements are there to condition how the courts construe the legislation . . .

This sort of clause might also convey something about the wider policy context of the legislation—the behaviour or consequences that Parliament wishes to encourage or promote by means of the legislation.[3]

This sums up precisely why a purpose clause would be appropriate, and would have legal effect, in the Freedom of Information Bill. It would make clear the government's underlying objectives for the legislation and would provide guidance for the interpretation of the various rights, duties and exemptions which, inevitably, have to be cast in general terms. A purpose clause would also serve a symbolic purpose with a clear legislative signal to all public authorities that cultural change, and a new relationship with individual and corporate citizens, is expected.

If a purpose clause does not find favour, a second-best approach would be to set out a series of objectives for the Information Commissioner, elaborating the balance between the public interest in disclosure and the public interest in withholding information. An analogy here is provided in the Financial Services and Markets Act which opens with objectives for the Financial Services Authority.

3. PUBLIC AUTHORITIES

The Bill is wide in its approach as to the public authorities which will fall within its scope. As well as government departments, local government, NHS and educational bodies and police authorities, Part VI of Schedule I sets out a fascinating A–Z of public bodies, going from the Adjudicator for the Inland Revenue to the Zoos Forum, by way of the Government Hospitality Fund Advisory Committee for the Purchase of Wine and the Marshall Aid Commemoration Commission.

The business community has a particular interest in ensuring that regulatory bodies are within the scope of the legislation from the outset, whether they are Non-Ministerial Government Departments (NDPBs) or otherwise constituted. Bearing in mind that exemptions will exist for their proper investigatory and enforcement activities, it is encouraging and welcome that all the main regulatory bodies fall within the scope of the Bill. Of particular importance are:

Financial Services Authority
Office of Fair Trading
Competition Commission
Utility regulators (Oftel etc)
Environment Agency
Health and Safety Commission and Executive
Independent Television Commission
Medicines Control Agency
Local authority enforcement functions.

[3] *Hansard*, HL (series 5) vol. 584, cols. 1596–7 (21 January 1998).

4. REDUCED ACCESS TO INFORMATION?

There are some anxieties that the Bill as drafted could have negative effects. There is a real fear that the process of getting information could become subject to bureaucratic procedures, and legalistic analysis, obstruction, and/or challenge. In some cases, the effect of the Bill could in fact lead to reduced access to information. Given that Clause 7 does not prescribe any form or procedure for a request, it can be foreseen that many—perhaps all—public authorities will treat all requests for information as falling within Clause 1.

This would mean that requests which are now routinely and quickly fulfilled, would in future:

- generate a 'fees notice' demanding a payment;
- be subject to detailed analysis and internal procedures to ensure that no exemption or other qualification applies;
- possibly take up to forty days to process; or
- be refused altogether if the Clause 11 financial limit (likely to be £500) would be exceeded.

This would be a very undesirable result for businesses. Any risk of such a result should be eliminated from the outset. This could be achieved by amending Clause 1 to make it clear that the legislation only applies to a 'request for information' explicitly made in accordance with the Act. In other words, any other request for information would be treated informally, and on its merits, without reference to the procedures and the substantive criteria introduced by the legislation.

5. EXEMPTIONS FROM THE RIGHT TO INFORMATION

It is difficult to disagree with the government that a single omnibus substantial harm test would be inappropriate for the full range of exemptions. There was also vagueness in the White Paper as to whether the harm 'will', 'would', 'could' or 'might' be caused. The precise wording of a harm test is important.

The Home Secretary, in his statement to the House of Commons on 24 May 1999, explained that one of the reasons for the use in the draft Bill of the word 'prejudice', rather than the word 'harm' as was used in the White Paper, is that the former is in greater statutory use. He referred to the use of the term 'prejudice' in the Local Government Act 1972 and the Contempt of Court Act 1981, although the term is not actually defined in either statute. The Home Secretary added that 'prejudice' has been subject to much judicial interpretation by the European Court of Human Rights, but there do not appear to be any cases in which the term is actually defined. *The Concise Oxford Dictionary* defines 'prejudice' as a noun as 'harm or injury' and as a verb as 'impair the validity or force of'. English legal dictionaries do not cast useful light on judicial interpretation of the word, but the *Dictionary of Modern Legal*

Usage (an Anglo-American publication) states that: 'prejudice is a legalism for harm'. The conclusion must be that in fact the terms 'prejudice' and 'harm' have similar meanings.

The policy set out in the 1999 Consultation Document was that: 'The prejudice must be real, actual or "of substance".' (para 36)

It is doubtful, however, that the Bill achieves this intended result. In particular the terms of the Bill make no reference to a need for the 'prejudice' to be substantial. The concept of 'substantial prejudice' is to be found in other statutes such as the Town and Country Planning Act 1990. Under such legislation, non-compliance with procedural requirements, which accompany the exercise of a statutory power, and which directly affect individual rights, will be disregarded unless the aggrieved person is *substantially prejudiced* by such non-compliance. The fact that the term 'substantial prejudice' is used in other legislation, runs the risk that simple 'prejudice' would make it easier to establish an exemption than suggested by the policy articulated in the consultation document.

There is accordingly a case for suggesting that the wording in the relevant exemption clauses should be recast to make clear that the exemption applies if: 'disclosure would substantially prejudice, or would be likely to prejudice substantially . . . [the relevant interest]'.

Turning to specific exemptions:

- *Clause 19. Accessible by other means*
  There are anxieties that information may only be available 'by other means' on payment of a very substantial fee, where the public authority is able to exploit its monopolistic control over the information without any safeguard or regulatory intervention. The government's consultations on Tradeable Information and Crown Copyright have created demands for price controls in this area.
- *Clause 25. International Relations*
  Businesses often find it very difficult to get access to information from the European Commission or other EU institutions. It is sometimes the case that the UK government has access to a paper which is in practice freely available to citizens and companies in another Member State (sometimes to US corporations), but denied to UK companies. This is an example where a stronger test than the simple likelihood of prejudice is required.
- *Clause 27. Economy*
  There are anxieties about the width of this exemption. Almost any disclosure could be said to prejudice the economic interests of the UK or the financial interests of the United Kingdom government. As well as a stronger prejudice test, a more precise formulation is needed. Alternatively, it may be appropriate for a certificate of a Treasury Minister to be required.
- *Clause 28. Investigations and Proceedings*
  This exemption is too wide. No company under investigation would want that fact to be disclosed publicly if no criminal or other proceedings resulted from the

investigation. Premature disclosure can also undermine regulatory effectiveness. But all companies benefit from knowledge about the policies, activities or decisions of prosecuting and regulatory authorities. Businesses themselves also need to be protected against dishonesty, malpractice or impropriety, with maximum knowledge about the activities of wrongdoers. Here, there is a need to draw the right balance between legitimate needs for confidentiality and the public interest in disclosure. The Clause effectively prescribes blanket confidentiality, even after proceedings have been successfully concluded.

The wording of this Clause needs modification to draw a better balance. The reference to 'at any time' should be dropped. Non-disclosure should be justified by clear rationales and a prejudice test should be introduced.

• *Clauses 33 and 34. Policy Formulation and Prejudice to Public Affairs*
It is fully appreciated that governmental decision-making requires space and time for private debate and reflection. But the class exemption of Clauses 33 and 34 are too wide. This is probably the exemption of greatest concern to businesses. In his Parliamentary Statement on 24 May 1999, the Home Secretary stated that:

> It is important that, so far as possible, background papers that inform policy considerations, but do not determine them, and whose publication would not prejudice the good workings of government, should be published.[4]

A test on these lines would be more acceptable than a wholesale exemption. This is provided as a factor in considering discretionary disclosure (Clause 13(6)) but this is not enough. At the very least, factual information should be made available on a mandatory basis after decisions have been taken. There is also a case for making it available earlier, except in those cases where there is good reason to keep confidential the fact or nature of a prospective decision.

• *Clause 43. Additional Exemptions*
An issue of constitutional principle is raised by the potentially retrospective effect of this Clause which can create an exemption to block a valid request which has already been made. If the Clause is to remain, the Secretary of State should be obliged to give reasons for his conclusion that the public interest in creating the exemption outweighs the public interest in allowing public access.

6. ACCESS TO A COMPANY'S OWN FILE

Businesses have a strong and legitimate interest in accessing and checking the accuracy of, information held about them by a government department or other public authority. The White Paper proposals may have gone a long way in that direction, but the draft Bill falls short of ensuring such access. This will not matter to individuals

---

[4] *Hansard*, HC (series 6) vol. 332, col. 27 (24 May 1999).

who have rights to access and correct their 'personal data' under Data Protection legislation. But the Data Protection Act gives an incorporated business no such rights at all.

This Bill provides an excellent opportunity to give equivalent rights for all companies to access information about them held by a public authority. It is therefore suggested that the Bill should contain a new clause, modelled broadly on the Data Protection Act, to give a company the right to access any factual information held by a public authority about that company and a corresponding right to secure the correction or deletion of inaccurate information. There would, of course, need to be safeguards and exemptions (again broadly modelled on data protection legislation) covering such matters as national security, the prevention or detection of crime, the apprehension or prosecution of offenders, and the assessment or collection of taxes.

7. INHIBITING DISCLOSURE OF BUSINESS INFORMATION

Freedom of Information is concerned with the openness, transparency and accountability of the machinery of government and with improving the quality of governmental decision-making. It is not about disclosure of information which could damage the commercial prospects and/or standing of individual businesses.

Although this might be characterized as a schizophrenic attitude, businesses should therefore have no difficulty in calling for greater openness from government at the same time as ensuring that commercially confidential information is safeguarded. It is important to avoid damage to legitimate commercial concerns or to competitiveness. Some businesses will be particularly concerned at the retrospective approach of the Bill—creating the risk of damaging publication of information passed to government many years ago.

The substance of Clause 41, which covers trade secrets and disclosure of information which would prejudice commercial interests, will certainly be welcome by most businesses and is unlikely to be controversial. In this quite separate context a stronger prejudice test would not be appropriate.

However, the following improvements are needed:

• a 'Reverse FOI procedure' is absolutely essential;
• the exemption should also apply to discretionary disclosures.

8. REVERSE FOI PROCEDURE

The main problem with Clause 41 is that civil servants or others making decisions about disclosure may not be aware of the confidential status of the information, or the nature or scale of the prejudice which disclosure would cause.

A mechanism is needed to allow businesses and other third parties to appeal against decisions to release information which they believe would cause substantial harm to their interests. (In the USA, these 'Reverse FOI applications' have played a prominent role in ensuring that businesses can prevent disclosure of genuinely commercial confidences.) The provisions in the proposed Code of Practice (Clause 44(2)(c)) about consultation with those affected by disclosure will not be sufficient. These provisions are not mandatory and they cannot confer adequate safeguards for businesses or others who fear improper disclosure about themselves.

There is therefore a strong case for arguing that the Bill should be modified so that:

- when a request for information is received and the public authority is minded to disclose (whether under the mandatory or discretionary provisions), it should be under a duty to notify any reasonably identifiable third party that information about them (or reasonably relevant to their activities) might be disclosed;
- a third party (whether or not so notified) should have the right to make representations against disclosure;
- if the public authority remains minded to disclose (notwithstanding such representations), the third party should have the right to appeal directly to the Information Commissioner or the Tribunal, who will review all the issues afresh. The information should not be disclosed until the end of the appeal period or (if an appeal is made) until the Commissioner or (if relevant) the Tribunal have ruled;
- the public authority and the Commissioner should have the power to decide in favour of partial disclosure (e.g. ordering disclosure, subject to deleting material of particular sensitivity);
- the third party should have the right to apply for judicial review if the Commissioner or Tribunal have acted improperly;
- the above considerations should apply to the existence, as well as the substance, of particular information;
- compensation should be available where commercially sensitive information has been improperly disclosed in breach of the statutory requirements.

9. PUBLIC INTEREST DISCLOSURES

The structure of the Bill (as revised at the Report stage in the House of Commons) is such that in many (but not all) cases where the circumstances will amount to an exemption, this will effectively raise only a presumption of non-disclosure. Clause 13 means that the public authority may still decide to disclose the information if it concludes that the public interest in disclosing that information 'outweighs' the public interest in maintaining the exemption. Perhaps more crucial, even if the public authority decides that the public interest in disclosure should not prevail, it will be open to the Information Commissioner to overrule that decision (Clause 49), though in turn a Minister will have a residual power (Clause 52) to veto such a ruling.

No guidance is given in the Bill as to how the competing public interests are to be identified and weighed, nor which factors are to be taken into account. This will create considerable uncertainty and it can be predicted that there will be lively arguments ahead as to whether or not sensitive commercial information should be disclosed.

Annex

This Annex, based on research from the sources documented below, sets out a brief summary of the nature and extent of business use of Freedom of Information legislation in other countries.

USA

The US has had a Freedom of Information Act for more than thirty years and the business community has benefited substantially from it. Indeed the US administration has actively encouraged the private sector to exploit public sector information commercially. American businesses have capitalized on the information that is available to them to seek competitive advantage, to assess possibilities for obtaining licences, government contracts etc. and to make sure that agencies are treating them fairly.

The business community is by far the greatest user of the Freedom of Information Act in the United States. NASA, for example, gets about 3,000 Freedom of Information Act requests a year. About 80 per cent of these are commercial and are concerned with contracts, proposals, and modifications to contracts and requests for proposals. Companies use the Act to get information about the business environment and learn more about the regulatory climate. Routine business use is made of the Act for marketing purposes, to obtain information about customers and potential customers. Other examples of business use of the Freedom of Information Act in the United States include the examination and re-examination of tenders and winning bids. Companies will ask for information to keep track of technology and to determine how to bid competitively as well as to learn about agency attitudes and strategies. Trade publications have used the Freedom of Information Act to get information about agency actions of interest to subscribers.

The US Freedom of Information Act has also been used effectively by business to uncover misconduct by federal agencies. For example ICI used the Freedom of Information Act to access documents which showed that Small Business Administration (a government agency) had committed a more serious violation of its own procedures than its official correspondence admitted. This led the Administration to terminate an illegal contract. Without a Freedom of Information Act, the only alternative would have been to sue the government—something most small businesses would not have the resources to even contemplate. The businesses that use the Act range from small, one-person companies to large multinationals. They include construction companies, real estate agencies, manufacturing companies, dredging companies, specialist publications, catering businesses, law firms etc.

Overall the Department of Defence and the Department of Health and Human Services have been the areas of government to receive the most number of requests under the Freedom of Information Act. About 80 per cent of all requests are granted fully. In 1993 there were 375,424 requests made to government agencies using Freedom of Information legislation.

Canada

The equivalent of a Freedom of Information Act was introduced in Canada in July 1983 giving a right of appeal to the Federal Court. Business use of the Act is increasing with nearly half of all requests now coming from the corporate sector. Specific areas of the business community have particularly appreciated the benefits of a Freedom of Information Act to access information about winning bids in government tender activities, and have also used it to look at meat inspection procedures, aircraft safety inspection procedures, nuclear power plants safety issues, and to challenge environmental impact assessments. The health industry has been a consistent user of the Act, requesting information on drug licensing and other trade mark and licensing issues. Originally the Act (the Access to Information Act) was used mainly by the media, lawyers and academics; however, there has been a marked uptake in the business community, with more than 5,000 requests coming from this sector each year. The most active business area relates to government tenders and contracts.

The Act, which covers central government and most agencies, gives a very wide right of access to records, even those which do not exist, but which can be produced from a machine readable record. It allows access to Federal Government records including 'letters, memos, books, plans, maps, photographs, films, microfilms, sound recordings, computerised data . . .'

The Act includes a requirement to provide written notice to any third party about whom confidential business information is requested. Requests may only be made by Canadian citizens or permanent residents.

Australia/New Zealand

Australia introduced a Commonwealth Freedom of Information Act in December 1982 and all the States have followed in due course. There has been only a low level use by business of the material potentially available. Only about 10 per cent of all requests (i.e. 3,400 each year) come from the business community, and it has been suggested that the reason for this is that managers of companies are concerned that if they seek information for example on a competitor it is probable that the competitor, will seek similar information on them.

The Federal Attorney-General has publicly expressed his disappointment that there has not been greater use made of the Freedom of Information Act by businesses.

Academic research has highlighted that one of the greatest advantages for businesses to come out of the Freedom of Information Act is a review and improvement in the record keeping procedures and practices of business. In general businesses have focused on protection rather than exploiting the advantages of having a Freedom of Information Act. The Australian Freedom of Information Act provides access to documents (not information), including computerized records. It includes reverse procedures which means companies are notified before information about them is disclosed to third parties and gives them the opportunity to make representations and challenges. An Ombudsman and an Administrative Appeals Tribunal are available for complaints and appeals.

New Zealand enacted its Official Information Act in 1982, which came into force in mid-1983. New Zealand differs from the other countries in this Annex by making 'information' rather than documents or records the subject matter of access, however otherwise it is similar to the Australian legislation. It gives very wide access rights to official information from Central Government, public bodies and corporations and is fully retrospective. A position of Information Ombudsman was created to deal with information complaints. His decisions are mandatory on the minister or department concerned.

Europe

The European Union is leaning more favourably toward open government decision making processes. The Amsterdam Treaty, effective from 1 May 1999, has introduced greater access to official documents produced by the EU institutions. The European Commission is currently consulting on its Green Paper on Public Sector Information in the Information Society. The Green Paper states in its introduction that public information is an absolute pre-requisite for the competitiveness of European industry. Further, that EU companies are at a serious disadvantage compared to their American counterparts which benefit from 'a highly developed efficient public information system at all levels of the administration'. Several of the Member States have their own Freedom of Information Act.

A non-retrospective Freedom of Information Act was introduced in Ireland in April 1998. It has been increasingly used by business. Figures from its introduction to December 1998 show that 14 per cent of all requests received were from business (377 from 2,750 requests).

The former Labour Party Minister who oversaw the introduction of the Act, Eithne Fitzgerald, said that the Act would become a very powerful tool for business organizations to get information about themselves held by government departments and agencies. It can also be used to get government policy papers and analysis of their sectors. All government departments and a number of public bodies such as local authorities and health boards are covered by the Act. The position of information commissioner, whose decisions are binding, has been created.

France has had a retrospective Freedom of Information Act since 1978 which provides the same access to individual citizens as corporations. The Netherlands introduced a Freedom of Information Act in 1991. Sweden has had a Freedom of the Press Act as part of its constitution since 1766. All official documents are available for inspection and copying but commercial organizations are excluded. Access to documents is free unless longer than nine pages.

Austria has a constitutional law, dating from 1987, which provides a minimum framework, namely that all officials at the federal, regional or local level should provide information where requested so long as this does not conflict with a legal obligation to maintain secrecy.

While Belgium has laws on civil transparency which provide a general right of access to documents held by a public authority, they cannot be used for commercial ends.

Italy has a general access law which provides information free of charge. Portugal, Greece and Spain also have a law providing general access to public sector information.

Sources

- Jim Amos, *Freedom of Information and Business* (The Constitution Unit, School of Public Policy, UCL, October 1998).
- Patrick Birkinshaw, *Freedom of Information: The Law, the Practice and the Ideal,* (2nd edn., Butterworths, 1996).
- *Public Sector Information: A Key Resource for Europe* (Green Paper on Public Sector Information in the Information Society, COM (1998) 585).
- *Freedom of Information: Consultation on Draft Legislation* (Home Office, May 1999).
- Colm Keena, 'Business world taps into freedom of information', *Irish Times,* 29 January 1999.
- Shane Scott, 'Freedom of Information Act used as business advantage', *Baltimore Sun,* 10 August 1997.
- R. S. Baxter, 'Public Access to Business Information held by Government' (1997) *Journal of Business Law* 199.
- *Proceedings of Seminar on Commercial Confidentiality* (1994).
- *Commercial Confidentiality* (National Consumer Council, 1998).

Index